CALV
A CLOS

Evangelicals, (
No One's Answering the Problem of Evil

by
Daniel Gracely

CALVINISM: A CLOSER LOOK
Evangelicals, Calvinism, and Why
No One's Answering the Problem of Evil

copyright 2006-2009 Daniel Gracely

(Note: an earlier and shorter printed version of this book has appeared under the title, *Hoodwinked and Happy?*)

The King James Version

Scripture taken from the NEW AMERICAN STANDARD BIBLE®, Copyright © 1960, 1962, 1963, 1968, 1971, 1973, 1975, 1977, 1995 by The Lockman Foundation. Used by permission. www.Lockman.org

The New King James Version © 1980 Thomas Nelson Co.

Grandma's Attic Press
eBook edition
2011

Acknowledgement

Without my brother David this book may not have been possible. Certainly it would have been weaker on particular points. His constant encouragement and insight during our long discussions often enabled me to get past some particular Scriptural difficulty. His suggestion, for example, that a child's inauguration into sin might coincide with that child's awareness of his nakedness (an awareness of nakedness first experienced by our first parents, Adam and Eve, at the Fall) is just one example which helped me to think through some biblical conundrum while trying to come to a rational and unified understanding of Scripture. Simply put, this book has been made better by his input.

In regard to other indebtedness, I will smile the next time I read of an author thanking his wife for allowing him time to complete a manuscript. I now know the long hours required to finish such a book as this, and I admit to the strain a wife feels while her husband is overly preoccupied with wondering if one sentence he is writing ought to be two. Many thanks, then, go to my wife, Alison (who also helped with some of the early formatting and proofing).

Several friends, Jim Rhynard and Drew Steiger, Dorothy Jones, Drew's mom, Lin Steiger, and my mother, Nancy Gracely, were also encouraging. Also, various resources were helpful, including Strong's Concordance, apostolic-churches.net/bible/strongs.html, scripturetext.com, and BlueLetterBible.com.

Finally, but first in importance, I thank the Lord for all His help and for sustaining me during the writing of this book.

In memory of

my father

Eugene Gracely

and

my uncle,
Elwyn Gracely

for Andrew

Preface

(A version of the following was submitted to the X-Calvinist Corner portion of the ArminianPerspectives website.)

    I was raised in a Methodist-background church that leaned heavily toward Baptist theology. As a child I attended Sunday School, a Good News Club, and AWANA club, and in all these venues the theology was Baptist throughout. I began college at 20 at Philadelphia College of Bible, then transferred to Glassboro (NJ) State College, and eventually finished my B.A. at Reformed-founded Geneva College in western Pennsylvania; later I attended Duquesne University and SUNY-Binghamton. So having matriculated at a Bible College, a State College, A Christian College, a Catholic University, and a State University gave me a relatively broad exposure to many different philosophical systems, both Christian and non-Christian. Among these, of course, was Calvinism, for while I attended Geneva College I frequently attended a Reformed Presbyterian church, and there I began to accept Calvinistic belief. Incidentally, by the term "Calvinism" I'm generally defining it for the purposes of this testimonial and book as the strong profession that God decrees whatsoever comes to pass.

    Although Calvinism never provided me the spiritual comfort it seemed to bring others, I believed in it for about six years or more. Simply put, I was convinced the Scriptures supported it. I think I was also impressed that Calvinism was rooted in a strong, intellectual tradition. Naturally I felt compelled to defend my views. I remember disagreeing with my Dad or uncle (or possibly with both of them), both of whom were ordained ministers, arguing in effect that God could only have foreknowledge about "whatsoever comes to pass" if He had also predestined all events in all their minutia. I also remember strongly espousing Calvinism during a graduate English literature class years later, encouraged by my fair-minded, agnostic Jewish professor, who believed that all viewpoints had a right to be heard, and that the class ought to hear the Calvinistic viewpoint, since it dominated the culture in which the American Transcendentalist authors (whom the class was studying) were active.

    Ironically, not too long after this I began to question my Calvinism. Numerous Calvinists, e.g., Jonathan Edwards, Martin Luther, James

Spiegel (in his book, *The Benefits of Providence*) have stated that whatsoever comes to pass **has** to come to pass, because God ordained it that way. Thus these authors conclude that every event *could never have been otherwise*. This assumption was the first one I questioned, and it happened one day as I read Matthew 11. There Jesus claimed events could have been different for Tyre, Sidon, Sodom, and Gomorrah, because those peoples would have responded differently had they seen His miracles. In other words, Jesus was saying that other histories could have been possible. Think about that. Yet Calvinists not only claim that God decrees everything, but that He does it *for His pleasure*. Yet if that were true, why was Jesus upset with Bethsaida and Chorazin, since God (according to Calvinism) was predestining their responses? Or again, if God's will was always being wrought during Jesus' ministry, why did Jesus weep for Jerusalem? Or yet again, if John Piper is right in claiming that man is "ultimately not self-determinative," who is it that quenches the Spirit? Numerous other examples could be given.

Indeed, Calvinism is so fraught with these kind of logical problems that Calvinist apologists, without exception, resort to justifying their theology by appealing to mystery and denying that such 'explanations' ARE contradictions. I take a cue from George Orwell, and refer to this approach as *doublethinking*. In layman's terms, this means that every one of Calvinism's definitions describing the nature of God, man, good, and evil, actually contradicts itself. This is why Piper, in the end, has to tell Calvinist disciples not to rely on logic or experience to explain Calvinism, but to make the explanation a textual issue every time. More on that in a moment.

Perhaps equal to any gain someone might receive from my particular testimonial would be what I would recommend to anyone evaluating Calvinism. First, **Realize that consistency of argument is no real test of the truth.** You can't 'one-upmanship' a Calvinist to concede your viewpoint by out-maneuvering him with clever arguments. As a general example, a Calvinist and I could look at a pair of salt and pepper shakers, and he could insist, against my objections, that what I properly recognize as the pepper shaker is really the salt shaker, that the stuff inside the shaker is really colored "white," and that it is "salt" which, put under one's nose, causes one to "sneeze." Arguments in favor of a false theology operate much the same way, though at a more sophisticated level. Fundamentally,

Calvinism always turns meaning on its head. (This is why the debate revolving around Calvinism never dies. Calvinism is able to offer philosophically irrational responses while remaining consistent, and many people assume that consistency of argument proves a position's truthfulness.) Let me show another example illustrating this non-meaning. If I said, "The man ate the apple that didn't exist," observe that, besides talking about a non-existent apple, I should not have said that a MAN ate such an apple, nor that a man ATE such an apple, since no subject and its predicate can be engaged with a non-thing. In other words, all the grammatical components in the sentence "The man ate the apple that didn't exist," have no meaning whatsoever. Technically speaking, such a 'sentence' is not even a sentence. There is an *appearance* of meaning, but no real meaning. Yet here's the catch: the hearer cannot help but think of a real apple when he hears the vocal-sound "apple" in that sentence. That's because of an association with real meaning that he has of the vocal-sound "apple" with real apples in the real world. This association was built over a lifetime, such as when, say, a waiter or waitress might have asked him if he wanted any fresh-baked apple pie, or when his dad told him to go pick apples at the local orchard.

    This leads to my second point: **Realize that a Calvinist and Non-Calvinist do not share the same meaning of words.** This is true even though probably neither one of them realizes they do not share meaning. Remember, Calvinism is merely the invoking of *associative* meaning, not real meaning. By "not real" I mean that the meaning is destroyed in the **overall** thought of the clause or sentence. For, of course, at one level the Calvinist understands the general meaning of words. But when he strings them together in such a way that it forms an *idea* that is false, then at another level he overthrows the meaning of such words.* For example, when a Calvinist uses the term 'God' in defending the absolute sovereignty of God, he is making nonsense statements. This is what I used to do as a Calvinist. I liken these nonsense statements, or propositions, to the riding of a rocking horse. As a Calvinist rider, I would throw my weight forward toward my belief in the absolute sovereignty of God until I could go no further, whereupon I would recoil backwards toward my belief in human freedom. Thus I would go back and forth in seesaw motion, lest on the one hand I find myself accusing God of insufficient sovereignty, or on the other hand find myself accusing

God of authoring sin. All the while, there remained an illusion of movement towards truth, when in fact there was no real movement at all. At length I would allow the springs of dialectical tension to rest the rocking horse in the
center, and then I would declare as harmonious propositions which, in fact, were totally contradictory to each other. Calvinist riders still ride out this scenario. This is why, among the Calvinistic writings of Van Til, Sproul, Boettner, A.W. Pink, etc., there are no unqualified statements about the absolute sovereignty of God or the free will of man. If one reads long enough, all forthright statements about them are eventually withdrawn by qualifying each statement with its exact opposite thought. This explains why every book and article advocating the absolute sovereignty of God ends with its terms unconcluded (though of course Calvinists claim them concluded). So when John Piper tells Calvinists to never mind logic and experience but to make the argument a textual issue every time, I must ask: Of what use is a 'textual' issue if the text has been deconstructed to a point where words have no definition, i.e., where the text is not a text? Calvinism is thus revealed as Zen philosophy (I'm not exaggerating), dressed up in Christian-sounding terms which merely evoke *associations* of meaning, not real meaning. (And so under Calvinism all terms of individuation are lost in favor of an illusory One.)

In the same sense, as long as the Bible student asks himself the doublethinking question, "Now how is it that I chose God, though He chose me irresistibly?" he will never arrive at the true biblical meaning of election. Nor, in the same vein, will the Bible student escape other biblical concepts that Calvinists have likewise overrun and redefined in most Evangelical minds, including the terms *predestination, adoption, foreknowledge*, etc. My personal opinion is that neither Calvinists nor Arminians really escape these kinds of questions (though I think the Arminian shows a certain or greater predilection of trying to). This is because, technically speaking, while both groups profess a belief in the absolute sovereignty of God and the free will of man, there *is* a difference of rhetoric in a relative tipping of scales. That is, the Calvinist speaks ***relatively*** more from the front rock of the rocking horse, and the Arminian ***relatively*** more from the back rock of the same. In other words, Arminians profess more frequently that man's will is not lost, or not AS lost.

Now observe that another striking example of doublethinking is when Calvinists use the word 'choice.' Calvinists will say (in defense of total depravity) "Man has choice, but he can only choose evil." But readers will note that this is merely a sophisticated way of saying than man has a choice that is not a choice. For obviously if a man can only 'choose' one thing, it is not really a choice at all. Yet this is where the Calvinist throws his weight backward on the rocking horse of his theology, insisting that we don't really understand his position, and that he ***does*** believe in choice. Sproul, for example, cites the 'explanation' given by Augustine, i.e., that man has freedom, but he has no liberty. Now in the everyday world that we inhabit, the words 'freedom' and 'liberty' are synonyms. But in the Calvinist world these two words are defined as opposites to justify Calvinism's doublethink. This is a trick that has fooled many people into becoming Calvinists. For Calvinists, by throwing aside lexical control groups that properly inform, e.g., a N.T. Greek verb like "foreknew," disregard how that particular verb was understood and used by the people of the 1st century in the Mediterranean Basin, and also how that same verb was used in the N.T. besides those instances when God is the grammatical subject of the sentence. In other words, such an attempt by Calvinists to circumvent historical lexical use is nothing more than special pleading. But in fact verbs don't change meaning just because God is the subject. Such special pleading by Calvinists is really no different in principle than the method of Mormon-founder Joseph Smith, when he claimed to have special glasses that enabled him to translate the pictorial symbols of hieroglyphics.

Third and finally, know that, **While the biblical autographa does not support Calvinism, the major English translations often do.** The examples are too numerous to mention, though this book includes considerable information on this point. Still, one example, that of Romans 5:12, might be helpful here. Romans 5:12 in Greek is in the format of a correlative conjunction, a point missed by most (if not all) major English translations. This correlative conjunction in the context of 5:12ff states that post-Adamic man sinned **similarly** to, not ***in***, Adam [the Greek *hosper* (Eng. ***just as***) finding its obvious grammatical completion in the *kai outws*, a two-word phrase that should have been translated ***also in this manner***, but was rendered instead ***and so***, which leaves the English reader with the wrongful impression of the causative ***and therefore***, a meaning *kai outws* never takes]. In fact, because the NAS (and possibly the KJV) doesn't recognize the correlative conjunction, it doesn't even grammatically conclude the verse, doubtless assuming the verse to be nothing more than another example of Paul interrupting himself before completing his thought. Yet the presence of this correlative conjunction challenges the very heart of the doctrine of original sin, a doctrine which has routinely been used to defend the idea of the lost will of man. [I actually do believe that man inherited something in the Fall, but this, I believe, was an extensive and (for man's lower form), *imprudent* knowledge (not a sin nature), a part, at least, which we allow to distract us from our focus upon God, even unto sin (see chap. 18). I believe that Gr. *sarx* (i.e., *flesh*) in the context of fallen man includes this knowledge.] As for myself, then, I tire of hearing comments from Calvinists that imply that Bible translation committees obviously know what they're doing simply because they're in agreement with each other. This is no more than valuing credentialism at the expense of logic and/or the historical-grammatical hermeneutic. In fact it can be shown that certain later translations subsequent to the KJV frequently defer to the very influential KJV in controversial passages, such as when the NAS follows the KJV numerous times in translating the Heb. *chazak* as "hardened" instead of "strengthened" in regard to Pharaoh's heart, or when the NAS mimics the KJV word "raised" in Romans 9:17 instead of rendering it as "fully roused," which is what Gr. *exegeiro* actually means. This latter mimicry once again leaves a wrong impression, in this case the notion that God raised Pharaoh from the cradle to the grave for the express purpose of reprobation.

Since there are various positions regarding Calvinistic arguments, I would urge someone who is truly searching the Scriptures to evaluate positional arguments carefully. And this should be done regardless of how offensive the speaker or writer might personally appear, and regardless of which side he or she is on. Most persons, myself included, like to read material from pastorally gifted people, because it tends to be more palatable. But I have found that many (I do not say all) pastors, despite their seminary training and general knowledge, are not necessarily gifted by the Spirit for the utterance of especial knowledge as outlined and implied in 1 Corinthians 12, i.e., the kind of utterance that stems from the critical analysis of things difficult of perception. In short, don't assume some admired commentator or your pastor couldn't be wrong.

Finally, remember that the Bible says that it is a shame and a folly for a man to answer a matter before he has heard it. This means persons ought to know both sides of an issue pretty well before taking it on. For most of us this will mean exhausting study and difficult work (in addition to sometimes having unreceptive hearers and persecution from opponents). But to lack diligence here is to not be fair to the general discussion. Could you represent to a fair degree your opponent's basic position in his absence and his reasons for it? That, I think, is the litmus test before engaging in much discussion on an issue. Let us all strive, then, to be relatively well informed on any issue to which God's Spirit has directed our attention, whether that issue is Calvinism or any other issue. And may we all find a church (sadly, I have yet to find one) which has a willingness to hear both sides in a genuine group setting, i.e., like that setting once provided by my fair-minded, agnostic professor.

Incidentally, if you have found my comments helpful, would you please pray for my own encouragement?
Daniel Gracely

Glassboro, New Jersey
November, 2008

*Similarly, whenever throughout this book I speak of the Calvinist invoking only the *appearance* of meaning, not real meaning, I refer to the **_overall_** thought of the clause or sentence.

TABLE OF CONTENTS

Chapter 1
The First Problem of Theology
    Charles Darwin and the problem of evil. How many Evangelicals assign all events to God's 'absolute sovereignty,' but then try to excuse Him from the problem of evil. Why a better answer is needed.

Chapter 2
Framing the Debate
    Why consistency of viewpoint is no test of the truth.

Chapter 3
Defining Doublethink
    The dangerous contradiction of believing two ideas that are diametrically opposed to each other. How Evangelical apologetics has resorted to this 'foundation' of doublethink. How doublethink is recognized even in some secular literature as a precarious problem.

Chapter 4
Dialecticism: Like a Rocking Horse
    How the positing of God's absolute sovereignty and man's free will form a contradiction, and how it parallels Hegelian relativism. Its similarity to a rocking horse ride, as described in my own experience as a former believer in God's absolute sovereignty.

Chapter 5
Man and the Origin of Sin
    The agenda of God and the addendum of man. How God wanted Joseph to be sold as a slave, but not through the sinful jealousy of his brothers. What the word "*it*" means in the statement, *Ye thought evil against me; but God meant it unto good.*

Chapter 6
Translation as Interpretation
    How the 'passive' participle "fitted" in Romans 9:22 (*vessels of wrath fitted for destruction*) is spelled the same way in the middle

voice in Greek, and what it suggests for interpretation. How the traditional interpretation of Romans 8:28 (in the KJV) is in conflict with 2 Corinthians 6:14-15. The biblical importance of maintaining the first principle of logic (*A* cannot equal *non-A*) when approaching the issue of God's absolute sovereignty.

Interlude: A Personal Journey

Chapter 7
Is Divine Sovereignty One or Two Wills?
How Calvinism is irrational, since it claims that God's sovereign will directs all events, but not sinful events. Examining Jerry Bridges's claim that God is blameless, since man's disobedience is merely against God's *revealed* will. How Calvinism thus posits the contradiction of two different wills, i.e., an absolute sovereign will and a revealed will, while saying there is only *one* (absolute sovereign) will.

Chapter 8
The Importance of Context
How false assumptions are made by taking Scripture out of context, and how they give an appearance of supporting the Calvinistic doctrine of divine, absolute sovereignty. Taking Lamentations 3:37-38 out of context, as seen in Jerry Bridges's book, *Trusting God Even When It Hurts*.

Chapter 9
The Limits of a Sovereign God
Job 1—2 discussed to show that God was incited by Satan, and that Job's trials were not God's 'perfect plan' for him. The Devil's specialty—presupposing and accusing his enemies of selfish motive. How God is thus accused of bribery if He blesses man, or accused of mean-spiritedness if He judges him.

Chapter 10
Does God Rule <u>OVER</u> or <u>IN</u> Everything?
Biblical passages explored where God is present but not directing specific weather events. The reason Calvinist-leaning pastors are content to promote God's sovereignty. The Church's dismissal of

certain gifts of the Spirit, such as proclamation and knowledge, which are designed to protect the Church from false doctrine. How Loraine Boettner and R.C. Sproul exemplify Christians who ought to operate within their own spiritual gifts and not try to usurp other gifts for which they are not fit.

Chapter 11
Does God Control Everyone's Heart?

More examples from Jerry Bridges designed to prove that God's sovereignty reigns over the hearts of kings and therefore over the hearts of everyone else. How the (generically considered) king of the Solomonic Proverbs and Cyrus, king of the Medes and Persians, are taken out of their biblical contexts to try to prove that God is absolutely sovereign.

Chapter 12
Does Voting Count in God's Election?

Comparisons in Romans 9 which show Paul's attempt to continue his Romans 4 argument about the distinction between grace and works. The contrasts are 1) unbelieving Israel with believing Israel; 2) Abraham's behavior prior to the birth of Ishmael versus Abraham's subsequent behavior surrounding the birth of Isaac; 3) Ishmael with Isaac; 4) Esau with Jacob; 5) Pharaoh with Moses; and 6) vessels of wrath with vessels of mercy. God's 'election' specifically stated as conditioned not upon works, but upon His calling. How this calling is biblically defined not as *bare calling*, for such calling must assume the provision of the Son, which Paul does not expressly state, but which must be assumed if the calling is be effective. So too, by extension, may it also be inferred that the Provision may be received, i.e., as demonstrated by Abraham's faith (Rom. 9:7-8), as suggested by the context.

Also, how Ray Stedman's quote about Jacob essentially ignores Jacob's personal faith. How personal faith in Christ is possible because man *can* choose between good and evil. How Jesus' statement in John 6:44 about a man who *cannot* come refers to 1) man's *actual* inability to provide his own atonement; 2) man's *willful* inability to come due to his stubbornness; and. 3) man's *possibility* of coming because of divine provision. Actual inability *vs.* willful inability distinguished. Paul's statement in Romans 8:5-8, meaning that the mind set on the flesh *cannot* come, and how this refers merely to the impossibility of seeking God and sin simultaneously. Thus, how *can* a man come, if he is *unwilling* to come (as exampled in principle by another question—How *can* a man be a good husband if he is *unwilling* to be a good husband?). Further, how *may* (Gr. *dunamai*) a man come to the Son unless it be according to the *Father's*, not *man's*, protocol? For the *Father's* protocol was that the Son should be lifted up on the cross to draw all men to Himself. This way man could take of the Manna from heaven and not live by physical bread alone. But *man's* protocol was (and is) far different. It is seen in the multitude described in John 6, who, having received a miraculous feeding from the Son, intended to take Him by force and lift Him up immediately to Kingship (apart from the cross). For, as Jesus noted, they sought to live by physical bread alone (see John 6, esp. vss. 15, 26-27).

Chapter 13
'We Had to Destroy that Village to Save It'

What the Bible really says about man's sinfulness. Simon the Pharisee as an example proving that all men do not sin uncontrollably nor intend to sin to the same extent. Acts 2:15-16 showing that even Gentiles justly *excuse* one another (in some sense) according to a proper conscience. Total Depravity (which denies the ability of a man to choose good) as an unbiblical view. Calvinism's meaningless distinction between Total and Utter Depravity. How the words *draw, drew,* and *dragged* in the New Testament and Septuagint show a distinction in forcefulness regarding God's drawing of men to a consideration of the cross (Jn. 6:44), compared to God's haling of a man before Him in judgment (Lk. 12:58). How the word *called* means "to invite" in the phrase, *Many are called, but few are chosen* (thus, who truly invites by irresistible coercion?). How Calvinists conversely believe that God's calling is a unilateral act of irresistibility (force). How this leads them to say that a man's desire has been changed, when it fact it has been *negated*. Thus, a man's new 'desire' is nothing other than the construct of God forcefully applied. How this defines 'man's mind' as merely God's constructs upon a certain physical creation. How the man, for that matter, could be a laundry basket for all the distinction that Calvinism requires. How such a view equates man's mind to God's.

Chapter 14
Pharaoh and the Hardened Heart

The Calvinistic doctrine of Reprobation examined. How God's foreknowledge actually includes contingent histories (Mt. 11:21), and how Calvin, Luther, Edwards, and Pink all conversely claim that God has foreknowledge solely because he has predetermined what shall come to pass. The clever but misguided lingual method of argument Calvinists employ to justify their general position.

Examining how three distinct Hebrew words were improperly reduced to meaning one English word, i.e., *to harden*, in the KJV exodus narrative. The idiomatic use of language that describes God as the causal agent in events where it is contextually understood He is merely allowing others to act in deference to His wishes (Job 1—2; 1 Ki. 22). The significance of God 'hardening' Pharaoh's heart at the exact point when Pharaoh's magicians could no longer stand before Moses. Two outlines showing the three Hebrew words that were translated 'to harden' as they occur in the exodus narrative.

Chapter 15
The Potter and the Pot

A.W. Pink in an extended quote describing Pharaoh and the doctrine of Reprobation. Why Pink's five points supporting Calvin's view of reprobation are unbiblical. How Pink (unwittingly) uses a subtle lingual method to achieve irrationality. How Calvinists ignore the detailed contexts of Isaiah 29, 45, and Jeremiah 18 when interpreting Romans 9. How the Old Testament metaphor of pots on a potter's wheel is contextually understood as God acting in *instances* of judgment against man's will, not in *eradicating* man's will through divine, irresistible force or decreeing all phenomena. The connection between 'yet' in Romans 9:19 (*Why doth he yet find fault*) with the word 'endured' in Paul's answer (*[So] what if God endured vessels of wrath…?*).

Chapter 16

Predestination Unto Adoption
   How the Bible defines "adoption" in Romans 8:23 as the future glorification of the body, which believers who *already* have the firstfruits of the Spirit await. The proper doctrine of adoption as explained by Andrew Telford and T. Pierce Brown in extended quotes. How adoption in Galatians 4 cannot mean 'a coming into God's family' without the term 'heir' flip-flopping in adjacent verses to mean an *unbeliever* in Galatians 4:1. How predestination pertains to the future glorification and inheritance of believers, not to unbelievers 'coming into the family of God.'

Chapter 17
Some Remaining Questions
   Certain important biblical passages not addressed elsewhere in this book discussed here in Q & A format. These include John 15:15 (*Ye have not chosen me, but I have chosen you*); Acts 13:48 (*As many as were ordained unto salvation believed*); and Acts 4:26-30, where a fine distinction is drawn between the idea that everything done by Herod *et al.* was predetermined by God, and the fact that God determined everything they should do. Also, what the phrase *to will* means in Philippians 2:13 (*For it is God who worketh in you to will, and to do of his good pleasure*), and what the Greek words *thelo* and *boulomai* respectively mean.

Chapter 18
The Freedom of the Will
   Examining whether man is born with a sin nature that 1) guarantees a deterministic condemnation and 2) predetermines his moral intentions. Observing whether there is any theoretical difference between man inheriting a sin nature and man inheriting the knowledge of good and evil. Romans 5:12-21 and the doctrine of Original Sin examined. The correlative conjunction and *epi ho* in verse 12. Pauline context of "flesh." Psalm 51:5 discussed.

Chapter 19
John 1:13 in its Historical-Grammatical Context
   Why the phrase in John 1:13 "not of bloods nor of the will of the flesh nor of the will of man" indicates three categories of *essential*

distinction, and how these categories are not maintained in traditional Evangelical interpretation. The importance in understanding that (a) the historical-grammatical approach to the biblical interpretation of John 1 is necessary, and (b) John's intended audience involved Greeks. Why, in one aspect of *flesh*'s polyvalent meaning, the word "flesh" ought to remain essentially consistent between verses 13 and 14. Why an accurate interpretation of this verse does not support the Reformed doctrine of Total Depravity.

Chapter 20
Calvinism and Other Pseudologies

The similarities between Calvinism and certain other mystical theologies and ideologies (pseudologies). How such ideological systems (when correctly critiqued) reveal that their propositions were put into an untestable realm, so that belief is based on belief's sake only. Some comparisons between Calvinism and certain ideologies, including Latter Day Saint theology, evolutionary theory, existentialism, Catholicism, multiculturalism, and Eastern mysticism. Also, the common problem all ideologies face—the problem of the One and the Many.

Chapter 21
Answering the Problem of Evil

A case history of whether God foreordains all human activity. Also, various arguments by Reformed professor James Spiegel considered, such as (a) whether God could have created a universe in which men could only choose good, and (b) the idea that evil does not have absolute being. The call for all Evangelicals to recognize that man is the uncaused, first cause of his sin, that God rules *over* all things, not *in* all things, and that only with this understanding can Evangelicals really know that God is removed from the problem of evil.

Supplement
On John Piper's article: "Are There Two Wills of God"

Piper's failure to distinguish between *the wicked* of Ezekiel, who have consciences that, though defiled, are still pliable enough to make it *able* for them to repent, and *the wicked* of Deuteronomy who are described as beyond remedy because of their unrelentingly stubborn will. Also, *the wicked* two sons of Eli whose worthless behavior in their positions of high responsibility made divine judgment appropriate. Similarly, the importance of understanding that "death" in the phrase "the death of the wicked" refers in Ezekiel to "the sinner's way" *prior* to divine judgment, whereas the context of Deuteronomy shows that the word "death" in the phrase "death of the wicked," if we are to introduce that thought into the context of Deuteronomy 28, would refer to "the sinner's way" *under* divine judgment. Examining Piper's view that God damns some *in order that* He might save others. The assumption by Calvinist commentators to take all appearances of Gr. *hina* (*that*) as referring to irresistible Divine decree. Why the use of irony in Scripture in cases involving fulfilled prophecy at God's expense requires the conjunction *hina* instead of *kai*. Piper's refusal to recognize contradiction by calling it "different," not "contradictory." Piper's definition of *not from the heart* (not really of the heart) as non-compassion. How Piper's theology of two divine wills enables Evangelicals to move toward ecumenicalism, since (as shown by Piper's irrational, theological method) a theology may contradict the Bible but merely be regarded as 'different,' not 'contradictory.' How Paul speaks of false teachers who were not even aware of what they affirmed.

Letter to Ravi Zacharias

To all readers, including my Brothers and Sisters in Christ:
To whatever extent I have erred in statements in this book, and/or, in God's sight, have been ungracious toward any, I ask forgiveness. I pray God's Spirit will help any false statements in this book to be either corrected or forgotten.

"The first question, almost anywhere, as it was at Harvard, too—'How can you talk about the existence of an all-loving and an all-perfect God, when there is so much of evil in this world? Does it not strike you as contradictory?'"

>—Christian apologist and university guest lecturer, Ravi Zacharias, responding to D. James Kennedy about the most frequently asked questions by university students.

"If the believer finally sees himself obliged to speak of God's 'inscrutable decrees', he is admitting that all that is left to him as a last possible consolation and source of pleasure in his suffering is an unconditional submission. And if he is prepared for that, he could probably have spared himself the *detour* he has made."
—Sigmund Freud, *Civilization and Its Discontents*

Chapter 1
The First Problem of Theology

When Anne Darwin died at age 10 after a two-year struggle with the aftereffects of scarlet fever and suspected tuberculosis, it had a tremendous impact on her father, the naturalist, Charles Darwin. According to the eminent Darwin scholar, E. Janet Browne:

> Anne was … the apple of her proud father's eye, his 'favourite child', he confessed to [his friend and cousin William Darwin] Fox. More than any of the other children she treated him with a spontaneous affection that touched him deeply; she liked to smooth his hair and pat his clothes into shape, and was by nature self-absorbedly neat and tidy, cutting out delicate bits of paper to put away in her workbox, threading ribbons, and sewing small things for her dolls and make-believe worlds.[i]

Charles was so overwrought with Anne's death that he could not bring himself to attend his daughter's burial or visit her grave.[ii] Brown, in fact, claims that the traumatic impact of Anne's death led Darwin to become an atheist.[iii] Seven years later, and despite his lingering regrets over how his Christian wife, Emma, might be affected, Darwin published his landmark book, *On the Origin of Species*. In it Darwin outlined his new theory of nature in which species evolved in a natural world through natural processes. Not at all confrontational himself, Darwin would leave it to his disciples to figure out the implications his theory would have on religion. But it was plain from the first that *Origin* left little necessity for a personal God who claimed to have an abiding interest and love for His creation.

Such tragedies as the death of Anne Darwin or of any child remind us that the first problem in life, as in Christian theology, is the problem of evil. The question persists: *Why do bad things happen in the world if God is truly sovereign and good?* Indeed, what answer can we Christians give to one who has lost a child to disease, a loved one to violent crime, a house to a flood, or a career to unjust office politics? How do we tell people that many Evangelicals believe that all these experiences are ordained and predestined by a loving Providence? Well-known Christian pastors and/or authors, such as James D. Kennedy, Charles Stanley, John MacArthur, Chuck Swindoll, R.C. Sproul [all of whose ministries, by the way, I have personally benefited from (esp. Dr. Stanley's)], and a host of others too numerous to mention, have represented a rising tide of pastors and theologians across the conservative, denominational spectrum who explain the problem of evil along the line of John Calvin and his disciples. For God to be God, the argument goes, He must be in control of everything at all times. *For God to allow someone or some thing to supersede His will at any point would mean that God ceased being God.* If the internet is any judge of the preponderance of this view among today's Evangelicals, John Calvin's view is by far the dominant one.

Calvin's view on the predestination of all events is not without its controversy, of course. Not many folks, Christian or otherwise, feel at ease with the idea that God has chosen some people for heaven, 'sovereignly passed over' others for hell, and is doing it all for reasons known only to Himself. Nor under the umbrella issue of God's sovereignty, in which the subjects of Foreknowledge, Election, Predestination, and Adoption have been debated, has the problem of evil gone away for the Calvinist. In fact, the idea of God's sovereignty is so problematic that its notoriety has sometimes reached beyond Christian in-house debates. Here I recall a certain multiple-choice SAT question during my high school days in the mid-70s. It asked me to define 'the paradox of Christianity.' I didn't feel comfortable with answering a question that assumed Christianity rested on a fundamental contradiction, though I knew the test answer was *B) the sovereignty of God and the free will of man.* So entrenched, apparently, was Calvin's view of the sovereignty of God, that even the public education-minded SAT examiners assumed no distinction between Christianity and Calvin's understanding of Christianity. It was as though other biblical interpretations did not exist.

When I said a moment ago that Calvin's explanation of evil is 'problematic,' I was only saying what at least one Calvinist himself has already stated. Popular speaker and Reformed theologian, R.C. Sproul, in his book, *Chosen By God*, admits with candor:

Surely the most difficult problem of all is how evil can coexist with a God who is both altogether holy and altogether sovereign. I am afraid that most Christians do not realize the profound severity of this problem. Skeptics have called this issue the "Achilles' Heel of Christianity." . . . For years I sought the answer to this problem, scouring the works of theologians and philosophers. I found some clever attempts at resolving the problem, but, as yet, have never found a deeply satisfying answer.[iv]

Elsewhere in his book, Sproul claims that he also came to discard such analogies as "parallel lines meet in eternity" that were being used by some Christians to explain the paradox of Calvinism.[v]

Regardless of whether one is an adherent or critic of Calvinism, the problem of evil is admittedly a tough question. Moreover, sometimes the Bible is hard to understand on difficult issues. The apostle Peter himself said that some things in Paul's writings were 'hard to understand,' and it is primarily in Paul's books that the subjects of Foreknowledge, Election, Predestination, and Adoption are discussed. But there is hope in Peter's phrase. The fisherman-turned apostle said that some of Paul's writings were *hard* to understand, i.e., he did not say they were *impossible* to understand. Unfortunately, today's evangelicals appear to believe that the problem of evil is *impossible* to understand. Doesn't the Bible, they say, tell us that evil is a mystery? Aren't God's ways inscrutable and His judgments past finding out? Shouldn't we just embrace the seeming contradiction that God decides what events shall happen, yet not be blameless for the *evil* events that happen?

Notwithstanding the widespread support for Calvin's theology among today's Evangelicals, this book contends that Calvin's teachings on the sovereignty of God and the problem of evil are biblically incorrect (and therefore dangerous to the Church). This book also argues that Calvin's views have so decimated Evangelical apologetics that rational debate on the issue of divine sovereignty is hardly understood within Evangelicalism anymore, even by many pastors and teachers. Furthermore, this kind of Calvinistic model has led to an inability to express true biblical Christianity to those outside (or even *inside*) the Evangelical faith. What is offered instead is a confusing amalgam of believing in Christ and believing for believing's sake, since, in the case of the unbeliever, he is asked to entrust his soul to the same 'caring' God who is said to have foreordained all the animus of human experience, including Hitler's fascism, Stalin's communism, religions that oppose Christianity, and whatever other atrocities and contradictions history may offer. Thus despite all the confident-sounding rhetoric Calvinists make about keeping God safely ensconced in His own sphere of Being, what has largely taken place within Evangelical apologetics is a complete breakdown of definition. The result is an Evangelical apologetic where God is no longer distinct in His person or His moral character.

Endnotes:

[i] Browne, E. Janet. [http://en.wikipedia.org/wiki/Anne_Darwin].

[ii] Desmond, Adrian, and James Moore. *Darwin: The Life of a Tormented Evolutionist.* (New York: W. W. Norton & Company; Reprint edition, 1994).

[iii] Browne, E. Janet. [http://en.wikipedia.org/wiki/Anne_Darwin]. [Note: Darwin himself claimed he was agnostic, not atheist.]

[iv] Sproul, R.C. *Chosen By God.* (Wheaton, Illinois; Tyndale House Publishers, 1994). p. 28.

[v] Sproul pp. 39-40 "The more I thought about the analogy the more I realized that it did not solve the problem. To say that parallel lines meet in eternity is a nonsense statement; it is a blatant contradiction… I don't like contradictions. I find little comfort in them. I never cease to be amazed at the ease with which Christians seem to be comfortable with them. I hear statements like, "God is bigger than logic!" or "Faith is higher than reason!" to defend the use of

contradictions in theology." Despite appearances, Sproul fails to spot contradictions consistently, and ultimately defines various terms (such as Augustine's bogus distinctions between "free will" and "liberty") irrationally, so that, in effect, "free will" equals (so to speak) *parallel lines*, while "liberty" equals the *intersection of parallel lines in eternity*. Much of Sproul's methodology follows a system whereby synonyms (*free will* and *liberty*) or chronologically simultaneous events (*becoming born again* and *becoming a son **upon** believing*) are defined differently in order to allow for dialecticism. In the former example, for instance, Augustine does not use the same exact word twice, and Sproul allows this trick to fool him into accepting Augustine's argument that free will exists in a system that is absent liberty. And so I find it ironic that Sproul is upset about the ease with which Christians accept contradictions.

Chapter 2
Framing the Debate

There is one truth that applies to all debates: consistency in itself is no real test of the truth. In one sense this is maddening. We naturally think that if we present enough evidence for our view the other person will eventually come around. We hope not only to survive a point/counterpoint discussion to outlast an opponent's best arguments, but also to one-upmanship him into a corner until he concedes that ours is the correct view. Setting aside for the moment whether we should even have such a competitive spirit, let us at least note that debates in real life seldom turn out so tidy. Most people are stubborn in their views and resist the idea of changing their minds even in trivial matters. When people are wrong they tend (wittingly or not) to adopt an additional lie to support the first lie, a.k.a. 'maintaining the fiction.' Reformed thinker Cornelius Van Til rightly points out how this additional lie is the adopting of a deeper, *consistent* irrationality in order to support an existing 'rationality.' [vi]

Consider the following example of maintaining the fiction. Suppose you meet someone who carries around an exact copy of your Bible and tells you he believes in God and everything written in God's Word. To your alarm, however, you discover that he thinks nearly every word in the Bible means the concept *God is a purple turtle in the sky*. Every word from Genesis 1 to Revelation 22 means this same thing to him except one verse, John 4:24: *God is a spirit, and they that worship him must worship him in spirit and in truth.* This verse troubles him. You point out that the word 'God' in the Greek is the same word used in other verses in the Bible, and so 'God' must be understood to be a spirit in other Bible verses where He is mentioned. Your new acquaintance faces a choice. Either he must believe the truth you've shown him and move toward a better understanding of the Bible, or he must adopt a deeper irrationality to support his existing irrationality. Suppose he chooses the latter. Instead of conceding your point, he decides at length that every word in John 4:24 means the same thing as all the other words in the Bible. Consequently, *every* word of the Bible to him now means *God is a purple turtle in the sky*. He has moved to a position where he is now totally immune to your argument that God is a spirit. So here's the question: *Is he any less consistent in his theology than you are in yours, even if you believe the truth of the Bible at every point, and he believes a lie?* No, he is not less consistent. Both of you can cite chapter and verse, discuss hermeneutics, profess to believe in the plenary inspiration of God, etc., and yet be equally consistent in presenting your opposing views.

As we delve, then, into the remainder of this book it should be remembered that both supporters and critics of Calvin can make rebuttals to every major and minor point the other side makes. Verses are interpreted with different meanings, and even the most fundamental qualities of God, including His moral character, are understood differently. As both sides offer opposite definitions of God's sovereignty, both sides cannot be right. I find it personally discouraging to think that *either* side has built an edifice of error, i.e., that one group is furthering the fiction each time their system is challenged. One would have hoped professing Christians would be of the same mind and arrive at the same definition regarding God's *sovereignty*, but such has not been the case since at least the time of Augustine in the 4th century. I urge my readers to therefore prayerfully consider the arguments in this book, since they will decide for themselves what is the Spirit of truth, and what is the spirit of error.

He Loves Me. He Loves Me Not.

My own journey in working through the issue of divine sovereignty took years. After graduating from a Reformed Christian college where I had come to believe that God could only foreknow history if He had predetermined it, I proceeded to graduate school where I soon faced a quandary. Periodically, I sat at a cafeteria table across from a friend of mine I'll call 'Susan,' and this young woman asked the same vexing question of us Christians every time we urged her to consider Jesus. Knowing we were Calvinists she concluded every discussion in the same melancholy way: *"But what if I'm not predestined to be saved?"* Her gaze was penetrating, a bit exasperated, and she always spoke with a dead earnestness that belied the possibility that her skepticism was tinged with any secret hilarity. What was I to say?—*Yeah, Susan, maybe you're right; maybe you are damned for all eternity and there's nothing you or I can do about it. In fact, all of this was settled long before you and I were born.*

Needless to say, this unsettling experience helped me to eventually make a *de novo* review of everything I believed about the sovereignty of God. And in the process of studying this issue I learned something else: I decided every Calvinist ought to forge his views while sitting across from someone claiming to represent the majority—i.e., the warm-blooded damned who may be no more worse than himself, before he accepts Calvin's theology in the detached, cooler climate of a seminary classroom. And so at length I began asking myself questions: Was God's control over all persons, events, and history as absolute as I had been taught? Was that idea really represented in the Bible? Or again, would God cease to be God if He allowed someone to supersede His will? Who indeed was God in the plainest terms, and how did He interact with His creation and people?

Despite being raised essentially as a free will Baptist in a Methodist-background church, I eventually understood as an undergraduate student why someone would become a Calvinist. The Scriptures supporting John Calvin's view of God seemed ironclad and inescapable. The list of passages teaching God's total and absolute sovereignty was a long and compelling list: *God worketh all things after the counsel of His will; All things work together for good to them that love God; For whom He foreknew He also did predestinate; Thou wilt say then unto me, Why doth he yet find fault? For who hath resisted his will? Nay but, O man, Who art thou to reply to God? Shall the thing formed say to him that formed it, Why hast thou made me thus?; I will have mercy on whom I will have mercy, and I will harden whom I will harden; …vessels of wrath fitted for destruction; As many as were ordained unto salvation believed;* etc. I had conceded in my early 20s that Calvin must be right, for how else could God foreknow history unless he had already predetermined what events should transpire? Ironically, after a handful of years I left Calvinism after examining more carefully this same 'reason.' I eventually came to understand that predeterminism, at least as John Calvin and his disciples understood it, led to a *theology of inconclusiveness*. By taking into account *all* of Calvin's statements about God's sovereignty, and not just *some* of them (*here* and then *there*), I found that nothing conclusive could be said about the moral character of God, the moral and existential statuses of man, or even whether good and evil were morally separable. As I now hope to show, the reason Calvinists do not come to these same conclusions is because they embrace a theology whose fundamental component is a contradiction that *cannot lead* to conclusions. As this statement is a serious charge against Calvinistic theology, we must see if it can be reasonably sustained.

Endnotes:

[vi] Van Til, Cornelius. *The New Modernism*. (Philadelphia: The Presbyterian and Reformed Publishing Company, 1947; 2nd edition). In his evaluation of Kierkegaard's effect on Barth and Brunner, Van Til notes that Kierkegaard intensified the pace of irrationalism brought on by Georg Hegel by a more consistent application. Says Van Til: "It follows that Kierkegaard's charge against Hegel, that he had placed movement in logic or formed an existential system, is tantamount to saying that Hegel had, in spite of his best effort, not made brute fact brute enough, or contingency contingent enough. And this logically includes the charge that Hegel had not made abstract logic abstract enough. That is to say, Kierkegaard sought to cure what he called Hegel's rationalism by an administration of still more irrationalism; but in order to make this administration, he must himself be a still greater rationalist than Hegel was." (p. 54). Hence, Van Til sees in the neo-orthodoxy of Barth the carrying through of Kierkegaard's consistent application of irrationality: "Each time a philosopher or theologian becomes more irrationalist than his predecessors, he becomes also more rationalist. Such, we have noted, was the case with Hegel and with Kierkegaard. Such is, we think, also the case with Barth."(p. 68).

Chapter 3
Defining Doublethink

John Calvin and his disciples have always maintained that God's sovereignty is total and absolute at all times. [Note: When I refer to Calvinism in this book, I am generally restricting its meaning to the doctrine that God sovereignly foreordains ***all*** phenomena. Likewise, when I use the term *Calvinist* (or *Reformed*) thinker, I generally mean someone who espouses strongly that God has foreordained all history, not generally someone who necessarily embraces all the tenets of Calvinism. The term, *absolute sovereignist*, seemed too cumbersome and unfamiliar for extended usage here, and many who believe in the doctrine of God's foreordination of all history often feel obliged to accept many or all of Calvin's most controversial points, anyway.]

Probably the best known statement that defines God's absolute sovereignty for the average Calvinist today is found in the Westminster Confessions of 1647:

God from all eternity, did, by the most wise and holy counsel of His own will, freely, and unchangeably ordain whatsoever comes to pass: yet so, as thereby neither is God the author of sin, nor is violence offered to the will of the creatures; nor is the liberty or contingency of second causes taken away, but rather established.

This sentence is a contradiction because it involves two ideas in which each idea makes it impossible for the other idea to be true. Yet under the Westminster Confessions these two opposing propositions form a 'system' (or *synthesis*) that is nevertheless held to be true. Let me give another example of a contradiction to make this clearer. Suppose I packed nothing but one apple and one orange for lunch. I might make the following statement:

Today I ate the apple before I ate the orange so I wouldn't get sick, yet not in such a way so that the orange was eaten last, which would have made me sick.

Suppose you heard me say this. It sounds like nonsense to you, but I insist that this is exactly what happened during lunch. Here is how our conversation might proceed:

<u>Me</u>: I feel sick.

<u>You</u>: Apparently you got sick by eating the orange first. Why didn't you eat the apple first?

<u>Me</u>: I *did* eat the apple first. Don't you remember what I said? "*I ate the apple before I ate the orange so I wouldn't get sick.*"

You: Then why are you sick?

Me: I believe I told you why. I said I didn't eat the orange last, which is why I feel sick.

You: I'm a little confused—which fruit did you eat first?

Me: I'll repeat myself entirely: *"Today I ate the apple before I ate the orange so I wouldn't get sick, yet not in such a way so that the orange was eaten last, which would have made me sick."*

You: But you're sick—is that right?

Me: Not at all. I said a bit earlier that *"I ate the apple before I ate the orange so I wouldn't get sick."*

As long as I respond with this 'logic' you cannot come to any conclusions about what I said. You cannot know whether I am sick or well, which fruit I ate first, or even if I ate at all. You cannot know what events happened because I affirmed everything, and yet denied everything. Consequently, *all the statements you heard are inconclusive.* In effect, I used language to say *nothing*. You could not even determine properly if I was actually describing myself in the above events, since nothing was being said about 'me.' I created this confusion by upholding two ideas that were in contradiction to each other, but which I claimed were simultaneously true.

In general, the shorter the statement of contradiction the more absurd it immediately appears. *I never ate the apple I ate*, is an example. Longer contradictions, such as the apple and orange analogy, or the Westminster Confessions regarding the sovereignty of God and the free will of man, will not always appear immediately irrational. This delay happens because our minds have more time to latch onto each idea separately. Paraphrasing can help identify contradictions more quickly. Consider the Westminster Confession's reference to *sin* in the phrase, "God is not the author of sin." Any sin is fundamentally a behavioral act of the mind and the will (often engaging bodily effect), and any act is also an event; so every sin by nomenclature may also be called a sinful *event*. Can you recognize more easily, then, the contradiction in the Westminster Confessions if I paraphrase it to say, "God ordains whatever events come to pass, but not in such a way so that God ordains the sinful events that come to pass?"

As long as people embrace contradictory premises that abandon logic it is impossible for them to arrive at the truth. Consequently, in theology it can be exasperating to show a person the contradiction of their Calvinism, since they *embrace* the contradiction. You are only pointing out what they already admit to. In fact, they do not even believe their contradiction is a real contradiction, but only a 'seeming' one. This is why a great division in Christian theology has continued to exist for centuries despite proponents from both sides appealing to the Bible. For centuries certain words in the Bible have been reinterpreted by some to fit the template of Calvinistic doctrine, and these followers of Calvin (in regard to all of their chief doctrinal distinctives) have read their Bibles through the lens of contradiction. Of course, the Calvinist would reply that it is *the other side* that is reinterpreting Scripture to fit their own template. This charge/counter charge leveled by Calvinists and non-Calvinists against each other is why all Christians themselves need to study the Scriptures. This way they will know which is the correct view and thus be "approved unto God, rightly *dividing* the Word of Truth."

Contradictionism Noted in Secular Literature

The dilemma over accepting ideological contradictions has not been restricted to the Church. In fact, the idea that accepting a fundamental contradiction is dangerous to one's understanding of things has also been noted by secular authors. Because their insights into this problem help explain the essence of Calvinism, as well as demonstrate why Calvin's apologetic regarding the problem of evil remains fundamentally false, we will briefly survey a few statements by these authors. Perhaps most telling of all, these statements will show how Calvinism has frequently hindered the evangelizing of intellectuals who have helped to set the pace of Western thought.

Perhaps the most famous of these statements against contradictionism is found in George Orwell's classic and futuristic, political novel, *1984*. Though a political socialist himself, Orwell worried about what might happen if a socialist state was abusive. He specifically feared how a contradiction could be used by the State to annihilate individual freedom and thought. Orwell referred to this contradiction as a *doublethink* (or *doublespeak*). This concept arises in the novel when Winston Smith, the main character in *1984*, violates the State's code by having a girlfriend and having sexual relations with her apart from State supervision. Another character, O'Brien, is a torturer for Big Brother (i.e., the State). O'Brien's job is to get Winston to repent of his individualism. This is accomplished by trying to torture Winston into accepting a doublethink.

O'Brien begins his interrogation by holding up four of his fingers and asking Winston how many fingers he is showing. When Winston replies "Four," O'Brien tells him that the answer is "Five" if Big Brother says it is five. Winston appeals to the absolutism that says four fingers must always be four fingers. O'Brien replies that truth is defined by what the State says it is. O'Brien then begins to 'work' on Winston, and eventually under pressure Winston changes his reply to "Five." "No, Winston," says O'Brien, and in effect tells Winston that he must not merely *say* there are five, he must also *believe* there are five. In fact, Winston must *know* there are five fingers even though he *knows* there are four. After more excruciating torture Winston finally *doublethinks*, i.e. *knows* there are five fingers, even though he *knows* there are four, and thus he cries out *"Five!"* [vii] The certainty of Big Brother's 'truth' lingers with Winston for about a half-minute. But then Winston challenges O'Brien about the difference between (a) the 'truth' of Big Brother's self-serving relativism, and (b) the truth of absolute facts that cannot change. Significantly, O'Brien asks Winston if he believes in God. "No," replies Winston. *"Then what is this principle,"* queries O'Brien, *"this principle that will defeat us?"* [1] [viii] Note here that Orwell views doublethinking as the instrument used by a more powerful entity to submerge and to subsume within itself the individual component. The result in *1984* is that Winston Smith is stripped of his identity, his ability to choose, and even his ability *to know*. At the last, he is resigned to act out the melancholy, puppet-like chorus-shouting of Big Brother slogans at State rallies with all the other citizen goons.

Another author, Herman Melville, directly addresses the contradiction of Calvinism in *Moby Dick*, America's most famous novel of the 19th century. Melville believes the entire world is subject to a contradictory existence because its Creator-God is a contradictory Being. Melville, who once referred to his novel, *Moby Dick*, as "a blasphemous book," ridicules the logic of the "infallible Presbyterian church" as early as the first chapter, then later mocks what he believes is *the* contradiction of Christianity in a chapter called "The Whiteness of the Whale." Melville speaks through the character of Ishmael to give a scathing indictment of the Christian God whom Melville understands in completely Calvinistic (i.e., contradictory) terms. Melville does this through a rambling account of how the color white has had contradictory associations throughout history and its religious symbolism, including Christianity:

> It was the whiteness of the whale that above all things appalled me. But how can I hope to explain myself here; and yet, in some dim, random way, explain myself I must, else all these chapters might be naught...
> ...among the Red Men of America the giving of the white belt of wampum was the deepest pledge of honour; though in many climes, whiteness typifies the majesty of Justice in the ermine drawn by milk-white steeds; though even in the higher mysteries of the most august religions it has been made the symbol of the divine spotlessness and power; by the Persian fire worshippers, the white forked flame being held the

holiest on the altar; and in the Greek mythologies, Great Jove himself being made incarnate in a snow-white bull; and though to the noble Iroquois, the midwinter festival of their theology, that spotless, faithful creature being held the purest envoy they could send to the Great Spirit with the annual tidings of their fidelity; and though directly from the Latin word for white, all Christian priests derive the name of one part of their sacred vesture, the alb or tunic, worn beneath the cassock; and though among the holy pomps of the Romish faith, white is specially employed in the celebration of the Passion of our Lord; though in the Vision of St. John, white robes are given to the redeemed, and the four-and-twenty elders stand clothed in white before the great white throne and the Holy One that sitteth there white like wool; yet for all these accumulated associations, with whatever is sweet, and honourable, and sublime, there yet lurks an elusive something in the innermost idea of this hue, which strikes more of panic to the soul than that redness which affrights in blood... Witness the white bear of the poles, and the white shark of the tropics; ...their smooth, flaky whiteness makes them...transcendent horrors...

    But not yet have we solved the incantation of this whiteness, and learned why it appeals with such power to the soul; and more strange and far more portentous—why, as we have seen, it is at once the most meaning symbol of spiritual things, nay, the very veil of the Christian's Deity; and yet should be as it is, the intensifying agent in things the most appalling to mankind... Is it that by its indefiniteness it shadows forth the heartless voids and immensities of the universe, and thus stabs us from behind with the thought of annihilation, when beholding the white depths of the milky way? Or is it, that as in essence whiteness is not so much a colour as the visible absence of colour, and at the same time the concrete of all colours; is it for these reasons that there is such a dumb blankness, full of meaning, in a wide landscape of snows—a colourless, all-colour of atheism from which we shrink?... and when we proceed further, and consider that the mystical

cosmetic which produces every one of her hues, the
great principle of light, for ever remains white or
colorless in itself, and if operating without medium
upon matter, would touch all objects, even tulips and
roses, with its own blank tinge—pondering all this,
the palsied universe lies before us a leper; and like
willful travelers in Lapland, who refuse to wear
coloured and colouring glasses upon their eyes, so the
wretched infidel gazes himself blind at the
monumental white shroud that wraps all the prospect
around him. And of all these things the albino whale
was the symbol. Wonder ye then at the fiery hunt? [ix]

Thus, in mocking criticism thinly disguised as reflective meditation Melville sees the universe as morally reflective of its Creator—heartless, void in its immensity, and backstabbing humanity with the thought of annihilation. Slyly, he couples *the very veil of the Christian's Deity* with *things most appalling to mankind*. Finally, he sees the color white as mired in contradiction, at once the void of all colors and yet also the combination of all colors—*a dumb blankness, full of meaning*—a contradiction that impossibly exists, and which would lead us to atheism were we not to shrink from our horror of the Void. Melville is stating what his contemporary, Charles Baudelaire, put more succinctly—"If there is a God," said the French poet, "He is the Devil."[x]

Again, Melville was not just writing a novel. Even according to today's academicians he was writing *the* American novel of the 19th century. The novel's influence upon the American Academy should not be underestimated, for it reflects the Academy's general objection against the Christian God. How many unbelievers across past centuries, I wonder, rejected the Bible and Christianity because they assumed, like Melville, that Calvin's position about the sovereignty of God represented the Bible's actual teaching? One can only guess at the extent of Calvin's effect on intellectuals of the past who wrestled with Scripture because they found the concept of an arbitrary God offensive. One ought not to think, then, that the dissent of certain New England intellectuals from the Calvinistic God of the Puritans was altogether misguided. Consider, for example, these lines from Emily Dickinson, America's best-known poetess of the 19th century:

> Papa above!
> Regard a Mouse
> O'erpowered by the Cat!
> Reserve within thy kingdom
> A "Mansion" for the Rat![xi]

The exact nature of Dickinson's faith is a little hard to determine from her various poems, since faith and accusation seem to alternate in a number of her poems; but again, the point here is that one cannot help but wonder how many people today continue to doubt Christ and the Bible because past intellectuals who have now become influential were miffed with the Calvinistic God, and because Evangelicals are still promoting the same errors of Calvin's contradictionism. People are understandably confused about the character of a God who arbitrarily picks some people for eternal life while leaving others to eternal damnation. Meanwhile, Evangelical Calvinists are left with the Petrine command to "give a reason of the hope" that is in them, which under Calvinism can only mean telling the unbeliever that God has already settled his fate in heaven despite his 'free will,' and that he cannot hope to comprehend the reasons for it. That Peter's command should mean something *else* in light of the disciple's other statement that "God is not willing that any should perish, but that all should come unto the knowledge of the truth," seems apparent. Instead, Calvin's most progressive followers have found in this latter verse an opportunity to interpret the words "any" and "all" as merely referring to the "elect" who under "limited atonement" are those referred to by the terms, "any" and "all." Indeed, the opportunities for biblical revisionism have led Calvinists to interpret the word 'world' as restrictively meaning 'the world of the elect' in some 20 New Testament verses, i.e., verses which otherwise would prove their theory of 'particular redemption' false. So, let me ask the reader at this point—which theology do you suppose is maintaining the fiction here with a twisted kind of *consistency*? They both cannot be right. Which group—Calvinists, or non-Calvinists—is being more creative, so that its interpretation of the Bible fits a preconceived template?

Footnotes:

[1] O'Brien also chides Winston regarding the empirical sciences, telling him that knowledge is defined according to the State's need for the moment. Says O'Brien: "The stars can be near or distant, according as we need them. Do you suppose our mathematicians are unequal to that? Have you forgotten doublethink?" (Part 3, Chapter 3).

Endnotes:

[vii] Orwell, George. *1984*. [http://www.online-literature.com/orwell/ 1984/19/].

[viii] Orwell, George. *1984*. [http://www.online-literature.com/orwell/ 1984/20/].

[ix] Melville, Herman. *World's Greatest Literature: Vol. XVII, Moby Dick*. (n.p. Spenser Press).

[x] Baudelaire, Charles.

[xi] Dickinson, Emily (edited by R.W. Franklin). *The Poems of Emily Dickinson.* (Cambridge, Massachusetts: The Belknap Press of Harvard University Press, 1998). Vol. 1, p. 190-191.

Chapter 4
Dialecticism: Like a Rocking Horse

We have already seen how the Westminster Confessions embraces a system of 'truth' made up of two ideas diametrically opposed to each other: 1) the absolute determination of God over all events, and 2) the freedom of human will. Now observe the following quote by Reformed thinker Loraine Boettner, in his book, *The Reformed Doctrine of Predestination*, an older Calvinistic work of a few generations ago:[2]

> But while the Koran and the (Mohammedan) traditions teach a strict foreordination of moral conduct and future destiny, they also present a doctrine of human freedom *which makes it necessary for us to qualify* the sharper assertions of divine Predestination in harmony with it. And here, too, as in the Scriptures, no attempt is made to explain how the *apparently* opposite truths of Divine sovereignty and human freedom are to be reconciled (emphasis added).[xii]

Here Boettner attempts a contrast between the Islamic Koran and Calvinistic doctrine. The statement above is his attempt to modify the absolute determination (sovereignty) of God so that people can be said to be the author of their own choices. Observe the language of Calvinism when Boettner says that predestination (i.e., for Boettner, the divine foreordination of everyone's activity, moral content, and future destiny) and human freedom are "apparently" opposite truths. The reason he prefers not to say that they *are* opposite truths is because to do so would be to admit to a final contradiction. Instead, he qualifies his assertion by implying that these concepts are "apparently" a contradiction, i.e., that they are a *seeming* contradiction rather than an actual one. As a result, conclusions about God and man are never finalized in definition, since Boettner's "divine Predestination" is 'qualified' with its exact antithesis. Thus, such an apparent contradiction that should be an *actual* contradiction to Evangelicalism is to Evangelical Calvinism only an "apparent" contradiction. In other words, for Evangelical Calvinists the 'apparent' contradiction is regarded as no real contradiction at all.

Calvinists attempt to solve their contradiction (as to who gets the final *say* in man's choices) by doublethinking, the common type of solution applied in relativistic Hegelian philosophy. Georg Hegel (1770-1831) was a German philosopher who increased the pace of relativistic philosophy brought on by his predecessors, especially Immanuel Kant. Kant had appealed to reason rather than to revelation as the doorway to understanding. The problem with Kant's philosophy from a biblical point of view is that man's reasoning is often foolish and leads to the most *outré* results. As Hegel followed Kant he furthered the principle of irrationality by believing that opposing ideas are never *either/or* issues to be resolved but are equally true realities that are 'qualified' by each other. This means that Hegel believed that a person should not seek one true answer in religion or philosophy, as though one tried many shops in order to find the right shoes; rather, one ought to embrace the whole process of 'shopping' itself. Thus, one shop is selling the idea that O'Brien is holding up four fingers, while another shop is selling the idea that O'Brien is holding up five fingers. "So what?" says Hegel, in effect. "Embrace the *whole*." Philosophically speaking, Hegel called this cultural process of 'shopping' the Spirit of History [*Zeitgeist*, literally *Ghost (Spirit) of History*]. Generally, philosophers refer to Hegel's concept as *dialecticism*. When seen for what it is, Hegelian dialecticism is nothing more nor less than an endorsement for relativity of viewpoint. Yet it is not fair to lay the blame for the beginnings of Western relativism at Hegel's feet alone, given the prior relativistic pantheism of Spinoza and German Idealism (or, arguably, even Heraclitus, *et al.*). And it is hard to say how much Hegel's philosophy was influenced by remnants of the sovereignty/determinism ideas of the influential German Lutheranism of Hegel's German predecessors (Luther was more of a 'Calvinist' than Calvin), or whether Hegel simply fertilized the ground in which the already existing Calvinistic contradiction lay planted (though rather dormant) in German congregants' minds. At any rate, it all has proved consequential to Evangelicals in the West, who have largely failed to understand the roots of their culture's philosophical relativism. Had they understood these roots, Evangelicals might have spotted the same *dialecticism* when it began appearing inter-denominationally within their own culture. Though saints we Evangelicals are, as sinners we ought to recognize how susceptible we remain to combining contradictory ideas with our faith. (As Jeremiah said—"The heart is deceitful above all things, and desperately wicked: who can comprehend it?").

My own personal experience (years ago) in embracing the doublethink of Calvinism was a frustrating one. I would liken it to riding a rocking horse. As a rider, I would throw my weight forward toward my belief in the absolute sovereignty of God until I could go no further, whereupon I would recoil backwards toward my belief in human freedom. Thus I would go back and forth in seesaw motion, lest on the one hand I find myself accusing God of insufficient sovereignty, or on the other hand find myself accusing God of authoring sin. All the while, there remained an illusion of movement towards truth, when in fact there was no real movement at all.

Calvinist riders still ride out this scenario. This is why, among the Calvinistic writings of Van Til, Sproul, Boettner, etc., there are no unqualified statements about the absolute sovereignty of God or the free will of man. If one reads long enough, all forthright statements about them are eventually withdrawn by qualifying each statement with its exact opposite thought. This explains why every book and article advocating the absolute sovereignty of God ends with its terms unconcluded. Thus, Boettner, bold enough to open the main body of his text by saying that God's sovereignty includes "all the activities of saints and angels in heaven and of reprobates and demons in hell"[xiii] is found later to say that the Koran's belief in "strict foreordination makes it necessary for us to *qualify* the sharper assertions of Predestination," so that God's absolute sovereignty will be in 'harmony' with human freedom (emphasis added).[xiv] Boettner's 'harmony,' of course, is his attempt, witting or not, to stake the tent of Evangelical apologetics within the camp of Hegelian dialecticism.

Like Hegelians, Calvinists simply *say* that their diametrically opposed principles are true. This 'affirmation' of all phenomena occurs in Calvinism because God in His sovereignty has to approve of all history. Like Hegelians, reality is rationality; *Whatever is, is right*. Consequently, all Calvinistically-oriented, 'biblical' exegesis is aligned with contradictory 'proof-texts' to support both sides of the dialectical argument. This way Calvinists can claim that God has ordained everything that has ever happened in history which men have chosen freely to do. When Boettner turns his attention from the sovereignty of God to the free will of man, man's freedom, despite the author's intense rhetoric, is shown to be just as inconclusive as God's sovereignty. Thus in one section about human freedom Boettner even remarks that, "In his fallen state he [man] only has what we may call *the freedom of slavery*" (emphasis added).[xv] To further this argument about 'the freedom of slavery,' Boettner also quotes Martin Luther:

> In another place [Luther] says, "When it is granted and established that Free will, having lost its liberty, is compulsively bound to the service of sin, and cannot will anything good; I from these words, can understand nothing else than that Free-will is an empty term, whose reality is lost. And a lost liberty, according to my grammar, is no liberty at all .... Free-will is thrown prostrate, utterly dashed to pieces .... it follows unalterably, that all things which we do, although they may appear to us to be done mutably and contingently by us, are yet, in reality, done

necessarily and immutably, with respect to the will of God."[xvi]

After these strong statements about 'the freedom of slavery,' which stress the *impossibility* of people ever authoring their own choices, one would think that the matter is settled for Boettner. But when such a destruction of human freedom is about to make God into the author of everything, including sin, Boettner retracts (i.e., 'reconciles') his position 16 pages later. Apparently, human freedom exists, after all:

> *A partial explanation of sin is found in the fact that while man is constantly commanded in Scripture not to commit it, he is, nevertheless, permitted to commit it if he chooses to do so. No compulsion is laid on the person; he is simply left to the free exercise of his own nature, and he alone is responsible.*[xvii]

This seesawing language in Calvinism is why the terms 'free,' 'freedom,' and 'choice' are all defined (though in appearance only) not merely along their 'proper' lines but also according to their 'opposite' meanings; consequently, they become meaning*less* terms.[3] How free, for example, are people in authoring their own choices in Boettner's following citation of B.B. Warfield?:

> It is He (God) that leads the feet of men, wit they wither or not; He that raises up and casts down; opens and hardens the heart; and creates the very thoughts and intents of the soul.[xviii]

As read, Warfield makes no concession to human freedom or even human *thought*. Yet, Boettner's approval of Warfield's freedom-of-slavery statement does not prevent Boettner from later saying that "God sets at nought the counsel of the nations." One wonders, in passing, how this counsel is said to be *of* the nations, since God is said to be creating the very thoughts and intents of souls. In fact, at one point Boettner himself says that "God rules and overrules the sinful acts of men."[xix] Thus, natural questions arise. Why would God create the very thoughts and intents of all people only to later overthrow them? Note that Boettner is not saying that God merely rules *over* the sinful acts of men, but that God *rules* the sinful acts of men, i.e. He *commands* them. Why God would rule and then overrule Himself, much less rule sinful acts, is never explained by Boettner. Needless to say, in Boettner's model, God must also *rule* the sinful acts of Satan and demons, or else God could not be sovereign. So the question remains: Is God set against Himself that He ordains that which He comes to abrogate?

If so, then how do we understand the principle that "God rules and overrules" in the area of Christ's opposition to demon possession? If language means anything, 'rules' and 'overrules' ought to be a contradiction for the Calvinist, for if God rules, how is it that He ever needs to overrule?

This view, that an absolute sovereign God rules, and yet overrules, produces a fundamental crisis in Calvinism. It is a crisis of God's identity. For example, we have already noted that Boettner believes that God foreordains *all* the activities of "reprobates and demons," yet Christ showed that He consistently stood *against* demon possession whenever He encountered it. In fact, Christ pointed out that demon possession was *always* the opposite of God's desire for an individual by rebuking those religious leaders who thought he was casting them out according to the will of the Devil. Christ also reproved these detractors because they failed to understand that consistency of behavior is a characteristic even of Satan, i.e., when He stated that if Satan were divided against himself then Satan's kingdom could not stand. The obvious implication is that neither is Christ divided against *His* kingdom. Despite such Scriptures, Boettner, since he claims that God ordains "all the activities of reprobates and demons," must ascribe to God both demon possession *and* exorcism. Boettner is no renegade Calvinist here; he is simply following his dialectical principles as far as he dares. Consequently, Boettner must view demon possession and exorcism as the ordained purposes of God. The freedom, then, that Boettner's Calvinism allots to God is really a freedom for God to act against Himself. The question here begs itself: Which group—the supporters of Calvin, or the detractors of Calvin—is maintaining a fictional theology with unbiblical statements about Christ's attitude (properly speaking, *attitudes*) toward demon possession? Apparently, for Boettner, God must ordain the demon possession that he might ordain its exorcism, that he might ordain its possession, that he might ordain its exorcism, etc., *ad infinitum*. We must ask, then, how God's *attitudes* towards demon possession can claim to be finalized or 'unified' apart from contradiction? To maintain the Boettner/Calvin model, God must be Someone who seesaws back and forth in a good/evil and love/hate relationship with man, since He ordains both the possession and exorcism of demons in regards to people. Thus, since God's actions are contradictory, nothing conclusive can be said about God's character. Now observe that this ambiguity in God's character is exactly the component of Christianity that Herman Melville was criticizing in "The Whiteness of the Whale." And what a shame it is that it takes a secular, mocking author to show the vast majority of Evangelicals what their God's character ought to be, and what the fundamental problem of their theology is![4] If Boettner's Calvinism is to believed, God even furthers the absurd by then insisting that men act according to concepts and ideals of absolutism and exclusivity, principles to which God does not even subject Himself. And even if, in defense of his view, Boettner were to quote, say, Psalm 100:5 to defend God's character, i.e., that "the Lord is *good,*" his argument would be meaningless, since the term 'good' ultimately finds its definition in God's character. And since God's character is revealed in His actions, the statement, *"God is good,"* can have no meaning, since under Calvinism God's moral character is itself contradictory and therefore inconclusive.

Despite Boettner's willingness to qualify Calvinistic statements in subsequent pages, paragraphs, or even the next sentence without showing a real sense of dilemma, other Calvinists have been more hesitant about the 'seeming' contradiction in Calvinism. R.C. Sproul, for example, also believes that the 'freedom of slavery' is due to the predetermination of God. Yet, Sproul knows that if men are not able to create their own choices, then a problem arises as to the origin of sin. For if God is truly the foreordainer of all events and experience, Sproul knows that God must "in some sense" be the agent responsible for sin.[xx] Sproul, it is assumed, would not be satisfied with the kind of arguments that Boettner proposes in a chapter sub-division called, "Calvinism Offers A More Satisfactory Solution of the Problem of Evil Than Does Any Other System," in which Boettner makes an assertion which seems incredulous even for him:

> . . . and while other systems are found to be wholly inadequate in their explanation of sin, Calvinism can give a fairly adequate explanation in that it recognizes that God is ultimately responsible since He could have prevented it.[xxi]

Thus Boettner actually states that God is responsible for sin! A few sentences later, however, Boettner again retracts his position on the absolute sovereignty of God in order to 'reconcile' his statement so that God is *not* responsible for sin:

> In regard to the first fall of man, we assert that the **proximate** cause was the instigation of the Devil and the impulse of his own heart; and when we have established this, we have removed the **blame** from God.[xxii] (author's emphasis)

So the reigns are pulled up after all, and we recoil back upon personal freedom, lest we jeopardize God's holy character by implicating him in sin. We are on the rocking horse in to and fro motion, but we fail to move because we are haltered between two opinions. This to and fro motion that Boettner demonstrates in the same paragraph is a never-ending ride. The tension of qualifying coils always limits the movement of the horse from going too far in either direction, and because the horse cannot stop to rest at either of its polar positions it must stop in the middle. Thus the Calvinist continues his ride *ad infinitum* until he has exhausted his energy in trying to ride out the contradiction. Finally, he declares the polar positions of the horse to be reconciled by tension, brings the horse to its synthesized (dialectical) center, and gets off. These long rides of to and fro motion is why Calvinistic treatises on the subject of predestination tend to be so repetitive. With the problem of evil, then, readers go back and forth while Boettner tells them that "we have removed blame from God" even though four sentences earlier he said that "God is ultimately responsible for it"!

The problem of keeping God's holiness intact is thus a problem taken more seriously by R.C. Sproul in his book, *Chosen By God*. Although I cited a more complete quote earlier, I think part of it is worth repeating:

> I am afraid that most Christians do not realize the profound severity of this problem. Skeptics have called this issue the "Achilles' Heel of Christianity." . . . For years I sought the answer to this problem, scouring the works of theologians and philosophers. I found some clever attempts at resolving the problem, but, as yet, have never found a deeply satisfying answer.[xxiii]

No doubt Sproul recognizes that such statements as Boettner's simply *state* that the contradiction is true rather than demonstrate it from the Bible. In passing, one should note that other analogies have also been devised to explain Calvinism: thus a coin, or a cross with a sign on it, is said to have on one side, "whosoever will may come," yet on the other side, "foreordained before the foundation of the world." Nevertheless, the problem with such analogies is that a two-sided coin, like a six-sided die, is not a contradictory object at all. Rather, in order to solve the standing contradiction one would have to devise a fictional object and explain it as (for example) one separate coins that are two separate coin in which the heads and tails are both on the only side! Did the syntax of that last sentence throw you for a loop? That was because the singular and the plural were indistinct in their reference to the nouns and verbs. This is actually the language hidden in Calvinism and in any other theology or ideology that builds itself around a contradiction. Regarding the dialectical method of Calvinism that we have been examining here, the concept of God's absolute sovereignty is grasped by the mind long enough so that even when synthesized with its exact opposite thought, i.e., man's free will, there is enough memory activated in our minds to imagine the premise of each idea, even though each premise logically cancels the other one out. Thus, it seems as though the two concepts exist as proofs against each other while remaining coexistent in the mind. The reason, then, that many Christians do not feel the pressure of their Calvinistic theology is because Calvinism's synthesis is presented slowly enough to facilitate memory. In effect, they are *imagined* to be true by being held in the mind by a multi-task mental operation, as though that act itself proved the principle of dialecticism. Jarring contradictions in Calvinistic statements are avoided (such as, "God causes all events, but not sinful events,") and so people are lulled to a rock-a-bye sleep on a dialectical seesaw instead of being jerked off the board.

In the Synod of Dort (ca. 1618, when the five points of Calvinism were codified) and in the Westminster Confessions (1647), this mistaken assumption, i.e., that because both sides of the contradiction can be separately imagined they are somehow proved, was aided by clever language. Notice, for example, the rather passive phrase, "whatsoever comes to pass," in the statement, "God from all eternity, did, by the most wise and holy counsel of his own will, freely, and unchangeably ordain whatsoever comes to pass…" As written, the statement, "whatsoever comes to pass" sounds like *whatsoever happens by itself*, as though *whatsoever* was a 3rd party besides God and man. Thus, the sovereignty of God is diminished lingually enough to allow for the free will side of the equation. I'm not saying here that the Westminster Confessors sat around *consciously* conspiring about what language to use. But certainly the natural tension of their ideological synthesis would have led them toward phrases that sounded less definite than those which could have been used. The phrase "God did…ordain whatsoever comes to pass" could have been put stronger, i.e. that "God causes everything that happens." But the game would be up with language so blunt, because Christians would reject that kind of theology out of hand. All of the Calvinist authors whose books or articles I have read use language that often avoids the word *"cause."* Instead, they usually bring to bear nearly every other possible word and phrase that means *cause*, but in a less direct way (i.e., as implied in the words *controlled, determined, ordained, decreed*, etc.). For to consistently use the word *cause* for the purpose of audience persuasion would mean rocking forward too hard on the rocking horse and ending one's ride with an embarrassing frontal somersault over the horse's head. No one (we certainly hope) would believe the Calvinists' contradiction if such unmitigated language was consistently used to support their doctrine of an all-sovereign God. Consequently, the language used is often subtler. Small wonder, then, that the Bible so strongly condemns the wrangling of words which brings destruction to its hearers.[5] [xxiv]

Footnotes:

[2] According to Discipleship Journal Magazine, Joni Eareckson (popular Christian inspirational speaker who, as a teenager, became a quadriplegic after a diving accident), when asked what one book besides the Bible she would recommend that someone read, answered, "*The Reformed Doctrine of Predestination*, by Loraine Boettner." Eareckson says the book gave her great comfort following her accident.

[3] Please chpt. 18, footnote 140, which discusses more exactly what I mean, in saying that the Calvinist's terms are *meaningless*.

[4] And what solution, on the whole, have Evangelicals offered in the 150 years since Melville has pointed out this fault?

[5] One marvels at the absence of dilemma which seems to attend (Calvinist author) Jerry Bridges's statement on page 84 of his book: "The second observation we can make is that God sometimes *causes* government leaders or officials to make foolish decisions in order to bring judgment upon a nation." If Bridges is right, by what moral authority does God Himself judge foolishness?

Endnotes:

[xii] Boettner, Loraine. *The Reformed Doctrine of Predestination*.
(n.p.: The Presbyterian and Reformed Publishing Company, 1968, 14th printing). p. 319.

[xiii] Boettner, p. 13: "God is seen as the great and mighty King who has appointed the course of nature and who directs the course of history even down to its minutest details. His decree is eternal, unchangeable, holy, wise, and sovereign. It extends not merely to the course of the physical world but to every event in human history from the creation to the judgment, and includes all the activities of saints and angels in heaven and of reprobates and demons in hell. It embraces the whole scope of creaturely existence, through time and eternity, comprehending at once all things that ever were or will be in their causes, conditions, successions, and relations."

[xiv] Boettner, p. 319.

[xv] Boettner, p. 212.

[xvi] Boettner, p. 213.

[xvii] Boettner, p. 229.

[xviii] Boettner, pp. 31-32.

[xix] Boettner, p. 228 "And while it is not ours to explain how God in His secret counsel rules and overrules the sinful acts of men, it is ours to know that whatever God does He never deviates from His own perfect justice." It remains a mystery to me why Boettner would feel that God's "perfect justice" involves the determination that men sin, regardless if God later "overrules" the sin.

[xx] Sproul, p. 31. As noted later regarding how James Spiegel states that the Bible student must not back away from either statement within the "compatibilist" view (but then immediately violates his own statement by using backpedaling

language so that God's sovereignty is at first called *complete*, but immediately afterward merely called *strong*), so Sproul, too, as soon as he states that God in some sense has foreordained sin, backpedals to stating that this merely means that God has "allowed" sin. Says Sproul: "We know that God is sovereign because we know that God is God. Therefore we must conclude that God foreordained sin. What else can we conclude? We must conclude that God's decision to allow sin to enter the world was a good decision. This is not to say that our sin is really a good thing, but merely that God's allowing us to do sin, which is evil, is a good thing."

[xxi] Boettner, p. 251.

[xxii] Boettner, p. 251.

[xxiii] Sproul, p. 28.

[xxiv] 2 Timothy 2:14.

Chapter 5
Man and the Origin of Sin

Because Calvinists accept a system that makes it impossible to say anything conclusive about the character of God, neither can they say anything *definite* about the character of man. For if God's character is the yardstick (so to speak) by which 'good' and 'evil' are measured, and yardstick markings too confused to read, then it is impossible to say whether man himself is doing good or evil. Morally then, man remains unfinalized, and it cannot even be stated that he sins. Indeed, even the idea that a man *could* sin in an act of self-determination is a problem for Calvinists. For the very presence of sin implies a will other than God's holy will at work. Thus in the following passage Boettner's view that sin is "illogical and unreasonable" is his attempt to put the discussion of sin, and especially the question as to who is responsible for its origin, into a realm that discourages discussion:

To begin with, we readily admit that the existence of sin in a universe which is under the control of God who is infinite in His wisdom, power, holiness, and justice, is an inscrutable mystery which we in our present state of knowledge cannot fully explain. As yet we only see through a glass darkly. Sin can never be explained on the grounds of logic or reason, for it is essentially illogical and unreasonable.[xxv]

To avoid a conclusion that would destroy God's absolute sovereignty, Boettner thus puts his explanation of sin beyond language and reason. We are told that sin is an "inscrutable mystery" which is "illogical" and "unreasonable." So the impression left by Boettner upon the reader is that man is not responsible for its causation (even as, indeed, man cannot be responsible for *any* causation). Thus man's moral character is never really granted a status. This loss in defining the identity of God, man, and sin, is what has produced blurred statements from Boettner such as the following:

The motive which God has in permitting it [sin] and the motive which man has in committing it are radically different. Many persons are deceived in these matters because they fail to consider that God wills righteously those things which men do wickedly.[xxvi]

The first thing that jumps out at us in the above passage is Boettner's backpedaling use of the word "permitting," in reference to God *permitting* sin. One wonders how divine 'permitting' fits in with God irresistibly ruling and overruling all phenomena! Then, of course, Boettner seesaws his language by saying that "God wills righteously those things which men do wickedly." Boettner here is proposing something different from what Genesis 50:20 means, when it gives us Joseph's reply to his brothers, i.e., "ye thought evil against me; but God meant it unto good..." For Joseph was not saying that God created the jealousy in his brothers' hearts—i.e., "it"—but that God had prompted them to sell him (Joseph) into slavery to the Egyptians. The selling of Joseph into slavery is the "it." (For note the preceding context of Genesis 50:15, in which the brothers express fear for "all the wrong which we **did to** him." People normally speak this way when describing their *actions* **done** *against*, not their *ill-feelings toward*, someone, though here of course the latter led to the former.) Taken by itself, it was not a wrong act for God to prompt Joseph's brothers to sell Joseph into slavery. Sin only arose when Joseph's brothers attached their own *additional* agenda of hatred to God's desire that Joseph be a slave. Designating Joseph for slavery was not an immoral act of God, since God had even commanded that Abraham sacrifice his own son. It is a hard saying, but every believer who has received the forgiveness of sins and stands to inherit the kingdom of God owes his very *life* to God—so, if God wishes that such a man be a slave in this life in order that good may result, it is no wrong to him. After all, God is not asking the man to sin, but only to serve. And such suffering of the man is not worthy to be compared with the glory that shall be revealed in him in the afterlife. (Easy to say, harder to believe and to live one's life with such faith accordingly!) The maliciousness, then, of Joseph's brothers was their *own* addendum that had nothing to do with God's desire that Joseph be sold into slavery. Joseph was not really excusing his brothers for their jealousy, because he later states that their intention was that his enslavement would cause him harm. (See chpt. 17 about the Assyrian King adding his own addendum to God's agenda). Because Boettner, however, believes that the very thoughts and *intents* of people's souls are created, he must also believe that God created the sinful jealousy within Joseph's brothers. Perhaps Boettner thinks God's agenda is dependent upon such jealously, though it seems to me that God's plan could have been conveyed, for example, through a divinely-given, shared dream. Thus, to excuse God, Boettner's apologetic becomes one of pure bias. In effect, he states that God is right because he is God, as though this were any real explanation of the origin of sin. And so Boettner's apologetic is simply reduced to a *pro Deo/ ad hominem* argument—i.e., God is right because He is God, and man is wrong because he is man. In fact, the essence of his Calvinistic argument is nothing more nor less than this.

The tremendous problems that arise from such a Calvinistic view regarding the absolute sovereignty of God, the problem of evil, and the moral indeterminacy of both God and man should be somewhat apparent by now. In order to solve these problems Calvinistic authors have appealed to the Bible, claiming support. The reason I have not focused as much attention on specific Bible verses disproving Calvinism up to this point in the book, is because I believed it would be useful to first point out that no one picks up the Bible without having certain presuppositions about the nature of God and His Word. These presuppositions influence the way we interpret and understand Scripture. These presuppositions, in fact, are why there are different theologies within Evangelicalism, and why Evangelicals are offering the world two very different views of God. Of course, the goal of the Christian should always be to realign his presuppositions with what the Bible really teaches. No one said this process would be easy, but until Evangelicals rightly divide the Word of Truth, their apologetic to the world will remain appallingly weak.[6] At the risk of sounding cavalier, if men are going to damn themselves in unbelief, Christians ought to at least make sure that what they disbelieve is the truth. It would be an ironic tragedy if an unsaved man rejected the Bible for what, in fact, proved to be an unbiblical idea.[7] Even so, to whatever extent men thus reject God because Evangelicals fail to give a biblically rational answer about why bad things happen in a world that God created, they become responsible for such men's damnation to that extent.

Footnotes:

[6] Unless the Word of God is rightly divided, it will affect not only the Christian, but also the Christian's effective use of his gift when attempting to minister to the Body.

[7] In his *Autobiography* Benjamin Franklin tells of his interest in the Christian religion, until its contradictory premises of divine predestination and human freedom led him to exasperatingly abandon it for more practical applications of knowledge. Thomas Paine, pamphleteer, and a Deist like Franklin, spoke approvingly of Franklin's abandonment in a scathing indictment of Romans 9:18-21, which Paine directed "to the Ministers of the Calvinist Church." Interestingly enough, Paine held the same mistaken assumption as his Calvinist contemporaries, i.e., that Paul espoused Reprobation in his use of the metaphor of the Pot and the Potter. In concluding his remarks Paine states:[1]

> Doctor Franklin gives a remarkable instance of the truth of this, in an account of his life, written by himself. He was in London at the time of which he speaks. "Some volumes," says he, against Deism, fell into my hands. They were said to be the substance of Sermons preached at Boyle's Lectures. It happened that they produced on me an effect precisely the reverse of what was intended by the writers; for the arguments of the Deists, which were cited in order to be refuted, appeared to me more forcible than the refutation itself. In a word I soon became a perfect Deist.

> Another famous Deist, Voltaire, similarly rejected the professing Christianity of his era, which he essentially took to be synonymous with both Catholicism and Calvinism. Following the great earthquake in 1755 that destroyed Lisbon, Portugal, Voltaire wrote a friend:

> One would have great difficulty in divining how the laws of movement operate such frightful disasters in the *best of all possible worlds*.... What will the preachers say, especially if the palace of the Inquisition has been left standing? I

flatter myself that the reverend father inquisitors will have been crushed like the others. That should teach men not to persecute men.

Thomas S. Vernon, commenting on this letter in his book, *Voltaire* (1989), describes the French philosopher's reaction against the religious assumptions of the Optimism of his day:[2]

The italicized phrase is a reference to Gottfried Leibniz, the German philosopher who, in 1710, had published a work explaining that the evil and suffering we witness are necessary features of a world which otherwise would not be as perfect as it is. This was a popular view among philosophers and theologians of the time: our limited minds cannot grasp reality as it is perceived by an infinite, benevolent, and all-powerful God who, out of an infinite number of possible worlds, has created the best that could be. This is one way of dealing with what is known in the history of thought as the problem of evil: ... Theodore Besterman reminds us that "in this context optimism has nothing to do with one's outlook on life; it is the belief that all that is and happens is for the best." Indeed to some thinkers, including Voltaire, the Leibnizian view makes for the deepest sort of pessimism, for if we were obliged to believe that the conditions of human life we see about us are the best that is possible—even under the management of an omnipotent and omnibenevolent God then we have good reason to be discouraged, not only about this life but about the life to come as well.

Hence Leibniz embraced the same Optimism which today goes under the name 'the greater good theodicy,' as described, e.g., by Calvinist James Spiegel in his book, *The Benefits of Providence*, which we will examine in a later chapter.

[1] [www.infidels.org/library/historical/thomas_paine/predestination.html].
[2] [http://www.positiveatheism.org/hist/voltvern.htm].

Endnotes:

[xxv] Boettner, p. 228.

[xxvi] Boettner, p. 229.

Chapter 6
Translation as Interpretation

All Evangelicals believe that the Bible is inerrant in its original autographa, and, indeed, the historical evidence for the reliability of the Bible far outweighs any other ancient document. Generally speaking, Evangelicals also trust how translators have handled the Scriptures. Bible translators must have language skills, a knowledge of how language and specific words were used in the contemporary culture in which the document was written, a feel for the author's voice, and an awareness of the danger of injecting their own personality and beliefs into the text.

It would be a mistake, however, to think that because translators are aware of these responsibilities it makes them naturally immune to any subjectivity in their own translations. Are journalists really objective in their political reporting or archaeologists unbiased in their interpretation of excavation findings? Like everyone else, translators are likewise prone to working their own presuppositions into their translation work, however unwitting.[8]

Consider also, for example, the tendency of many pastors you and I know in our respective locales. These men study to preach the Bible weekly, and like many other Evangelical pastors outside our local regions, they appear to believe what the Westminster Confessions states about God's absolute sovereignty existing alongside human freedom. Suppose, then, that any one of these pastors had been a proofreading translator under King James I of England at the beginning of the 17th century. And suppose too that in the course of proofing the translation they read the rendering of Romans 9:22: "What if God, willing to show his wrath, and to make his power known, endured with much longsuffering the vessels of wrath fitted to destruction…" Do you suppose as believers in God's absolute sovereignty (sometimes called God's *providence*) these pastors would render the verse any differently from what, in fact, the actual King James translators did? Note the phrase in verse 22: "…[God] endured with much longsuffering vessels of wrath fitted for destruction…" In this verse the King James translators rendered the verb "fit" in the passive voice, since the spelling of the verb appears as a perfect passive participle. Yet the exact Greek spelling of this verb is rendered the same way in the middle voice, which means that the verb "fitted" in the phrase "fitted for destruction" could just as easily have been translated to reflect a state of being which the vessels brought upon themselves (especially given the context). Now supposing further that these pastors knew that the Greek verb "fitted" was spelled the same way in the middle voice as in the perfect passive, and thus *could* be translated differently, i.e., "vessels of wrath who fitted themselves for destruction"—

do you suppose they would have translated it thus? What compelling reason would they have for choosing to put the verb in the middle voice? In fact, to do so might imply that man was self-determinative and that God was not really absolutely sovereign over people's choices. Naturally, as translators under the influence of Calvinism faced with a ticklish passage like Romans 9, they would want the verb rendered so it would be consistent with what they believed the Bible taught. Furthermore, even if they were not a follower of Calvin and *were* to translate it correctly, they would still have to know that Greek participles, like "fitted" in Romans 9:22, are spelled the same way in the middle voice as they are in the perfect passive.

But this same spelling in the middle voice seems as ignored today as it was then. I myself only know about this spelling because someone shared it with me from a radio program he had heard. Admittedly, all of us Christians—pastors and translators included—have gaps in our knowledge, and we should not be overly faulted for not knowing everything there is to know. But why the general ignorance about "fitted vessels?" The point here is that I don't know of even *one Bible translation* that renders Romans 9:22 in the middle voice. In fact, I don't even know of one Bible version that mentions the middle voice as a *possibility* in a *marginal* note. How many translators does *that* represent? The monolithic agreement with the Calvinistic view that vessels are "fitted for destruction," i.e., as though *God* had fitted them, is universal in all extant English Bible translations, so far as I know. No wonder why Christians are so adamant about their Calvinistic leanings; their responsibility is to believe the Bible, isn't it? Even Spiros Zodiates in his generally helpful *Greek-Key Study Bible* fails to mention this possible rendering in Romans 9:22, though verbs in the text have coded abbreviations that are referenced back to a prefix page which shows that he includes the middle voice indication.[9] In light of all this, I must admit I smiled a bit when an online Calvinist, discussing the phrase in Acts 13:48, i.e., "And as many as were ordained unto salvation believed," remarked that the overwhelming preference by translators retained the word "ordained," and that the only real preference in translation for "predisposed" was the New World Version by the Jehovah's Witnesses! Such unbounded confidence in Christian translators might be understandable, but in light of how Romans 9:22 has been translated, it does not appear prudent. In fact, a few years later, I discovered that the word "ordained" in Acts 13:48 is also, like "fitted" in Romans 9:22, a 'perfect passive participle,' and should have been translated in the middle voice.

One might imagine, then, what I used to think as a Calvinist when reading the phrase "vessels of wrath fitted for destruction." It appeared to me that God didn't see fit to extend His mercy to certain people (for reasons unknown to me). Naturally, I had to brush off the paradox this verse implied, i.e., that God had to *endure* these vessels that He Himself had ordained for destruction according to His own self-satisfied plan. (Calvinists claim that since God ordains all things, everything that comes to pass is according to His good pleasure).

I view Romans 9:22 differently now. It just seems biblically *logical* that the verse should read, "What if God...who endured with much patience vessels of wrath which fitted themselves for destruction..." *Biblical* logic is not a bad thing, though admittedly *logic* has taken a fall in reputation among Christians for a long time. In general Christians have questioned *logic* at least since the time of the Enlightenment. During that period of history, man's reason was often extolled as the final authority in matters of science *and* religion. Of course, in one sense Christians have been right to be skeptical about man's logic, for history has shown that such 'logic' as applied to the interpretation of archaeology and history has hardly been objective or supportive of the Bible. Yet, it remains true that God is the author of all real logic. Thus when translators rendered Romans 9:22 to read that God *endured* those vessels that He Himself fit for destruction, how did they come to find logic in that? Should not that contradiction of logic have caused them to examine further the Greek possibilities for a non-contradictory rendering?

Consider, too, how God defines logic in Isaiah 5:20: "Woe unto them that call evil good and good evil, that put darkness for light and light for darkness, that put bitter for sweet and sweet for bitter." The logic defined by this verse means that evil cannot also be good. A university class in formal logic would put it thus:

A cannot equal non-A. Paul repeated the same thought when he rhetorically asked in 2 Corinthians 6:14b-15a: "what fellowship hath righteousness with unrighteousness? and what communion hath light with darkness? And what concord hath Christ with Belial?" So the question begs itself: Why would God tell us to think in *either/or* terms but then settle our apologetic on the kind of *both/and* dialectical statement held by the Westminster Confessions? The *both/and* (doublethink) of Calvinism affects one's interpretation of the Bible in many places (technically in all places). I believe it also affected the way KJV translators translated certain other phrases in the Bible besides Romans 9:22.

Though we will discuss portions of Romans 8—9 in more detail later, consider for now one more example of a questionable translation—the well-known phrase in Romans 8:28: "all things work together for good to them that love God." How many Christians (including myself) memorized this verse toward the latter end of the 350+ years in which the KJV was used in every place from Anglican High Church pulpits to American backyard children's Bible clubs? Many people similar to me grew up believing that somehow, inexplicably, all things worked together to produce good for the believer. Again, that would mean *everything*. And everything includes Christ and Satan, light and darkness, righteousness and unrighteousness. Did someone lie about your reputation at work? Has college ruined your son or daughter so that he or she now finds your Christianity embarrassing and meaningless? Did your spouse finally admit to a long-term affair? Not to worry—for if the King James translators are to be believed, then all these things are working together for your good. (At least that's what mainline, Evangelical commentary has accepted as the KJV's intent.) So, taking into account Isaiah 5:20, Romans 8:28, and 2 Corinthians 6:14b-15a, what are we left with?—apparently a Bible that claims in 1 Corinthians 6 that righteousness and unrighteousness can have *no* communion, while stating in Romans 8 that good and evil are working *cooperatively* to produce good for the believer!

This contradiction of good and evil things working together is not something that is likely to bother the Calvinist very much. After all, if God foreordains all events there *must* be a sense in which God approves of all history, since it is ordered after the counsel of His good will and pleasure. Again, in effect, *Whatever is, is right*, as the poet Alexander Pope expressed it (apparently even when it *isn't* right!). To what kind of 'Romans 8:28 theology,' then, does John Calvin actually invite me as a follower of God? Just this—one where I find myself at the end of most days not worrying too much about anything I did, since all the means of all my actions are ultimately working for my good anyway. In fact, despite Paul's admonition in Romans 6 that I ought not to sin for the purpose of making grace abound, I see no reason to worry *that* much if I grow lackadaisical in my moral behavior, since even sin serves the purposes of God. I might even conclude that grace *necessitates* sin, since grace wouldn't have any opportunities to exist were it not for sin. Perhaps this explains why I recently heard a president of a major Reformed seminary state on the radio that the sin of man praises God.

EXAMPLES OF SOVEREIGNTY?

Perhaps that president's attitude also explains the behavior of two Christian men I knew who once justified their behavior by appealing to an all-sovereign God. One of these men was a pastor of the church in which I had been raised. This pastor had graduated from what many would consider is the 'Harvard' of Evangelical seminaries, though his Calvinistic perspective upon his arrival at our church was relatively new to many of the church's Methodist-influenced parishioners. At one point, however, this pastor fell into an adulterous relationship with another woman in the church. Moreover, the pastor and the woman with whom he was having an affair each had a spouse and children, and so their sin affected two entire families (not to mention the church). When the pastor was eventually confronted by two of the church's elders his reply was enigmatic. How, he asked, could he have really done otherwise? Could he actually have frustrated God, who, in some sense, had already predestined every event that had come to pass?

The second example of a man I knew who appealed to God's sovereignty was the president of the small Reformed Christian college I attended. During one particular spring semester (many years ago) he proposed budgeting the college's future resources by reorienting monies away from the Liberal Arts departments to help fund the Engineering and Science departments. Apparently, he thought the college should depart from its long-standing commitment to the humanities in order to respond to the growing market of technologies, thereby drawing more students into the college. His new proposal led to great dissent among many of the faculty and students on campus. A question and answer session between the president and students was arranged in hopes to quell the unrest. At the appointed day, students crowded into the upper lobby of the student center. The atmosphere was tense. After numerous questions were raised the president concluded one of his answers by appealing to the sovereignty of God. "Even if the new proposal is put into motion with misgivings, or in some sense is found wanting," said the president, "we can still rest in the knowledge that God is sovereign over the decisions of men." Hearing this statement, Mick,[10] an older student, immediately shot out from where he had been standing near a side wall, and, pointing at the president, cried out with an intense voice, "This is *man's* will and *man's* decision; don't make this out to be God's will!" Despite his anger the point was made, and it was met with loud, spontaneous applause and approving shouts (all this, by the way, at a *Reformed* college). Though Mick later confessed to me that he felt terrible about chastising the president in public and believed he had been wrong to do so, his remarks underscore, I think, the continuing frustration many of us feel as we confront an Evangelical mindset that has been locked in doublethink and doublespeak for far too long. Mick was right; God's will is *not* being perfectly worked out in all of man's decisions; indeed, God's will is *not* being done on earth as it is in heaven, as the Lord's Prayer plainly tells us.

So what do we do with Romans 8:28? Was the president of the college correct to imply that God works *everything* according to His plan for those who love Him? Are we forced to accept this verse as teaching the idea that good and evil work together, even though Paul says elsewhere that certain things cannot have *any* communion with each other? Says seminary professor, Tim Geddert, regarding the general impression Romans 8:28 once made on him:

...there was a time when I interpreted this verse to mean that there really are no "bad things" that happen to believers. If things *seem* bad, but really serve to fulfill God's purposes, then even these things are ultimately good... (as though there is some deep magic in the universe that somehow creates the hidden "good" pattern out of all the "bad" pieces.)[11]

Geddert points out that since the beginning of the 17th century English translators have differed about whether the subject noun of Romans 8:28 was 'God,' or 'all things' (both are grammatically possible). The KJV settled on "all things," the NIV on "God." Geddert explains how Romans 8:28 could have been translated differently. He believes the NIV treatment is a more accurate translation than the KJV, i.e., "In all things, God works for the good of those who love him..." But Geddert notes something else in Romans 8:28. The verb *sunergei* (from which we get the English word *synergy*) is used four times in the New Testament (Mk. 16:20; 1 Cor. 16:16; 2 Cor. 6:1; Ja. 2:22) and always means two or more entities or parties working together as a team. The first three passages show God working with people or people working with each other cooperatively. The fourth is used metaphorically to describe how faith and works work together in consort. Says Geddert:

> I have before me a new edition of the NIV. It contains two footnotes to this verse...The second says this: "OR...works together with those who love him to bring about what is good..." This way of reading the verse still views "God" as the subject of the verb "works together." However, on this reading "those who love God" are not the *beneficiaries* of God interventions; they are God's *co-workers*! Romans 8:28 is not about God working to bring about good things *for us* (though God also does that!); Romans 8:28 is about God working *with us* to bring about good things...
>
> There is yet another possibility. Sometimes the grammar of a Greek sentence is ambiguous (technically it is called polyvalent). More than one grammatical option is possible and both meanings are intended. Perhaps the verse is about God working both *with us* and *for us* to bring about good things in tough situations.

So, then, as Geddert points out, the traditional interpretation of the key phrase "all things work together" in Romans 8:28 as found in the AV (Authorized Version, i.e., KJV) was never really biblical.[12] For if all things without limitation worked together, that would mean righteousness works with unrighteousness, Christ works with Belial, and light works with darkness, etc., when, in fact, these persons or acts of persons are moral opposites which have no shared goal. It is surprising, is it not, that as well known as Romans 8:28 and 2 Corinthians 6:14-15 are to many churchgoers, not to mention the average translator, that the discrepancy between these verses has received very little attention? Many Christians seem to have sided with Calvinism so long that contradictions in logic no longer bother them. It's rather like the purple-turtle-in-the-sky theology all over again (see chpt. 2). Christians come face to face with a biblical discrepancy that forces them in one of two directions. Either they will solve the KJV's Romans 8:28/2 Corinthians 6:14-15 contradiction with irrationality and allow the contradiction to remain, *or* they will look further into Scripture to see what went wrong in the translation and interpretation of one or both of these passages, to prove there is no contradiction. So far, mainline Evangelicalism has taken the uncritical route.

IS A KEY PRESUMPTION FUELING THE DEBATE?

Frankly speaking, Calvinism has gotten a lot of mileage out of readers' inference from the AV's rendering of Romans 8:28. I once knew an elderly Presbyterian woman who said that she hung onto this verse for all it was worth, after her son, a young WWII veteran, unexpectedly committed suicide while in his mid 20s. Her son, raised in church where he heard many sermons from the pulpit, though apparently none that explained the Hebrew distinctions in the Old Testament words 'kill' and 'murder,' went away to war at age 17 convinced that killing the enemy was still a violation of the sixth commandment ('Thou shalt not kill'). Apparently at some subconscious level he believed there was no such thing as a 'just war.' He then fought in three companies where every soldier but him was either killed or wounded out of action. When the war was over, he came back to the States and eventually developed signs of post-traumatic stress. Finally, he moved from the East Coast to California, and one day someone found him in a closed-up garage with the car running and with a suicide note next to him on the car seat. Now I ask you—What caring pastor six months after this young man's death wouldn't want to be able to tell the still grieving mother that somehow even this tragedy would somehow ultimately work together for her good? What biblical counselor wouldn't have wanted the KJV rendering of Romans 8:28 in his back pocket when trying to comfort this same woman five years later because her infant granddaughter died after a two-year battle with liver disease? Perhaps this woman had even learned of Romans 8:28 from *her* mother who had once lost three small children to scarlet fever within a month. This woman—like other Christians who seem to have a penchant for practical daily faith—will find some way to get through the day. But not all Christians are so inclined. Indeed, a few end up in garages with the car running, having committed the kind of act that Dietrich Bonhoeffer once described as someone's last attempt to give human meaning to what has become for them a meaningless human existence.

To be sure, tragedy still mocks even those who know their trials are tied to the fact that they live in a fallen world in which God did not necessarily design the circumstances they face. Yet I wonder how many of us would still pose the "Why God?" question if some personal disaster came knocking on our door. Personally, I think almost certainly I would. And so I find myself praying "O Lord, I believe that Romans 8:28 does not mean what the traditional interpreters say it does about all things working together; help thou mine unbelief." Yes, I want to be done with candy-coating the Bible, because such gloss-overs have never really led anyone to the truth. Today the Church wonders why some Christians sail through difficulties full of 'faith' while others cool off in their spiritual ardor at an almost imperceptible pace and for reasons not even clear to themselves. The problem may be that the Bible is perceived by these latter folk as guaranteeing to meet their needs, though, we note, only on an illogical basis [since Romans 8:28 (KJV) remains (as traditionally interpreted, at least) in standing contradiction to 1 Corinthians 6:14-15]. And so this dilemma gnaws at such persons' minds until the raw nerve-ends of doubt are exposed. Yet in one sense what is actually happening to these believers is that their faith is being tested in the midst of what they imagine is a withdrawal from God. And in fact they are withdrawing from a *false* view of God rather than embracing it, though they simply do not realize it. Instead they find themselves depressed, separated from the assembly and wondering what has happened to their faith. Yet, had they followed the Evangelical party line about the absolute sovereignty of God, it would merely have led to their worshiping something else in addition to the God of the Bible. Despite, then, what other illegitimate reasons there may be for the 'cooling off' of some Christians, it would appear in such cases these persons are closer in their walk with God than many of us imagine. Meanwhile, the Church has yet to test a truly biblical model that *fully* ministers truth to such grieving persons facing the problem of evil.

Footnotes:

[8] And yet Christians so often quote controversial passages as though translations were as infallible as the autographa.

[9] The problem, of course, is that the average reader won't realize that participles coded as perfect passive appear the same way when spelled in the middle voice.

[10] Not his real name. These statements are given in their essence and according to memory.

[11] "Another Look at Romans 8:28." [http://mbseminary.edu/main/articles/geddert1.htm], 1999.

[12] A third possibility of translation may be that "all things" refers to the list of things Paul immediately gives in 8:29-30, i.e., God's foreknowledge, predestination to conformity to the Son, calling [naming **out** from among (Gr. *ekalese*)], justification, and glorification of the believer, all of which could be said to be working together for the same goal, i.e., the good of the believer. In such a case the period at the end of Romans 8:28 would require a colon in translation (the autographa of the New Testament was without punctuation) so that the "all things" could be contextually understood to have this limited meaning, as opposed to "all things" in the world, which would include sin, the Devil, etc., none of which or whom share any commonality (in the synergistic sense) with Christ or His cause. Observe that absent punctuation in the autographa sometimes makes it possible for the Spirit to lead the reader into a multi-leveled understanding of certain passages. One such result is that Romans 8:28 could be considered polyvalent in meaning.

Interlude: A Personal Journey
Why I Wrote This Book

If you're a Christian who has had little or no New Testament linguistic training (or, like me, barely a year of Classical Greek), you can still evaluate many Calvinistic arguments if you have a good working knowledge of the Bible and apply it logically. This is not to say that knowing the original biblical languages is unimportant. I am merely saying that one does not need to have such knowledge to know that dialectical conclusions are always false, regardless of what appeal to Scripture a theologian may claim. Unfortunately, in today's relatively unchurched generation many Christians are prone toward accepting contradictions in their theology. To add to the problem, society's emphasis on relativism has clouded many people's judgment into accepting ideas uncritically. Thus in the jungle of today's competing philosophies and theologies, more Christians ought to be taking the attitude of the philosopher Socrates, who believed his mission in life was to test every statement to see if it were true. Yet seemingly the opposite has happened. Indeed, I continue to be amazed that certain Evangelical authors put forth statements *as though* they were hardly familiar with the Bible, or as though logic and reason were less important to Christian thinking than an apologetic appeal to divine 'mystery.'

One of the books whose Calvinistic premises I recently felt ought to be challenged was *Trusting God Even When It Hurts* by Christian author, Jerry Bridges. This book came to my attention through somewhat peculiar circumstances, and my reaction to it caused the writing of this book. We will examine the writings of a number of Calvinist authors but will park ourselves for some time on certain claims which Bridges makes about the absolute sovereignty of God. Some of his conclusions seem to draw specifically from Arthur W. Pink, a well-respected Reformed writer of a few generations ago. (We will address some of Pink's views in considerable detail in later chapters.) We will also consider in further detail the Reformed views of various authors, including Loraine Boettner, R.C. Sproul, Jonathan Edwards, and the philosophy/theology of James Spiegel (a Reformed philosophy professor). I chose these authors simply because they happened to come to my attention in the course of this study, and because they represent many of the main arguments of Calvinism.

First, we will look at some statements by Jerry Bridges. My introduction to Bridges's book began shortly after the only friend of mine with whom I discuss a full range of subjects—Christianity, art, music, philosophy, literature, and writing—told me that he no longer believed in the inerrancy of Scripture. This news shook me, but at the same time I understood that he had been facing some very difficult circumstances in life that had tried his faith. He had also become disenchanted with a well-known Reformed church in our area. Thus when I asked a certain pastor what book he would recommend for my friend, he suggested Bridges's popular book, *Trusting God Even When It Hurts*. I read through it and found most of Bridges's book devoted strongly to the Calvinistic doctrine of divine absolute sovereignty. Bridges feels this doctrine is beneficial for a person to believe, that is, if he is to understand the immanency of God's design in everything he faces. For me, however, the book had much the opposite effect. It dredged up the Reformed arguments that had caused me to write an opposing essay about Calvinism some 15 years ago, after coming out of my own Calvinistic experience. I thus felt strongly that *Trusting God* would only further my friend's disillusionment with God, and after some discussions about Bridges's book with my brother David, who felt the same way as I, we both thought a fuller statement in the form of a book ought to be written to challenge many of the Reformed assumptions about the absolute sovereignty of God. (Of course others had done this from other desired angles, but it did not seem to me that enough such books had been written.) Perhaps Jerry Bridges, R.C. Sproul, etc., are men who deeply care about people. That fact alone, however, should not exempt them or any author from critical review, especially if such persons are having considerable impact on the Christian public.

I mention all this to chiefly explain the *as we go* critical format of much of the rest of this book. Primarily, there are two approaches an author may use when trying to reach the reader. One is to map out one's position with an outline, so that the investigation follows a fairly strict sequence of points and sub-points. Of the two methods this is the more classical approach, the easiest for the reader to follow, and the one which comes naturally to those with an especial gift for teaching. Sometimes associated with this method is the modern, scholarly distaste for colored statements designed to evoke emotion in the course of argument or that would show anything of anger on the part of the writer. By avoiding such prose the author is thought to appear more objective to the Western reader, because patience is assumed to safeguard the scholar against hasty thinking and false conclusions. It should be observed, however, that such a dichotomous chasm between conviction and emotion is often absent in biblical writings. At any rate, I realize I do not have the especial gift of teaching.

The other method, the method of this book, is more in the manner of a personal, prophetic[13] warning where the message is urgent and therefore less formally structured. Here the urgency of the moment overrides the kind of left-brain approach that would take the reader upon a natural step-by-step accounting of the argument. Therefore the remainder of this work is more of a reflection of my own personal journey of discovery, especially in the past six months.[14] Neither the left-brain nor the right-brain method of presentation is superior to the other; the method preferred is simply a result of the author's particular tendencies, his specific spiritual giftedness, and what the moment calls for. Discovering truth *as we go* is somewhat analogous to what Michelangelo would do when he 'released' a statue from a slab of marble. The Renaissance sculptor would 'see' a statue encased in the marble before him, and gradually reveal it by *default*, i.e., by removing everything that was *not* the statue. Even so, by making some use of the *as we go* approach, it is hoped that the chiseling off of shavings of theological error will eventually reveal a 'statue' of truth.

Footnotes:

[13] While writing this book, I believed that "prophet" and "prophecy" had a different meaning in the N.T. than in the Old (something along the lines of "proclaimer" and "proclamation," neither necessarily divinely inspired, as in the O.T.). However, since the completion of this book and after further study, it does not appear to me that these words have changed meaning in biblical or extra-biblical writings of the Testamental periods. It appears, then, that a "prophet" was thought to be a divine spokesman, i.e., one who spoke *in front of* the one for whom he spoke; and that "prophecy" was thought to be a divinely-given message. However, I have left uncorrected and in situ other statements pertaining to prophets and prophecy in this book. One other note. It appears that the prophetic gift is closely allied to the gift of knowledge (implied in 1 Corinthians 13:2, where a link is suggested between prophecies and knowledge into mysteries). Now although I am personally uncomfortable with the idea of prophecy in today's Church, I concede the fact. And I do not agree with various arguments put forth for this gift's cessation. In fact, Paul indicates that the gift will not cease until "that which is perfect is come," namely, when we shall see "face to face." This would be that time when we are irrevocably in the presence of the bodily Christ. It is not, as some may think, when the early Church experienced a maturity derived from the completion of apostolic and apostolic-influenced writings. Rather, it is when we are "face to face." The term is derivative of the Old Testament experience of being face to face with God.

Chapter 7
Is Divine Sovereignty One or Two Wills?

In a chapter called, "Is God In Control?" Jerry Bridges (in *Trusting God Even When It Hurts*) makes a few assertions, but one which seems so obviously unbiblical to me that I wonder how it slipped by its Evangelical publisher (or was it left there intentionally?). In an extended section that supports the idea of God's absolute sovereignty, Bridges says:

> God rules as surely on earth as He does in heaven. He permits, for reasons known only to Himself, people to act contrary to and in defiance of His revealed will. But He never permits them to act contrary to His sovereign will.[xxvii]

Even occasional churchgoers, some of who attend service and say the Lord's Prayer but twice a year on the Christian holidays, may immediately observe a problem in the above quote. Despite Bridges's claim that "God rules as surely on earth as He does in heaven," the Lord's Prayer states the very opposite thought. Jesus instructs Christians to pray to the Father, "*Thy will be done on earth, as it is in heaven*" (Mt. 6:10). How much plainer could Jesus have stated the fact that the Father's will is *not* being carried out on earth as it is in heaven? Indeed, in the same prayer Jesus even instructs us to ask for forgiveness for our sins, so obviously the presence of sin on earth is enough to conclude that the moral state of earth is hardly that of heaven. According to the verso of my copy of Bridges's book, *Trusting God* has gone through 18 printings. How, I wonder, could such statements that obviously contradict the Lord's Prayer be left intact by an Evangelical author and his Evangelical publisher for 15+ years without further explanation? On the other hand the reason is not hard to grasp if we realize that Bridges, as a Calvinist, will feel compelled to maintain God's sovereignty even at the cost of having to make such a statement.

Another statement less obviously wrong but just as disturbing as the one that contradicts the Lord's Prayer, is given immediately afterward.[xxviii] Here Bridges claims that there is a 'revealed will' which men disobey, but not in a way that is contrary to God's *sovereign* will. Bridges's term, 'revealed will,' occurs for the first time in chapter 3 and remains undefined throughout the rest of the book. Presumably, by 'revealed' will, Bridges is referring to revelation, i.e., the Bible and its specific commands, such as "*Thou shalt not steal*" and/or to creation through which God reveals His power and nature such that man is responsible to Him. At any rate, Bridges certainly attempts to draw a distinction between God's *revealed* will and God's *sovereign* will, since he says that a man can act contrary to the former while not acting contrary to the latter. But therein lies the problem. For throughout his book Bridges claims repeatedly that God's sovereign will rules *every* act that takes place in the world. How, then, we ask, can it be understood that *another* kind of will other than God's *sovereign* will exists, much less be disobeyed?

The off-hand manner in which Bridges introduces the idea of God's 'revealed will' without ever defining it, as though its existence and his readers' understanding of it were already taken for granted (despite the fact that God's absolute sovereignty logically makes a *different* will of God impossible), shows how doublethinking can become so unconscious among its users that logical dilemmas are simply not felt.[15] The reason, of course, that Bridges is forced to introduce the idea of a *revealed* will of God is because he doesn't want it supposed that the *sovereign* will of God has caused men to sin. Yet Bridges knows he must admit that men sin against God, since it is obvious that sin exists. How, then, does Bridges 'solve' or 'reconcile' this problem? Simple—by *saying* that there is another will of God (i.e., a 'revealed will') that is *different* from that sovereign will of God which Bridges had repeatedly assured us earlier in his book covered every possible circumstance in regard to all the activity and will of man. Hence, we find out that God's 'revealed will' *is* apparently an exception to God's sovereignty after all.[16]

But observe that in this attempt to keep God from being blamed for sin, Bridges ends up pitting God against Himself, and so much so that we can't tell from Bridges's description *what* will of God is really in play regarding the acts of men. This inconclusive way of expressing God's will as one will and yet two different wills is something we should have anticipated of Bridges as a Calvinist, since one (and only one) will of God can account for God's absolute sovereignty, while two different wills are needed to additionally explain the existence of man's free will which causes sin. Thus Bridges has subtly changed 'rocking horses' on us, so that we hardly notice him jumping from the contradictory one with its 'polar' positions of *The Sovereign Will of God* and *The Free Will of Man* to another of the same breed, i.e., *The Sovereign Will of God* and *The Revealed Will of God*. <u>The Calvinist problem is thus recast so that the question about man and his sin becomes a discussion now seemingly centered entirely *within God*. This 'buzz' around God leaves the subtle impression that perhaps there is no contradiction about the absolute sovereignty of God, after all.</u> This is nothing more than a clever argument based on a dishonest use of language [though to Bridges's credit (if credit it be) I am certain he is unaware of it].

There is yet one more important aspect to Bridge's statement about a 'revealed' will of God. Insofar as distinctions are made by Bridges between God's *revealed* will and God's *sovereign* will, such that man's will is positionally incongruent with the one will of God *while at the same time* positionally congruent with the other will of God, a question begs itself about the nature of God's sovereignty.

For instance, assuming that the term 'revealed will' (i.e., God's revelatory will), includes Bible commands like, "*Thou shalt not steal*," then of what moral quality is God's *sovereign* will were I to steal my neighbor's TV, thereby breaking God's *revealed* will? Just this—my *in*congruency with God's *revealed* will *is* my *con*gruency with His *sovereign* will. In fact, Bridges himself says that man's defiance is never contrary to God's sovereign will. It follows logically, therefore, that God's *sovereign* command must be, "Thou *shalt* steal." By extension, then, Bridges as much as says that God's *sovereign* will is exactly *opposite* of everything the Bible teaches! At this point some of my readers are no doubt thinking to themselves, "Well, that whole thing sounds too silly. Bridges would certainly tell us that the sovereign will of God is not opposite of what the Bible teaches." But I would challenge this assumption. What **is** Bridges saying, then? Will he not as a Calvinist slip out of every one of our logical, biblical conclusions by an irrational appeal? At all times one must keep in mind that whenever a Calvinist attempts a foundational, apologetic statement about God or man, what appears to be said isn't really being said at all. All crucial statements by the Calvinist about God or man will eventually be withdrawn and replaced with its very opposite thought in any discussion about sovereignty. Were I Bridges, for example, I would further my viewpoint about God's 'revealed' will with another irrationality. I would claim that although God's *revealed* will is, in fact, a separate consideration, it is nevertheless ultimately and indistinguishably submerged within God's *sovereign* and mysterious will. Thus I would use language in gobbly-gook fashion to invoke the idea of 'a separate consideration' which I would undo seconds later with the phrase 'indistinguishably submerged.' I would also state that God's revealed will and sovereign will, though seemingly contradictory, form a mysterious truth (or more cleverly put, a *difference*) that finds its final explanation in God's inscrutable judgments and unfathomable decrees which are past human discovery.

I hope my readers will see that the term, *revealed will* actually adds nothing new to the Calvinist's contradiction. Bridges is still going back and forth adopting irrational statements that follow from his original, irrational premise, except that now he is adding an additional contradiction since another subject has arisen. In effect, instead of him eating an apple before eating an orange which he ate first, he has eaten the apple before eating a pear which he ate first. Once again, nothing is *actually* being said, and it is upon *this* kind of logic that Calvinists tell other Christians they ought to trust God in the face of evil.

Footnotes:

[14] And thus this book is not an exhaustive exposé of Calvinism's distinctive elements. Incidentally, much of the revised and enlarged portions of this later edition (constituting about 35-40% of this book) were written about 2 to 3 years later.

[15] I believe this happens when a person thinks (or *says* something aloud) while alternately thinking something else. For example, one might say, "God is in some sense responsible for sin," while repeating in his mind (virtually subconsciously) "But God is not guilty, but God is not guilty, but God is not guilty…." in an attempt to appease the guilt which the first premise demands.

[16] John Piper, quoted in the Supplement to this book, uses the word "different" in an attempt to convince readers that his contradictory interpretation of Scripture is "different," but "not contradictory."

Endnotes:

[xxvii] Bridges, Jerry. *Trusting God Even When It Hurts.* (Colorado Springs, Colorado; NavPress) pp. 37-38.

[xxviii] Bridges, p. 38.

Chapter 8
The Importance of Context

We have now seen two ways in which Calvinists convince others that God is absolutely sovereign in the world. One way is to make bold statements that actually contradict Scripture, such as "God rules as surely on earth as He does in heaven." Another way is to get Christians to doublethink (a tactic we will continue to observe throughout this book as other theological subjects are discussed). There is yet another method of Calvinist argument beside these two—that is, one in which the Calvinist takes Bible verses out of their context (also known as *proof-texting*).

A good example of this *uncontextualized support* is the argument found in Bridges's first chapter of *Trusting God,* in which there appears a crucial first-chapter set-up passage:

> The sovereignty of God is asserted, either expressly or implicitly, on almost every page of the Bible…. We are going to look at many of these passages in later chapters, but for now consider just one:
>
>> Who can speak and have it happen if the Lord has not decreed it? Is it not from the mouth of the Most High that both calamities and good things come? (Lamentations 3:37-38)
>
> This passage of Scripture offends many people. They find it difficult to accept that both calamities and good things come from God. People often ask the question, "If God is a God of love, how could He allow such a calamity?" But Jesus Himself affirmed God's sovereignty in calamity when Pilate said to Him, "Don't you realize I have power either to free you or to crucify you?" Jesus replied, "You would have no power over me if it were not given to you from above" (Jn. 19:10-11). Jesus acknowledged God's sovereignty over His life.[xxix]

Leaving the question about Pilate's power for a later chapter (17), let us consider the above quote from Lamentations. When Bridges cites calamities, he means it in the broadest sense of human experience. As a case in point, in his next chapter he appeals to God's sovereignty as foreordaining all accidents where people are paralyzed from the waist down.[xxx] Later, while commenting on Ephesians 1:11, he even says:

…God makes all events of history; all the decisions of rulers, kings, and parliaments; and all the actions of their governments, armies, and navies serve His will.[xxxi]

After reading this statement I cannot help but wonder why Bridges would suppose that God *makes* all the events of history without needing to be accountable for them? It should not surprise us, then, that those who see no real dilemma in such statements should also see in certain Bible verses doctrines that are not really there. This is what Bridges does with Lamentations 3:37-38 in an attempted *tour de force* at the beginning of his book. His treatment of these verses is an attempt to prove God's total and absolute sovereignty at the very outset. But herein lies the problem, for Bridges's appeal to Lamentations 3:37-38 is never explained against the historic background of Lamentations, i.e., God's *instance* of judgment against the inhabitants of Judah and Jerusalem. This theme of judgment, along with the prophet's response to God's decision to bring judgment, is dominant throughout the entire book of Lamentations and also through much of Jeremiah.

God's judgment and Jeremiah's declamatory mourning are both evident from Lamentations's first sentence: "How doth the city sit desolate, that was full of people!" Again, this is the dominant theme throughout the book. So, when 3:37 says, "Is it not from the mouth of the Most High that both calamities and good things come?" the calamity in specific view is *the instant* God speaks judgment upon Jerusalem and Judah (Lam. 3:7). And *if* a general application ought to be made, then it must implicitly refer to any judgment against a nation that God decides to carry out because of that nation's sin (see also Is. 29 and 45). The idea that God brings "calamities and good things" in verse 37 hearkens back to Jeremiah 18:3-10, where the prophet is given a picture of God deliberating about whether He will bring destruction or blessing upon a nation:

> ³Then I went down to the potter's house, and there he was, making something at the wheel. ⁴And the vessel that he made of clay was marred in the hand of the potter; so he made it again into another vessel, as it seemed good to the potter to make. ⁵Then the word of the Lord came to me, saying: ⁶"O house of Israel, can I not do with you as this potter?" says the Lord. "Look, as the clay is in the potter's hand, so are you in My hand, O house of Israel! ⁷The instant I speak

> concerning a nation and concerning a kingdom, to pluck up, to pull down, and to destroy it, ⁸if that nation against whom I have spoken turns from its evil, I will relent of the disaster that I thought to bring upon it. ⁹And the instant I speak concerning a nation and concerning a kingdom, to build and to plant it, ¹⁰if it does evil in My sight so that it does not obey My voice, then I will relent concerning the good with which I said I would benefit it.

Note that it is *"the instant"* following a nation's probationary period that God speaks His judgment or blessing. It is not upon *every* instant that God says that He cannot be resisted. *Furthermore, even in divine judgment God's irresistibility does not negate whatever a man's or nation's intentions (choices) might be, but merely the* **effects** *of such intentions.*

Jeremiah was an empathetic prophet, and though not personally culpable in the sense that other individuals were (who because of their acts, made divine judgment on Israel a necessity), nevertheless identifies himself with his nation. Thus at the beginning of Lamentations 3 Jeremiah is a witness to God's *judgment*. "I am the man who hath seen affliction by the rod of his wrath." Thus, after describing God's judgment upon Jerusalem in the book's two previous chapters, he comes in chapter 3 to personalize Jerusalem's desperate situation, seeing in it something of his own position. For he describes the affliction which he bore as the Lord's prophet and, in effect, mediator, stating the he was derided by the people and their (mocking) song all the day. In another place he states "we have transgressed," thus identifying himself with his nation. In the former sense his statements appear to be Job-like in their pathos, yet Messianic insofar that the sufferer feels estranged from God because of his identity with his people. As chapter 3 progresses Jeremiah says he is hedged in by God's judgment, but he later reflects on how his own deserving misery has had a humbling effect. Thus, he hopes that his contrite spirit might find eventual relief, since God is a God of mercy. Let us note the actual context of Lamentations 3:37-38 by reading verses 19-40:

> ¹⁹Remembering mine affliction and my misery, the wormwood and the gall. ²⁰My soul hath them still in remembrance, and is humbled in me. ²¹This I recall to my mind, therefore have I hope. ²²It is of the LORD'S mercies that we are not consumed, because his compassions fail not. ²³They are new every morning: great is thy faithfulness. ²⁴The LORD is my portion, saith my soul; therefore will I hope in him. ²⁵The

LORD is good unto them that wait for him, to the soul that seeketh him. ²⁶It is good that a man should both hope and quietly wait for the salvation of the LORD. ²⁷It is good for a man that he bear the yoke in his youth. ²⁸He sitteth alone and keepeth silence, because he hath borne it upon him. ²⁹He putteth his mouth in the dust; if so be there may be hope. ³⁰He giveth his cheek to him that smiteth him: he is filled full with reproach. ³¹For the LORD will not cast off for ever: ³²But though he cause grief, yet will he have compassion according to the multitude of his mercies. ³³For he doth not afflict willingly nor grieve the children of men. ³⁴To crush under his feet all the prisoners of the earth, ³⁵To turn aside the right of a man before the face of the most High, ³⁶To subvert a man in his cause, the LORD approveth not. ³⁷Who is he that saith, and it cometh to pass, when the LORD commandeth it not? ³⁸Out of the mouth of the most High proceedeth not evil and good? ³⁹Wherefore doth a living man complain, a man for the punishment of his sins? ⁴⁰Let us search and try our ways, and turn again to the LORD.

The term *evil* has been changed in most modern translations, since the Hebrew word in this context of judgment is better translated 'calamity' (as rendered by the NAS and NIV). The preference for 'evil' instead of 'destruction' by the KJV, however, is just another example of how a translation can influence Christians for centuries to think that sin itself is somehow *comprehended* within God (i.e., that even evil comes forth from the Most High). Of particular note in the above passage is the thought that follows verses 37-38. Observe that the word *commandeth* in verse 37 specifically refers to the word *punishment* in verse 39. Thus, what God is commanding is His *punishment*, i.e., *not* the thoughts and intents of men's souls as Bridges (and other Calvinists) would like us to believe. In fact, the entire the chapter that surrounds verses 37-38 is chiefly about God's authority to judge an unrepentant people, that is, if God's merciful program during their probation has been ignored.

Of course, the reason for God's judgment was in large part due to the false prophets of Judah and Jerusalem. It was they who encouraged Israel's rebellion against God and continued to speak deceptions to the inhabitants of Jerusalem during the siege of the city. Jeremiah would later recall their activity in Lamentations 2:14: "Thy prophets have seen vain and foolish things for thee: and they have not discovered thine iniquity, to turn away thy captivity; but have seen for thee false burdens and causes of banishment." Jeremiah himself had asked King Zedekiah during the final stage of the Babylonian siege of Jerusalem: "Where are now your prophets who prophesied unto you, saying, The king of Babylon shall not come against you, nor against this land?" (Jer. 37:19). These false prophets had ignored the warnings of God in Deuteronomy about how continued sinfulness would result in Israel's exile from the land. When the exile became immanent these prophets hid themselves, for they were powerless to prevent God's decreed hour of judgment. Thus, when Jeremiah writes in Lamentations 3:37: "Who is he that saith, and it cometh to pass, when the LORD commandeth it not?," this verse, when understood in its proper context, is a rhetorical question about who can resist the instances of God's *judgments* following probationary periods. The false prophets had promised one thing (blessing), but God declared another result (judgment) because of the people's sin. And only the latter of these would prove irresistible. Thus, the immediate specific context is about the judgment of Jerusalem and Judah. And *if* verses 37-38 *are* intended to be applied beyond their immediate context, the responsible Bible student is still obligated to understand these verses in a context of betimes divine *judgment,* for that is what the Lamentations 3 passage and the book of Lamentations primarily addresses. *God's decrees, then, which are said to be irresistible, are those instances of judgment which affect men and nations in history.* They are not, as Bridges implies, God's foreordination of every iota that men write down in the pages of their histories both individually and corporately, i.e. God's *making* of all history. The context of Lamentations simply does not bear out such an interpretation. Thus Bridges can only use verses 37-38 to serve his theology by quoting them out of context.

To thus read into verses 37-38 something far different, such as the idea that God *makes* every decision of man, is an irresponsible use of Scripture. Imagine, for example, what havoc would result if someone took verse 31 out of its context. It reads: "For the LORD will not cast off for ever." One could form an entire doctrine of purgatory or universalism by interpreting other verses to say that God inevitably abates His anger. One could state, for example, that even as God's judgment upon Jerusalem was eventually mollified as evidenced by the returning remnant to the land of Judah 70 years later, even so do we have a biblical picture here that, as Revelation says, "He (God) makes all things new." Following this we might quote Psalm 103:9: "He will not always strive with us, Nor will He keep His anger forever." One could then add the idea that eternal punishment is a monstrous one, especially as the Christian comes to a better understanding of Jesus' message of forgiveness. That's what one could do if one took Lamentations 3:31, Revelation 21:5, and Psalm 103:9 out of their contexts and added some feel-good statements about Jesus and forgiveness. To ensure such a view, one could then read false definitions into every other Bible verse and passage that would seem to oppose it. Every cult uses such a method. Calvinism uses such a method also. That's how these systems of thought remain consistent and fool people. Indeed, exposed to such a process the uninitiated often feels intimidated and stupid, supposing he knows so much less than he thought. After all, the person trying to convert them seems to have thoughtful, consistent answers for everything.

How can we Christians (and especially the true apologist) combat such renegade interpretations? By *looking around* at the verses and chapters that surround the verse in question (i.e., specific, or near context), as well as understanding the message of the Bible as a whole (i.e., general, or far context). To see, then, Lamentations 3:31 ("For the LORD will not cast off for ever") in relation to other contexts is to understand that this verse refers *specifically* to Jerusalem's eventual restoration, and *generally* to the principle that God's mercy is eternally upon the *living* who repent of their sins. Failing to contextualize Scripture is an incredibly powerful tool of the Enemy, and Christians ought to have nothing to do with it. Indeed, when Satan tried to convince Jesus that He ought to have enough trust in God to cast Himself off the tower of the Temple, he did this not only by omitting part of Psalm 91:11a-12, but also by taking the Old Testament passage out of context. [The Devil stated: "If thou be the Son of God, cast thyself down: for it is written, He shall give his angels charge concerning thee: and in their hands they shall bear thee up, lest at any time thou dash thy foot against a stone" (Mt. 4:6)]. Let us, then, leave the job of *a*contextualizing the Bible to the Devil. Whenever Christians employ the same methodology it merely promotes unbiblical ideas and a theology of error.

Endnotes:

[xxix] Bridges pp. 18-19.

[xxx] Bridges, pp. 24-25.

[xxxi] Bridges, p. 76.

Chapter 9
The Limits of a Sovereign God:
Understanding Job 1—2

A few days ago, my wife and I happened to catch a local news story on TV about a church we once attended. As a thunderstorm had passed through the Philadelphia region where we live, a building owned by this church suffered a lightning strike through a top portion of it. No one was hurt, but the damage was hardly insignificant. An elder of the church who was interviewed by the TV reporter wondered aloud why the Lord had the lightning bolt strike the building, when He could just as easily have had it strike a nearby tree. The possibility *in theory* that the lightning *could* have had a different source than God didn't seem to have occurred to this elder. In effect the elder was saying, 'Lightning *from God* has fallen from heaven.' I noted with some irony that the church had undergone a major split over Reformed doctrine just a year or two earlier, and, since the Reformed view was hardly discredited at that time, it seemed odd to me that any elder of the church would still feel the need to wonder about lightning bolt strikes.

It is indeed difficult for most Christians to think of God as giving over any of His control. They say that for God to allow someone to supersede His will at any point would mean that God ceased being God. God must not simply rule *over* the acts of men, but *rule* the acts of men. Such Christians also wonder how God could maintain His glory if He yielded His will to another creature. Thus God must direct all things after the counsel of His own will in order to prevent chaos from entering man's individual experience and corporate history. However, as we examine the first two chapters in the Old Testament book of Job, we will see that this view of God is not really supported by the Bible. In fact, though God knows everything about the future, He is not so *causally* behind everything as many Christians think.

In approaching the poetry of Job, it is important to understand that Job is a historical book. The prophet Ezekiel speaks of "Noah, Job, and Daniel" as three outstandingly righteous people (Ezek. 14:14, 20). Also, the apostle James tells Christians to "remember the patience of Job" (Ja. 5:11). To those Christians—and there are some—who think that Job was not a historical person, we can only reply that we find it doubtful to suppose that the best example of patience from which Christians are to draw encouragement is a fictional character who never really existed or endured anything at all.

The book of Job is believed by most scholars to be the oldest book of the Bible. One reason for this assumption is because Job lived to a great age. While we don't know the patriarch's exact age, we are told that he lived 140 years after his trial. This means a lifespan that places him chronologically between the Flood of Noah and the time of Abraham. This also means that the book of Job predates Moses and the Pentateuch. Assuming Job is the first book of the Bible, I think it is entirely possible that God wanted to deal first with the oldest problem of theology for our sakes—the problem of evil. Indeed, until a Christian can get past this difficult issue it is hard to understand how he can trust God more fully and grow effectively in the Christian life.

The position we have been advancing in this book is that God is a free will Person, and that He has made other free will persons. We also want to press forward the idea that all free will persons whom God has made, both angelic and human, have retained their free will. In fact, humans have retained it despite the Satanic activity which has affected human history, and also despite the unlawful acquiring by Adam of the knowledge of good and evil (a knowledge we inherit in seed through the male, Adamic line). In short, we believe the book of Job will show that God does not choose the choices of other persons.

Satan and his underlings have used their free will to considerable advantage over men. We will consider in a later chapter the plausible roll that the Enemy [Satan and/or other fallen angels (demons)] played in furthering the hardening of Pharaoh's heart. We will also look at the *de facto* roll that the demonic underworld once played in King Ahab's ruin (1 Ki. 22). It seems prudent, therefore, to pause for a few moments to consider how free will, specifically the Devil's use of free will, has operated against God in the past. This is the great conflict of the ages. Humans may occupy the pages of their history, but Satan is said to be the god of this world, and his influence has compelled men negatively. At length, the lesson we hope to show in this chapter is that God does not operate His free will at the expense of annihilating the free will He has given other persons (as though that were possible without annihilating the person himself). By free will we mean the ability to choose between good and evil, not that alleged 'other' kind of merely 'choosing' between one evil and another evil (which is not a choice at all).[17] Further, by free will we do not mean that one necessarily *obtains* the fruition of one's will, but merely that one *intends* to obtain it. In short, by free will we mean *bare intention*.

Now observe that despite the uncommon integrity in Job none of his friends would concede that he was a righteous man, nor would Satan concede that fact. For his own part Job never mentions Satan in any of his conversations, and he seems unaware of the role the Devil played in bringing about his ruin. Naturally, Job experienced the kind of fear, terror, and anxiety that any of us would experience under the same circumstances (were we to enter such trials, having such faith). Chief among Job's problems was his lingering question as to why God seemed so indifferent to his suffering. In many ways Job's exasperation seems quite understandable to us. For at least one renowned poet in Modern Western culture it seemed a little *too* understandable. New England's Robert Frost saw his own life in the story of Job. The list of tragedies that attended Frost's life was considerable: two of his six children died in infancy, his youngest and favorite daughter, Marjorie, died from complications after giving childbirth, his wife died unexpectedly (Frost would outlive her by nearly 25 years), his son Carol committed suicide a few years after his mother's death, and another daughter suffered mental anguish (as did his sister Jeannie who was eventually institutionalized).[xxxii] Frost came to write a play called *A Masque of Reason* based loosely on the biblical book of Job. In the play, God puts Job through all sorts of trouble for no other reason than to settle a callous bet between Himself and a cantankerous Devil. Frost's statement remains the general objection echoed everywhere by those who believe that God cannot be good, since there is evil in the world. Frost's complaint embodies the first type of objection any critically thinking unbeliever asks: 'If there's a God, why is there evil?' This is why Evangelicals need to understand the lesson of Job, so that they can answer their fellow man on this very point.

Now, the book of Job opens with the sons of God giving an account of their activity before their Creator. The phrase "sons of God" means any offspring of God in physical or spiritual form, and here means angelic beings (including fallen ones):

> [6]Now there was a day when the sons of God came to present themselves before the LORD, and Satan also came among them. [7]The LORD said to Satan, "From where do you come?" Then Satan answered the LORD and said, "From roaming about on the earth and walking around on it." [8]The LORD said to Satan, "Have you considered My servant Job? For there is no one like him on the earth, a blameless and upright man, fearing God and turning away from evil." [9]Then Satan answered the LORD, "Does Job fear God for nothing? [10]"Have You not made a hedge about him and his house and all that he has, on every side? You have blessed the work of his hands, and his possessions have increased in the land. [11]"But put forth Your hand now and touch all that he has; he will surely curse You to Your face." [12]Then the LORD said to Satan, "Behold, all that he has is in your power, only do not put forth your hand on him." So Satan departed from the presence of the LORD.

Notice Satan's reply when God asks him to consider Job's integrity—"Does Job fear God for nothing?" Thus in one fell swoop Satan accuses Job *and* God. Satan accuses God of bribing Job for his worship, and Job is accused of being the type of person who accepts such a bribe, i.e., someone who only worships God for what he can get out of Him. The Devil's reply is a fascinating one and reveals much about his own view of God. His disagreement with God over the assessment of Job implies that Satan doesn't believe that God knows or speaks the truth. This may strike many of us odd when we first consider it. Many of us have grown up thinking that Satan hates God because he knows Him to be good. But notice that Satan actually thinks *he* is correct in the question of Job's motive and God's motive, i.e., he is *truthful* where God is *lying*. *Thus, it appears that Satan actually believes that God is evil and therefore must be fought.* It follows that Satan would think that all of God's motives are suspect, and that therefore God's protection of Job was merely a bribe. Thus it is always catch-22 for God. If God is gracious to a man, Satan assumes God is bribing him for his worship; conversely, if God brings chastisement or judgment upon a man (the former upon the believer, the latter upon the unbeliever), Satan assumes God is angry because his bribe is being resisted. Satan's responses in all cases are constant accusations that demonstrate the kind of *consistency* in argument that we discussed earlier in chapter two.

This accusative posture is *the* method of the Devil. Naturally, then, Satan claims that the reason Job didn't curse God after the loss of his children and possessions was because Job was not personally molested. All evidence throughout the Scripture suggests that Satan, since the time of his rebellion, has always believed the worst about God and His children. Furthermore, if Satan has no grounds to attack a believer by pointing to his behavior, he will accuse him in his motive (as he did with Job). This is a very effective strategy by the Devil, since purity of motive appears impossible to prove without subjecting the one in question to extreme circumstances. Indeed, how can any of us regularly prove purity of motive? For example, one can sing a solo in church because of wanting to worship God or because of wanting to be seen and applauded. Parents can have children because of wanting to care for them or because they hope their children will take care of them when they are old. Motive is very slippery, and one can have mixed motives in these matters. The Devil does not appear to be double-minded, however. By being single-mindedly set against God, Satan is all the more effective because he never gives his opposition—God and the believer—the benefit of the doubt. He always assumes the worst about God and us, and this assumption informs his protest. Even Satan's original rebellion in heaven almost certainly followed this line of argument; for we see his method at work in the way he crafted his accusations in Genesis 3 and Job 1—2. Prior to Genesis 3 he appears to have coerced a third of the angelic host to join his rebellion against God (see Rev. 12:4). Thus based on Genesis 3 and Job 1—2 we can imagine that his original conversation with the angels might have gone like this: *"Has God really given you positions of honor? Yea, are they given you for nothing? Does he not bid you to worship him and to accept his rule? For he knows if you stopped worshiping him his rule would be over, and you yourselves would rule in that moment. Reject his 'love' now, and you will discover his anger; for his 'graciousness' is only a ruse to buy your loyalty. Why do you continue to accept his rule without testing his character? For his true character cannot be known until you stop worshiping him."*

Again, this debate about motive is the Devil's specialty because he can accuse God and His servants whenever he wants. I think the Bible makes it fairly clear that Satan believes his own lies, and that he regards God and His followers as inauthentic. Perhaps this explains why the Enemy presumed to believe the worst about Jesus, and why the demonic world was astonished when they learned that Christ had risen from the dead. In fact, the Bible tells us that had the demonic world known about Jesus' resurrection they would not have crucified Him. What does this say, except that the Enemy must have assumed that Jesus was too selfish to *willingly* undergo death, especially death by crucifixion?[18] I personally think it also suggests that Satan does not believe in the Creatorship nor power of God unto resurrection.

So we were mistaken if, after the first set of Job's trials, we expected Satan to bow his head and sheepishly admit, "Well, You were right, after all, God! I really didn't think Job would respond the way he did, but I see that I'm wrong!" For Satan will do and say anything he can to maintain his fictions. Thus, when Satan was proven wrong after the first round of Job's trial, he adopted a deeper irrationality to support his original accusation against Job, saying, "Skin for skin, yea, all that a man hath will he give for his life." This Satanic accusation against man was the Devil's assessment of all humanity. And though Satan's statement may have been generally true, he was applying it universally without exception; and Job, of course, would prove to be the exception.

The Greek word for devil, *diabolo* (*Strong's* #1228), means slanderer or traducer. Traducer means 'to lead across,' and this description of Satan is implied in Genesis 3, in Eve's reply to God that she was *beguiled* by the serpent, i.e., led astray by deception to cross a prudent boundary. This is what the Devil does with the majority of men, leading them across God's prudent boundary like a kind of pied-piper toward a land for which the children of men have a desire to go, but never so much as when they hear the sounds of the pied-piper's flute. From Job we learn that Satan even incited God to do something He wouldn't have done otherwise. Of course, I don't mean that Satan has ever led God into sin or forced God to do something wrong. Rather, Satan incited God to act according to His *permissive* 'will' rather than His *direct* will. As a result, God removed His hedge of protection from around Job. It is clear from a plain reading of the text that God would not have removed the hedge if Satan had *not* incited Him to do so—(as God said to Satan: "though you have incited me to ruin him without cause"). Someone might say, "But this was all part of God's plan to teach Job more patience." Well, certainly it is true that Job learned more patience because of his trial, but the question remains: Did God actually indicate that these circumstances of Job's suffering at this time and in this manner was His plan for Job? No, much to the contrary. God removed the hedge because He was incited to do so. God's motive and his servant's reputation had been questioned before the entire angelic host, and God decided not to let this particular accusation pass unchallenged. Thus, the particular trials that Job suffered in chapters 1—2 were not part of God's design for pruning character. Indeed, it would not be like God to direct hammer blow upon hammer blow on the anvil of Job's life to get a point across in the quickest and severest possible manner. God does not collar the believer up against the wall in order to get the most spiritual growth out of him in the shortest period of time. He is more merciful than that, a fact proved by God's restoration of Job by the end of the book (cp. Ja. 5:11). Had God thought that Job needed to be chastened to learn more patience, He would have done it at a more gradual and gracious pace than that recorded in chapters 1—2. But God did allow Job to suffer in order to vindicate His servant and Himself before all the heavenly host. Thus, when God says to Satan the second time, "Hast thou considered my servant Job, that there is none like him in the earth, a perfect and an upright man, one that feareth God, and hateth evil?" He reproves Satan by repeating the exact words He used to describe Job at the beginning, as if to say to the Devil that *every* word spoken and assessment made by *Elohim* shall stand. Observe, then, that Job in his suffering did not experience these awful things by God's design.

Thus, according to the Bible, God took all of Job's possessions, including Job's children, and put them into Satan's power. God did this without directing Satan toward any specific end. God is not the causal agent for any of the disasters brought against Job, even though God speaks in an idiomatic way *as though* He were responsible for Job's ruin by having removed His divine protection. Again, from the text itself we understand that it is Satan, not God, who brings about all these horrific disasters upon Job. This is clear from Job 1:12, "And the LORD said unto Satan, Behold, all that he hath is in thy power; only upon himself put not forth thy hand." This is further clarified in Job 2, when we are specifically told that Satan left the presence of the Lord to smite Job with boils over his entire body. Here it is implied that Satan had an ongoing desire to destroy Job, hence his earlier complaint to God—"You have put a hedge about him." This serves to show the difference between Satan's free will (intention) and the *effects* of his free will. Satan was never denied his autonomy in *intending* to ruin Job but merely denied the *obtaining* of this particular object of his will for some time.

It is interesting to see that Job's three friends assigned all of Job's troubles to the direct work of God. Like the servant who cried, "Fire *from God* has fallen from heaven and devoured all the sheep," Job's friends found it natural to assign all weather events to God. Satan worked in conjunction with this mindset, trying to persuade Job that some of his trials were completely God's doing. Thus when Satan destroyed Job's most treasured possession—his children—the Devil was careful to do it with a great *wind*, so that it might point to God. Had the Sabeans, for example, killed Job's children, Job might have rationalized the event as having been caused by the sinfulness of man; but the *wind?*—the question begged itself: *Couldn't God have controlled the wind?* Job himself seems to believe that God is behind all of these disasters. "The LORD hath given, and the LORD hath taken away, blessed be the name of the LORD." The servant of the Lord does not always say what is true.[19] Again, a plain reading of the story shows that it was *Satan* who destroyed Job's children and possessions, not God. [Furthermore, Job seems to have entertained the possibility of his friends' arguments (when he says of God, "Though he slay me…")]. One other possible interpretation of the phrase, "The LORD hath given, the LORD hath taken away" is that Job is referring to God's *hedge of protection* being given and then taken away (such that in the interim Job had merely applied himself according to sound domestic and financial principles, which led him to success). But the balance of Job's bewilderment seems to point to a conviction that his suffering was caused by God, especially since he seems unaware of Satan's causative role. Furthermore, even though Job was familiar with the Adamic Fall (Job mentions Adam hiding his transgression in his bosom), there is nothing in the Fall narrative which would have led Job to believe that Satan could control the weather upon receiving God's reluctant permission.[20] Thus Job is in the crucible of trial, and he inquires into the problem of evil. To add insult to injury Job's three friends assume *a priori* that Job cannot be a man of integrity because of all the things he has suffered. "Who ever perished, being innocent," asks his oldest friend, Eliphaz, "or where were the righteous cut off?" (Job 4:7). Eliphaz' argument is based on a false presupposition. Even if someone pointed out to Eliphaz that, hypothetically, righteous men of past generations also had suffered to significant degree, Eliphaz would have had a fool-proof, tautological answer—"Ah, Friend, but if the man had suffered, he could not have been righteous!"[21]

Our survey of Job 1—2 has been a cursory one, but a few things have been suggested. It is hard to read the narrative of Job and see how one could conclude, along with the Calvinist, that God is *ruling* the Devil's accusations against His own self, *ruling* the responses of Job, *ruling* the acts of the Sabeans, and so forth. One can only hold this position by doing violence to the plain meaning of the text. God's statement, for example, that He is putting all of Job's possessions into *Satan's* power, i.e., to do with them as *Satan* wills, loses all meaning if God is really ruling what Satan does.[22] Nor can we write off the word 'incited' as a mere idiom of speech in God's aggravated statement to Satan, i.e., "you have incited me to ruin him without cause."[23] Again, it is the context of the narrative that determines that "incited" be taken literally, while God's statement about His role in 'ruining' be taken as idiomatic. God *was* incited and allowed Himself to be led by His permissive 'will' to put Job's possessions into Satan's power. It is disappointing that so many commentators of the Bible generally describe God in such sovereign terms that one would think God could never be incited or change His feeling of expression. If Job 1—2 is any proof, however, God certainly *does* experience an intensity of feeling, and this despite his foreknowledge of what the future will be. For God is a person, and though He is sinless, He has feelings like any other person. Despite the fact that God *foreknew* Satan would incite Him, He naturally felt more upset at the Devil during the actual moment of His conversation with him, e.g., in the same way that we ourselves would feel more upset in an actual moment of confrontation with someone, though we might have anticipated a meeting with that person for days.

At this point someone will object, "But if God gives Satan power to do something which He doesn't really want the Devil to do, then Satan is ruling a part of the universe in which God is not absolutely and totally sovereign." *Exactly! In fact, that's an example of what free will in the universe looks like when God allows its physical effects. But even regardless of physical effects, men and angels exercise their own will (intention). Therefore God cannot be accused in their sin, and thus He is removed as a factor from the problem of evil.* This does not mean that God ceases to be God, as some claim. God ultimately brings all angels and men into judgment for their intentions and actions. But we must allow *God* to describe Himself, not some theological system that differs from the Bible. As a friend of mine has pointed out, when Christians allow the latter, they end up going to church and worshiping *theology* (i.e., so called) rather than the God of the Bible. The point here is that Job teaches us that God is not sovereign *in* everything, but rather sovereign *over* everything. To be sovereign *in* everything would mean God foreordains 'whatsoever comes to pass.' To be sovereign *over* everything means God will ultimately judge how others have been sovereign in their own sphere of decisions.

God's sovereignty, as properly (biblically) understood, means that God rules over men and angels and sometimes limits the *effects* of their free will. This means that God is sovereign in the same sense that a human king is sovereign, only on a much grander scale. A king does not *make* the choices of people; rather, people make their own choices but are subject to the king's punishment if they do evil (or conversely, subject to the king's blessing if they are righteous). Unfortunately, many in Evangelicalism have taken the word 'sovereign' and changed its meaning so that God *makes* the events of history. Again, this is not how the Bible defines the concept of divine sovereignty in the first two chapters of Job, that is, once they are understood in their proper context. Thus, true biblical sovereignty could be defined as the following:

> God foreknows everything, but does not *make* all the events of history.
> God may limit the *effects* of a person's free will upon another person or thing, but He never limits any person's *intention* (free will).
> God limits the degree and duration of every trial facing the Christian, so that the believer need not be tried above his endurance.
> God, because of what He prepares for the believer's future, knows that the suffering of the Christian in this world is not worthy to be compared to the glory which He shall reveal in the believer in the hereafter.
> God will condemn the sin of every fallen man and fallen angel at a future and final judgment. No one can avoid or resist these judgments.

Redefining God's sovereignty so that it lines up with the Bible's teaching is critical. Evangelicals cannot present their faith fully and accurately unless they accept a correct definition of God's sovereignty. Job 1—2 clarifies this definition. Sadly, alarmingly even, it appears that many Evangelicals have drawn no such proper lessons from the book of Job regarding either the unqualified *fact* of free will (intention) or the difference between free will and whether God shall allow its *effects*.

Footnotes:

[17] It is important here to mention why Calvinists believe that post-Adamic man can only choose in the direction of sin. Jonathan Edwards, the well-known 18th century Calvinist, believed that a man always willed his choice in the direction of his greatest desire. Since man (in the Calvinistic view) is born a sinner, he will always choose to act according to his strongest desire. Thus a man cannot choose other than to sin. Furthermore, it should be noted that Edwards's argument does not seem to demand a particular prerequisite moral condition (i.e., Fallen *vs.* Unfallen) for man to choose according to his strongest desire. But how (we ask), upon the former point (i.e., the claim that man can only choose according to his strongest desire), can Edwards explain Jesus' statement to the Father in Gethsemane, "Not my desire, but thine be done?" (Gr. *thelo*, i.e., *desire*, (which, depending upon context, either means *bare desire*, or *a will congruent with desire*, or *a will **in**congruent with desire*). Christ (i.e., the Son) is clearly stating that His strongest desire is to avoid crucifixion, while the Father's strongest desire is that He

undergo crucifixion. Edwards's response presumably would be that Christ ultimately had a greater *desire* to please His Father than He had *desire* to avoid the cross. But this argument renders Christ's statement about His strongest desire meaningless. Moreover, if Christ so desired to obey the Father as to make insignificant the experience of crucifixion, why then does the writer of Hebrews state that Christ *endured* the cross? Christ should have *desired* the cross if He *desired* the Father's will. Again, however, Christ said "Not my **will**" (Gr. *thelo*, contextually here, *desire*). Thus Christ bent His will in a direction *opposite* of His desire and did not follow His strongest desire. Properly speaking, then, Christ *willed* the Father's desire; He did not *desire* the Father's desire. That is, He chose it. On this basis we may conclude Edwards's argument false (i.e., that a man always chooses according to his strongest desire). Indeed, how else is the Christian to also understand Christ's statement that the one who wishes to follow Christ must *deny* himself? That is, how can one follow Christ *while* denying himself? The conflict in Christ to will something other than His strongest desire is, in fact, the whole basis for Christ's agony in Gethsemane.

Therefore when R.C. Sproul and other Reformed thinkers attempt to draw a distinction between 'regeneration' and man's strongest desire—a desire in which man 'chooses' to follow the divinely regenerated desire if/when God implants it in him—it should be noted that, according to Reformed theology's own criteria of defining man's will and desire, there is no distinction being made between the two. Any Reformed attempt at distinguishing between *man's will* and *man's desire* is thus meaningless, since these terms are put forward (unwittingly) by Calvinists as synonyms, except in these terms' relation to *time*, which in salvific contexts, is *irrationally defined*. In other words, their assumption is that one can define the (properly and biblically understood) *instant* (indivisible point) of one's belief as a *process of stages* (which by biblical definition is irrational), involving early and latter stages of time, a process divided into its early stage of 'divine desire given' (that which Calvinists call "regeneration") and its latter stage of 'man, having received the new desire, rushing to Christ.' In this manner Calvinists make it appear as though their theology can involve both the "will of God" and "man's belief" because of the psychological associations which all people invariably have about God and man as distinct persons of wills. A pretty trick. Thus (to return this observation back to the main point) Sproul, like Calvinist author Jerry Bridges, who (unwittingly or not) attempts to make distinctions between God's "sovereign" will and God's "revealed" will in order to posit 'God's will' and 'man's will' (and therefore *God* and *man*) as distinct from each other and yet the same as each other, defines 'God's changing of man's desire' and 'man rushing in accord with his new desire' as the same thing (i.e., "*belief*," insofar as the Calvinist 'understands' that such belief is caused unilaterally by the sole Determiner of acts in the Cosmos), and yet distinct things ("regeneration" and "belief," so that the particulars of the Cosmos are not swallowed up in the One). Incidentally, man's 'choice' in following God's implanted and irresistible desire would not, under Calvinism, be a choice at all, but merely the flip side of saying that depraved man can 'choose,' but can only choose evil. Thus the words "choose" and "choice" take on a different meaning than that which God intends and which is often (if not always) the commonly accepted or understood meaning of those words as used by average people in everyday life. <u>Observing this phenomenon of arbitrary</u>

change is crucial for the true apologist. ***For the way to spot false theology is to see whether words (predicates, direct objects, etc.) ever change meaning merely depending on the grammatical subject.*** This is true whether the subject is God, man, or something else. This is a key thing to be observed.

For example, Sproul claims that God changes the man's strongest desire so that the man will desire Christ. This is a clever way of changing meaning. For in effect this makes the words "God" and "man" change back and forth, first to synonyms, then returning to non-synonyms. Again, the 'his' of the man in the man's desire has been completely extinguished. It may be **_called_** "*man's* desire" or "his desire" by Sproul, but in fact the man's desire has been *negated* in order that God might replace it with His desire. Indeed, had not man's desire been negated it would have remained as it was. Thus man (rather, 'man') cannot be distinguished from a computer or any other kind of inert material which God could animate, according to the definition the Calvinist provides us. And so the attempted distinction between the created person and the Creator, as following the alleged distinction between the 'creature's will' and the 'Creator's will,' turns out to be irrationally defined.

This Calvinistic doublethink regarding man's nature has entered Evangelical lingo, affecting even the way many Evangelicals speak of Christ—even, we might contend, to the unwitting denial of Christ's Incarnation. For observe the misguided explanation that Christ, regarding sin, was "tempted in His flesh but not in His deity." What does such a statement imply? For to put it this way is to suggest that Christ in Gethsemane could have been disobedient to the Father in the flesh, while, at the same time, not have been disobedient in His deity, i.e., to sin with one part of Himself without sinning with another part of Himself. [In passing, we grant here the underlying condition necessary for this argument—that Christ *could* sin had He chosen to (i.e. as He expressed that possibility of His choice in Gethsemane)]. But this idea of Christ sinning with only one part of Himself makes no sense, for would not Christ *also* sin in His deity if He sinned in His flesh? An objector might answer us thus: "Christ *could* have (failed), but *would never* have." But here we contend that such an explanation is merely a doublethink, for if Christ *would never* have, i.e., theoretically have done otherwise under any possible circumstance(s), then He also *could not* have. What should rather be stated is that Christ could have sinned, but *would not* (i.e., *chose not to*). I say "would not" rather than "would never have" because the latter phrase (at least to me) seems to imply the theoretical impossibility of Christ ever sinning (as though Christ could choose, but could only choose right—i.e., the flip side of man in his alleged Depravity), rather than state an inability of Christ to sin *because of His willingness* to remain obedient. Thus for some to say that "Christ was tempted in His flesh but not in His deity" is to employ a doublethink that makes Christ *able* yet *unable* to be tempted, and thus separates Christ's flesh from His deity in an irrational way, which is really to deny the Incarnation. When genuine Christians make such statements, they obviously do so ignorantly.

Lastly, it should be noted that Thayer's lexicon shows that extra-biblical writings define "regeneration" not at all as the Calvinist. Rather, it consistently means "restoration," as shown in e.g., Cicero's *restoration* to his former rank and fortune. It is something Cicero *assents* to, not something irresistibly done *to* him.

This meaning of restoration is in every extra-biblical example Thayer offers. Moreover, the word occurs but twice in the N.T., and, except for its biased use of it by Calvinists in its single occurrence in the book of Titus, expresses in Luke the same idea of restoration as found in extra-biblical writings. The idea in the gospel is that of Christ's kingdom restored back to Christ. In short, Calvinist's have simply hijacked a Greek word which occurs extremely rarely in the N.T. They have ignored the lexical-control group of extra-biblical writings and even its use in the gospel, in order to make a case of special pleading. Thus Calvinists assert a definition which has no basis in that word's historical usage. Conversely. once the word is given its proper meaning, i.e., that of "restoration," it actually argues *against* the idea that all sin (or are guilty of sin) in Adam (see chpt. 18), pointing instead to the restoration of a person to his former state of non-guiltiness.

[18] Calvinist John Piper, in an article called, 'Is God for Us or for Himself?' concludes at the end of his article:

> God is the one Being in the entire universe for whom self-centeredness, or the pursuit of his own glory, is the ultimately loving act. For him, self-exaltation is the highest virtue.

Although in his article Piper also mentions God glorifying Himself in the redemptive process, his remarks miss the fact of God's self*less*ness seen in the Godhead's individual Persons. For the Son would in fact do only that which the Father showed Him to do, and the Father was committed to support only that which the Son requested in return (even if to the point of willing to rescue Christ in Gethsemane and to the breaking of Scripture). Thus for Piper to speak of God as *"one* Being" who seeks His own glory is false, unless a strong qualification is asserted to show that the term, 'one Being' is understood corporately and thus as the separate Persons of the Godhead willing to allow the other Two Persons of the Godhead their own decision at the expense of Himself. For this is the actual position of Scripture. Note that Jesus said, "The Spirit shall not speak of himself, but whatsoever he shall hear, that shall he speak." Where in Piper's article is such a distinction pointed out? For Piper speaks of "God's intention in sending his son," instead of "The *Father's* intention in sending His son," which would have stated the matter more clearly, given his term "one Being". For Christ Himself said He came not on His own but because the Father sent Him. Piper thus misses the point, i.e., that the motive of the Father is to glorify the *person* of the Son, and that the motive of the Son is to glorify the *person* of the Father, and that as Each does so, the *person* of the Spirit (who supports the work of the Son as designed by the Father) is also glorified. That is different than stating that God's motive is to glorify God, and that God is *one* Being. In the end, then, Piper's view of the Persons of the Godhead is divine musketeerish—all for one, and one for all—but in which one's *motive* is not merely for the benefit of others but also for himself. While it is true that glory ultimately redounded to the Father for having sent His Son, this realization did *not* inform the Father's motive, as the Bible makes clear. The Father has never been selfish in that sense, i.e., in the sense that Piper means. Piper uses the term 'self-centeredness,' but there is a 180° difference between God *centering* and orienting the world properly according to Himself as the Creator and Final Judge of the creature man, and what Piper is describing, which in fact would be divine *selfishness*.

To support his view that God is justifiably *selfish* (we recognize the actual definition of Piper's term 'self-centeredness' as we have given it above, and not as Piper nomenclatures it) Piper quotes Ayn Rand about inauthentic people who despise others for superficial reasons (e.g., what Piper cites as style of dress, etc.):

> They are what Ayn Rand calls "second-handers." They don't live from the joy that comes through achieving what they value for its own sake. Instead, they live second-hand from the praise and compliments of others. We don't admire second-handers, we admire people who are composed and secure enough that they don't feel the need to shore up their weaknesses and compensate for their deficiencies by trying to get as many compliments as possible.
> [http://www.crosswalk.com/11574813/page4/]
> (May 8, 2008).

Note that Piper, by analogy, implies that the justification for God's 'self-centeredness' is simply because God is composed and secure within Himself. Nowhere here or in Piper's entire article does Piper state anything about the sacrificial nature of the individual Persons within the Godhead or how such self*less*ness informs the definition of who God really is.

[As a side note here (and lest some readers be troubled in mind), this activity within the Godhead does not mean (by anyone attempting to extend the principle) that men, at the horizontal level, are likewise to encourage and allow other men whatever decisions they choose, such as criminal acts. For at all times man must first orient himself to God as his Creator and Judge.]

[19] Technically speaking, Job may have been expressing this statement idiomatically to say that God had caused his loss (even as God expressed it Himself), but Job seems not to understand that it was Satan who caused his loss. Thus, while Job unwittingly expressed his loss in a way that could be understood to be idiomatically true, it seems very unlikely that he intended his statement to be understood in this way.

[20] As readers enter chapter 14, it should be noted that even as Job was presumably familiar with the narrative of the Fall, so too may Moses have been familiar with the book of Job. This familiarity with Job may have extended to other Israelites and helped early Jewish readers of the Pentateuch piece together what may be Mosaic allusions to 1) the Enemy's activity upon Pharaoh's heart, and 2) the way the Lord speaks as though He is the causative agent in certain circumstances, when contextually it is evident that He is not.

[21] It may also be that none had suffered like Job in Eliphaz's lifetime because none had been so conscientious as Job, and that therefore Eliphaz had no experience with which to compare his friend's suffering.

²² Nor in such a case would any transfer of power from God to Satan have been needed.

²³ This is the sense in which Job 42:11 must be understood, in which it says that Job's relatives and friends comforted him "over all the trouble which the LORD had brought unto him." This statement is a synopsis about God's *allowance* for trial, much like the Lord's synopsistic statement in Exodus 4:21, in which the Lord states that He would harden Pharaoh's heart, the difference in Exodus being that the Lord uttered the statement about Pharaoh *a priori* to the events that led to Pharaoh's hardening—events that we suggest in chapter 14 were successive allowances for the Enemy to augment Pharaoh's already rebellious heart. These two statements (Job 42:11 and Ex. 4:21) are subject to the detailed accounts of the narratives themselves for their explanations, and, in the case of Exodus, also dependent on the book of Job for its description of Satanic method (again, see chapter 14). In both cases God is understood to be *allowing* these events, not *causing* them. Even with so little imagination as we might possess, we can imagine what it would be like for God to have to grant permission to the Enemy for every trial that befalls mankind, such that He would feel responsible for such trials, even though He were merely allowing it and therefore *not* responsible for it (see also 1 Kings 22). There is yet one further consideration. Especially as Job is a poetic book, there is certainly the possibility that in its summation Job 42:11 is intended as a tongue-in-cheek comment, and that the writer of Job—whether it were Job himself or someone else—would have seen the absurd, ironic element in Job having assessed God wrongly throughout much of his trial.

Endnotes:

[xxxii] [www.english.uiuc.edu/maps/poets/a_f/frost/life.htm].

Chapter 10
Does God Rule <u>OVER</u> or <u>IN</u> Everything?

"The worst thing a parent can experience," runs the saying, "is the death of a child." In a chapter entitled, "The Wisdom of God," author Jerry Bridges discusses the problem of human experience with a truly tragic story:

> At 9:15 a.m., just after the children had settled into their first lesson on the morning of 21 October 1966, a waste tip from a South Wales [coal mine] slid into the quiet mining community of Aberfan. Of all the heart-rending tragedies of that day, none was worse than the fate of the village Junior School. The black slime slithered down the man-made hillside and oozed its way into the classrooms. Unable to escape, five teachers and 109 children died.
>
> A clergyman being interviewed by a B.B.C. reporter at the time of [the tragedy, in response]…to the inevitable question about God [said], 'Well…I suppose we have to admit that this is one of those occasions when the Almighty made a mistake.'
>
> True Christians will be appalled at the clergyman's flippant and blasphemous statement about God. But do we not sometimes wonder, when a calamity of some kind strikes us, if God has not made a mistake in our lives? I think of another statement—not flippant but heartfelt—made by a sincere Christian watching a child struggle with cancer, "I sure hope God knows what He's doing in this." Anyone who has dealt deeply with adversity can probably identify with the doubts this person struggled with.
>
> When we stop and think about it, we know in our heart of hearts that God does not make any mistakes in our lives or the villages of South Wales or anywhere else. God does know what He is doing. God is infinite in His wisdom. He always knows what is best for us and what is the best way to bring about that result.[xxxiii]

Thus, in his entire discussion about South Wales, Jerry Bridges makes no mention about whether it were even *possible* that Satan could have been involved in this tragedy. Rather, he assumes *a priori* that God is behind everything. A page or so later, Bridges uses the long-standing interpretation of Romans 8:28 to support his view, saying that everything that happens to the believer is working together for his good. Consequently, the collapse of the man-made hill at Aberfan is in some sense just another example of God's loving hand. (Why, then, I wonder, does Bridges describe it as a "heart-rending" tragedy?) And so whatever happens on earth happens to the glory of God, including all the circumstances surrounding the deaths of all children. It should be noted that conspicuously missing from Bridges's list of God's sovereign activities is any mention of America's great national sin—abortion—and how *it* exactly fits into that plan of history which God makes with His loving hand (especially when we consider God's statement to Jonah about His natural inclination to have mercy upon those who cannot tell their right hand from their left). For though such abortions are done by men, Bridges elsewhere implicitly assures us that all men (presumably abortionists as well) are under the all-sovereign direction of God and His loving hand.

How Bridges's interpretation of the event in South Wales squares with the book of Job is indeed puzzling. A great wind smote the house and killed Job's children as they were celebrating the birthday of one of their own.[24] The Devil uses the occasion of one of these birthdays to destroy all of them, adding irony in the process by killing them during a celebration meant to commemorate life and its continuance. It is clear from the Bible, as we have already noted, that the deaths of Job's children were a direct result of Satan inciting God to remove His hedge of protection from around Job. But where do these opening chapters of the book of Job figure into Bridges's understanding about the children of South Wales dying? In fact, he makes no recognition of it. Please note that I'm not saying here that Satan is responsible for *every* destructive thing that befalls children and adults in the world. God did indeed tell Adam that if he ate the forbidden fruit he would surely die, and the fallout resulting from Adam's sin has continued to affect the earth and every person in it. The book of Job does, however, provide an example where the Devil is allowed to exert his free will over wind, lightning (KJV: *fire from heaven*), and disease for a limited time and application. Incredibly, however, Bridges never discusses these diabolical activities from the book of Job, except to say that Satan had tried to get Job to curse God. Instead, Satan's activity is apparently dismissed with overarching, breezy statements made elsewhere in Bridges's book implying God's sovereignty over every force in the world. At no time are the opening chapters of the book of Job truly taken seriously by Bridges or, for that matter, by any other Calvinist author I have read. In short, the problem for Bridges, as for all Evangelical Calvinists who approach Job, is that *a verse like Romans 8:28, which allegedly teaches that all things work together for the good of the believer, ends up informing the book of Job, rather than the book of Job informing Romans 8:28, so that the latter's translation might be examined for accuracy.*

The unfortunate reality is that Romans 8:28 remains part of a coterie of playing cards (Romans 9:22, i.e., "fitted for destruction," etc.), forming a trump suite against all other problematic verses to the Calvinistic view, allowing Calvinism to ante up in its hand in the game of biblical interpretation. The result is an erroneous doctrine that defines God's sovereignty as total and absolute. When Evangelical authors fail to account for the fact that Satan has had the ability to destroy a man's house and his children, they can be expected to make statements like the following one by Bridges:

> The truth is, *all* expressions of nature, *all* occurrences of weather, whether it be a devastating tornado or a gentle rain on a spring day, are acts of God. The Bible teaches that God controls all the forces of nature, both destructive and productive, on a continuous, moment-by-moment basis.
> Whether the weather merely disrupts my plans or destroys my home, I need to learn to see God's sovereign and loving hand controlling it.[xxxiv]

Where is the lesson of Job in all this grand statement? It is not to be found. This is because the Bible doesn't support Bridges's conclusions at all. So the question remains: Where is the critical thinking of so many Christians (let alone theologians) on this point, that they should not come rallying to the statements of Job 1—2 to vindicate God in the death of Job's children?

We have already noted that God's transference of certain powers to Satan is never attended with how that power shall be used. Prior to removing His hedge of protection from Job, God directs the wind, lightning, and disease so that Job and his family do not fall victim to any of them. God then allows Satan to direct the wind, lightening, and disease as *he* (the Devil) will. Certainly God knows how the Devil will use these newly acquired powers, for His foreknowledge is perfect. But if we note the actual conversations between God and Satan, it is obvious that God is never *making* Satan choose how he shall use these powers, i.e., anymore than God is *making* the events of Job's history. All along, in fact, God is quite upset with how Satan uses his power.

Throughout history, many men (such as the poet Robert Frost in *The Masque of Reason*) have been angry at God for not stopping evil from happening in the world. The only way, however, that God could have prevented evil from happening in the world, were if He had eliminated free will at the beginning of creation (i.e., by creating merely a plant-and-tree, stars-in-the-heavens creation). But God wanted certain created things to have free will, and so he made angels and men; and these have demonstrated that they have always wanted their free will. Indeed, would Frost be content not to have the choice to be angry with God and so write *The Masque of Reason*? The hypocrisy of man is this: Whenever he raises the accusation—i.e., 'If God is good, why does He allow evil in the world?'—he has already shown his argument to be false, for he has used his free will to feel angry and accusative toward a fair God, thereby demonstrating that he wishes to retain his free will to a point of sinfulness. And such a result, when added to the sinfulness of all men, has given us the present moral condition of the world. Why then doesn't a man like Frost also complain against God for allowing his disobedience? Well, in fact, that is just what he is doing, though unwittingly! He is blaming God for how free will has been used, including (by implication) his own. Yet he wants the free will to be able to raise an objection against God. The very act therefore of a man raising an *accusatory* question about why God would allow evil merely exposes his own hypocrisy.

Again, free will is a part of God's own nature, and God chose that free will be a part of sentient creation—including angels and men. (However, this does not mean that all things sentient are made in God's image, nor able to disobey unto eternal liability after the fashion of men and angels.) Free will is that part of us that thinks thoughts and chooses our moral course. Sadly, each man has chosen to use his free will to act foolishly by choosing to sin. Certain angels, including the Devil, have also made the choice to think that God is evil. We forget, however, that just because Satan (for example) *does* choose to do evil, he must always continue to do so. He is still, even now, a free will person able to choose otherwise. The problem, of course, is that the Devil never chooses to do good because he hates God and thinks God is evil. God, on the other hand, knows Himself to be benign and gracious and that to relinquish any area to Satan will always result in that area's ruin. Thus God was simply placing the welfare of Job's possessions at the disposal of another person's free will. "That seems cruel," someone might say by way of objection. "If I had a child, I would never subject him to such horrors, especially just to prove a point." Of course, these thoughts are understandable until we realize that God saved men at greatest expense to Himself, thus proving the Trinity's selfless nature. "Easy for the Father to say, who wanted the Son to do all the hard work," someone may think. But many an earthly father who has given his son to die in a worthy cause has wished that he himself could have died in his son's place. In the midst of Job's trial, the plan of God remained steadfast—He would one day glorify Job as one of His children, knowing that Job's suffering in this present world was not worthy to be compared to the glory that would be revealed in His servant. Furthermore, the issue at stake in the book of Job was not only God's reputation, but Job's as well.

WHETHER THE WIND

While the opening chapters of Job show that God is not causing the events that befall Job, they also disprove another of Jerry Bridges's claim that we have touched on but now more fully treat—i.e., that *all* weather occurrences are of God.

First, we recall from Job that the wind which blew the house down on Job's children and the fire that burned up all the sheep were directed by Satan as *he* willed. The reason the Devil is not mentioned specifically by name as the sequence of destructive events unfolds in Job 1 is a literary device meant to bring the reader into experiencing the disaster from Job's point of view.

Yet, Job is not the only book of the Bible that disproves the notion that God is behind all weather occurrences. Another example is found in 1 Kings 19:9b-12, in which Elijah is told to leave the cave where he had been hiding from Queen Jezebel, and to stand on the mountain of God (Mount Sinai):

> ..and behold, the word of the LORD came to him, and he said unto him, What doest thou here, Elijah? [10]And he said, I have been very jealous for the LORD God of hosts: for the children of Israel have forsaken thy covenant, thrown down thine altars, and slain thy prophets with the sword; and I, even I only, am left; and they seek my life, to take it away. [11]And he said, Go forth, and stand upon the mount before the LORD. And behold, the LORD passed by, and a great and strong wind rent the mountains, and brake in pieces the rocks before the LORD; but the LORD was not in the wind: and after the wind an earthquake; but the LORD was not in the earthquake: [12]And after the earthquake a fire; but the LORD was not in the fire: and after the fire a still small voice.

The fact that God's presence goes *before*, and is not *in*, the devastation, is the comforting thought offered to the believer. God goes before us so that we can be assured of His presence during certain terrifying events which He Himself does not cause. This passage is so blunt about God **not** being in the events of wind, earthquake, and fire on this particular occasion, that no further comment is really necessary for us to make, except to add that it would have been interesting to see how Bridges would have explained these verses. Although six pages in *Trusting God* are devoted to the subject of God's sovereignty in weather, *no mention* is made of 1 Kings 19, an obviously problematic passage for any Calvinist trying to make statements about God's sovereignty in nature. Even assuming Bridges's oversight was unintentional, how do we explain this omission? For it hardly points to a thorough study of the subject.

Nor does Bridges mention Mark 4 where Christ *rebukes* the wind which was causing the waves to nearly swamp the boat which held Jesus and His disciples. The very fact that Christ rebuked the wind implies that He was not directing it just prior to his rebuke, for why would Christ *rebuke* the wind if it were already under his absolute sovereign control? In any particular situation Jesus may first command the wind to blow in one direction and later command it to blow in another direction; but to *rebuke* the wind? A rebuke implies that Jesus stood in contrariness to an existing circumstance fueled by ungodly activity.[25] How much plainer must these passages be to tell us that God is not the cause of every weather occurrence? Therefore if weather brings destruction we should not automatically attribute it to God, as the Calvinist asks us to do.[26]

Perhaps someone will raise an objection here. Why, in Mark 4, would God allow the Enemy to cause a violent wind to blow, if He knew Christ would rebuke it? Wouldn't that mean that God was acting against Himself? But the Bible does not support this objection because *to allow* something is not *to cause* it. God is not ruling the wind at the time Jesus rebukes it. While it is true that God allowed the Enemy to control the wind for a time prior to

Christ's rebuke and foreknew that it would cause trouble for Christ, that circumstance is not the same as if God commanded it (anymore than as if God commanded the wind in Job 1, or the lying spirit in 1 Kings 19). God didn't send the wind against Christ any more than He sent Satan to tempt Christ in the wilderness. In Mark 4 Christ rebukes the wind after being awakened to circumstances that would have proved terrifying for any other man. His faith in God was firm, however, and He rebuked the wind that had been driving the waves. (Certainly, the storm also tested the disciple's faith.)

Another reason to assign this storm to demonic activity is to realize where Jesus was heading. Mark 5 reveals that after Jesus calmed the storm he arrived at the country of the Gaderenes. There He confronted an unclean spirit named Legion who was possessing and tormenting a man. (Scripture refers to this entity as Legion, i.e., with both singular and plural pronouns. Probably they were a group of demons under the leadership of one demon, or perhaps a group that acted as though it was of one mind. At the least, it was a corporate entity.) The name, "Legion" indicates a great number of demons, since a legion of Roman soldiers was approximately 4,000 to 5,000 persons. (Perhaps their name also suggests a warrior-like temperament.) The devils were upset at having to leave the man because of

Jesus' command, and they asked Him for permission to enter a nearby herd of swine. Jesus granted them permission, the devils entered the animals, and the herd of 2,000 swine ran violently down a steep hill into the sea. Prior to the confrontation, Legion was no doubt aware that Christ was heading toward him in a boat and suspected he would be exorcised. It is reasonable to assume (indeed, *necessary*, if we are to maintain a theology in which God is not divided against Himself) that Legion or some other demonic force (the Devil perhaps) had asked God the Father (not *his* Father, of course) permission to direct the winds in this region, and so brought about the storm. The demonic control over this intense wind would explain why Jesus' disciples, many of whom were experienced fishermen on this very Galilean lake, failed to anticipate this sudden, violent wind. Again, all this evidence points to weather occurrences that were powered by demons, not by God. Their power, however, was but for a time and perhaps for an amount of time unknown even to the Enemy himself. (Presumably, God is not, or always not, under obligation to say for how long He will grant the Enemy rule over a given area.)

And so one must ask why an Evangelical book trying to prove God's sovereignty would fail to discuss the weather phenomena of Job 1—2 or mention whatsoever Mark 4—5 or 1 Kings 19? These passages naturally suggest themselves as contrary proofs against the Calvinistic view of God's total sovereignty in weather occurrences, yet all these Scriptures are completely ignored. How do we account for this? Of course, we may eliminate any *purposeful* deception on the part of the author, but then what is left? Neglect perhaps, but if so, such neglect is not fair to a Christian readership struggling to understand the problem of evil. My concern is that such books which advocate God's total and absolute sovereignty (e.g., as authored by Bridges, Sproul, Boettner, etc.), when augmented by many other similarly-minded seminary classes, books, sermons, and commentaries, wrongly influence the majority of Christians. Evangelicalism has embraced Calvinism for some time now and therefore slipped into a theology that promises the Christian a benign unity to everything he experiences. Christians have largely forgotten that their faith is not about finding unity in the experience of man's history, but about finding unity with *Christ*. Doubtless, those who believe that everything happens by divine design can relax more readily in life, even as persons do who use transcendental meditation to melt away their anxieties by embracing the One of what *is*. In fact, arguably, one who meditates agreeably upon Calvinistic principles is merely practicing a certain form of yoga meditation. And because Calvinism's dominance is so strong in today's Church culture, one suspects that the doctrine of God's absolute sovereignty will be the great 'Christian' lullaby for the foreseeable future.[27] Moreover, as the world gets scarier, the retreat into Calvinism will become more attractive. The question, then, is whether the 'sweetness' of this lullaby has settled over the Church to where a correcting message to the Body is an unwelcome interruption that will not be heard. Indeed, if my own experience is any gauge, I would say that the answer is *yes*. (In my case, for example, with one church's leaders there appeared to be a certain reluctance to address the problem of Calvinism as I tried to raise the issue with some of them.) Meanwhile, many Evangelicals simply seem to submit themselves uncritically to Calvinistic doctrine, a doctrine which promises to make God and the gospel irrational in definition and explanation.

THE CHURCH: EQUAL JUSTICE FOR ALL?

We have only explored in part why so many Evangelical books and magazine articles continue to endorse the idea of God's absolute sovereignty. Another reason seems to be that the Church has not been paying attention to Christians who have been warning them against false doctrine. In the Old Testament the job of warning God's people (Israel) against false doctrine fell to the prophets, and today it would appear that a similar prophetic gift may operate in the New Testament church, though I am not arguing here for an extended *Bible*. By 'prophet' I mean 'proclaimer,' not foreteller—though it is true that proclaimers generally have a greater sense of what *future* consequences lay ahead for the Church if it ignores certain truths.[28] Christians with the gift of proclamation may frequently also have some measure of the gift of knowledge into *mysteries* (i.e., included here would presumably be things that at first glance appear contradictory and therefore difficult of perception), so that their warnings have a greater sense of urgency. Thus the prophet prophesies according to the measure of his faith. Like the tone of Old Testament prophets, the tone of today's warnings can sound abrupt and severe. This is because the proclaimer senses an immediacy about some divine warning to the church and understands that God is warning the Body against some disastrous course or doctrinal disease. When we consider the messenger's severe tone to the lukewarm church at Laodicea in Revelation 3 (*"and knowest not that thou art wretched, and miserable, and poor, and blind, and naked"*), we can imagine how that kind of message would be received by a 21st century American Evangelical church. Yet God is the same, His attitude about sin is the same, and the degree and prevalence of sin in the world is the same, if not worse, than it was in the first century. Why then, does the Church expect that the prophetic gift should sound any different? Today the Church seems to expect warnings to be *winsome*, as though they came from diplomats, not prophets. And while winsomeness might be found in the gifts of hospitality, evangelism, helps, pastoring, teaching, etc., this characteristic is *relatively* absent in the case of prophecy. Where, for example, is *winsomeness* found in the many calls for repentance in the Old Testament prophetic books? It does not occur often. While we would grant that an unbeliever must be approached with care, concern, and with tempered speech, why does the Church act as though God has not reserved for Himself certain persons to be His voice of exasperation to His own people? Has He reserved for Himself pastors, teachers, helpers, evangelists, etc., but not proclaimers with knowledge to warn the Church in properly applicable circumstances?

While spiritual gifts make most people feel they are helping to build community, the proclaimer who relays a blunt-sounding message from God can feel considerably marginalized within the Church. I have been involved in local churches most of my life, and have yet to personally experience the church which has taken seriously the gifts of prophecy or the utterance of knowledge, or made a proper venue for them. The practical effect is that some members are saying to other members within the Body, "We have no need of you." Perhaps that's because most people, Christians included, don't like to be told that their thinking ought to change. If you're a Christian with the gifts of proclamation and/or knowledge, you may often feel estranged after attempting to use your gift(s) to help the Body. Probably you are reduced to making some brief comment in Sunday school. Yet Paul's implication that men **can** ask questions at an appropriate time **during the formal worship service** is habitually ignored.[29]

Instead, often the pastor determines the parameters of discourse, and, intentionally or not, monopolizes the information process. And any man wishing to ask a dissenting question about something the pastor says is almost certainly resigned to the non-public venue of the pastor's office at the pastor's convenience. This 'presenter-to-audience' format, conveying the one-way pipeline of information from pastor to congregation, is the near universal experience for most Evangelicals in American churches. As a result, parishioners are mere receivers of information (or what *poses* as information). As such, they are not expected to question the 'authority' of the pastor [i.e., the term 'authority' here seems to represent to the congregation whatever ideas the pastor happens to present]. Indeed, many parishioners seem to be suspicious of any man wishing to critically question something the pastor has said.

Nevertheless, your job (if you are a proclaimer) is to be the scout on the other side of the hill, for few others see what God is showing you—this is simply your job in the church.[30] Yet many of today's proclaimers, or those gifted with the utterance of knowledge, either find no venue in church for their gift or the effort of using their gift too discouraging. Other people with different gifts, such as encouragement, hospitality, or helps, seem relatively welcome in the church and feel less conflicted (at least ideologically) while ministering. This is because everyone appreciates the guy who mows the front lawn of the church or the amateur electrician who knows how to wire a three-way switch between the basement and the sanctuary. Such persons, while they might come into *relational* conflict with others—the kind of conflict which pastors seem naturally adept at handling—rarely come into *doctrinal* conflict with church leadership for obvious reasons. If you are a proclaimer, however, you are almost certain to feel that you are on the outside looking in. Most Christians become guarded whenever you go into a mode of proclaiming, and I don't mean into a mode of public address *per se*, but even when the warning is simply offered in private conversation. For example, Proclaimer *A* says something to Person B that invites a response, but often *Proclaimer A* receives only a short and polite, non-committal reply. No outward disagreement is expressed by Person B (he might even *appear* interested), but the response seems clear—'Don't talk to me about it,' or 'This makes me feel a little uncomfortable.' The proclaimer's persistent attempt at dialogue often earns him the reputation for being somewhat unpredictable—a 'loose cannon on the deck,' a 'difficult' person who is rarely satisfied with the ideological direction of the Church in one way or another. Hence, the proclaimer remains a puzzle to those congregants who do not recognize the need to acknowledge his message. And the same general reaction is directed toward the knower (person gifted with the utterance of knowledge).

And so enters Evangelical Calvinist 'thinkers' who operate in the vacuum of the prophetic gift.[31] These have gained influence for their ideas chiefly from 1) having the gift of especial faith (a gift that is different than the prophetic gift which is used according to the *prophet's* faith), and 2) having the sheer ability to teach and communicate their ideas in a positive-sounding way. Many of these authors do, in fact, have extraordinary abilities to teach, to pastor, and to encourage others. Because most of them have fine intellects and are caring, positive-minded people, they are uncritically listened to in the Church. Most pastors seem to have a special faith like Job, who was prepared to trust God even when it looked like God was punishing him. This is what the gift of faith often looks like among Christians. The gift makes it easier for them to exercise daily, practical faith and to encourage greater faith in the church.[32] In many respects, the gift of faith commends these believers to God and, of course, to many Christians. For people are naturally drawn to faith-filled individuals. When we pause to think of faith-filled people, we realize that a common denominator in them is a deep-seated confidence in God that bears up under public scrutiny. They find it *natural* to believe, and many Christians admire this ability and wish it for themselves. In short, the gift of daily, practical faith is a *winsome* gift. It often attracts people, and again, this gift is absolutely vital to the Church because it encourages others to believe God regardless of the circumstances.

On the other hand, Christians who do not have this *especial* gift of practical faith find it *natural* to be somewhat skeptical. You would never want to settle on the naturally skeptical person as the rightful example of what it means to take God at His word on a moment-by moment basis. Consequently, Christians (like myself) with a natural turn for skepticism are more able to 'identify' with those who believe any one of a hundred false religions or ideologies, because we see in ourselves the human tendency (or temptation) to disbelieve God through a non-biblical idea that can prove just as verbally and argumentatively consistent. Though we are believers, this empathy nevertheless means we entertain more objections against our faith than most other Christians. But as Christian proclaimers with a strong turn for knowledge (or visa versa, knowers with a secondary gift of proclamation) we feel keen concern for whether the Church will maintain the absolute authority of Scripture. This concern often causes us to delve into why the Christian (biblical) faith is the correct one, and why other religions and philosophies are not true. People with the gift of practical faith—and I'm speaking very frankly here—usually do not make the best apologists, because they don't particularly identify with how easy it is for some people to disbelieve, and this often leads them to a lesser interest in examining the Scriptures to combat false ideas (because the concern or emphathy simply isn't there). By the same token most prophets would be lousy pastors because their often blunt and serious approach can leave people feeling they are impatient and unsympathetic. So, there is often no necessity driving the person of faith to seek answers to certain difficult issues. If people with the gift of faith come to a conundrum in the Bible they find it easy to say to themselves, "Well, I can't figure that one out, but obviously God and His Word are true anyway." I know someone who is like this, and he once told me that regardless of whether evolution were true it didn't really impact his Christian faith. Conversely, a person like myself sees the same conundrum and understands why the skeptic might disbelieve the Bible, eeling compessed to adopt the despairing position that he is nothing more than highly evolved sea goo. Another way of expressing this difference in giftedness is to understand that a Christian gifted with evangelism, especially if he is also gifted with practical faith, will more likely be used by God to open a dialog and "close the deal" in evangelizing a person, whereas a Christian with the gifts of proclamation and knowledge may occasionally be used by God to argue down the initial philosophical objections of the unbeliever, far in advance of the arrival of the evangelist. Thus the evangelist may reap the seed that another has sown (and of course, as Paul says, God gives the increase).

What is often misunderstood in the Evangelical church, then, is that the gift of pastoring does not automatically come with the gifts of (*especial*) proclamation and (*especial*) utterance of knowledge, which help the church to better understand the conundrums that affect one's view of God. This is not to say that a pastor/teacher may not be strong in another and complimentary gift. But the especial gift of knowledge to understand difficult, analytical and critical arguments should be expected infrequently among pastors, because the relational temperament generally needed for a pastor to nurture, encourage, and practically instruct others is somewhat different than the temperament generally needed for proclaiming intense, urgent warnings stemming from critical analysis. By "gift" here, I mean that God not only gives a special ability for a Christian to minister to the Body but also—and this is important—*a propensity toward having certain concerns* about the Body. The person with the gift of faith is concerned that other Christians have more faith. By the same token, the one gifted with knowledge about biblical conundrums is concerned that Christians have more understanding about the nature of God, or of eschatology, etc. The one gifted as a pastor is concerned that others be more caring of one another in love and truth, to maintain unity, and so forth. I believe one of the problems in today's Evangelical Church (i.e. regarding the issue of defining the exact nature of God's sovereignty, properly expressed) is that many books have been published by many faith-filled, caring pastors and teachers who, in fact, have **not** had an *especial* gift for knowledge.

I have to be blunt here. What else besides this confusion of gifts would explain why such persons often nibble at problematic passages without really digesting them? They simply believe God is sovereign regardless of what certain Scriptures say. This is why Calvinist apologists are always appealing to 'mystery' in order to explain such a diversity of things—from the problem of evil to the moral character of God. Any person prone to running up the flagpole of conundrum the banner of explanation that reads "God's inscrutable decrees" either 1) does not have the gift of knowledge, or 2) *potentially* has the gift of knowledge but is not walking in the Spirit and so cannot give a proper explanation.[33] Please understand, some of these are men (particularly in the former instance) with a caring nature who don't want to see the faith of Christians overthrown by life's circumstances. Hence, they write long treatises trying to convince Evangelicals to maintain their faith in a God whom they claim guides and governs all the decisions of all the governments, kings, and mad tyrants that have ever lived, some of whom have even blasphemed the name of Christ. Well-meaning men (at least let us hope they are well-meaning) make these Calvinistic statements, but when such statements are taught at our seminaries and preached by nationally recognized pastors, they set the pace for a false apologetic in the Church that is not Christian at all. The most recent example I heard of this was from a well-known Evangelical radio pastor who gave the standard Calvinistic explanation about the tension between the election of sinners by God and the free will of man. After a brief 'explanation' he added the caveat that the conundrum between divine election and human freedom shouldn't bother us overly, "For if God were that small, He wouldn't be big enough to worship." This interpretation about *election* puts the issue of election under the banner, *God is sovereign **in** everything*, including persons' predestined ends, and it may sound impressive—but what does this radio pastor mean, except that God cannot be understood in a rational way? Are we not being told, in effect and by extended application, that God is big enough for us to trust *today* and also big enough to trust that He knew what He was doing in *history* when He foreordained 1930s German politics and the Holocaust which flowed out from it? Personally, this leaves me feeling that God could *afford* to be a little smaller, so that I could thank Him for my salvation without having to glorify Him for His foreordination of the Nazi party. Perhaps this particular preacher would nay-say this alleged implication. Certainly one presumes he is unaware of what he is doing. But as Evangelicals we seem to have forgotten that when the Bible says that God's thoughts and ways are as high above our own even as the heavens are to the earth, this means in *degree*, not in *fundamental kind*, such that a proper logic would no longer be applicable, except in rare cases in which the normal meaning of words would lead to those few antinomies which attend every ideology (e.g., in Christianity's case, a God who—despite having an eternal past, which according to one of Zeno's paradoxes ought to mean God cannot predicate—nevertheless inhabits Time). We are, after all, made in God's image, and so much so that even sucklings and children are able to praise Him. So while it is true that God cannot be understood in His full comprehensiveness, the Bible *does* teach that God can be known *fundamentally*. [Calvinists John Piper, Justin Taylor, and Paul Helseth in *Out of Bounds* show the kind of scriptural backing they imagine supports the idea that God is not merely *quantitatively* different, but also *qualitatively* different. In support of their view they quote the Lord's own statement from Isaiah: "For as the heavens are higher than the earth, so are my ways higher than your ways, and my thoughts than your thoughts." But again, note that God is comparing himself in *degree*, not in *fundamental kind*. This quotation used by Piper et al does not argue for a *qualitatively* different God at all. Moreover, when they make the claim that language descriptive of God is not equivocal nor univocal, but rather analogical, and that, for example, the numerous masculine pronouns referencing God cannot be understood literally, this too is without Scriptural support. For doubtless Piper et al must chiefly have in mind the N.T. statement that God is a Spirit, and therefore without physical, bodily form (except for the Incarnation and possibly O.T. theophanies). But in Greek there is no indefinite article "a"; there is only the definite article "the". Therefore it may be rendered, "God is spirit," i.e., even as man is spirit, though he inhabit bodily form. And as for the possible objection that Christ is said in Hebrews to have remarked of His Father, "Thou has prepared me a body," and that therefore this was an inauguration of a Divine Person into bodily form (or a mere continuation of O.T. theophanies) prior to which Divine Persons had no bodily form, is simply an argument from silence, on the assumption that the only kind of body the Divine Persons can ever inhabit is flesh.]

Incredible damage to Evangelicalism has resulted from seminary professors, pastors, and teachers who for generations have failed to understand when and when not to appeal to "mystery" as a theological explanation. Because these Christians are like the rest of us Christians who still sin, these men are prone to believe in God's goodness even when their interpretations of disastrous events would be legitimate reasons not to trust a God who is alleged to be directing everything. The problem, again, is that many of these men have usurped the office of especial knowledge and/or especial proclamation, and consequently (though perhaps unintentionally) marginalized those who truly do have these gifts. For example, in the Church we have missionary conferences (emphasizing evangelism), marriage seminars (emphasizing nurturing, helps, encouraging, etc.), and even pastor conferences (emphasizing pastoring), but whenever did you hear of a local church seminar concerned with understanding knowledge about conundrums (eschatology excepted)? The proclamation of especial knowledge is simply assumed to be exercised from the pulpit. In the case of Calvinism spawned, the result has been theological error rigorously applied. Take the doctrine of God's absolute sovereignty, for example. Spiritually speaking, it is as though such pastors, teachers, and professors copy out a math problem from a textbook but fail to copy a positive or negative sign, which consequently affects the entire equation. In many respects the deductions of Calvinists *per se* are flawless and in-depth, but because a false, opening premise about the sovereignty of God affects all the deductions that follow, their entire equation, process, and conclusion are wrong. That type of error is not a matter of general intelligence but of specific knowledge (or of a willingness to be open to that knowledge). The situation is like trying to balance a checkbook and transcribing the wrong penny amount from the very first check, and then subsequently carrying that error throughout all the subsequent calculations and balances. Furthermore, all this theological error happens amidst an already bewildering atmosphere of worldly, moral decline affecting the Church—a Church already trying to keep apologetic pace with a score of bizarre, philosophical slants demanding its attention. Naturally, if the Church does not regard prophetic warnings in this climate, it will unwittingly grow accustomed to doubtful ideas. This is what is happening today, and it has been happening for a long time. The result is a Christianity that is watered-down in understanding, so that the Living Water is not presented as refreshing as it (rather, *He*) once was. Of course the principles of consequence that govern the neglect of explaining certain conundrums also govern the neglect of all other spiritual gifts. If the evangelist is undervalued in the Church, the Church will lack missionaries and new converts. If the pastor or teacher is undervalued, the church's nurturing and spiritual education, respectively, will suffer. If helpers are undervalued the church facility will be untidy and work poorly. So, too, if the gift of understanding conundrums (including those about God's character) is undervalued, the church's early warning system against false doctrine is compromised. Indeed, would not today's lack of appreciation for the gifts of prophecy and knowledge go far in explaining why so many false theologies are gaining footholds in the Church?

Is God All-Sovereign in Creation?

If one wanted evidence why someone *not* utilizing the gift(s) of prophecy and/or knowledge should stay away from taking a leading role in apologetics, there are numerous examples. Again, not the least of these (as already demonstrated, but to which we now add a further example) is found in Boettner's book, *The Reformed Doctrine of Predestination*. My study of Boettner was an interesting and disturbing one, for I found a great many assertions in his book urging the reader to concede that God was absolutely sovereign. For example, Boettner speaks of the absolute sovereignty of God over all creation, including the animal kingdom. He begins with examples no one would likely question. Thus we are told that God's eye is on the sparrow, that He provides food for the birds that neither sow nor reap, gives food to the young lions, takes cattle away from the devious Laban in order to give them to Jacob, and shuts the mouths of lions that otherwise would have hurt Daniel.[xxxv] But obviously one finds these examples lopsided; for Boettner[34] makes no mention of the baby sparrow that the cat kills, the crushed animal at the side of the road, or Caesar's lions (or dogs) which masticated upon the faces of early Christians. But why this censoring if indeed God is absolutely sovereign? And what about the human realm? Why not cheer the daily body-count of victims reported on the local evening news as much as the biblical miracles of old? Are not all these the acts of an all-sovereign God? Evidently, the reason for these omissions is because Boettner, though a Calvinist, is one in whom the Spirit of God is still trying to convince of his theological errors. Thus, Boettner has a latent feeling within him that wants to perceive God in terms of kindness. Boettner is not really prone toward seeing God as equally involved in all of man's history and experience, despite his professed willingness to do so.

As I widened my research I came to Sproul's book, *Chosen By God*, which I have previously mentioned. Sproul likewise selects examples that are geared toward gaining our sympathy with God's sovereignty, using evidence one would unlikely question. Here is one such example:

> If there is one single molecule in this universe running around loose, totally free of God's sovereignty, then we have no guarantee that a single promise of God will ever be fulfilled. Perhaps that one maverick molecule will lay waste all the grand and glorious plans that God has made and promised to us. If a grain of sand in the kidney of Oliver Cromwell changed the course of English history, so our maverick molecule could change the course of all redemptive history. Maybe that one molecule will be the thing that prevents Christ from returning.[xxxvi]

Notice here how Sproul appeals to English history and the Protestant reformer Oliver Cromwell as examples of God's sovereignty over 'maverick molecules.' Sproul has thus picked a non-controversial, much-admired figure to pull on the heartstrings of Evangelical Protestants. But imagine the dubiousness of Sproul's argument if his example were that of Adolf Hitler and Nazi policy. On such a footing one might wish that maverick molecules *had* escaped God's foreordained plans in order to run around loose in *Der Fuhrer's* kidney's and change all of German history. Why is it, then, that Sproul is not as prone to use the example of Hitler as he is of the Protestant, Cromwell? Are not both the acts of an all-sovereign God? The reason, apparently, is that Sproul has a desire to perceive God in terms of kindness. Sproul does not really see God as equally involved in all of the affairs of man's cruel history and experience. Thus he feels the pressure to give a *sympathetic* example, despite his eventual appeal to dialectical mystery. Evidently, it has been easier for Sproul to persuade Evangelicals to believe in the absolute sovereignty of God by talking about Reformers who reportedly never entered battle except with a prayer on their lips, rather than by talking about the foreordination of gas ovens and the SS.

The truly astonishing thing about the above statements by these Reformed authors is that neither Boettner nor Sproul express any sense of dilemma in these passages. We wonder what has happened to the kind of concern Sproul mentioned early in his book about the problem of evil not really being appreciated by Christians for its difficulty. Yet where is *his* appreciation of this difficulty at the end of his own book, when stating that he has taken a "great comfort" in the idea of an all-sovereign God? And yet we find a further question—Why would either of these men even suppose that their examples of God's sovereignty fairly represented all of man's history and experience? Indeed, why would they think that such biased examples as they use had any apologetic value at all? For us to surmise the reason or reasons for this is admittedly speculative. Yet let us eliminate purposeful deception; and we also ought to correct any notion that these men lack diligence *per se*, for witness the earnest efforts at writing books that attempt answers. But again, the question is begged—what *then* is left? The only answer I can give is that they do not have the gift of the utterance of knowledge aimed at understanding the particular conundrum we are discussing (despite their giftedness as communicators), and are not listening to those who have it. Remember what 'sovereignty' means to the Calvinist. For him it is not that God is sovereign *despite* history but that God is sovereign *in* history. Unfortunately, Calvinism's grave, mistaken assumption passes largely unnoticed by the Church. Thus Evangelicals continue to embrace Calvin's philosophical model but are without a biblical apologetic. '*Without,*' I say, because the only apologetic that Boettner, Sproul, etc., can offer is history itself, and history as it stands is hardly a compelling argument for a caring God. Indeed, men like Charles Darwin and his followers have always known that such an 'answer' was not a compelling argument. Yet many Christians *still* don't know this, and it's now 150 years *after* the appearance of *On the Origin of Species*. The ideological and evangelizing ground that Christians have lost is simply staggering.

I'll admit that prophetic warnings given to the Church are hard to hear. After all, are there any *nice, winsome* ways to tell a professor, an author, or a pastor that he is wrong? The error will need to be pointed out, and the person will have to realize their mistake. In the case of certain persons it will be incredibly awkward for them. The person in error might have already published in support of divine absolute sovereignty and enjoyed the favor of a national audience. Probably he will have come to his conclusions after studying the Bible and the subject of sovereignty for long hours as a young seminarian or self-educated Bible student. And now we ask him to *repent* of his thinking?! Realistically speaking, what is the likelihood of that? Nevertheless, if the Church is to move forward at all possible speed, then repentance from wrong thinking will need to take place. Even for the Church to move forward at *any* speed toward a correct apologetic about the nature of God will mean recognition by *some* Christians—*more* Christians—that Calvin's view on the sovereignty of God is not biblical, and that it falls woefully short of giving any kind of satisfactory answer to the problem of evil.

Footnotes:

[24] Job 1:4 says that Job's sons "feasted in their houses, every one his day [i.e., birthday)] and sent and called for their three sisters to eat and to drink with them." This verse explains why all of Job's children were in the same place at the time of their deaths. Note that Satan waited to bring disaster until it was the eldest son's birthday, a day symbolic of divine blessing and the beginning of Job's patriarchal strength. Following the tragedy, doubtless Job imagined that these birthdays now promised to be but grim reminders of that terrible day. No

wonder when Job finally spoke out of his depression and sense of survivor-guilt, he first cursed his own day and wished it off the calendar.

[25] The same Greek word in Mark 4:39 translated *rebuked* is used when Jesus rebukes a demon in Mark 1:25 and 9:25. No word translated *command* or *rebuke* appears in Mark 5, as the emphasis instead is on Jesus' permission for the devils to enter the swine. Mark uses other words which have been translated *command*. Thus, Jesus' rebuke of the wind is an act of *contrariness* to the existing circumstance.

I once asked a Reformed thinker about the implication of Jesus *rebuking* the wind. He replied by gesturing with his hands in one direction, then the other, saying we might understand it as Jesus commanding the wind *this* way one moment, then directing it *that* way the next moment. Such a response is a clear example of what Thomas Edgar, in his article on foreknowledge, shows to be the reading of one's theology into the meaning of words when God is [grammatically] the subject of the passage. This Reformed thinker, instead of allowing the historical-grammatical lexical evidence to lead him to a proper understanding of the distinct meanings of 'rebuked' and 'commanded,' chose simply to read his theology into the passage. Thus, since Christ [God] was the subject of the passage, and because this Reformed thinker needed to uphold his doctrine of divine absolute sovereignty, the words 'rebuked' and 'commanded' were forced to be synonyms.

Along these lines I am compelled to say something additionally here. I originally wrote this book in response to Jerry Bridges's book, *Trusting God Even When It Hurts*. This came about (as already noted) because one of my pastors at the church I was attending suggested I give Bridges's book to a close friend of mine who no longer believed in biblical inerrancy. As I read Bridges's book, however, I saw that it was hyper-Calvinistic, and so I never passed it on. Now, in retrospect, I wonder if my friend wasn't being more honest than this pastor (unwittingly) proved to be, for my friend was forthright in his denial of biblical inerrancy, whereas this pastor stood by an author who takes biblical terms and makes them errant. Pray tell, what is the difference, then, between these two acquaintances of mine regarding biblical inerrancy in a certain regard? For if this pastor takes key terms and concepts in the Bible only upon the condition of the terms he accepts, and those terms are in error, then it seems to me his *apologetic understanding* is, at the best, that of a doubleminded Christian, or, at the worst, even Buddhist in nature (since all Reformed terms are flatlined down to meaninglessness). I certainly grant the former, not the latter, but it gives me small comfort to think of the continued influence such Christians wield when expressing their apologetic.

[26] Obviously my statement is not meant to include future divine judgments of God involving weather as foretold in Scripture.

[27] As Arthur Pink says in *The Attributes of God* (p. 27): "Rightly did the late Mr. Spurgeon say in his sermon on Matt. 20:15, "There is no attribute more comforting to His children than that of God's sovereignty. Under the most adverse circumstances, in the most severe trials, they believe that Sovereignty has ordained their afflictions, that Sovereignty overrules them, and that Sovereignty will sanctify them all. There is nothing for which the children ought more

earnestly to contend than the doctrine of their Master over all creation...." "
Hence according to Pink (who follows Spurgeon), God "ordains" that which He "overrules."

[28] Two spiritual gifts that supplement the effort in exposing false doctrine are the gift of prophecy and the gift of knowledge (see spec. 1 Cor. 13:2, but also chpts. 12—14 for a general discussion of spiritual gifts). Paul appears to link these two gifts with explaining mysteries. Peter is an example of someone who probably did not have the gift of (*especial*) knowledge, since his own epistles are fairly straight-forward, and because he speaks of Paul's writings as containing some things hard to understand (difficult of perception). (Arguably, he had the gift of prophecy, however.) Some might argue that these two gifts are related only to canonicity and no longer exist. This argument seeks support from 1 Corinthians 13, in which Paul states that when the complete (KJV *perfect*) thing is come, the partial shall be done away. But Paul is making a general point about completeness, and he offers the example of putting away childish things once he became a man. More to the point, Paul states that when that which is complete arrives he shall know even as he is known. Being in the presence of Christ, not the completion of the Scriptural canon, would seem to be the more likely event referred to here. Granting this, the gifts of prophecy (evidenced today as proclamation) and knowledge are still in operation today.

[29] A fact deduced from a **woman** (or perhaps, *wife*) not being allowed in the formal worship service to ask questions (at least, as the text may be stating, in relation to prophetic evaluation and apart from her husband's authority). Thus any habitual failure on the part of church elders to recognize a man's right, in due order, to question something said in the formal worship service *during the worship service*, is also a failure by such elders to embrace sexual distinction as intended by God regarding this particular area.

[30] While this does not make the proclaimer more special than anyone else in the Body, neither does it make him *less* special. As Paul says, all the gifts of the Spirit in the Body are necessary for the proper working of the whole. Yet in 1 Corinthians 12 Paul does say that the gift of prophecy is greater (weightier) than all others except for the apostleship that was then extant in the early New Testament church. Unlike other lists of spiritual gifts in Paul's other epistles, in which gifts are arranged in no particular order, Paul's assignment of a specific order to the spiritual gifts in 1 Corinthians is given to combat a problem peculiar to the Corinthian church, i.e., that church's tendency to exaggerate the importance of the lesser spiritual gifts. Furthermore, the gift of prophecy is *akin* to the gift of knowledge which understands mysteries (1 Cor. 13:2) and things difficult of perception (2 Pet. 3:16). Further, unlike Old Testament prophecy, New Testament prophecy was to be evaluated. Thus prophets like Agabus were transitional figures between the old and new dispensations, living in the new, but having the kind of ability to foretell events seemingly absent from that activity (of prophecy) in which Paul urged every believer in the Corinthian church to participate, and in which certain ones were especially gifted. Note, then, that the Corinthian text can hardly mean that Paul was urging every believer in the Corinthian church to *foretell* events. Nor should it be assumed that the

"prophecy" which the Corinthian *prophets* spoke was of an Old Testament variety and therefore fundamentally different than that "prophecy" to which all other Corinthian saints were encouraged to use according to their own gifts, since such an assumption would rely on the false hermeneutic that even in the same non-idiomatic context a word (in this case "prophecy") may change meaning depending on the subject. For these reasons proclamation ought to still be considered operational in Christ's church today, though we realize it is somewhat different in form than that found in the Old Testament.

Incidentally, when prophecy or the utterance of knowledge is spurned by the Church, such as explaining how God and His goodness are removed from the problem of evil, it would seem that the Christian's reward stemming from the using of his gift(s), if he does so with deliberate spurning of such gifts in the Body as prophecy and knowledge, will be in vain relative to the extent which his understanding has become false. In other words, if 40% of one's motive in preaching the gospel is based on one's desire that people know God according to the principles of Calvinism, then 40% of one's work is vain in terms of it personally profiting him. That is, God cannot reward him for that part. In addition, his effort in that regard may cause much harm to others.

Also, and incidentally, 1 Corinthians 13:2 is not teaching that a person with the gift of knowledge will have knowledge into *all* mysteries. That is, one ought not to fault a knower for not knowing everything. Indeed, Paul said that we know in part. Simply defined, the Christian knower is the one demonstrating a greater propensity for understanding knowledge than most Christians. Paul is thus stating hypothetical cases in 1 Corinthians 13 to make a general point about love. Thus when Paul says that if he spoke with the tongues of men and of angels, it is doubtful he is implying that it would be possible for him to speak with angelic tongues, for if Paul spoke such languages as a man, angelic languages would cease to be so exalted, since they would no longer be of special angelic domain but accessible also to man (who was made lower than the angels). Rather, Paul is simply making a point in 1 Corinthians 13 by using hyperbole to prove that even the greatest hypothetical accomplishments, if attached to wrong motive, would be without any godly merit.

[31] ...as well as in the vacuum of the gift of knowledge.

[32] A question may be raised here as to how faith of any kind may be said to be given by God, since it must be the believer himself who exercises *his* faith, not God exercising the faith 'on behalf of' the believer. The answer lies upon this fact: the faith described in 1 Corinthians as "the gift of faith" is not *irresistibly* given but is given in the sense of being offered. In the case of the person God wishes to gift with faith, the believer, if willing, is specifically strengthened by God toward that end *via a greater thought presentation*, i.e., according to that which God says is true. This divine mode of Spirit-giving is really true in relation to all the gifts. In other words, spiritual gifts are not irresistible. The Christian who is gifted with mercy is the one walking in the light of Christ and exercising mercy, but clearly that Christian can quench the Spirit in that regard if he wishes to. Even so, the person gifted with faith is not gifted irresistibly against his will. In

fact, probably we all tend to waffle to one degree or another about allowing or resisting the Spirit regarding our gift(s).

As a sidebar point here, let us remember that God in His foreknowledge understands when a person's faith in the work of Christ is of such degree that it shall persevere to the end. And because God has this knowledge, He can declare that such a person is eternally saved upon the instant that person truly trusts Christ. (Incidentally, this fact refutes the notion that we would disbelieve and lose our salvation in the future. God knows whose faith among men is of a persevering kind (i.e., *belief*) and consequently gives His Spirit only unto those who truly (irretractably) believe. Thus God's bestowal of the Spirit is a seal of their salvation.) Note also Christ's statement to his disciples, when He said that the Spirit is willing, but the flesh is weak. He did not say that the flesh was utterly incapable of choosing to do the correct thing in a given situation, but that it was *weak* to do it (see chapter 18 for a true definition of man's fallen nature). Therefore the flesh is not helpless, but weak, i.e., weak in the sense that it *will* not (I do not say *can* not) diligently act unless it is encouraged by God to do so. The point here is that God (in the case of the one being offered the spiritual gift of faith) opposes the believer's weakness in the flesh by presenting to his mind and spirit His divine thoughts, so that the flesh (Gr. *sarx*), which presents to the believer a regular stream of thought (knowledge) telling him of the pleasures of good *and evil*, is interrupted by the divine presentation that seeks to have us live after the Spirit only. God has decided that His interruption of the presentation of the believer's old nature (Gr. *sarx*) *via divine thought-presentation* shall be more pronounced in some believers than in others, i.e., *of faith* to one, *of knowledge* to another, *of how to pastor* to yet another, etc. Incidentally, the wise Christian will see that this divine activity in his life eliminates any boasting in the using of his gift.

[33] Ironically, those who do not have the gift of knowledge but purport that they do, make frequent appeals to the *absence* of knowledge as the basis of explanation. We ought to remember that such persons in their theology will promote a seducing spirit of doctrine that may feel good to the Body but is, in fact, deadly. If it is true that we are living in the last days, then one ought to look for a popular doctrine that *sounds* like it is Christian, but is not (i.e., Calvinism); for presumably Satan is clever enough to know that believers will not discard biblical doctrine for another gospel unless it *appears* biblical.

[34] I first came across Boettner's work after it was recommended to me some 20 years ago in the basement bookstore of a large, well-known, Presbyterian church whose membership I nearly joined. I had come within a week of completing my membership classes, when I came to realize I no longer felt comfortable enough with the doctrine of the absolute sovereignty of God to join the church. Nevertheless, I wanted to study a book about Calvinism that was authored by a Calvinist in order to better understand the Calvinist's argument. When I asked the elderly clerk of the church bookstore (who seemed long on experience) if there was a standard work on the subject of *predestination*, he recommended (with little hesitation) Boettner's work, *The Reformed Doctrine of Predestination*.

Endnotes:

[xxxiii] Bridges, pp. 117-118.

[xxxiv] Bridges, p. 96.

[xxxv] Boettner, p. 39.

[xxxvi] Sproul, pp. 26-27.

CHAPTER 11
*Does God Control Everyone's Heart?:
Understanding Proverbs 21:1*

One of the suppositions used by Calvinists to say that God is directing every man towards a particular, unalterable end is the argument about God's all-controlling activity in human government. In his book, *An Exposition of the Book of Proverbs*, author Charles Bridges advances the argument that God directs all the affairs of men. Jerry Bridges, in his book, *Trusting God Even When It Hurts*, endorses Charles Bridges's commentary regarding a key biblical passage both men believe supports the doctrine of God's absolutely sovereignty:

> Perhaps the clearest biblical statement that God does sovereignly influence the discussions of people is found in Proverbs 21:1, "The king's heart is in the hand of the Lord; he directs it like a watercourse wherever he pleases." Charles Bridges, in his exposition of Proverbs, states, "The general truth [of God's sovereignty over the hearts of all people] is taught by the strongest illustration—his uncontrollable sway upon the absolute of all wills—the king's heart."
>
> In our day of limited monarchies in which kings and queens are largely figureheads, it may be difficult for us to appreciate fully the force of what Charles Bridges is saying when he speaks of the king's heart as the most absolute of all wills. But in Solomon's time the king was an absolute monarch. There was no separate legislative body to make laws he wouldn't like or a Supreme Court to restrain him. The king's word was law. His authority over his realm was unconditional and unrestrained.
>
> Yet God controls the king's heart. The stubborn will of the most powerful monarch on earth is directed by God as easily as the farmer directs the flow of water in his irrigation canals. The argument, then, is from the greater to the lesser—if God controls the king's heart surely He controls everyone else's. All must move before His sovereign influence.[xxxvii]

Note in the above passage how God's sovereignty is described (directly or as metaphorical type) first, as an *influence.*; second, as *directing* ; third, as an *uncontrollable sway* ; fourth, as *absolute* ; fifth, as *unconditional and unrestrained* ; sixth, as *controls* ; seventh, as *directed/directs* ; eighth, as *controls* ; and ninth (as at the first), *influence*. Observe, then, how God's sovereignty is discussed at the beginning and end of this quote as merely an *influence* (which leaves the reader with the opening and closing subconscious impression that the king is acting in free will), yet in the interim is described in the much more forceful terms of divine *irresistibility*, since God supercedes the king's authority which is said to be *absolute, uncontrollable, and unrestrained.* Such language, we note, makes synonyms out of non-synonyms. For example, in the sentence: "The teacher had a positive influence over the students," no one would suppose that the teacher's influence was anything of the forceful and coercive kind implied in the terms *uncontrollable and unrestrained*, i.e., such that the word *influence* should be thought to have these same meanings. In other words, no English dictionary in common use has, for the word *influence*, a basic definition such as "absolute control," "unrestrained authority," or other words or phrases implying *irresistibility*, which is the 'forward rock' of meaning Charles Bridges uses to convey his doublethink. Thus Calvinism's seesawing language of combining non-synonymous words to form such dialectical phrases like *uncontrollable sway* or *sovereign*[35] *influence* (which, in fact, unlike simple oxymoronic phrases, are invoked to genuinely endorse the dialectic), is all part of the nonsensical language that Calvinists so habitually use that they have become unaware of how they use dishonest language when discussing theology. Thus for Charles Bridges, "all **must** move" (emphasis mine) when the subject is God's sovereignty. Note also the subtle word "move," by which is really meant "irresistibly follow."

As the primary proof of Charles Bridges's point, Jerry Bridges cites the example of Cyrus. Cyrus began his reign by uniting the two Iranian tribes of the Medes and Persians (in the early 6th century B.C.). King Cyrus then proceeded to become emperor and, in the course of his reign, made authoritative decrees that affected many peoples, including the Jews. Says Bridges:

> We see it also in the account of Cyrus, king of Persia, when he issued a proclamation to allow the Jews to return to Jerusalem to rebuild the Temple. Ezra 1:1 says,
>
> > "In the first year of Cyrus king of Persia, in order to fulfill the word of the Lord, spoken by Jeremiah *the Lord moved the heart of Cyrus* king of Persia to make a

> proclamation throughout his realm and to put it in writing." (emphasis added)
>
> The text clearly says that King Cyrus issued the proclamation because God moved his heart. The destiny of God's people was, humanly speaking, in the hands of the most powerful monarch of the day. In reality, though, their destiny was completely in God's hand, because He had the ability to sovereignly control the decisions of that monarch.
>
> God, speaking through the prophet Isaiah, gives us another helpful insight into His working in Cyrus's heart: "For the sake of Jacob my servant, of Israel my chosen, I summon you by name and bestow on you a title of honor, *though you do not acknowledge me*...I will strengthen you, *though you have not acknowledged me*" (Is. 45:4-5, emphasis added). It is not necessary for a person to acknowledge God's sovereign control in his heart or to even acknowledge the existence of God. Neither the Egyptians nor Cyrus intended to obey any revealed will of God. They simply acted as their hearts directed them, but their hearts were directed by God.[xxxviii]

I must confess that I was not very familiar with the details of the story of King Cyrus when I first read the above passage by Jerry Bridges. Certainly the argument sounded pretty convincing for the Calvinistic side of the argument. Nevertheless, I decided I ought to read more of the story of Cyrus in Ezra 1 and Isaiah 45. To my amazement I discovered a very different history for Cyrus than the impression left by Bridges's summation. After reading Bridges's comments one would think that God's will was being carried out *despite* any conscious or intentional cooperation from King Cyrus. In fact, Bridges never suggests that Cyrus ever acknowledged God at all. He even claims that the king did not intend to obey any revealed will of God. [Again, we see that Bridges mentions that (Calvinistic) 'other' kind of will (i.e., *revealed will*) besides God's supposed *all-encompassing/ no exceptions* sovereign will to account for man's disinclination from God, e.g., in Cyrus's alleged non-acknowledgement of God.] Thus, Bridges leaves the impression that Cyrus is nothing more than a heathen king directed unknowingly by God to do something which the king did not intend. According to Bridges, then, Cyrus does not acknowledge God, does not have relationship with Him, does not want to obey Him, and essentially wants nothing to do with God. You would certainly never guess from reading the above passage by Bridges that Cyrus ever *knew* God and, in fact, had a personal relationship with Him. Nor would you ever suppose that Cyrus's relationship with God would naturally lead him to favor the return of the Jewish exiles once God raised the subject with him. Let us read the following two passages in context about Cyrus: (Is. 45:1ff)

> [1]Thus saith the Lord to his anointed, to Cyrus, whose right hand I have holden, to subdue nations before him; and I will loose the loins of kings, to open before him the two leaved gates; and the gates shall not be shut; [2]I will go before thee, and make the crooked places straight: I will break in pieces the gates of brass, and cut in sunder the bars of iron: [3]And I will give thee the treasures of darkness, and hidden riches of secret places, that thou mayest know that I, the Lord, which call thee by thy name, am the God of Israel. [4]For Jacob my servant's sake, and Israel mine elect, I have surnamed thee, though thou hast not known me: [5]I am the Lord, and there is none else, there is no God beside me: I girded thee, though thou hast not known me: [6]That they may know from the rising of the sun, and from the west, that there is none beside me. I am the Lord, and there is none else.

And from Ezra 1:1-3:

> [1]Now in the first year of Cyrus king of Persia, that the word of the Lord by the mouth of Jeremiah might be fulfilled, the Lord stirred up the spirit of Cyrus king of Persia, that he made a proclamation throughout all his kingdom, and put it also in writing, saying, [2]Thus saith Cyrus king of Persia, The Lord God of heaven hath given me all the kingdoms of the earth; and he hath charged me to build him an house at Jerusalem, which is in Judah. [3]Who is there among you of all his people? His God be with him, and let him go up to Jerusalem, which is in Judah, and build the house of the Lord God of Israel, (he is the God,) which is in Jerusalem.

We see, then, in the above Scriptural passages a more complete and *very different* history of Cyrus than what Bridges conveys in his book. Of course, we see that Bridges is right when he says that Cyrus had not known nor acknowledged God—but what of it? It is clear from Psalm 14:2-3 that this kind of statement is initially true of *any* man: "The Lord looked down from heaven upon the children of men to see if there were any that did understand, and seek God. They are all gone aside, they are all together become filthy: there is none that doeth good, no, not one." We should hardly be surprised that a Gentile king who grew up in a heathen nation without the benefit of the Mosaic Law should especially begin by not diligently seeking God. The Bible tells us, though, that God granted Cyrus military successes so that the king would understand that it was He (God)—the God of the Hebrews—who gave him these victories.

Thus Cyrus was already predisposed toward obeying the God of the Hebrews when he commanded the Jewish exiles to return to Jerusalem, since Cyrus understood that God had proved Himself in prophecy.[36] So when Ezra tells us in 1:1 that the Lord *moved* the heart of Cyrus, the word "moved" in Hebrew does not convey any sense of unilateral action on God's part, as though Cyrus were a kind of puppet unaware of God's plan when he issued the proclamation for the return of the Jewish exiles. Rather, the word *moved* means *to stir up* (cp. KJV), as one roused from sleepiness.[37] God was stirring up Cyrus toward a specific end regarding the Jewish people, and Cyrus was already predisposed toward listening to the Hebrew God. Isaiah, in fact (speaking in the prophetic present), states that Cyrus "knew" God. It would be natural, then, for Cyrus to 'get aboard' with God's plan involving the Jewish people. Hence, we see Cyrus making a bold proclamation about "The Lord, the God of heaven, (who) has given me all the kingdoms of the earth" before proceeding to personally encourage the Jews to return to Judah and Jerusalem. There is no indication, here, as Bridges claims, that Cyrus intended to go his own way irrespective of God *as the Egyptians had done*, i.e., in Bridges's statement that *Neither the Egyptians nor Cyrus intended to obey any revealed will of God. They simply acted as their hearts directed them, but their hearts were directed by God.* That Cyrus needed to be roused to make a proclamation involving the Jews hardly proves Bridges's point, unless we are to suppose that the rest of us as believers never need to be roused from our own spiritual sleepiness to do God's will!

One also wonders what Bridges would do with the word *move* as given in the KJV in Job 1, when God says to Satan:

> Hast thou considered my servant Job, that there is
> none like him in the earth, a perfect and an upright
> man, one that feareth God, and hateth evil? And still
> he holds his integrity, though you move me to destroy
> him without cause.

Here God says that He was *moved* by Satan to destroy Job without cause.[38] But according to Bridges, supposedly only God moves hearts. So, what is all this about God saying *He* was moved (and by no less a person than Satan)? This would certainly seem to lead to a quandary about exactly who is moving whom. Interestingly enough, the Hebrew meaning of the word *moved* in Job 1 means *to prick*, and the word properly translated by the NAS is *incited* (i.e., "though you incited me to destroy him without cause"). The verb *moved* (KJV) in Job 1 is arguably a more intensive verb than the word 'moved' (NIV) found in Ezra 1:1, the argument being that one would prefer to be roused awake rather than be pricked.

Given, then, the consideration of Ezra and Isaiah in their contexts, how can Cyrus be thought prototypical of the king who rules with no intention of obeying God? Or again, why would Bridges assume that Cyrus made a proclamation involving the Jewish people with no intentional regard for their welfare? The Scriptures simply do not support Bridges's conclusions regarding the matter.

The main reason offered by Bridges for coming to his conclusions regarding Cyrus is his interpretation of Proverbs 21:1—"The king's heart is in the hand of the Lord; he directs it like a watercourse wherever he pleases." Bridges agrees with author Charles Bridges that the king is meant to be understood as the representative head of his subjects; thus, if God directs the king's heart, surely He directs everyone else's heart. Unfortunately, this interpretation is another example of a verse being taken out of its proper biblical context to try to prove the notion of divine irresistibility. For Bridges's argument fails when one considers both the near and far contexts of the Solomonic proverbs. First the near context: Proverbs 21:1-4: ¹The king's heart is like channels of water in the hand of the Lord; He turns it wherever He wishes. ²Every man's way is right in his own eyes, But the Lord weighs the hearts. ³To do righteousness and justice is desired by the Lord more than sacrifice. ⁴Haughty eyes and a proud heart, The lamp of the wicked is sin.

Consider Bridges's theology in light of some of the statements in these four verses. God is said to direct the king's heart, and Bridges claims that this means that all men have hearts that are likewise directed just like water is channeled this way or that way according to whatever pleases the Lord. But if this is true, why does verse 2 tell us that every man thinks he is right in his *own* eyes? Moreover, a dilemma arises when verse 3 tells us that the Lord desires justice more than sacrifice. This implies that some men think sacrifice is sufficient even when they are not merciful. But how could such men with such hearts exist, since God (according to Bridges) is the One moving everyone's heart? For if God *desires* justice more than sacrifice and is also moving everyone's heart, why wouldn't *every* man's heart consequently *desire* justice more than sacrifice? Or again, why would some men have "a proud heart," have haughty eyes, and love wickedness if God is the One responsible for where their hearts have been channeled? At this point I can imagine what the Calvinist would say. Proverbs 21:1-2 must be the perfect expression of the 'seeming' contradiction in the Westminster Confessions, i.e., that God moves every person's heart, *yet so, as thereby neither is God the author of sin, nor is violence offered to the will of the creatures*, with the result that every man does that which is right in his *own* eyes.

Though such a reply might be clever, its assumption is not supported by the wider context of Proverbs 21, which we will look at in a moment. But notice first that both Jerry Bridges and Charles Bridges treat the king's heart in the abstract, as though it awaits God to move it into whatever directional channel God desires. Bridges's view is not that the heart can desire wicked things, which is what Christ stated about a man's heart in Matthew 15:19ff. I find it interesting that although Calvinists attempt to uphold the two principles of God's absolute sovereignty and man's free will (the latter through betimes subtle, ambiguous phrases, like 'man is permitted,' instead of 'God permits man' (i.e., the former of these phrases presented in the same spirit as stating *'whatsoever comes to pass'*), Calvinists seem more concerned that man's freedom be an expression of God's sovereignty rather than God's sovereignty be an expression of man's free will. In theory one should not have ascendancy over the other if both are as inviolate as Calvinists need them to be when discussing the origin of sin. This is a very crucial problem for the Calvinist and, in fact, causes him an unsolvable dilemma when trying to account for the problem of evil. But to return to our main discussion, the king mentioned in Proverbs 21:1 is not a king to be viewed in the abstract but rather a king who is already listening to God, as the verses in Proverbs about "king" and "kings" teach.

Before we list every one of the Solomonic verses referring to a king, consider that Solomon's experience of kingship was in many ways a positive one. His father was David, the great and godly king of Israel, and by the time Solomon was just an infant David was past that season of his life when he had transgressed against Uriah the Hittite by committing adultery with Uriah's wife, Bathsheba, and arranging Uriah's murder. He was thus a more chastened and obedient king when Solomon was raised. Solomon also saw the attempted usurpation of his father's throne by his stepbrother, Absalom, and understood how a man could rise to become an evil ruler. As for himself, Solomon would remain uninterrupted in his reign as long as he lived. Even at the political level he generally had successful relationships with rulers of other nations (though he sometimes did the wrong thing). He married Pharaoh's daughter and was at peace with the Egyptian pharaoh. He had peaceful, business relations with Hiram, king of Tyre, with whom he bargained for cedar and cypress wood and for gold to build the Temple in Jerusalem. He even had a good rapport with the Queen of Sheba, who admired Solomon's wisdom and the proceedings of his court. Many or all of these experiences are reflected in how Solomon understands the idea of kingship in Proverbs. The following is an exhaustive list[39] of all the Solomonic verses in Proverbs describing the character and role of a king: In the multitude of people is the king's honour: but in the want of people is the destruction of the prince (14:28).

The king's favour is toward a wise servant: but his wrath is against him that causeth shame (14:35).

A divine sentence is in the lips of the king: his mouth transgresseth not in judgment (16:10).

It is an abomination to kings to commit wickedness: for the throne is established by righteousness (16:12).

Righteous lips are the delight of kings; and they love him that speaketh right (16:13).

The wrath of a king is as messengers of death: but a wise man will pacify it (16:14).

In the light of the king's countenance is life; and his favour is as a cloud of the latter rain (16:15).

The king's wrath is as the roaring of a lion; but his favour is as dew upon the grass (19:12).

The fear of a king is as the roaring of a lion: whoso provoketh him to anger sinneth against his own soul (20:2).

A king that sitteth in the throne of judgment scattereth away all evil with his eyes (20:8).

A wise king scattereth the wicked, and bringeth the wheel over them (20:26).

Mercy and truth preserve the king: and his throne is upholden by mercy (20:28).

The king's heart is in the hand of the Lord, as the rivers of water: he turneth it whithersoever he will(21:1).

He that loveth pureness of heart, for the grace of his lips the king shall be his friend (22:11).

My son, fear thou the Lord and the king: and meddle not with them that are given to change(24:21).

It is the glory of God to conceal a thing: but the honour of kings is to search out a matter (25:2).

The heaven for height, and the earth for depth, and the heart of kings is unsearchable (25:3).

Take away the wicked from before the king, and his throne shall be established in righteousness (25:5).

Put not forth thyself in the presence of the king, and stand not in the place of great men (25:6).

The king by judgment establisheth the land: but he that receiveth gifts overthroweth it (29:4).

The king that faithfully judgeth the poor, his throne shall be established for ever (29:14).

Again, note how Solomon generally views the king in positive terms as a ruler in God's stead. Only one verse in more than 20 describes a negative king, and even this one begs the question why God (if Bridges is right) would turn a king's heart towards something that was abominable to Himself. Otherwise, Solomon speaks confidently and optimistically about the king, describing him as though certain ideal traits are to be expected of him. Thus, the king favors the wise servant but is angered against shameful persons (14:35), the king executes godly sentence and does not trespass in judgment (16:10), the king scatters the wicked with his eyes (20:26), and the king's friend will be one who loves pureness of heart (22:11). In all these instances the king is *assumed* to be a righteous king. The king will also allow himself to be tempered by a wise man on certain occasions when he is angry and thinks to exercise the law without mercy (16:14).[40]

Needless to say, though Solomon's perspective in Proverbs assumes the king is righteous, many kings and rulers in history have been quite evil. Numerous examples come to mind from the Bible and throughout human history. A partial list would include the Egyptian pharaohs in Exodus, Og (Bashan), Ahab (Israel), Manasseh (Judah), all the other kings from Israel and various kings of Judah, the Caananite kings who fought against Joshua, Herod the Great, Nero, Ivan the Terrible, Napoleon, Hitler, and Stalin. These kings and rulers were obviously unrighteous and consistently demonstrated none of the godly characteristics Solomon assumes for a king. So when we come to Proverbs 21:1 and read that the king's heart is in the hand of the Lord and that He directs it wherever He wants, it must be understood that this verse cannot be *universally* applied to all the crazed despots in human history. Rather, God influences kings who understand righteousness and have a predisposition for godly rule. King Cyrus, in fact, is the perfect example of Proverbs 21:1, though not in the way Bridges describes him. It is not true for Bridges to imply that Cyrus was going on his own way irrespective of God, and that God laid his arm upon him to unwittingly accomplish His will in returning the Jewish exiles to their homeland. Rather, Cyrus was already in relationship with God when he was spiritually roused to do God's work. The heart of Cyrus was in the hand of the Lord, and the Lord turned it in whatever direction He wanted for a simple reason—because Cyrus was already predisposed toward doing what God wanted.

Proverbs 21:1 is a good example of why it is important that great care be used in interpreting the Bible so that wrong conclusions are not reached. Look what happens to the strength of Bridges's argument, for example, when we apply his universalizing hermeneutic to other Solomonic proverbs regarding *the king* in Proverbs. In Proverbs 16:10 we are told that the king's mouth does not transgress in judgment, and in 22:11 that the king will accept as his friend all who love pureness of heart and have grace upon their lips. *Thus, if we follow Bridges's universalizing hermeneutic about "the king" in Proverbs whose heart a good God moves, we must also say that every king who has ever lived has never transgressed in judgment, nor failed to befriend the pure in heart!*[41] That such a benign description does not fit every king who has ever had occasion to reign is beyond debate. These examples show the obvious error in universalizing the king of Proverbs 21:1 to mean anything more than a king who has a relationship with God and is therefore predisposed to following Him. The selection by Bridges of Proverbs 21:1, to prove that God sovereignly directs and controls every activity and decision of man, is what happens when a Christian author who believes in the absolute sovereignty of God lifts a verse out of its near and far contexts to make it say whatever he needs it to say in order to maintain his particular brand of theology.

Footnotes:

[35] Obviously, by the term *sovereign*, the Calvinist always means all-sovereign (insofar as it can be said that he actually means anything while on the forward rock of the dialectical rocking horse).

[36] The Jewish historian, Josephus, tells us that Cyrus became convinced that the Hebrew God was the one true God when he became aware of Isaiah's prophecy about him. The prophecy was written generations before Cyrus was born. Says Josephus:

"This was known to Cyrus by his reading the book which Isaiah left behind him of his prophecies; for this prophet said that God had spoken thus to him in a secret vision: "My will is, that Cyrus, whom I have appointed to be king over many and great nations, send back my people to their own land, and build my temple." This was foretold by Isaiah one hundred and forty years before the temple was demolished. Accordingly, when Cyrus read this, and admired the Divine power, an earnest desire and ambition seized upon him to fulfill what was so written; so he called for the most eminent Jews that were in Babylon, and said to them, that he gave them leave to go back to their own country, and to rebuild their city Jerusalem…" (Josephus. Antiquities of the Jews, Book XI, chapter I)

[37] See *Strong's Concordance*, word #5782.

[38] God, in allowing Job's trial to result in proving His and His servant's motives, also proved His foreknowledge of the future by showing that He could predict accurately Job's response. Satan, on the other hand, was proven false. One wonders what impact, if any, this event has had on the fallen angels, i.e., whether a foreboding exists among them regarding their future and eternal abode (which is a divinely prepared hell) as prophesied in Scripture, since God has proven to them that He knows the future accurately.

[39] Not included here are those of King Lemuel as taught to him by his mother (see Proverbs 31); for some believe that Lemuel is a diminutive form for the name Solomon. Interestingly enough, if that is the case, then Bathsheba was the one who taught Solomon about the 'Proverbs 31 woman.' At any rate, nothing in Proverbs 31 relevant to kingship, such as the statement that kings ought not to drink strong wine and forget the rights of the afflicted, affects whatsoever the above argument in the main text, unless it be said to strengthen it.

[40] This does not necessarily mean, however, that the king would be doing evil were he to hold people to a stricter accounting of the law on certain occasions. Even the Lord was pacified by Moses when the Lord thought to destroy the children of Israel for their disobedience.

[41] An additional example supporting our contention is Proverbs 16:13, "*Righteous lips are the delight of kings; and they love him that speaketh right.*" Are we to really to suppose, then, that Tyndale at the fire stake and Bonhoeffer on the gallows are examples of those in whom kings delighted for speaking right?

Endnotes

[xxxvii] Bridges, pp. 58-59.

[xxxviii] Bridges, pp. 59-60.

Chapter 12
Does Voting Count in God's 'Election'?

It is exactly one week before Christmas, and earlier today an announcement was made in my church that one of our young congregants, Cameron, a 26-year old husband and father of three young daughters, died from injuries suffered in an accident. The crash itself happened about a week earlier, when, in the early morning hours after Cameron helped a friend and was returning home, his vehicle hit a patch of black ice and he lost control of it. Since then, Cameron had lain in the hospital, and the congregation was told that despite the severity of the crash there was no major head trauma or damage to the spinal column. In short, Cameron was expected to recover. But again, that was last week. The man who made the announcement today added as compassionately as possible that this was apparently the time God had "determined" to bring Cameron home. This kind of statement was meant to offer consolation to the family, but, of course, it was also meant to calm the anxieties of those who might be tempted to wonder where God was in the midst of this terrible circumstance. Couldn't God, we are tempted to ask, have done something to prevent this awful tragedy? Couldn't the weather have been different so that the roads were in better shape? Couldn't the young man have taken a different way home, so he wasn't in that exact place on that particular part of the highway? These are natural questions for people to ask, but they pale into insignificance if one truly believes that God *determined* to take this young man home. After all, who are we to tell God that Cameron should still be here with us? (*Shall the thing formed say to him who formed it, Why hast thou made me thus?*) And so the traditional explanation prevailed of "whatever the Lord wills," as yet another tragedy was generalized into a God-approved event to reassure nervous Christians of a Final Providence in a frightening world.

No doubt the age-old idea presented today, that man proposes but God disposes, has led many Christians throughout the centuries to wonder just what kind of a God they serve. Of all the chapters in the Bible (in this regard), Romans 9 seems to trouble Christians more than any other passage. This is because Romans 9 appears to add fuel to the fire of the argument about persons' divinely appointed ends. So at this fundamental level, there is this question of whether God 'conducts' his relationships with people so that some men receive eternal mercy while others are "sovereignly passed over" (if not outrightly reprobated). Says Dr. Bob Deffinbaugh, a Reformed thinker trying to understand the biblical issue of election in Romans 9, while trying to figure out what God is doing:

If Romans 8 has the distinction of being the high-water mark of the New Testament, chapter 9 has the dubious honor of teaching one of the most emotionally volatile doctrines of all the Bible, that of election. This chapter is so troublesome to some Bible teachers that they would prefer it not to be in Scripture. One of the pastors I regard most highly in terms of his ministry in my life told me that he would try not to teach on chapter 9, even if he were teaching through the Book of Romans chapter by chapter.[xxxix]

Probably every Christian (including myself at one time) has wondered why God's nature appears so different in Romans 9 compared to elsewhere in the Bible. The Psalms, for example, tell us that God is merciful and good, and certainly we see these divine traits exercised throughout the Old Testament as God enters into relationship with people. In the New Testament we also see God in the person of His Son as similarly benign: Jesus invites little children to come to him, feeds multitudes of people to prevent their becoming faint on their way home, walks on the Sea of Galilee to comfort His disciples during a storm, forgives the heinous sin of a repentant adulteress, heals the sick and the maim, raises the dead, and preaches the gospel to the poor. But all this benevolence of character seems suddenly cast aside as we read through the infamous examples of Romans 9. Indeed, God seems to choose Jacob over Esau for no particular reason, even while the twins are still in their mother's womb. He also appears to raise up Pharaoh for the purpose of destroying him in order to bring glory to Himself. God even appears to decide individual eternal destinies in such a complete way that the only image strong enough to convey the idea of divine, unilateral activity is the Potter forming the clay into whatever the Potter wants.

It appears that a careful study of Romans 9, however, yields a different conclusion than the typical explanation about God's unconditional election of some persons to be saved, and the reprobation of the rest to be lost. Here, Paul, in comparing one thing or person with another, uses Old Testament history to clarify God's nature and work in the world. As we come to better understand this difficult chapter we will find that a chief theme is not that God is inscrutably wrathful toward vessels of destruction, but that He is patient with all and everlastingly merciful to those who trust Him.

As we begin, then, to examine Romans 9, note the many contrasts made (or implied) by Paul. They are: 1) unbelieving Israel to believing Israel; 2) Abraham's behavior prior to the birth of Ishmael to Abraham's subsequent behavior surrounding the birth of Isaac; 3) Ishmael to Isaac; 4) Esau to

Jacob; 5) Pharaoh to Moses; and 6) vessels of wrath to vessels of mercy. Let us consider verses 1-24 (with a notation at verse 16):

> [1]I say the truth in Christ, I lie not, my conscience also bearing me witness in the Holy Ghost, [2]That I have great heaviness and continual sorrow in my heart. [3]For I could wish that myself were accursed from Christ for my brethren, my kinsmen according to the flesh: [4]Who are Israelites; to whom pertaineth the adoption, and the glory, and the covenants, and the giving of the law, and the service of God, and the promises; [5]Whose are the fathers, and of whom as concerning the flesh Christ came, who is over all, God blessed for ever. Amen. [6]Not as though the word of God hath taken none effect. For they are not all Israel, which are of Israel: [7]Neither, because they are the seed of Abraham, are they all children: but, In Isaac shall thy seed be called. [8]That is, They which are the children of the flesh, these are not the children of God: but the children of the promise are counted for the seed. [9]For this is the word of promise, At this time will I come, and Sara shall have a son. [10]And not only this; but when Rebekah also had conceived by one, even by our father Isaac; [11](For the children being not yet born, neither having done any good or evil, that the purpose of God according to election might stand, not of works, but of him that calleth;) [12]It was said unto her, The elder shall serve the younger. [13]As it is written, Jacob have I loved, but Esau have I hated. [14]What shall we say then? Is there unrighteousness with God? God forbid. [15]For he saith to Moses, I will have mercy on whom I will have mercy, and I will have compassion on whom I will have compassion. [16]So then it is not of him that willeth (Gr. *thelō*), nor of him that runneth, but of God that sheweth mercy. [17]For the scripture saith unto Pharaoh, Even for this same purpose have I raised thee up, that I might show my power in thee, and that my name might be declared throughout all the earth. [18]Therefore hath he mercy on whom he will have mercy, and whom he will he hardeneth. [19]Thou wilt say then unto me, Why doth he yet find fault? For who hath resisted his will? [20]Nay but, O man, who art thou that repliest against God?

Shall the thing formed say to him that formed it, Why hast thou made me thus? ^{21}Hath not the potter power over the clay, of the same lump to make one vessel unto honour, and another unto dishonour? ^{22}What if God, willing to show his wrath, and to make his power known, endured with much longsuffering the vessels of wrath fitted to destruction: ^{23}And that he might make known the riches of his glory on the vessels of mercy, which he had afore prepared unto glory, ^{24}Even us, whom he hath called, not of the Jews only, but also of the Gentiles?

Leaving the discussions of (a) Pharaoh; and (b) the pot and potter metaphor for later chapters (detailed esp. in chpts. 14 and 15); let us for now consider the acts of Abraham. Again, as Paul begins chapter 9 he has just finished one of the loftiest passages of the Bible (as Deffinbaugh notes). It is one in which he states that the believer shall never be separated from God (Rom. 8:38-39). The segue of Paul's thoughts now naturally turn to those who *are* separated from God, i.e., the great majority of Israelites—"My kinsmen," says Paul, "according to the flesh." The question at hand is the same as that taken up by Christ in the gospels, namely, whether or not salvation is based upon being a physical descendent of a blessed ancestor, i.e., Abraham. Paul agrees with Christ that physical ancestry does not save, answering the question by saying,

…Neither, because they (Abraham's physical descendents) are the seed of Abraham, are they all children: but, In Isaac shall thy seed be called. ^{8}That is, They which are the children of the flesh, these are not the children of God: but the children of the promise are counted for the seed. ^{9}For this is the word of promise, At this time will I come, and Sara shall have a son.

Paul has said in verses 2-3 that he has great heaviness of heart because the majority of Israelites remain under the curse of God due to their unbelief. He is especially grieved because Israel, his own nation, was the vehicle God used to give His Word. God's promises, covenants, and intended glory were all for the Jewish people, and so the shortcoming of Israel has been all the more tragic. Paul notes, however, that some Israelites have not followed the wrongful course of the greater part of the nation. These are Abraham's true spiritual children because they are like Isaac whom Sarah bore—children born of God's promise and intervention. The allusion here is that God's promise to Abraham of a son was *not* realized when Abraham willfully took Hagar (his barren wife's handmaiden) as a concubine to try to make God's promise a reality. This act of Abraham is a picture of *works*, of man striving on his own to achieve some end he imagines to be good. Though Abraham was a believer at this time, his failure to wait on the Lord is parabolic of the unsaved man striving to reach God's promises through his own will and effort. Consequently, the Lord told Abraham that the resulting child, Ishmael, was not the son God had promised. Abraham thus learned to be more patient, and so exercised his faith in this matter by now waiting diligently upon the Lord. Finally, at age 90, Sarah gave birth to Isaac.[42]

Note here how Paul's allusion to Abraham's faith in Romans 9 hearkens us back to the principle of Abrahamic faith which Paul discussed earlier in Romans 4:

> [1]What then shall we say that Abraham our father has found according to the flesh? [2]For if Abraham was justified by works, he has something to boast about, but not before God. [3]For what does the Scripture say? "Abraham believed God, and it was accounted to him for righteousness." [4]Now to him who works, the wages are not counted as grace but as debt. [5]But to him who does not work but believes on Him who justifies the ungodly, his faith is accounted for righteousness, [6]just as David also describes the blessedness of the man to whom God imputes righteousness apart from works: [7]"Blessed are those whose lawless deeds are forgiven, And whose sins are covered; [8]Blessed is the man to *whom the Lord shall not impute sin.*"

This passage, as well as Romans 7 (where the emphasis is on the believer's struggle between following the flesh or following the Spirit) is complimented in Romans 9 by Abraham's example, which first shows the patriarch in failure but then shows his restoration to faith. Again, Abraham's failure with Hagar is a picture of the man who mistakenly tries to accomplish God's will through inappropriate means. In other words, it appears that Abraham was double-minded in his intentions. Thus in one sense he acted with some purpose toward wanting God's promise to become a reality (i.e., the promise that he would be the father of many nations) by taking Hagar to wife, but in doing so he acted from the presumption that God could not use his barren wife to fulfill the divine promise. Such a motive was not born of faith. Hence, Galatians tells us that Abraham's son, Ishmael, was the fruit of *Abraham's* desire, not *God's* desire. The main lesson here is that any assumption by man that his human striving is sufficient before God is wrongheaded. One can only *receive/take* God's promises by faith apart from works. [The word 'receive' is of the kind described in John 1:12 ("received") and Matthew 26:26 ("take"), the Greek word being the same in these passages, i.e., *to receive by taking*.] Thus, observe in particular Romans 4:5: "Now to him who does not work but believes on Him…" The Bible is talking about faith, and this is faith that a *man himself* produces *ex nihilio* (by which I mean, without prior cause). Nothing is in view here about God *making* the man believe. (The difference between these two thoughts will be examined further as we cover Romans 9.) Any normal reading of Romans 4 fails to leave such an impression about any alleged impotence of man to have faith. Despite certain other verses that Calvinists try to use to claim that man *cannot* believe (which we will also address later in this chapter), the statement here in Romans 4:5 says that *Abraham believed God*. This statement leaves no ambiguity about who is the causal agent of faith. The faith is produced by Abraham, not God. Note, too, that Abraham's belief is not boastworthy. Calvinists often make a contrary claim. They say that if a man were self-determinative and could receive Christ, he would be able to do something he could boast about. But that idea is refuted by Romans 4, which actually defines what **is** boastworthy. It says that works by some men are boastworthy when compared *relative* to the works of other men. Before God, however, no works are boastworthy or acceptable. And yet we see that Abraham's belief **is** acceptable before God. *Thus logically speaking, Abraham's faith is not boastworthy, and on this basis we may say that faith is not a work.* Furthermore, even in the claim by Calvinists that Ephesians 2:8-9 describes grace *and* faith as the gifts of God, the Calvinist ought to admit that within the Ephesians 2:8-9 sentence structure the phrase, "grace…through faith" is posited as a *contrast* to works. The Calvinist seems to want to stop reading after the word *God* in order to say that faith is not of ourselves, thus, '*For by grace are ye saved through faith; and that not of yourselves: it is the gift of God,*' rather than allow Paul to finish the thought of what he means by the term 'yourselves'—"not of works (i.e. the works of yourselves), lest any man should boast." The substitution of the word *yourselves* for what Paul means is *works* is known as a *metonymy*.[43]

Whenever Paul uses the terms *work* or *works* in the book of Romans where the immediate context is about justification *vs.* judgment, he always defines them according to his definition in Romans 4. When therefore in Romans 9 Paul discusses Abraham's belief in God to provide him a son through Sarah, Abraham's belief has nothing to do with works. <u>And it is in this context (i.e., the example of Abraham's faith vs. works) that the next verses in Romans 9 concerning Jacob's **election** over Esau are intended to be understood</u>. Let us pick up the reading with verse 10:

> ¹⁰And not only this; but when Rebekah also had conceived by one, even by our father Isaac; ¹¹(For the children being not yet born, neither having done any good or evil, that the purpose of God according to

election might stand, **not of works**, but of him that calleth;) [12]It was said unto her, The elder shall serve the younger. [13]As it is written, Jacob have I loved, but Esau have I hated (emphasis added).

What exactly do these verses mean when understood in their near context about Abrahamic faith? What, but that God wanted to make evident that election would *not* be based upon works (as pictured in Abraham's wrongful striving for a son), but upon His calling as apprehended by faith (as pictured in God's call for Abraham to believe God and to wait patiently until God opened the womb of Sarah). Thus God so established 'election' (rather, lit. *the naming out of from among*), by defining it prior to the births of Esau and Jacob, so that no one would suppose that Jacob had been 'chosen' on a works-based comparison between he and his brother. For the natural tendency is for men to link God's favor to positive[44] human behavior. But God does not want any to suppose that the 'selection' of Jacob was due to any works that Jacob had done. Rather, the 'election' (*naming out of from among*) of Jacob is based upon God's foreknowledge of what Jacob *himself* would do in exercising Abrahamic-type faith in God's Provision (note: compare 1 Peter 1:2: "Elect *according to the foreknowledge* of God the Father..."). Divine *election*, then, is merely the naming out of, from among the persons in the world, those whom God knows in advance will believe in Him. This has nothing to do with "irresistibility." The matter is similar to a boss of a company making an announcement of whom he will *select* from among a larger group of applicants. (This analogy is not to be pressed; one should not suppose it endorses a works-based salvation.) And as is the nature in such cases, every announced hiring is contingent on the hir*ee's* agreement to the conditions set by the boss. Biblically speaking, God's conditions for those who will follow Him are belief in Christ and confession of that belief. Note again that God's naming out of these individuals is NOT anything like the kind of "selection" or "election" that is defined by the Calvinist. In fact, the same Greek verb translated "to elect" is used when Stephen *was named out from among [others]* by the church for special service, or when the Pharisees *named out from among [others]* the most prestigious seats during feasts, or when Christ *named out from among [others]* those who would be His 12 disciples. The same root word is also used when Paul named out Silas from among and *over* others to accompany him on his missionary journey. Obviously, Silas and Stephen, as objects of the subject, could have declined to go along with the proceedings of the naming out of themselves from among others. In fact, Judas Iscariot ultimately **did** reject Christ's naming out of him, i.e., his '*election.*' So, when the Bible tells us that God (KJV) "elects" us, the word does not change meaning just because God is the grammatical subject. As we have already noted, words do not change meaning based on the subject of the sentence, even when that subject is God. The difference involving believers, of course, is that God's *naming out of from among [others]* is in a context in which He foreknows who will believe and not shrink back unto perdition. So then, when we read the word "election" in an English translation, we must keep in mind its proper definition. Indeed, we must do our best to resist the definition of Calvinists, who, during the course of overrunning and redefining in Evangelical minds key words like "election" (or "predestination," "foreknowledge," "adoption," etc.), always employ a kind of twisted, Farragutean strategy to gain more of the opponent's territory—i.e., damning the lexical history to move full speed ahead. Thus Calvinists change a verb's meaning and then marry it off to some noun, usually "God," as done here in Romans 9 with "election." In fact they perform this kind of ceremony every time they face a passage that contradicts their theology.

The naming out of some from among others (i.e., regarding believers' "election") might be better understood if we give an analogy. I once heard the story of a football coach who had his entire team run a sprint. He decided ahead of time that the fastest 11 guys would be his *defense*. Now suppose that football coach is God, but that instead of God having his players run a sprint, He puts them through a series of drills to see if they will make the team. Furthermore, let us suppose that the young men trying out for the team are a stubborn lot. Often they do not obey the Coach when He tells them to run drills. One day, after a difficult double session of practice that exposes every man's weakness, God lines them up and says, "None of you are worthy to play on My football team, but if you want to accept Me as your Coach, take one step forward." There is considerable hesitancy, but at length 11 guys step forward. The rest believe that their performance should have satisfied the Coach. Disgusted, the ones who did not step forward head back to the locker room to clear out their gear and leave. The Coach (God) had already circled the 11 names of the guys who ended up stepping forward from a roster of everybody who had tried out for the football team. In fact He circled their names before any of them were born. He did this simply on the basis that He knew beforehand who would step forward to accept Him as their Coach. That is, they were 'chosen' according to His foreknowledge.[45] Yet the Coach's 'selection' ahead of time in no way made them decide to play or not to play. Nor in any way did it determine that some would clear out their lockers and go home. Again, the 'selection' was simply based on the Coach's foreknowledge of who would, and who would not, decide to accept Him as their Coach; it impinged nothing whatsoever on the choices of each young man.

Let us now take the analogy one step farther. The Coach decides that, when these 11 young men grow up and get married and have families, He will give their children special instruction about the game of football. He does this because He loves these children, but also because He especially loves their fathers who had accepted Him as their Coach. The instruction the Coach will give these children does not guarantee that they too will accept Him as their own Coach when they grow up. Regardless of what the children will decide for themselves in upcoming years, they are in a place of special privilege, because their fathers had accepted the Coach so many years ago. The Coach knows already which children will come to accept Him as their Coach, and He has already circled their names on a roster, i.e., named them out from among others. Meanwhile, the children who were born to those players who walked off the field many years earlier are not in a position of special privilege. Nevertheless, they have heard of the Coach. They even know something of what is expected of those who are on the Coach's team. Nearly all of these underprivileged children will grow up disinterested in the Coach based on what they know the Coach will expect of them, and based on their fathers' negative stories about the Coach. Nevertheless, the Coach will contact them about joining His team. And if any of them want further information about joining, the Coach will provide even more details.

This analogy helps to explain what Romans 9 is saying about God's 'selection' of people. Men like Abraham, Isaac, and Jacob were sinners like everybody else, but when God's invitation was given to all men, they accepted God as their 'Coach' (Savior). The Bible makes clear that these men decided to have a personal relationship with God. For this reason God had a special affinity for their descendants, and He decided to enter into relationship with them (i.e., the Jewish people) by giving them special instruction. God has not been pleased, however, with the overall response of these children to His instructions. As a result, He has decided to make His instructions known to the children of all men everywhere. The ultimate hope is that the first group of children will become jealous of the relationship which the second group of children has with God, so that they too might decide to accept Him whom they had forsaken. Even so, Paul, in the book of Romans, is discussing the circumstances surrounding the Jewish and Gentile nations. Thus one should not lose sight in Romans 9 of the back-story of Abraham, Isaac, and Jacob. The faith of these individuals helps us to understand the current relationships which God has with the Jewish and Gentile nations.

So the view by many non-Reformed commentators, that Jacob and Esau in Romans 9 ought to be viewed *primarily* as nations, is an argument we would grant (based in part on the fact that "Jacob have I loved, and Esau have I hated" is from Malachi 1:2-3 and refers to the *descendents* of Jacob and Esau). In this regard we should note that Moses tells the Israelites in Deuteronomy that God was pleased to have a special relationship with them, not just because He loved them, but because of what He swore unto their fathers (Deut. 7:8). The implication here is that Abraham, Isaac, and Jacob believed God's promises about their descendents inheriting the land, and acted with faith accordingly.[46] Note Romans 11:28b in this regard: "As concerning the gospel, they [Jewish people] are enemies for your [*you Gentiles'*] sakes: but as touching the election (the naming out of some from among others), they are beloved <u>for the fathers' sakes</u>." Thus, Romans 9 has in view the "selection' of Israel unto the place of special privilege to be God's intended vehicle for communicating His good news of salvation to all peoples (see Rom. 9:4). This 'selection' was a result of their fathers Abraham, Isaac, and Jacob, who met the condition of divine selection by believing in God. So then, to see the individuals mentioned in Romans 9 as *merely* nation states is an unnecessarily forced interpretation. Such an unlayered interpretation, i.e., that Jacob and Esau merely represent nations, is the one traditionally held by non-Calvinists. While I would probably agree that nation states are primarily in view in verse 10, there is certainly a lesson about grace vs. works regarding the individual that informs the entire passage. Thus the conditional selection is not just of nations, but also of individuals unto a place of special privilege. It is, in fact, a confluence of thought stemming from chapter 4 where Abraham and David are discussed as individuals who had faith. The believer, after all, has his individual identity in Christ but lives out his faith in the corporate community of the church; and observe that Paul has both the individual and corporate experience of the believer in view throughout much of chapters 4, 6, 7, and 8. Note too that in chapter 9 the climax of illustrative examples culminates in *vessels* of mercy and *vessels* of wrath (plural, not singular), which, though it indicates nations, may also indicate *persons*, i.e., the individual components that make up the Jewish and Gentile nations that are otherwise in view. Also, the pot/potter metaphor hearkens back to the same metaphor in Jeremiah and Isaiah (discussed in chapter 15 of this book in detail), and while we admit that these pots are metaphors primarily meaning nations, Jeremiah also uses the metaphor to urge the men of Judah to repent, and of course such men are expected to repent of personal sin, not just their national sin. Furthermore, Pharaoh is cited as an individual ("For this purpose have I fully roused <u>thee</u>"). Given these considerations, the individual aspect ought not to be *entirely* set aside when attempting to understand Romans 9.

Picking up where we left off (with the story of Jacob), then, Genesis 24—49 shows that in the course of his life Jacob came to exercise faith in God. Initially, there does not seem to be much moral difference between Jacob and his brother. Esau despises his birthright, but Jacob steals his brother's blessing; thus neither is stellar in his behavior. But then begins their different paths which God foresaw in His response to Rebekah's inquiry about why her unborn children were struggling in her womb. " 'Two nations are in thy womb,' the Lord had said, 'and two manner of people shall be separated from thy bowels.' " According to *Strong's* the word *manner* comes from a primitive root meaning *tread* and means *a road (as trodden)* and therefore figuratively means *a course of life*. Most of the time the word appears in the Old Testament it means "way." That the lives of Jacob and Esau diverged unto different ways becomes evident in the course of Genesis. This process begins when Rebekah realizes that Esau plans on killing Jacob for stealing his birthright. Fearing for Jacob's safety, she sends him away to her brother, Laban. Jacob journeys to Bethel while traveling toward Laban's house, and there passes the night in sleep. It is here that he has a remarkable dream of angels ascending and descending on a ladder that reaches from earth to heaven. Jacob awakes with the realization that "Surely God is in this place," and builds an altar and makes a vow that he will make the Lord his God if the Lord will provide him life's necessities and return him to his father's house in peace. He then continues his journey and finally reaches his uncle's house, where he works for many years.

Meanwhile, Esau is moving away from God by taking a wife from the surrounding heathen people. From a human standpoint we can understand why Esau has chosen a different path to tread. Esau observed his father, Isaac (who, through no intention of his own, nevertheless gave Jacob the blessing), give specific instructions to Jacob about avoiding the Caananites in marriage. Esau sees that Jacob has departed to obey their father, but Esau decides to displease his father and marry a Caananite woman anyway. So despite Esau's profession to Jacob upon their reunion some 20 years later, that "The Lord has blessed me," the New Testament does not support the idea that Esau really followed the Lord. The New Testament gives us the sure word about Esau's moral character in a succinct synopsis, calling him a "fornicator" and a "profane person" (Heb. 12:6).

When Jacob and Esau are about to meet again, Jacob is very worried that his brother might harm him and his family. The night before they meet, the angel of the Lord wrestles all night with Jacob in a prolonged test of strength and wills. Finally, Jacob asks the Lord to bless him, and the Lord replies by asking Jacob his name. This is the moment of truth for Jacob. He had stolen his brother's blessing illegitimately by telling his father, "I am *Esau*." Now he asks the Lord for a legitimate blessing. But, of course, God is not in the habit of blessing a dishonest man who has cheated another. The Lord thus tests Jacob by asking him to admit to his name *Jacob*, which means *supplanter*. Jacob admits, "I am *Jacob*", i.e., confesses that he is a *supplanter*, and the Lord changes Jacob's name to Israel, which means *one who rules as God as a prince*. The Lord Himself explains the name's meaning in Genesis 32:27: "Thy name shall be called no more Jacob, but Israel: for as a prince hast thou power with God and with men, and hast prevailed." In effect, even as Jacob has had power with God (i.e., in a physical sense), so will he prevail with men. While Jacob's descendants would eventually prevail over many of the people groups of Caanan in a physical sense, the reason for their military successes would really be the result of their spiritual strength—the same trust in God first evident in their fathers, Abraham, Isaac, and Jacob. Even as Jacob finally humbled himself before God by admitting that his true nature was that of a supplanter, even so would the nation of Israel prosper so long as it humbled itself before God. The all-night wrestling match with the angel of the Lord was thus a turning point in Jacob's life. We see this not only in Jacob's request for God's blessing but also in his naming the site *Peniel*—"for I have seen God face to face, and my life is preserved." Though Jacob would suffer many things during the rest of his life, he would continue to grow in the fear the Lord—indeed, even prophesying about his sons at the end of his life.

The point here is that Jacob understood that only God could guarantee spiritual blessing, and would only do so for the man who humbled himself before Him. This type of trust in God is the mark of the believer. Should we yet doubt that Jacob was a believer we should remember that God would repeatedly refer to Himself in the Scriptures as "the God of Abraham, Isaac, and Jacob." As for Jacob's father, Isaac, we have not treated him at any length here, but suffice it to say that he is also included in the *I am the God of Abraham, Isaac, and Jacob* statement. By implication, Isaac is contrasted in Romans 9:7-9 with Ishmael, the child of Abraham's ungodly striving.[47] Note that God said that Ishmael would be a donkey of a man who would have his hand against every man, while every man would have his hand against him (Gen. 16:12 NAS). Such a description of Ishmael hardly befits that of a believer. We see then that Paul continues to draw out his argument that God's choice for blessing is based upon His provision of salvation as received humbly by faith. Thus God's calling unto election (lit. *bidding unto the naming out of some from among others*) is by His own provision and one *conditioned* by a man's faith (and therefore not of works). Note that this conditional nature of election is exactly opposite of the Calvinist's definition, which insists that faith *is* a work if it finds its origin in man.

At this point the Calvinist may argue that election is according to God's *calling*, and that man's belief is not in view. There are two faults with this argument. First, if it truly be according to God's calling *alone*, i.e., without any other phenomena attending it, then neither can it involve God's *provision* through His Son, which Paul does not expressly state, but which obviously he must be implying if God's calling is to be effectual. By this logic we conclude that *calling* is meant by Paul to embrace more than just *bare calling*.

Second, by extension, as God's *provision* is implied in the term *calling*, so too is *man's belief* in response to God's calling, i.e., as Romans 4 tells us,

"*Abraham believed God*, and it was counted unto him for righteousness." How then, we ask, could God's calling of Abraham be effectual without Abraham's positive response, that the Calvinist should claim such a calling to be *un*conditional? The picture of *calling* here brings to mind Christ's statement about his sheep. "My sheep hear my voice, and I know them, and they follow me, and I give unto them eternal life." The Eastern custom was for shepherds to corral sheep at night into a place of safety, such as an enclosure of stone walls. This would prevent them from wandering off or from running away during a thunderstorm. A single opening allowed one of the shepherds to block the doorway from predators. In the morning the sheep would be let out, and each of the shepherds would call his sheep from out of the herd unto himself. Sheep are known for recognizing the voice of their master, and in this manner are properly separated. Thus, in Romans 9 when Paul refers to God's *calling*, the apostle is not implying just the Shepherd's *calling*, but also the Shepherd's *provision* of Himself <u>and</u> the *response* of the sheep to the Shepherd's voice (all of which form the familiar illustration used by Christ). But of course regarding all these considerations, the Calvinist casts them aside, singing the same *chason* about how a verb, in this case "calling," has a special meaning because of its relation to the noun "God" when the elect are in view. And thus by special pleading [including the assumption that only the elect are in view, as only those objects that can be unconditionally bid (called), Calvinists put forth their necessary supposition, lest, e.g., the lexical case of Judas Iscariot, who rejected his election by Christ, proves Calvinism false].

Furthermore, to understand the language of Romans 9, it is also important to understand that Paul is addressing a proud readership. These were world-conquering Romans, after all. Like those Israelites who thought their ethnicity guaranteed God's approval, so would these Romans have been tempted to think their ethnicity was something pretty special. Throughout the book of Romans Paul will repeat the argument that blessing comes through belief, not through ethnicity or human striving. Someone else has stated it succinctly: "Salvation is not dependent on race, but on relationship." Paul stresses God's provision as opposed to man's striving, and this is true even in Romans 4, where the discussion involves Abraham and David's faith. For though the book of Romans upholds the ability of man to have faith in God, the book is really a treatise *against* the kind of self-confident hubris that people have in themselves, their ethnicity, and their works. This is why some statements in Romans might, at first glance, appear to be speaking of God's unilateral activity, i.e., the call of the one baby, Jacob, as opposed to the other baby, Esau—that is, of what sounds (at least to modern ears) like a forced reprobation of Esau, etc. This is why it is so important to study the near and far contexts of Paul's statements. When working through Romans 9 this means looking at the stories of Abraham, Sarah, Ishmael, Isaac, Rebekah, Jacob, Esau, Moses, Pharaoh, Christ's statement about His sheep in the gospel of John, the pot/potter metaphors in Isaiah and Jeremiah, and so forth. Until (or unless) one considers all these passages which are indicated or implied in Romans 9, some of Paul's statements are likely to appear to have meanings other than what they really do have, and the language of the chapter may be misunderstood. I have to say, that in all the Calvinistic literature I have personally read, a great deal of assertive force is given to the immediate and very narrow context within chapter 9 itself (though not as we have properly contextualized it here), while essentially none of the force of the argument is about the detail of near and far contexts. This is especially true of Calvinists regarding the definition of works in Romans 4 and also of the pot/potter metaphors in Isaiah and Jeremiah, whose contexts of the *instances* of judgment are entirely ignored.[48] Hence, what is sometimes offered in Calvinist books are clipped phrases from verses, or mere soundbytes, such as Jesus saying of His sheep, "I know them," or of Cyrus, of whom it is claimed had no intention to obey God, etc., i.e., the kind of statements that appear at first to support the Calvinistic view of God, that is, of God *unilaterally* knowing persons apart from their acknowledgement. But again, a fuller context shows the very opposite thought, i.e., "My sheep hear my voice, I know them, and they follow me," etc.[49]

The result of misunderstanding the *conditional* nature of election is that Calvinists have accepted a doctrine of *un*conditional election. This view has led to considerable confusion, because man's faith (properly defined, not as the Calvinist 'defines' it) is not seen as a factor in God's calling. Note again Romans 9:11-12:

> [11](For the children being not yet born, neither having done any good or evil, that the purpose of God according to election might stand, not of works, but of him that calleth;). [12]It was said unto her, The elder shall serve the younger.

Now let us consider the standard Calvinist interpretation of these verses, represented here by the prolific Reformed writer, Arthur W. (A.W.) Pink:

> The Sovereign exercise of grace is illustrated on nearly every page of Scripture. The Gentiles are left to walk in their own ways while Israel becomes the covenant people of Jehovah. Ishmael the firstborn is cast out comparatively unblest, while Isaac the son of his parents' old age is made the child of promise. Esau the generous-hearted and forgiving-spirited is denied

the blessing, though he sought it carefully with tears, while the worm Jacob receives the inheritance and is fashioned into a vessel of honor. So in the New Testament, Divine Truth is hidden from the wise and prudent, but is revealed to babes.[xl]

One almost wonders what Bible Pink is reading, that he should leave the impression that in the course of their lives Esau should be so applauded and Jacob so condemned! Indeed, where in his life do we see Esau exercising real faith? In forgiving Jacob after receiving large gifts of livestock? In seeking the blessing with tears instead of *repenting* in tears? Granted that Jacob stole the blessing; may he not have returned to Esau (following a life-changing wrestling match with the Lord) as much portion of that blessing which God could allow to a man neither interested in God for Himself nor willing to apprehend the blessing which required faith? Indeed, should Isaac have blessed his eldest son whose heart despised his own birthright, a son who likely believed in his own self-sufficiency such as he already perceived was evident in his hunting skills—i.e., even that which he likely presumed would help him make his own way in the world in so great a fashion as to render the question relatively meaningless as to whether he should receive a double portion of inheritance from his father (even such inheritance of physical and material blessing which implied the blessing of God)? Is not Esau called a "vain person" in the New Testament? Better, we think, had Isaac broken tradition's protocol and intentionally blessed the younger son whose mother was told would have a different manner of life than his elder brother. But Isaac didn't do this, though he himself had once been the younger son of his own father and the one favored over his older brother. Pink, however, makes no concessions to any of these facts, insisting that God simply chose (irresistibly) one over the other according to His own good pleasure. For Pink, Esau's lack of repentance and Jacob's eventual turnabout unto faith (neither of which he seems to recognize) would presumably be little more than God's predestinated ends for these individuals. However, Pink seems not to cite the argument we might expect of him but speaks instead of the "generous-hearted and forgiving" Esau on the one hand, while referring to the "worm" Jacob on the other. Pink, by the way, is not alone among Evangelicals who see Jacob as a rascal. A general online search brought me to a similar viewpoint as expressed by Christian author, Ray Stedman:

> Moreover, neither is it on the basis of God's foreknowledge of what men will do that he chooses them. This is where many people feel that we have an explanation of why God chooses some and not

others. They say he looks ahead and sees what they are going to do, and, because of his foreknowledge, he chooses them. No, it is not that! Paul says so! Before Jacob and Esau were born, when they had done no good or evil at all, God chose Jacob and not Esau—and these were twin boys. You see, it is not a question of what man's character, or his work, may be. While these boys were yet in their mother's womb, God chose to bless Jacob and accept him, and to reject Esau and allow him to remain under the curse of the Adamic sin in which he was born. Well, you say, he foreknew that Jacob would be a good man and that Esau would be a bad man. No, he didn't. If you read the record very clearly, you can see that, in many ways, Esau was a much better man than Jacob. If we had our choice of which one to live with, I certainly would choose Esau rather than Jacob. Jacob was a schemer, a rascal, a usurper, always working underhandedly to see what advantage he could take of someone—and he did this all his life. No, God didn't choose them because one of them was better than the other. Both of them were equally depraved at this point, and they were equally lost. Yet God chose to save Jacob but not Esau. Therefore he says, "Jacob I loved, but Esau I hated."

I know that this quotation is taken from the book of Malachi, the last book of the Old Testament, and it has been pointed out that this was written long after Jacob and Esau had lived, and that this was God's conclusion after he had seen all that they were going to be and all that their descendants were going to be. But that is, of course, to ignore God's foreknowledge; he knew that all along. No, that is putting the cart before the horse:

Men are not good and then God chooses them,
Men are good only because God has chosen them —
that is the point.[xli]

I find it fairly incredible that anyone could read the story of Jacob in its entirety and conclude so severely, as Stedman does, that *Jacob was a schemer, a rascal, a usurper, always working underhandedly to see what advantage he could take of someone—and he did this <u>all his life</u>* (emphasis added). Any fair-minded reading about Jacob shows that his understanding of faith developed slowly throughout much of his life, until at last he gives spiritual prophecy concerning each of his sons just prior to his death. Indeed, if Jacob were a supplanter *all his life,* as Stedman claims, why does God change Jacob's name from *supplanter* to a 'prince with God'? Are we to suppose that nothing in Jacob's character changed, that God would so rename him? Indeed, where in the Bible does Jacob *supplant* anyone after his personal wrestling match with God?

The rest of Stedman's apologetic regarding "election" appears to be based upon the Calvinistic assumption that faith is a work. Thus, when Stedman says, "Men are not good and then God chooses them, Men are good only because God has chosen them—that is the point," a man's faith is no where in view, or, if it is, Stedman is including the man's faith as a work, which Romans 4 shows it is not. For his own part, Stedman does not even say whether the *good* he refers to is a work, faith, or a combination of both. Presumably, it is what he would call imparted faith—faith that a man cannot produce whatsoever (i.e., the same kind of 'faith' that, presumably, Stedman would have to assume activated Jacob to admit "I am *Jacob* "). Nevertheless, biblically understood, both faith and works are predicated by man—the difference being that a believing man's faith is in the work of *Christ,* not in the work of himself.

Cannot or Will Not?

Finally, although we have been saying much about a man's faith (i.e., by definition, faith that is unilaterally brought into being by the man himself), Calvinists object to such an idea. They claim that man *cannot* have faith unless God gives it to him. A number of passages are cited to support this view. John 8:43-44 is representative of the Calvinist argument in the main, which says that man *of himself* cannot believe. Calvinists take these two verses to mean that God has decreed all men not to believe in order that He may impart to some a desire to believe. As the meaning of "cannot" has often been used to great effect by Calvinists, let us consider the word 'cannot' in John 8:43 in some of its surrounding context:

> [40]But now ye seek to kill me, a man that hath told you the truth, which I have heard of God: this did not Abraham. [41]Ye do the deeds of your father. Then said they to him, We be not born of fornication; we have one Father, even God. [42]Jesus said unto them, If God were your Father, ye would love me: for I proceeded forth and came from God; neither came I of myself, but he sent me. [43]Why do ye not understand my speech? even because ye cannot hear my word. [44]Ye

> are of your father the devil, and the lusts of your father ye will do. He was a murderer from the beginning, and abode not in the truth, because there is no truth in him. When he speaketh a lie, he speaketh of his own: for he is a liar, and the father of it. ⁴⁵And because I tell you the truth, ye believe me not.

Another verse sometimes cited is Romans 8:7, which we again show in some of its context:

> ⁵For those who are according to the flesh set their minds on the things of the flesh, but those who are according to the Spirit, the things of the Spirit. ⁶For the mind set on the flesh is death, but the mind set on the Spirit is life and peace, ⁷because the mind set on the flesh is hostile toward God; for it does not subject itself to the law of God, for it is not even able to do so, ⁸and those who are in the flesh cannot please God. ⁹However, you are not in the flesh but in the Spirit, if indeed the Spirit of God dwells in you. But if anyone does not have the Spirit of Christ, he does not belong to Him.

Note how Paul describes the carnal mind as that which is *upon*, i.e. (KJV) *set upon*, the flesh. I believe this explains the circumstance in which a man *cannot* come to Christ. If a mind is *upon*, i.e., *determined* that it shall not move from its position of unbelief regardless of what spiritual light God may give it, then by definition it *cannot* also be set toward the Spirit. In other words, *how can a man respond to God if he will not*? Again, by analogy, if a man *will* not be a good husband, how *can* he be a good husband?[50] Indeed, such activity is confined to the sphere of the individual will in such cases. For example, imagine a man whose mind is set upon driving from Chicago to Philadelphia to meet his parents at 7:00 p.m. on Christmas Eve. Since his mind is already made up to drive to Philadelphia, it cannot also be made up to drive to San Francisco to meet someone else at the same hour on the same day. Paul's point is one of formal logic: *A* cannot equal *non-A*. "Well, that is obvious," someone will say, "and Paul wouldn't waste our time with such obvious examples." Oh, but *have* such Pauline arguments proved obvious to Christendom? Has not an entire philosophy known as Calvinism been dressed up in theological-sounding terms while standing upon a bold contradiction? And does not this same Calvinism make the skeptic's statement in Romans 9:19-20 (*For who hath resisted His will*) to mean that God's will cannot be resisted whatsoever, thereby putting such an interpretation at conflict with Paul's immediate rejoinder that such a rhetorical accusation by the skeptic is *against* God? (In other words, how can the skeptic's reply be considered *against* God if Paul has just gotten done saying that the man is unable to resist God in any way?)[51]

We would grant that John 8:43-44 teaches that man *will* not seek God, but to where does such an argument bring us? It only proves that man is unable to seek God so long as he has determined that he *will not* seek Him.[52] [53]

Footnotes:

[42] Sarah's faith also played a part in Isaac's birth, for Hebrews 11 tells us that God miraculously helped her to conceive because of her faith.

[43] Bullinger in his *Figures of Speech* gives many examples, but for our purposes here we cite just one. In Psalm 51:7 David says, "purge me with *hyssop*." Hyssop was a moss-like shrub which was used to sprinkle the atoning blood for ceremonial cleansing. It was not the actual *hyssop* that effected purging in the symbolic ceremony, but the *blood*. Thus the use of the word *hyssop* in Psalm 51:7 is a metonymy—a word substitution in which (in this case) one noun is given to mean another.

[44] Regarding "positive human behavior," the following clarification needs to be added. Although there may be a positive aspect to a person's act, such as loving one's neighbor as himself in a given circumstance, there is no sense in which "positive" behavior can be assigned to any man's life as a whole. This is because his works are judged as an entire whole.

[45] Likewise, we may presume God's foreknowledge is in view in John 6:39, when Christ says, "And this is the Father's will that hath sent me, that of all that he hath *given* me I should lose nothing, but should raise it up again at the last day." Thus, the Father *gives* the Son those whom Christ said He should not lose. Let us consider this statement in light of the above football metaphor. We might say that God the Father, knowing in advance which men would accept God as their Coach, gave these men to Christ (God the Son) according to His foreknowledge. The problem in verse 39, however, is that some interpreters give the word *given* an undue force to say that God accomplishes man's salvation *irresistibly* by forming the man's will, thus applying to the word *given* in verse 39 the kind of force implied in the phrase, *he was given a black eye*, or again, as Paul actually uses it in 2 Corinthians 12:7, "*There was given unto me a thorn....*" Note that the term *give/given* behaves in English as it does in New Testament Greek, having a wide latitude of meaning but always determined by the context, sometimes implying irresistibility, but often not. For example, Christ also refers in Matthew 7:11 to earthly fathers who, though evil, nevertheless *give* their children good gifts. But note here that such gifts obviously could have been refused by these children *because of the nature of giving* as described in the particular context of Matthew 7:11; in other words, it is a giving that can be refused. Nor is Matthew 7:11 an exception, since the word *give* in certain other New Testament passages conveys this same meaning without implying anything of irresistibility. Hence, the

meaning of *give/given* is determined by the particular **context** in view, and obviously this matters a great deal in theology when the exact nature of God is being expressed. For if God is such that He gives to Christ those men whose choices God Himself has formed, then human freedom is annihilated. In other words, the verb *give/ given* is one whose historical-grammatical history shows a wide latitude of meaning regardless of its subject. Moreover, the meaning of verbs and object nouns do not change with the subject. To insist otherwise is special pleading; for it is the general context that determines meaning. In regard to this point one ought to consider the remarks of Thomas Edgar, which, though they specifically have in view the Greek word *proginwskw* (Eng. *to foreknow*), are relevant to the study of all theologically controversial words (such as *give*) when used in reference to God. Says Edgar, regarding the practice of restricting the lexical study of such words to only those passages where God is the subject:

"It is exegetically incorrect to consider only those passages where God is the subject. Still, this approach is common. The subject involved in so restricting the study is that the meaning is *different*, and not merely modified, when God is the subject. Several reasons show this approach to be incorrect: (1) The meaning of a verb is not dependent on, not does it vary with the subject of the verb. (2) Other words do not have a different meaning when used of God. How do interpreters know that this one does? (3) God has given Scripture to communicate to humans. He uses human language with its normal meanings. If words have different meanings when God is the subject, the interpreter cannot know what they are, nor if our concepts about God are accurate. (4) Why would God deliberately make the communication difficult? Why would He use words with different meanings than normal when He could use readily available words that clearly communicate? If this term normally means "foreknowledge," but when used of God, it means "electing love, intimate knowledge, or determining choice," why use it here? Why not say, "electing love." Such an approach is illogical. (5) If words do not have their normal meaning when used to describe God, there can be no objective control on interpretation, leaving each interpreter to read in his theological opinions. Thus, to study only those uses of proginwskw where God is the subject is defective hermeneutically and logically."

Now consider the word *give/given* in light of Edgar's comments. The lexical meaning of *give/given* is not automatically restricted in John 6:39 to mean an irresistible giving, simply because God is in view. Rather, the precise meaning depends on the context in which the word appears. And in John 6 the context of God's giving is that of an *offer* to which men are asked to respond willingly. Specifically, the *offer given* to men is that of God's provision, contextually shown here to be Jesus as the Bread from heaven which corresponds to 1) God's provision of manna to the children of Israel in the wilderness, as echoed by 2) Jesus' feeding of the 5,000 mentioned earlier in John 6. In both instances food was divinely *given* to a people, but not in the sense in which a thorn was *given* to Paul (that is, involuntarily). Note that no Israelite at the time of Moses, nor any among the 5,000 whom Jesus fed, *had to* accept God's *offered* provision. While certainly it would have been foolish for them *not* to accept God's provision, they *could* have chosen to refuse the food. To put it another way, the Lord did not make the food automatically appear *involuntarily* in the stomachs of those he wished to feed. His *giving* was not of that irresistible sort, and this is the context of *giving* in John 6.

So note again the conditional nature of God's giving in John 6:39. Though God is giving certain ones to Christ, the giving is nevertheless also dependent on Christ's decision as to whether He will do the will of the Father to confirm the Father's giving. The word "will" in the phrase " the Father's will" is the Greek word *thelo*, i.e., contextually here, *desire unto plan*. (See chpt. 17, question about Phi. 2:13.) It was the Father's *desire* and *plan* that Christ *should* (the KJV here properly recognizes the subjunctive mood) lose nothing, but should raise it up again at the last day. The matter is subjunctive. For note that Christ *could* have refused to do the Father's will. In fact, He states in the Garden of Gethsemane that He could call 12 legions of angels to rescue Him and His disciples from danger (one each for He and his 11 disciples?). Thus, in John 6:39, the exact nature of *giving* by the Father to the Son is not of an *irresistible* kind, either in regard to *that* which is given or even in regard to *Whom* it is given. To claim otherwise, as Edgar might explain it, is to read into the text one's own theological opinions.

[46] —thus the verse that follows Deuteronomy 7:8, which speaks of "the faithful God, which keepeth covenant and mercy with them that love him and keep his commandments."

[47] In Genesis 21:12 God tells Abraham "In Isaac shall thy seed be called." This is not meant to imply that only those whom God foreknows He invites. Rather, it implies a *successful* calling, and in this sense it parallels the assumption in John 6:44, i.e., that him who *successfully* responds to the Father's drawing shall also be raised by the Son at the last day. (See chpt. 18, footnote 142)

[48] One observes this unfortunate consistency in Calvinist writings.

[49] We ought to be vigilant in pointing out the dangers of Calvinism to fellow believers who are searching. The Calvinist is an example of one who, as Proverbs 18:17 tells us, comes first in his explanation and seems to be right. But then his neighbor *searches* him [i.e., lit. *penetrates* (his argument)]. May we be a neighbor to those who have ears to hear.

[50] When Christ states in John 6:44 "No man can (Gr. *dunamai*, i.e., *is able to*) come to me, except the Father which hath sent me draw him," it should be noted again that the use of *can* is tied to *will*. Hence an example from the same writer, John, who says in 1 John 3:9 "and he (i.e., whosoever is born of God) cannot (negative of same Gr. root, *dunamai*) sin, because he is born of God." Here in the context of his first epistle, John is saying that we cannot sin because we have exercised our will to a point of repentance (a changing of the mind in which we receive Christ) from the lie (that Christ is not come in the flesh), a repentance of mind from which the true believer never departs because he *will* not. Moreover, God's Spirit witnesses with the believer's spirit that the believer is a child of God. **A statement about the word 'can' in the New Testament is relevant here. I believe the word 'can' (Gr. *dunamai*, commonly claimed to mean 'to be able to') can be misleading to English readers in contexts about intention, and should in such cases be understood as "to be able by means of the**

will," i.e., 'powers the will to.' This is not the exact same thing as "do," if by "do" is meant "to bring the will unto an effect besides itself." Carl Conrad notes the following about *dunamai*:

"As for DUNAMAI, it is an intransitive verb functioning as an auxiliary requiring a complementary infinitive in normal usage. Be careful about classification of active and passive and by no means assume that a verb that is not active must be passive. Perhaps it is a truism and not very helpful to say it, but I think that Voice in the ancient Greek verb is at least as slippery a phenomenon as Aspect. Particularly tricky is the Middle voice, and many of the forms that are traditionally categorized as passive in Greek are really, in my opinion, middle."

Conrad also notes that middle-passive verbs are not middle OR passive; thus, the matter is not merely expressed by saying "The boy was baptized," but also, "The boy allowed himself to be baptized." Similarly, though not exact (owing to the object's subject being the person himself), as regards *dunamai*, then, we note that a man's own spirit (his will) is the subject that renders his own soul (his desires, thoughts, and deliberation) passive regarding the matter at hand. In short, man's spirit renders his soul passive whenever the spirit acts. Thus, for example, Christ in Gethsemane, after lengthy deliberation upon His desire to avoid the cross, nevertheless acted in His spirit (willed Himself) to submit to His Father, and, in so doing, rendered His soul passive unto the Father's desire. That is, Christ ruled His soul by His spirit. And his passions, though they remained in some degree present and even contrary to the Father, proved (because of Christ's will) not active unto ruling. Even so, the disciple of Christ is called to *deny* himself and follow Christ. This means that our spirit is to deny our soul's greatest desire of avoiding the persecution that arises from following Christ, and follow Christ nonetheless. Thus (again), the spirit of man, when it acts, renders his own soul passive. Put another way, the man puts his soul passive in relation to his will. Observe also that this is the case even when a man's soul is congruent with what his will chooses, because it is a man's own will—not his soul—that actually rules himself, for better or worse. This is simply the nature of what man is. Note the distinction in Hebrews 4:12 between the soul and the spirit, as represented by the thoughts and intents, respectively: "For the word of God is quick, and powerful, and sharper than any two-edged sword, piercing even to the dividing asunder of soul and spirit, and of the joints and marrow, and [is] a discerner of the thoughts and intents of the heart." Just as a skilled surgeon can separate the joints and marrow when operating, so God's word exposes the difference between our desires on the one hand, and our will on the other, which involves our motives. It is, in fact, man's *motive of will* that God judges. If this were not the case, then the Father would have judged Christ guilty for having different *desires* in His soul than that of the Father. But Christ was victor in His will and motive, which is why God has given Him a name above all names, so that every knee [*ought to* (subjunctive mood)] bow, and every tongue [*ought to* (subjunctive mood)] confess, that Jesus is Lord.

So then, in turning our attention again upon John 6:44, the spirit of man ***wills***, i.e., is actively rendering his thoughts, desires, and emotions passive, *with the result that* [and *in order that* (the ecbatic and telic sense are both apparent here in the middle-passive)] he is not coming toward Christ apart from the Father's pulling. This is how the matter stands as a brute fact. Thus in John 6:44, **though** the complimentary infinitive for *dunamai*, as grammarians would normally describe it, would be "coming," since *dunamai* is a verb that does not take an object and therefore requires an infinitive, which, in this case takes the object "Son"—***yet*** it must also be understood in another sense that *dunamai* is a *transitive* verb insofar as man (his spirit) takes himself (his soul) as the object. Therefore, as *dunamai* is a middle-passive verb (which means that at least in some sense (in fact, in the *soul* sense) the person is the subject of his own actions), we could woodenly translate the opening phrase in John 6:44 thus: "No one wills himself to be coming to the Son…" Again, however, the KJV, instead of using *to will* or *to power (one's self)*, here translates Gr. *dunamai* as "can" in the context of a man's *own* will. The resulting traditional interpretation is that man, besides his inability to provide an atonement for himself, also cannot even *receive* God's provided atonement of Christ's blood unless the Father drags the man's will into a place where the man 'receives' it. But unfortunately for the Calvinist, the surrounding context and examples of John 6 simply do not justify the Calvinistic idea that man cannot choose good (see John 6:44 in Scripture Index for further comments). Therefore, one may come to the conclusion that the verb "can" in (KJV) John 6:44 (i.e. "no man *can* come to me except the Father which hath sent me draw him,")—besides meaning "to be able to," which at one level of meaning means that man cannot come to the Son for reconciliation because of his *de facto* inability to provide his own atonement—must be understood at another level to mean (even if it be not literally translated as such), <u>the verb *will*</u>, i.e., ["*can* (by virtue of the will)"]. Thus "will" is preferred (or at least understood within this verse's polyvalent meaning), lest it be thought that *total inability* is in view, in which unfortunate case other key passages might be similarly misunderstood, and so lead to the thought that man has no real freedom of the will. In fact, a proper understanding of "can" as "will" clears up considerable confusion in certain other passages, even in which Jesus (as One Person of the Godhead) is the subject. For example, when Christ speaks in the present tense to state that, "The Son *can* do nothing of himself, except what he seeth the Father do," the real meaning must be "The Son ***will*** do nothing of himself [lit., if expansively, *wills himself to be doing nothing of himself*] except that which the Father shows Him;" for otherwise the word "cannot" would mean that Christ had no free will choice of His own in the matter. Yet Christ's remark in Gethsemane (i.e., "not my desire, but thine be done") and His *de facto* choice of whether to call for angels to rescue Himself, clearly shows that He <u>could</u> have subverted the Father's plan, broken Scripture, and not have drunk of the cup of death. Along these lines, note also how the following verse [(Int.) Mt. 26:54]—"How then *should* the Scriptures be fulfilled, that it **must** happen this way?"—is actually used by some theologians to argue that Christ *could not* have failed. This assumption comes from reading the KJV's "shall" (or the NAS's "will") instead of the Interlinear's "should." But observe that even here the word "must" is still subject to the word "fulfilled," which is in the subjunctive mood, and therefore makes the matter contingent, i.e., in effect, "**IF** the Scriptures are to be fulfilled, it **must** be in this way." But of course to the dedicated Calvinist there really is no such thing as the Subjunctive Mood when

God or His Word is the grammatical subject of the sentence. Calvinists simply assign all such occurrences of the subjunctive to idiomatic expression. This is all part of the Calvinists' rigorous program of special pleading whenever God (or His Word, etc.) is the grammatical subject, as necessary. Again, however, and for the reader's sake, we will repeat the following to a point of *ad nauseam*—***words don't change meaning depending on the grammatical subject.***

So the Calvinist's substitution of "can" for "will" is a major problem affecting key doctrine in all commonly used English translations. This is because in English translations the word "can" is often inferred to mean that even certain *de facto* acts which *are* possible of the human will are *not* hypothetically possible. The danger of this problem can hardly be overstated. In short, there is (especially) no single **formal** English *quid pro quo* word for Gr. *dunamai*, since *formal* English divides *dunamai* into "can," "will," and "may." Only in **informal** English do we gain something of *dunamai*'s other meanings besides "can", e.g., "Teacher, *can* I get a drink of water?"

So then, as part of its polyvalent meaning, John 6:44 means that men ***will*** not come, for to insist here on the English formal "can" instead of "will" would be to make the verse of private interpretation at the expense of numerous other detailed biblical passages (involving both near and far contexts) which affirm an uncorrupted human will (see *Hoodwinked*, chpts. 12, 13, 18, & 20). Thus, whether *dunaami* should mean "can" or "will" or even "may" depends on the context. (The only exception for John 6:44 would be if "can" refers only to man's inability to produce his own atonement.)

Furthermore, a polyvalent meaning of "can" and "will" is also possible in at least one passage, e.g., Matthew 6:27, in which Jesus, besides asking the following question plainly, may also be using rhetorical humor to reply to the idea of mind-over-matter, when he asks who it is, that, by taking thought, 'can,' i.e., or *chooses* (*wills*) to add a cubit to his stature? Note too, and perhaps more importantly, that when Jesus is asked by his disciples and the father of the demoniacal son why the disciples (Gr.) *ou dunamai* (KJV Eng.) *were not able to* cast out the demon, Jesus replied that this generation was faithless and perverted, i.e., that the disciples (who could cast out demons because Christ gave them the power to) *could not because they **would not**,* i.e., ***chose not*** to have faith through the exercise of earnest prayer, but were rather perverted in this instance, in which they typified the generation of His poor hearers (Mk. 9). Finally in this regard, note also the "may" aspect of *dunamai* in Scripture, exampled when the Athenians (Acts 17:19) asked Paul, "May (*dunamai*) we know…?" Observe how especially the word "can" makes no sense here. In fact, this verse shows the ignorance of R.C. Sproul's implicit argument that *dunamai* always means "can," but never "may." Or are we to suppose that Sproul thinks the Athenians were asking Paul if they "can" know, i.e., have the mental capacity to understand an argument! But if we wait a little, perhaps Sproul can (will) either 1) change the meaning of the verb *dunamai* in John 6:44, so that it has the restrictive meaning of "to be able to" when man's coming to God is the subject; or 2) at the expense of his previous argument [i.e., "Who has not been corrected by a schoolteacher for confusing the words *can* and *may*?"], allow the word "may" but insist on a God who answers *No* to the question of "May we…?", i.e., does not *allow* men to come apart from His *pulling*, so that all glory for man's salvation goes to God (as though man having predicative ability to come to God would somehow nullify God's glory). In other words, while arguably there IS a subjunctive aspect of the verb *dumanai* present here, pointing to the contingency of God providing atonement, Sproul, to follow Calvin, would take the subjunctive aspect (insofar as it can be said that Calvinists even grant God subjunctive contingency), to refer to the Calvinistic definition of "regeneration"; or 3) allow the word symbol "will" but imply (via a point about the "deadness" of man) that man has no more predicative possibility than a plant. But regardless of which of these three options Sproul may take—*wood, hay,* or *stubble*—we anticipate that if he becomes aware of our argument but remains deaf to it, he will step down into a darker, deeper irrationality in order to keep a retreating pace from the sunbeam of the Spirit's truth that exposes more of his method. But by proceeding this way, Sproul can at least undergird his already false lexical assumptions with more of the same. And incidentally, note in the last sentence how "can" means both "can" and "will."

But moving on, if the English reader will understand that "can" encompasses all the above proper considerations for *dunamai* as we, not Sproul or those like him, have explained it—that is, essentially like its <u>informal</u> English use—then "can" would appear to be an acceptable translation. Historically, I believe cultures blur the words "can" and "may" lexically to hide motive or to soften rejection. No one likes to say, "I ***will*** not come to your party," nor even ask the question, "***Will*** you come to my party?" Simply put, societies have found the word "can" easier on their souls.

There is another thing here, regarding John 6:44, and that man cannot come, for I recently saw something additionally in my last reading. It appears to me that the essential issue in John 6 is about whether man will live by bread alone. Thus, Jesus perceived that the people whom He miraculously fed would COME and take Him by force, to make Him king (v. 15), because (as He told them later) they wanted physical bread alone, not the spiritual bread (Manna from heaven) which they also needed (see v. 26ff.). This kind of intended coming to the Son speaks of man's protocol. But that is not the Father's protocol. The Father's protocol for coming toward the Son is through the Son on the cross. For it is the Son, lifted up, who will draw all men unto Himself. And so, the Father sets the protocol for approach like a king did in ancient times. This is the context of John 6:44, i.e., that man cannot come according to his own protocol—which is to live by bread alone. Thus, at the layer of meaning in John 6:44 regarding protocol, dunamai means may, i.e., no man may come to the Son except via the Father's protocol—i.e., His drawing—which is through His Son's lifting up which will draw all men. The reason this is called the Father's drawing is because Christ came not on His own. [Note that, conversely, man's (the human) protocol hearkens back to that which Satan claimed was Job's modus operandi in serving God—bare self interest. And observe further that Jesus, being God, exhibited the opposite nature compared to that which Satan claimed of God in the book of Job, and chose self denial and the path of the cross, instead of offering bribery to ensure man's following. For physical bread alone is what the crowd wanted, thus their challenge to Jesus to perform a daily miracle of physical bread as they believed Moses had done.

One last thought here about the "may" aspect of *dunamai* in John 6:44. It might be objected that "may" is not in view at all, or else the Greek would have spelled *dunamai* to show subjunctive. But the counterargument is this. Even as in English the word "can" may be used in a polyvalent sense so that the formal "can" and informal "may" aspects of meaning are both present, though the spelling (i.e., "can" instead of "may") only indicates one of the meanings—the formal meaning, so likewise in Greek. For since in Greek a verb like *dunamai* will only take one of those endings to show either indicative or subjunctive (or other tense), the indicative and subjunctive aspects may both be meant, though only the indicative be indicated by the verb's spelling. For example, I might say in English, "I cannot go the company's party to receive a gift from the boss," for more than just one reason. I might not go because I have no means of transportionto get to the party to receive the gift—therefore I *cannot* come and receive the gift, but also because I am unwilling to receive a gift from the boss because I do not like him—therefore I *may not come and receive a gift*. The first is beyond my control (provision of transportation and provision of the gift), the second is not (reception of the gift). Even so, a man both *cannot* come to Christ unless the Father provides the means of coming— even Jesus Christ the Righteous One (understood metaphorically in John 6 to be the Manna from Heaven), *nor may he come* if, when the means have been provided, he refuses to come. Thus may the word "can" be used to express both formal and informal aspects of meaning in English, even as the Greek verb "dunamai" may express both aspects of meaning, though solely with its indicative spelling, **that is, if the context justifies it**. And in my opinion the context of John 6 does justify both the indicative and subjunctive aspects of meaning.

Finally, in all the discussion from Calvinists about John 6:44, it appears overlooked by them the clarification given in John 6:65. The verse reads: "Therefore said I unto you, that no man can come unto me, except it were given unto him by my Father." The key words refuting the Calvinist interpretation are the actual Greek meanings of "can" and "it were given unto him". Let us take them in order. Checking Blueletterbible.com, the word "can" is a "middle or passive deponent" verb. Here we anticipate Carl Conrad's opinion about "deponent" being the most useless term in Greek grammar (see Chpt. 18 footnote 142). This is because "deponent" is traditionally defined as an active verb but in a passive position, an oxymoron. Rather, as Conrad shows, such "deponent" verbs are best understood as action done to a person(s) with that person(s) consent. "He gives "to baptize" as an example. The action is done *to* a person but the person, though in a passive position to receive baptism, would not be receiving the action apart from his consent, i.e. his *active* consent. Likewise, when Christ says in John 6:65 that no man "*can* come", the "deponency", so to speak, of the verb "can" actually means that the man *by consent* agrees to the action of the Father (to him) to come to the Son.

Second, the phrase "except it were given unto him" was assumed by the KJV (and later translations) to mean that man has total inability of will. However, the words "except *it* were", ("were" is in the subjunctive") apparently intended by translators to refer to "except *the coming* [of the man] were", may instead be translated "except *he* should [ought, or may]. In other words, the word "it" may be rendered "he" in the subjunctive phrase. Just as importantly, the words translated "given unto him" may be instead rendered " given unto him *by himself* (i.e. by the man). Blueletterbible.com lists this verb as a Perfect Passive Participle. But as will be seen in footnote 142 of Chapter 18, a "Perfect Passive Participle" in Greek is spelled the same way as in the a *middle* voice, and therefore may mean that the action is self-reflexive. And so, taking the whole verse of John 6:65, we see that it could have been rendered thus: "Therefore said I unto you, that no man by consent agrees to the action of the Father (to him) to come to Me, except he should give it unto himself from my Father." This makes perfect sense in the context of John 6, in which Christ uses the analogy of men taking unto themselves (middle or reflexive action) the Manna from Heaven which the Father alone supplies.

I suppose the objection by the Calvinist to this alternate rendering would be that man only consents because his desire has been regenerated from a will that is totally disabled. Somewhere I remember Thayer remarking in one of his lexicon's entry (I paraphrase here) that if it be in doubt whether the action is of man or God, one should understand that *all* action ultimately originates from Providence alone. I think it should be evident such a hermeneutic as Thayer's refuses to believe man capable of even the most basic elements of *self*-action, such as that of the Jews in the Wilderness, when their *own* hunger followed their *own* desire to go outside their tents to take the Manna God provided. For the Calvinist, then, to refuse to grant that man has any will at all is to deny any separation of the Divine and Human Mind. And that ought to strike the Christian believer—he who is not equal with God but must humble himself before his Creator and repent of heart *and mind*—as absurd.

[51] The Greek word translated *against* is *antapokrinomai*, from the primary particle *anti*, thus *Strong's* primary definition is: *over against, opposite to, before* (Rom. 9:19-20). The NASB seems to understand the dilemma of how the Calvinistic interpretation leads to a contradiction and thus prefers a translation that says the skeptic *answer[s] back*, rather than the KJV's *repliest against*. Thus the NASB translates the skeptic's question *connotatively* without sufficiently conceding the *denotative* reality to the skeptic's arrogant reply, which in fact is *against* God. In other words, the NAS somewhat treats the verse as though the skeptic merely returns a reply, rather than replies *against*. Yet the skeptic's arrogance is implied not only in the skeptic's question when the meaning of the question is properly understood [that is, *Why does God delay judgment if He is able to bring it?*], but also in Paul's abrupt and severe censure.

[52] Gordon Olson makes a most interesting and helpful observation here (*Getting the Gospel Right*, p. 36-37): "Many Christians base their view of inability on the English of Romans 3:10-11: **"There is none righteous, not even one; There is none who understands, There is none who seeks for God."** In Paul's paraphrase of the Septuagint of Psalm 14, he was careful to use the intensified verb *ekzētein*, rather than the simple *zētein*. From its usage in Acts 15:17; Heb. 11:6; 12:17; and 1 Pet. 1:10, it is clear that Paul is not referring to an indifferent seeking, but a 'diligent seeking' for God. So Paul was not affirming that no one

ever seeks God at all, but rather *that no one diligently seeks God*. It is also significant that this verb is a present participle, which likely has a customary force. This would refer to a regularly recurring action, and thus, could be rendered, "**no one customarily and diligently seeks God.**" Otherwise, if neither of the above were true, Scripture would be in contradiction with itself. *There are only fifty verses which contradict a superficial reading of Romans 3:10-11!* Why do people ignore the fifty and focus on the one? William A. Butler got it right: "*We hold a few texts so near the eyes that they hide the rest of the Bible.*" "

Incidentally, James White takes the position that the 50 texts Olson cites in defense of his position are but divine commands, directed either to the regenerated who **will** obey, or to the reprobated who will **not** obey, and thus these 50 offer nothing in support of the idea that man himself can generate saving faith. White's argument thus assumes that man, if 'regenerated,' can choose—but only choose right, while man, if 'unregenerated,' can choose—but only choose evil. This is merely a sophisticated way of saying that man has a choice that is not a choice. Thus, like Piper, White dismisses logical definition based on his assumption that man is not self-determinative (that is, while White is on the front rock of Calvinism). Thus, for White, *to seek* and *to diligently seek* have the same essential grammatical range, and the difference implicit in the prefix *ek* all but nullified, and *absolutely* nullified for any passage that, we note, *de facto* contradicts Calvinism. This explains why White defines *choice* irrationally. Furthermore, it would seem that White concedes only salvific or reprobative contexts for these 50, as though *nothing* in *any* of the verses could be directed to backslidden believers to repent and to stop quenching the Spirit's influence in their lives. In short, contingency by man appears to be simply dismissed by White, and the meaning of words 'rehabilitated' until man is not self-determinative and thus bankrupt of will.

[53] God confronted this stubbornness of man (in man's less than diligent seeking of Him) when He sent Christ into the world. Christ's incarnation, His manner of life, His performing of miracles, His death followed by His resurrection—all these raised the status quo of the old, if ongoing, revelation of creation. These made it harder for man to reject God. Once Christ accomplished the ordeal of the cross and the miracle of His own resurrection, God commanded with even greater intensity that every man repent. For it had been one thing for God to command repentance prior to the cross, quite another thing for Him to command it afterward. For prior to Christ's first advent God "winked" at the sins of past generations without insisting as fully as He would come to do (following the resurrection of Christ), that all men should repent. Therefore when Christ accomplished His ministry, God obtained a fuller moral authority (from man's point of view, at least) to insist on man's repentance: "Let not him who puts on his armor boast like him who takes it off," said an Old Testament king. It was one thing for God to speak of His salvation to men before Christ put on His armor to battle Satan, sin, and death, but quite another thing for God to command it after Christ was victor over all three. Thus, while the old revelation was enough to make unbelieving man inexcusable before his Creator, the further revelation of Christ makes unbelieving man inexcusable before God his Savior. And that is a significant difference.

Endnotes:

[xxxix] Deffinbaugh, Bob. *Reasoning in Romans.* "The Sovereignty of God in Salvation." (Romans 9). [http://www.bible.org/page.asp?page_id=1175].

[xl] Pink, Arthur W. *The Sovereignty of God.* [http://www.sovereign-grace.com/pink/chapter01.htm], Chapter One: "God's Sovereignty Defined."

[xli] Stedman, Ray. Romans (Series #1), Message No: 16, Catalog No: 20, "Who Chose Whom?" [http://www.pbc.org/library/files/html/0020.html].

Chapter 13
"We Had to Destroy That Village to Save It"

Having examined the faulty Calvinistic definition of "election," we now turn our attention to Calvinism's related argument about Depravity—the idea that all men are depraved in their choice, and by nature intend to sin unrelentingly. In fact, this underlying assumption about man by the Calvinist makes divine, "irresistible" election necessary, since man cannot even meet the condition of having a will of his own that can receive Christ.

As for Depravity, then, it is important that the passages in the New Testament allegedly claiming man's inability to believe [e.g., "ye cannot hear my word" (Jn. 8:43)] show a context where men have set their minds determinedly away from Christ in a way not generally described of every unbeliever. We saw this at the end of the last chapter, especially in footnote 53, regarding *dunamai* in Greek verses usually translated "can." [The reader is strongly recommended to read this footnote if he has not done so. Now recalling our final point in the main text in the last chapter, remember that the specific audience which Christ addressed in John 8 was to *would-be Christ killers* to whom Jesus said, *'ye seek to kill me...ye cannot hear my word.'* This was not Christ's attitude toward the average unbeliever during His ministry. Jesus didn't speak parables to the common people who "heard him gladly" (Mk. 12:37) and then end such sermons by saying they wanted to kill him and could not believe. Nor did He treat them as if they had no will. Rather, he said to them, *'He that has ears to hear, let him hear'* (Mk. 4:9; cp. Mk. 4:23). Thus God does not describe every unbeliever as those men of John 8, who were doubtless like the stubborn men of Zechariah 7:9-13:

> [9]Thus speaketh the Lord of hosts, saying, Execute true judgment, and show mercy and compassions every man to his brother: [10]And oppress not the widow, nor the fatherless, the stranger, nor the poor; and let none of you imagine evil against his brother in your heart. [11]But they refused to hearken, and pulled away the shoulder, and stopped their ears, that they should not hear. [12]Yea, they made their hearts as an adamant stone, lest they should hear the law, and the words which the Lord of hosts hath sent in his spirit by the former prophets: therefore came a great wrath from the Lord of hosts. [13]Therefore it is come to pass, that as he cried, and they would not hear; so they cried, and I would not hear, saith the Lord of hosts:

A natural reading of this passage shows that man's reprobation begins with man himself. God specifically says that the men of Zechariah 7 have not hearkened to do what He cried out for them to do. To what position must we contort Christian theology, then, to agree with the Calvinist that verse 11 means the opposite view, i.e., that God does *not* want these people to hearken to Him because He has ordained it? Again, notice the order of rebellion, "they refused to hearken, and pulled away the shoulder, and stopped their ears, that they should not hear. Yea, they made their hearts as an adamant stone…Therefore came a great wrath from the Lord." Note how these people were virulent in their rebellion *before* the Lord brought forth His wrath. They are described as having turned the shoulder and having shut down the eye gate and ear gate so they didn't have to see or hear the truth. I would encourage readers to take the time to stand up and imitate the kind of body language described of these stubborn men of Zechariah 7:11. One will find that the shoulders actually begin turning before the feet can change position to walk away. Thus, the description is one where men have gotten so accustomed to not wanting to hear God's Word that their spiritual body language has become one of *instinctual* rejection. They have seared their consciences in regard to the truth of Christ. Thus they don't even want to see the message of the Lord *mouthed*. Clearly, this is not how the Bible has described *every* unbeliever who rejected God's Word upon hearing it. The unbelieving Gentiles in Acts 13 who heard Paul preach at Antioch made an express commitment to hear him again during the next Sabbath. They had become dissatisfied with their spiritual life and were determining to believe the truth. The following week many believed. In contrast to these men at Antioch, the Athenians who heard Paul preach about salvation on Mars's Hill (Acts 17) can arguably (according to the Greek Interlinear text) be compartmentalized into two groups—those who believed, and those who stopped up their ears while turning their shoulders away. Two groups, we note, because Luke says that some of them "mocked *and* (Gr. *kai*, possibly *yet*), said, 'We will hear you again on this matter.' " A literal picture of unbelievers stopping up their ears is described in Acts 7, in which many of the crowd rushed upon Stephen and killed him. Those who wanted to kill Christ in John 8 also stopped up their ears (metaphorically speaking). In fact, they had been in the *habit* of accusing him—"Say we not well that thou art a Samaritan, and hast a devil?" (Jn. 8:48). Again, this was not the average response of those unbelievers among the general public whom the Bible says "heard him gladly" (though sadly, we note, but for a time).

    The point here is that not all men respond the way that Calvinistic theology says they uncontrollably must. Calvinism makes the further claim that God foreordains Satan's blinding activity upon such unbelievers. But if that is so, why does the Bible tell us that Satan is the *god* of this world? For

God to sovereignly ordain that a man shall be subject to the evidence of Himself in the creation, but merely for the express purpose that Satan be sovereignly directed by God to blind that man to that very evidence, is to argue for a God that is monstrous and is Himself the ruler of this world. Simply put, such a view is neither biblical nor logical. Granted, we suspect how the Calvinist will respond to our appeal for logic; as A.W. Pink says:

> Once more, we say, it is not for us to *reason about* the Gospel; it is our business to *preach* it.[xlii]

Different Degrees of Sinfulness

Moreover, if it is true that men intend to sin uncontrollably (as Calvinism implicitly suggests), then all men ought to be intending to sin to the *greatest degree* possible, and therefore should be judged equally guilty in the afterlife. That nations, however, receive different degrees of punishment in the afterlife is proof that all men in their intentions do not sin equally. Yet the Calvinistic reply that God is restraining some, while allowing others to sin relatively unhindered, explains nothing about why all men are not judged equally guilty in the afterlife. Indeed, to go the heart of the matter, how is the Calvinistic idea of God's common grace a credit to man? For it is the mindset and heartset which concern God. Christ implied this fact in the Sermon on the Mount, when he said that if a man was given to lust, though he have no opportunity to engage it, he was nevertheless guilty before God (i.e., by reason of his intention). So if the Calvinist is right about all men being utterly depraved apart from the common grace of God, why are not all judged as equally guilty by reason of their intentions? Instead, Christ showed that one people could have a lesser sinful intention than another people. Christ points out this fact when discussing the judgment of certain cities, i.e., that the reason some unbelieving cities would receive a lesser condemnation than others in the coming judgment is because they would have responded positively had they been given the latter's circumstances. For example, in Matthew 11:21-23 Christ claims that Tyre and Sidon would have repented in sackcloth and ashes a long time ago if they had seen the same miracles as those done in Bethsaida and Chorazin. He also says that Sodom would have remained to the present day had it seen the miracles done in Capernaum. This prompts Christ to pronounce a special "Woe!" upon these hard-hearted cities of His generation, the kind of which was not pronounced upon Tyre, Sidon, or Sodom. In another instance Christ said that the Queen of the South who heard Solomon, and the men of Nineveh who heard Jonah, would rise up and condemn the generation of Christ's unbelieving listeners, since these former ancients had repented at the teaching and preaching of Solomon and Jonah respectively, both of whom were lesser figures than Christ (Lk. 11:31-32). How, we ask, can these statements be understood regarding the different judgmental outcomes of peoples, if the heartset of all men and women are at all times equally sinful, as Calvinistic theology claims? Again, if God was the sole factor in seeing that the Queen of the South and the men of Nineveh repented, how is that a basis for judgment against Christ's own generation? Such an explanation defies any normal reading or explanation of the text. Thus, Calvinists fail to see that some men choose to sin where others do not, and that God will make a difference in judgment because of it. This is the *biblical* explanation of what constitutes the basis of God's judgment, and it is a *reasonable* one. Unfortunately, the Calvinist will not accept this explanation. He wants to say that all men have done (or would do) an equal amount of wickedness because their heartsets are the same. But again, this is simply not a position the Bible supports.

Simon the Pharisee

Let us further consider what the Bible says about some people not sinning as much as others. For there is another passage besides those of Matthew 11:21 and Luke 11:31-32 in which an inequality of sinfulness is assumed, and it is the parable Jesus spoke to Simon the Pharisee. As we recall, Jesus is eating at Simon's house when a woman comes in and washes His feet with her tears. Apparently, it was public knowledge that this woman was a sinner. This probably meant she was a prostitute, for it is unclear in New Testament culture what else besides prostitution would cause others to label her a *sinner*. Thus, Simon wonders why Jesus, if He were a real prophet, would allow such a woman to touch even His feet. Jesus knows what Simon is thinking and turns the event into a teaching moment:

> [37]And there was a woman in the city who was a sinner; and when she learned that He (Jesus) was reclining at the table in the Pharisee's house, she brought an alabaster vial of perfume, [38]and standing behind Him at His feet, weeping, she began to wet His feet with her tears, and kept wiping them with the hair of her head, and kissing His feet and anointing them with the perfume. [39]Now when the Pharisee who had invited Him saw this, he said to himself, "If this man were a prophet He would know who and what sort of person this woman is who is touching Him, that she is a sinner." [40]And Jesus answered him, "Simon, I have something to say to you." And he replied, "Say it,

Teacher." ⁴¹"A moneylender had two debtors: one owed five hundred denarii, and the other fifty. ⁴²When they were unable to repay, he graciously forgave them both. So which of them will love him more?" ⁴³Simon answered and said, "I suppose the one whom he forgave more." And He said to him, "You have judged correctly." ⁴⁴Turning toward the woman, He said to Simon, "Do you see this woman? I entered your house; you gave Me no water for My feet, but she has wet My feet with her tears and wiped them with her hair. ⁴⁵You gave Me no kiss; but she, since the time I came in, has not ceased to kiss My feet. ⁴⁶You did not anoint My head with oil, but she anointed My feet with perfume. ⁴⁷For this reason I say to you, her sins, which are many, have been forgiven, for she loved much; but he who is forgiven little, loves little." ⁴⁸Then He said to her, "Your sins have been forgiven." (Lk. 7:37-48)

Simon was a rare bird. He was actually a believing Pharisee. This is made plain by Christ symbolizing him as a forgiven debtor. Spiritually speaking he was a debtor of 50 denarii. (A single denarius was one day's wage, so even 50 denarii was not an inconsiderable sum.) But like so many who find themselves with Pharisaical baggage after their conversion, Simon too is seen judging others without proper understanding. While Christ actually confirms Simon's belief that this woman was a considerable sinner—10 times, in fact, the sinner that Simon was (presumably, Christ was speaking in general terms), Simon is told that because his debt to God was not as great, so neither will be his gratitude and love. Christ, however, cancels all debts, and so the woman stands with Simon on an equal footing. Because of God's forgiveness Simon is to realize that the woman he regarded as too unclean to touch Jesus' feet ought rather to be *embraced as a sister*. In fact, in terms of Christian service, this would mean that Simon should wash *her* feet.

Some interpreters have suggested that this parable does not teach an inequality of sinfulness among men, and that Simon's debt is said to be less because Simon *perceived* it to be less. Nothing in this parable supports this claim, however. Rather, Christ assumes the very opposite premise when He states that this woman's sins were many in number. Thus, Jesus confirmed the accuracy of Simon's comparison in principle, though we hasten to add that Simon, as a legalist, may have thought he was not even 1% of the sinner the woman was! (Perhaps this is why the Bible tells us comparisons are not wise, since everyone tends to think they are less sinful than they really are).

This parable of the Lord, besides whatever other lessons are intended regarding indebtedness, gratitude, and love, also teaches us that all men are not equally in debt regarding their sins. Yes, all men are debtors, all are headed for eternal punishment in hell, and all are in need of a Savior. To put the parable into a modern setting, certainly a boss is not going to call into his office an employee who stole $5,000 from his company and tell him how commendable he is for not having stolen as much as someone else who stole $50,000! Neither one is commendable, but the fact remains that one stole 10 times that of another. (Incidentally, the one who stole $5,000 may have something to boast about to the man who stole $50,000, but not before the boss). The Calvinist will not explain this difference in sinfulness. Perhaps, I should say the Calvinist *cannot* explain this difference so long as he is *unwilling* to set his apologetics on something other than a doctrine of depravity, which says that all men have dug themselves to the same level of pig-slop sinfulness because of their inability to choose the good. Rather, it is correct to say that no man can be seen as righteous by reason of the sinfulness that completely covers all men, while also noting that some men have dug themselves deeper into the pig slop of sin than others.

God's Drawing of Man—What It Is; What It Isn't

Before we leave the subject of what man *can* and *cannot* do, we must consider the word *helko* in John 6:44, translated "draw." [This will compliment what we have already seen in footnote #53 regarding what the word "dunamai" means in this verse. (Incidentally, for further information about interpreting John 6:44, see Scripture Index.)] Let us look at verse 44 in the context of its prior verses:

> [41]The Jews then murmured at him, because he said, I am the bread which came down from heaven. [42]And they said, Is not this Jesus, the son of Joseph, whose father and mother we know? how is it then that he saith, I came down from heaven? [43]Jesus therefore answered and said unto them, Murmur not among yourselves. [44]No man can come to me, except the Father which hath sent me draw him: and I will raise him up at the last day.

The Greek word for *draw* here is the same word which Christ uses in John 12:32 when He says, "If I be lifted up I will <u>draw</u> all men unto myself." This word *to draw* (the *intensity* of the verb varying, according to context), means *to pull;* though often Calvinists claim that *helko* means *to drag* in all of its occurrences (or at least in those occurrences necessary to affirm their Calvinism). In the New Testament it seems to occur in contexts in which there is a *lifting.* (I do not mean to suggest, however, that such verticality is necessarily part of *helko*'s lexical meaning, due at least to its Septuagint use. Nevertheless, it is an interesting observation.) Taking into consideration what we have learned the word "cannot" means in regard to free will persons (again, see footnote #53), let us consider the meaning of John 6:44 and John 12:32. All men have chosen to set their minds upon evil and thus against spiritual things, and therefore they *cannot* come to Christ. They are unable to come because they are unwilling to come. Again, expressed another way, how *can* a man come if he is unwilling? God has left the matter of a man's ultimate response entirely within that man's own will. If, then, a man is unwilling to respond to God's outreach, there is no other recourse that can effect his coming, and the matter is over.[54] **Moreover**, a man *cannot* effect his own atonement. In using the word "cannot" in the last sentence we mean it in the sense of *actual* (or *de facto*) inability, not *willful* inability. This means that man must rely upon God to provide him an atonement for his sin.

Christ gives a description of the Father in John 6:44 to show by what exact means God brings about man's salvation, i.e., "the Father which hath sent *me.*" It is the One the Father has sent who will provide the way of salvation for men. It is the Father who will lift men up to a place where, like the thieves on the cross on either side of Jesus, they can gaze (so to speak) upon Christ and decide if they will believe in His work for them. Some men will look upon Christ without any sense of urgency or submission of heart, as did the unrepentant thief. Others will ask for a place in Paradise with Him, as did the repentant thief who cried out for mercy. During the course of these two thieves' lives, both had allowed their feet to set in the thick ooze of the sludge of their will, so that their faces might always gaze more intently in the direction of evil. The longer they stayed in this position the greater became the sucking power of the mud upon their feet. God, however, through the Sun (Son), turned the mud into dry ground and lifted their feet to a place upon the soil so that they could walk more easily in a new direction if they but chose to do so. But each of these men had to choose for himself what he would do. Notice in John 6:44 that Christ does not say that man cannot come to Him unless the Father *makes* the man come. Rather, the problem lies in getting the man to a place where he is under more influence to exercise his will to receive Christ. Thus toward this place the Father draws a man, i.e., to the foot of the cross, where he might consider the Savior who died for him.[55] This kind of *resistible* drawing agrees with the nature of man's will as Christ implicitly described that will to Nicodemus in John 3:14-15, "As Moses lifted up the serpent in the wilderness, even so must the Son of Man be lifted up," i.e., so that "whosoever believeth in Him should not perish." One could choose to look at the serpent, but one did not have to. Thus, Christ's sacrifice solved the problem of our *actual* inability and encourages us in the problem of our *willful* inability. In fact, *helko* is the Greek word used by the Septuagint translators for the idea of persuasive *wooing*, found in Song of Solomon 1:4. Arguably, this wooing was done publicly (note the 'we') and may have run to and fro between gentleness and stronger exhortation. "Draw (*helko*) me, we will run after thee." This use in the Septuagint shows that the contemporary culture of Jesus understood that *helko* had some latitude of meaning depending on the context. <u>Thus the English *pull*, not *drag*, IF only one word were used in translation for *helko*, works for both passages, i.e., for a maiden asking to be pulled toward her lover so that she might run after him, and the pulling of a net ashore.</u> Thus nowhere *must* the Bible student take *helko* to mean the kind of irresistibility that Calvin's theology demands, that is, as long as the passage in question suggests another meaning. Furthermore, if, say, in a novel one read the word "drag," in which its meaning was non-literal, i.e., *Mom had to drag Jason from bed every morning to go to school,* the same author might use the word *drag* in a literal way in other portions of the same book. Similarly, no conservative Protestant, for example, would take the words of Christ literally in John 6:54, i.e., when Jesus tells His hearers that whoever *eats* His flesh and drinks his blood has eternal life, even though 5 verses earlier Jesus uses the word *eat* in a literal sense. Even so, it should be understood that the Father does not drag a man irresistibly in some spiritual sense unless the biblical context demands it, which it never does. Thus, with a verb having some latitude of meaning, one must examine the near and far contexts to determine the meaning that Scripture intends for each of that verb's given appearances.

The best biblical example of pulling a man all the way to the foot of the cross, at which point man himself must exhibit faith, is probably that of the Jewish people during the exodus narrative. God, *pulls* (Gr. *helko*, i.e., *woos and admonishes*) the children of Israel safely through the first nine plagues toward the goal of delivering them, even as a shepherd might his sheep. But observe that the children of Israel must exercise faith by trusting the Lord's word regarding the Passover meal, that is, if God is to deliver them from the 10th plague (and ultimately from Egypt). Deliverance will fail them if they do not exercise faith at this point. Even so, a man must exercise faith after God has pulled him toward the cross of Christ.

Now needless to say, we can expect the Calvinist to claim that God dragged the hearts of Israel into a state of regeneration, so that they would observe the Passover. We anticipate this argument from the Calvinist, since he is unwilling to state unqualifyingly that man decides anything on his own. For to admit such a thing would be to threaten his entire Calvinistic paradigm—a paradigm which denies any meaning to human freedom. Consequently, the Calvinist will apply Scripture irrationally (by stating contradictory propositions). The result is that man remains the puppet that he must, in order that God might remain absolutely sovereign. Thus, regarding the present discussion of the Israelites, '*man's choice*' to believe the Lord regarding the Passover and be saved, is redefined by the Calvinist, so that it is neither *man's* nor a *choice*, yet claimed to be both. Even so, such '*regeneration*' (as defined by the Calvinist, i.e., with a view *toward* salvation) would be claimed by Sproul to *precede* (Sproul, "leads to") the renewed life, even though it is also claimed to mean 'rebirth,' (i.e., life itself). (We must note here that 'regeneration' of man's desire cannot itself be the renewed spiritual life if man must still rush to Christ in order to have that life.) Make no mistake—such irrational arguments are indeed sophisticatedly drawn, and if this were not the case the Church would not continue to struggle with such 'theology' after 16 centuries. What the Calvinist has done is this: he has taken *helko* and insisted that it means "to drag" in verses where the meaning *to drag* is obvious, i.e., 'Peter dragged the net ashore,' then made that meaning of private interpretation (that is, exempted it from lexical controls and other differing contexts in which the word also appears) and then applied that private meaning to every salvific context, while ignoring everything else in those salvific contexts which disproves his theology. Such a method would be like that of a reader of a memoir finding in one place the sentence, "I love horseshoes," and finding in another place the sentence, "I love my wife," and, by absolutizing the context about horseshoes, insisting upon the inference that the author was stating that he loves to throw his wife around, preferably upon a stake. Even so, the dragging of a fishnet is not the same as dragging the fishes' will to a place of change, and the dragging of Jason and certain brethren was the dragging of their *bodies*, not their *wills*, unto a place not of their choosing. Nowhere in the Bible is the will of one thing ever dragged irresistibly to a place of change.

Appearance is Everything

Because this method of misapplying contexts (initiated by private interpretations) is something vitally important to note, we will need to examine it at some length before returning to a discussion of *helko*. For the real strength of Calvinistic argument is redefined definitions which are subtly introduced as something other than redefined definitions. Thus the one exposed to Calvinistic arguments *thinks* he shares the same meaning of words when conversing with the Calvinist. But in fact the Calvinist is using definitions that are no definitions at all. For example, although early in life we hear phrases like, "That was a good report card," "That apple pie sure tasted good," "The orchestra sounded good," etc., and therefore learn from these experiences the proper and logical definition of the word "good," the Calvinist uses the word "good" in a very different way to mean *the moral quality of whatever happens in history*. I am convinced that at least many Calvinists themselves (and remember, I once counted myself among them) are unaware of what they do.

The strength of Calvinism is thus twofold. First, the person encountering Calvinism who has formerly understood the true meaning of words like "good," has previously built up in his mind an association between the *vocal-sound* "good" and its *correct meaning*. But now, in encountering Calvinism, this association of the vocal-sound "good" will be used against him (as will the vocal-sounds of all key terms in theology). For as he now encounters the word "good" *as used by the Calvinist*, he assumes he knows what the Calvinist is saying, but in fact he assumes incorrectly, because he really has no shared *meaning* with the Calvinist. Therefore, because of his association of the vocal-sound "good" to the true meaning of "good" in past experiences, he may *think* he knows what the Calvinist means by the vocal sound "good" when he hears that word, but he is mistaken. For the Calvinist means something entirely different when he uses the vocal-sound "good." In brief, the Calvinist and the non-Calvinist do not mean the same thing by the vocal sound "good," and therefore they have no shared meaning. Yet *it will appear that they share meaning, since they use the same vocal sound.*

To give an analogy of this, suppose two brothers grew up eating apples and knew what apples really were, but then years later one of the brothers (having ruined his mind through false philosophy) says to the other, "I ate an apple that has never existed." The still sensical brother, hearing this, will nevertheless picture an apple in his mind upon hearing his brother's statement, even though such an "apple," which the ruined brother proposes, could never be eaten. That is, the vocal-sound "apple" will bring a picture of a real apple to the sensical brother's mind because of his past associations between the vocal-sound "apple" and its correct meaning. Yet at this point in the brotherly dialogue something else happens. The ruined brother now adds even more confusion to the conversation by reminding his brother about the apples they used to eat when they were kids. Thus it seems to the sensical brother that his ruined brother is talking sense again. Only it doesn't last long; for the ruined brother soon returns to talking about the apple he ate which never existed. This goes back and forth until the sensical brother doesn't know *what* to make of it all.

Now let me offer an actual example of this kind of dialogue to show how absolutely similar Calvinism is to other false religious systems, in this case Buddhism (which *de facto* treats all terms as having illusory meaning). Recently I tuned into a National Public Radio show called "Fresh Air," in which I heard hostess Terry Gross say[56] to her guest Pico Iyer (a journalist covering the Dalai Lama during the Chinese oppression of the Tibetans) that while she (Gross) understood how the Dalai Lama's response to oppression, i.e., that "one does not have to be unhappy," might make sense on some spiritual level, it was difficult to see how it could really intersect with the political realm (i.e., was relevant). Iyer replied by admitting that certainly there was political oppression going on against the Tibetans. But then Iyer immediately added that the Dalai Lama was "not simply handing out placebos," when he told his people they did not have to be unhappy, because in fact there were "many freedoms" in life, and in whatever circumstances one found himself, one could still "remain with an open heart."

Observe, then, that Iyer replied to Gross's question first by a *rational* statement, conceding Gross's point that real political oppression did exist against Tibetans. *Or at least Iyer appeared to concede Gross's view with a seeming rational statement.* For I contend that Iyer immediately backed off the *reality* of such oppression by stating that the Dalai Lama was "not handing out placebos" but merely recognizing that there are "many freedoms," and that in the midst of oppression one can still remain with "an open heart." But note that to state the matter this way is to state a doublethink. For we ought to contend that the Dalai Lama **is** handing out placebos, since he advocates a state of mind that does justice neither to the reality of political oppression nor to the emotion of anger that all fair-minded citizens ought to feel against oppression. In other words, his rational appeal is a sham. Indeed, will the Dalai Lama suggest next that such a response would have been appropriate for the Jews in Auschwitz? Yes, what a shame the Germans did not hang up signs in the gas showers to help alleviate the suffering of Jews- "You do not have to be unhappy while you die." Wisdom will certainly perish with the Dalai Lama. Well, enough of this nonsense. By now we see that the Dalai Lama recognizes no real political oppression against his people *despite the appearance that he does*. He has, in effect, merely taken the vocal-sound "political oppression" and played a clever trick on a naive journalist by convincing her of his 'profound' utterances, so that she in turn can enlighten the Western world about how to handle suffering. Indeed, as every Buddhist knows, one does not have to be unhappy about suffering as long as that suffering takes place in a world of illusion. Iyer, in effect, was merely the Dalai Lama's mouthpiece, first reminding us of the apples we ate as kids, before promising that we can eat apples that don't exist; and so these statements, <u>when taken together</u>, mean that we can eat "rotten apples" with "worms" in them and at the same time not be unhappy, since such "apples" and "worms" have existence only as vocal sounds, not real things. Technically in fact, and as already observed, such a statement about "eating non-existent things" is meaningless in all its grammar, since predicates and subjects cannot engage non-existent things. Thus the trick in Buddhism, as in Calvinism, is to speak the irrational, but claim it is rational.

So then, let me ask a question of my readers: How is the Calvinist response to the problem of evil any different than the Dalai Lama's? As my readers ultimately move into the last chapter of this book (*The Problem of Evil*) we will see a Calvinist who <u>appears</u> to admit *with rational sounding statements* that there **is** real oppression and evil in the world, but will then quickly add the statement that evil has no "ontological being." Thus in one breath (so to speak) he will tell us that evil exists, yet in a way in which it has no being! And, of course, this Evangelical will deny handing out placebos to us.

Second, and this point is actually similar to the first, Calvinism's irrational 'theology' redefines reality in a seductive way so that, regardless of circumstances, a kind of bliss reigns; or at least we are told we can assume this, since even attacks done *to us* as believers is claimed to be done *for us*, regardless of their origin. Indeed, if God (according to the Calvinist) creates the very thoughts and intents of all souls, how can anything be truly against the believer even if the activity is from the Enemy? Thus, the Enemy is merely the 'Enemy,' i.e., a word which for the Calvinist merely reflects another kind of God's construct that is working itself out in the world and for '*our good*,' which, as my astute readers will now see, is actually neither *ours* nor *good*.

Various Forms of *Helko*

Now I confess I have gone somewhat far afield in these observations, though, of course, they are relevant in showing the method Calvinists use to overthrow the meanings of key words, like *helko*. But now let us compare some of the various words which are translated *draw*, *drew*, and *dragged* in the New Testament, realizing that basically the only *quid pro quo* word that works in English translation in all instances is "to pull," not "to drag." Now not in view in our discussion here is the word *draw* used in John 2:8 and John 4:7, 11, and 15, which specifically relates to the drawing of water, as from a well, or as in the bailing of a ship's hold (the etymology for this particular word translated *draw* actually comes from a word meaning *a ship's hold*). There are, then, three remaining Greek words to consider. Two of these are commonly translated as *draw*, *drew* or *dragged* and are more similar in meaning to each other than to the third. These two are exchanged in at least one example in the New Testament where Peter is said to have *drawn* his sword: Matthew and Mark choose a word for *draw* whose root (Gr. *spao*), means *to draw*, or *draw out*, and which seems to emphasize the drawing *out* of Peter's sword. John chooses a word for *draw* (Gr., *helko*, meaning *to draw, to pull*) which happens to occur in a context of lifting, thus Peter drew out (pulled out) his sword in an *upward* motion to strike Malchus's *ear*. (Observe that we do not think of a sword being *dragged* out, but *pulled* out.) Interestingly enough, the word that John uses for the drawing of Peter's sword is the same word for *draw* in John 12:32, where Jesus says that if He is lifted up He will *draw* all men unto Himself, i.e., in this case, *up* to Himself. The occurrences of *helko* in a context of vertical lift appear to be found in all of the other New Testament passages in which *helko* appears. Thus, the disciples could not *pull* the net of 153 fish (*up*) into their boat, Peter *pulls* this same net of fish to shore (and thus presumably *up* onto the shore so that it was out of the water), and Paul and Barnabas were *pulled* by certain angry Philippi merchants from Lydia's house in Thyatira (*up*) to the Philippian marketplace (the latter, I believe, being of a higher geographical elevation). Again, though, this observation of *helko*'s vertical aspect does not include the history of other lexical control groups, such as the Septuagint. Nevertheless, there does appear to be the suggestion of verticality in all of the New Testament passages in which the Greek word *helko* (*to pull*) is used. On the other hand, verticality does not appear to be a contextual element for *spao*, unless the form *anaspao* is used, as it is in Acts 11:10, where it is said that the sheet in Peter's vision was *drawn* back up into heaven, or in Luke 14:5, where it talks of drawing out an ass that has fallen into a pit. The form of *spao* in Matthew 23:51 (of Peter's sword) is *apospao*, meaning *to draw (pull) out (in separation)*. It might be argued here that John would have used *anaspao* instead of *helko* if he had really intended to give the sense of verticality and ***irresistibility***.

At any rate, a third word for *draw* in the form of *drew* (Greek, *suro*) is used to refer to an even greater intensive and coercive activity, and occurs in the New Testament without decided prejudice regarding *lifting*. It is used to describe those who failed to find Paul and Silas at Jason's house, and so *pulled* Jason and certain brethren before the rulers after setting the entire city of Thessalonica to an uproar. It is also used to describe Paul's body being *dragged (pulled)* out of the city of Lystra by those who had stoned him until they supposed him dead. It is also used in Revelation to describe the dragon which *drew* a third of the stars with his tail. This passage in Revelation is understood by most biblical scholars to refer to the Devil pulling along a third of the angelic host into his rebellion. Note in this case that the word for *draw* suggests an opposite directional meaning than upward, as Satan's rebellion caused a betimes departure from heaven, and so presumably *downward*, where he became the fallen god of this world. Implied here is that the angels who joined in the rebellion approved of Satan's intention (i.e., will). But note especially in this last example how the word *drew* used to describe Satan's activity does not have the same shade of meaning as the word *draw* used to describe Christ's wooing and admonishing of all men toward a consideration of Himself. Nor should the meanings of these words be the same if we consider the actions and distinctive personalities of each in their respective attempts to gain persons' allegiances. While *Strong's* suggests that *helko* and *suro* are probably akin to each other etymologically, the evidence seems speculative, and further, one cannot deny a certain difference in meaning as used in the New Testament. Furthermore, the word used of Satan's *drawing* away of the angels (Revelation 12:4) is also used parabolically for Christ's *haling* of rebellious men to judgment, because they did not pursue peace with Him (Lk. 12:58). Thus by the use of different verbs, Christ is showing that the haling of someone before the judgment court of Christ (as expressed by *suro*) is of greater intensity than that which attends the Father's drawing (*helko*) of men (Jn. 6:44) or of the Son's drawing (*helko*) of all men toward (Gr. *pros*) Himself (Jn. 12:32). Is it little wonder, then, why one word for *pull* is used of the Father who pulls men toward the Son, while another word for *pull* is used to describe the greater intensity and more coercive manner of Christ in judgment, or of the Devil in his rebellion?[57]

The point here is to ask why, if the Calvinistic view is correct, God should not have to act with equal intensity to foreordain every act of man? For the question is naturally raised: Is the Calvinist God less sovereignly involved in some of the acts of man than in others? Plenty of Calvinistic statements about man's 'freedom' seem to point otherwise, but at the full tilt of the forward rocking-horse position regarding the absolute sovereignty of God, no-exception statements are made about God acting unilaterally. The Calvinist, then, leaves us without an explanation about why different verbs implying different intensities are used of God's activity toward man, the one unto a consideration of salvation, and the other unto judgment. One objection the Calvinist might offer is that the different verbs merely show an attitudinal difference on the part of God and not a difference of force applied. To this objection we can reply again that, though the force of God be strong against man's *willful* inability to believe, the extent of God's force must be consistent with the kind of *invitation* (KJV, *calling*) that Christ described, even though this invitation is also a command to repent. To draw a parallel here, even as a parent would pull aside a child to command him for his own sake not to cross the street without looking both ways (or else suffer the consequence of parental punishment), so too is this coercion of the parent somewhat less when *instructing* the child not to cross the street, than it shall be if the parent brings the child to judgment for disobeying his instructions. In other words, the parent does not walk the child up to the edge of the street and grab the top of the child's head in his hand and coerce it first this way and then that way to make sure the child will 'obey' safety rules, as though such 'obedience' could then be said to be a matter of the child's will. Even so, God gives man grave warnings for man's own sake apart from the kind of coercive force that will be brought to bear in judgment if the man acts foolishly. To the Calvinist who would reply that God's judgment is always upon those He reprobates, we would remind him that while John 3:36 teaches that all men are under the judgment of God before any are saved, Hebrews 9:27 says that it is *after* a man's death that the *final* judgment of God is exercised.

A further point barely touched on earlier, regarding the degree of force implied in *helko*, is to note the Greek preposition *pros* in both John 6:44 and John 12:32. The KJV renders *pros* as the word *to*, but in English the word *to* is often inferred by the reader to mean completed action, such as in the sentence, *Bob went to the ballgame*. The impression in English is that Bob is *in* the ballpark watching the ballgame. But the Greek word *pros* in the above passages in John simply means *toward*. Therefore when John states that the Father pulls a man *toward* the Son, it means something quite different than if John had said that the Father pulls a man *into* Christ.[58] Thus no man can come *toward* Christ except the Father pulls him. Why? Simply because of the brute fact that the man demonstrates his *unwillingness* to come. [That is, technically speaking, man **can** come toward the Son, but apart from the Father's encouragement he **won't**. (Indeed, even **with** the Father's encouragement many **will** not come.)] Similarly to the Father, if Christ be lifted up He will **pull** all men *toward* (Gr. *pros*) Himself.

Now I suppose it is conceivable that Calvinists might grant our argument about *pros* and add their own spin on it. Perhaps they would argue that God does draw a man *toward* Christ in the process of changing the man's will, whereupon the man rushes *into* Christ. Or perhaps they would prefer to say that a man rushes *to* (*toward*) Christ (though we ought to ask the Calvinist at this point, Does he mean that *man* rushes by his own predication!) and is placed *into* Christ by the Father? But such a Calvinist argument regarding man's *will* (so called by them) nevertheless makes indistinct the terms 'God' and 'man' in any meaningful way, as already noted. The result is that man is regarded as nothing more than a will*less* plant receiving a kind of divine construct of *will* from outside himself. The Calvinist does not understand his own illogic, and so will hardly admit to it. But all his definitions affirm this illogic, insofar that such definitions can be said to affirm illusory meaning.[59]

Having somewhat surveyed the verb *helko*, ie., *to pull* in the New Testament, let us now consider the general context of John 6:44 (where Jesus states that a man cannot come to Him unless the Father draws him). First, Christ describes Himself as the Bread of Life in John 6. This Bread is what the Father has sent down from heaven for the benefit of man. In this sense Christ is the spiritual reality that answers to the physical manna which God had sent down to sustain the Israelites during their days in the wilderness (the O.T. manna was a point of discussion between the Pharisees and Christ in John 6). To the Israelites in the wilderness, the manna was God's provision, something only He could miraculously provide. But note that God didn't impart to their stomachs or bodies the food they needed regardless of their desire. Each man had to have a submissive and receptive spirit. Each one had to decide to leave his tent and go receive that which God had provided for him.[60] This physical manna in the Old Testament is thus symbolic of the spiritual manna which God gave men in the New Testament (i.e., His Son), which men are called upon to *receive by taking*. Again, the word *received* in John 1:12, "But as many as received him (Christ), to them gave he the power to become the sons of God," means to receive *by taking*, and is actually translated *take* in Matthew 26:26 "Take, eat; this is my body." It is an active, not passive, type of receiving.

The Bible also describes *receiving* (as in receiving manna) in terms of looking (with belief) upon Jesus. We are like those in Moses' time who were commanded to look upon the serpent on the pole if they desired to live. Note that God didn't command Moses to drag the Israelites to the bronze serpent so that the priestly Levites could then use their thumbs to force open the people's eyelids so that the people couldn't help but see the serpent on the pole whether they wanted to or not (and so be healed). That is the picture of God the Calvinist wants to overlay upon John 6:44, i.e., one of irresistible coercion. But that is not how the Bible describes looking with belief. Rather, Moses lifted up the serpent on the pole so that all those who were *willing to receive* God's method of healing would believe and look upon it by faith. Yet many did not believe and so died in the wilderness. Clearly, then, while man *cannot* raise himself to heaven through an atonement of his own because of *actual* inability, he **can,** if God provides an atonement for him, come to Christ by exercising his will to take and receive Him. So the Father must provide an atonement if man is to be saved, but man must willingly receive this atonement which he cannot provide for himself. Thus, God graciously gives us His Son, the Bread of Life, and all who receive Him live. A sense of *lifting* carries through the last phrase of John 6:44: "and I will raise him up at the last day." God makes the work of the cross potentially effective for all men, so that even at the last day the risen Christ might raise up those who have believed in Him. All who receive the Bread of Life will one day be raised from the dead; and their final abode will be that same place from where the Bread of Life came down.

The problem of Calvinism, then, is its failure to understand Jesus' implicit statement about receiving in John 6. And the concept of receiving in John 6 is the very same as that of John 1:12. Yet the word *received* in John 1:12 means nothing intelligible to a Calvinist. This may sound harsh, but it is putting the matter frankly. Nowhere in verse 12 or in the surrounding context is it suggested that God imparts a new nature so that men can be said to *passively* receive Christ. The word simply does not mean that. The Calvinist may make much ado about man "rushing to Christ" upon his 'regeneration,' which they claim precedes the man's belief, but that is not the sequence of events as described in John 1:12.[61] The chronological order surrounding belief is: 1) God has further enlightened every man's proper conscience through a) creation, and b) the incarnation of His Son who has provided atonement for man; 2) a man decides to receive (take) Christ; 3) *whereupon* a man is given the right by God to become His child. I do not mean to suggest here than a man *earnestly* seeks God apart from God drawing him up to behold the work of the Son. As Psalm 14:1-3 says, no man *diligently*[62] seeks God. Rather, I am only saying that a new nature cannot be imparted to man *prior* to his belief, since the Bible states that the man *himself* believes. (Again, cp. Rom. 4:5, which says that *Abraham* believed God.) Furthermore, remember the words of John 10:27, "My sheep hear my voice, and I know them, and they follow me." This is the Great Shepherd's call, and the sheep who recognize His voice are the call*ees* who act upon the voice of the Great Shepherd and follow Him. This means a response is necessary on the part of the hearer—a bleating of the voice for the Shepherd. But, of course, a sheep, if he wished, could bite the hand of the would-be rescuing shepherd. For the sheep might fear that it would be too painful to be pulled through the thorny bush to safety. While it's actually hard to imagine a sheep choosing such a foolish end, this type of foolishness is characteristic of the man who refuses God's grace because he wants to remain in the thorniness of his sin.

Utter Depravity, Utter Oneness, Utter Bliss

Calvinists *appear* to take the thorniness of sin very seriously, but in fact they have forsaken a sound understanding of the nature of sin. R.C. Sproul, for example, following the classic argument of the famed, 18th century Calvinist, Jonathan Edwards, argues that man is so completely dead in his sins that any response on man's part is impossible. Sproul argues that God alone must *entirely* change a man's desire if the man is to be saved. To show how God is the sole participant in changing a man's desire, Sproul contrasts his Calvinism with the Arminian position:

> In this (Arminian) view fallen man is seen as a drowning man who is unable to swim. He has gone under twice and bobbed to the surface for the last time. If he goes under again he will die. His only hope is for God to throw him a life preserver. God throws the lifeline and tosses it precisely to the edge of the man's outstretched fingers. All the man has to do to

be saved is to grab hold. If he will only grab hold of
the life preserver, God will tow him in. If he refuses
the life preserver, he will certainly perish. Again in this
(Arminian) illustration the utter helplessness of sinful
man without God's assistance is emphasized. The
drowning man is in a serious condition. He cannot
save himself. However, he is still alive; he can still
stretch forth his fingers. His fingers are the crucial link
to salvation. His eternal destiny depends upon what he
does with his fingers. (But) Paul says the man is dead.
He is not merely drowning, he has already sunk to the
bottom of the sea. It is futile to throw a life preserver
to a man who has already drowned. If I understand
Paul, I hear him saying that God dives into the water
and pulls a dead man from the bottom of the sea and
then performs a mouth-to-mouth resuscitation. He
breathes into the dead man new life. [xliii]

We should note here to what extent Calvinists take the man to be 'dead' at the bottom of the lake. To understand the extent of this deadness, we must further consider what the doctrine of total depravity means, since to the Calvinist the term *total depravity* equals this deadness. Sproul defines it as the following:

Total Depravity is a very misleading term. The
concept of total depravity is often confused with the
idea of utter depravity. In Reformed theology total
depravity refers to the idea that our whole humanity is
fallen. That is, there is no part of me that has not been
affected in some way by the Fall …(but) Total
depravity is not utter depravity. Utter depravity would
mean that we are all as sinful as we possibly could be.
We know that is not the case. No matter how much
each of us has sinned, we are able to think of worse
sins that we could have committed. [xliv]

Thus Sproul appears to define a man's total depravity as horizontally comprehensive (i.e., affecting every area across the spectrum of life) but not vertically comprehensive (i.e., not affecting any area to a total saturation of its depth). Boettner likewise concurs with Sproul that a difference exists in the 'deadness' of Total Inability and Utter Depravity:

> This doctrine of Total Inability which declares that men are dead in sin, does not mean that all men are equally bad, nor that any man is as bad as he could be . . .[xlv]

But despite such statements about total depravity not equaling utter depravity, the two are soon confused with each other in Calvinistic theology, as shown here in Boettner's view:

> The unregenerate man can, through common grace, love his family and he may be a good citizen. He may give a million dollars to build a hospital, but he cannot give even a cup of cold water to a disciple *in the name of Jesus*... All of his common virtues or good works have a fatal defect in that his motives which prompt them are not to glorify God; a defect so vital that it throws any element of goodness as to man wholly into the shade.[xlvi]

Thus Boettner states that if a man gives the appearance of acting righteously, it is only because God's common grace is involved. Remove the common grace, then, and the man would be utterly depraved, since all of man's motives (according to Boettner) are wrong. But this raises a question. Why doesn't Boettner see a contradiction in stating that 1) *no man is as bad as he could be* (as evidenced, says Boettner, by man being found in total, not utter, depravity), while yet stating that 2) *no man has any correct motives* whatsoever? For we must ask: Wouldn't the definition of *utter* depravity mean that man does not have any correct motives whatsoever? Boettner seems unaware that Paul states in Romans 2:14-15 that even Gentiles who lived apart from the Mosaic law did by nature the things contained in the law, even to the point of accusing or *excusing* one another. The fact that a Gentile could *excuse* even one thing in a fellow man, i.e., by realizing in that man an act which was ethically and justifiably excusable in some sense, would indicate that such men, though unsaved, were *able* to do something good. As for Boettner's objection that all of a man's motives or good works have the fatal defect of not wanting to glorify God, we would say it is doubtful whether any *Christian* is fully free of this same defect. Even Paul said "I am the chief of sinners" well into his ministry, and he was given a thorn in the flesh to prevent his pride from asserting itself after he was caught up to the third heaven and given a special vision. Indeed, even Christians may deceive themselves into thinking they are loving God with all of their heart, soul, mind, and strength, when in fact they are not. As John says, "If we say we have no sin, we deceive ourselves, and the truth is not in us." Whatever the motives of men may be, the truth of Romans 2:14-15, i.e., that even Gentiles *can* do something good and sometimes do act in some sense ethically *excusable*, must always be maintained. Thus Boettner's point cannot be supported when he says that "*any* element of goodness as to man [is put] wholly into the shade" (emphasis added) simply because man does not keep the Great commandment. Man may, and indeed does at times, obey the 2nd (neighborly) command of the New Testament in some sense, or else Paul could not have said that Gentiles sometimes act excusable [in some way and in some sense].

Nevertheless, since Boettner claims that all of man's motives are self-directed, one wonders why he draws a distinction between total depravity and utter depravity. Suppose, for example, that there are a total of four apples on the grocery shelf. An utterly depraved man would steal all four apples. Boettner is saying that if a man were to steal only three apples, two, one, or even none at all, the only reason he has done so is because God's common grace is restraining him. But since Boettner is suggesting that the only reason a man gives the appearance of right doing is because of common grace, then if the common grace were removed from the man, it would reveal his utter depravity. Take away the common grace *of God*, then, and all men would be stealing four apples. So for the Calvinist, the only difference between total depravity and utter depravity is the intervention of God's common grace. Such grace (again, according to the Calvinist) is the only reason why men are not all equally bad or doing every possible evil thing they can. How then, we ask, can a man be *totally* depraved without the nature of that depravity also being *utter*? For Boettner, the introduction of God's grace comes to a man when he is already in his natural state of intending to steal all four apples. Any attempted distinctions by Calvinists between total depravity and utter depravity are therefore meaningless, because latent within Calvinism's concept of total depravity is always utter depravity, since anything short of stealing four apples relies accordingly on some supposed version of God's grace. The extent, then, to which our man is spiritually dead at the bottom of the lake is as radical as Calvinists can imagine, since they would claim that the intention of any man, left to himself, is to steal four apples.

Not surprisingly, then, Sproul's conclusion about the drowned man is that the man's deadness is so irreversible that God must, apart from any human participation whatsoever, 'regenerate' the man. There is nothing which the man can do, *or even to which he can respond*. He is totally functionless and inoperative. *To suggest that the man is functional or operative in any spiritual way is, for Sproul, nothing less that the ascription of works. Sproul's definition of 'works,' then, is the spiritualized version of the physicist's definition—that of movement, enactment, or response. Even man's receiving of Christ is, according to Sproul, a <u>work</u>.*

But Sproul's idea of what constitutes work is obviously problematic, since he includes faith as a work. An analogy can serve us here. Suppose a father were to buy a dress for his five-year old daughter and hand it to her on Christmas day in a gift-wrapped package of ribbon and bow. Let us assume that the small girl receives the gift gladly, opens the box, and is delighted at having the dress. Would we say that she has earned the garment in any way? No—certainly not. Furthermore, she is incapable of entering the work force as a laborer to earn money to buy the dress for herself. Would we say, then, that in receiving the gift of the dress, she had worked for it? Again, no. But if this is the case, why does Sproul insist that a man's reception of the gospel has to be considered working for it? Apparently, Sproul has forgotten that Paul's discussion of Romans 4 is a contrast between grace and the wage earner, not grace and non-predication.

Nevertheless, because Sproul accepts *works* as meaning any form of faith-predication whatsoever, a natural question arises about the man at the bottom of the lake said to be absolutely dead and inoperative. Namely, if God brings this man up to sit with Christ in heavenly places, how can we say that this man has participated in his conversion, i.e. to the extent that he has *taken* Christ (Jn. 1:12)? That is, how is it that *he* has faith? For if God does the work of faith in the man's heart without man allowing or disallowing that act, then it must be God who is doing the believing rather than the man. For if the man is in a completely inoperative mode, then God is doing the surrogate believing on behalf of 'him.' Sproul attempts an explanation by defining the *desire* and *will* of man so that they appear different, when, in fact, he demonstrates no essential distinction in meaning. Indeed, if a man *must* choose according to his strongest desire, how is the meaning of the word "desire" different from the meaning of "will," except that it describes an 'earlier' stage in the same phenomenon? Or how is *man's will* different from *God's implanted desire*? To so define *desire* and *will*, and *God* and *man*, as indistinguishable, is all part of the irrationality subtly advocated by Sproul and Edwards. *With Sproul and Edwards, then, it is not that the man has faith* (if we grant any meaning whatsoever to the *individuation* of these terms for the moment), *but that faith has been found in the man. It is not that the man believes, but that belief has been found in the man. Thus, for the Calvinist, man 'receives' Christ as a fighter might 'receive' a bloody nose or a child might 'receive' a spanking, i.e., in a totally passive way apart from any willingness to receive it.*

Furthermore, because of Sproul's definition of *desire*, any attempt at saying that man "rushes to Christ" upon receiving a new implant from God is an attempt to maintain the dialectical side of human "freedom" and "choice" within Reformed theology, not to mention a defense Sproul needs in order to explain the active form of the verb 'receive' in John 1:12. In any final analysis, all such Reformed-defined terms are reversible (man's choice/God's construct), and therefore no real distinctions are being made between God and man.

To understand the implications of this Calvinistic view, consider that I am in a chair writing this page. All of the molecules that make up my being (according to Sproul elsewhere in his book) are in sovereign control by God. According to Sproul and Boettner (who follow Edwards) any faith that I have has been a result of God putting a new desire in me apart from my willingness. Indeed, had God not implanted a new desire in me, I would have remained as I was. But the question arises—If Calvinism says that God has placed His desire in Dan *against* Dan's desire, then Dan's desires have been negated in order to receive the construct of God. That is, without God's forceful and coercive removal of Dan's *own* desires, Dan would simply remain as he is. How then, for example, can Sproul or Edwards say that this new desire is *Dan's* desire? For if I now say the sentence, "God has changed my desire" there is an illusion of meaning because there is no more 'my.' God has overthrown the 'my.' He has negated the 'my' and replaced the vacuum with His desire. The only way, then, that 'Dan' could say that "God has changed my desire" is if we reduce the 'my' to particle physics. Thus, in place of Dan's essence is now a bio-organic automaton that, in effect, calls up a program that God has put within him to give the illusion that when the automaton speaks saying, "I am Dan, and my desire has been changed," Dan and his desire are still present, when in fact they are not. In reality 'Dan' must only be a bio-computer which God has made out of material creation. So the mass of collective molecules in process that sits in a chair, which we call 'Dan,' has been the object of God's construct. 'Dan,' for that matter (as previously noted), could be a laundry basket for all the distinction that Calvinism requires. The 'my' enacts no final thinking or willing as a separate entity distinct from God. Thus 'man' is a non-predicated being, and the uniqueness that distinguishes him from a laundry basket is lost. For God could just as well sustain the being of a laundry basket, a plant, or an automaton in His presence, and cause it to echo back His constructs as will*less* computers with no consciousness. Either way it is God's continuation of an object's being in His presence—and that is all. We see then that under Calvinism the result is a total annihilation of the person, because to say that "God chooses another person's choice" is the same type of irrationality that would say that "somebody else is me."

There is a disturbing implication in Calvinistic theology here. The consistency in accepting this paradigm is to see the 'my' as a mere extension of God's thought. The 'my' is seen as the Logos or Idea of God. And since in Calvinism every 'my' is the construct of God, there is no final thought identity of the 'my' apart from God. Every 'my' has been dissolved in God and has become an expression of His Godhead. The 'my' is God, and God is the 'my,' and so the entire Cosmos becomes the expression of a God who moves molecules about to receive His constructs.

The implications of the Edwardian view for the Creation now become plain. Since Calvinism confuses God with the 'my,' distinctions between the Creator and sentient creation become lost. And if all ideas and will in the creation are only those of the Creator, then we are all part and parcel of God, having no *thought* and *will* identity apart from Him. Thus in some sense we are all participants with God in His all-sovereign activities. We were with Him in the Creation, in the Fall, in the sacrifice of Christ—indeed, in any and all history, and in eternity past. All thought experience and mental and spiritual being is comprehended in Us (rather, 'Us'), for we 'persons' and God are One.[63]

Such a conclusion of indivisible oneness with God is always the result of those authors and thinkers who apply such a dialectical 'solution' to their Calvinistic assumptions. The result are 'definitions' of *desire* and *will*, and *God* and *man*, that are indistinguishable in their pairings. Is it any wonder, then, that it was from within *Calvinistically* influenced denominations[64] that there arose during the twentieth century certain influential neoorthodox theologians, such as Rudolph Bultmann, Paul Tillich, and Karl Barth, who amalgamated their beliefs with various secular philosophies until they believed that God could become His opposite and yet remain true to Himself? Such teachings by these thinkers proved that these were merely the consistent conclusions that follow from Calvin's dialectical theology. Thus Christianity, which is suppose to uphold that *A cannot equal non-A* [i.e., as in bitter cannot be sweet (Is. 5:20) and righteousness cannot be unrighteousness (2 Cor. 6:14)] as well as that Christ is mutually and exclusively the Savior of the world, instead is succumbing to a rigorously applied Calvinism until all meaningful distinctions are lost. For whenever Calvinism is applied, definitions are no longer definitions, and so anything may at the same time be its *otherness*.

Yet despite the position on total depravity to which the Edwardian position leads, Calvinists would certainly call the above conclusions caricatures of their views. In any Calvinistic treatise they would point to many statements where man is said to be fully responsible for his sin and therefore a free moral agent who acts apart from outside coercion. (Indeed, one wearies of online Calvinists making such claims on the internet about their opponents misrepresenting them.) Man is far from being a laundry basket, they would say, and always maintains his particularity. But if one would tell them that their view of human freedom thus eliminates the absolute sovereignty of God, the same Calvinists would point out many other statements in the same Calvinist treatises where the absolute sovereignty of God is asserted with equal conviction. So the two principles are held in contradiction. This is why it is difficult to convince Calvinists of their God/'my' amalgamation; i.e., because in fact they have unwittingly accepted an *illusion* of separateness and therefore an illusion of meaning (because, we note, the proper meaning of thing**s** demands *separateness* of definition). Because Calvinists believe that God constitutes all thought experience, yet maintains a respective distance from Man's thought and will, it is always Catch-22 for the non-Calvinist in debate.

Footnotes:

[54] Apparently, Sproul does not see the possibility of a connection between *can* and *may* under *any* biblical circumstances. Thus Sproul: "Who has not been corrected by a schoolteacher for confusing the words *can* and *may*?" (Sproul, p. 67). Regarding this point of *can* versus *may*, it is again interesting to note that Christ Himself said that "The Son *can* (Gr. *dunamai* i.e., *powers to*) do nothing of himself, but what he seeth the Father do" (Jn. 5:19). But as previously noted, the experience and statements of the Son during His hour of agony in Gethsemane show that the Son indeed *did* have a will capable of doing what was opposed to what the Father wanted, even to a point of calling down rescue by legions of angels. Thus Christ's point in John 5:19 is that the Son, *at the time he spoke this*, powered not to act on His own because of His absolute *unwillingness* to do so, and because His desire was the same as His Father's *at that time*, and thus not because of any general disablement of the will relating to possibility.

[55] Note: interestingly enough, B.F. Westcott takes the cognate *ekelko* in James 1:13 to mean *to lure out* (*by bait*), in a hunting sense; hence, *to entice*.

[56] Terry Gross put it more diplomatically than I am putting it here.

[57] The word for 'draw' in John 12:32, which is also used in James 2:6: ("Do not rich men oppress you, and draw [pull] you before the judgment seats?") does not necessarily imply the same force as that found in Luke 12:58, where the rightness of the adversary (as parabolically pointing to Christ) is assumed to be upright and *earnest*, whereas the moral authority of a rich man (if 'authority' it be called) lies chiefly in his riches, a fact not lost upon the rich man himself. Therefore, while a rich man would hope his (probably often dubious) charges in court would be accepted with no small force, it would (we hope at least) hardly carry the conviction than that of those poorer than he whose arguments were often given with the knowledge that they had been truly wronged. But another solution seems more probable than this one IF James was using hyperbole to make a point about pulling in the sense of dragging, even as the tongue, for example, is said to be "a world of iniquity." In all likelihood rich men did not literally drag, or have others drag, their adversaries by the heels into court. But the real point here is that men were dragged against their will, not in a sense in which their will ever changed. The biblical context is key when interpreting the force of *helko*, even as with the word 'give,' which we explained in an earlier footnote. As a side note, it should be observed that the judgment seats of some cities were likely at an elevated place relative to the city's popular dwellings (in order to symbolically convey the loftier, formal decisions for which civic courts were responsible), and

so the James 2:6 passage may still be considered supportive of the verticality at least generally evidenced in the New Testament's use of the Greek word *helko*.

[58] Thus while we are told elsewhere that we are placed in the heavenlies, this action of the Father must be congruent with all other statements about the process of a man coming to be reconciled with God, *whereupon* that man is placed in Christ.

[59] [See footnote 63 (which begins on p. 228), detailing yet again how the word 'man' in the term 'the will of man' ceases to have meaning in Calvinist theology.] As C.S. Lewis has stated the matter in a similar context, God can do all things, but they must be *things*; they cannot be *non*-things.

[60] The objection that might be proposed by Calvinists here, that God irresistibly controls even the people's decisions and actions to obtain the manna, is rank eisegesis, i.e., the arbitrary reading of one's theology into the text. Such an 'answer' attempts to lengthen, so to speak, the strings on the marionette to a point where it becomes a total mystery to man how the Puppeteer could exert absolute manipulation of him. But the various Old Testament examples of the Israelites' faith (or at other times unbelief) point to man's own role of response.

[61] Says Sproul (pp. 61-62): "Edwards and all who embrace the Reformed view of predestination agree that if God does not plant that desire [for God] in the human heart no one, left to themselves, will ever freely choose Christ." But the question for Sproul is how such a "desire" would be the man's and not God's? That is, how is such an implanted desire a result of a man who "freely chooses Christ?" The 'his' in "his desire" is no longer present for the one receiving the implant (against his will), for the 'his' would be exterminated by the implant. Needless to say, the man's 'his' is kept around for the Calvinist's convenience in order to make it appear that the Calvinist still accepts *man* as a distinctive.

Thus Sproul believes that God enables a man in the state of total inability, and he quotes Augustine's attempted distinction between "free will" and "liberty." Says Sproul: "Augustine got at the problem by saying that fallen man has a *free will* but lacks *liberty*." Thus, Sproul claims that fallen man has a choice, but evidently (we note) only of *one* thing (which readers of common sense will recognize is not really a choice). Non-Reformers rightly regard such definitions as irrational. (Indeed, I wonder how 'free' any American would feel if his U.S. representative knocked on his door to tell him that although he still had freedom, the President and Congress decided he would no longer have liberty. Would he really feel that such a statement was *congruent*? But dress up the door knocker in theological dress and the statement becomes 'profound'! Thus, this is mere rocking horse methodology on the part of Augustine—using the synonyms *freedom* and *liberty* but defining them as antonyms in order to maintain an irrationality of definition. Unfortunately, Sproul falls prey to accepting Augustine's contradiction despite his professed distaste for *parallel lines that meet in eternity* type explanations. Because Augustine doesn't use the exact same word, Sproul is deceived. Had Augustine said, 'man has freedom but he has no freedom,' presumably Sproul would have seen the nonsense of it all. But Augustine's use of the *difference of vocal sounds* of these synonyms ("freedom" and "liberty") *while defining them as antonyms*, passes unchecked.

Sproul himself does something similar, taking a pair of words (*receive*, and *regenerate*) and defining them as near antonyms to support his soteriology. I say "near" because, while both terms properly refer to the instant one is born again, *receiving* is the instant *man* takes Christ, whereas 'regeneration,' though occurring the same instant, is one in which *God* (according to His foreknowledge which makes it possible for him to anticipate the instant of man's choice) declares the one believing to be a child of God. Thus biblically speaking, receiving and regeneration happen simultaneously. If this were not the case, then one could believe *prior*, or *subsequent*, to becoming a child of God, which is illogical, since in the former case this would mean that one could believe without being a child of God, or, in the latter case, that one could be declared a child of God without believing. Sproul, however, takes the vocal sound "*regenerated*," and the vocal sound "*receiving Christ*," and attaches unbiblical meanings to them by defining them as happening upon different instances. For observe that he states that *regeneration* is God's implant in a man for a new desire for God, which allegedly happens *prior* to that man's belief, whereupon the man then "rushes" to *receive* Christ. Sproul believes that such a man **must** rush to Christ, and thus, as man cannot be properly understood by us to have a choice in the matter, we must here, if we are to remain consistent in argument, state that the man as defined by Sproul is merely moved materially **as God's construct, and nothing more**. Sproul has simply taken the word "regeneration" and given it his own meaning apart from sound biblical theology, i.e., as it ought to be biblically, historically, lexically, and contextually defined. But again, a proper understanding of biblical regeneration is that a man is saved *upon* belief, i.e. upon the *instant* of belief, for John 1:12 states that (Int.) "But as many as received Him, He gave to them authority to become children of God, to those believing into the name of Him." Nothing of divine empowerment that "leads to" (as Sproul words it) the childship of the believer is suggested in the Bible prior to man's faith. Yet, further, in one place Sproul actually states (p. 117) that "Rebirth *produces* new life" (emphasis added), when it should be understood that rebirth, as defined in John 3, *is* the beginning of life, not something that *leads to* life. Sproul is forced to these kind of irrational definitions and expressions not from any proper Scriptural exegesis, but because his Reformed interpretation of other scriptural passages demands it. In this way he gives the <u>appearance</u> that the salvation of man is *only* of God's will, yet of man's will, too.

[62] Again, the Greek word 'seek' that Paul uses when quoting Psalm 14 is a word suggesting a customary and diligent form of seeking, as contrasted to the *possibility* of seeking. Note that Calvinists always regard the *deadness* of a man who is dead in sin to be more radical that the *aliveness* of a man who is alive in Christ; for the one alive in Christ may nevertheless still sin, while the one dead in sin is assumed by Calvinists not to be capable of any goodness whatsoever. [See Ephesians 2, in which Calvinists apply more force to the deadness of being dead in sin, than to the aliveless of being alive in Christ. I use the term 'more force' with the reader's understanding, since, technically speaking, the Calvinist's view of deadness is irrational, having (unwittingly) defined man as annihilated in will and therefore unable to believe and be alive in Christ.]

[63] I once had an exit meeting with a pastor from one of the churches I attended in which we discussed the doctrine of Irresistible Grace. (For those readers wishing to skip the details of this conversation and a related discussion about Foreknowledge and Irresistibility, please forward past this footnote.) The problem, of course, with the doctrine of Irresistibility is that God and man are treated as One and not maintained as distinctive beings. This oneness is achieved (according to the Calvinist) through God's will being performed through the spiritually dead or blind one. Thus during the meeting, this pastor emphasized the deadness and blindness of the sinner and claimed that God had to remove the blindfold for a sinner to see. On the other hand I contended that I did not think this description supported John 1:12, i.e., that those born of God *received*, that is, *took*, Him. I referred the pastor to Matthew 26:26, in which the same Greek word rendered *received* in John 1:12 is rendered *take* ("Take eat, for this is my body"). Nevertheless, the pastor seemed to resurface the blindfold analogy during the conversation. At one point I asked him why God showed such exasperation in the Old Testament prophetic books if the people He addressed really had no ability to respond? (Why all the exasperation if only God could remove the blindfold?)

Anyhow, it didn't occur to me until over a week later that the blindfold analogy the pastor had chosen was really an attempt to use a dialectical object to support his argument of Irresistibility. It was designed to make it appear that *God chose* that man would see, but in a way where *man chose* that he would see. Thus the causal agent behind the decision *to see* was blurred beyond distinction. And yet the words *God* and *man* seemed to remain, at a psychological level, distinct terms in our conversation because of the normal way in which everyone, including this pastor and I, thinks of these words. But in fact the only real distinction one could infer from this pastor's blindfold analogy was an aural difference in the vocal sound '*God*' and the vocal sound '*man*.' And so during our conversation about the blindfolded man, the pastor was (unwittingly) taking the concept 'man' and apologetically defining it to be synonymous with the concept 'God,' until neither term had any real meaning (though of course these words *appeared* to have meaning).

In other words, a man who is as dead as Sproul defines him to be (i.e., *drowned*), cannot *see* simply because God takes the blindfold off. After all, he's dead, isn't he? Sproul's description of God going down to the bottom of the lake and bringing the man up and breathing life into him is suggestive here. It means that God must—if we are to be consistent with an analogy of a blindfold, i.e., be faithful in expressing the kind of *deadness* that Sproul describes (and which is obviously implied if man needs *irresistible* grace)—*not merely remove the blindfold, but also open the eyes of the sinner, give him sight, and give him the will to look.* So where, I ask, is a man's predicating faith in any of that? The pastor was assuming that man has the will to look, yet because of blindness could not look at anything except the inside of the blindfold. But that is not the kind of radical deadness which this pastor's Calvinistic theology really demands of him, i.e., as exampled by Sproul's *drowned* man. (Indeed, since when does removing a blindfold from a drowned man do something for the drowned man's *sight?*) For as we have previously shown, it is impossible to point to a time in Sproul's analogy of the drowned man when the *man* exercises faith. It is all God's doing. For notice that the man (according to Sproul) is dead until *God* gives him 'life.' [Remember that the words 'life,' 'seeing,' and 'faith' are each defined dialectically by the Calvinist, since these things must be considered '*man's*,' yet also the result of '*God's*' *unilateral* activity. Yet note in this regard that Christ said, "one must see the Son *and* believe." (Jn. 6:40)] It is not simply a matter of God taking off the blindfold when we are stubborn about it. We must also believe (have faith). Thus a man taking Christ (placing his faith in Christ) is nowhere possible in such analogies as that offered by Sproul or by my former pastor. In other words, if a blindfold (or drowned man) analogy is offered that cannot say *when* a man could exercise his faith, then I contend it has not provided that a man *could* exercise his faith. Indeed, if the man is really as dead as the Calvinist claims, then man is a will*less* thing that cannot take Christ by faith (I use the word 'thing,' I dare not use the word *man*, since *man* implies *decisional ability* and therefore special dignity and *sentient being*, all of which the Calvinist denies by implication).

Sproul, facing this dilemma of trying to account for a man's belief, actually gives an additional analogy elsewhere in his book, in which the man "rushes to Christ" after God has allegedly given the man the desire to receive Christ (a desire which Sproul, though he does not admit to doing it, equates with *the will* [that is, in its latter stage (as though it *could* have a latter stage)]. But where, we ask, is man "rushing to Christ" in Sproul's *drowned man* analogy? It is nowhere to be seen, because obviously the analogies contradict each other. Such chaos was inevitable in any analogy Sproul could have invoked. This is because Sproul is on the dialectical rocking horse of Calvinistic theology trying to go in two directions, first forward, then backward. And since he will not recognize a man's absolute sovereignty over his own decision to accept or reject Christ, Sproul can only imply the kind of combined, absurd analogy of a drowned man rushing to Christ! (This betimes emphasis on "deadness" is why Dave Hunt, for example, says that the Calvinist confuses spiritual death with physical death whenever he draws this inappropriate parallel; for if a dead man cannot respond to God, neither can a dead man sin nor be held accountable for sin.) (Incidentally, I highly recommend Dave Hunt's 90-minute youtube presentation on Calvinism. Hunt has a real grasp of Calvinism, and he has the kind of clarity in presentation only possible for someone with the teaching gift.)

Now, the fact of man's absolute sovereignty over his own decision to follow or not follow God's plan for himself is dramatically seen in a passage often overlooked in the Calvinist debate—the story of God's vineyard in Isaiah 5. In fact, this is why I brought this passage up to my pastor. Isaiah tells us that God planted a vineyard on a fertile hill, cultivated it, removed the stones, planted the choicest of vines, made a tower, and prepared a wine vat.

> "Then He expected it to produce good grapes, but it produced only worthless ones. And now, O inhabitants of Jerusalem and men of Judah, judge between Me and My vineyard. What more was there to do for My vineyard that I have not done in it? Why, when I expected it to produce good grapes did it produce worthless ones?"

As a result God says He will bring judgment upon His vineyard—the house of Israel (v. 7) and the men of Judah, His delightful plant (v. 7). Why, then, in all this description cannot the Calvinist see that God is *expecting* man to respond? That is, why is God's rhetorical question not taken at face value, so that it is conceded that God did all that was necessary to *expect* a proper response of good grapes? To continue to speak of Irresistibility in the face of the Vineyard story in Isaiah 5 (as this pastor did in the meeting I just alluded to) surprised me. But, in fact, that is what happened during my exit meeting. For once I raised the subject of this parable, this pastor reinterpreted it, claiming that God *would* do more, that is, provide His Spirit, and further suggested that a parallel be understood between Isaiah 5 and the New Testament parable of the Sower. In retrospect I now see even more clearly that the point of the Vineyard parable is not whether God *would* do more (i.e., offer His Spirit), but whether He *should* have done more before expecting a positive response. The text's answer in Isaiah is an emphatic *No*. God Himself states that He *expected* (i.e., had the just expectation of) the vine to bring forth good grapes. It was thus *reasonable* that God should get the response His investment deserved (even though it would be hundreds of years before the Spirit of God was given to those who believed in Christ). Yet obviously, such a response could only be the case if man's will were free. Such human freedom brings to mind a classic passage regarding man's will, i.e., Romans 1, which shows that God's power and nature was so evident in creation that God *expected* (that is, had a right to expect) Gentiles to respond differently than they did. Why? Because their will was free.

As to this pastor's statement that a parallel existed between the Vineyard story and the New Testament Parable of the Sower, I also see now upon further reflection that the fertile, cultivated field in Isaiah 5 represents **God's** *offered provision*, whereas the soils in the New Testament Parable of the Sower represent a *variety of* **human** *predispositions towards God's provision*. A tightening of definition also shows that Isaiah's message is addressed to a nation comprised of both believers and unbelievers, whereas the New Testament parable of the Sower is about all men in need of salvation (Lk. 8:12). Because my pastor did not make this distinction about what the ground represented in each story, he could not accept the plain meaning of God's rhetorical question in Isaiah 5. In fact, his conclusion was the only conclusion possible as a Calvinist, i.e., that both soils represented the activity and will of God, and that man was non-predicative. Thus he merely mish-mashed the representative elements of the parables into the kind of definitions which his Reformed view required, so that divine irresistibility might be thought represented in these parables, so that God could be thought to choose man's choices.

Now, moving away from my discussion with my former pastor for a moment, let us consider that another and very serious problem regarding the doctrine of Irresistibility is that it relies on a false lexical appeal regarding *foreknowledge*. Thomas Edgar clearly exposes the misguided attempt by Calvinists to redefine *foreknowledge* so that it fits the template of their theology (the reader is greatly urged to Google *Thomas Edgar foreknowledge* to read Edgar's article). For observe that God would need to have <u>*non-determinative foreknowledge*</u> if the terms *God* and *man* should remain properly distinct from each other and not be treated as synonymous in meaning. God would need such foreknowledge for Him to declare that a person was born of God *upon the instant* of a man's faith, so that God could impart to him the Spirit *upon* the man's belief. That is, God would need *foreknowledge* as we have defined it in this book, not as the Calvinist defines it, who applies a different meaning to the word than lexically justifiable, owing to his refusal to allow New Testament lexical definitions to also be informed by 1) *extra-biblical, contemporary sources* and 2) *biblical passages where God is not the grammatical subject*.

A rather disturbing example of how far a Calvinist can go in trying to force-fit the lexical evidence into a preconceived Calvinistic template is found in the youtube presentation of Romans 9 by well-known Reformed apologist, James White. During White's prologue in part-1 (of a 5-part download presentation) in which White sets up the main body of his speech with some comments on Romans 8:28ff, he argues (to the effect) that *foreknowledge,* **in its (active) verb form, not its noun form, when God is the subject, in the New Testament, has to mean 'intimate knowledge,'** since the object is <u>personal</u> in nature and not of mere actions, and thus *to foreknow* (according to White) cannot be understood as merely meaning *to know in advance* (as Arminians argue). We give White's statement below, conceding that, though it is impossible to fully render into text the totality of any speaker's voice inflections so that primary, secondary, tertiary, etc., emphases are all properly conveyed, we have tried to italicize what words White himself seems to give particular vocal emphasis to:

> "Let me just stop long enough to *challenge* in the minds of anyone who thinks that this term, *'foreknew,'* as a *verb*, is the same thing as the *noun*—(to simply have foreknowledge)—that you are *wrong*, and that you need to *look* at the text of Scripture and realize this is an *active verb*—this is something God is doing. And every time *God* is the subject, and *this* is the verb–*in* the N.T.–the object is *personal*, it's never *actions*. To simply say, 'God knew who was going to believe,' *there is no example of that statement in the N.T.—it's not there.*"
> [http://www.youtube.com/watch?v=kiTxBftvqnM]

Now, though I have personally found White's book on the KJV controversy (a separate matter) very helpful (incidentally, I recommend the book), and recognize White as a serious thinker, what is the listener to make of White's argument regarding foreknowledge? That is, why the lexical split in fundamental meaning between a verb and its own noun? Are we really to infer from White's comments that, for example, when Peter tells us that God's election of us is according to His *foreknowledge* (noun), that this noun's lexical meaning (i.e., '*knowledge in advance*') is a fundamentally different one than the related verb form which Paul refers to in Romans 8:29, when he states that [God] *foreknew* (verb) (i.e., according to White's general view, *intimately knew*) whom he would predestine? We grant the obvious superficial distinction between a verb and its companion noun, but what of it? For example, a man *throws* (verb) a baseball, and thus has made a *throw* (noun) of a baseball, but where is there any fundamentally different sense between these two words beyond the superficially grammatical one?

One argument that *at first glance might seem* to truly advance White's position is if the verb *foreknew* and the noun *foreknowledge* in Greek have lexical histories that show fundamentally different meanings (besides their obvious grammatical difference). For example, hypothetically, one might by analogy (in defense of White) argue that the words 'social' and 'socialist' are *both* adjectives which can either mean the same thing or have different meanings depending on *who* is in view. Thus, in the two phrases, 1) 'the leader's social policy,' and 2) 'the leader's socialist policy,' only the former phrase using the word 'social' could refer to, say, Ronald Reagan as a fiscal Conservative, but both the former and the latter phrases could refer to a communist like Joseph Stalin (since Stalin's social policy was also socialist). Thus one could never say 'Ronald Reagan's *socialist* policy,' but one *could* say 'Joseph Stalin's *social* policy.' In type, this is really White's argument about why his definition should be accepted regarding *foreknew*. That is, White believes that God intends this kind of special-pleading definition (my term, not White's) which he and other Calvinists accord God, because they believe that God Himself defines *foreknew* that way in the New Testament when God is the subject. Our objection to White's assumption, then, is what Thomas Edgar points out in his argument about language, i.e., Why use the word 'foreknowledge' when 'electing love' would have sufficed (or, by extension, the argument as would follow from the verb form *foreknew*) so that a non-ambiguous phrase could have been used? That is, why would God deliberately make the language difficult to understand? Why obscure meaning? This point by Edgar thus throws the whole matter back upon the issue of lexical use, though unfortunately for White, the desired lexical history he wishes to see for the word 'foreknew' is just not there, i.e., not there in the extra-biblical sources (or in the New Testament when God is not the subject) which act as the control groups against theologians seeking to make a special pleading for a particular word's lexical use. In other words, the whole kind of argument based on making synonymous the terms "social" and "socialist" is a false one. For the only reason "social" might seem to mean "socialist" in the case of Stalin is if the writer has, in the course of his essay, *connotatively* implied these terms to be synonymous once he describes the *social* policy of Stalin to be *socialist*. But in fact these terms are **not** synonymous, denotatively speaking (i.e., according to standard lexical and dictionary use, which examines the width and breadth of the word's historical-grammatical use). In other words, the writer telling about Stalin is attempting to change the definition of "social" with the result that the reader infers *also* a connotative, not strictly denotative, meaning. The writer has merely read his own definition into the word "social" apart from standard lexical use. Consequently, and in the same essential manner, White has to either invent a lexical history for *proginwskw* to support his argument or follow the lead of someone else (like that of the Reformed commentator, Baugh, i.e., Edgar's foil) whose lexical revisionism is already in play. This is because the biblical writers have not demonstrated any such connotative definition for "foreknew" even in the normal evolution which language sometimes demonstrates with certain words. For we note that the word "foreknew" was never part of such an evolutionary change, except insofar that an Augustinian minor subculture has taken a word like "foreknew" and redefined it for so long a time that a reader might imagine the mistaken definition to be the normal one.

Looking at this question of connotative versus denotative from another angle, consider, say, the word "act" in the phrases "the act of the sinner" and "the act of the righteous." A Calvinist might argue that in such phrases the word "act" changes meaning based on the noun of the prepositional phrase, so that the word "act" in the phrase "the act of the sinner," obviously means something bad, whereas in the phrase "the act of the righteous," the word "act" means something good. So again the question ought to asked: Do words change meaning based on the noun? The answer is *No*, according to the word's denotative definition, though of course allowances can be for figures of speech intended by the author. For though a Calvinist might be convinced that the word "act" in the phrase "the act of the sinner" implies something bad, observe that the phrase "the act of the sinner," when conveyed by a Calvinist while on the front rock of the dialectical rocking horse, in fact means nothing whatsoever. But regarding cases of exception involving figures of speech, note, for example, the term "tender mercies" in the Proverbs 12:10 phrase, "the tender mercies of the wicked are cruel." Here the term "tender mercies" really means the word "cruel" on a scale of things going from cruel to crueler to cruelest, and thus acts as a metonomy [a kind (form) of figure of speech]. Now there are many kinds of figures of speech, as Bullinger has pointed out. [Sidebar note (as observed previously): Furthermore, some words in Koine Greek have a closer *quid pro quo* relationship to informal English words than formal, such that its normal everyday use had a wider latitude of meaning than what might be inferred by an English reader today. The point here is that the term "tender mercies" doesn't cease to have its denotative definition in the normal course of how that term is understood in everyday social use, though here in Proverbs 12:10 we recognize that the writer is using the term to serve as an idiom of speech, so that it means "cruel." The writer does this to state that really the wicked do not exhibit tender mercies at all. Even so, idioms of speech occur in the Bible, but one of the problems in Calvinism is that idioms of speech or a word's latitude of meaning is not recognized when man's will is determinative, such as when John 6:44 tells us that God *pulls* (Gr. *helko*) man toward the Son. Here the word "pulls" refers to God's positive thought-distraction in which He betimes interrupts man's own thought process to present His own thought, such as, "You need to come to My Son for the forgiveness of sins." Such "pulling" is within the latitude of meaning for *helko*, in the same sense as if I were to say, "My wife hates baseball, but I pulled her toward the ballpark." Of course, Calvinists deny misinterpreting such latitude, and turn to the only kind of general framework which supports their dialectical, frontward-rock premise that man is always non-self determinative— that of lexical special pleading. (This method runs hand in hand with another of their related methods—finding where a verb is used denotatively upon a passive object and inappropriately claiming the same force of meaning in a passage where man's will is the object.) Thus in the apologetics that stand behind their policy toward speech idioms, "choice" really doesn't mean choice, and, further, God's one and only will is really two wills, which, when 'perceived' by our 'limited understanding' as two wills, is (we observe) defined *de facto* as mutually opposite, yet claimed by the Calvinist to be "different," "not contradictory," and so forth and so on—the whole gist of Calvinistic argument thus appealing to "mystery" because of its irrational nature.

But again, and to return our discussion back to the word "foreknew," and moving somewhat past the above discussion of speech idioms, there is no reason not to accept the biblical use of "foreknew" along the lines which the New Testament-era lexical control groups support, both prior to and following the New Testament writings. So, the Calvinist can only make his case by insisting on special pleading, i.e., eisegesis. Can we *prove* White and Baugh wrong? Yes, as long as we accept the normal rules of language (i.e., the commonly understood definition of what words meant to people living during the New Testament era) as rationally upheld by the Spirit (just like the Spirit affirms the mathematical language of $2 + 2 = 4$), i.e., by Him who seeks to affirm in the hearer/reader's mind the correct definitions of words. As Jesus said, 'He who has ears, let him hear.' For, as we have already noted, consistency by itself is no real test of the truth, and words can be used just as consistently by the one opposing truth as the one telling truth.

Expect, then, more spin from Calvinists if they become aware of the additional arguments we raise against their position. Indeed, such spin is why each generation of true apologists has to combat the ongoing trek of Calvinistic spin on somewhat newer turf, since each Calvinistic generation faces new challenges from truthful apologists and responds by taking another step backward into a deeper irrationalism of increasingly bizarre 'explanations.' And so the Calvinistic discourse devolves into ever stranger forms. Doubtless this explains one youtube presentation which I first assumed was a sarcastic joke by an Arminian, until I realized it was, in fact, a presentation by an earnest Calvinist who purported to show **in a 2-D cartoon** the justification of God's reprobation of the damned, i.e., by insisting that a cartoonist, in determining the action of the cartoon character he was drawing, was an appropriate parallel to God in His determining of a man's will! Can such Calvinistic 'proofs' really become more pathetic that this? And yet some Calvinists claim we misrepresent them when we point out that their theology makes man a puppet! Would it sooner soothe their nerves if we said that their theology makes God a cartoonist? Dare I say it—when one considers that John Calvin killed some 400 persons who disagreed with him, and considers further that Calvinists in mid-17th century England imprisoned some non-Calvinist, non-Catholic Christian 'heretics' who subsequently died and (at least in some cases) left behind widows and orphans, and considers yet further that in the 21st century the echoes of such hate can now be found in the kind of vitriolic, unsparing, blue-blood responses of younger online Calvinists who are being groomed for the fight against non-Reformed Protestants—one can imagine just how guilty such a Calvinist as this cartoonist might likely feel if he found himself with the political power to persecute those who disagreed with him, especially since he equates the damned and their destiny as hardly more substantial than sheet acetate and paint. I don't say every Calvinist is the same [they certainly are not (and perhaps even this cartoonist is not)], but it goes a long way toward explaining the anonymous, online, Calvinist brouhaha aimed at stifling books like Dave Hunt's *What is This Love?*, in which Calvinist groupies rack up one-star, negative 'reviews' against such books as Hunt's, which have gotten above the radar and dared to question the wisdom of John Calvin's irrationalism which makes God and man the same. These latest disciples of Calvin, twice the children of fervor as their immediate forbears, are acting out the kind of behavior which presumably stems from the kind of idealism generally found only among the young. Upon these, perhaps, one may have pity. But upon the rest....?

At any rate (and to return to the subject of *foreknew*), White, a keen public debater, ought to know (and presumably does know) that in a debate one answers one's opponent's strongest argument first, before proceeding to build one's own position. Presumably, this is why White anticipates an objection about *foreknew* based on (it would appear) Thomas Edgar (or someone else of similar mind), and this may account for why White begins his statement (quoted above) within the first minute of his 45+ minute presentation. Nevertheless, White's 'explanation' is non-lexical and thus unproven; and yet we see in his method a very aggressive act that goes beyond the mere stratagem of an Augustine and a Sproul who used the synonyms 'freedom' and 'liberty' to doublethink their way out of having to explain the nature of personal choice and the problem of evil. Instead White employs a more audacious irrationalism, asking us to assume that the noun which derives from its own verb (or, we note, the verb which derives from its own noun—take your pick) has a fundamentally different meaning from its grammatical fellow. Of course, we don't deny White's claim, abstractly considered, that God knows the elect intimately, but as Thomas Edgar has shown, such a fact has nothing to do with the lexical meaning of *foreknew/foreknowledge* as observed across the whole spectrum of that term's lexical use. White's failure to show real lexical evidence, a failure stated with the kind of confidence and impressive rhetoric that gives his 'explanation' the likelihood of it persuading uncritical minds, typifies the Calvinist's error of ignoring broad lexical controls that should properly inform the definition of Greek (and Hebrew) words. Thus by restricting his meaning of the verb foreknew to "*God, in the New Testament,*" he eliminates any extra-biblical sources, the Septuagint, and even New Testament sources where God is not the grammatical subject. In short (and again), White's technique is special pleading. It is no more than a kind of textual 'Rorschach test' in which the individual imposes his own meaning upon a word symbol. In degree of irrationalism, White's approach is somewhere between Augustine/Sproul's 'freedom' and 'liberty,' which uses two synonyms, and President Clinton's 'explanatory' statement ("It depends on what **is 'is'**"), in which the former President doublethought the same verb in immediate succession. Again, White, by restricting the lexical relevance of *foreknew* to (1) the New Testament occurrences; (2) when *God* is the grammatical subject; and (3) when the verb takes a personal object, is able to read his Calvinistic definition into the verb 'foreknew,' so that it means something like *intimately loved* or *intimately loved and therefore chosen*. As Edgar wryly notes in a similar context about the use by Calvinists of such lexically unauthorized meanings: 'This selective approach is seldom used where the customary meaning agrees with the interpreter's point of view.' Thus we see that such Calvinistic special pleading is really only a theological form of literary deconstruction. And, as the apostle Paul stated with unmincing words, all such unsound doctrine finds its inspiration from, and ultimate origin in, demons (fallen angels). I do not say this lightly, for White has, in fact, suffered injustices from the professing Evangelical community in certain matters (i.e., the KJV controversy), and so one can understand a considerable exasperation on his part; but the ultimate source of origin regarding the bogus matter (of falsely defining foreknew) under review here, i.e., from which White draws inspiration apart from sound lexical evidence, must be labeled for what it is. As to the finer point of White's assumption, i.e., that the verb "foreknew" has a different meaning depending on when God is the subject in the New Testament and the object is personal, not actions, Thomas Edgar explains why, lexically and logically, this cannot be the case:

> "In [Acts] 26:2-4, the Apostle Paul testifies before Agrippa and reminds him that "all the Jews" know Paul's life from a youth, from the beginning among his nation and in Jerusalem (26:4). He continues, "Since they know me from before (proginwskontes), from the beginning (if they want to testify), that I lived according to the strictest sect of our religion, a Pharisee" (translations are the author's unless otherwise indicated). We should note several aspects: (1) proginwskw refers only to knowledge. There is no implication in the Jews' words of a choice or predetermined plan. Neither is there an implication of affection or intimate and loving relationship. The Jews referred to were Paul's enemies. (2) Several phrases establish a chronology, i.e., "from a youth, from the beginning, before."[22] (3) The most significant facet for this study is the syntax. The object of the verb proginwskw, "to foreknow," is the personal pronoun, "me" (me). The passage is clear. Paul says, "foreknowing me . . . that I lived according to the strictest sect of our religion, a Pharisee." The "that" (*hoti*) clause expresses the content of the concept "foreknowing me." The apostle asserts "They knew me before; that is, they knew that I lived as a Pharisee."[23] Thus, to "foreknow" a person means to *know something about that person beforehand*. The personal object does not imply any personal, intimate ramifications, nor does it imply any deterministic concept such as election. In addition, Greek verbs commonly take an object with an idea such as "about" or "something about" implicit in the Greek verb itself, yet we must specifically supply it in English. For example, Hebrews 6:9 (NKJV) says, *But, beloved, we are confident of better things concerning you*. The verb, "we are confident" takes the object "better things" and could be woodenly translated, "We are confident better things." However, the Greek verb does not need the additional word "of," as in English, to translate "I am confident *of* better things." The verb itself means "to be confident *of*." This also occurs with the verb ginwskw ("know"). "The tree is known (ginwsketai) by its fruit" (Matthew 12:33) does not mean there is an intimate relationship or electing love of the person for the tree. The

tree is known *as to its character*; something about the tree is known by its fruit. Neither the context of Acts 26:5 nor the use of a personal object gives the slightest implication that proginwskw means anything other than "to know before," specifically to know something about Paul beforehand. Thus, the verb proginwskw with a personal object means "to know something about the person beforehand."

"*1 Peter 1:20*. Referring to Christ, 1 Peter 1:20 says, "Foreknown before the foundation of the world; however, manifest in these last times for your sakes." Baugh argues that the interpretation of "foreknown" is "a loving, committed relationship." He says, "Here neither Christ's faith nor any other action or attribute of his is the object of foreknowledge; rather, it was Christ himself foreknown."[24] Thus, he concludes that the verb cannot mean "prescience." This is an all too common argument based on the personal object.[25] This argument is erroneous. Acts 26:5 is particularly clear that, when this verb has a person as the object, it does not change meaning. It still means "to know before." It specifically means to know beforehand *something about* PROGINWSKW *that person*; e.g., an action or attribute. Both the syntax of proginwskw as revealed in Acts 26:5 and normal Greek usage (including other verbs) directly contradict the argument that a personal object requires or even implies a meaning other than prescience.

"Proginwskw is commonly interpreted with a deterministic meaning in this verse.[26] However, the passage and context are contrary to this nuance. The severe chronological contrast in this verse between a manifest *now* and foreknown *before* should not be overlooked.[27] Aligning the statements in parallel will help clarify this since the parallel is particularly evident in the Greek:

proegnwsme,nou me.n pro. katabolh/j ko,smou

fanerwqe,ntoj de. evpV evsca,tou tw/n cro,nwn diV

u'ma/j i.e., "foreknown before the foundation of the world

but manifested in the last times for your sakes."

[22] This verb and the corresponding noun have a strong temporal aspect (*NIDNTT*, 1.692).

[23] Hans Conzelmann, *Acts: Hermeneia* (Philadelphia: Fortress, 1987), 186, 208; *EDNT*, 3:153; Richard Longenecker, *Acts*: EBC (Grand Rapids: Zondervan, 1995), 348; Moo, *Romans*, 532; Johannes Munck, *Acts*, vol. 31: AB (New York: Doubleday), 239-41; Ben Witherington, III, *The Acts of the Apostles: A Social Rhetorical Commentary* (Grand

Rapids: Eerdmans, 1998), 740; and an older work, H. A. W. Meyer, *Acts* (New York: Funk and Wagnall's, 1883), 463. The fact that the foreknowing concerns Paul's life; that is, something about Paul, is commonly recognized by interpreters. Cf. Bruce W. Winter and Andrew D. Clark, *The Book of Acts in its First Century Setting*, vol. 1: *Ancient Literary Settings* (Grand Rapids: Eerdmans, 1993), 329-30.

[24] Baugh, "Foreknowledge," 196. However, Baugh gives no evidence to show why it means "loving, committed relationship." Many interpreters prior to Baugh have asserted this.

[25] This erroneous argument states that since Christ, a person, is the object, it does not refer to something about Christ but to Christ himself.

Thus Edgar states, in effect, that the result is that the *something about* is missed by Calvinists, and so *proginwskw* is taken to mean something *different*, not merely modified, from its actual meaning. Of course, for the Calvinist, too much is at stake to abandon the personal object argument which has given them their windfall of different meanings for *proginwskw*, e.g., 'to elect in love' or 'to determine in choice,' etc. In short, such arguments have allowed Calvinists one small step for their definition of 'foreknowledge,' one giant leap for their assumption of '*irresistibility*.' And from there it is the tiniest step to defending Augustine's theology of One Will, i.e., a Will that operates under the various activities of 'God,' 'man,' 'angels,' 'demons,' etc., to a point where individuation of will, and therefore all personal meaning (at least besides that found in the Trinity), is lost.

But to return to the conversation I had with my Calvinistic pastor, this kind of spurning of proper lexical evidence is why my pastor read his dialectical definition into how spiritual blindness is overcome, until he embraced One Will under varying names. This dialectical trump card could then trump every other card (biblical passage) that might have been used against his Calvinism. Thus, in so doing, this pastor employed the same *method* that cultists use, as when the Christian Scientists, for example, insist on taking a Bible verse like "In the grave there is no remembrance of thee" and *a*contextualizing it until all the Scriptures that support the physical resurrection of Christ fall aside like so many dominoes, making room in the process for bizarre explanations like "the shared hallucinatory vision by the disciples," etc. Please know I am not saying that this former pastor of mine does not believe in the physical Resurrection—he certainly does. I am merely saying his *apologetic explanation* stressing man's blindness is based on the same *method* as cultists. As a result, his apologetic annihilates man as a distinct person from God, since man is considered unable to take Christ by faith, yet is said to *have* faith. (Remember that the term 'faith' is defined dialectically by the Calvinist.) Once more we state it: a man's *decision* (the decisional instant itself) to take Christ must be unaided, or it cannot be said to be the *man's* faith (i.e., *his* taking Christ). (This is equally true for all decisional instances of man.) So beware! For whenever a pastor, teacher, apologist, etc., goes from talking about God's *influence* to talking about God's *irresistibility*, or makes these two terms synonymous, he has gone over to speaking about One will, not two.

There is one other thing to be observed here (relevant to the blindfold analogy) about sinners' "minds," which are said to be blinded by the Devil (see 1 Cor. 3-4). The word in Greek is *nousmata*, meaning *"thoughts,"* not *"minds,"* the latter being that which the Calvinist-influenced KJV translators chose to render. So the question is this: Is there a difference between saying that the god of this world has blinded the *mind* of the unbeliever, as opposed to his *thoughts*? In fact, yes, there is. For the Scripture does not say that the god of this world has blinded people *in order to* produce unbelief. Rather, it implies that unbelief is already present (even as, in the Parable of the Sower, the hardness of the receiving ground is already present when the good seed is cast upon the stony path, making it easier for the Devil to remove the seed). The KJV's use of the word *mind* is taken by many readers to mean *the will*, leaving these readers to conclude that the Devil has *disabled* man's ability so that he cannot will good. But the Greek word 'mind' (if we assume merely for the moment and sake of argument that the mind **is** synonymous with the will) is not in the autographa. Rather, the Bible teaches that a man's unbelief is a result stemming from the will of *himself*, not the will of the Devil. That the Devil (we anticipate the objection here) is stated in Scripture to capture such men (lit.) "into (at) his desire" speaks only to those opportunities he seizes to remove good seed from those whose heart-soil, by reason of its hardness, have made them *a priori* susceptible to the Devil's suggestive *thoughts* to reject the seed. In other words, the Devil captures them into his desire because they themselves desire to reject the seed. The Devil is simply urging them along the path of desire they are accustomed to tread. In short, thoughts do not a will make. Rather, thoughts not originating from a man (though presented to him) are an influence upon that man's will, whether they are bad thoughts from the Devil, or good thoughts from God, or thoughts of his own, which in any case are subject to the man's mind for sole deliberation and sole decision. A final curiosity in all this is why an unbeliever rejects the seed to begin with? For in such a case the man wills himself to unbelief rather than belief, and therefore acts against his own best interest. This, I think, is the least of what the Bible must mean by the phrase, "the mystery of iniquity."

In the end, though my exit meeting with the pastor stayed cordial I found it quite deflating. This pastor had helped me at various other times in important ways, but now the knowledge I wished to share about the dangers of Calvinism was essentially regarded as false. And since I had no room to apply my gift as Christ intended that I should use it for this particular local Body, I judged it was time to move on. The various evidences I cited (Jn. 1:12, Mt. 26:26, and Is. 5) became, for the most part, unsought opportunities for my pastor to obligatorily put a Calvinistic spin on them. At one point he posed the hypothetical question as to whether I would submit to the elders' authority (within the context of church discipline) if all the elders came to the conclusion that I was wrong (a process that appeared as though it would have stemmed from only one of the elders informing himself about my book and then reporting on it to the other elders). At length I asked in return if that is what Martin Luther should have done (i.e., does one yield one's conscience to the leadership of men, even when such an opinion of the leadership is opposed to God)? He replied that Luther's situation was different, for it involved church tradition, etc. I replied that I believed his own position was church-tradition based. Frankly, I am not a quick thinker on my feet and generally did not present my case nor answer as well as others would have done in such a meeting (indeed, that is one reason I wrote a book on the subject of sovereignty and wished it had been read through by this pastor). But I nevertheless warn those readers, who are more able than I at thinking on their feet when conversing with Calvinists, not to expect much from engaging church leaders who have believed in Calvinism most of their lives. I know very few persons besides myself who believed in the absolute sovereignty of God for years but then came to the opposite conclusion. Thus the situation at large does not encourage me, in fact it depresses me, and it remains a mystery to me why people, especially church leaders, seem generally content to be unmindful of the Scriptural and logical evidence against Calvinism. Indeed, it seems as though the hypothetical import of Calvinism being false were somehow less important to these Calvinist leaders than certain other priorities within their ministries, even when such import might mean that, e.g., some of the pastor's teaching would be blasphemous. At the least, it certainly makes one wonder if the Evangelical Church is properly jealous of its own God's reputation.

[64] Bultmann had a Lutheran background, Tillich had been an ordained minister in the German Lutheran Church, and Barth had been a Reformed pastor in Switzerland.

While we're on the subject of the neoorthodoxy of Barth, let us examine briefly its dialectical methodology. Of Barth's theology Wikipedia states:

> "The relationship between Barth, liberalism and fundamentalism goes far beyond the issue of inerrancy, however. From Barth's perspective, liberalism, as understood in the sense of the 19th century with Friedrich Schleiermacher and Hegel as its leading exponents and not necessarily expressed in any particular political ideology, is the divinization of human thinking. This, to him, inevitably leads one or more philosophical concepts to become the false God, thus attempting to block the true voice of the living God. This, in turn, leads to the captivity of theology by human ideology. In Barth's theology, he emphasizes again and again that human concepts of any kind, breadth or narrowness quite beside the point, can never be considered as identical to God's revelation. In this aspect, Scripture is also written human language, which bears witness to the self-revelation of God in Jesus Christ. Scripture cannot be considered as identical to God's self-revelation, which is properly only Jesus Christ. However, in his freedom and love, God truly reveals himself through human language and concepts, with a view toward their necessity in reaching fallen humanity. Thus Barth claims

that Christ is truly presented in Scripture and the preaching of the church, echoing a stand expressed in his native Swiss Reformed Church's Helvetic Confession of the 16th century."

Thus we note that Barth, by insisting on a 'transcendence' of "God" that makes all human statements short of being ***identical*** to the revelation of "God," including ***narrowness*** [of definition] quite beside the point, has subtly stated that language cannot describe God *whatsoever*. For (it follows) no matter how narrow, i.e., 'atomized,' so to speak, humans wish to understand God even in the simplest terms—Creator, Redeemer, Person, etc.—since these terms are humanly comprehendible they therefore do not describe "God." But we note that to speak of something that is not identical in meaning based solely (or sufficiently) on its being linguistically comprehendible to humans, is to imply that humans have 'almost meaning,' which, readers should observe, is not to speak of meaning at all. Again, one is reminded of novelist Lloyd Douglas' complaint of the critic who accused him of being "almost ungrammatical," to which Douglas stated his familiarity with what *grammatical* was, and *ungrammatical* too: but what was "almost ungrammatical"? Thus Douglas saw through the ludicrous demand for the compromise that some philosophers claim is rightfully *synthesis* ($A = non\text{-}A$). Naturally then, Barth, as a philosopher who *does* embrace the dialectic, plows the furrow of synthesis by dragging up muddiness on both sides of it. And so on the one hand language is compartmentalized so that 'human language' is defined so wholly other to a point where it cannot describe God. And so obviously the Bible, in the Barthian view, cannot be *identical* to the revelation of God (i.e., describe God), since humans wrote it. (Again, by "identical" we note that Barth means *deficient* en masse *in all of its parts*, though of course he would deny that this is his definition.) Such a Barthian approach, we note, is essentially like that error of Philo (the influential, Jewish first century philosopher who derived his thought from Plato), and therefore antichrist in principle, since it regards God and man as so fundamentally different *in kind* as to deny that they can practically inhabit shared realms—realms which make not only Spirit-breathed inspiration possible through a media of language comprehendible both to God and man, but the Incarnation of Christ (the Logos) as well. (Nothing would hardly seem sillier to Platonists than the idea of the Incarnation, which to them would mean the ridiculous idea of Reality became its shadowy form.)[1] So while Evangelicals would admit that "humans wrote" the Bible, they contextualize that event in non-Barthian terms as having taken place under the inspiration of the Spirit of God in unequivocal language. But moving on, *on the other hand* Barth also claims that God nevertheless reveals himself in human concepts! For note Wikipedia's continuing synopsis of Barth, which requires the immediate doublethink which follows, stating that "in *this* aspect" the human language of Scripture "*bears witness…of God*" (emphasis mine). But we must ask how human language (Scripture or no, as Wikipedia notes) can bear witness of God when that very human language is *wholly other in meaning* to the revelation of God! Indeed, doubtless Barth is forced to this other side of the dialectical rocking horse lest 1) the religious and philosophical discussion simply end then and there; and 2) it be thought that his own statement refutes itself, since the act of stating that human language cannot describe God is itself a way of partially framing the definition of God by way of negation, and therefore even in this manner is self-refuting. Therefore Barth's long-standing complaint that the liberal, biblical criticism of the 19th century had followed Hegel to a point of embracing the complete divinization of human thinking, i.e., until there was no appreciable distinction between the mind of man and the mind of God, while true, nevertheless rings hollow in Barth. For the dialecticism of Barth, like that of Hegel, cannot be inferred by readers as having any meaning. Therefore the *perceived* difference between Hegel and Barth is only that!—merely an *appearance* of difference. In either case the reader ought to properly infer only a meaning of Zero, of nothing, because the 'meaning' of word symbols evoked in the reader's mind arise only because of the words' psychological *associations*. And so the deconstruction has been a *fiat accompli* upon the very outset of Barth's premise. Thus in Barth's case "Jesus Christ" becomes the term that rehearses the kind of Medievalist theology that believed that God was so 'wholly other' that no human description of God could properly be made, again, a statement that refutes itself [that is, insofar as it can be said (with my readers' understanding) that dialectical systems contain *statements*]. So Barth fails to escape the endless Hegelian loop, since he implicitly makes the absurd claim that human concepts are wholly other in meaning to the revelation of God, a statement which demands that he would know who or what God is. The only real escape here for Barth, it seems to me, is to claim a possession of knowledge given irresistibly by the Divine which he did not initiate or willingly retain (hello, Calvinism), since it cannot be anything of human.[2] But of course if that is the case then individuation of Mind is lost, and so Barth is no different than Hegel (or Calvin, for that matter) in proclaiming the divinization of man. Thus in such a case all boundaries of individuation are erased, and so the idea of the infinite Logos becoming the Second Adam is denied.

I think we may safely assume that Barth's defenders, like Calvin's, will attempt to refute our criticism with its own version of beneficent-sounding, post-Modern deconstruction, i.e., in the same manner we noted of Pico Iyer, or of the critic who thought I misrepresented Gregory Koukl (see endnote lxxvii). Such criticisms begin by making the opposing side suppose that both sides in the discussion share the same meaning of terms, when in fact they do not. And yet in one sense perhaps this veneer of diplomacy is wearing thin. For this would seem to explain the recent observation by Wikipedia that some critics now discount the 20th century understanding of Hegel's philosophy as *thesis-antithesis-synthesis*. After all, just who did those 20th century critics think they were, invoking such absolutist terms like "thesis" and "antithesis," rather than judge Hegel on his own terms? Ought we not to apply dialectical criticism to dialectical philosophy! And so we observe that the cat continues to chase its tail, whether in dialectical philosophy or dialectical theology. As Van Til (in effect) properly observed about dialectical systems through a consideration of their founders (if failing to note the same about his own Calvinism): each thinker, whether Hegel or Kierkegaard, accused his predecessor of not making brute fact brute enough, or contingency contingent enough. It seems to me, then, that from Barth's defenders we are destined to hear how much we misunderstand Barth, while they seem to commit the same error that Barth accused others of, when he claimed that 19th century religious liberals had made human thought idolatrous. And if we live to see the younger generation of critics begin to take on Barth, we may expect to find them likewise feeling scandalized that neither did Barth make brute fact brute enough, or contingency contingent enough.

> [1] Observing Barth's theology even closer, we see the hallmark characteristic of all progressive neoorthodoxy—for whereas the apostle John used a cultural contact point, the Logos, to go from the abstract and *im*personal to the specific and personal, today's neoorthodox theologian does the opposite—using a cultural contact that is specific and personal, i.e., the Logos as defined since John, and driving it backward toward the abstract and *im*personal. In this way the neoorthodox theologian avoids the rancor of traditional arguments, like those between Calvinists and Arminians, and moves immediately to agendize whatever (esp. social) concern he feels is more important than a personal Savior, such as poverty or global warming or same sex marriage, etc. Hence God so loved the **world** becomes God loving *equally* the whole of the environmental **cosmos**, not primarily persons, and salvation becomes the vague goal of "bringing healing to that which is broken," a phrase ambiguous enough to serve the needs of socialized, ecumenical theology. This new vision (not so new, really) is the result of overthrowing the historical meaning of words, and mythologizing Scripture into enough abstraction to serve the social moment. Now, note that all such conclusions arose from neoorthodoxy's *selective* attack on language, claiming on the one hand that human concepts are *wholly other* than those which can describe God, yet also something God makes use of to explain Himself. I guess we're just suppose to take the neoorthodox theologian's *word* for it, i.e., that we have it backwards, and he front, right, and center. That is the difference—the Bible's historical-grammatical approach as compared to his special pleading.
>
> [2] [I think this is basically what N.T. Wright (Bishop of Durham) is unwittingly after, when he talks of the *possession* of Torah as symbolic of the kind of *possession* of justification which he alleges Paul is teaching, a view, we note, which denies that man predicates his own faith, a predication which Wright implicitly derides would mean a *getting into* justification. No surprise to us that Wright finds that this view of possession works *consistently* in other alleged difficult passages.]

Endnotes:

[xlii] Pink, Arthur W. *The Sovereignty of God*. [http://www.sovereign-grace.com/pink/chapter11.htm]; Chapter 11: "Difficulties and Objections."

[xliii] Sproul, p. 116.

[xliv] Sproul, pp. 103-104.

[xlv] Boettner, p. 61.

[xlvi] Boettner, p. 67.

CHAPTER 14

Pharaoh and the Hardened Heart

On the evening of March 9, 1898, a French Egyptologist, Victor Loret, entered a burial tomb that his workers had discovered a month earlier in Egypt's Valley of the Kings. Throughout that night Loret combed the corridors and chambers amidst many objects, some of which had been vandalized by ancient robbers. Yet some 2,000 objects had survived the thefts intact or partially intact, including a number of royal mummies. One of these mummies was found within its coffin inside its sarcophagus, and today some Egyptologists believe it to be Amenhotep II. If the archaeologists' identification is correct, this is quite possibly the Pharaoh of the biblical exodus.[65]

The reigning chronologies of Egyptian Pharaohs at this time is not known for certain, but some of the circumstances surrounding Amenhotep II and his father, Thutmose III, would seem to be in agreement with what we know of the two Exodus Pharaohs. First, the Pharaoh at the time of Moses' flight from Egypt (Ex. 1:22) appears to be the same Pharaoh whose death is mentioned in Exodus 2:23. The biblical narrative requires a reign that covered a greater span than Moses' 40-year sojourn in the Midian wilderness. The only monarch whose reign was long enough to cover so lengthy a period just prior to 1445 B.C. (the conservatively estimated date of the Israeli exodus) was Thutmose III, who reigned for 54 years. Second, Amenhotep II's son, Thutmose IV, states in an inscription that he was not the legitimate heir. Presumably, the firstborn son of Amenhotep II was the heir but had died before a natural succession could take place. This statement by Thutmose IV would agree with the Bible's statement in Exodus 12 that Pharaoh's firstborn son died in the 10th plague. Finally, history suggests that Amenhotep II was prevented from carrying out military campaigns for a handful of years near the beginning of his reign, and this would certainly have been the case if Amenhotep II had lost his army in the Red Sea.[xlvii]

If this speculation is correct, Amenhotep II was the Pharaoh before whom Moses stood and upon whom God brought the 10 plagues. In fact, God's judgment of Pharaoh and the Egyptians pre-figures the judgment which God will someday exercise over every people, tribe, and nation when earth's present history is over. In Pharaoh's case divine judgment in this life came in a series of stages. It is important to understand that if a *series* of judgments comes upon a man (or nation) during this life on earth, God's aim, at least in the initial stages, is to turn him from his wicked way, not to destroy him (or them). This is true *even while* God takes no pleasure in the way of the wicked. "I have no pleasure in the death of the wicked, saith the

Lord God, but that the wicked turn from his way and live" (Ezek. 33:11). Here the "death" spoken of is spiritual, not physical, since those spoken of are described as able to repent (see Supplement). And yet we know from John 6:44 that no man will (i.e., 'bothers' to) repent unless God draws him.[66] These wicked of Ezekiel are not (yet, at least) of a type who have placed their hearts into a position where there is no practical remedy regarding their repentance (cp. 2 Chr. 36:16), though they are, in fact, currently under the condemnation of God because of their unbelief (Jn. 3:36). During the approximate first half of the exodus narrative, we may insert Pharaoh's name to personalize the sense of the verse, i.e., 'I have no pleasure in the death of Pharaoh, says the Lord God, but that Pharaoh turn from his way and live.' How Ezekiel 33:11 squares with the Calvinistic idea that God reprobates men (such as Pharaoh) according to His good pleasure would seem to be a contradiction left for Calvinists to explain. Presumably, Calvinists would appeal to the idea that the 'wicked' in this verse are the elect who will be saved, since the verse implies they are able to repent. This means that Calvinists would still maintain that God *does* take pleasure in the death of the wicked who are 'non-elect,' i.e., the great majority of men whom they hold to be reprobated. With Calvinism there is often this turning of Scripture on its head by inserting redefinition into Scripture whenever their doctrinal distinctives make it necessary. Again, such a forced conclusion is brought into play because Calvinists hold to the idea of divine reprobation. They believe, for example, that every decision Pharaoh ever made during the 10 plagues was foreordained by God, and that it pleased God to foreordain not merely the plagues, but also Pharaoh's responses to them.

So before we enter into a detailed examination of the 'hardening' of Pharaoh's heart, a further introductory word ought to be said about the so-called divinely ordained histories of men. As for my former Calvinistic viewpoint, I too once believed that God had somehow foreordained all human history, whether Egyptian or Jewish, or modern day Gentile or Jewish. At some point, however, I found myself slipping away from the idea that God had foreordained all human activity, and the one biblical passage responsible for drawing me away from Calvinistic error was a statement about divine judgment; (in fact, it was one that Christ uttered when He was particularly angry, which implies His good pleasure was *not* being realized):

> Woe unto thee, Chorazin! woe unto thee, Bethsaida!
> for if the mighty works, which were done in you, had
> been done in Tyre and Sidon, they would have
> repented long ago in sackcloth and ashes (Mt. 11:21).

As a Calvinist I had always believed that God knew the future because he had predestinated history. This is the standard reason Calvinists give. For example, Reformed philosopher James Spiegel states in his book, *The Benefits of Providence:*

> Martin Luther emphatically reiterated the classical doctrine of God, saying, "it is…essentially necessary and wholesome for Christians to know that God foreknows nothing contingently, but that he foresees, purposes and does all things according to His immutable, eternal and infallible will."[xlviii]

…The Puritan theologian Jonathan Edwards…affirmed the doctrine of exhaustive divine foreknowledge, which includes the voluntary actions of human beings. And divine foreknowledge of all events, Edwards argues, implies the predetermination of all things. For if the prior knowledge of the event in infallible, "then it is impossible it should ever be otherwise…and this is the same thing as to say, it is impossible but that the event should come to pass: and this is the same as to say that its coming to pass is *necessary.*"[xlix]

Arthur W. Pink likewise concurs with Luther and Edwards:

> Few…are likely to call into question the statement that God knows and foreknows *all things,* but perhaps many would hesitate to go further than this. Yet is it not self-evident that if God *foreknows* all things, He has also *foreordained* all things? Is it not clear that God foreknows what will be *because He has decreed what shall be?* God's foreknowledge is not the cause of events, rather are events the effects of His eternal purpose. When God has decreed a thing *shall* be He knows it *will* be. In the nature of things there cannot be anything known as what shall be unless it is certain to be, and there is nothing certain to be unless God has *ordained* it shall be.[l]

But despite what Reformed thinkers like Martin Luther, Jonathan Edwards, and A.W. Pink believed, Matthew 11:21 states that Jesus knew what the future *could* have been. This means that Christ knew (and knows) history *contingently.*[67] So, in my own *de novo* review as a Calvinist (see chpt. 3), I realized that God didn't have to predetermine history in order to know what would happen. In fact, occasionally non-Calvinists had told me that divine foreknowledge was not determinative, but I stubbornly disbelieved them, perhaps in part because they shared no Scripture with me that pointed to contingent histories, such as Matthew 11:21. Once I discovered this truth about Christ knowing contingent histories, it was still largely a mystery to me, of course. I could not explain how Christ knew such things, but clearly He did, and clearly Matthew 11:21 was stating that He did. This discovery offered me the hope that answers could be found outside the Calvinistic model. (This was important to me, for if man's will were not free, then how could God justifiably judge him?) At last, I saw a proposition about foreknowledge that involved mystery apart from predetermination. No longer, then, did I feel compelled to believe in the contradictory premise that God foreordained everything while somehow not foreordaining sin. True, the statement of Matthew 11:21 was *fairly* beyond my understanding, i.e., like another fact I likewise couldn't grasp which posited God as an uncreated Being. But these facts about God's foreknowledge and His eternal existence stayed within appropriate biblical bounds because of the lexical evidence. That is, they appealed to Scriptural mysteries based on a proper historical-grammatical hermeneutic, not on lexical special pleading, which would have led to an irrational *mysticism* about God's moral nature (and therefore quite another thing).

    I sometimes ask myself how I would explain a particular Bible passage were I still a Calvinist. I can imagine my reply to Matthew 11:21 if that were still the case. Jesus, I would say, was merely implying that He would have imparted new natures to the people of Tyre and Sidon in order that they would have responded in faith to His miracles. These are the kind of 'explanations' I'd be left with as a Calvinist. Of course, the whole force of Matthew 11:21 is undone with such an unnatural explanation, because clearly Christ is angry that Chorazin and Bethsaida are not *choosing* to repent as other cities would have done under the same circumstances. This comparison of cities goes to the whole point about why Chorazin and Bethsaida would receive greater condemnation. But again, were I a Calvinist, I would also have to explain why Christ is angry in this passage, since in the Calvinist view everything Providence does is suppose to accord with His good pleasure. I think I would begin by claiming that if Christ was angry at man's sin, it was simply because it pleased Him to be angry. Everything is pleasurable for God, even His anger. In other words, I would frame the debate Calvinistically so that all divine anger would actually be *pleasure*. Thus, since the Bible says that God takes no pleasure in the death of the wicked, then the tone of Matthew 11:21 must mean that God is not taking pleasure in 'pleasure', but pleasure in 'anger.' In effect, there is nothing that truly displeases God, it is only that it *appears* to displease Him. Therefore even sin serves God's purposes and plans in some sense; and thus all things do work together for the good of the believer, even the believer's sin, as necessary.

Second, (were I a Calvinist) I might add that Christ, in expressing His 'anger,' was at the same time expressing it idiomatically. On the one hand He would have to be angry at sin because He is holy and recognizes that man can only choose sin, while on the other hand His 'anger' is a mere idiomatic expression of the fact that He understands that His sovereignty ordains all the final decisions which men decide on their own. Yes, it is a mystery how Christ can be angry while at the same time express it in an idiomatic way to state that He cannot be angry at His sovereignty, but our job is to accept Scripture, not explain it. God doesn't expect us to understand everything, but only to trust Him. The carnal-minded man will always suppose he can unwrap the unfathomable judgments of God in order to give others a 'reason' for his faith. All he offers us, of course, is man's reason, not God's reason. God's reason is different. This is a mystery to us, but if God were so small that we could understand Him, He wouldn't be big enough to worship.

Let me now stop my Calvinistic persona. As I reread the last sentences of the preceding paragraph, I have to admit I sound like I'm exalting God, debasing man, and sounding pretty humble, overall. There I was, proceeding to tear down every absolute statement about God and man, pleasure and anger, and good and evil so that they were indistinct from each other, yet doing it in a way so that readers would find it winsome and encouraging. But in reality this depresses me, so I need to make a brutally honest statement about books on Evangelical apologetics addressing the sovereignty of God. If I wanted to write a 'successful' book to help people through their problems, I wouldn't write the kind of book I'm writing. Instead I would write about the problem of evil through the lens of Calvinism, because that's the kind of books Evangelicals are largely reading (i.e., *buying*) today. I'm not saying that Calvinistic books are written because their authors want to make money, because I believe these Calvinist authors genuinely think they are helping people understand the Bible and the nature of God. Nevertheless, I look at Evangelicalism and then at the only response to Calvinism that has been getting much attention these days—Open Theism—and wonder what is happening. Here's the only Christian response to Calvinism that seems 'above the radar' these days, and it's a theology that believes God can be mistaken about the future! So, as I again consider Matthew 11:21 and the positions of Calvinists and Open Theists, I feel disconcerted. Are these Christians reading the same Bible I am? *Is this really the best we Christians are willing to believe?*

Part of God's judgment of us, His own house, is a result of how we understand the nature of God and His judgments, i.e., what we believe. The Bible tells us that "the time is come that judgment must begin at the house of God: and if it first begin at us, what shall the end be of them that obey not the gospel of God?" (1 Pet. 4:17). As we now look further into God's judgment of those who disobey the good news of God—and Pharaoh will be our test case—it is important to understand the Bible correctly, lest we invite a certain judgment of God upon ourselves for teaching that His nature and judgments are something other than what they are.

And Whom He Will He Hardeneth

> For the scripture saith unto Pharaoh, Even for this same purpose have I raised thee up, that I might shew my power in thee, and that my name might be declared throughout all the earth. Therefore hath he mercy on whom he will have mercy, and whom he will he hardeneth (Rom. 9:17-18).

This well-known passage in Romans 9 regarding Pharaoh has troubled many Christians and invited many explanations down the years. For a long time Calvinists have not needed to do much explaining about God hardening a man's heart, since the KJV translation has long seemed self-explanatory: God hardened Pharaoh's heart, and Pharaoh hardened his own heart. For the Calvinist this has been a clear demonstration that God has already disposed what man will come to propose—a perfect example of the two statements of the Westminster Confessions. And certainly Calvinists are right to point out that Exodus seems to state that the Lord would harden Pharaoh's heart, that afterward He hardened Pharaoh's heart, and that finally Pharaoh hardened his own heart. In fact, the hardening of Pharaoh's heart appears some 20 times within the space of 11 chapters. Nevertheless, a closer examination of the exodus narrative will reveal some interesting points about what the Bible really means when it says, "the Lord hardened Pharaoh's heart." For the main problem regarding this phrase lies in the translation, not the autographa.

To begin with, it is essential to note that three different Hebrew words are used in the biblical text for the 'hardening' of Pharaoh's heart. Of the KJV appearances of *hard/harden* in the exodus narrative, one of these three Hebrew words is generally used to refer to those instances when the Lord 'hardens' Pharaoh's heart; a second word usually alternates with this first word to state that either Pharaoh's heart was 'hard' or that Pharaoh 'hardened' his own heart; and a third word is mentioned but twice, once in Exodus 7:3 and again in Exodus 13:15, *forming a kind of introduction and summary*[68] to what God said *would happen*, and, in fact (as events proved), *what did happen* regarding Pharaoh's heart in the course of the plagues. In both instances this 3rd Hebrew word appears to have a meaning of *hard, tough, stubborn,* or *indurate*. In fact, only this third Hebrew word really has a meaning of *hard/hardened*.

The root of the first word (Heb. *chazaq*)[69] [li] (pronounced *khaw-sak*) comes from a root that literally means *to fasten upon*; hence, *to seize, be strong* (figuratively, *courageous, causatively strengthen, cure, help, repair, fortify*), *to bind, restrain, conquer*, and is thus a verb thought by translators to have various meanings both figuratively and causatively. The variations of all these words maintain an augmented aspect to them, such as to *make strong, courageous, prevail*, etc. Some rabbis, for example, have interpreted the word *chazaq* to say that God *strengthened* (not *hardened*) Pharaoh's heart so that Pharaoh would not fail in courage, in which case Pharaoh's choice would have been disabled. While I agree that *chazaq* means "strengthen," I think the Rabbinical view is faulty on at least two accounts: 1) the Bible teaches that man's will is capable of exerting its choice either for or against God under any circumstances (see Chpt. 17); and 2) The biblical narrative does not describe Pharaoh as fearful, but rather *unimpressed* both with Moses' sign[70] and first plague prior to the Lord's 'hardening,' which begins after plague six., i.e., "(Pharaoh) set not his heart upon it" (Ex. 7:23). However, the idea that *strengthened* ought to have been used by the KJV instead of *hardened* has at least Robert Young's approval in his long-regarded Literal Translation (Exodus 4:21):

> And Jehovah saith unto Moses, 'In thy going to turn back to Egypt, see — all the wonders which I have put in thy hand — that thou hast done them before Pharaoh, and I — I strengthen his heart, and he doth not send the people away;[71]

Young appears to be alone among translators in advocating that *strengthen* ought to be the rendering instead of *harden*. Indeed, the Hebrew word *chazaq* does, in fact, have a meaning of "strength" or "strong" as it appears in the Old Testament. In fact, the idea of "strength" is implied in nearly all, if not all, of the remaining 'chazaq' words in the Old Testament. The breakdown in the KJV is as follows: "strong" 48 (occurrences), "repair" 47, "hold" 37, "strengthened" 28, "strengthen" 14, "harden" 13, "prevail" 10, "encourage" 9, "take" 9, "courage" 8, "caught" 5, "stronger" 5, "hold" 5, misc. 52; total—290 occurrences. The word "repair" is found 35 times in Nehemiah 3 in the record of Jewish families who worked side by side to rebuild Jerusalem's walls; thus, even in the description of "repairing" there is the aspect of *strengthening* (the wall). As for *chazaq* being translated as "harden," it appears this way 13 times and is almost exclusively restricted to Exodus (again, among the *290* occurrences in the Old Testament). A rare exception might be argued for Jeremiah 5:3 "they have made their faces *harder* than a rock," but even here it may simply mean "stronger," as in "stronger than steel," i.e., "stronger than rock." In fact, the best way to get a real sense of how often the word *chazaq* means *strength* or *strong*, or is implied to mean *strength*, such as "lay hold" (in which case perhaps British understatement has hindered the reader from seeing the idea of *seizing*, or *fastening*), is to go through a hardbound copy of Strong's Concordance (or, more easily, do an online BlueLetterBible.com search and read each reference in which *chazaq* appears). Thus, by looking up in *Strong's* the various English words which the KJV rendered for *chazaq* (i.e., *strong, repair, hold, strengthened, strengthen, harden, prevail, encourage, take, courage, caught, stronger, hold*, etc.), one gets a real sense of what *chazaq* truly means.[72] For example, the Lord tells Joshua four times in Joshua 1 to be *strong* (*chazaq*) and courageous, and in Exodus God is said to have delivered the Israelites "with a *strong* (*chazaq*) hand" (13:9) which He did by sending a "mighty *strong* (*chazaq*) west wind" which divided the Red Sea. *Chazaq* also appears some 42 times as *strength*, such as when Samson prays for the Lord to "*strengthen* me, only this once*." The meaning of *seize* or *fasten* (hence, implying *strength*) is present in Judges 19:29 ("[the Levite] took a knife, and *laid hold* (*chazaq*) on his concubine"); 2 Samuel 1:11 ("David *took hold* (*chazaq*) of his clothes, and rent them"); Isaiah 4:1 ("seven women shall *take hold* (*chazaq*) of one man"), 2 Samuel 18:9 ("and his [Absalom's] head *caught hold* (*chazaq*) in the oak"), etc.

Thus whenever one reads Exodus and finds the word *harden* for the Hebrew word *chazaq*, it is an exception to the way *chazaq* is always, or nearly always, translated in the Old Testament even by the King James translators themselves. Presumably, the translation resulting in *harden* in Exodus was thought to be justified by the context of the Lord's dealings with Pharaoh. For it is much less awkward (or is it?) to say that "The Lord *hardened* Pharaoh's heart," than to say, "the Lord *strengthened* Pharaoh's heart." Indeed, to say that the Lord 'hardened' Pharaoh's heart is to say that God hardened Pharaoh *in advance* of any choice Pharaoh himself made. And that would mean God was arbitrary in judgment. The more meaningful question, therefore, is to ask why Young's Literal Translation rendered Exodus 9:12 the way it did, i.e., "The Lord *strengthened* Pharaoh's heart." The answer, first, is that one must remember that though the word "strengthen" in English has positive and good *connotations*, its *definition* is not restricted to such connotations. For example, we would all recoil from the statement, "Adolph Hitler had strength of character," yet, *denotatively* understood, Hitler did, in fact, have strength of character in the sense of having a strong character. We hasten to add that Hitler's strength was guided to evil, but I give this example to show how a word often has a connotative (associated) 'definition' besides its denotative (actual, technical) definition. I believe this will explain why the KJV translators chose "harden" over the more exacting and transliterated term "strengthen" in the Exodus narrative.

Second, it must also be understood that the strengthening of Pharaoh's heart ascribed to the Lord (as we will argue in the rest of this chapter) is merely that of *allowance*. That is, the Lord strengthened Pharaoh's heart *by allowing the Enemy to strengthen Pharaoh's heart*. Such strengthening by the Enemy would have been done by an intense campaign of thought-suggestion. And yet we must remember that, as strong as the Enemy's thought suggestions are, Pharaoh himself decided upon his own heart's intention (i.e., his will). Indeed, one must remember at all times that it is **Pharaoh's** heart that is strengthened, not some *negated vacuum* merely *called* Pharaoh's heart by certain theologians who, audaciously, would retain *Pharaoh's heart* in name only. That is, it cannot be called *Pharaoh's* heart unless *Pharaoh himself* makes his own choices. Unfortunately, translators other than Young seem not to grant this common sense definition, and thus they apparently think that saying "God *hardened* Pharaoh's heart" is somehow more palatable than saying "God *strengthened* Pharaoh's heart." Thus, while many translators have substituted "harden" for "strengthen" to describe God's activity upon Pharaoh's heart, the overwhelming use of "strong" and "strengthen" for the Hebrew *chazaq* throughout the rest of the Old Testament would argue that the translators' preference for *harden* in the Exodus narrative was due more to editorializing upon the word *chazaq*, rather than from any straightforward, denotative treatment of the word. Apparently, the reason for such editorializing was because the translators felt compelled to use "harden," or else the passage would appear to be saying that God was strengthening Pharaoh's evil heart, i.e., rather than hardening him to a point where Pharaoh chose rebellion for himself (as though that made sense). Doubtless, the other reason "harden" was chosen by translators was that God's manner of speaking was not understood to be idiomatic. <u>Thus they failed to see that God is speaking **as though** He is the causal agent when the context shows that He is merely acting in deference to His wishes.</u> Readers of the Bible should imagine what it must be like for God to express Himself when confronted by a king like Pharaoh who is no more than a speck within the *dust* on the scales that represent the nations of the earth (Is. 40:15). To such an audacious Pharaoh God speaks *as though* He Himself, not the Enemy, shall be the one strengthening the king in the king's own course. But, in fact, the *fermenting* process of Pharaoh's stubbornness accelerates during the plagues, because (we will argue) the *Enemy* adds his influence which Pharaoh ultimately regards as the truth, and so Pharaoh further augments his own heart against God. As to *why* Pharaoh should do this, rather than to respond **to a** fair and just God, is Pharaoh's own contribution to what the Bible elsewhere calls "the mystery of iniquity." The point here is this: we must always remember while reading the Exodus narrative that God's realm of *causal* activity is the bringing of plagues, not Pharaoh's responses.

Later in this chapter we will give additional reasons for why neither God Himself nor the Enemy could be the causal agent behind Pharaoh's heart. For while God intensifies Pharaoh's conscience so that Pharaoh might do right (through the influence of Moses' speeches and His own further thought-suggestion), the Enemy, it appears, gains God's permission after the 6th plague to attempt to *sear* Pharaoh's conscience thoroughly, so that Pharaoh should do intensive wrong (the Enemy plans to accomplish this through thought-suggestion, though presumably it will be done with greater intensity than what God feels is just when promoting His own thought-presentations to men). Again, Pharaoh alone ultimately decides the final condition of his own heart in either case. The example of another Old Testament king, King Ahab, in his stubborn persistence in listening to his false prophets (1 Kings 22), will be reviewed later in this chapter to show how God sometimes speaks idiomatically to say that He is the causal agent, when, in fact, the context shows that He is merely acting in deference to His wishes. Whether therefore one prefers to translate *chazaq* to read '*strengthen/strong*' or '*harden/hard*,' the main thing to be understood is that God is speaking idiomatically of the Enemy's activity. However, though God speaks idiomatically as the casual agent who strengthens Pharaoh's heart, it is true, at least, that in Pharaoh's case God had come to a point where the Egyptian king had so spurned God that the Lord desired to give him up.

The meaning of the second Hebrew verb rendered by the KJV as "harden" is the word *kabad* (pronounced *kaw-bad*). The word *kabad* literally means to *be heavy* (from a primitive root meaning *liver*, because the liver was held to be the heaviest organ in the body), in a bad sense (*burdensome, severe, dull*) or in a good sense (*numerous, rich, honorable*), and may also mean *abounding with, more grievously afflicted, glorify, boast*, etc. The meaning of the two verbs *chazaq* and *kabad* in the plague narrative of Exodus 4—14 do not therefore have the same exact meaning. Nor do they have the same primitive root. The point here is that if God hardened Pharaoh's heart in the way Calvinists claim—unilaterally and apart from any ability for Pharaoh to act in any other way than 'freely' and in perfect conformity with God's will—why, then, throughout Exodus does Scripture predominately use one word (*chazaq*) to describe the kind of 'hardening' the Lord does, but two different words (*chazaq* and *kabad*) to describe the kind of 'hardening' Pharaoh does? If, as Calvinists claim, Pharaoh is merely receiving the construct of God, why isn't the *same* word always used in both cases to tell us this? Certainly, if God wanted to convince us that Pharaoh did nothing but receive God's constructs, Scripture could have been clearer on the point. One would think, for example, that the Bible would have rendered matching verbs in those statements about Pharaoh that are paired with the Lord's statements. Thus, "the Lord '*kabad*' Pharaoh's heart," should be followed by, "Pharaoh '*kabad* ' his heart," or again, "The Lord *chazaq* Pharaoh's heart" followed by, "Pharaoh '*chazaq* ' his heart." Numerous times in Exodus, however, different verbs for *harden* are used within these paired statements. The point for the Calvinist is not whether the verbs *ever* match, but why they should not *always* match. This, in fact, ought to be the case if Calvinism is correct. That is, like Earth's moon which does nothing but reflect that element of the sun it receives and gives to the earth, so Pharaoh, too, if the Calvinist is right, ought likewise to reflect naught but the construct of God in whatever he does. But simply put, the Hebrew language does not bear this Calvinistic assumption out. There are at least two suggestions the Calvinist may offer for why the verbs in Exodus do not always match within these paired statements (besides their argument of 'sovereign' will *vs.* 'revealed' will, which tries to pass off God's will as *one* will while being *two* wills). The first is that these must be Hebrew synonyms that are used to alleviate word redundancy for the reader. This suggestion, however, is hardly plausible, since *Strong's* concordance shows that multiple uses of one of the words (*chazaq*) is used six times within a succession of seven occurrences of 'harden,' and also because one of the two main words for *harden* is used almost exclusively when 'hardening' activity is referred to the Lord. The other objection the Calvinist may offer, one that is legitimate, in fact, is that the two Hebrew verbs have somewhat different meanings. Thus they might claim that the intent of the passage is *not* meant here to be a *tour de force* example proving the Calvinistic doctrine of total sovereignty, *vis-à-vis*, such that God has already disposed what Pharaoh will come to propose. With this objection— that the words are lexically different—we would agree, but where does that leave the Calvinist? Not only would Calvinists have to give up their example of God allegedly hardening Pharaoh's heart, which they claim supports a doctrine of reprobation, but it would also suggest that the discussion of Pharaoh in Romans 9 (with its supposed view toward reprobation) ought to be looked at anew. In fact, I would say that a fresh translation reflecting the words' different meanings *ought* to be the case. At any rate, if one truly understood Hebrew as the Hebrews did at the time of the Pentateuch, one would certainly not be left with the same impression which the KJV translation has been leaving upon English readers for centuries.

Now I find this tampering of God's Word by the King James's translators disturbing. One does not even have to be trained in translation work to see the problem. For example, since the Hebrew language of Exodus primarily uses two different words for the verb translated 'to harden,' why didn't the KJV at least choose synonyms, such as *to harden* and *to stiffen*, in order to alert English readers that something was going on in the Hebrew language which they might want to investigate for themselves? Instead, all *three* Hebrew verbs were reduced in translation to one word, *hardened*, and this is undoubtedly the chief reason why English readers have thought for centuries that Pharaoh simply hardened himself along the same lines to which God had supposedly ordained him. For centuries, this translation error in the KJV has been promoting the idea that Pharaoh was little more than a marionette on strings acting out debase behavior for which he would be blamed, even though he was arguably under the command of an all-controlling Puppeteer. In the end, Calvinists simply promoted the idea that God could be exonerated in the process because He was God, and that man could be condemned in the process because he was man. And in this manner the Calvinistic doctrine of reprobation has survived up to today, i.e., the Puppeteer pulls all the strings, but the marionette gets all the boos.

The Mistranslation of Exodus 7:13

Perhaps the most unfortunate translation in Exodus regarding the Pharaohic aspect of the exodus narrative is found in 7:13, a verse that has misled Christians for a long time. While the NAS is an improvement over the KJV, we will see that it too leaves something to be desired. One of the morbidly fascinating things I have observed, during my personal study of the exodus narrative, is how the KJV and NAS appear to approach Exodus 7:13 with a prejudice toward a Calvinistic interpretation. The KJV, for example, blunders with a total mistranslation: "And he hardened Pharaoh's heart." All major translations today, including the New King James Version (NKJV), as well as major Reformed authors like A.W. Pink, recognize that the original KJV (Authorized) translation of this phrase in this verse was a bastardization of the Hebrew. The New King James Version reads, "But Pharaoh's heart grew hard," and the NAS reads, "But Pharaoh's heart was hardened." Notice that the word "he" was added into the KJV, indicating that another party besides Pharaoh was strengthening Pharaoh's heart. The necessary correction to the Authorized Version has been made in later translations, including the NKJV, since the verb, although active here (not passive), nevertheless indicates no other agent as the cause. Therefore (and unfortunately), when the KJV renders "And he hardened Pharaoh's heart," it introduces 1) a *specific and exclusive* second person ["he" (God)] and 2) describes this 'he' as the causal agent hardening Pharaoh, both of which concepts are without any support in the Hebrew language. This unsupported assumption by the KJV of God's involvement at this point in the narrative is especially evident in the Hebrew. As can be seen in the chart toward the end of this chapter, God's statement in Exodus 4:21, that he will *strengthen* Pharaoh's heart, shows that the verb in this instance has a Piel stem [Intensive form (note: Hebrew verbs have seven different type stems)] in the Imperfect Mood (incomplete action), and the fulfillment of this prophetic statement is dramatically seen in Exodus 9:12, when for the first time since 4:21 we are told that the Lord actually does strengthen Pharaoh's heart, and note this quite remarkable thing—that the verb *strengthen* takes the Piel stem in the Imperfect Mood just as it did in 4:21. Thus the beginning of the fulfillment of the Lord's statement in Exodus 4:21 does not occur until 9:12 (after the 6th plague), and the fulfillment continues with succeeding statements about the Lord strengthening Pharaoh's heart, with the verb *strengthened* taking repeatedly the Piel stem and Imperfect Mood in Exodus 10:20, 10:27, 11:10 and 14:8 (after the 7th, 8th, 9th, and 10th plagues, respectively). [Incidentally, in Exodus 14:4 the mood is Perfect (completed action) as the Lord seems to be announcing a *strengthening* of Pharaoh's heart unto a certain completion, and this completion occurs not after the 10th plague but before it. This is because there is also the subsequent hardening of the Egyptians stated in 14:17, among which Pharaoh is apparently accounted as one of them. For the Imperfect form of the verb *will strengthen* stated prior to plague 10 (found in 14:8) is a strengthening of Pharaoh's heart still not complete, since Pharaoh continues to strengthen his heart even after Israel's departure. For note that Israel's ultimate and final deliverance as *fiat accompli* will not occur until Pharaoh's army is drowned in the sea. Presumably, then, the incomplete strengthening of Pharaoh's heart mentioned in 14:8, prior to plague 10, is fulfilled in the strengthening of Egyptians in 14:17.] So, then, while it is true that prior to Exodus 7:13 the Lord says "I *will strengthen* Pharaoh's heart," the narrative doesn't actually *state* that "the Lord strengthened Pharaoh's heart" until Exodus 9:12.[73] Again, this is very clear in the Hebrew but absolutely lost in existing English translations (especially since there are no marginal notes in these translations to alert readers of the Hebrew's grammatical significance). Thus, the KJV blunder in Exodus 7:13 is even more unfortunate because it is the first description of Pharaoh's heart and sets the tone for the entire narrative. Thus by implying that the Lord hardened Pharaoh's heart, the KJV leads its readers to conclude that the Lord *actively* hardened Pharaoh's heart from the very onset of the plagues. Personally, I find it unlikely that the KJV simply made a mistake inadvertently. I think it is more reasonable to conclude that the KJV translators interjected their own thought because they believed the general context supported this idea, even though the original Hebrew didn't state it. (Indeed, a more careful review of the Hebrew should have led them to the opposite conclusion.) The KJV allegedly italicizes words it interpolates, but it did not do it here with 'he' in Exodus 7:13. This mistranslation by the KJV raises an interesting question. How many people (like myself) grew up in KJV-influenced homes and therefore naturally came to conclude that God hardened Pharaoh's heart from the very outset of the exodus narrative, with the result that Pharaoh couldn't repent? Everyone? Certainly all but a select few would have reached this conclusion unless they owned commentaries and had taken the time to study them. Frankly speaking, for many years I've sat in Evangelical churches heavily oriented toward the KJV, and yet I never remember having heard a challenge raised against the KJV for its Calvinistic assumption that God actively hardened Pharaoh's heart at the time of the very first plague.

Unfortunately, it appears that the KJV has proceeded to transfix even some translators who ought to have known better. The NAS, for example, doesn't seem to intend much of a difference in its overall approach to Exodus 7:13. The NAS's phrase, "And his heart was hardened" fails to really give the true meaning of the word "strengthened." Thus we are confused about what was really happening in Pharaoh's heart. Lest it remain ambiguous, however, the NAS study version I have in front of me has a verse footnote reference meant to be helpful. It occurs at the end of Exodus 7:13 and refers the reader back to Exodus 4:21. There we read, "The Lord said to Moses…I will harden his heart so that he will not let the people go." The citing of Exodus 4:21 is thus stated in the NAS verse footnote to be the *referenced* fulfillment of Exodus 7:13. This verse, in turn, supports the Calvinistic assumption that another party, i.e., God, is the cause of Pharaoh's hardening of heart. The NAS is thus trying to convince the reader that the *Lord* hardened Pharaoh's heart, even though (as we have already noted) Scripture makes no reference to the Lord actually hardening Pharaoh's heart until Exodus 9:12! Hence the NAS verse footnote *should* have referred the reader back to Exodus 3:19 as the fulfillment of 7:13, i.e., "But I know that the king of Egypt will not let you go, except under compulsion." That is, Exodus 7:13 has God's *foreknowledge* of Pharaoh's decision in view, not His 'hardening' activity. Yet, the linguistic pointers in Hebrew which the NAS ignores (even as the KJV did), tell us that the Lord is referring back to his previous statement in Exodus 3:19 to show his foreknowledge of what Pharaoh will do in his *existing condition*. Here, then, is the path of verse to footnoted-verse the NAS asks the reader to take (Ex. 7:13, cf. Ex. 4:21):

> *Yet Pharaoh's heart was hardened, and he did not listen to them, as the Lord had said…* (supposedly refers to) *The Lord said to Moses…I will harden his heart so that he will not let the people go.*

Here is the path of verse to footnoted-verse to which the NAS reader *should* have been taken (Ex. 7:13, cf. Ex. 3:19):

> *Yet Pharaoh's heart was hardened, and he did not listen to them, as the Lord had said…* (actually refers to) *But I*

know that the king of Egypt will not permit you to go, except under compulsion.

When Exodus 7:13 is properly understood, it changes the whole tenor of the exodus narrative. Again, remember that the phrase, "The **Lord** hardened his heart" does not appear until Exodus 9:12 (after the sixth plague). This means that the Bible states *seven* times that either Pharaoh's heart was *strengthened* (i.e., KJV "hardened") or that Pharaoh strengthened his own heart, before it ever states that the **Lord** strengthened Pharaoh's heart. Would not this fact suggest, when we arrive at Exodus 9:12 to find the Lord strengthening Pharaoh's heart, that this activity of the Lord is, while at the least, the Spirit's ceasing to strive with Pharaoh any longer, also and arguably more than just this—namely, the Lord's allowance of the Enemy to more intensely affect Pharaoh's heart? That the Lord is not described as strengthening Pharaoh's heart until Exodus 9:12 raises a serious problem for the Calvinist. Who is strengthening Pharaoh's heart prior to that time? The answer is found in Scripture. It tells us plainly that Pharaoh's heart is strengthened, and proceeds to show us that, with each divine miracle, Pharaoh only furthers the strengthening of it. Even if the Calvinist wants to point out the numerous times from Exodus 9:12ff where Scripture says that it was the Lord who 'hardened' (strengthened) Pharaoh's heart, he can point to no such scripture to support the same conclusion *prior* to Exodus 9:12. Therefore to imply that the Lord hardened (*strengthened*) Pharaoh's heart from the very beginning of the narrative is to make an argument not merely from silence but also from a gross ignorance of the Hebrew. In fact, one could argue that the omission of any suggestion that the Lord 'hardened' (*strengthened*) Pharaoh's heart prior to Exodus 9:12 is really an argument for Pharaoh acting in unqualified free will. The Calvinist is thus left with giving us the tired explanation upon our ears that the Lord must have done it anyway, and that the Almighty is not obligated to explain Himself because our carnal minds cannot hope to comprehend His unfathomable judgments.[74]

Apparently, it is not convincing enough to Calvinists that the reason the Bible is silent about the Lord strengthening Pharaoh's heart until after the sixth plague is because that is exactly what happened. When the Calvinist offers his own kind of explanation to claim the presence of the Lord's activity in hardening Pharaoh during the course of the first six plagues, he places the Lord's character in contradiction to other places in Scripture which speak of God, at the first, being merciful to all men. Of course, the Calvinist makes his claim for absolute divine sovereignty nonetheless (bolstered by the KJV and NAS), in an attempt to support his doctrine of Reprobation. Thus, when the Calvinist claims that such conundrums about God's nature are beyond our understanding (e.g., in God commanding

Pharaoh to let the children of Israel go but hardening Pharaoh so he could not obey), the Calvinist effectively places his doctrine into the realm of mysticism. He is going beyond what Calvinists and non-Calvinists would both hold to be true, i.e., that Scripture teaches that men cannot know God *comprehensively*, to claiming that neither can men know God *fundamentally*. This is a very dangerous position. The Calvinist is implying that we cannot really know the *nature* of God nor explain it to anyone else. This flies in the face of 1) Romans 1, which tells us that God's nature is *indisputably knowable*; and 2) the biblical command that we are to give a reasonable explanation to everyone who asks us about the hope that is in us. Of necessity, then, this sharing of the gospel should involve a reasonable explanation about the nature of God who so loved man that He sent His only Son to die for him. And this biblical command to give a reason for our hope also implies that Scripture *can* be reasonable to the man who responds to God's invitation to reason with Him. Thus God obviously has a nature that must be fundamentally understandable.

The Calvinist, however, can offer no *reasonable* explanation of God's nature, since he claims that God is hardening Pharaoh's heart from the very beginning for the purpose of reprobation. And so he attempts an explanation at the expense of the Scripture, which says that God does not take pleasure in the *death* (understood here as *path*) of the wicked (Ezek. 33:11). Moreover, the Calvinist cannot explain how Pharaoh has the will to harden his own heart without relying once again on his dialectical method which 'explains' that God's absolute sovereignty is creating Pharaoh's thoughts and intents despite Pharaoh's own choices. And if we were to object to this 'reasoning,' the Calvinist is likely to offer a further 'explanation' involving Romans 9:19-20, which follows on the heels of Paul's discussion of Pharaoh's hardening a few verses earlier, in which Paul states that "the thing formed cannot say to the One who formed it, 'Why have you made me thus?' " The problem with the Calvinist, then, stated briefly (though explained in more detail later), is that he misinterprets Romans 9:19-20 by failing to understand the far (though *referred*) context of Romans 9, which speaks of God's irresistibility in *judging* men and nations, not in *eradicating* their wills so completely that questions can never be asked. This error in Calvinism arises because Calvinists have not considered carefully the three Old Testament passages which speak of the pot/potter metaphor to which Paul is referring, i.e., Isaiah 29, 45, and Jeremiah 18. The same analogy is there used in these Old Testament passages to describe pots upon the Potter's wheel which, far from being the willy-nilly, divinely acted-upon vessels which the Calvinist in Romans 9 depicts them to be, are shown in speech and behavior to be their *own willful selves*, thus speaking to the general theme of Romans 9 regarding irresistible *judgment*.[75]

A few more thoughts should be offered here to show again that the Lord did not actively cause Pharaoh's heart to be hardened at the beginning of the narrative. That is, we have not emphasized enough that the 2nd Hebrew word we cited earlier (*kabad*), which the KJV translates as *hardened*, as in the phrase, "The Lord hardened Pharaoh's heart" (Ex. 10:1), is claimed by *Strong's* to be a verb of *variable* nature. That is, it does not (according to translators) invariably describe negative action, such as *to harden*). While many translators believe it *can* mean *to harden* or *to stiffen*, they also feel it can mean *to make stouthearted* or *to make courageous*, etc. At any rate, the word carries with it a sense of *weightiness*. Perhaps a more accurate translation would have been "I will make Pharaoh's heart (heavily) pronounced," and so also, "The Lord made Pharaoh's heart pronounced," and again, "Pharaoh's heart was pronounced." God, in effect, would cause Pharaoh's heart to become pronounced by allowing (not commanding) a lying, demonic spirit to augment what Pharaoh wanted for himself, i.e., to resist God with ever greater intensity. By definition a man like Pharaoh, whose heart increases its rebellion against God, will become pronounced against additional light. It *becomes* augmented *during* repeated opportunities (thus, *is made heavy*), and *is* augmented (weightier) *afterward* as a state of the heart (thus, *is heavy*). As God gave Pharaoh spiritual light, he rejected it; and then when God gave Pharaoh additional light, he rejected this also, etc. Ultimately, as more light was given, more rejection resulted, and the stronger and weightier Pharaoh's heart became. Thus Pharaoh's heart grew weightier during the process, and afterward was heavy.

Bearing that thought in mind, i.e., that Pharaoh grew fully *roused* even while God gave him great light, consider this: the word *raised* in Romans 9:17 literally means *to rouse fully*, a meaning hardly apparent in the KJV:

> For the scripture saith unto Pharaoh, "Even for this same purpose have I raised thee up, that I might shew my power in thee, and that my name might be declared throughout all the earth."

Again, many readers have read this verse without realizing that *raised* in the Greek literally means to *fully rouse*, Gr. *exegeiro*, Paul even departing from the Septuagint here. While Pink notes Paul's departure from the Septuagint, he nevertheless completely fails to realize that *exegeiro* means "to fully rouse," not "to appoint." Perhaps most of us, when we first became familiar with Romans 9:17, assumed, like Pink, that God orchestrated events so that Pharaoh would become a ruler in Egypt and live a puppet-like existence that was divinely decreed from the cradle to the grave. While it is true that God sets up the thrones of men or allows men to set up their own thrones to rule over others, neither of these is in view in this verse. A more appropriate translation of Romans 9:17 should therefore read:

> And in very deed for this cause have I fully roused thee, to show in thee my power; and that my name may be declared throughout all the earth.

Keeping this more accurate translation in mind, let us recall that there are three different Hebrew words in Exodus that were translated to the same English word (*harden*) by the KJV translators, and thus given the same meaning. The result has been a very Calvinistic-sounding passage in Exodus where Pharaoh is depicted as merely mimicking the kind of constructs God had already determined upon him. When one considers that Romans 8:28 (as already seen) was likewise translated in a way that made it biblically incompatible with other passages, while at the same time sounding more Calvinistic, so also in Exodus have the KJV translators remained true to Calvinistic assumptions at the expense of certain other linguistic considerations. Frankly, the translation of Exodus 9:16 ("for this cause have I raised thee up") is careless, because the KJV translators saw no relevance in Paul's citation of this very same statement which God made to Pharaoh in a clearly marked passage in Romans 9. Sadly, the NAS has not fared any better in translating Romans 9:17, opting for the inferior *raised* instead of stating the transliteration, "For this purpose have I *fully roused* thee."

Furthermore, Paul, in his use of *fully roused* in Romans 9:17, is not simply *discussing* the Exodus passage, but is quoting what Scripture records God *actually said* to Pharaoh in Exodus 9:16. Thus, the translators should have used the more exact Greek word in Romans 9:17 to inform the more variable[26] Hebrew verb *to stand*, so that it was understood that God was speaking figuratively to Pharaoh about 'standing him,' i.e., about raising Pharaoh's *spirit* in the sense of rousing him. This is a far cry from suggesting that God had raised Pharaoh from the cradle to the grave for a specific reprobative purpose, as, for example, A.W. Pink insists. As for whether the verb *rouse* was used during the era of the KJV translators so that it would have been available for use in the 17th century KJV translation, it should be noted that the word *rouse* occurs over 30 times in the 16th century works of Shakespeare.[27]

Moreover, we should not miss the implication in Exodus 7:3 when the Lord says to Moses that He will harden Pharaoh's heart and *multiply* signs and wonders. In this regard note that the verb 'harden' is in the Imperfect Mood, while 'multiply' is in the Perfect. The idea appears to be that God will still be 'hardening' Pharaoh's heart, though He will have *finished* (brought completed action to) the multiplying of signs and wonders. This Imperfect Mood for 'harden' and Perfect Mood for "multiply" speaks of a 'hardening' of Pharaoh after a certain hardening had already been completed, which the signs and wonders (i.e., of the plagues, not the dividing of the Red Sea) had accomplished.

Does God Work *in* Pharaoh's Sin, or *Despite* It?

Before moving on, we must pause here to consider a certain assumption about God held by many Christians who read through the Exodus narrative. It is unfortunate that some Christians believe that God *wanted* Pharaoh to reject His light so that the Lord's name might be proclaimed in all the earth. For God is not the type of Person to employ such means, even for so glorious an end. Indeed, God would not have been any less glorified in a repentant Pharaoh than in a stubborn one (cp. the story of Cyrus). Sadly, it seems that some Christians believe that God is equally or more glorified in the work of sinners, than by the faith of believers. But again, God does not need the darkness of sin to make a greater contrast to the light of His righteousness to gain a greater glory for Himself. For this would make God *dependent* upon sin in order to effect the greatest expression of His holiness. As such, it would also diminish the degree of perfect glory He always had in Himself prior to creation. This idea of sin redounding to God's glory should be shunned as readily as that attitude which Paul denounces among Christians who rationalized sin on the basis that it resulted in more of God's grace and glory (see Romans 6). God is put upon, not glorified, when we sin. Nor, to give another example, would God have been less glorified in Adam and Eve's continued obedience than in the path of sin they chose. Their disobedience simply resulted in God deciding to provide an atonement for them through the death of Christ. In other words, *God did not need an opportunity to prove His love for Adam and Eve, for His love was already so. Man's rebellion simply compelled God into a show of it.* This goes to the point that God's moral character was already established *regardless* of the compelling opportunity which led Him to demonstrate His character. In a sense the same is true, albeit often negatively, for men. For a man, for example, not to commit adultery only because the opportunity does not present itself, is no virtue. Jesus says that such a man is already an adulterer because his heart is already committed to the act. Pharaoh is of this committed sort regarding his *intention* to disobey and defy God. The nature of such rebellion is pointed out in the gospel of John to explain why the Light (Christ) was rejected by men when the Light came into the world, i.e., because men loved darkness rather than light because their deeds were evil. In effect, then, Pharaoh is like a man sitting in the darkness upon whom God throws light via a switch. Because Pharaoh prefers darkness he gets up and switches off the light, and then he sits down again. But God turns on another light that is even brighter than the first. Yet because Pharaoh still prefers darkness, he is even more annoyed at this brighter light, and so he gets up in a greater huff to switch off this greater light. But yet again God turns on another light, this one brighter than the previous two. Thus Pharaoh grows even angrier as he gets up from his chair to turn off the light yet again. This kind of rebellion repeats itself in the exodus narrative until Pharaoh is fully roused at a point following the 6th plague. Yet we note that Pharaoh *could* have light in the room (of his soul) if he merely allowed God's light to remain shining, but this he will not do. Consequently, his heart is darkened more and more as he sears his conscience with additional rejections of God's light. Notice, then, that however harsh God's plagues were upon Egypt, they were also acts of spiritual light. We tend to forget that God's initial desire was to show mercy upon Pharaoh and the Egyptians. We seem to think that **all** of Egypt's plagues, including the earlier ones, were unvaryingly angry expressions of a God determined to have vengeance upon a nation that had enslaved His people. Yet even God's *latter* plagues, in which he no longer actively strove with His Spirit to dissuade Pharaoh from his foolish course, were, hypothetically at least, also acts of spiritual light that could have led Pharaoh and the Egyptians to the truth.

Pharaoh and the Lesson of Ahab

God's program for all men begins as one of mercy. In fact, God is no respecter of persons, and His Spirit works to convince every man of his need for a Savior. And God will keep doing this unless He gives up on a man because that man has hardened his heart in prolonged, virulent rebellion. At that point such a man, to use an older phrase, 'has sinned away his day of grace,' not theoretically, but in a willfully determined and final way, and in this sense irrevocably. Such a man is probably that which Elihu described in Job 36:13: "But the godless in heart lay up anger; They do not cry for help when He binds them." (NAS) This means that the wicked man is not humbled by life's difficulties. Instead, he strengthens himself and feels he has no need of God. History has shown that often the worst men in this regard are political rulers, like Pharaoh. Perhaps more accurately stated, we should say that such offenders have merely had more opportunity than others to allow power to "go to their heads."
Now the Bible has much to say about the special encounters—pro and con—which God has had with both Jewish and Gentile rulers. One of these encounters (told in 1 Kings 22) is the story of King Ahab of Israel, and it bears directly upon our consideration of Pharaoh and the 'hardening' (strengthening) of his heart:

⁶Then the king of Israel gathered the prophets together, about four hundred men, and said unto them, Shall I go against Ramothgilead to battle, or shall I forbear? And they said, Go up; for the Lord shall deliver it into the hand of the king. ⁷And Jehoshaphat said, Is there not here a prophet of the Lord besides, that we might enquire of him? ⁸And the king of Israel said unto Jehoshaphat, There is yet one man, Micaiah the son of Imlah, by whom we may enquire of the Lord: but I hate him; for he doth not prophesy good concerning me, but evil. And Jehoshaphat said, Let not the king say so. ⁹Then the king of Israel called an officer, and said, Hasten hither Micaiah the son of Imlah. ¹⁰And the king of Israel and Jehoshaphat the king of Judah sat each on his throne, having put on their robes, in a void place in the entrance of the gate of Samaria; and all the prophets prophesied before them. ¹¹And Zedekiah the son of Chenaanah made him horns of iron: and he said, Thus saith the Lord, With these shalt thou push the Syrians, until thou have consumed them. ¹²And all the prophets prophesied so, saying, Go up to Ramothgilead, and prosper: for the Lord shall deliver it into the king's hand. ¹³And the messenger that was gone to call Micaiah spake unto him, saying, Behold now, the words of the prophets declare good unto the king with one mouth: let thy word, I pray thee, be like the word of one of them, and speak that which is good. ¹⁴And Micaiah said, As the Lord liveth, what the Lord saith unto me, that will I speak. ¹⁵So he came to the king. And the king said unto him, Micaiah, shall we go against Ramothgilead to battle, or shall we forbear? And he answered him, Go, and prosper: for the Lord shall deliver it into the hand of the king. ¹⁶And the king said unto him, How many times shall I adjure thee that thou tell me nothing but that which is true in the name of the Lord? ¹⁷And he said, I saw all Israel scattered upon the hills, as sheep that have not a shepherd: and the Lord said, These have no master: let them return every man to his house in peace. ¹⁸And the king of Israel said unto Jehoshaphat, Did I not tell thee that he would prophesy no good concerning me, but evil? ¹⁹And he said, Hear thou therefore the word

of the Lord: I saw the Lord sitting on his throne, and all the host of heaven standing by him on his right hand and on his left. [20]And the Lord said, Who shall persuade Ahab, that he may go up and fall at Ramothgilead? And one said on this manner, and another said on that manner. [21]And there came forth a spirit, and stood before the Lord, and said, I will persuade him. [22]And the Lord said unto him, Wherewith? And he said, I will go forth, and I will be a lying spirit in the mouth of all his prophets. And he said, Thou shalt persuade him, and prevail also: go forth, and do so. [23]Now therefore, behold, the Lord hath put a lying spirit in the mouth of all these thy prophets, and the Lord hath spoken evil concerning thee. [24]But Zedekiah the son of Chenaanah went near, and smote Micaiah on the cheek, and said, Which way went the Spirit of the Lord from me to speak unto thee? [25]And Micaiah said, Behold, thou shalt see in that day, when thou shalt go into an inner chamber to hide thyself. [26]And the king of Israel said, Take Micaiah, and carry him back unto Amon the governor of the city, and to Joash the king's son; [27]And say, Thus saith the king, Put this fellow in the prison, and feed him with bread of affliction and with water of affliction, until I come in peace. [28]And Micaiah said, If thou return at all in peace, the Lord hath not spoken by me. And he said, Hearken, O people, every one of you. (vss. 6-28)

By comparing the circumstances of Pharaoh in Exodus with the story of Ahab in 1 Kings 22, it seems *quite reasonable* to suggest that the Lord, at some point, allowed an evil spirit to incite Pharaoh toward the rebellion to which Pharaoh had already committed himself. We know it is the nature of the demonic world to so interfere in human events. "For we wrestle not against flesh and blood," said the Apostle Paul, "but against principalities, against powers, against the rulers of the darkness of this world, against spiritual wickedness in high places" (Eph. 6:12). The Bible does not often highlight these situations in which the Enemy gains the Lord's reluctant permission, but we may consider them implied (cp. 2 Sam. 24:1ff with 1 Chr. 21:1ff). Indeed, what other situation for involvement would the Enemy have preferred, if not one where God's people might continue in bondage under the hand of an oppressive and godless ruler? It would be naive indeed to imagine that Satan (whom the Bible refers to as the *god of this world* and as the *prince of the power of the air*) would quietly lay aside, while so much was at stake between Pharaoh and the children of Israel.

Even so are there two choices of interpretation facing the reader of 1 Kings 22. The first is the Calvinistic view in which God is thought to send lying spirits to deceive men because He (though blameless!) has pleasure in watching wicked men perish in their own foolishness. This view reduces the Bible to a ridiculous book by depicting an arbitrary God who is pleased to put humans into impossible predicaments which God Himself decrees and in which there is no escape. In effect, this is Robert Frost's view of the Christian God in the *Masque of Reason*. Sadly, many people conclude that God is exactly this kind of controlling and uncaring Being. This is not a correct view, of course, and thus no necessity is laid upon the Bible student to so interpret 1 Kings 22 along Calvinistic lines. Rather, because the Bible tells us that God takes no pleasure in the death of the wicked but that the wicked turn from his way and live, we ought to understand that 1 Kings 22 and Job 1—2 (the latter as earlier discussed) show that God takes no pleasure in allowing the Enemy to wreak havoc with men. Therefore God rules *over* the demonic powers so that they need not overwhelm man. Remember, there is all the moral difference in the world between God ruling *over* the activity of demons and God *ruling* the activity of demons. The former means that God reluctantly *allows* demons to afflict men (and only then upon certain conditions), while the latter means that God *commands* demons to 'their' unrelenting, evil activities. Calvinists believe that God *commands* demons to do what they do, and that such demonic activity is used by God and somehow inexplicably accords with His good pleasure.

A fairer reading of 1 Kings 22 shows that God simply acceded to what King Ahab already wanted, i.e., to listen to his false prophets. Twice, in fact, King Ahab of Israel complains to King Jehoshaphat of Judah that the Lord's prophet, Micaiah, never says anything good about him but speaks of calamity only. Ahab, far from being thankful for God's warning, is resentful once Micaiah gives him the word of the Lord. The question, then, is why God should be patient with Ahab at all, since the king had rejected His messenger repeatedly? Yet 1 Kings 22 shows God extending even *more* patience toward Ahab by having Micaiah tell the king exactly what evil spirits had been doing to plot his downfall. Here, then, is *another* warning by God, and Ahab likewise rejects this further warning, even as he rejected the first. Thus the whole tenor of this passage is certainly against the Calvinistic interpretation that God is commanding demons after His good pleasure to do his bidding. *Indeed, if God's real intent was to command demons to lie and deceive Ahab, why would He bother warning Ahab about it?* That would mean God was trying to warn Ahab against the very disaster to which he was trying to entice him! And if that were the case, then God would be acting against Himself.[78] Despite what conclusion about God's nature the Calvinist is forced to embrace (because of his theology), God is not divided against Himself, as Christ made clear.

Like the warning given to Ahab, God's mercy in Exodus is extended to Pharaoh in divine warnings about upcoming plagues. After a certain point in the course of the plagues, it may have been that the warning was more for the Egyptians' sake than for Pharaoh's, as some of the Egyptians (though not Pharaoh) heeded God's warning and removed their livestock from the open fields prior to the 7th plague. In short, God's acts of patience with Pharaoh and Ahab show to what incredible lengths God will go on behalf of sinful men. In fact, Ahab was the only king in Scripture who was ever told of impending disaster in a way that so exposed demonic activity. *We should observe in particular that 1 Kings 22:23 describes God in language <u>as though</u> He is the direct, causal agent, when the context of the entire passage shows that He is not.* Says Micaiah to Ahab: "Now therefore behold, the Lord hath put a lying spirit in the mouth of all these thy prophets, and the Lord hath spoken evil concerning thee." (Remember that the word *evil* in Hebrew may also be translated *disaster* or *calamity*; it comes from a root word that properly means *to spoil*, literally, by *breaking* in pieces). The point here is that the Lord is described by Micaiah as Someone who has put a lying spirit in the mouth of the false prophets, while the context shows that God is doing this by *permission*, not *commandment* (even warning Ahab in the process). The lying spirit helps the false prophets to speak lies into Ahab's ear about all that the king wants to believe about his future. As for God, it appears that He feels so grieved, just by being permissively involved, that He describes Himself as though He were the direct, causal agent. Again, it is an idiomatic way of speaking, which the entire context of 1 Kings 22 demonstrates. In reality, then, God is not sending Ahab what *He* wants, but rather what *Ahab* wants.[79]

Idiomatic Language in the Phrase, 'The Lord Hardened'

Based on our review, the relevancy of 1 Kings 22 to the situation of Pharaoh in Exodus is more than suggestive. The Lord says in Exodus 7:3 (note: not 7:<u>13</u>) that He will *harden* Pharaoh's heart [rightly translated here from *qashah* [80] (Strong's #7185), the third Hebrew verb mentioned earlier], yet such a statement must be understood in the same idiomatic sense as when the Bible tells us that God sent a lying spirit to Ahab. Both passages use idiomatic language to achieve the sense of Who truly oversees the universe. "The Lord hath sent a lying spirit" in 1 Kings 22 is a stronger way of stating God's overall governing of the universe than merely stating "God has allowed a lying spirit (etc.)." This subtlety and especially the extent of such idiomatic language is generally foreign to the concrete, Western mind.[81]

But to return again to a consideration of the first Hebrew word, *chazaq* (*Strong's* #2388), note that: 1) it occurs for the first time in Exodus 9:12 regarding the Lord's activity upon Pharaoh's heart; and 2) that it appears between the sixth and seventh plagues. (See the two charts, beginning p. 296, at the end of this chapter.) As we have seen, this particular Hebrew word is sometimes properly understood as *fasten* or *seize*. Thus, an additional meaning for *fastened* (or *seized*) beyond the primary meaning of *strengthened*, which we have already observed for *chazaq*, may perhaps be implied for Exodus 9:12. This would yield an additional meaning of "*the Lord fastened (i.e., seized) Pharaoh's heart.*" What exactly does this mean—to *seize*, or *fasten*? In one sense it seems as though it should mean that God *seizes* Pharaoh with His plague judgments in an inescapable confrontation. Personally, the picture that comes to my mind is that of a cowboy breaking a bronco. The cowboy has fastened himself upon the animal's back—seizing the horse's spirit, so to speak, and forcing it into an inescapable 'showdown.' The fact that the man owns the horse is not even understood by the horse. Instead, the horse is incited against the cowboy for trying to subject him to obedience. Thus the horse does not recognize the cowboy's authority and so tries to throw him off by trickery and force. If the horse never comes to recognize the authority of the cowboy he may continue to buck until he dies. The main incongruence with this analogy, of course, is that most horses come to accept the will of their master, while most men do not accept the will of their own Creator in heaven nor acknowledge him as Master. And Pharaoh, to be sure, was as most men. As the one in Egypt who stood to lose the highest position and most power, Pharaoh refused to yield to God's demand for obedience, even when his servants told him, "Knowest thou not that Egypt lies in ruins?" Pharaoh would, in effect, go down bucking.

Nevertheless, although in one sense it is true that God *seized* Pharaoh insofar as removing His Spirit from striving with him [therefore relegating Pharaoh to the practical (though technically not hypothetical) impossibility of repentance (i.e., allowing Pharaoh to self-destruct)], it appears here that the primary meaning of *chazaq* is something different given the context. That is, while the above is true in one sense, i.e., that the Lord fully roused Pharaoh with the bringing of plagues, this is not, at the least, primarily what is being specifically referred to, when the Scripture says that the Lord *chazaq* Pharaoh (mentioned in 9:12). We may grant this conclusion because the Hebrew verb, with its Piel stem in the Imperfect Mood showing the beginning of the fulfillment of 4:21, had not occurred up through the 6th plague. In other words, up through plague six it has not yet been stated that the Lord strengthened Pharaoh's heart, despite the fact that the Lord's activity was, of course, generally present in the sense of His having brought the plagues. Moreover, Pharaoh was given opportunities up to the 6th plague to irretractably repent prior to the Lord's 'strengthening' of him. Thus, by default, it appears that the *'strengthening'* referred to in 9:12 is meant to be idiomatically understood as *God allowing the **Enemy** to seize* Pharaoh on repeated occasions after each latter plague event (the Enemy being somewhat like an uncaring cowboy driving his spirited horse to a greater distance in a shorter period of time than what the animal would even have done on its own). Thus all the above reasons are why we may suggest that 1 Kings 22 speaks into Exodus 9:12 here, and that the Bible is implying that this is the point at which God sends a lying (or rebellious) spirit (or spirits) to influence Pharaoh. Again, as in 1 Kings 22, God does this by permission (not commandment) at the behest of the Enemy. The particular strength of this argument is to notice that the Lord 'hardened' Pharaoh's heart at a point in time when *the Egyptian magicians could no longer stand before Moses*. For note in particular that 9:12 is the first appearance of *chazaq* insofar as it relates *de facto* to the Lord's activity in the entire exodus narrative, and that this appearance comes immediately after we are told in 9:11 about the magicians' inability to stand before Moses. I believe this fact is very suggestive, since presumably Pharaoh was now without these regular advisors, i.e., those who, sick with boils and having 'lost face' (and therefore their moral authority), proved unable to contest with Moses and resist the effects of the Lord's plague upon their own selves. (We will take up the full significance of this point about the absence of Pharaoh's advisors in a moment.) Note also that now with the Enemy's influence Pharaoh would be fully roused, a stated condition to which the Lord gives witness four verses later.

Now it should be observed that another idiomatic statement follows on the heels of the 6th plague. For in the contiguous passage of Exodus 9:34-10:1, the Hebrew word *kabad* (*made heavy*) is used in reference not only to Pharaoh and the Egyptians "hardening" (Heb. *kabad*, i.e., *honoring, making heavy*) their hearts (Ex. 9:34), but also in reference to the Lord who hardened" (*kabad, honored*) their hearts (Ex. 10:1). At first, the Scripture's use of *kabad* might strike us as strange, for what could be meant when the Bible tells us that the Lord *honored* the hearts of Pharaoh and the Egyptians? To answer that, we must look at the lexical meaning of the Hebrew word *kabad*. And in fact it *is* most frequently translated as *honour* in the KJV, thus: "Honour (*kabad*) thy father and thy mother." Even more notably for our present discussion is Exodus 14:17: "I will get me honour (*kabad*) upon Pharaoh, and upon all his host." Thus God strengthens Pharaoh's heart according to Pharaoh's own course, and by so doing, *honors* Pharaoh's heart. Again, it seems awkward to say that God would 'honor' an evil Pharaoh, but what is merely being stated here is that Pharaoh's heart has been strengthened to a heavier state, and that God has thus honored Pharaoh's heart by deferring to it for a time (in the sense of allowing him to rule over

His people Israel despite his not letting Israel go), even though He does not approve of what Pharaoh is doing. That is, God defers to Pharaoh's heart for the purpose of allowing Pharaoh's choice to exalt itself **unto effect** over God's own ideal plan.[82] (Again, this has nothing whatsoever to do with God *approving* of Pharaoh's decision.) Thus Pharaoh was one of those willful vessels whom Paul says God endured with much longsuffering, obviously not because God Himself ordained that His own patience be so tried(!), but rather that other vessels might erstwhile receive mercy, and perhaps also that it might be shown evident that man is the god that Christ said he was—a god who decides his own intention in all matters unto eternal liability (see Jn. 10:34); for in fact that is part of the unchanging definition of man. (Yet it should be noted that we, as creaturely gods, are still subject to the eventual and inescapable judgment of the Creator God Himself—the *King of kings and Lord of lords*, who alone has an eternal past and upholds all *forms*[83] by His own power.) Now observe that these two statements about the Lord strengthening (*chazaq*, Ex. 9:12) Pharaoh's heart and the Lord honoring (*kabad*) Pharaoh's heart (Ex. 10:1) occur on either side of a very specific warning that the Lord gives Pharaoh in Exodus 9:13-19, in which He warns the Egyptian king to put his men and cattle under cover to save them from an upcoming plague of hail. Some of the Egyptians heed the warning, but Pharaoh refuses to listen and the seventh plague ends in great disaster for Egypt. Note the timing here, for it was immediately prior to this warning that the Lord stated the effect of His strengthening of Pharaoh's heart in 9:12, which apparently effected Pharaoh's servants, too. Thus God states in 10:1 that He has 'hardened' (*kabad*, i.e., *honored*) Pharaoh's heart and the hearts of his servants. This statement in 10:1 as rendered by the KJV makes God appear as if He were hardening, and therefore forcing, Pharaoh and his servants to disbelieve Him. Calvinists would certainly hold this position, i.e., that Pharaoh and his servants simply mimicked the constructs of disbelief which God had already determined upon them.

Calvinists apply the same kind of deterministic interpretation implied in the KJV's Romans 9:18: "Therefore hath he mercy on whom he will have mercy, and whom he will he hardeneth." The NAS gives the accurate lexical rendering in this case, changing 'will' to 'desire,' thus stating that God *desires* to harden certain people, such as Pharaoh. On the surface this sounds like God wants these people to be damned according to His desire (good pleasure). Thus the NAS renders it, "So then He has mercy on whom He desires, and he hardens whom He desires." On the surface of things, this sounds like some men are predestined to be damned. Though a Calvinist will often (to state it colloquially) 'talk out of both sides of his mouth' in order to dance around this issue of how God, if He hardens people, is not then responsible for the evil actions of those He hardens, the Calvinist nevertheless believes that men are hardened and therefore never really have a chance at receiving God's mercy. (Indeed, if this assessment of the Calvinist is not true, then why is there a doctrine of Reprobation?) The question, then, is whether the Bible really teaches that God *desires* to 'harden' people without ever giving them repeated chances of repentance?

I believe a first step in understanding what the (NAS) Scripture means when it says that the Lord *desires* to harden people (such as Pharaoh) is to consider whether God 'desires' to do everything He 'does.' Take Job 1—2, for example. When God places Job's children into Satan's power to do unto them as Satan himself wishes, is it right for us to say that what subsequently happened to Job's children was something God *desired*? No, it is clear from the entire context of Job 2 that God merely allowed this event because He was incited to do it. He even *says* He was incited to do it. So the only sense in which God could be said to *desire* that Satan have power over Job's possessions (including his children), is in the sense that God *desired* to *allow* Satan to have such power, which (in this case) is as much to say that He did not at all desire that Satan use his power as he did. Thus, when God says that He 'ruined' Job, He speaks idiomatically as though He were the causal agent, when, in fact, the narrative shows He is not.

An example, here, will further clarify how idiomatic expressions work. Let us say that a parent tires of telling his child not to touch the electric element on the family's kitchen stove. Yet one day he sees the child about to burn his finger on a heating element that was accidentally left on at its lowest setting. But rather than intervene, he allows the child to do what he wants. Soon the child is crying in pain (due more to surprise than actual hurt), and the parent attends to the slight wound. Would we say that the parent *desired* that the child hurt himself? No, certainly not. The parent would have preferred that the child be obedient. He might even describe the finger-burning incident to another parent by saying, "My son kept trying to touch the hot stove at our home, so finally *I set his finger to it*." Here the parent is using language in an idiomatic way. What is being said is understood in the context of the conversation not to have literally taken place. Rather, the parent allowed the child to hurt himself slightly, so that a greater danger would be avoided when the parent was outside the house or in a far corner of the home where the child could not be as immediately watched. Now, the way Bible students know when idiomatic expressions are being used is to understand what is being communicated in the entire context of a given passage and in the general message of the Bible. And we have now seen what "hardening" means in context. Thus, **were** the Bible to state that God 'desires' to harden certain men, it could only mean that God would desire to allow men to harden themselves (which may include their acquiescence to the augmenting work of the Enemy). But, in fact, the Bible never states that this is the case with God at the beginning of His relationship with any man. It would appear that God only desires to indurate a man if that man has spurned God repeatedly to a point of instinctual rejection. So, when God does allow a man to become indurate He does so for a simple reason, because it pleases Him that His Spirit should not always strive with man. Therefore, to claim that a man is damned from the very beginning is to deny that God has love for every man and is no respecter of persons (see Rom. 2:11). Further, the Scripture states repeatedly in the prophetic books that sinners should repent, and elsewhere states that God does not desire the death of the wicked (Ezek. 33:11), and that God "is longsuffering to us-ward, not willing that *any* should perish, but that all should come to repentance" (2 Pet. 3:9).[84]

Again, the idiomatic expressions of God's permissive will in Job 1—2 and 1 Kings 22 (the latter speaking of God 'sending' a lying spirit) thus help us to understand Exodus 10:1. When the Lord says that He hardened (*honored*) the heart of Pharaoh, we understand that it doesn't mean that God *made* the Egyptian king reject Him. Pharaoh had been on the path of disbelief for a long time before God ever used Moses to confront him. The Egyptian king could have responded differently at any one of many points but chose not to repent; "Who is the Lord God that I should obey his voice?" Pharaoh wanted to believe what Pharaoh wanted to believe, and God upheld the form of Pharaoh in his choice. By "form" I mean that God sustained Pharaoh's earthly body despite Pharaoh's disobedience. God also allowed the Enemy (the Devil and/or his demons) to influence Pharaoh because Pharaoh had *continually* shown that he wanted to rebel against God. That is what Pharaoh wanted for himself. God will often keep evil spirits at bay until a person's own will has become very, very determined. Furthermore, because Pharaoh hardened his own heart he cannot be excused as simply a victim of demonic activity. Indeed, he has no more excuse than would King Ahab of Israel. When we further consider that Pharaoh was a man who actually claimed *to be* of deity (this belief was part of the structure of Egyptian religion) and subjected with great cruelty an entire race to slavery for his own aggrandizement—a race, in fact, that suffered partial genocide only a few generations earlier (see Exodus 1)—we have to admit that Pharaoh and his predecessors had been in the process of searing their consciences and strengthening their hearts against God long before God ever appeared to Moses in the burning bush. When Moses appears in Pharaoh's court, the Egyptian king still believes he is in control. God instructs Moses to perform a miraculous sign to show the Egyptian king that he will not be in control of any contest with Yahweh, the God of Israel. Pharaoh, however, foolishly refuses this chance to avoid judgment. God then strikes Egypt with a series of six plagues, offering Pharaoh a window of repentance after each one of them. Still, Pharaoh will not listen. At this point (as we have been contending here in this chapter) God 'strengthens'[85] Pharaoh's heart, i.e., releases him to his own wayward decision by deciding not to strive further with him and, presumably, to allow demonic forces to augment what Pharaoh has been desiring all along. (There will still be opportunities for repentance, but they will not be realistic ones, *per se*.) In effect, God has been asking Pharaoh in the course of the first six plagues, "Is rebellion what you *really, really, really* want?," and Pharaoh has been replying, "Yes, rebellion is what I *really, really, really* want." So finally God says, "So be it." As C.S. Lewis has stated this matter of man's will in opposition to God's: "Either man says to God, 'Thy will be done,' or God says to man, 'Thy will be done.' " So Pharaoh grows ever more stubborn until the Lord uses the 10th plague to kill his firstborn son. At that point Pharaoh lets the Israelites go, though a short time later he changes his mind and chases after them.

The further commands that God gives to Pharaoh about letting His people go are still commands which God would delight in seeing obeyed. But now, in the absence of obedience, and because divine patience is exhausted, God will now take pleasure (albeit a lesser pleasure than were the man to repent)[86] in allowing Himself to cease from striving against Pharaoh with His Spirit, even unto the man's own hardening.

Let us consider, then, the overall mercy which God showed to Pharaoh, and how Pharaoh nevertheless stubbornly rejected *en masse* all of God's offers for leniency. As we do, we feel no obligation to believe, as Calvinists insist, that the Lord *hardened* (*chazaq*) Pharaoh's heart in the sense of designing his destruction from the very beginning, i.e., of seeing that Pharaoh cooperated with a divine plan for his own reprobation. Rather, the idiomatic way in which God sometimes speaks, as in the phrase, "The Lord *strengthened* Pharaoh's heart," must be remembered as a pronounced decree. And such a pronouncement does not nullify God's *greater* desire to see Pharaoh repent and obey, though in fact no man chooses to come to God apart from divine merciful urging. At any rate, idiomatic references must be recognized for what they are. And in short, active verbs (e.g. Romans 9:17 "I *harden*") do not always indicate causality. Indeed, the process of man's *self*-reprobation, as seen in Pharaoh, is what Romans 1 actually teaches us. Men knew God but glorified Him not as God. They also refused to thank Him for His blessings and worshipped the creation instead of the Creator. Therefore God finally gave them up to their own desires. Even so, Pharaoh knew God but refused to glorify Him. Consequently, he grew futile in his imagination and served the creation (e.g., numerous Egyptian gods, including Ra the Sun god) instead of the one true Creator God. Notice again with what mercy God approached the hard-hearted, unsaved Egyptian king. He did not demand at the first that Pharaoh bend his knee and worship God, but merely that Pharaoh recognize within his own mind that a God of Israel existed. Even this Pharaoh would not do. Plague upon plague arrived by divine command as God ratcheted up the tension on

Pharaoh. Finally, because of their boils, the magicians could no longer stand before Moses nor presumably also before Pharaoh. No longer, then, could Satan make use of these courtiers who had stood by Pharaoh's side and often incited the Egyptian king with tricks, and by giving chorus to Pharaoh's roused indignation against Moses and Aaron. These magicians were now absent from Pharaoh's presence, as those whose boil-infested bodies argued their own counteracting ineffectiveness and loss of moral authority. Surely this change in circumstance would hardly have been lost upon the Devil. Other means must be found to replace the influence of the magicians—(the false prophets, so to speak, of Pharaoh's court). As we contemplate Satan's methods, and how hundreds of years afterward he (or his underling) would act to harden the heart of King Ahab of Israel (not to mention the Enemy's much earlier attempt to harden the heart of Job), is it, indeed, so far-fetched to presume that Satan would use whatever means God would allow him, in order to incite Pharaoh to greater rebellion? Remember, when Exodus 9:12 states for the first time that the Lord *strengthened* Pharaoh, this statement occurs *in the very next verse* after we are told the Egyptian magicians could no longer stand before Moses. We can imagine, then, what likely argument the Devil presented to God when asking to commence direct activity upon Pharaoh's mind. "Will you deny Pharaoh any advisors and overwhelm him? Have you not robbed the king of his counselors—counselors to whom he is entitled? And if boils make it impossible for a man to stand before Pharaoh, shouldn't Pharaoh have counselors like those whom he himself would choose?" Thus, in Exodus 9:12 I am contending that God gave Satan permission to directly influence Pharaoh's heart. Satan may have used the magicians previously, but now his direct influence would presumably be even greater. Granting this, the appearance of *qashah* (the third Hebrew word in this study) in Exodus 7:3, which precedes the entire narrative of plagues, serves as a kind of marker of introduction (the word will not return until its reappearance in 13:15), in which God states (by His foreknowledge) the *synopsis* regarding Pharaoh, due to Pharaoh's own responses after demonic activity *seizes* and *fastens* him to his own miry path following the latter plagues of 7, 8, and 9. The final result we observe is that Pharaoh "would *hardly (stubbornly refuse to)* let the children of Israel go" (Ex. 13:15). There is one other noteworthy feature about Exodus 7:3. It is the only time this particular Hebrew verb (*qashah*) is used in the Exodus narrative to refer to God's activity. In fact, it is God Himself who says He will *qashah* (*harden*) Pharaoh's heart, and note again that we do not come across this word referring to the Lord's activity until its fulfillment in Exodus 13:15 (again, see charts beginning on p. 296). Let us remember that *qashah* literally means *dense, tough, severe, cruel, fierce,* etc. When the Lord says that He will *qashah* (make dense, tough, severe, i.e., *harden*) Pharaoh's heart, I believe He is synopsizing the entire process of

'His'[87] strengthening and honoring of Pharaoh's heart, according to Pharaoh's own hardness.

Further Similarity Between Exodus and Job

Now, note further that the only time the 2nd Hebrew word, *kabad*, refers to the Lord's honoring of Pharaoh's heart (Ex. 10:1) is *after* the first time we are told that the Lord *chazaq (strengthened)* Pharaoh's heart in Exodus 9:12. An interesting, approximate parallel can thus be observed between Satan's activity in Exodus and his activity in the book of Job (which we examined earlier). The form of attack is somewhat different, since Satan's primary goal for Pharaoh is to strengthen a heartset already publicly manifest, while with Job the goal was to remove the supporting superstructure of his possessions so that Job's real character (according to Satan) would emerge publicly, thus putting God to shame. For Satan the difference between the two men is merely one of profession, not of actual heart. But the main point in Job 2 is to note how God idiomatically states to Satan that He is the causal agent of events, when contextually it is understood that He is merely allowing Satan to act in deference to what He truly wants. *Now observe further that this statement of God to Satan in Job 2:3 (about being incited to ruin Job) occurs in the* **immediate aftermath** *of Satanic activity, which commenced when Satan received permission to attack Job for the first time.* In other words, the process is:

> 1) Satanic activity is undertaken against a target after the Lord grants Satan permission (compare Job 1:12 with Ex. 9:12). Also, compare the Satanic activity of Job 1:13-19 (aimed at suggesting to Job that God ought to be rebelled against) with the Satanic suggestion that led to the 'hardening' (strengthening) of Pharaoh and his servants (see Ex. 9:34).
> 2) The Lord speaks idiomatically to say that He was the direct causal agent, even though the overall biblical context shows that He is *not* causally responsible (cp. Job 2:3 with Ex. 10:1 and Ezek. 33:11).

The following comparisons of Satan's activity should help to explain some of the similarities between Exodus and Job:

First Comparison

Job 1:12 Satan gains permission to 'emerge' the character of Job in an attempt to *demonstrate* its hypocrisy and rebellion.
Ex. 9:12 Satan gains permission to strengthen Pharaoh's heart to augment the rebellion already demonstrated.

Second Comparison

Job 1—2 The result of Satan's activity leads God to idiomatically say that *He* had ruined Job. The context, however, shows that God was incited and merely *allowed* Satan to do what he wanted.
Exodus 10:1 The result of Satan strengthening Pharaoh's heart leads God to idiomatically say that *He* had done the strengthening. Indeed, we also know this statement must be idiomatic since the book of James tells us that God tempts no man to sin (1:13).

Granting our argument thus far, note further that the word appearances describing the Lord's hardening of Pharaoh's heart involving *Strong's* word #2388 (*chazaq*) form separate instances, and, according to the principle we find in Job, would likewise presumably be *separate* instances in Exodus, i.e., in which the Lord granted the Enemy direct and further access to influence Pharaoh by strengthening his already rebellious heart.[88] Moreover, note carefully in the book of Job how Satan had to be granted *separate* permission for the two rounds of trial which he brought upon Job. Thus Satan could do nothing without God granting the permission to allow him his activity upon two *separate* occasions. Even so, in Exodus Satan would have presumably had to petition God during (or after) each *separate* plague (each of which constituted further, divine positive testimony) before hoping to intensify the *strengthening* of Pharaoh's heart against God through Satanic suggestion, and this would explain the repeated idiomatic statement that "the Lord *chazak* (*strengthened*) Pharaoh's heart."

To continue the comparison, we may also reasonably presume that God responded to Satan after the second round of Job's trial even as He did following the first. That is, presumably, God again pointed out to Satan that Job had maintained his integrity and not cursed God, despite Satan's inciting of Him 'to ruin' Job's *health* without cause. The Bible leaves many such statements merely implied, and while I am not at all arguing that such presumptions ever be granted the status of Scripture, it remains to be shown by any who would deny us the use of such presumptions how they are not biblically informed. Thus, granting the above assumption, we may further hypothesize that the reason the exodus narrative does not tell us that God *kabad* (*honored, made heavy*) Pharaoh's heart other than the one appearance found[89] in Exodus 10:1, is because such subsequent idiomatic utterances by God, while not explicitly stated in the biblical record, may nevertheless be taken as implied, as coming after each plague and after the activity of the Enemy, even as presumably God likewise similarly replied to Satan after Job's 2nd round of trial even as He did after the 1st round, that is, when God said He had 'ruined' Job. Again (and at any rate), the culmination of all the influential activity of the Enemy and even of Pharaoh himself upon himself is Pharaoh's induration (hence *Strong's* #7185, *to render stubborn, indurate, obstinate*). <u>This *synopsis* is arguably why Paul chose the Greek word *skleruno* (i.e., *to indurate, to render stubborn*), since it equates in Greek to the 3rd Hebrew word we have been studying, i.e., *qashah*, that is, when, in Romans 9:18, Paul speaks of God *hardening* Pharaoh. In other words, Paul is simply following the idiomatic and synopsistic usage of *qashah* as it appears in the exodus narrative.</u> To prevent any contradiction within true biblical theology, we must always maintain that God's intent and greatest desire for Pharaoh, while remedy was realistically possible, was that spiritual death of this wicked man be prevented.

The Process of Hardening

Although much discussion in this chapter has revolved around the strengthening, honoring, and hardening of Pharaoh's heart, we will nevertheless return to the subject of Pharaoh in the next chapter in order to critique A.W. Pink's view of Pharaoh's hardening within the context of the doctrine of Reprobation. At this point, however, it might be helpful to review the definitions of the three Hebrew words we have been studying, and to show from *Strong's* Concordance the actual order of their appearances in the exodus narrative. Remember that all three words were translated by the KJV and NAS as *hard/harden*).

> (*Strong's* #2388: *chazaq*), from a primitive root meaning *to fasten upon;* hence, *to seize, be strong* (figuratively, *courageous, causatively strengthen, cure, help, repair, fortify*), *obstinate, to bind, restrain, conquer, sieze, fasten*. (Note; although *Strong's* lists "harden" among the definitions, I have omitted it here, based on my argument that it is unwarranted, even as it is in #3513.)
> (*Strong's* #3513 and related word #3515; *kabad*), meaning *heavy, weighty, honored*.
> (*Strong's* #7185: *qashah*) meaning *dense, tough, severe, hard, cruel, fierce*.

Note below in the chart the first appearance of *chazaq* (#2388), and also the only appearance of *kabad* (#3513), as both relate idiomatically[20] to the Lord's activity, the former occurring immediately prior to the seventh plague, the latter occurring just after it.

Note also that Exodus 7:13 has here been changed to reflect the correct translation; thus, '*The heart of Pharaoh was strengthened*.' Observe also that the word "that" in the phrase, "I will harden Pharaoh's heart, *that* he shall follow after them [(i.e., follow after the children of Israel)]" is assumed by the translator. This treatment of '*that*' may, in the minds of some readers, lead them to infer that God is the causal agent, when, in fact, it should be taken idiomatically as a connective referring only to the Enemy's purpose in his activity.

Finally, where it says below that Pharaoh strengthened himself, it may be assumed that other human agencies—the magicians and sometimes Pharaoh's servants—helped in this process, though presumably to a lesser degree of intensity than that which God allowed the Enemy to commence between the 6th and 7th plague. In addition, the Hebrew verb stem and mood are given where applicable:

Ex. 4:21 (#2388) but I will *strengthen* his heart, that he
   Piel (Intensive); Mood Imperfect (Incomplete action)

Ex. 7:3 (#7185) I will *indurate (harden)* Pharaoh's heart,
   Hiphil (Causative); Imperfect (Incomplete action)

Ex. 7:13 (#2388) And Pharaoh's heart was *strengthened*
   Qal (simple, causal, active); Imperfect (Incomplete action)

Ex. 7:14 (#3515) Pharaoh's heart is *weighty* [*honored*]
   No Tense Given,[21] hence, presum. a stated condition (i.e., adj.)

Ex. 7:22 (#2388) Pharaoh's heart was *strengthened*
   Qal (simple, causal, active); Imperfect (Incomplete action)

Ex. 8:15 (#3513) *honored (made weighty)* his heart, and hearkened
   Hiphil (Causative); Infinitive (object -ing; hence, "he, giving weight to his heart, hearkened not....")

Ex. 8:19 (#2388) Pharaoh's heart was *strengthened*
   Qal (simple, causal, active); Imperfect (Incomplete action)

Ex. 8:32 (#3513) And Pharaoh *honored (made weighty)* his heart at
   Hiphil (Causative); Imperfect (Incomplete action)

Ex. 9:7 (#3515) heart of Pharaoh was *honored (made weighty)*
Qal (simple, causal, active); Imperfect (Incomplete action)

Ex. 9:12 (#2388) Lord *strengthened* the heart of Pharaoh
Piel (Intensive); Mood Imperfect (Incomplete action)

Note: Seventh plague occurs

Ex. 9:34 (#3513) sinned yet more, and *honored (made weighty)* his
Hiphil (Causative); Imperfect (Incomplete action)

Ex. 9:35 (#2388) the heart of Pharaoh was *strong*
Qal (simple, causal, active); Imperfect (Incomplete action)

Ex. 10:1 (#3513) I have *honored (made weighty)* his heart,
Hiphil (Causative); Perfect (Complete action)

Ex. 10:20 (#2388) the Lord *strengthened* Pharaoh's heart,
Piel (Intensive); Mood Imperfect (Incomplete action)

Ex. 10:27 (#2388) the Lord *strengthened* Pharaoh's heart,
Piel (Intensive); Mood Imperfect (Incomplete action)

Ex. 11:10 (#2388) the Lord *strengthened* Pharaoh's heart,
Piel (Intensive); Mood Imperfect (Incomplete action)

Ex. 13:15 (#7185) Pharaoh would *hardly (stubbornly refuse to)* let us go
Hiphil (Causative); Perfect (Complete action)

Ex. 14:4 (#2388) I will *strengthen* Pharaoh's heart,
Piel (Intensive); Perfect (Complete action)

Ex. 14:8 (#2388) So the Lord *strengthened* the heart of
Piel (Intensive); Mood Imperfect (Incomplete action)

Ex. 14:17 (#2388) will *strengthen* the hearts of the Egyptians
Piel (Intensive); Participle (unbroken continuity, emphasizing *to be*; i.e., "I will be strengthening to the strengthening of")

We should observe that the occasions when the Enemy was given permission to strengthen Pharaoh's heart (i.e., granting our argument) are occasions when the Piel stem indicating an *intensive* activity would be appropriate (and in fact are present).

Below is another chart showing the occurrence of the three Hebrew words (Eng. *strengthen, honor, harden*) in relation to the chronology of plagues:

> 4:21 And the Lord said unto Moses, When thou goest to return into Egypt, see that thou do all those wonders before Pharaoh, which I have put in thine hand: but I will *strengthen (seize)* [Piel (Intensive); Imperfect (Incomplete action)] his heart, that he shall not let the people go.
>
> 7:3 And I will harden *(indurate, harden)* [Hiphil (Causative); Imperfect (Complete action)] Pharaoh's heart, and multiply my signs and my wonders in the land of Egypt.

God turns Moses' rod into a serpent in the presence of Pharaoh, has it eat the magicians' snakes, then turns it back into a rod again.

> 7:13-14 (corrected from "And he hardened Pharaoh's heart") And Pharaoh's heart was *strengthened* [Qal (simple, causal, active); Imperfect (Incomplete action)], that he hearkened not unto them;[92] as the Lord had said. And the Lord said unto Moses, Pharaoh's heart is *weighty (honored)*, he refuses to let the people go.

Moses lifts up his rod in the sight of Pharaoh and smites the Nile's waters; the Nile and its tributaries become blood (1st plague).

> 7:22 And the magicians of Egypt did so with their enchantments: and Pharaoh's heart was *strengthened* [Qal (simple, causal, active); Imperfect (Incomplete action)], neither did he hearken unto them; as the Lord had said.

God brings frogs to cover Egypt (2nd plague); Pharaoh promises to free Israel if God will remove the plague; God removes the frogs.

> 8:15 But when Pharaoh saw that there was respite, he *honored (gave weight to)* [Hiphil (Causative); Infinitive (object -ing; hence, "he, giving weight to his heart, hearkened not...")], his heart, and hearkened not unto them; as the Lord had said.

God brings gnats to cover Egypt (3rd plague).

> 8:19 Then the magicians said unto Pharaoh, This is the finger of God: and Pharaoh's heart was *strengthened* [Qal (simple, causal, active); Imperfect (Incomplete action)], and he hearkened not unto them; as the Lord had said.

God brings a swarm of flies to cover Egypt (4th plague); Pharaoh promises to free Israel; God removes the flies.

> 8:32 And Pharaoh *honored (gave weight to)* [Hiphil (Causative); Imperfect (Incomplete action)] his heart at this time also, neither would he let the people go.

God strikes the livestock of Egypt, and all the cattle die (5th plague).

> 9:7 And Pharaoh sent, and, behold, there was not one of the cattle of the Israelites dead. And the heart of Pharaoh was *weighted (honored)* [Qal (simple, causal, active); Imperfect (Incomplete action)], and he did not let the people go.

God strikes the Egyptians and the animals of Egypt with boils (6th plague). The magicians are not able to stand before Moses because of their boils.

> 9:12 And the Lord *strengthened (made strong, or seized, and so similarly below)* [Piel (Intensive); Imperfect (Incomplete action)] the heart of Pharaoh, and he hearkened not unto them; as the Lord had spoken unto Moses.

The Lord sends hail mingled with fire (7th plague). The nature of this plague is unprecedented in Egypt. Pharaoh promises to free Israel if God will stop the plague. God stops the plague.

> 9:34-10:1 And when Pharaoh saw that the rain and the hail and the thunders were ceased, he sinned yet more, and *gave weight to (honored)* [Hiphil (Causative); Imperfect (Incomplete action)] his heart, he and his servants. And the heart of Pharaoh was *strengthened* [Qal (simple, causal, active); Imperfect (Incomplete action)], neither

would he let the children of Israel go; as the Lord
had spoken by Moses. And the Lord said unto
Moses, Go in unto Pharaoh: for I have honored
(*made weighty*) [Hiphil (Causative); Perfect
(Complete action)] his heart, and the heart of his
servants, that[93] I might show these my signs
before him:

God sends a plague of locusts (8th plague). Pharaoh promises to free Israel. God removes the locusts with a great west wind.

10:20 But the Lord *strengthened* [Piel (Intensive);
Imperfect (Incomplete action)] Pharaoh's heart,
so that he would not let the children of Israel go.

God sends three days of darkness upon the land of Egypt (9th plague). Pharaoh promises to let Israel go if they will leave their livestock behind. Moses replies that the livestock are needed for sacrifice.

10:27 But the Lord *strengthened* [Piel (Intensive);
Imperfect (Incomplete action)] Pharaoh's heart,
and he would not let them go.

God instructs Moses to tell Pharaoh that He will kill the firstborn of Egypt (10th plague), from the throne of Pharaoh to the (lowly) maidservant behind the mill. The firstborn of Egypt's beasts will also die.

11:10 And Moses and Aaron did all these wonders
before Pharaoh: and the Lord *strengthened* [Piel
(Intensive); Imperfect (Incomplete action)]
Pharaoh's heart, so that he would not let the
children of Israel go out of his land.

Note: The phrase in the above verse ("these wonders") appears to refer only to the first nine plagues, since the Lord had yet to bring the last plague. Pharaoh and the Egyptians are defeated by the 10th plague (death of their firstborn sons and beasts). The Hebrews avoid the death of their firstborn by believing God regarding the Passover, a special meal which involved the slaying of an unblemished lamb (which, as esp. the gospel of John shows, pointed to the coming Messiah, the Lamb of God).

13:(14)-15 And it shall be when thy son asketh thee in
time to come, saying, What is this? that thou shalt

> say unto him, By strength of hand the Lord brought us out from Egypt, from the house of bondage: And it came to pass, when Pharaoh would *hardly (stubbornly refuse to)* [Hiphil (Causative); Perfect (Complete action)] let us go, that the Lord slew all the firstborn in the land of Egypt, both the firstborn of man, and the firstborn of beast: therefore I sacrifice to the Lord all that openeth the matrix, being males; but all the firstborn of my children I redeem.
>
> 14:4 And I will *strengthen* [Piel (Intensive); Perfect (Complete action)] Pharaoh's heart, that he shall follow after them; and I will be honored upon Pharaoh, and upon all his host; that the Egyptians may know that I am the Lord. And they did so.

The firstborn in every Egyptian household and the firstborn among Egyptian beasts die in the 10th plague. The Egyptians, gripped with terror that they might all die, plead with the people of Israel to get out of their land. After the Israelis leave, Pharaoh and his servants regret that they have let Israel go.

> 14:8 And the Lord *strengthened* [Piel (Intensive); Imperfect (Incomplete action)] the heart of Pharaoh king of Egypt, and he pursued after the children of Israel: and the children of Israel went out with an high hand.
>
> 14:17 And I, behold, I will *strengthen* [Piel (Intensive); Participle (unbroken continuity, emphasizing *to be*; i.e., "I will be strengthening to the strengthening of")] the hearts of the Egyptians, and they shall follow them: and I will get me honour upon Pharaoh, and upon all his host, upon his chariots, and upon his horsemen.

The Egyptian army pursues Israel into the Red Sea and is drowned.

The Mercy of God

One of the lessons we can learn from the exodus is that God does not remain unknown to the Egyptians just because Pharaoh acts foolishly. In the end Jehovah's name and power is demonstrated at considerable cost to Pharaoh and the Egyptians. But this is never the preferred way of God. He does not *prefer* the death of the wicked in the process of making His name known, but prefers that they recognize Him and obtain His mercy. Moses chose to heed the sign of the burning bush in the Midian wilderness, but Pharaoh refused to heed much greater signs and wonders in the heavens. Nevertheless, God is not mocked, and His power and mercy will not be subject to anonymity just because a ruler or a nation does not wish to retain Him in their knowledge.

As we look back upon the example of Pharaoh, perhaps the most important lesson to understand is that God is not arbitrary in His dealings with men but is patient with all. He gives all men opportunity for repentance before ever thinking to bring upon them irreparable destruction. In short, God's judgments, when they finally come, are fair because they are in accord with His good nature.

Finally, we tend to think the story of the exodus stops with Pharaoh's death, but in a sense it does not. Hundred of years later the Enemy is described in 1 Kings 22 as still relentlessly trying to defeat the children of Israel, this time by persuading King Ahab, ruler of the northern tribes of Israel, to go to an ill-advised war. Pharaoh, Ahab, and many other men throughout history have met incredibly tragic and unnecessary ends because of allowing the Enemy to feed into their own foolish desires. What sadness God must feel to know that He can deliver a ruler and people if only they will look to Him. The examples of Sidon, Chorazin, Bethsaida—all were cities that Christ said needlessly perished. Even the city of Jerusalem could have averted its destruction in 70 A.D., had only it recognized its Messiah. As Christ said:

> O Jerusalem, Jerusalem, thou that kills the prophets, and stones them which are sent unto thee, how often <u>would I have</u> gathered thy children together, even as a hen gathers her chickens under her wings, and <u>ye would not</u>! (Mt. 23:37).

Biblical stories about cities and nations are so old that we practically forget that these histories could have been different. Indeed, the book of Exodus, too, could have turned out different: it didn't have to read the way it does. God has a plan for good for every nation, but so often a ruler and nation reject that plan. Sadly, this is what Pharaoh and the Egyptians did. As we look back upon the exodus narrative and think about the nature of God, each one of us ought to ask the question: Does God really *cause* a person's heart to be hardened? And what will one believe about the Lord *strengthening* Pharaoh's heart if one refuses to take such a statement as idiomatic expression? The only alternative I personally see is to accept the contradiction that God commands repentance from certain persons whom

He predestines unto disobedience. Unfortunately, this conclusion is exactly what the Calvinist accepts. He embraces this contradiction along with certain other contradictions in his general apologetic, *calls* them non-contradictions, and then proceeds with great ingenuity to defend these contradictions. This is the methodology of Calvinism—to *embrace* contradictionism without naming it as such (nor admitting to it). Furthermore, Calvinists attempt to defend their contradictionism with (of all things!) *Scripture*, such as when they allege that 'God hardened Pharaoh's heart.' The result of their influence has played a significant part in formatting the current, distressing state of today's Evangelical apologetics. For Calvinist theology makes it impossible to have a consistent *and true* biblical hermeneutic, i.e., *the general guiding principle that when two statements are in direct conflict with one another*[94] *at least one of them is figurative or idiomatic*. To the extent that Calvinists have taken idiomatic phrases to be literal, and literal phrases to be idiomatic or figurative, their theology has strayed. The current result is that the logic of Scripture has been cast aside regarding the nature of God, though of course *consistency* of argument has been maintained. The problem is grave—to wrongly assign idiomatic or literal phrases in key verses is to potentially cast away every truth in the Bible regarding God's nature. Thus, to reinterpret Scripture for the purpose of justifying a contradiction, such as the alleged co-existence of God's absolute sovereignty with human freedom, is to lay the foundation for 'biblically' justifying other contradictions using the same irrational method. It just becomes a matter of inventiveness and willingness.[95]

Footnotes:

[65] Exodus 9:15 (KJV) speaks of Pharaoh being "cut off from the earth," which would make it appear that Pharaoh died in the Red Sea with his army. However, (Robert) Young's Literal Translation (YLT) for Exodus 9:15 reads: "for now I have put forth My hand, and I smite thee, and thy people, with pestilence, and thou art hidden from the earth." If this translation is correct, it would seem to leave open the possibility that Pharaoh might have survived the plagues. In fact, the Bible does not definitively state that Pharaoh was with his army when his men and horses drowned in the Red Sea; nor is Pharaoh mentioned in the Israeli song of victory in Exodus 15. (See footnote 100)

[66] This is a very sobering thought. Most men are in the habit of hardening their hearts against God every day. As they do so, they move ever closer to a point where God may give up struggling with them, in which case there would then be no realistic chance that they would ever be saved. This ought to motivate us toward developing sensitivity toward sharing the gospel with others whenever the Spirit leads us to, as well as motivating us to lead a more godly life in general. I suspect all of us, at one time or another, need encouragement and greater determination to do this.

[67] Consider also Matthew 11:23: "And thou, Capernaum, which art exalted unto heaven, shalt be brought down to hell: for if the mighty works, which have been done in thee, had been done in Sodom, it would have remained until this day." Note that for Christ to have made such a statement about Sodom remaining to the present day, He would have had to foreknow what generations of Sodomites would believe, as well as what activities and movements would take place regarding the surrounding people groups in that particular geo-political area over the course of 2,000 years. Although it may be conceivable that Christ, as the Son (and one Person of the Trinity), chose during the Old Testament era to limit His foreknowledge of *certain* events and human choices (such as *perhaps* implied in the statement regarding Abraham's willingness to sacrifice Isaac, "*Now I know that you will withhold nothing from me....*"), this does not mean that the Father (at least) did not know in advance what Abraham was willing to do. It is possible that Christ, in wanting to demonstrate to man a fuller expression of His desire to identify with humanity from humanity's own viewpoint, chose to limit for a certain time His foreknowledge about *certain* future events and human choices *at certain times*. Note in the New Testament that Christ voluntarily limited His foreknowledge of the Father's set day for His (the Son's) Second Coming, and therefore total foreknowledge has not extended to all the Persons of the Trinity (by choice). Yet, Christ was not always ignorant about the future or even its contingent possibilities, as seen in His observation that Sodom would have been preserved to the present day had they seen the miracles He had done in Capernaum (as Matthew 11:23 makes clear). This would suggest that Open Theism, for example, is mistaken to suggest that God exhaustively knows the past and present, but has no foreknowledge about what human choices will be in the future.

[68] —regarding events through the ninth plague.

[69] Hebrew verbs are shown in their basic forms.

[70] i.e., the turning of Moses' rod into a serpent and back into a rod.

[71] Though I agree with the minority translation Young gives for *chazaq*, I believe the future tense of the majority translation should have been preserved, since 9:12 *et al.* show 4:21's fulfillment.

[72] Obviously, reviewing these other English words will be restricted to Strong's numbered word for *chazaq* (#2833). The website [www.blueletterbible.com] actually has a feature to allow for a Hebrew or Greek word's reversible look-up.

[73] Furthermore, the remainder of 9:12 indicates that it is the fulfillment of 4:21, for 9:12 reads, "And the Lord strengthened Pharaoh's heart, and he did not listen to them; *just as the Lord had spoken to Moses.*" As for the NAS claim (see argument on pp. 262-263 in this chapter) that 7:13 is the fulfillment of 4:21, it will be shown later why the fulfillment of 7:13 is 3:19, not 4:21.

[74] To support Calvinism's deterministic view of reprobation, G. K. Beale actually foregoes an immediate explanation of mysticism and takes a different approach in his article, "An Exegetical and Theological Consideration of the Hardening of Pharaoh's Heart in Exodus 4—14 and Romans 9" (in which he discusses the three Hebrew words translated *to harden*). He suggests that God was hardening

Pharaoh's heart prior to the first time Scripture actually records that God hardens Pharaoh's heart. Thus, he states: "*Although the 4:21 hardening is integrally related to the performance of signs, it is even more related to [the] refusal of Moses' request to release Israel. The hardening of 4:21 is not conditional on the performance of signs. Hence, signs could be absent and hardening present. The argument rests with the one attempting to prove an absolute and strictly necessary relation between hardening and "sign reaction.""* The burden of proof, however, is very much on Beale's end, since all the biblical statements that actually state that God hardened Pharaoh's heart obviously follow Pharaoh's reactions to successive *plagues*. Moreover, Beale, to support his argument, cites Moses' complaint as recorded in Exodus 5:22, as though it must be true and not the mere biblical recording of a saint's *opinion* about God in the midst of his impatient, accusative exasperation, thus Beale: "Another argument for God's control of Pharaoh is found in 5:22-23. In 5:22 it is said that Yahweh had brought harm to Israel…." But (contrary to Beale) we note the actual passage: "Then Moses returned to the Lord and said, 'O Lord, why have you brought harm to this people? Why did you ever send me? Ever since I came to Pharaoh to speak in Your name, he has done harm to this people, and You have not delivered Your people at all.'" Finally, one wonders how repetitive the Scriptures must be, regarding the Lord's 'hardening' of Pharaoh's heart (in its successive statements which follow plagues 6,7,8,9, and 10), in order for Beale to think that his criteria has been met for "an absolute and strictly necessary relation between hardening and 'sign reaction.'" One is reminded of the Scottish philosopher David Hume, who kept insisting that there was no strict proof of causal relationship just because one always saw that trees bent away from the direction of the wind, and then only when the wind was blowing. Also, Beale, as someone trying to tie divine reprobation to the exodus narrative, does not appear to **interpret** the Hebrew *chazaq* to mean *strengthen* in the Pharaohic context but follows instead the usual translators' bias of *harden*.

[75] Incidentally, one wonders why the Calvinist seems to treat his own position as though finding a proof-text for God's absolute sovereignty *over here* in the Bible, and then finding a proof-text for human freedom *over there* in the Bible, formed a sufficient explanation. Why is it not understood by Calvinists that *any* biblical passage about the subject of sovereignty, such as Isaiah 29, 45, and Jeremiah 18 in their extensive, contextual detail, ought to affirm both sides of Calvin's 'antinomy'? Or have Calvinists really given up the hope for a unified field of intelligible knowledge?

[76] (in the hands of some translators, that is).

[77] Expect the Calvinist to claim that God *roused* Pharaoh by *raising* him expressly for reprobation. Thus one expects that the Calvinist (if he becomes aware of our argument) will resurrect his old trick of using irrational argument and thus treat yet another word, in this case, *rouse*, as merely one more activity of divine irresistibility. Doubtless, this method of redefining terms to fit the Calvinist template will be used by Calvinists against any book that gets 'above the radar' in exposing Calvinism. In other words, any book that makes it into the repertoire of books exposing the Calvinistic misdeeds of defining synonyms as non-synonymous, and non-synonyms as synonymous (resulting in eisegesis), may

likely be turned on its head by Calvinists, and its author accused of doing the very thing of which Calvinists themselves are guilty.

[78] It would also mean that God was tempting Ahab to do evil, which could not have been the case, since God tempts no man (see Ja. 1:13).

[79] Even as a Christian I may be tempted to ask why God permits this, i.e., the existence of anything outside His will. But if I so object, I condemn myself in the question—for again, I accuse God with the very same free will that I claim ought not to exist! The answer as to why God permits evil is evident, nonetheless. God has desired that men and angels have free will to decide the spiritual course of their own lives regardless of the outcome. (Incidentally, there is a general effect of calamitous outcome not always in line with a theory of individual *quid pro quo* that works itself through the world because of man's sin.) The worship God desires is that of people freely choosing to respond to Him in love. As Christian thinker Paul Little has stated about God's desire to bring free will into creation: it is even as a man who would prefer a wife over a car, even though a wife will not always do as he pleases, and though the car can be steered according to his whim.

[80] —suggested pronunciation: *kaw-shaw*.

[81] God appears to have revealed to Ahab more about the (behind-the-scenes) judgment process than to Pharaoh, perhaps because Ahab, though evil, was king over the northern tribes of Israel, God's people, and had humbled himself on one occasion when the Lord pronounced a curse against his male descendents (because of Ahab's acquiescence in the murder of a man whose property Ahab had then confiscated).

[82] That is, God's ideal plan would have been the release of Israel prior to the plagues, but failing that, then as early as possible during the course of plagues.

[83] —by 'forms,' I mean (for example), that God upholds a man's *form* as the Sustainer of creation, though He never decides man's *content*, whether good or evil. While it is true that God preserves both the form of the world in which sin takes place and also the eternally forward existence of man, man alone commits sin and sustains it unless it becomes remitted in Christ by God's grace which we accept by our faith.

[84] A.W. Pink offers the argument that the pronoun *us* in the phrase *to us-ward* in 2 Peter 3:9 must refer to the elect, since Peter's salutation at the beginning of the epistle is addressed only to saints. This is a forced argument for the following reasons. First, if Peter is speaking of the elect *who are already saved*, by what grammar do we understand that such elected *saints* (i.e., those who are *already* saved and to whom the epistle is addressed) should come toward this knowledge of the truth, i.e., should *yet* come unto the knowledge of the truth of salvation? For by definition the elect, contextualized here in this passage as "saints," are those who *already* have come to the knowledge of the truth. I suppose, then, that Pink is referring to the future elect. But note in 2 Peter 3 the *judgment* context prior to verse 9. Peter observes that men were willfully ignorant of the watery judgment (that came in Noah's day), even as they now resist the Spirit by mockingly stating, "Where is the promise of His coming?" Peter then states that

God is not slow regarding His promise, as some men define slowness, but is long-suffering toward us, not willing that anyone should perish, but that all should come to repentance. Furthermore, Peter states in verse 16 that Paul also mentions these things in all his epistles, "in which are some things hard to be understood, which they that are unlearned and unstable wrest, as [they do] also the other scriptures…" Observe then, that Peter's reference about divine long-suffering, judgment, and mercy in Paul's writings would certainly include Romans 9, a chapter universally conceded by theologians to be difficult of perception. And note especially that Paul states in Romans 9:22-23 that God is long-suffering with *those who disbelieve,* while other vessels receive (i.e., take the proffered) mercy. Thus Paul states that: "God, desirously willing to make his wrath known, endured with much longsuffering the vessels fitting themselves to destruction, *and* [Gr. kai, *also,* i.e., *also (for the reason)*] that he *might make known* [note: Gr. subjunctive mood, showing the following matter to be contingent on the vessels' decisions (and therefore obviously not on the 'irresistible' activity of an all-sovereign God)] the riches of his glory on the vessels of mercy, which He has before prepared unto glory." Even so, the *us* in 2 Peter 3:9 corresponds to all those toward whom God has exhibited long-suffering, **which, the reader will observe, are the wicked** (which, contextually in Rom. 9, includes Pharaoh), among whom some become righteous through their belief in God's mercy. Thus the "anyone" and "all" of 2 Peter 3:9 may be understood as universal, lost man, especially as we consider our second point. To wit, observe that any preacher may, in a sermon addressed to believers, use the pronoun *us* to urge his hearers as members of the larger community of the world to consider an abstract argument. Paul actually does this in Romans 4:24 when he says "But for us also, to whom it shall be imputed, if we believe on him that raised up Jesus our Lord from the dead." By using the conditional future tense ("shall…*if* we believe") and the pronouns *us* and *we,* Paul is obviously asking his Christian readers to imagine for the moment (and for argument's sake) that they are general members of the larger, unbelieving community of the world. Observe, then, that the pronoun *us* in Romans 4:24 is used to mean a group other than the saints at Rome to whom Paul specifically cited in his salutation. Even so, though Peter does not use the conditional tense as does the more philosophically-minded Paul when the latter addresses his Roman audience, nevertheless Peter expects his own hearers to understand that as vessels of mercy they are nevertheless part of the *us* of universal man with which God has been long-suffering.

[85] If God took equal pleasure in avenging the blood of Christ as in bestowing grace upon sinners, then God, following the resurrection of Christ, may as well have saved the Spirit the trouble of trying to convince the world of sin, since the same amount of divine pleasure could have been realized either way. This is not the case, of course, because God's beneficent nature is preferential to, as the hymn says, both "giving and forgiving."

[86] If God took equal pleasure in avenging the blood of Christ as in bestowing grace upon sinners, then God, e.g., following the resurrection of Christ, may as well have saved the Spirit the trouble of trying to convince the world of sin, since the same amount of divine pleasure could have been realized either way. This is not

[87] Again, the word is in single quotation marks to show the idiomatic nature of the phrase, "The Lord strengthened Pharaoh's heart," i.e., to show the non-causal nature of the divine permission which granted Satanic activity to commence.

[88] That God did so because He was willing to be glorified among the Egyptians, even if judgment were the only way to achieve it, does not mean that such divinely granted permission to the Enemy was tantamount to what *God* would have preferred for the Egyptians. Nor does it mean that God was insincere when He commanded Pharaoh to repent and humble himself (see Ex. 10: 2-3).

[89] i.e., as it refers to the Lord's activity upon Pharaoh's heart during the plague events.

[90] It might be argued, with some justification, that the idiomatic nature we claim for *chazaq* and *kabad*, as it relates to the Lord's activity upon Pharaoh's heart, is in some measure due to the connotative meaning of the words *strengthen* and *honor* as used in the English language. In other words, perhaps the idiomatic nature of these words in Hebrew was more (or very) readily understood, such that it seemed to the Hebrews a more natural way of expressing the matter in such contexts.

[91] According to the source I have available, i.e., Blueletterbible.com

[92] "them" refers to Moses and Aaron.

[93] Again, if by the word 'that,' the translators meant to imply *in order that*, their view should be discarded. For God never desires that man sin.

[94] i.e., granting that the translation of both statements is correct.

[95] For example, this confusion of definition is exactly what the Catholic Church came to embrace because of their amalgamation of grace and works, a view made possible by the irrational method.

Endnotes:

[xlvii] Turner, Allan. "Who was the Pharaoh of the Exodus?" [http://www.allanturner.com/pharaoh.html].

[xlviii] Spiegel, James S. *The Benefits of Providence*. (Wheaton, Illinois, Crossway Books, 2005). p. 23.

[xlix] Spiegel, p. 25.

[l] Pink, Arthur W. [www.reformed.org/books/pink/pink_sov_06.html]; Chapter Six: "The Sovereignty of God in Operation."

[li] For all the occurrences of the three Hebrew words translated 'hardened,' see online at [http://www.apostolic-churches.net/bible/strongs.html]. Also, Strong, James. *Strong's Exhaustive Concordance of the Bible*. (Nashville: Abingdon Press, 1986) lexical section. BlueLetterBible.com is also helpful and fairly easy to use.

Chapter 15

The Potter and the Pot

If Romans 9 is the most troubling chapter of the Bible to most Christians, the illustration of the potter and the pots is the most troubling analogy. The unmitigated force of the King's English makes the illustration particularly striking, especially with Paul's prior statement about Pharaoh's hardening:

> [17]For the scripture saith unto Pharaoh, Even for this same purpose have I raised thee up, that I might show my power in thee, and that my name might be declared throughout all the earth. [18]Therefore hath he mercy on whom he will have mercy, and whom he will he hardeneth. [19]Thou wilt say then unto me, Why doth he yet find fault? For who hath resisted his will? [20]Nay but, O man, who art thou that repliest against God? Shall the thing formed say to him that formed it, Why hast thou made me thus? [21]Hath not the potter power over the clay, of the same lump to make one vessel unto honour, and another unto dishonour? [22]What if God, willing to show his wrath, and to make his power known, endured with much longsuffering the vessels of wrath fitted to destruction: [23]And that he might make known the riches of his glory on the vessels of mercy, which he had afore prepared unto glory, [24]Even us, whom he hath called, not of the Jews only, but also of the Gentiles? (Rom. 9:17-24).

Many Christians throughout the centuries have taken the pot and potter metaphor to mean that man cannot resist God whatsoever. The upshot to this thinking is the belief that many men are damned according to God's mysterious choice. In a chapter on Reprobation in his book, *The Sovereignty of God* (from which we quote a few lengthy passages below), Reformed thinker A.W. Pink explains how the Westminster Confessions implies that God chooses to send some people to hell. He follows up this statement with Calvin's view of reprobation, and then adds some additional points of his own. Later, he explains the metaphor of the common pot upon the Potter's wheel as man formed by the sovereign Potter into a vessel of damnation. Although in previous chapters we have already answered many of the arguments presented in the following quote by Pink, we will analyze some of them a bit further, and answer in more detail the claim by John

Calvin that the word *raised* in Exodus 9:16 means *appoint*. All word emphases below are from Pink:

> **(Pink quote)**
> In the Westminster Confession it is said, "God from all eternity did by the most wise and holy counsel of His own will, freely and unchangeably *foreordain whatsoever* comes to pass". The late Mr. F. W. Grant—a most careful and cautious student and writer—commenting on these words said: "It is perfectly, divinely true, that God hath ordained for His own glory whatsoever comes to pass." Now if these statements are true, is not the doctrine of Reprobation established by them? What, in human history, is the one thing which *does* come to pass every day? What, but that men and women die, pass out of this world into a hopeless eternity, an eternity of suffering and woe. If then God *has* foreordained *whatsoever* comes to pass then He must have decreed that vast numbers of human beings should pass out of this world unsaved to suffer eternally in the Lake of Fire. Admitting the general premise, is not the specific conclusion inevitable?
>
> …We cannot do better now than quote from Calvin's comments upon this verse (Romans 9:17). "There are here two things to be considered, —the predestination of Pharaoh to ruin, which is to be referred to the past and yet the hidden counsel of God, —and then, the design of this, which was to make known the name of God. As many interpreters, striving to modify this passage, pervert it, we must first observe, that for the word 'I have raised thee up', or stirred up, in the Hebrew is, 'I have appointed', by which it appears, that God, designing to show that the contumacy of Pharaoh would not prevent Him to deliver His people, not only affirms that his fury had been foreseen by Him, and that He had prepared means for restraining it, but that He had also thus *designedly ordained it* and indeed for this end, —that he might exhibit a more illustrious evidence of His own power." It will be observed that Calvin gives as the force of the Hebrew word which Paul renders "For this purpose have I raised thee up,"—"I have appointed". As this is the

word on which the doctrine and argument of the verse turns we would further point out that in making this quotation from Exodus 9:16 the apostle significantly departs from the Septuagint—the version then in common use, and from which he most frequently quotes—and substitutes a clause for the first that is given by the Septuagint: instead of "On this account thou hast been preserved", he gives "For this very end have I raised thee up"!

...First, we know from Exodus 14 and 15 that Pharaoh was "cut off", that he was cut off by God, that he was cut off in the very midst of his wickedness, that he was cut off not by sickness nor by the infirmities which are incident to old age, nor by what men term an accident, but cut off by *the immediate hand of God in judgment.*

Second, it is clear that God raised up Pharaoh *for* this very end—to "cut him off," which in the language of the New Testament means "destroyed." God never does anything without a previous design. In giving him being, in preserving him through infancy and childhood, in raising him to the throne of Egypt, God had one end in view. That such was God's purpose is clear from His words to Moses before he went down to Egypt, to demand of Pharaoh that Jehovah's people should be allowed to go a three days' journey into the wilderness to worship Him—"And the LORD said unto Moses, When thou goest to return into Egypt, see that thou do all these wonders before Pharaoh, which I have put in thine hand: *but I will harden his heart*, that he shall not let the people go" (Ex. 4:21).

...Third, an examination of God's dealings with Pharaoh makes it clear that Egypt's king was indeed a "vessel of wrath fitted to destruction."

...Fourth, God "hardened" his heart as He declared He would (Ex. 4:21). This is in full accord with the declarations of Holy Scripture—"The preparations of the heart in man, and the answer of the tongue, *is from the Lord*" (Prov. 16:1); "The king's heart is in the hand of the *Lord*, as the rivers of water, He turneth it *whithersoever He will*" (Prov. 21:1). Like all other kings,

Pharaoh's heart was in the hand of the LORD; and God had both the right and the power to turn it whithersoever He pleased. And it pleased Him to turn it *against* all good.

...Finally, it is worthy of careful consideration to note how the *vindication* of God in His dealings with Pharaoh has been fully attested... Again; we have the witness of Moses who was fully acquainted with God's conduct toward Pharaoh. He had heard at the beginning what was God's design in connection with Pharaoh; he had witnessed God's dealings with him; he had observed his "long-sufferance" toward this vessel of wrath fitted to destruction; and at last he had beheld him cut off in Divine judgment at the Red Sea. How then was Moses impressed?

Does he raise the cry of injustice? Does he dare to charge God with unrighteousness? Far from it. Instead, he says, "Who is like unto Thee, O LORD, among the gods? Who is like Thee, glorious in holiness, *fearful* in praises, doing wonders!" (Ex. 15:11).

...We must believe, therefore that the Judge of all the earth did right in creating and destroying this vessel of wrath, Pharaoh.

...IN CONCLUSION, WE WOULD SAY THAT IN FORMING PHARAOH GOD DISPLAYED NEITHER JUSTICE NOR INJUSTICE, BUT ONLY HIS BARE SOVEREIGNTY. AS THE POTTER IS SOVEREIGN IN FORMING VESSELS, SO GOD IS SOVEREIGN IN FORMING MORAL AGENTS.

...That which is most repellant to the carnal mind in the above verse is the reference to *hardening*—"*Whom He will He hardeneth*"—and it is just here that so many commentators and expositors have adulterated the truth. The most common view is that the apostle is speaking of nothing more than *judicial* hardening, i.e., a *forsaking* by God *because* these subjects of His displeasure had *first* rejected His truth and forsaken Him. Those who contend for this interpretation appeal to such scriptures as Romans 1:19-26—"God gave them up", that is (see context) those who "knew God" yet glorified Him not as God (v. 21). Appeal is

also made to 2 Thessalonians 2:10-12. But it is to be
noted that the word "harden" *does not occur* in either of
these passages. But further. We submit that Romans
9:18 has no reference whatever to *judicial* "hardening".
The apostle is not there speaking of those who had
already turned their backs on God's truth, but instead,
he is dealing with *God's sovereignty*, God's sovereignty as
seen not only in showing mercy *to whom He wills*, but
also in hardening *whom He pleases*.

…Verse 18: *"Therefore hath He mercy on whom He will have
mercy, and whom He will He hardeneth"*. This affirmation
of God's sovereign "hardening" of sinners' hearts—in
contradistinction from judicial hardening—is not
alone. Mark the language of John 12:37-40, "But
though He had done so many miracles before them,
yet they believed not on Him: that the saying of Isaiah
the prophet might be fulfilled, which he spake,
LORD, who hath believed our report? and to whom
hath the arm of the LORD been revealed? *Therefore
they could not believe* (why?), because that Isaiah said
again, *He hath* blinded their eyes, and hardened their
hearts (why? Because they had refused to believe on
Christ? This is the popular belief, but mark the answer
of Scripture) that they should not <u>see with their eyes, nor
understand with their heart, and be converted, and I should heal
them.</u>" NOW, READER, IT IS JUST A QUESTION
AS TO WHETHER OR NOT YOU WILL
BELIEVE WHAT GOD HAS REVEALED IN
HIS WORD. IT IS NOT A MATTER OF
PROLONGED SEARCHING OR PROFOUND
STUDY, BUT A CHILDLIKE SPIRIT WHICH IS
NEEDED, IN ORDER TO UNDERSTAND THIS
DOCTRINE. [lii]

At this point A.W. Pink explains the illustration of the pot and the potter.
He does this because of his view of the hardening of Pharaoh's heart.
Notice in the passage below that no attempt is made to correlate the pot on
the potter's wheel with the pot and potter metaphor found in Isaiah 29, 45,
or Jeremiah 18:

Verse 19: *"Thou wilt say then unto me, Why doth He yet find
fault? For who hath resisted His will?"* Is not this the very
objection which is urged today? The force of the

apostle's questions here seems to be this: Since everything is dependent on God's will, which is irreversible, and since this will of God, according to which He can do everything as sovereign—since He can have mercy on whom He wills to have mercy, and can refuse mercy and inflict punishment on whom He chooses to do so—why does He not will to have mercy on all, so as to make them obedient, and thus put finding of fault out of court? Now it should be particularly noted that the apostle does not repudiate the ground on which the objection rests. He does not say God *does not* find fault. Nor does he say, *Men may* resist His will. Furthermore; he does not explain away the objection by saying: You have altogether misapprehended my meaning when I said 'Whom He wills He treats kindly, and whom He wills He treats severely'. But he says, "first, this is an objection you have *no right* to make; and then, This is an objection you have *no reason* to make" (vide Dr. Brown). <u>The objection was utterly inadmissible, for it was a replying against God.</u> It was to complain about, argue against, what *God* had done!

Verse 19: *"Thou wilt say then unto me, Why doth He yet find fault? For who hath resisted His will?"* The language which the apostle here puts into the mouth of the objector is so plain and pointed, that misunderstanding ought to be impossible. Why doth He yet *find fault*? Now, reader, what can these words mean? Formulate *your own* reply before considering ours. Can the force of the apostle's question be any other than this: If it is true that God has "mercy" *on whom He wills,* and also "hardens" *whom He wills,* then what becomes of human responsibility? In such a case men are nothing better than *puppets,* and if this be true then it would be *unjust* for God to "find fault" with His helpless creatures. Mark the word "then"—Thou wilt say *then* unto me— <u>he states the (false) inference or conclusion which the objector draws from what the apostle had been saying.</u> And mark, my reader, the apostle readily saw the doctrine he had formulated *would* raise *this* very objection, and unless what *we* have written throughout this book provokes, in some at least, *(all* whose carnal minds are not subdued by divine grace) the *same* objection, then it must be either because we have not presented the doctrine which is set forth in Romans 9, or else because human nature has *changed* since the apostle's day. Consider now the remainder of the verse (19). The apostle *repeats* the *same* objection in a slightly different form—repeats it so that his meaning may not be misunderstood—namely, "For who hath resisted His will?" It is clear then that the subject under immediate discussion relates to God's "will", i.e., His sovereign ways, which *confirms* what we have said above upon verses 17 and 18, where we contended that it is *not* judicial hardening which is in view (that is, hardening because of previous rejection of the truth), but *sovereign* "hardening", that is, the "hardening" of a fallen and sinful creature for no other reason than that which inheres in the sovereign will of God. And hence the question, "Who hath resisted His *will?*" What then does the apostle say in reply to these objections?

Verse 20: "*Nay but, O man, who art thou that repliest against God? Shall the thing formed say to him that formed it, Why hast thou made me thus?*" The apostle, then, did not say the objection was pointless and groundless, instead, he rebukes the objector for his *impiety*. <u>He reminds him that he is merely a "man", a creature, and that as such it is most unseemly and impertinent for him to "reply (argue, or reason) against God". Furthermore, he reminds him that he is nothing more than a "thing formed", and therefore it is madness and blasphemy to rise up against the Former Himself.</u> Ere leaving this verse it should be pointed out that its closing words, "Why hast thou made me *thus*" help us to determine, unmistakably, the precise subject under discussion. In the light of the immediate context what can be the force of the "thus"? What, but as in the case of Esau, why hast thou made me an object of "hatred"? What, but as in the case of Pharaoh, Why hast thou made me simply to "harden" me? What other meaning *can, fairly,* be assigned to it?

It is highly important to keep clearly before us that the apostle's object throughout this passage is to treat of God's sovereignty in dealing with, on the one hand, those whom He loves—vessels unto honor and vessels of mercy, and *also*, on the other hand, with those whom He "hates" and "hardens"—vessels unto dishonor and vessels of wrath.

…Ere passing to the next verse let us summarize the teaching of this and the two previous ones. In verse 19 two questions are asked, "Thou wilt say then unto me, Why doth He yet find fault? For who hath resisted His will?" To those questions a threefold answer is returned. <u>First, in verse 20 the apostle denies the creature the right to sit in judgment upon the ways of the Creator</u>—"Nay but, O man who art thou that repliest against God? Shall the thing formed say to Him that formed it, Why hast Thou made me thus?" <u>The apostle insists that the rectitude of God's will must not be questioned.</u> Whatever <u>He</u> does *must be* right. <u>Second, in verse 21 the apostle declares that the Creator has the right to dispose of His creatures as He sees fit</u>—"Hath not the Potter power over the clay, of the same lump, to make one vessel unto honor, and another unto dishonor?"

…"Hath not the potter power over the clay of the same lump, to make one vessel unto honour, and another unto dishonour?" Certainly God has *the right* to do this because He is the Creator. Does He *exercise* this right? Yes, as verses 13 and 17 clearly show us—"For this same purpose *have I* raised thee (Pharaoh) up".

…ONE POINT IN THE ABOVE VERSE REQUIRES SEPARATE CONSIDERATION—"VESSELS OF WRATH <u>FITTED</u> TO DESTRUCTION". THE USUAL EXPLANATION WHICH IS GIVEN OF THESE WORDS IS THAT THE VESSELS OF WRATH <u>FIT THEMSELVES</u> TO DESTRUCTION, THAT IS, FIR THEMSELVES BY VIRTUE OF THEIR WICKEDNESS; AND IT IS ARGUED THAT THERE IS NO NEED FOR <u>GOD</u> TO "FIT THEM TO DESTRUCTION", BECAUSE THEY ARE ALREADY FITTED BY THEIR OWN DEPRAVITY, AND THAT THIS *MUST* BE THE REAL MEANING OF THIS EXPRESSION. Now if by "destruction" we understand *punishment*, it is perfectly true that the non-elect *do* "fit themselves", for every one will be judged "according to his works"; and further, we freely grant that *subjectively* the non-elect *do* fit themselves for destruction. But the point to be decided is, Is *this* what the apostle is here referring to? And, without hesitation, we reply it is not. <u>Go back to verses 11-13: did Esau fit himself to be an object of God's hatred, or was he not such before he was born? Again; did Pharaoh fit himself for destruction, or did not God harden his heart before the plagues were sent upon Egypt?</u>—see Exodus 4:21!

Romans 9:22 is clearly a continuation in thought of verse 21, and verse 21 is part of the apostle's reply to the questions raised in verse 20: therefore to fairly follow out the figure, it *must* be God Himself who "fits" unto destruction the vessels of wrath. Should it be asked *how* God does this, the answer, necessarily, is, *objectively*, —He fits the non-elect unto destruction by His fore-ordinating decrees.[26]

Since A.W. Pink gives such strong affirmations of God's sovereignty, it should not surprise us that toward the close of his essay he turns his attention to the problem of evil and man's free will. At this point Pink has thrown his weight so far forward on the rocking horse of dialecticism (i.e., toward emphasizing the unilateral activity of an all-sovereign God), that he dare not throw his weight anywhere but backward. Hence, even though Pink has repeatedly been claiming that the Potter forms every moral essence of wrathful vessels designed unto damnation, man is now claimed to be responsible for how the vessel turned out. Thus, verses like Ecclesiastes 7:29 are now presented as proofs against the very arguments Pink himself had been making just moments before. Says Pink:

> Having thus stated the doctrine of Reprobation, as it is presented in Holy Writ, let us now mention one or two important considerations to guard it against abuse and prevent the reader from making any unwarranted deductions: —…the doctrine of Reprobation does not mean that God purposed to take innocent creatures, make them wicked, and then damn them. Scripture says, "God hath made man upright, but they have sought out many inventions" (Eccl. 7:29). God has not created *sinful* creatures in order to destroy them,

for God is not to be charged with the sin of His creatures. The responsibility and criminality is man's. God's decree of Reprobation contemplated Adam's race as fallen, sinful, corrupt, guilty. From it God purposed to save a few as the monuments of His sovereign grace; the others He determined to destroy as the exemplification of His justice and severity. In determining to destroy these others, God did them no wrong. They had already fallen in Adam, their legal representative; they are therefore born with a sinful nature, and in their sins He leaves them. Nor can they complain. This is as *they* wish; they have no desire for holiness; they *love* darkness rather than light. Where, then, is there any injustice if God "gives them up to *their own* hearts' lusts" (Ps. 81:12)!

…God does not (as we have been slanderously reported to affirm) compel the wicked to sin, as the rider spurs on an unwilling horse. God only says in effect that awful word, "Let them alone" (Mt. 15:14). He needs only to slacken the reins of providential restraint, and withhold the influence of saving grace, and apostate man will only too soon and too surely, of his own accord, fall by his iniquities.[liii]

One reason I cite these quotes is to show how persuasive Calvinist arguments can at first appear to the reader because of an author's adamant and consistent argument. This is because readers do not usually take the time to critically process what they read. Nevertheless, my readers will see that most of A.W. Pink's assertions in the above quotes have already been answered in earlier portions of this book. And yet I think that some further comments are advisable as a review and also as a rebuttal to certain other points raised by Pink in his support of Calvin.

First, Calvin's explanation of Exodus 9:16 is offered as evidence of God's sovereignty over Pharaoh. Pink notes that in Exodus 9:16 Calvin translates, *I have raised thee up* to mean, *I have appointed thee*, treating it as the true, and apparently *only* meaning of the Hebrew word. In fact, Pink states that "this is the word on which the doctrine and argument of the verse turns." He does so without citing any real lexical evidence of the Hebrew word (*'amad*), and without suggesting it could have any other meaning than *appoint*. There are, in fact, *over 20 other possibilities* according to *Strong's* concordance. The word *appoint* is simply one of these in *Strong's* long alphabetical list:

'a prim. root; to *stand*, in various relations (lit. and fig., intras. and trans.):-abide (behind), appoint, arise, cease, confirm, dwell, be employed, endure, establish, leave, make, ordain, be (over), place, (be) present (self), raise up, remain, repair + serve, set (forth, over, -tle, up) (make to, make to be at a, (with-) stand (by, fast, firm, still, up), (be at a) stay (up), tarry.

The Hebrew word *'amad* (which Calvin takes to mean *appoint*), as it actually appears in the KJV Old Testament, is rendered as the following words: "stood" 171, "stand" 137, ("raise, stand…) up" 42, "set" 32, "stay" 17, "still" 15, "appointed" 10, "standing" 10, "endure" 8, "remain" 8, "present" 7, "continue" 6, "withstand" 6, "waited" 5, "establish" 5, misc. 42; (total) 521. The King James translators chose to render the Hebrew word *'amad* into the word "appoint" about **2%** of the time in the Old Testament. *'Amad* is rendered as "raised up" in Exodus 9:16. Choosing *appoint* from what appears to be many word possibilities, Calvin builds huge inferences by then applying it irrationally, i.e., in such a way so that it contradicts other statements in the Bible. When abstractly considered apart from the biblical context, it is right to say that "raised" **may** mean *appoint* (again, when *abstractly* considered), but it must be pointed out that Calvin *completely* ignores Paul's use of *fully rouse* in Romans 9:17 when quoting Exodus 9:16. Furthermore (as already noted), Paul even deviates from the Septuagint in order to use the word "exegeiro," giving the word *'amad* a very particular meaning, one which Calvin and Pink obviously missed.

Incidentally, though in the last chapter I expressed my belief in the idea that the Enemy led Pharaoh to be fully roused, the mere decision of God to leave Pharaoh to himself as a fully roused ruler, *regardless of whether the Enemy's influence contributed to this state*, would be enough to account for all that our argument demands (regarding God's 'hardening' of Pharaoh's heart) as laid out in the last chapter, **if necessary**. By accepting Ezekiel 33:11 at face value ("God has no pleasure in the death of the wicked but that the wicked turn from his way and live"), we may say with confidence that God attempts to actively restrain a man from evil for a prolonged time and perhaps in some or many cases up to the man's death. He does this by presenting to the man's mind thoughts about what he should believe and do (i.e., encouraging the man's proper conscience). Our suggestion about the Enemy, then, was not from any *necessity*, but from a desire to show the dovetailing richness of Scripture by appealing to other relevant and circumstantially suggestive passages. (In fact, in my opinion the passages together are circumstantially *conclusive*.) When Pharaoh demonstrated his preference for rebellion repeatedly, God finally walked away from Pharaoh. The result was that Pharaoh was then completely *undistracted* toward his commitment to evil, and so he became fully roused in his rebellion against God. Whether Pharaoh actually traveled his remaining path of rebellion with the Enemy for his companion may not be absolutely known, but if the Enemy was not present, we may say that Pharaoh's own spirit proved equal to the task of fully rousing itself, i.e., at that point in which God stopped trying to repair the Egyptian king's conscience.

For some may think our suggestion about the Enemy's presence in the exodus narrative is taking too much license, and so this issue of appropriate assumption should be discussed here. For example, I recently talked with a Christian instructor who felt I was taking too presumptive an approach with Job 1. We had been discussing the opening scene in Job to determine if God had foreordained all history. I pointed out that God Himself said He had been incited by Satan to 'ruin' Job. The instructor, on the other hand, queried if God Himself had not thrown down the gauntlet to incite Satan, since God was the One who first broached the subject of Job. After all, he argued, if God foreknew how Satan would respond, wasn't it God, not Satan, who started the whole chain of events that led to Job's ruin? I responded by suggesting that God had probably waited until Satan had finished his accusations against believers to bring up the more faithful example of Job (we know from the New Testament that Satan accuses the brethren *'day and night'*). The instructor, in effect, replied that one ought not to make such presumptions where Scripture is silent. Of course, his concern (and one that I shared) is that people sometimes read into Scripture their own ideas and grant them an equal status to Scripture. And so for the rest of that day I thought upon the nature of presumptions and who it is that holds them. In the end I wondered if such instructors (or preachers, professors, etc.) who would lay against some of us the charge of presumption (when we are really only struggling to solve alleged contradictions in the Bible by demonstrating in these difficult passages a subtle, scriptural harmony along biblically internal and circumstantial lines), have ever themselves taught *what* it was, for example, that Jesus prayed on the one occasion when we are told that He spent all night in prayer before choosing His 12 disciples (Lk. 6:12-13):

> [12]And it came to pass in those days, that he [Jesus] went out into a mountain to pray, and continued all night in prayer to God. [13]And when it was day, he called unto him his disciples: and of them he chose twelve, whom also he named apostles;

I imagine that every Christian teacher or pastor who has taught a lesson or given a sermon from this passage has assumed that Jesus prayed about which of His disciples should be the 12. Yet the Bible does not actually tell us what Jesus prayed about when He prayed all night. Shall we not, however, make the obvious *inference* that He prayed about who He should pick as His 12 disciples? Or again, have any of these instructors ever taught that the animal skins with which God clothed Adam and Eve following the Fall almost certainly came from animals that had been sacrificed by God to make an atonement offering for the guilty pair? Indeed, have they not presumed this idea as well, though, technically, Scripture is silent about it?

The point, then, is that Bible instructors, though not claiming that such presumptions are themselves Scripture, also make presumptions based on circumstantial evidence to explain the Scriptures and to bring harmony to them. While I would grant that the biblical implication about Jesus praying for which disciples He should choose is more plain than whether the Enemy augmented Pharaoh's rebellion in Exodus 9, the latter suggestion is at least *reasonable* if we take Job 1—2 and 1 Kings 22 as circumstantial evidence. Interestingly enough, those who point out our circumstantially evidenced presumptions seem not to see the presumptions *they* hold which treat alleged contradictions in the Bible *as though they were true*. In fact, it appears to me that these latter presumptions are much more egregious. Indeed, if a paradigm-shifting *presumption* is being held by either party, it is by those who hold to the idea that God in some sense has predetermined every human happenstance of sin in the world, and that God in doing so should *not* be blamed, while man in doing so *should* be blamed. Thus, after being told that I should not *presume* that Satan had been accusing other brethren prior to when the Lord brought up the more faithful example of Job, the Bible instructor himself (unwittingly) presumed that God had thrown down a gauntlet *in order to* incite Satan, an assumption which meant that God had designed His own temptation at the hands of the Devil. "Temptation," I say, because observe that Satan doesn't say to God, "Remove your hedge of protection and let *me* touch all that Job possesses," but rather that God *Himself* ought to touch all that Job possesses: ("But put forth thine hand now, and touch all that he hath, and he will curse thee to thy face.") Thus, for the instructor to maintain his argument that God designed the activity of Satan was to assume, among other things, that God's *motive* in mentioning Job was more than simply pointing out a truth regarding Job's integrity. It presumes that God incited Satan so that Satan in turn would incite God. I hasten to add that such an interpretation is at odds with the plain language of God saying to Satan that *He (God)* had been the one incited. The problem here is that the instructor equated God's foreknowledge of all the world's events with *planning* them all. This is indeed a *presumption*,[27] i.e., that because God foreknew how Satan would react, He must have therefore *planned* that the Devil so react. Accordingly, for the Calvinist, God foreordains not merely the ends of all history, but the *means*, as well. In fact, this was exactly the Bible instructor's point, i.e., that

God was absolutely sovereign and had to remain the Lord *in* all history. But again, to argue such a point from Job 1 is to argue that God wanted to be tempted. Someone may object here to say that the Bible teaches that God cannot be tempted with evil. However, this objection is incorrect. First, this statement (addressed more fully in a later chapter) refers to God's *willful* ability to refuse temptation, not the theoretical impossibility of God sinning. Second, the Bible tells us that the children of Israel tempted the Lord (1 Cor. 10:9). Then thirdly, of course, there is also the commandment that Jesus gave Satan, "Thou shalt not tempt the Lord thy God," which implies He *was* being tempted.[98]

We will continue, then, to maintain that certain presumptions are admissible, certainly not as Scripture, but at least as plausible explanations, that is, if they stay within scriptural bounds in order to attempt a more harmonious understanding of certain difficult passages in the Bible, including not only the stories of Job and Ahab, but of Pharaoh, as well.

Observe *presumably* then, how Pharaoh, in becoming fully roused, may have believed that the Egyptian gods were in control of the situation despite what was happening. It may seem crazy to us that Pharaoh might still be trusting Egypt's own gods to secure his rule by removing the plagues that affected Egypt, since Pharaoh himself had to make appeals to Yahweh for the removal of each plague; but again, man is prone to such contradictory thinking. Did not Ra, the Sun god, finally exalt himself to overcome the darkness of three days? Did not the Nile restore herself, though evil afflicted her for a time, etc.? Such conclusions would be in keeping with the then Mediterranean pagan belief about the nature of things: for in such cultures there was no simple concept as, say. one tripping over a stone while walking a path; rather, *the stone had made its presence known.* Even so, the Sun and Nile may have been regarded as having first hid, then subsequently revealed, themselves. Thus each of God's stays of mercy may have been to Pharaoh simply another proof that he and the gods of Egypt were ultimately more powerful than the Plague-bringer. Sinful man always seeks a *rationale* to justify his stubbornness and contradictory thinking. (Compare Proverbs 27:22, which tells us: "Though you pound a fool in a mortar with a pestle along with crushed grain, Yet his foolishness will not depart from him.") As if to answer Pharaoh's assumption about the gods of Egypt (or, if our presumption is wrong, *whatever* wrong assumption it was which Pharaoh held was the reason he had remained king), God informs Pharaoh that the real reason he has remained behind as a ruler is because God has allowed it so that His power will be known and that His name might be declared in all the earth. In effect, God is willing to endure with much longsuffering (cp. Rom. 9:22) a pharaoh who has fitted himself for destruction, in order that He might have opportunity to bestow mercy upon all those who fear Him.

The result of God's demonstration of His power was naturally aimed toward benefiting the children of Israel, but it also resulted in the Egyptians coming to know Him: "And the Egyptians shall know that I am the Lord, when I stretch forth mine hand upon Egypt, and bring out the children of Israel from among them" (Ex. 7:5). Indeed, Exodus 9:20 tells us that some of these Egyptians were already learning to fear the word of the Lord: "He that feared the word of the Lord among the servants of Pharaoh made his servants and his cattle flee into the houses" (i.e., to avoid the hail). Furthermore, when Israel finally left Egypt there was a "mixed multitude" that went out (Ex. 12:38), which means that some Egyptians exited Egypt with the Israelis. Apparently, some of the Egyptians had decided that Yahweh was God, or at least more powerful than the gods of Egypt. Because God does not prefer the death of the wicked, God would have preferred that the Egyptians had learned of Him through an obedient pharaoh. But since Pharaoh proved uncooperative, the Egyptians learned of God through the divine judgments brought upon their nation, as under the stewardship of Pharaoh.

In review, then, there appears to be a very solemn thought here regarding Pharaoh in Exodus 9:12. It is that God will no longer engage Pharaoh as he did previously. Verse 12 tells us, "And the Lord 'hardened' (*honored, gave weight to*) the heart of Pharaoh." God had finally decided to allow Pharaoh to set in the cement of his choice. Thus, God ceases to strive with Pharaoh's spirit toward the goal of repentance. What a solemn thought to picture God walking away from Pharaoh, leaving him to his just desserts. For such a divine vacuum the Enemy is always prepared to petition God for involvement. In fact, because the purposes of God and the Enemy are distinctly opposite, the Enemy cannot gain divine permission for *special* involvement to indurate an already stubborn man until God decides to suspend His own plan of striving against that man's obstinacy. Until now Pharaoh must have had his private moments of reflection despite the many voices of magicians and servants he heard during the day. But presumably that time was over, and a lying spirit had come to coerce Pharaoh toward an even greater ferocity of rebellion with a *constant* onslaught of suggestion. Even as many Egyptians had followed Pharaoh out of the natural inclination which countrymen often have for their ruler, so too could Pharaoh now be expected to follow suit under the influence of *his* master, i.e., Satan, "the god of this world." Thus, when granting this context, God's withdrawal from Pharaoh can be said to have fully roused the king's spirit. We may even grant that God '*appointed*' Pharaoh to abide behind and suffer the consequences of his decisions as a fully roused ruler, so long as the Calvinistic baggage which so readily attends the average Christian's association with the word 'appoint' is not applied, and if by 'appoint' we understand instead that God unilaterally decided to allow Pharaoh an undistracted, seared conscience.

Conversely, Calvin's definition of 'appoint' is very different than the one we offer. In passing, let me say again that as long as one defines words like *predestination, election, adoption, foreknowledge*, etc. along the irrational lines of Calvin, one can never escape the Calvinistic model. This statement may seem too obvious to mention, but I found myself doing this very thing while writing this book and trying to define *election* along the irrational lines I had unwittingly always accepted. At one point I had been thinking at length about the doctrine of election and consequently found myself encountering a considerable amount of interpretative difficulties. Finally, I caught my error; I was defining the concept of election irrationally. I had been thinking to myself, "Now how is it that I choose God in such a way that God nevertheless chooses me irrevocably?" Such words as *election, foreknowledge, predestination, adoption*, etc., have incredibly strong Calvinistic associations for many of us Christians, and until we discard the irrationality of Calvin's definitions we cannot arrive at the true, biblical meaning of these words. As for 'election' I came to correctly understand that God's choice was not one where He 'chose my choice,' but rather one in which He 'chose' us in the sense of 'selecting' those he knew ahead of time would agree to the conditions of His selection, i.e., that I be his child upon the condition of my faith in the work of Christ [and thus apart from works (Rom. 9:11)]. This is a choice He knew I would make according to His foreknowledge (1 Pet. 1:2). When considering the word 'appoint,' then, we must seek the true definition of the word, such as we have just given it regarding its appearance in Exodus 9:16 (granting for the sake of argument that the word 'appoint' should even be *used* in translation here). Again, though, when Calvin says that God 'appointed' Pharaoh, he means to define it with all the trappings of his particular brand of dialectical theology. Thus, for Calvin, Pharaoh is 'appointed' in the sense that God is fashioning the vessel, Pharaoh, along the exact lines of reprobation which God the Potter had predetermined before the creation of the world. All of Pharaoh's history, including his ignoble end, is held by Calvin to be predestined by God, and Calvin believes it cannot be otherwise.

Such a Calvinistic definition of 'appoint' raises several other issues. First, there is the problem of God's commands being divided against themselves. As we have already noted, on the one hand the Calvinist says that God hardens Pharaoh's heart so that he (Pharaoh) will not let the people of Israel go. On the other hand, we have numerous statements where God tells Pharaoh, "Let my people go." Thus the question is this: Which command of God shall Pharaoh's history not be in accord? If Pharaoh's history will be in accord with God's command that he be hardened, then it is impossible for him to obey God's command to let the children of Israel go. On the other hand, if Pharaoh obeys God and lets the children of Israel go, then his experience is not in accord with God's decree that his heart be hardened. Such a dialectical expectation of Pharaoh is impossibly demanded of him under a Calvinistic interpretation, yet the Calvinist assumes that God has made it so.

There are perhaps two 'explanations' that the Calvinist can offer to solve his problem of why God would demand of Pharaoh an impossible response. The first is that man (in this case, Pharaoh) cannot disobey God's 'sovereign' will, but can disobey God's 'revealed' will. We have already shown the irrational nature of this Calvinistic 'explanation,' but we should add here that such a dualistic response from the Calvinist was inevitable once he defined God in terms where God would have to be divided against Himself. A God who is double-minded and undependable in all His ways will of necessity have two opposing wills. So the Calvinist, while insisting that God is unified in His being, nevertheless manages to observe what he calls the 'sovereign' (absolute) will of God and the 'revealed' will of God, and defines these two divine wills such that compliance with the one *must* mean non-compliance with the other. These form a natural contradiction because God's sovereignty is claimed to be absolute, yet treated as limited, and let us remember how the Calvinist treats contradictions which support his particular doctrinal distinctives—he *calls* such contradictions *non-contradictions*. Accordingly then, the Calvinist's description of God's two opposing wills is *called* one unified will, and this non-explanation is *called* an explanation.

A second, or additional, 'explanation' the Calvinist may use to 'explain' the conundrum of how Pharaoh's experience can accord with God's two opposing commands, is to say that God is being sarcastic when he commands Pharaoh to let the children of Israel go. In effect, God is merely taunting Pharaoh to do that which he cannot do, i.e., as though God said, "Go ahead, Pharaoh, let my people go! Just see if you can do so in order to escape my judgment!" Our objection to this appeal to idiomatic expression is to ask why God would observe to Moses that "Pharaoh *refuses* to let the people go," indicating that God's command to Pharaoh was meant to be understood in its normal sense. To maintain this explanation of sarcasm, the Calvinist would have to add another 'explanation' and say that God was speaking idiomatically to Moses about Pharaoh 'refusing' to let the people go, i.e., as a humorous deprecation about Pharaoh's inability. This then is how the contradiction would presumably be 'solved.' Note that both non-determinists *and* Calvinists have to appeal to idiomatic language to maintain a consistent argument. It is not an honest assumption, then, to imagine that only the non-Calvinist needs to rely on idiomatic speech to resolve the alleged inconsistency of God's character (e.g., as when the Bible tells us on the one hand that God *strengthens* Pharaoh's heart to the disobeying of His command, yet elsewhere tells us that God has no pleasure in the death of the wicked). Thus, the Calvinist *also* must at times rely heavily on argument based on idiomatic language.

As a general observation, then, we should note that there are three ways theologians may handle an alleged contradiction in the Bible. Take the alleged contradiction currently under consideration, i.e., one in which the Bible states on the one hand that God hardened Pharaoh's heart but on the other hand states that God takes no pleasure in the death of the wicked but that the wicked turn from his way and live. The first way a reader may handle such an alleged contradiction is to state flatly that the Bible *does* have contradictions as evidenced in this example, and therefore the Bible's origin cannot be divine, or solely divine. This is the skeptic's response. The second way a reader may handle an alleged biblical contradiction is to embrace the alleged contradiction *as* a contradiction, but *call* it a non-contradiction. This is the Calvinist's response. The needed resolution is claimed to occur in the mind of a transcendent God whose ways cannot be fundamentally understood even by the believer (at least on this side of life). The third way a reader may respond is that which this book advocates ought always to be the way a Christian responds (whenever and wherever the Bible gives him the authority to do so), namely, that of believing an alleged contradiction to *not* be a rational contradiction, and therefore something to be examined further to see why the two statements are not in actual conflict. Such a resolution will be:

1) along the lines of idiomatic, sarcastic, figurative, or exaggerative language, or
2) no real conflict once the contexts of each statement are better understood, or
3) recognized as not really in conflict once rigorous logic is applied. An example of this sort is when one understands that "will not" can equal "can not" when "can not" means inability that is *willfully* caused.
4) A genuine mystery that remains despite a rigorous application of contexts and the historical-grammatical method. Generally speaking, this will be very rare.[22]

To return, then, to Calvin's meaning of 'appoint,' we would say that Calvinists embrace the contradiction of a God who is *not* pleased at the death of the wicked but *is* pleased at the death of the wicked. (In fact, this is Calvinist apologist John Piper's view as discussed in the Supplement at the end of this book.) Again, Calvinists are prone to *call* this contradiction a non-contradiction. In fact, they call this 'apparent' contradiction an *antinomy*, which presumably can only be resolved by:

1) an appeal to a higher logic understood only by God,
2) an idiomatic use of language so that what God says about the wicked in Ezekiel 33:11 isn't really what it appears to mean, or
3) asserting that 'the wicked', since they are described as able to turn from sin, are the elect of God who have not yet had imparted to them a new nature to believe (i.e., the Calvinist's definition of "regeneration").

Because this theology alleging a divine Sovereign *at odds with Himself* never expressed this way by its adherents, of course) has been endorsed by notable thinkers, such as Augustine, Calvin, Luther, Edwards, etc. (and this despite its confusing nature to many Christians), the sad result has been centuries in which an irrational, indeed, *immoral* Church apologetic has merely exasperated the skeptics of Christianity who have repeatedly asked the same question—Why does evil exist if God is all-sovereign and good? Today, the Church's presentation of the gospel is geared more for attracting those who manage to believe the gospel despite this oft-used, irrational (and therefore meaningless) apologetic of Evangelicals about the nature of God. The inevitable result is a certain dumbing-down of the Body, not to mention a failure to engage certain unbelieving skeptics who otherwise might conceivably have become defenders of biblical Christianity. Instead, these skeptics have been left to their own melancholy corner of the world to brood upon the meaninglessness of life, including the irrationality of Christianity. For today's Church is one in which the gospel appeals more to those people to whom faith comes naturally. Indeed, today's church is one in which its apologetics are all but assigned to a realm of unfathomable mystery, with the 'happy' result that the faith-filled don't have to think very much about their dialecticism. And so the dumbing-down of the Church continues, as words like *foreknowledge, election, predestination, adoption*, etc., remain defined along irrational lines. And doubtless it is in this spirit that Calvin accepted the idea that God hates certain men, and so decided upon the word "appoint" in Exodus 9:16.

Pink's Reasons for Supporting Calvin

In regard to embracing irrational definitions, we should examine the five points that A.W. Pink gives in defending Calvin's view that God reprobated Pharaoh.

First, Pink concludes that Pharaoh did not die of natural causes or an accident, etc., "but *by the immediate hand of God in judgment.*" (Pink thus seems to think that Pharaoh received no mercy at any point). One wonders, however, what Pink means by "immediate [*judgment*]?" Does he mean 'immediate' in the sense that God immediately killed Pharaoh after He witnessed the king's enslavement of the children of Israel before He ever appeared to Moses in the burning bush? Or does Pink mean 'immediate' in the sense that God struck Pharaoh dead after the king refused to consider the initial miracle-sign of Moses? Perhaps by 'immediate' he means that God killed Pharaoh after one of the ten plagues. No, apparently, none of these are it. Apparently, Pink means 'immediate' in the sense that God caused Pharaoh to die with his host in the midst of the Red Sea after a very lengthy period of divine patience. (Yes, that seems to be it!) Perhaps it should be pointed out again that Pharaoh is not even said to have perished in the Red Sea. One of the most definite implications we have of Pharaoh's fate is from Psalm 136:15, where Pharaoh and his army are said to have been "overthrown" in the Red Sea. Whether this refers to Pharaoh's own person or merely to his power is a remaining question. Therefore even Pink's assumption that Pharaoh died in the Red Sea is not necessarily correct, especially when one considers that the Israeli song of victory makes no mention of the death of Pharaoh specifically, but only of his horse.[100] While this may be a poetic metonymy for Pharaoh, perhaps the horse alone attended the Egyptian host as a symbol of Pharaoh's presence, and so without actually jeopardizing the king.

Second, Pink claims that God *raised up Pharaoh…preserving him through infancy and childhood…raising him to the throne of Egypt*. It is clear from this statement that Pink understands "raised" in the normal English sense of raising a child. Hence, he believes that Pharaoh was "raised" from the cradle to adulthood and kingship, and likewise on through to destruction. Pink (like Calvin) thus entirely misses Paul's point that Pharaoh was *fully roused*. He simply assumes the normal meaning of the *English* word given in Romans 9:17 and assumes this is the meaning in the Greek text. We would agree with Pink if, by 'raised,' it was understood that Pharaoh was *raised in full spirit* (of agitation), but obviously this is not Pink's point, nor the KJV's.

Third, Pink declares that *Egypt's king was indeed a 'vessel of wrath fitted to destruction.'* Toward the end of his essay Pink seeks support for this idea by citing like-minded "*Dr. Hodge—perhaps the best known and most widely read commentator on Romans.*" Despite this appeal, we have noted earlier the theological clarity that comes into view once it is understood that the Greek participle *fitted*, in the phrase, "fitted for destruction," is spelled exactly the same way in the middle voice as in the perfect passive in Greek. This would mean a translation of *fitted themselves for destruction*. Pink makes no mention of this possibility, and neither does Hodge.

Fourth, in making the argument that the *heart of the king is in the Lord's hand,* Pink is arguing that everyone's heart is directed by God just like every king that has ever lived. We have already shown that Proverbs 21:1 cannot be arguing for universal applicability, i.e., or the extension of that thought as it might be applied to men in general.

Fifth, and finally, note the language Pink uses to support his argument for a Calvinistic interpretation:

> ...*We must believe, therefore that the Judge of all the earth did right in creating and destroying this vessel of wrath, Pharaoh.*
> ...IN CONCLUSION, WE WOULD SAY THAT IN FORMING PHARAOH GOD DISPLAYED NEITHER JUSTICE NOR INJUSTICE, BUT ONLY HIS BARE SOVEREIGNTY. AS THE POTTER IS SOVEREIGN IN FORMING VESSELS, SO GOD IS SOVEREIGN IN FORMING MORAL AGENTS. (emphases Pink's).

This is a lot of verbal nonsense, but for the sake of language itself we should observe Pink's use of it. Note here that Pink is claiming 1) that God is *the Judge of all the earth*, and 2) that God formed Pharaoh as a *moral agent*, but in such a way (claims Pink) that it involved neither *justice nor injustice*. Our question, then, is as elementary as it can be: How can God be called a *judge* if in regard to Pharaoh He is not declaring what is just and unjust? Isn't that what any judge does, i.e., declares what is justice and injustice? Isn't that, in fact, the *meaning* of the word *judge*? As for Pharaoh, then, *someone* must be *justly* accused in Pharaoh's sin, for otherwise Pharaoh would not be a vessel of wrath. Presumably, Pharaoh would naturally be responsible for his own sin. Yet this raises a dilemma for Pink (as it does for any Calvinist). For if *Pharaoh* is *justly* credited for his sin, then he is autonomous in deciding that moral content for himself, and that means God could not be truly sovereign nor *rule* (command into being) the activities of all men. On the other hand, had Pink said that *God* should be appropriately credited with Pharaoh's sin (as the Creator and Destroyer of such reprobate vessels like Pharaoh, whose thoughts and intents He creates) that would mean the Almighty was responsible for the sinful content of Pharaoh's heart. That, too, Pink cannot allow. Consequently, Pink is stuck with the old Calvinistic problem of wanting to say that God has ordained *all* that shall come to pass, yet not in a way where He has ordained sin. What is Pink's 'answer'? As a Calvinist Pink must keep man's autonomy and God's sovereignty in dialectical tension. This way it can be said that God chooses Pharaoh's choices but not in a way where God chooses Pharaoh's choices. This is why Pink's conclusion (shown above) ignores the *either/or* biblical language which maintains God and man as distinctives, and uses instead the kind of *both/and* mystical gibberish which voids words of their meaning. Hence, Pink's 'Judge' of all the earth is not judging at all (i.e., as Pink says of God in relation to Pharaoh, *neither displayed justice nor injustice*), and a vessel's *wrathful end* is not said to be a result of any process involving "justice" or "injustice." So, the vessel's sinful content which makes it deserving of God's wrath is not said to be *caused* by the vessel itself, much less by the Potter. Simply put, Pink's theology on this point is wholly indefinite in meaning. How indeed, then, can even the content of the vessel be called sinful if no one has caused the content of the vessel? Whenever Christian thinkers have employed such doublethinking, it has always led to this kind of indefinite and inconclusive theology. Thus, Pink's reason (if *reason* it be called) for a vessel's damnation is an appeal to God's 'bare sovereignty,' i.e., which by default is defined as an apparent no-man's land of ethical neutrality (as though such a land could exist) where justice and injustice are not operative. This is Pink's additional '*either*' which he brings into the discussion to solve the already present *either/or* logical problem that confronts him. In other words, it is his *either/or* OR *either* 'solution'. And thus do we properly understand Pink's 'solution' to be irrationalism. Pink's wish for an ethical no-man's land might indeed exist for *plants*, which do no good or evil, but such a 'land' cannot exist for men said to be *moral agents*. As Christ expressed it in an argument against even the *possibility* of neutrality, "He that is not against me is for me, and he that is for me is not against me." There is no third possibility in a good God's either/or universe, despite Pink's Calvinistic longing for it. The only explanation Pink offers is a mystery involving God's 'bare sovereignty,' as though somehow this phrase ([God's] 'bare sovereignty') makes plain all the irrationality of his position which cannot allow justice on the one hand nor injustice on the other in any discussion about sin. As someone has said, "Calvinism sweeps all of its dirt under a rug called *'God's sovereignty.'* " Hence Pink leaves us in a paralysis of unknown definitions. What, then, is 'God,' or 'man,' or 'justice,' or 'injustice,' or 'sovereignty,' or 'wrath,' or even a 'vessel'? None of Pink's readers nor Pink himself seem to know. The strength of Pink's argument lies in his reader's *association* of these words with their real meanings, for such meanings cannot be derived from Pink's own descriptive use of these words. In other words (and to briefly review an earlier point), if I said, "I ate the apple I didn't eat," it is impossible for a hearer not to picture an apple in his mind, even though the statement was non-sensical and therefore absent of meaning in all of its grammatical components. Thus there is only an illusion of meaning which Pink believes *is* meaning, but only such meaning which he claims God can understand. Thus, Pink falls into that group observed by his contemporary, Sigmund Freud, i.e., that some men feel "obliged to speak of God's *inscrutable decrees*."

In short, whenever a Calvinist comes to expressing his conclusions, look for an increased ambiguity in language. Even though Calvinists will use religious and emotionally-charged terms, they have stepped away from a real discussion involving key definitions, such as that for sin. Sin is a problem for the Calvinist because it implies accountability and *cause*. Hence, Pharaoh is called a 'moral agent' and a 'vessel of wrath,' but conversely also just a 'form' which God engages in his 'bare sovereignty' apart from any 'justice or injustice'. I really don't think Pink himself understands how he discusses Pharaoh as though the Egyptian king were anything more than a *plant*. For it is with *plants* that one is neither just nor unjust. It is *plants* that are created and destroyed in their 'forms.' It is about plants that Pink's supporters need not worry about giving a detailed explanation of what it means to be a 'moral agent.' Gone, in Pink's summarizing but ambiguous fifth point, is the kind of dogmatic, B.B. Warfield type of statement about God "creating the very thoughts and intents" of men's souls (such as Pharaoh's). For Pink to invoke such forceful statements here would all but accuse God of sin, and now that a conclusion is being drawn, Pink, as a Calvinist, must back away from meaning-loaded language statements. We readers tend to miss this shift. The tendency for most of us is to read quickly, whether a light novel or a more serious work. Even in theological works readers often plunge forward when reading over a confusing statement, assuming the author will clarify his point in the next paragraph or two, or give other examples to show what he means. Consequently, little critical thought takes place when encountering the first conundrum. With Pink, as with any Calvinist author, readers progress from one irrationality to another and begin to assume, along with the Calvinist author himself, that consistency is proving the author's point. As a result, Christians imagine that lofty things are being said about God, though they are not, and that responsibility is being laid at man's feet for sin, though it also is not. What is offered instead is a confusing amalgam of statements: first, Pink justifies Pharaoh's hardening on the basis that God is the '*Judge* of all the earth' (emphasis added). One sentence later he denies the role of any *justice and injustice* in the damnation of Pharaoh (i.e., principles whose absence would obviously not necessitate a *judge*). A bit later he attempts to buttress the same claim about the absence of *justice and injustice* by saying that Romans 9:18 ("…and whom He will He hardeneth") "has no reference *whatever* to *judicial* 'hardening.' " How anyone can read through the exodus narrative and come away with the feeling that Pharaoh was not at least *also* judged, is truly amazing. Pink tries to convince us with a delay of doublethink. Rather than state in one thought, "God is a judge who is not a judge," he divides his doublethink into two thoughts and uses language coyly. Thus, God is a judge. God does not employ justice nor injustice.

Conclusion of Pink's Argument

Pink's next comment stays consistent with his *ad hominem/pro Deo* approach of condemning man because he is man and exonerating God because He is God. From Pink's comments I find that my prolonged searching and profound study into the difficulties of Calvinism has (according to Pink) been misguided, and that I should rather have had a childlike spirit of acceptance. Apparently such a spirit is necessary to understand the awe-inspiring doctrine of God's arbitrary damnation of men. If Pink is right, some men (such as myself) have perverted what God reveals in His Word about reprobation:

> Mark the language of John 12:37-40, "But though He had done so many miracles before them, yet they believed not on Him: that the saying of Isaiah the prophet might be fulfilled, which he spoke, Lord, who hath believed our report? and to whom hath the arm of the Lord been revealed? *Therefore they could not believe* (why?), because that Isaiah said again, *He hath* blinded their eyes, and hardened their hearts (why?) Because they had refused to believe on Christ? This is the popular belief, but mark the answer of Scripture) that they should not <u>*see with their eyes, nor understand with their heart, and be converted, and I should heal them.*</u>" *Now, reader, it is just a question as to whether or not you will believe what God has revealed in His Word. It is not a matter of prolonged searching or profound study, but a childlike spirit which is needed, in order to understand this doctrine* (emphases Pink's).

Again, the NAS study version before me refers the reader of John 12:37-40 to the appropriate Old Testament passage, Isaiah 6:10. From John we learn that this Isaiaic passage is also a prophecy foretelling Israel's rejection of Christ's ministry. Beginning with Isaiah 6:9, God tells Isaiah to speak a message to the people:

> [9]..."Go, and tell this people: 'Keep on listening, but do not perceive; Keep on looking, but do not understand.' [10]Render the hearts of this people insensitive, Their ears dull, And their eyes dim, Otherwise they might see with their eyes, Hear with their ears, Understand with their hearts, And return and be healed."

In verse 9 we see God instructing Isaiah what to say to the people: "Keep on listening, but do not perceive. Keep on looking, but do not understand." Pink interprets this literally as do many *non*-Reformed commentators. For the latter group this leads to insuperable difficulties for obvious reasons. For Pink it is wonderful stuff. What better way for the Bible to prove that God hardens people than to show His successive commands for people to hear but not to obey? In verse 10 God furthers His instructions by telling Isaiah what to do, i.e., to render stubborn the hearts of the people, etc.

But the key to understanding Isaiah 6:9-10 is to realize that it reveals God's *exasperation* with His people. As sometimes expressed in Jewish culture (as well as other cultures), there is a way of speaking which shows at the same time one's disapproval and exasperation—namely, *sarcasm*. The whole tenor of the above two verses cannot be understood properly without realizing that this is the manner here in which God speaks. Lest someone should think that sarcasm is unworthy of a holy God, we have only to look at Christ's own comment to those who wanted to kill Him: "I showed you many good works from the Father. For which of them are you stoning me?" In Isaiah 6:9 the effect of God's sarcasm can be paraphrased thus: "Go tell this people, 'By all means keep on listening! But whatever you do, don't perceive. Yes! Great! Keep on looking! Just make sure you don't understand!' " God then tells Isaiah to render their hearts stubborn. This instruction floats between sarcasm and literalness, for stubbornness will result, though hardly because of God! Thus, God is telling Isaiah to keep preaching, even though His word will inevitably result in more rejection by those already predisposed to receiving it contemptuously, as though *God* had made their hearts stubborn and not they themselves from their own responses. God slides back into a fuller tone of sarcasm toward the finish of verse 10 to again express His frustration. In effect, God tells Isaiah, *"Make their hearts insensitive, their ears dull, and their eyes dim, because otherwise, well, they might actually believe! And horror of horrors—what would that mean except their healing!"*

Sarcasm occurs when someone speaks in an 'insincere' tone of voice to show that he means the opposite of what he says. Again, the purpose of sarcasm is to make a statement while revealing one's justified exasperation with the other party. That this clever form of expression has been used to great effect by Jewish people to our own day need hardly be stated. It is, in fact, a betimes characteristic of some of their humor even when self-deprecatory, and is also used on occasion in conversational and/or legal argument to great effect. As for the Bible, a few examples come to mind. Paul used sarcasm to make a point to those Corinthians who were puffed up with their own self-importance (1 Cor. 4:10): "We are fools for Christ's sake, but you are prudent in Christ; we are weak, but you are strong; you are distinguished, but we are without honor." All of Paul's phrases can here be presumably understood, at least at one level, as sarcastic *double entendres*, since Paul implies that a relative few Corinthians were of the noble class, and therefore (we suppose) in one sense were distinguished as nominally religious citizens of a sophisticated, cosmopolitan culture, though in another and truly spiritual sense the Corinthians in general (presumably the noble included) were hardly distinguished, as the Corinthians' factious behavior so plainly showed.

The previously mentioned passage in 1 Kings 22 gives us another example of what also may have been sarcasm. There Micaiah appears to have answered Ahab in a manner which told the Israeli king he was being facetious. In effect, Micaiah may have been sarcastically affirming the voice of the false prophets, *"Sure! That's right, Go up to war. Not to worry. Victory's already in the bag."* This invites the censure of the king. Thus, Ahab *chides* Micaiah for his tendency to be sarcastic ("How often have I told thee to speak only what the Lord has told you?") If we are right in thinking that Micaiah was sarcastic, then he annoyed Ahab every time the king wanted to hear what the Lord's prophet had to say. For what else besides sarcasm would have tipped off an exasperated Ahab that Micaiah was not really giving the word of the Lord? Actually, if Micaiah was speaking sarcastically, he *was* giving Ahab the word of the Lord, including the Lord's exasperation! The only other explanation of Ahab's comment against Micaiah is if the prophet had a reputation of being too timid to speak what the Lord wanted him to say. This is certainly possible, for despite their calling, prophets were sometimes afraid to give out God's warning. Yet Micaiah's parting exhortation to all present, that they should mark these words of the Lord, may argue against a general timidity in Micaiah.

Whenever the Bible student fails to recognize sarcasm in the Scripture, the inevitable result is an interpretation exactly *opposite* of what the Bible is stating. Similarly, to whatever extent the Bible student misunderstands sarcastic, double entendres (e.g., 1 Cor. 4:10) either *all* or *half* of the meaning will be lost. Isaiah 6:9-10 is generally of the former kind. As a result, Pink misunderstands the sarcastic point of the passage *entirely*. Far from these two verses supporting the Calvinistic claim that God ordains men into hardness, they actually teach that God's reason for feeling exasperated is because His hearers will not *respond* as they should. Indeed, how else does one explain the oft-repeated description of God's exasperation with His chosen people that runs throughout so many of the Old Testament prophetic books? Why all this upsetment on God's part unless the prophets are assuming that the children of Israel *can* repent? Isaiah 6:10 is actually quoted five times in the New Testament, including John 12:37-40 which Pink cites. Again, one must always return to those Old Testament passages that are alluded to in the New Testament if one is to understand them properly.

Interestingly enough, the verses preceding John 12:37 describe the same kind of hard-heartedness among Christ's hearers as was evident among Isaiah's hearers. Both groups had long exposure to God's revelation of Himself, and this condition appears to be a requisite for justified sarcasm. Unfortunately, these New Testament hearers were truly children of those of their fathers who were rebellious: in both instances of Isaiah 6 and John 12, it is Israel's *own* hard-heartedness in the face of God's overwhelming patience that leads the Almighty to speak with exasperated sarcasm. I have to essentially agree with a comment by a Christian counselor who once told me that sarcasm is the last step God often uses before He gives up trying to communicate to His people.[101]

The Potter And the Pot

Pink finally moves his discussion of reprobation to the Romans 9 example of the pot on the Potter's wheel. Calvinists have gotten a lot of their doctrinal mileage out of this metaphor. According to Pink, the gist of Paul's argument is twofold. The first is that God forms each vessel (i.e., *man*) to function exactly as He [God] wills ("Therefore hath He mercy on whom He will have mercy, and whom He will he hardeneth"). The second argument Pink claims of Paul is that God is not answerable to man as to why He doesn't form all men to avoid reprobation.

The problem with Pink's interpretation of Romans 9:18-24 is that Pink fails to show how the same metaphor of the pot/potter is treated in the Old Testament. Such scriptures should naturally be considered, yet nowhere in Pink's chapters on the hardening of Pharaoh's heart and man's alleged reprobation (nor in any of the writings or presentations of any of the Calvinist books or speeches I have personally read or heard) do I remember these Old Testament passages ever referred to in their contextual detail. Frankly, the evidence of these Old Testament passages is so damning to the Calvinistic view that I would think *every* Calvinist book would attempt an explanation of them. That they have not done so is simply a proof of how, even within Evangelicalism, error is propagated through biblical ignorance.

As already noted, the three most detailed examples of the metaphor of the pot on the potter's wheel are found in Isaiah 29, 45, and Jeremiah 18. In Isaiah 29 God raises a serious complaint against Judah and Jerusalem because his people are making an *appearance* of worshipping Him, though really they have forsaken Him. They are talking the talk but not walking the walk, and so they have deceived themselves into thinking their worship is real:

> [13]Wherefore the Lord said, Forasmuch as this people draw near me with their mouth, and with their lips do

> honour me, but have removed their heart far from me, and their fear toward me is taught by the precept of men: ¹⁴Therefore behold, I will proceed to do a marvelous work among this people, even a marvelous work and a wonder: for the wisdom of their wise men shall perish, and the understanding of their prudent men shall be hid. ¹⁵Woe unto them that seek deep to hide their counsel from the Lord, and their works are in the dark, and they say, Who seeth us? and who knoweth us? ¹⁶Surely your turning of things upside down shall be esteemed as the potter's clay: for shall the work say of him that made it, He made me not? or shall the thing framed say of him that framed it, He had no understanding? (Is. 29:13-16)

Notice the *Forasmuch (v. 13)…Therefore (v. 14)* construction of the passage. Forasmuch as men did evil, *therefore* God judged them. This chronological order of man's reprobation aligns with Romans 1 and 2 Thessalonians 2. Men persist in their *own* stubborn disobedience *after* which God gives them up. Furthermore, the work of the Potter's hand is making very specific *willful* comments directed against its Maker. Thus the rhetorical question of the prophet is not *whether* the Potter's work can talk back to Him, but whether it *ought* to talk back to Him. Calvinists have over-literalized the pot/potter metaphor in Romans 9 because of assuming (while in the forward position upon the dialectical rocking horse) that the parable is stating that clay found in the real world cannot talk back to the Potter while on the Potter's wheel—thus, man, as represented by the clay, cannot effect his will except as God decrees. Such an interpretation entirely misses the point, since the Old Testament itself uses the metaphor to present clay that **is** talking back to its Maker (cp. especially Isaiah 45, in which it states plainly that the pot *is* quarreling with its Maker). The point of the Old Testament is to show the *assumptive* absurdity of the clay's argument (that God is weak and/or powerless to judge), not the *impossibility* of argument. The clay, after all, is a *metaphor*.

Similarly, the metaphor of the pot and the potter is used in Isaiah 45 to describe man in rebellion before his Creator. This chapter begins with a prophecy declaring that God will give the kingdom of Babylon into the hand of Cyrus, ruler of the Medes and Persians. In the process Cyrus will come to know that the God of Israel was responsible for giving him this particular victory, as well as other victories. Since God is the author of Cyrus's victories, Cyrus's rule is unable to be resisted. As Isaiah 45 progresses, Cyrus is shown to be a foreshadowing example of Messiah and His kingdom. Christ, too, will one day rule the nations with a rod of iron, and He too will not be overthrown in His position. In the meantime, by command or allowance, God sets up kings and kingdoms, and they are fully responsible to Him. In this regard Cyrus makes an interesting monarchial contrast to the Pharaoh of the exodus. Both Cyrus and Pharaoh were given considerable positions of stewardship, but only one of them acted responsibly. Historians have noted Cyrus's reputation for generosity and kindness toward those he conquered, whereas the Bible shows Pharaoh to be cruel and obstinate toward the nation he enslaved. Whereas Cyrus came to understand that God was the One who had granted him power and authority, Pharaoh refused to acknowledge God in any genuine way. Thus, Pharaoh's oppression compelled the visitation of God's judgment upon Egypt. But again we would not agree with certain non-Reformed commentators who think Romans 9 is using the term 'Pharaoh' as merely a metaphor of the entire nation he ruled. Pharaoh is treated in Romans 9 as an *individual*, much like Jacob and Esau are treated earlier in the chapter, and not merely (though perhaps primarily) as the representative head of a nation. For example, the phrase, "Jacob have I loved, but Esau have I hated," is an Old Testament reference from Malachi 1:2ff, which refers to the *nations* which descended from these two men; yet Romans 9:16 states that the matter of salvation is not of *him* that desires, nor of *him* who runs, but of God who shows mercy. As for Jacob and Esau, these were individuals whose relationship with each other would be largely representative of the kind of struggle experienced by their respective descendents.[102] Thus we ought not to follow certain (non-Reformed) scholars into concluding that the "vessels of wrath" refer only to nations, not individuals, as we have earlier noted. It should be observed further that Romans 9:17 is certainly speaking of Pharaoh as an individual. Moreover, it is Pharaoh *the individual* who serves as the example of divine judgment which prompts the skeptic's question in Romans 9:19, which in turn prompts Paul's general answer via the pot/potter metaphor in verses 20 and 21. *But again, the chief question at hand is whether the vessels of wrath in the Old Testament are described as merely the recipients of God's constructs upon them, or whether they are willful nations/persons acting in rebellion of their own accord.* The answer seems plain enough in Isaiah 45:1-19 and Jeremiah 18:1-17:

> ¹Thus says the Lord to Cyrus His anointed, Whom I have taken by the right hand, To subdue nations before him And to loose the loins of kings; To open doors before him so that gates will not be shut: ²"I will go before you and make the rough places smooth; I will shatter the doors of bronze and cut through their iron bars. ³"I will give you the treasures of darkness And hidden wealth of secret places, So that

you may know that it is I, The Lord, the God of Israel, who calls you by your name. ⁴ "For the sake of Jacob My servant, And Israel My chosen one, I have also called you by your name; I have given you a title of honor Though you have not known Me. ⁵"I am the Lord, and there is no other; Besides Me there is no God. I will gird you, though you have not known Me; ⁶That men may know from the rising to the setting of the sun That there is no one besides Me. I am the Lord, and there is no other, ⁷The One forming light and creating darkness, Causing well-being and creating calamity; I am the Lord who does all these. ⁸"Drip down, O heavens, from above, And let the clouds pour down righteousness; Let the earth open up and salvation bear fruit, And righteousness spring up with it. I, the Lord, have created it. ⁹"Woe to the one who quarrels with his Maker—An earthenware vessel among the vessels of earth! Will the clay say to the potter, 'What are you doing?' Or the thing you are making say, 'He has no hands'? ¹⁰"Woe to him who says to a father, 'What are you begetting?' Or to a woman, 'To what are you giving birth?' ¹¹Thus says the Lord, the Holy One of Israel, and his Maker: 'Ask Me about the things to come concerning My sons, And you shall commit to Me the work of My hands. ¹²It is I who made the earth, and created man upon it. I stretched out the heavens with My hands And I ordained all their host. ¹³I have aroused him in righteousness And I will make all his ways smooth; He will build My city and will let My exiles go free, Without any payment or reward,' says the Lord of hosts. ¹⁴Thus says the Lord, 'The products of Egypt and the merchandise of Cush And the Sabeans, men of stature, Will come over to you and will be yours; They will walk behind you, they will come over in chains And will bow down to you; They will make supplication to you: "Surely, God is with you, and there is none else, No other God." ¹⁵Truly, You are a God who hides Himself, O God of Israel, Savior! ¹⁶They will be put to shame and even humiliated, all of them; The manufacturers of idols will go away together in humiliation. ¹⁷Israel has been saved by the Lord With an everlasting salvation; You will not be put to shame or humiliated To all eternity. [18]For thus says the Lord, who created the heavens (He is the God who formed the earth and made it, He established it and did not create it a waste place, but formed it to be inhabited), 'I am the Lord, and there is none else. [19]I have not spoken in secret, In some dark land; I did not say to the offspring of Jacob, "Seek Me in a waste place;" I, the Lord, speak righteousness, Declaring things that are upright' (Isa. 45:1-19).

[1]The word which came to Jeremiah from the Lord, saying: [2]"Arise and go down to the potter's house, and there I will cause you to hear My words." [3]Then I went down to the potter's house, and there he was, making something at the wheel. [4]And the vessel that he made of clay was marred in the hand of the potter; so he made it again into another vessel, as it seemed good to the potter to make. [5]Then the word of the Lord came to me, saying: [6]"O house of Israel, can I not do with you as this potter?" says the Lord. "Look, as the clay is in the potter's hand, so are you in My hand, O house of Israel! [7]The instant I speak concerning a nation and concerning a kingdom, to pluck up, to pull down, and to destroy it, [8]if that nation against whom I have spoken turns from its evil, I will relent of the disaster that I thought to bring upon it. [9]And the instant I speak concerning a nation and concerning a kingdom, to build and to plant it, [10]if it does evil in My sight so that it does not obey My voice, then I will relent concerning the good with which I said I would benefit it." [11]Now therefore, speak to the men of Judah and to the inhabitants of Jerusalem, saying, "Thus says the Lord: "Behold, I am fashioning a disaster and devising a plan against you. Return now every one from his evil way, and make your ways and your doings good. [12]And they said, 'That is hopeless! So we will walk according to our own plans, and we will every one obey the dictates of his evil heart.' [13]Therefore thus says the Lord: 'Ask now among the Gentiles, Who has heard such things? The virgin of Israel has done a very horrible thing. [14]Will a man leave the snow water of Lebanon, Which comes from the rock of the field? Will the cold flowing waters be forsaken for strange waters?

¹⁵Because My people have forgotten Me, They have burned incense to worthless idols. And they have caused themselves to stumble in their ways, From the ancient paths, To walk in pathways and not on a highway, ¹⁶To make their land desolate and a perpetual hissing; Everyone who passes by it will be astonished And shake his head. ¹⁷I will scatter them as with an east wind before the enemy; I will show them the back and not the face In the day of their calamity.' " (Jeremiah 18:1-17)

Notice the strong similarity between Isaiah 45:9 ("Woe to the one who quarrels with his Maker—An earthenware vessel among the vessels of earth! Will the clay say to the potter 'What are you doing?' ") with Romans 9:20 ("...who are you, O man, who answers back to God? The thing molded will not say to the molder, 'Why did you make me like this,' will it?"). The preceding verse (Is. 45:8) explains what prompts men to accuse God with such belligerent questions. It is, in fact, their *resentfulness* against God and His righteousness. They would not have God ("He has no hands") nor His righteousness which drips down from heaven and pours itself out on the earth ("What are you doing?... What are you begetting?"). God's righteousness is an effrontery to man because it shows the *standard of measurement* by which he (man) shall be judged. Man resists any outside system of accountability and wants to believe that his responses to life are always justified. And he wants to justify himself so that divine mercy can be regarded irrelevant. Putting the matter as a kind of financial metaphor, we might say that a man wants to be his own accountant, his own IRS, his own government, and his own judicial system. Naturally, then, man resents and replies against any other system. The Bible even indicates that a man's death will not alter his rebellious attitude in this regard. Note those, for example, whom Christ said would make a reply against Him in the afterlife while still calling him 'Lord': "Many will say to Me on that day, 'Lord, Lord, did we not prophesy in Your name, and in Your name cast out demons, and in Your name perform many miracles?' And then will I profess unto them, 'I never knew you: depart from me, ye that work iniquity.' " In effect, people will be saying, "Are we not righteous, Lord? Surely the good works we have done are also regarded favorably in *Your* system of reckoning, are they not?"

Jeremiah 18:1-17 likewise gives us the metaphor of the pot and potter to show how all vessels are subject to God's standard of righteous judgment. The pot is found marred *in* the potter's hand, not *by* the potter's hand. Despite the strong language God uses in verse 6 ("Can I not, O house of Israel, deal with you as this potter does? declares the Lord. Behold, like the clay in the potter's hand, so are you in My hand, O house of Israel"), the pot is not regarded at any time as *unable in will* to resist God, but unable in will to resist the *judgment* of God. This is made plain by the context. God says if a nation repents of its evil He will change His mind regarding the destruction He had thought to bring. Conversely, if a nation does evil He will reconsider the blessing He had intended to bestow. God is thus seen here as responding to what a nation itself decides will be its moral course. This manner in which God speaks of *changing* His mind does not affect the argument that God will respond according to what men do. God can change His intention despite His foreknowledge, for His foreknowledge is not tantamount to predestination (as Calvinists would understand and define *predestination*). At any rate, clearly, these pots are not void of exerting their *will*. This is made even plainer with the examples of Judah and Jerusalem who *displeased* God and were therefore admonished to turn back to Him. Their decision to remain rebellious is shown in Jeremiah 18:12 and echoes the same attitude of the belligerent vessel of Isaiah 45: "It's hopeless! For we are going to follow our own plans, and each of us will act according to the stubbornness of his evil heart." Where, we ask, is the Calvinistic doctrine of divinely appointed reprobation even suggested in all this?

As we turn again to the skeptic's two-fold question in Romans 9:19 we find the following:

> *Why doth he yet find fault? For who hath resisted his will?*

The Calvinistic view of this verse is as follows: First, Paul responds rhetorically by telling the skeptic that he has no right to question God, i.e. "*.Can the pot say to the potter, 'Why have you made me thus?*' " For the Calvinist, Paul's response is the great *period*. End of story. End of apologetic. Paul is saying that God doesn't have to answer the skeptic because the Creator doesn't have to give an explanation to His creatures. Calvinists might cite the last part of the book of Job here in an attempt to support their argument. Elihu says that God cannot be questioned, and God Himself repeatedly rebukes Job by asking him to dare give a response to the Almighty's doings. But in reality, the point of God's rebuke of Job is that the orderliness of God's creation does notably demonstrate God's power and divine nature. Thus Job should have understood God's divine nature and goodness as an observer of creation and not have imagined that God was the cause behind the chaos of his suffering, even when he had no other answer to explain the cause behind his trial. For Job to do so was to flirt with the doublethink that God was at the same time a God of order in creation and yet also a God of chaos who brought destruction in trial. In fairness to Job, it is probably right to assume that every man other than this unique servant of God would have understood the point even less if subjected to the same terrible circumstances.[103]

Second, the Calvinist claims that Paul furthers his argument by not refuting the skeptic's assumption. Paul does not say, "No, you misunderstand me; you're not stating the problem correctly." Rather, Paul upholds the man's own exasperated statement that man cannot resist God whatsoever.

Our first objection to the Calvinistic view is a straightforward one we have already given: If the verse is really stating that man cannot resist God whatsoever, why does Paul immediately respond in the very next verse by saying that the man's reply is *against* God? That is, how can any man make a reply *against* God if no man can resist God's will? Note that Pink at one point completely misses Paul's follow-up statement that the skeptic's reply is *against* God, claiming, "Nor does he [Paul] say, *Men may* resist His will" (emphasis Pink's). What, then, does Pink think the word "*against*" means! The point here is that the skeptic's question as understood by the Calvinist cannot therefore be correct. Note, however, that there is no conflict if one takes the view that the skeptic is complaining about being unable to resist God's will regarding divine *judgment*.

Our second objection to the Calvinist is that he misinterprets the pot/potter metaphor and also Paul's statement that the thing created cannot ask questions of its Creator. In advancing his interpretation, the Calvinist has ignored at least three Old Testament passages about the pot and potter, all of which agree with each other in similar interpretation and take place in a similar context of judgment. *Rather, we would say that to properly understand the two-fold question of the skeptic is to see how Paul answers it.* As Jesus did so many times in His own ministry, Paul first gives an analogy and follows it with its meaning. Thus, Paul's analogy of the pot and potter is really a kind of parenthetical illustration which is ultimately explained in verse 22: "What if God, willing to show his wrath and to make his glory known, endured with much longsuffering vessels of wrath who have fitted themselves to destruction; And that he might make known the riches of his glory on the vessels of mercy, which he had before prepared unto glory..." If for a moment we eliminate some of the parenthetical thoughts found in Paul's main answer, we can see that the apostle's reply to the skeptic is: "What if (i.e., *so what* if) God *endured* vessels of wrath who were fitting themselves to destruction in order that He might show mercy to other vessels?" Paul's reply, especially his use of the word "endured," answers to the word "yet" in the skeptic's question, "Why doth (God) yet find fault?" The skeptic is asking why God should *still* find fault with man if His will in judgment cannot be resisted? The skeptic's argument is thus: Why does God *continue* to allow sin if He is truly upset about it and has the power to subject it to judgment? *Why the delay? Why does He yet find fault?* The skeptic's question is not expressed in naivete or the genuine puzzlement of curious inquiry as Reformed (and non-Reformed) commentators sometimes suggest. Rather, the tone is accusatory and hostile, as Paul plainly understands by saying the skeptic is *replying* (that is, giving an *answer*) with an accusation that is *against* God. The skeptic's question is thus a rhetorical challenge: *Perhaps God is not even able to bring judgment!* That Paul understands the skeptic's reply to be antagonistic (i.e., "against God") implies what the skeptic had, at the least, already concluded about God, i.e., that God, though powerful enough to judge, is unjust and perhaps even a sadist who delays judgment so that man might accrue additional judgment upon himself. If this is not the skeptic's accusation, then it goes to the more fundamental claim that God is not *able* to bring man into judgment. Perhaps both accusations are implied, that God *thinks* to be sadistic, but will prove impotent in the end. If the latter (double accusation) is the correct interpretation, then the former of these two Satanic-like accusations is aimed at God's *motive*: thus, delay equals sadism, not mercy. To this Paul replies that God is not obligated to bring *immediate* judgment since He desires to show patience to those vessels who in time will come to recognize their need for divine mercy.[104] Thus, the vessels of wrath, which incline themselves to a greater judgment, is not God's fault simply because God's righteousness is at work in the world upon vessels of mercy. Indeed, Paul says that God has been extraordinarily patient with the vessels of wrath.

One wonders, then, why Calvinists claim that God ordains all things which come to pass according to His pleasure. Where, we ask, is God's pleasure in the words "endure" and "longsuffering" when the Scripture tells us that God *endured with much longsuffering* vessels of wrath? It is simply not there. In fact, the idea that God endures vessels who are fitting themselves for destruction sounds to me like a Pauline observance of human freedom. Were I still a Calvinist, I would certainly trot out some explanation at this point along the lines of idiomatic expression. And while doing so, I might as well apply it wholesale to the voluminous prophetic passages in the Old Testament that show the same longsuffering God who *endured* sinners. The problem, of course, is that an appeal to an idiomatic expression to explain the words "endured" and "longsuffering" has the same result of misunderstanding sarcasm (cp. Isaiah 6:9-10)—it leads to an interpretation exactly *opposite* of what the Bible is really teaching. Which theology is here building irrationality upon irrationality in Romans 9 because of a willful ignorance of the authorial referred, Old Testament contexts which demand a straightforward understanding of phrases like "*endured with much longsuffering?*" The irony of Calvinism is that it begins with an illogical (dialectical) premise of a good God who shows arbitrary favoritism but then proceeds with *ruthless logic* to change the meaning of any Scripture that would contradict this premise. One is thus reminded of the technique of interpretation used by the early church thinker, Origen. As Renald Showers observes in his book, *There Really Is A Difference*:

> ...Origen developed a new method of interpreting the Bible. This method has been called the allegorical or spiritualizing method, and it stands in contrast to the literal historical-grammatical method. This permitted him to read almost any meaning he desired into the Bible, and it led him into heresy in certain areas of doctrine (for example, he rejected the idea of physical resurrection and believed in universal salvation for all human beings and fallen angels). Concerning this approach by Origen to the interpretation of the Scriptures, [Philip] Schaff has written,
>
>> "His great defect is the neglect of the grammatical and historical sense and his constant desire to find a hidden mystic meaning. He even goes further in this direction than the Gnostics, who everywhere saw transcendental, unfathomable mysteries...His allegorical interpretaion is ingenious, but often runs far away from the text and degenerates into the merest caprice."[liv]

While Evangelical Calvinist believers do not reject the Resurrection or believe in universal salvation for all men, as Origen did, nor form *all* their statements by "merest caprice," they nevertheless hold to a theology of mystical indefiniteness in their *apologetics* about the nature of God, man, good, and evil. This has led them to a technique of apologetic interpretation where idiomatic expressions are wrongly applied to certain biblical passages is a confusing theology where key terms are never defined or properly understood. Again, technically speaking, the apologetic of the Calvinist cannot lead to any meaning whatsoever. Words like 'God,' 'man,' 'good,' 'evil,' 'justice,' 'injustice,' etc. merely *seem* to have meaning in Calvinistic theology because all readers of Calvinistic treatises have previous associations of these words in other contexts *involving real meaning* which they have encountered in their pasts. (We have already seen an example of this in an earlier chapter, in the analogy of the two brothers, one of whom claims to have eaten an apple that didn't exist.) So when the Calvinist says, 'God is good,' we understand that the Evangelical Calvinist is confessing to believe what every Evangelical believes, i.e., that the statement, 'God is good' is to be understood as a child would properly understand the word *good* in its normal sense. Yet the Calvinist has also embraced an interpretation of 'good' that makes it impossible to have a childlike understanding of the statement 'God is good.' Thus, Calvinistic language is being used in a similar way to how some people use the word 'pantheism.' The word 'pantheism,' as Christian apologist Francis Schaefer once observed, comes from two Greek words, 'pan' meaning 'all,' and 'theism' meaning 'God.' So, the word 'pantheism' literally means 'all is God.' But Schaeffer noted that the word 'God' actually means a hierarchical Being, and therein lies the problem with the word "pantheism," for if one is saying that everything is God, then really *nothing* is God. Schaeffer thus notes that a better word would be "paneverything-ism." But "pantheism" remains popular with its adherents because the 'theism' part of the word in 'pantheism' inspires a psychological reaction of acceptance, whereas the word 'paneverything-ism' inspires no one about anything.[lv]

Even so does the language of Calvinism entice its followers by reason of strong, emotional attachments which Evangelicals have made with words like 'God,' 'man,' 'good,' 'evil,' etc. In reality Calvinistic apologetics reduces the word 'God' into meaning *nothing* when it discusses its doctrine of the absolute sovereignty of God, for it does not refer to the one true God of the Bible anymore than it does to a flower or a building. A lie, in other words, has no reality except for its existence as a sinful act against God. Someone might ask why such a book as they are reading now would therefore bother to attack *nothing*. Well, of course, when I say that the Calvinist has defined God as *nothing* in his apologetics, I merely mean it is *nothing of the truth*. A lie is always *something*. It is sin, and sin *is* something, and something bad. It must be resisted for the same reason Christ bothered to reply to the lies of the Devil during the Temptation—for though Satan's lies had no reality concerning the way things really were, they always had reality as sin and rebellion. Thus, it is only because of the shared terms used by Reformed and non-Reformed believers that this book has undertaken to argue as it does. The goal for all Evangelicals is to remember what Paul said about the language believers are to use: "Wherefore putting away lying, speak every man truth with his neighbour: for we are members one of another."

Footnotes:

[96] Nowhere in Pink's discussion of Pharaoh's reprobation does he mention that more than one Hebrew word for *to harden* is used in the Old Testament autographa, nor what implications such Hebrew words might have for the exodus narrative's interpretation.

[97] And note that this presumption is based on defining the word 'foreknowledge' as meaning "divine, relationally intimate knowledge," which is incorrect according to the lexical evidence of what *foreknowledge* means.

[98] That Jesus was led up into the wilderness *by the Spirit to be tempted of the Devil* is merely an expression to tell us that the Devil was *allowed* to tempt Jesus. The Devil only tempts man by God's permission (not commandment). If it were otherwise, then when Jesus told the Devil not to tempt the Lord, He would have been at odds with the leading of the Spirit (if the Bible really meant to tell us that the Spirit *wanted* Jesus to be tempted by the Devil).

[99] The chief mystery I have personally found, relevant to the general debate addressed in this book, is God's foreknowledge apart from divine determination. I personally think, however, that the lexical and contextual evidences are quite solidly in favor of the non-deterministic view.

[100] Similarly, Nehemiah 9: 9-10, as rendered by Young's Literal Translation, does not state specifically that Pharaoh was among those who pursued the Israelites into the Red Sea, i.e., if the reader naturally understands the 'them' in verse 11 to refer to the Israelites (since *them* is stated as having *their pursuers*):

> [10] and dost give signs and wonders on Pharaoh, and on all his servants, and on all the people of his land, for Thou hast known that they have acted proudly against them, and Thou makest to Thee a name as [at] this day. [11] And the sea Thou hast cleaved before them, and they pass over into the midst of the sea on the dry land, and their pursuers Thou hast cast into the depths, as a stone, into the strong waters.

[101] After sarcasm, presumably chastisement.

[102] Observe that God says to Rebekah in Genesis 25:23, "two nations are in thee." This does not mean that Jacob and Esau's descendants were pre-existing souls waiting for ensoulment in history's due course, as some might suggest, but merely that God foreknew that two nations would arise from these two unborn babies. Again, this is not language meant to be understood by strict, literal means.

[103] If someone here objects that orderliness is absent in creation, such as evidenced in the ostrich which God says He has bereft of even such wisdom as would prevent a mother ostrich from stepping on her own eggs (Job 39:13), we may say that death of any sort, even of an animal in its embryonic state, would not have been allowed by God in an unfallen creation, and that if there is a wisdom of God that has responded to the consequences of Man's fall and creation in general, it is not one according to His original intention for His creation.

[104] even as the Prodigal son who, despairing, finally "came to himself," i.e., came to his senses.

Endnotes:

[lii] Pink, Arthur W. The Sovereignty of God. [www.sovereign-grace.com/pink/chapter05.htm]; Chapter Five: "The Sovereignty of God in Reprobation."

[liii] Pink, Arthur W. The Sovereignty of God. Chapter Five: "The Sovereignty of God in Reprobation." [www.sovereign-grace. com/pink/chapter05.htm].

[liv] Showers, Renald E. *There Really Is A Difference! A Comparison of Covenant and Dispensational Theology.* (Bellmawr, NJ: The Friends of Israel Gospel Ministry, Inc., 2009. Ninth printing). p. 130.

[lv] Schaeffer, Francis A. *The God Who Is There.* (Downers Grove, Illinois: Intervarsity Press, 1968).

Chapter 16

Predestination Unto Adoption

One of the disheartening things I came to realize after studying the biblical subject of adoption was the near universal misunderstanding of this doctrine among Christian commentators. My study began with a working definition of adoption I first encountered years ago from a short book called *Subjects of Sovereignty* by Andrew Telford, a one-time professor at Philadelphia College of Bible.[105] Telford stressed a definition based on Romans 8:23, which defines the word "adoption" as the future redemption of our *body*, and therefore not to our present and general redemption *per se*, except in terms that our spiritual redemption makes our future, bodily redemption possible. Recently, however, I wrestled with Paul's discussion of "adoption" in Galatians 4 and began second-guessing Telford's conclusions. I think it is a natural tendency for someone like myself who has no formal seminary training (and but little, formal Greek language study) to yield to the person of superior qualifications. Viewing it from the other end, I understand this tendency for the credentialed person to inwardly *scorn* (not too strong a word if we are to be honest) the thoughts of another who has not endured the same rigors and expense of specialized education. We are all too human. Even as a composer I have to admit of this tendency to *scorn* the music critic who can't play an instrument but who has much to say about the structure of music on the back of a classical CD. Imagine, then, the seminarian who is discussing eschatology with a non-seminarian and finding out that the word "chilianism" means nothing to the person with whom he's talking. The seminarian will find it hard to accept the amateur's thoughts simply upon that basis. Along these lines I remember an elderly, if annoyed, Catholic layman who once confided to me that his priest presumed to understand religion, when in fact he didn't even know that the etymology of the word "religion" came from the Latin *religio*, which means *to bind*. I said little, of course, since I, too, was ignorant of the etymology of "religion." I mention this as an example of how all of us can have a decided *attitude* about, or be influenced by, credentialism and in-house jargon.

Thus, because I too sometimes find credentialism intimidating, I was recently tempted to defer to the commentator who exposited Galatians 4 in *The Pulpit Commentary* (while studying the subject of adoption). I was completely bowled over by the commentator's Greek parsing in Galatians 4 that seemed to leave no corner of the passage's syntax untouched. My own edition of *The Pulpit Commentary* is a WWII era edition that hearkens back to the original late 19th century edition by British theologians,[lvi] and some of the writers in this multi-volume work think nothing of interrupting their exposition with a typical comment such as, "Erasmus says…" and then reeling off eight to ten lines in Latin, none of which, of course, I understand (especially since my high school Latin was nearly thirty years ago and never very good). So then, I have habitually found it natural to think I ought to defer my interpreting skills to one who has mastered all the tools of study. After all, it would seem that one so diligent in the treatment of Greek prepositions in Galatians 4 would almost certainly not misinterpret the *essence* of the passage.

How this commentator interpreted Galatians 4 in *The Pulpit Commentary* seemed to coincide with what other commentators thought. Nearly all seemed to agree that the "child" of Galatians 4:1 is a picture of a man who *becomes* redeemed and therefore adopted into God's family. This happens through a process in which the man comes into a greater realization of his sinfulness because of the law, which rouses him to a greater awareness of his conscience. The man is thus more markedly shown his sinful shortcomings which helps him to understand his need for a Savior. Again, all of the traditional commentary resources I surveyed interpreted Galatians 4:1-7 in this manner—that is, they treated it essentially as a reiteration of the argument Paul gives in the previous chapter. To give us a proper idea of the flow of Paul's argument, let us look at the contiguous passage of Galatians 3:19-4:7:

> [19]Wherefore then serveth the law? It was added because of transgressions, till the seed should come to whom the promise was made; and it was ordained by angels in the hand of a mediator. [20]Now a mediator is not a mediator of one, but God is one. [21]Is the law then against the promises of God? God forbid: for if there had been a law given which could have given life, verily righteousness should have been by the law. [22]But the scripture hath concluded all under sin, that the promise by faith of Jesus Christ might be given to them that believe. [23]But before faith came, we were kept under the law, shut up unto the faith which should afterwards be revealed. [24]Wherefore the law was our schoolmaster to bring us unto Christ, that we might be justified by faith. [25]But after that faith is come, we are no longer under a schoolmaster. [26]For ye are all the children of God by faith in Christ Jesus. [27]For as many of you as have been baptized into Christ have put on Christ. [28]There is neither Jew nor Greek, there is neither bond nor free, there is neither male nor female: for ye are all one in Christ Jesus.

> [29]And if ye be Christ's, then are ye Abraham's seed, and heirs according to the promise (Gal. 3:19-29).
>
> [1]Now I say, That the heir, as long as he is a child, differeth nothing from a servant, though he be lord of all; [2]But is under tutors and governors until the time appointed of the father. [3]Even so we, when we were children, were in bondage under the elements of the world: [4]But when the fullness of the time was come, God sent forth his Son, made of a woman, made under the law, [5]To redeem them that were under the law, that we might receive the adoption of sons. [6]And because ye are sons, God hath sent forth the Spirit of his Son into your hearts, crying, Abba, Father. [7]Wherefore thou art no more a servant, but a son; and if a son, then an heir of God through Christ (Gal. 4:1-7).

Again, most scholars and commentators take the position that Paul is essentially repeating his argument of chapter 3:19-29 in 4:1-7; thus, a man is trained by the law to recognize his sinfulness in order that he might receive the work of Christ and be adopted into God's family. The idea here, according to one Calvinistic thinker, is to imagine a man in court being acquitted for some crime. That is one thing. But imagine if the judge were then to say, "Yes, I've dismissed your crime—but now I'm going to adopt you as my son." Such would be an astonishing gesture of kindness.

Now, in one sense I would agree that God adopts us into His family once we receive the work of Christ. In this sense we might say we are adopted by God. But is this the "adoption" of which Paul speaks in Galatians 4:1-7? I don't think it *can* be—and hopefully this will also be evident to my readers as we biblically evaluate the passage. You see, *to agree with most scholars and commentators that Galatians 4:1-7 is essentially a repeat of the argument in Galatians 3:19-29 would mean that the word 'heir' in Galatians 3:29 is a <u>redeemed</u> person, while in the very next verse the word 'heir' would have to mean an <u>unredeemed</u> person.*

Consider the culmination of Paul's argument in Galatians 3. He talks of the man whose exposure to the law quickens his conscience until at last he believes in Christ. His spiritual journey has resulted in redemption, and he now stands with faithful Abraham to receive God's promises and inheritance. Thus this promise of inheritance makes him an *heir*, and this is the concluding thought of Galatians 3. In the next verse, however—indeed, in practically the subsequent phrase—Paul is still talking about an *heir*. As we follow out the *heir* of 4:1 through the verses that follow, virtually all commentators agree that the *heir* is in bondage to the elemental rudiments of the world (i.e., the *law* mentioned in Galatians 3) until he experiences redemption. If, then, they hold the *heir* of 3:29 to be saved (and we have no argument with that), how is it that they hold the *heir* in 4:1 to be *unsaved*? In other words, what sense would there be for Paul to make such an inconsistent use of the word "heir"? Are we to believe that the apostle Paul is such a poor teacher as to further confuse the already confused Galatians with a hermeneutic that defines the *heir* of 3:29 to be a saved man (living above the law), to defining an heir in 4:1 to mean an *un*saved man (living under the law)? What is the likelihood of that? And yet this flip-flopping definition of "heir" is what scholars and commentators say we ought to believe, since "adoption," they claim, means the *coming into* the family of God. Or again, we must ask how one could be an heir awaiting inheritance in a family and not yet have entered the family itself? Keep in mind that in the 1st century there were no verse or chapter divisions in the original New Testament autographa, and so the whole passage about *heir* in Galatians 3:29-4:7 has an even greater sense of continuity than that found in the Bibles we have today. Thus, it seems beyond credibility that such a flip-flopping interpretation of 'heir' by these scholars and commentators can be correct.

Thankfully, a more reasonable explanation of Galatians 3:29-4:7 can be given. To do so we must return to a biblical definition of "adoption" that we considered earlier, one that promises to logically work in all the passages in which the word "adoption" occurs. We will consider first how the word "adoption" is defined in Romans 8:23. Second, we will examine how the believer's suffering in Romans 8 mirrors the very groanings of creation, a suffering from which adoption will one day release the believer. Finally, and perhaps most importantly, we will see how the sons are described as *already having* the first fruits of the Spirit as they eagerly *await* their adoption which has not yet taken place:

> [12]Therefore brethren, we are debtors—not to the flesh, to live according to the flesh. [13]For if you live according to the flesh you will die; but if by the Spirit you put to death the deeds of the body, you will live. [14]For as many as are led by the Spirit of God, these are sons of God. [15]For you did not receive the spirit of bondage again to fear, but you received the Spirit of adoption by whom we cry out, "Abba, Father." [16]The Spirit Himself bears witness with our spirit that we are children of God, [17]and if children, then heirs—heirs of God and joint heirs with Christ, if indeed we suffer with Him, that we may also be glorified together. [18]For I consider that the sufferings of this present time are not worthy to be compared with the glory which shall

be revealed in us. ¹⁹For the earnest expectation of the creation eagerly waits for the revealing of the sons of God. ²⁰For the creation was subjected to futility, not willingly, but because of Him who subjected it in hope; ²¹because the creation itself also will be delivered from the bondage of corruption into the glorious liberty of the children of God. ²²For we know that the whole creation groans and labors with birth pangs together until now. ²³Not only that, but we also who have the firstfruits of the Spirit, even we ourselves groan within ourselves, eagerly waiting for the adoption, the redemption of our body. ²⁴For we were saved in this hope, but hope that is seen is not hope; for why does one still hope for what he sees? ²⁵But if we hope for what we do not see, we eagerly wait for it with perseverance. ²⁶Likewise the Spirit also helps in our weaknesses. For we do not know what we should pray for as we ought, but the Spirit Himself makes intercession for us with groanings which cannot be uttered (Rom. 8:12-26).

Now, as we explore this subject further, I doubt we can do better here than to offer Andrew Telford's very thorough explanation of adoption, and what adoption means for the believer. We give his explanation here in its entirety from his book, *Subjects of Sovereignty*:

I. The Meaning of Adoption

What does Adoption really mean? It does not mean what we usually take it to mean. Neither does it mean the "adopting of a child." Adoption in the Bible does not mean the same as the word Adoption when used in relation to the legal transaction of receiving into the family as a son or daughter, a child who has been born of other parents. Evidently the translators failed to find a word in the English language that would express to us clearly, the full meaning of the transaction of God Almighty, when God by a divine act, placed a certain destination and position for the believer. The translators have used the word Adoption as the only word at their disposal, to express this act of God.

Adoption means to be "Son Placed", not "son made". You are made a Son the moment you are saved by God's grace. Now, as a son there are certain privileges and benefits God by His sovereign[106] acts has provided for those who are saved. No one has been son placed as yet. One time you will be. You belong to the Lord Jesus Christ now, just as much as you ever will. You have not arrived at the goal which God has predestinated you to—which goal is Adoption.

> Ephesians 1:
> *6. "Having predestinated us unto the adoption of children by Jesus Christ to himself, according to the good pleasure of his will,"*

In the early days of the Roman Empire when a boy was born into the family, he was cared for by his parents till be was twenty-one years of age. At the age of twenty-one, they took the child and there placed him in the market place before the public. He was son-placed. From that time on he could sign his own name to legal documents, and went forward with the full authority of a man. This act at the market place did not make him a son; he was a son when he was born into his parents' family. At the age of twenty-one he was son-placed.

Adoption in the Bible means "son placed." I want you to notice Ephesians 2:7

> *7. "That in the ages to come he might shew the exceeding riches of his grace in HIS kindness toward us through Christ Jesus."*

That unfolding of the riches of His grace will be experienced by redeemed men when we are son-placed…

II. The Time of Adoption

Did you ever notice the word Adoption as set forth in Romans 8:23? Here in this verse we read:

> *23. "And not only they, but ourselves also, which have the firstfruits of the Spirit, even we ourselves groan within ourselves, waiting for the adoption, to wit, the redemption of our body."*

...What is that something that Paul and the saints in Rome were waiting for? It is called by the Spirit of God in this verse the Adoption. He then tells us when it will take place—at the redemption of our bodies. This verse gives us two reasons which tell us that the time of Adoption is future. The first proof or reason that Adoption is still future is that we are waiting for the Adoption to wit. It could not have taken place if they were waiting for Adoption to happen at some future time. In the closing part of the verse, it tells us that it will take place at the redemption of our bodies. We now have redeemed souls in unredeemed bodies. We see here that the matter of Adoption or being son-placed is in the future. Many teach that the new birth and Adoption mean the same thing. This is not the teaching of the Word of God. As a Christian, the new birth took place when I received Christ and became a child of God. Adoption will take place when I receive my glorified body.

III. The Certainty of Adoption

Let us now turn to Ephesians 1:4, 6

> *4. "According as he hath chosen us in him before the foundation of the world, that we should be holy and without blame before him in love:"*
> *6. "Having predestinated us unto the adoption of children by Jesus Christ to himself, according to the good pleasure of his will."*

...For our blessing, and for our comfort, and that we might have full assurance, God has made a tremendous statement in this Scripture regarding the certainty of our Adoption. Notice this verse: "Having predestinated us unto the Adoption." Our Adoption is in the predestination purpose of God for the Church which is His Body. Remember that the word

"Predestinate" always carries with it certainty and surety. Our Adoption is certain since it was predestinated that every believer shall arrive at that goal. Let us look up and thank God, that one day we shall be Son-Placed. Bless God for the assurance of it, and let us daily live in anticipation of this coming experience. God has given us this truth to strengthen our faith and deepen our hope. God says we will be Son-Placed, and please remember that God cannot lie.

IV. The Desirability of It

May we turn again to the Word of God to find what the Spirit of God makes known to us in relation to this matter in Romans 8:23

> *23. "And not only they, but ourselves also, which have the firstfruits of the Spirit, we ourselves groan within ourselves, waiting for the adoption, to wit, the redemption of our body."*

Thousands of God's dear saints would rather be in Heaven than on earth today. Hundreds of them suffer as they live in bodies that produce pain and groanings. They need to be released from the world of sin and wickedness, and know something of the relief from pain and affliction that will come when they see Him at the redemption of their bodies.... Remember that this world is not the sweet Beulah Land that we sing about in the hymns. This is a world of sin and chaos. Paul tells us in Philippians 1:23

> *23. "For I am in a strait betwixt two, having a desire to depart, and to be with Christ; which is far better."...*

than to continue living in a world that is doomed for judgment. Paul desires to be with Christ. In Romans 8:18 to 32, Paul speaks about the glory that is to come. He tells us there is something better on ahead for the child of God, something better than even the best that we have ever enjoyed or expressed down here while in our bodies of humiliation. He tells us in Roman 8:22

that all creation is groaning for something better to come. In verses 22 to 25 he tells us that the Christian is groaning also. He says in verse 23, that not only they, but even we, ourselves, groan within ourselves; waiting for, wishing for, longing for, and wanting that better portion that God has provided for his children. In Philippians 1:23 Paul says,

> *23. "For I am in a strait betwixt two, having a desire to depart, and to be with Christ; which is far better:"*

Here Paul is thinking of the redemption of his body. He is looking and longing for that day to come when he shall leave his body of humiliation behind him and rise to be with Christ. Adoption will never take place until that day when the trump of God will sound. Somehow, there is a tug in every believer's heart that pulls that way. Paul here uses that verse, we ourselves groan within ourselves to show the desire of saints for that better portion. The saints of God desire, they wait, and hunger for the Adoption to take place. Oh, to be like Him, to be like the Lord!...

V. THE PRESENT MANIFESTATION OF ADOPTION

We read in Romans 8:15

> *15. "For ye have not received the spirit of bondage again to fear; but ye have received the Spirit of Adoption, whereby we cry, Abba, Father."*

We thank God that we have received the Lord Jesus Christ as our personal Saviour. Notice in this verse that these believers in Rome had also received the Spirit of Adoption, and the Spirit of Adoption is the Holy Spirit. In this verse he is designated as the Spirit of Adoption. He is in your heart and life now. Do you see this as your present experience of Adoption? As a believer, you have not yet been adopted but you do have the Spirit of Adoption. This verse does not teach that Adoption took place when you were saved, for this verse does not inform us concerning your present experience of Adoption but the present manifestation of Adoption. All believers are indwelt by the Spirit of God and they have the Spirit of Adoption here and now.

VI. THE PARTICIPANTS IN ADOPTION

Notice carefully the closing verse found in Paul's statement in Galatians 4:5

> 5. *"To redeem them that were under the law that we might receive the adoption of sons."*

Let us notice the phrase "that we might receive the adoption of sons." By the use of the word "we", Paul identifies himself with the believers in Galatia, and here we notice that believers are the ones who will be adopted. Adoption belongs only to sons. Let me refer again to the custom in ancient Rome. The father took his boy, that one who was his son to the market place, and that son was son-placed or Adopted. Only those who are sons will ever be adopted. Have it clear in mind that when you are saved you are made a son. Now because you are a son, you shall be son-placed. This is another of the benefits of being a son of God. What benefits are you now receiving as a Christian? True it is, we have experienced the pardon of our sins. We have the knowledge of our salvation in Christ. We have daily communion with Him. We have the privilege of service, and all of this with persecution.The things that I am receiving and enjoying here and now while I am in this body are manifold, but as a son of God there are better things to come. The Bible says in 1 John 3:2

> 2. *"Beloved, now are we the sons of God, and it doth not yet appear what we shall be: but we know that, when he shall appear, we shall be like him; for we shall see him as he is."* [lvii]

Notice again what it says in Galatians 4:4

> *4. "But when the fullness of the time was come,*
> *God sent forth his Son, made of a woman, made*
> *under the law,"*

That was the time when the divine clock in the future purpose of God struck. Let me ask you something. Why did Jesus Christ come? Why was he born? Why did he come into this world at that definite time? In Galatians 4:5, we find the answer.

> *5. "To redeem them that were under the law, that*
> *we might receive the adoption of sons."...*

VII. THE ONE THAT PROCURED OUR ADOPTION

In these closing remarks I just want to emphasize some of the things in Galatians 4:4, 6 that are clearly set forth concerning the purpose of Christ's coming. We notice in these two verses that the Lord Jesus Christ is the One who procured our adoption for us. He made Adoption possible. Surely our hearts should go out in praise to Him who came to make possible all future blessings. "But when the fullness of the time was come, God sent forth his Son." "That we might receive the Adoption of sons." The Lord Jesus left the glory that was His with the Father. He was born as a babe in yonder manger, that we might receive the Adoption of sons. Jesus Christ did not merely come into this world to save you from the drink habit; to save you from blowing cigarette smoke through your nose and mouth, to save you from swearing, or stop you from stealing, or pardon your sins, . . . that was not the main purpose. There is a higher and greater purpose in His coming than that. Christ came not only to save you from the penalty and power of your sins, but He came that you might be son-placed. On the cross He died to take care of my sins, and when I see Him another great miracle shall take place. I shall be "son-placed."

We as believers will be an amazement to the angels as they stand back with a gaze that shall be unbelievable and indescribable. They will behold the wonderful

grace of the Lord Jesus son-placing saved sinners.
Ephesians 2:7

> 7. *"That in the ages to come he might shew the exceeding riches of his grace in his kindness toward us through Christ Jesus."*

We may not be like Jesus now. Oh, we are so much unlike him. Thank God, some day every saint will be like him. That is the real purpose of the Saviour. God had in mind to have sons who would be like his Son. To be son-placed is to be like the Lord Jesus. Friend, that is just what the Gospel does. The man who turns to the Lord Jesus Christ, who puts his faith and trust in the Lord Jesus, can have this abiding hope. Heaven and the likeness of Christ lies before him. This is inexpressible. This is the clear teaching of the Word of God regarding the matter of Adoption. Adoption is a definite act of God whereby God sets a goal for the believer. It will take place when we are son-placed.
Romans 8:23

> *"And not only they, but ourselves also, which have the firstfruits of the Spirit, even we ourselves groan within ourselves, waiting for the adoption, to wit, the redemption of our body."*

When I am son-placed, I will have a new body. It is future, it is certain, it brings perennial joy to think about it. Then we will be there.
If a man is not saved, he will never be there when the son-placing takes place, but if a man receives Jesus Christ as his Saviour he will not miss being son-placed.
This subject has to do with the sovereignty of God. Adoption is one of the future blessings for the man who believes in Christ as planned by the wisdom of the Triune God. No child of God need ever be afraid of losing his Adoption papers. The word of God is eternally settled in Heaven. You will never be allowed to go out into the blackness of darkness forever. What a joy, what a hope, what a satisfaction to know that *"we shall be like Him, for we shall see Him as He is."*

Note in particular Telford's distinction between a son receiving the *Spirit* of adoption versus a son receiving the adoption itself. Newer translations often put the word *Spirit* in lower case, i.e., *spirit* (e.g. Rom. 8:15 NAS), leaving the impression that one is somehow already experiencing the beginning of adoption whose completion will occur in the future at the time of the redemption of one's body. Here, for example, is the NAS:

15For you have not received a spirit of slavery leading to fear again, but you have received a spirit of adoption as sons by which we cry out, "Abba! Father!" 16The Spirit Himself testifies with our spirit that we are children of God,

This opposing view implied with the word *spirit* in lower case offers an interesting thought, but we must ask whether it is truly biblical. Much of the argument over whether *spirit* (Gr. *pneumos*) should be capitalized has appeared to rest on the discretion of the translators. We should first understand that there are no small case *vs.* large case distinctions in the original Greek. The earliest copies we have of the Greek New Testament were written in all capital letters with no punctuation and with no division between words. For example, the sentence, "He went to the store to buy eggs," would have been written,

HEWENTTOTHESTORETOBUYEGGS

Thus, whether or not the word "SPIRIT" is capitalized in translation depends upon what translators believe the context is teaching. All translations seem to agree that the word *spirit* in the phrase, "you have not received a spirit of slavery" should be in lower case. Not all translations, however, agree about capitalizing the word "Spirit" (as given in the KJV) in the next phrase, i.e., "but you have received the Spirit (a spirit) of adoption," or even if the article "the" or "a" should precede it. I personally think that an analysis of the surrounding verses argue that "*spirit*" ought to be capitalized to read "Spirit," but that the article should be "*a*." First, the idea that we have received a *Spirit* of adoption, and not the actual adoption itself, seems plain from the fact that the sons of God, as noted by Telford, already have the first fruits of the Spirit *but are awaiting their adoption,* as verse 23 tells us.[107] Furthermore, the fact that the article is missing in front of the word 'Spirit' does not mean that the translation must read, '*a spirit of adoption,*' anymore than it should have to read, '*a Spirit of adoption.*' We might say that the phrase, "a Spirit of adoption" is preferable for the same reason that the phrase, "We serve a God of miracles," is better than the phrase, "We serve the God of miracles." This latter phrase practically leaves the impression that there are other Gods in existence, but that we serve the particular God who does miracles. (The near and far contexts of Scripture would obviously prevent that the term (Gr. *pnuema*), if translated "a Spirit," were arguing for a plurality of Gods.) Thus, by using the phrase "a God of miracles," the emphasis of the sentence is upon the *attribute* of God, rather than upon God Himself. For these reasons I think a better translation than the KJV or NAS would be to render the phrase in Romans 8:15 as "a Spirit of adoption," rather than "the Spirit of adoption" (KJV) or "a spirit of adoption" (NAS) (that is, if one's responsibility as a translator is to render *either* "a" or "the," i.e., instead of "a/the" which would show a possible polyvalent emphasis on both points, i.e., the *attribute* of *the* (that is, the one and only) Spirit of God.[108]

We can only suppose that the NAS and the NIV chose to render the phrase "a spirit of adoption" with the lower case "s" for "spirit" because the article was omitted in front of "SPIRIT," and because it kept a certain parallelism with the small case of 'spirit' in the preceding phrase ("the/[a] spirit of slavery"). All of these considerations lead us to ask the question: What other corroborating evidence in Scripture might justify the translation that suggests that "adoption" happens upon conversion? In other words, since verse 23 describes "adoption" as something the sons of God eagerly await while already having the Spirit's first fruits, what scriptural evidence does the Calvinist present for his view beside commentator opinions? It would appear that the answer is none at all, at least none I have been able to find. Rather, as author T. Pierce Brown exasperatingly states in his article, "Born or Adopted," the evidence cited by the opposing view relies on the translators' insistence upon the English dictionary meaning of "adoption:"

> The Greek term translated "adoption" is "huiothesia" about which Thayer says, "The nature and condition of the true disciples of Christ, who by receiving the Spirit of God into their souls become sons of God." He adds, "It also includes the blessed state looked for in the future life after the visible return of Christ from heaven—i.e., the consummate condition of the sons of God which will render it evident that they are sons of God." We wish that we and our readers were always able to differentiate between a casual opinion expressed by an "authority," and a scholarly, definitive conclusion, arrived at and proven by the proper analytical methods. Also, we wish the authority or the student would make a proper distinction between the meaning of a term and the thing to which the term refers in a particular context. For example, "baptizo" means "dip, plunge, immerse, overwhelm, etc." It may refer to immersion in water for the remission of sin,[109] being overwhelmed with

grief, suffering, etc., or in some denominational terminology, "a water ritual by which one is designated a member of a religious group."

So, we suggest to you that the term "huiothesia" means "standing as sons." Whether it refers to some 'standing' or 'position' which sons may have in a particular situation, or whether it refers to a *coming into* a position as a son depends on how we actually find it used in the Bible. The only clear statement of which we are aware which indicates its use in the New Testament is the one in which Thayer says "it *also* includes" in Romans 8:23, which says, "And not only so, but ourselves also, who have the firstfruits of the Spirit, even we ourselves groan within ourselves, waiting for our adoption, to wit, the redemption of the body."

As far as we know, it is not used in the Septuagint, and as far as our limited ability and resources allow us to check, we find no case from Herodotus to the "church Fathers" (including the New Testament) where the word clearly means "coming into a family." We admit that all the reference works to which we have access define the word "adoption" as "an act by which a person takes another person into his family," or words to that effect. But a careful student may notice that *none* of them in that definition gave as a reference the word "huiothesia" and shows that *it* was used in that way. In *every* case we have checked, the "authority" takes the English word, "adopted," and applies *it* to what has happened, such as Jacob adopting Ephraim and Manasseh, or Mordeciah adopting Esther, or the daughter of Pharaoh adopting Moses. But the word "huiothesia" is never used about these cases.

We have no objection to the use of the word "adopted" in those cases, but we *do* have serious objections when a "scholarly authority" makes a group of statements about "adoption" and *assumes*, and allows his readers to assume, that he has somehow defined the term "huiothesia" which God used, and which men have erroneously translated "adoption." The reason we say this is because the word, in any use we have found, *never* clearly refers to what the term "adoption" means to us—"the act by which a person takes a stranger into his family."

The etymology of the word suggests that it literally means "standing as a son," and probably most of us, including the "authorities," have *assumed* that means "becoming a son." Keenly aware of my limited ability, training, and resources for scholarly research, I am still forced to conclude, at this moment, that the word refers to one who *is* a son coming into a certain standing *as* a son, but in *no* case, simply *becoming* a son, equivalent to what we mean by being born, or adopted. In *every* case, we think it is not "sonship," per se, that is being considered, but the standing or position to which the sonship entitles one.

The only verse I know that clearly defines one such aspect of "adoption" is Romans 8:23, to which we previously alluded. The "redemption of the body" *cannot* refer to our *present salvation,* for it is "we who have the firstfruits of the Spirit" who are "waiting for our adoption, the redemption of our bodies." There are four other times the word is used in the New Testament, *none* of which violates the basic meaning of the term. It is true that they do not as clearly express the idea as this passage, but if *one* passage sets out what a term means, and no other passages show any other meaning, how better can we discover the meaning of *any* term?

In Romans 8:15, we find, "For ye received not the spirit of bondage unto fear, but ye received the spirit of adoption, whereby we cry, 'Abba, Father'." It is apparently assumed by most of us that Paul means, "When you *became* a son, you received the spirit of a son, whereby you can now say, 'Father.'" My judgment is that the "spirit of adoption" is the spirit of one who *is already a son*, now looking forward to what Paul expresses in the next two verses—the glorification with Christ when we come into our inheritance as heirs of God and joint heirs with Christ. Is there anything wrong with the concept that one who *is* a son should have the "the spirit of sonship"—the spirit in which he yearns for a particular standing as a son (which is what the word "huiothesia" means)?

In Romans 9:4, the Israelites are mentioned as those "whose is the adoption." Most commentators, I presume, would admit that the term has nothing whatever to do with "being born again," but refers to their standing as sons. Yet, no commentary of which I am aware does any more than make a statement about the meaning of the English word "adoption" as if it were the meaning of "huiothesia" which all scholars admit means "standing as sons" not "becoming a son." The point I am making is that "huiothesia" *never* refers, as far as we can tell, to *coming into the family*, as being "born again" or literally, "being generated from above" does. It *always* refers to the standing or position of a son who has the rights and privileges of the inheritance—whatever they may be. In our case, they involve the redemption of the body, and whatever glorification we shall have with Christ.

This seems to be very close to the idea found in Galatians 4:1-4. The Israelites were heirs, but it did not do them much good as long as they were like bondservants. But God sent forth his Son to redeem them that they might receive the "adoption of sons." Most of us have apparently *assumed* that he meant "that they might be adopted *as* sons." But it does not say that. Although I do not approve of the NIV in general, I happened to notice right now that it is here translated, "The full right of sons." I do not know how the translators arrived at the conclusion that this is the correct idea, but I suppose even a blind hog can occasionally find an acorn. Instead of Paul saying that Christ came to redeem the Israelites that they might *come into* the family of God, he is saying that he came to redeem them that they might receive the "adoption *of* sons"—the full right of sons—a special position that an adult son will receive as an heir, as verse 7 suggests.

In Ephesians 1:5, we are told that he "foreordained us unto adoption as sons." This has been understood (or misunderstood) to mean "adopted *into* the family of God that we might *become* sons." It does not say that. What it actually teaches is that he chose us before the foundation of the world that we, who have chosen to be holy and without blemish—sons of God—might receive the "adoption as sons"—the standing or position AS adult sons, to the praise of the glory of His grace, or as verse 14 climaxes it, "Unto the redemption of God's own possession."

…I am willing to stick with Paul's definition in Romans 8:23, unless someone can show that God somewhere gives another one. So far I have not found it[lviii]

Thus as Brown points out, no commentary regarding the word "adoption" which he resourced defined the translation by the autographa, but rather defined the autographa by the translation, i.e., the tail has been wagging the dog. As a concluding thought upon Brown's article, perhaps we ought to concede one aspect of the *adoption* argument to those commentators who have reached a conclusion other than that of Telford and Brown. *Huiothesia*, or "son placement," in Roman culture *could* happen simultaneously, it seems, in the case of a slave who had come of age. In the movie Ben Hur we have such an example as taken from Roman culture, when Judah Ben Hur is publicly declared a son by the centurion whose life Judah saved. In such a case the slave, like Judah Ben Hur, would become the man's son while at the same time come into all the rights and privileges pertaining thereto. As a concession to the opposing view I believe it *may* be correct to observe that *huiothesia* can refer in Roman culture to *the entering into a family*. This might at first appear to be somewhat in deference to Telford and Brown. The point, however, is which of these two definitions (if we grant that there *are* two definitions) of "adoption" are used *in the Bible*, or are both definitions in view? T. Pierce Brown's conclusion is that the biblical contexts which discuss *huiothesia* never contradict "son-placement" *as* a son, but do contradict a meaning of *becoming* a son, and I think his argument is correct in light of Romans 8:23 and Galatians 3:19-4:7. Clearly, in Romans 8, Paul is using the example of a son who is already demonstrating the first fruits of the Spirit. The same holds true for the *child* of Galatians 4:1. It is the *child* who is *de facto* an heir, a "lord of all," though in a practical sense he differs nothing from a slave. He is subject to the rule of others as though he were a slave despoiled by the world, i.e., he is under guardians and household managers who act at the behest of the father to safeguard the child's interests. In time it should be natural that the child (Gr. *nerion*, an *infant*, or *child*) should mature and take his place by his father. A different word is used in Galatians 4:5-7 to describe the *nerios* of verse 1. The *nerios* has matured into a *huio*, i.e., a *son*.[110] Note that Ephesians 4:4-5 is another passage describing adoption along these same lines:

> ⁴According as he hath chosen us in him before the foundation of the world, that we should be holy and without blame before him in love: ⁵Having predestinated us unto the adoption of children by Jesus Christ to himself, according to the good pleasure of his will,

Here it does not speak of "the *children* of adoption," as the KJV would have us conclude from its translation, but rather, as the NAS has since properly rendered it, "the adoption of *sons (huios)*." (Once again the KJV shows a strong predilection for Calvinistic definitions.) The "adoption" of sons is what God shall give all believers. He intended it first for Israel, but not all Israel believed. The gospel was thus opened to the Gentiles, and now all who receive Christ stand as heirs ready to receive the "*adoption as sons.*" The apostle, then, puts the term "son-placement" in a context of believerhood, or, as would have been the case with Israel, the believerhood God had intended for them. Within the Church there appears to be some "children" (i.e., those who are presumed to be new believers), whose behavior puzzles us. This in turn raises questions about their spiritual paternity. Are they really the children of God, or still the children of wrath? (Eph. 2:3). This question only comes to the forefront if the child remains a child. Presuming the former, the Galatians nevertheless had the appearance of infant, spiritual children (*nerios*) instead of mature sons (*huios*), and therefore Paul fears that his labor for them may have been in vain.

The distinction between an infant (*nerios*), a dependent and somewhat older child (*tekna*), and a mature son (*huios*) are important distinctions that Paul maintains whenever these words are present in his discussion of the believer's position in Christ. Again, Paul's use of "adoption" in Romans 8:23 cannot be logically understood to mean "an act by which a person takes another person into his family." The great majority of commentators have merely fed the cause of Calvinism by failing to think logically about these key passages regarding the believer's future glory. Their influence has made many to suppose that God's predestination of the believer unto adoption means that some people are chosen for heaven before they are born, while others are 'sovereignly passed over.' Not only has this error added more chaos to the already existing quagmire of Christian apologetics, but it has sacrificed an opportunity for all Evangelicals to reflect upon the hope of the believer's future glorification. And so we watch the tail wag the dogma instead of seizing the opportunity to teach the subject of adoption properly. This is the unfortunate direction of the Church, at least the status of the American Church at present. And the same spirit which animates the failure to discern true wisdom in this matter has compounded many other similar errors. In short, all this goes a long way toward explaining the weakness of proper thinking in today's Evangelical Church and of key doctrines that have ended up redefined in the Calvinist's hands.

PREDESTINATION

We will say but a few words regarding "predestination,"[111] since we have largely treated the subject via a backdoor discussion about *son-placement*. The verses about "predestinate" (or, as Gordon Olson points out regarding the lexical evidence based on over 30 appearances by early church fathers, a word better understood as *preappoint*),[112] which have been such a bane to some, and yet such a weapon for others in promoting a doctrine of absolute divine sovereignty, is the well-known passage of Romans 8:29-30. Let us begin with verse 22, and I will take the liberty of inserting the essence of Tim Geddert's understanding into verse 28:

> [22]For we know that the whole creation groans and labors with birth pangs together until now [23]Not only that, but we also who have the firstfruits of the Spirit, even we ourselves groan within ourselves, eagerly waiting for the adoption, the redemption of our body. [24]For we were saved in this hope, but hope that is seen is not hope; for why does one still hope for what he sees? [25]But if we hope for what we do not see, we eagerly wait for it with perseverance. [26]Likewise the Spirit also helps in our weaknesses. For we do not know what we should pray for as we ought, but the Spirit Himself makes intercession for us with groanings which cannot be uttered. [27]Now He who searches the hearts knows what the mind of the Spirit is, because He makes intercession for the saints according to the will of God. [28]And we know that in all things (situations) God works together with those who love him for the good, for those who are called according to His purpose. [29]For whom He foreknew, He also predestined to be conformed to the image of His Son, that He might be the firstborn among many brethren. [30]Moreover whom He predestined, these He also called; whom He called, these He also justified; and whom He justified, these He also glorified (Rom. 8:22-30).

First, note that God foreknows whom He predestinates (preappoints). Calvinists claim that foreknowledge means something more than knowing the future—that it implies the kind of intimate knowledge only a Creator could have for His creation, i.e., the kind which Adam, for example, had for his wife Eve, when he "knew" her (i.e., in Adam's case, intimately and sexually). Again, however, the Greek word *foreknowledge (proginwskw)* in extra-biblical sources contemporary with the New Testament era never implies such an attached understanding, but simply means, *to know ahead of time*.[113] I will admit to feeling dubious about what such a Calvinistic definition of *absolute and decreed* foreknowledge actually means for Calvinistic theology with its implied parallel message about Adam 'knowing' Eve in sexual union (again, when one considers those statements within Calvinism which stress God's *complete* sovereignty), i.e., that the more powerful party does subject the weaker party to all of the greater party's means and ends, according to the unilateral design of the greater party. How such a view of absolute sovereignty thus escapes the charge of the spiritual rape of human freedom remains to be answered. Or are we mistaken to think that Calvinists are describing persons as something more than computers, which likewise are said to *do* tasks, when in fact such activities are the mere programmatic responses (i.e., '*choices*') predetermined by the Programmer? At any rate, following this Calvinistic line of reasoning (i.e., that foreknowledge means more than just knowing what shall happen in the future), God's foreknowledge is therefore thought by Calvinists to include all the means and ends of believers and all the means and ends of unbelievers. What the Calvinist fails to properly see, then, is that God's foreknowledge is a complete foreknowledge of history apart from determining it. God doesn't have to control history to foreknow it, as Jesus plainly stated in Matthew 11:21.[114] The point here is that God has never needed to sin or to have partaken in sin in order to understand the experience of sin. His knowledge includes the knowledge of good and evil, yet He Himself has never sinned to obtain that knowledge. On the other hand, Adam and Eve could only gain the knowledge of good and evil by sinning [because as man (i.e., as being in the state of mannishness) they were persons of a lower order]. This is shown in Genesis 3:22-23:

> And the Lord God said, Behold, the man is become as one of us, to know good and evil: and now, lest he put forth his hand, and take also of the tree of life, and eat, and live for ever: Therefore the Lord God sent him forth from the garden of Eden, to till the ground from whence he was taken.

When God said that Adam had now come into the knowledge of good and evil He was not describing Adam's sheer ability to know anything right or wrong. Before the Fall Adam would have had to know it was wrong to partake of the forbidden fruit, or else he would not have understood God's command. In Hebrew the word "knowledge" in the phrase "knowledge of good and evil" means a higher, or hidden, or exalted type of knowledge. But the basic element of knowledge was simpler in pre-Fallen Adam. Still, Adam's conscience told him what was right or wrong. Again, then, the possession of the knowledge of good and evil for Adam was something he obtained by sinning, whereas God has always had the knowledge of good and evil apart from sinning. Yet the Calvinist makes God into a God of sin by insisting that God's foreknowledge is based upon, nay, even *dependent* upon, His determination of all history—a history which decrees that men sin. Furthermore, the Calvinist believes that God's determination of history is only possible if He has *experienced* history. Thus, to maintain this view that God's foreknowledge is solely based on determinative *experience*, I have even seen Calvinists insist that God is outside time and space and therefore *experiences* history before it happens. James Spiegel, for example, even endorses the idea that God is outside time, space, *and* emotion. In all this irrationality, one wonders how the Calvinist can also suggest that Adam was really made in God's *image*, if on the one hand God is not a being of time, space, or emotion, but Adam *is* a being of time, space, and emotion. Indeed, what realms are more elementally shared than these?[115] This is the irony and irrationality of the Calvinistic position, i.e., that Calvinists decry others of holding a dim view of God's sovereignty, when, in fact, it is the Calvinist who finds himself forced to view God as small enough not to be able to have foreknowledge unless He controls everything about the future in all its means and ends (and which *means and ends* in the physical time/space world have to be irrationally understood, since God is said *not* to inhabit time and space). It would almost be amusing, were it not sad, that Calvinists can swallow so many contradictions while simultaneously holding the line on one conundrum, i.e., God's non-determinative foreknowledge. But unless one accepts the fact that God's foreknowledge of history is *truly* separated from history itself (i.e., not 'separated' as the Calvinist would define it), one will define foreknowledge so that God is a control monger who unilaterally determines the destinies of both believers and unbelievers. For example, one confused thinker on the internet (who failed to truly separate God's foreknowledge of history from history itself) so completely stripped Romans 8:29-30 out of its surrounding context about God working with the *believer* in his earthly life of trial, while also failing to understand Paul's synopsistic ellipsis that those "whom God foreknew" refers to those whom God foreknew *would believe*, that he attempted to claim that because God justified those he foreknew, it was impossible that foreknowledge could mean foreknowing only, since God foreknows what everyone will do in the world but not everyone is saved. (Yeah—don't worry if you didn't follow that one!) We must understand that a proper, biblical definition of foreknowledge is that God knows everything there is to know, both actually and contingently. This defines *foreknowledge* as the following: *God knows exhaustively what will happen and what could happen without predetermining anyone else's choices.*

But moving on, the ultimate end of the believer is to be with his Lord and to be like Him, and someday the believer will quit the groanings of this life for a life with Him in glory. This is what Paul meant when he said that we are predestined (preappointed) to be conformed to the image of His son. Note how Paul speaks first about the "adoption" (glorification) of our body in Romans 8:23, then proceeds to discuss our conformity to the image of God's Son *in toto* in verse 29. Arguably, the adoption might itself constitute this conformity; at the least, it is a part of it. This anticipated state of our bodily glorification is a chief thought behind Romans 8. And the same conclusion in Romans 8:23 about son-placement is again in view when Paul speaks in Ephesians 1 about our predestination (preappointment) unto son-placement, *not* salvation:

> [4]According as he hath chosen us in him before the foundation of the world, that we should be holy and without blame before him in love: [5]Having predestinated us unto the adoption of children [lit. *huiothesia*, thus, 'adoption of sons'] by Jesus Christ to himself, according to the good pleasure of his will, [6]To the praise of the glory of his grace, wherein he hath made us accepted in the beloved.

Positionally in Christ we are holy and without blame, but experientially we still struggle with sin. The original Greek demands no colon after the phrase, "before him in love," hence the connective thought may be stronger than what the colon implies, so that it could just as easily translate to the idea that God wants us to be "holy and without blame before him in love—having predestinated [preappointed] us unto the placement of sons," etc. Even so, the apostle John likewise tells us in 1 John 3:2:

> Beloved, now are we the sons [huios] of God, and it doth not yet appear what we shall be: but we know that, when he shall appear, we shall be like him; for we shall see him as he is…

Again, when the concept of "predestination" (preappointment) is raised in Ephesians 1:10-12, Paul puts it in the context of our future glorification: [10]That in the dispensation of the fulness of times he might gather together in one all things in Christ, both which are in heaven, and which are on earth; even in him: [11]In whom also we have obtained an inheritance, being predestinated according to the purpose of him who worketh all things after the counsel of his own will: ¹²That we should be to the praise of his glory, who first trusted in Christ.

Observe here how the believer in Christ is said to be predestined (preappointed) to obtain an inheritance. This is a long way from saying we are predestined to be saved. While salvation is necessary to obtain an inheritance, the Bible (KJV) never says we are predestinated unto salvation, but only unto <u>conformity to the son</u>, predestinated <u>unto son-placement</u>, and predestinated to <u>*[obtain] an inheritance*</u>. Thus, the same essential thought is expressed each time the word *predestinate* or *predestinated* is given in the Scriptures.

Incidentally, many Calvinists like to cite another thought from the Ephesians 1 passage in an attempt to support their theology:

> *Who* [God] *worketh all things after the counsel of his will.*

Notice, however, that "all things" is contextualized in verse 10 to be merely "all things *in Christ*, both which are in heaven, and which are on earth, even *in him.*" Where, then, is that point of Calvin's theology, that would tell us that a doctrine of predestination unto salvation is found in any of the passages we have examined? We cannot find such a definition except from commentators who are so convinced that these verses teach Calvinistic doctrine that they are prepared to have Calvin's terms interpret the translation which then interprets the autographa. This is the sad state of Christian apologetics, because Calvin's definitions have been accepted regarding *foreknowledge*, *predestination*, and *adoption*. Calvinism teaches that God foreknew us based upon His predestination of us, and that God chose us unconditionally to be in his family before we were ever born. In Calvinism, the Divine will is accomplished without any real choice-based participation of the man. This elimination extends to man predicating his faith, which Calvinists allege is imparted to man apart from his will (though the Calvinist would deny this view of his theology, urging instead that we accept his attempted distinctions between *desire* and *will*, terms which, in fact, we have already shown he treats synonymously, if irrationally). Frankly stated, Calvinism has succeeded in fooling many Christians about the real meaning of foreknowledge and predestination because of redefined meanings which culminate in a feel-good theology. Regardless of whether a Christian has good moments or bad moments God, in the Calvinistic view, has already predestined everything that is going to happen to him. I cannot think of a more blissful thought for the Christian. Here every trouble is seen as a good that God is giving us—where even sin itself bows its knee to serve the purposes of God and His pleasure. Well, enough of that view. Calvinism has been a theology of *panacea*, if we would just be honest about it for a moment. Grown-up Evangelicals cling to this idea of God as ardently as children cling to a belief in Santa Claus, and for pretty much the same reason. And so I am reminded of what Paul told Christians they ought to do in a circumstance where a greater maturity is needed.

> When I was a child, I spoke as a child, I understood as a child, I thought as a child: but when I became a man, I put away childish things.

This verse reminds us of what Paul said to the Galatians—*When we were once children*. So we are heirs and lords of all, but we haven't yet seized some of the adult things of our faith. Instead we have counted off a long string of chaotic, red-letter days for Christian theology and apologetics by allowing the doctrines of *foreknowledge, election, predestination,* and *adoption* to be handled by theological determinists to a point where nothing of true biblical definition has remained. Rather, this ought to be a time for truth-telling in theology about the Lord's coming and our redemption that "draweth nigh"—a time when we await our adoption as *huios*, not *nerios*—*mature sons*, not *infants*.

Footnotes:

[105] —since renamed *Philadelphia Biblical University*

[106] As the context of Telford's remarks show, by the word "sovereign" Telford does not mean "sovereign" as the Calvinist would define it.

[107] Compare Philippians 3:20-21: "For our citizenship is in heaven, from which also we eagerly wait for a Savior, the Lord Jesus Christ; who will transform the body of our humble state into conformity with the body of His glory, by the exertion of the power that He has even to subject all things to Himself."

[108] A qualifier should be added here for additionally allowing the phrase to be rendered as "a spirit of adoption," but only because of the reason given by T. Pierce Brown in the article that shortly follows.

[109] T. Pierce Brown appears to belong to the Church of Christ. Although some in the Church of Christ believe that water baptism is necessary for the forgiveness of personal sins, I do not believe this doctrine is true. For according to Romans 10:9-10, "with the heart man believeth unto righteousness; and with the mouth confession is made unto salvation." Nowhere here, nor in any other biblical passage once it is properly understood, is water baptism implied to be necessary for personal salvation.

[110] *When we were children* is in the past tense. But Paul is not really stating that they are no longer children (and therefore mature sons), because elsewhere he states his fear that their bondage to works is so severe that he wonders if his former ministry to them has been in vain. Rather, Paul's expression is a manner of face-

saving speaking so that the Galatians will reconsider their view of works to which they have entangled themselves. To the strong Paul is strong, and to the weak Paul is weak: whatever was the state of the hearts of the Galatians, it does not appear that it was attended with that degree of hubris which caused Paul to take a severer line with the Corinthians. Paul's manner of speaking—*'we were children once'*—would be (for example) like a college senior who had gotten his spiritual walk straightened out with the Lord and was about to graduate with his former college drinking buddies, all backslidden Christians, and who now says to them encouragingly: 'C'mon guys! We filled our days with drinking once, but we're graduates now!' Technically speaking, his college buddies had not yet gotten their walk with the Lord straightened out, nor had any of them graduated yet, but the point is made (by the one rehabilitated) that all of them as impending graduates should now be thinking and behaving differently.

Regarding Galatians 4:1-7, note the following. The fullness of the time of adoption, which the one who is a practical slave is awaiting, was accomplished by the birth, life, death, and resurrection of Christ. The emphasis on Christ's work which provided salvation for the believer is no doubt a main reason why so many have interpreted the word "adoption" as meaning a "coming into the family of God." But the resurrection of Christ is also what makes the future glorification of the believer's body possible. We must remember that the "practical slave" has already been established as an *heir* who stands with faithful Abraham to receive the promises of a faithful God (Gal. 3:29). If we understand *huiothesia* to be *son placement*—which Romans 8:23 defines as the redemption of the believer's body—it enables us to take a different interpretation than that which is usually advanced about this passage. What Paul is really saying is that our adoption was all but *effectually* accomplished when God's word of promise about the redemption of the believer's body was fulfilled by divine deeds, i.e., by the coming of the Messiah who offered himself to God for man's redemption in the fullest sense, a promise guaranteed by Christ's resurrection. Thus Paul is not actually stating that our adoption has already *de facto* taken place, but rather that God by His own deeds has *de facto* accomplished all that is necessary, so that the son-placement of believers (i.e., the glorification of believers' bodies) is now a future certainty. For the believer this presumably means that one day he will no longer have to endure the *perverse* state in which he currently finds himself—that is, living with an intensified knowledge of good and evil. It does not appear that death will similarly deliver the unbeliever from this fallen nature which all men have inherited from Adam. Furthermore, living in the 21st century has given us a somewhat different perspective on this verse. It would have been easier for Paul to have spoken in the manner he did 2,000 years ago, than if he were living today, for Paul lived at a time when nearly all believers who had ever trusted in God had lived and died *prior* to Christ's first coming. This is essentially Paul's perspective, that the son-placement of the majority of believers who had lived up to the time of his writing had to look *forward* to what God would accomplish through the Messiah in order to make their son-placement a future certainty; thus, "when it pleased the Father." By expressing the matter of son-placement thus, Paul gains another opportunity to drive home the main point of his epistle to the *justification-by-works*, flirting Galatians—i.e., that it was the work of Christ alone that had provided their atonement, apart from their works.

[111] Olson (pp. 267-273) shows that "predestination," a rare word found only once in Classical Greek (Demosthenes, *laid claim*), really means "preappointment." Olson also cites G.H.W. Lampe [*A Patristic Lexicon of Greek* (Oxford, 1961)] who noted that the word *proorizein* is used by the early church fathers in 30+ occurrences, yet never with a likely sense of "predestination," but rather of "preappointment." Says Olson: "From an examination of its six occurrences in four contexts in the New Testament and the meaning of its cognates *horizein* and *aphorizein*, as well as these rare secular usages, a meaning like "to preappoint" emerges."

[112] Perhaps one reason Olson (following G.H.W. Lampe) has accepted the conclusion that "predestinate" really has a meaning like "to preappoint," may be that he subconsciously senses that the word "predestinate" has been defined irrationally (and therefore falsely) by Calvinists. One can only imagine what impulse toward *irresistibility* Lampe might have 'found' in the patristic usage of *proorizein*, had he been a Calvinist.

Thus, as "predestinate" has been tainted with Calvinistic definition to a point where the word's proper rehabilitation in Evangelicalism is, from a practical standpoint, all but impossible, it is simply easier to find a relative synonym without all the Calvinistic trappings of association. For in English it must be admitted that, e.g., there is not a very great difference in the statements, "He was predestined for greatness," and "He was preappointed for greatness." The chief difference would seem to lie in connotation. Thus I believe the reason Olson has had to settle on "preappoint" is because Calvinism has destroyed the original meaning of 'predestinate' as intended in the Greek. This destruction appears to have chiefly come through extensive commentary. This is where the true apologist must try to put his finger in the hole of the theological dyke to stop the Calvinistic flow of irrationality. Indeed, maintaining an honest use of words is the ongoing challenge of those trying to be true to language. For certainly if all translations today substituted the word "preappoint" for "predestinate," it would be a short time until "preappoint" would come to mean the same thing in Christians' minds as "predestinate" already does, since only a short time is required for a little leaven of Calvinistic revisionism to affect the whole lump of a particular word's definition. Meanwhile, there is only the occasional blip on Evangelicalism's radar that would suggest something is wrong with its general appearance of smooth-sailing, Calvinist-based, theological language. When the radar does 'blip,' a more winsome term is sought, which means there is an adoption of some new Calvinistic term and a disinheritance of the old one. The snuggly term 'compatibilism,' to describe the alleged *antinomy* of what we recognize to be Calvinism's doublethink, comes readily to mind.

Now regarding this phenomenon of negative association on the 'uncozy' side of the equation, I heard just this week from a friend that a certain Mr. X says he is not (or says he should not be called) a *Calvinist*, though Mr. X apparently agrees with Calvin's doctrine. We presume the reason Mr. X wishes to avoid this label is the same kind of reason (i.e., negative association) that political liberals no longer like to be called "liberals," though the term was once widely used without so much negative implication. For in American politics the term 'liberal' appears to have once had the *positive* connotation of being generous hearted, but it came to mean in many person's minds something much different and *negative*. And since politicians seek labels with positive associations, the solution became a matter of change and marketing.

The same is true about Calvinistic language. The true Christian apologist of the future will need to spot linguistic revisionism, not only of those words whose definitions were changed in some murky past (and yet still manage to serve effectively the cause of irrationalism), but also of those words now being discarded for ones more positive and winsome-sounding.

The true apologist's battle is less with Calvinists than with the Enemy. (Indeed, the true apologist is not to regard any Calvinists who are his brothers as enemies). When the Devil, who seems to have the ear of so many Calvinist-leaning Christians today, finds that his revisionism of, say, *a-b-c* is exposed, he will find it convenient to remind Calvinist-leaning Christians of their growing discomfort with that term, and that a truer reflection of their position (demeanor included) is really found in *x-y-z*. In reality, the Enemy's *a-b-c* doctrine equals x-y-z doctrine, but the marketing change tends to pass unnoticed. [The Emergent Gospel (to cite an example in the non-Calvinist realm, though even here one might argue that in spirit the Emergent Church is Calvinistic in the one sense of committing itself to the ridding of distinctives), repackaged as the Social Gospel, is one such example.] In the spirit of this adventure, the NIV has now begun to use the term "*sovereign* Lord," (emphasis mine) which for many Christians will mean a sovereignty of absolute degree, a term sounding more benign, personal, and protective than the mere brute term, "the Almighty." Yet for some strange reason theological terms seem to have a longer 'shelf life' than the label assigned to the protagonists who defend them. That is, though Calvinists try to avoid the label 'Calvinist,' they seem to feel less antagonized when making dogmatic statements about Calvinistic *doctrine*. Probably the reason for this strange state of affairs is because people are generally more hypersensitive about the names they are called than about the labels applied to the doctrines they believe. Apparently, there just isn't the same emotional investment across the board.

Still, not all theological terms have remained unscathed. Again, 'limited atonement' has been taking a particular fall in favor of late, probably because it sounds too *excluding* (and maybe even *bloody*) for today's 'tolerance' environment, and probably also because the large and vocal Baptist contingency in America seems to find the 'L' in TULIP a particularly objectionable and loathsome letter. The Calvinistic revisionist result? The much more winsome-sounding, "particular redemption," with its suggested focus on the *benefit to the believer*, rather than on that *arbitrary damnation of the lost*. And thus the dance of language continues.

[113] For an exegesis of foreknowledge (Gr. *proginwskw*), see Thomas R. Edgar's article at [http://www.chafer.edu/journal/back_issues/ Vol%209-1%20ar3.pdf]. The subject of foreknowledge has been so thoroughly treated by Thomas Edgar in his article, that I can only (again) urge that the reader study Edgar's unparalleled treatment of proginwskw (foreknowledge) and his masterly critique of the Calvinist's defective hermeneutic arising from the Calvinist's failure to employ sound lexical practice.

[114] The failure to understand that God knows contingent (alternate possible) histories apart from predetermining them has been a real obstacle in understanding God, not only for Calvinists but also for Open Theists. Thus while Open Theists believe that God has exhaustive knowledge about the past and present, they do not believe that God has foreknowledge of the future, except regarding His own determination to enter man's history at certain points to effect His work in the world. As Thomas Edgar points out, this is the great similarity between Calvinists and Open Theists: both believe that divine foreknowledge is not possible unless God has also determined it. Thus, this belief that man is not really free to choose his choices if God knows what his choices will be, is a defining doctrine of the Open Theistic movement. Matthew 11, however (as we have already seen), shows that Christ knew the alternate possible histories of specific cities.

[115] Regarding time and space, God has the ability to perform an act upon every one of the smallest points of time, or *indivisible* points, according to 1 Corinthians 15:52, Greek *atomeros* for "moment" ("uncut-able atom of time") *"in a moment, in the twinkling of an eye,"* contextually understood by the phrase "twinkling of an eye" to be an indivisible moment, rather than a non-moment (the Greek "a" negating the word, or putting the word in apposition), whereas man, though existing during these smallest points of time, is only able to perform an act upon points of time greatly spaced apart from one another. How greatly spaced apart are these acting points for man in relation to God's acting points? They are as the earth is to the height of the heavens. As the Lord says, "As the heavens are higher than the earth, so are my ways than your ways, and my thoughts than your thoughts, saith the Lord." God is different than man in chiefly three ways: 1) He is uncreated and sustains the form of His own being, and the being of all His created forms, 2) He exceedingly exceeds man's degree of power, and 3) He chooses to remain morally upright ("The Lord is not as a man, that He should repent [i.e., change his mind]."

Endnotes:

[lvi] Spence, H.D.M. and Joseph Excell (editors). *The Pulpit Commentary*. (London and New York; Funk & Wagnalls Company, new edition).

[lvii] Telford, Andrew. *Subjects of Sovereignty*. (Philadelphia: Berachah Church).

[lviii] Brown, T. Pierce. "Born or Adopted" [http://www.oldpaths.com/Archive/Brown/T/Pierce/1923/adoption.html].

Chapter 17
Some Remaining Questions

Up to this point I have attempted to reply to certain arguments that are generally believed to prove Calvinism, and to show in contrast what is a true, biblical understanding of God, man, good, and evil. There are, however, other passages Calvinists sometimes use to argue God's sovereignty that we have not addressed. Furthermore, there are other questions related to divine sovereignty and human freedom not normally discussed in debate (such as whether a man is denied his free will if he spends eternity in hell). My goal here is not to answer every conceivable argument, nor address every Scripture that has been cited in an attempt to support Calvinism, nor give an explanation of every question that could arise in a discussion about human freedom (an attempt that would plainly be impossible). Rather, my goal is merely to answer certain of these remaining questions I think are especially worthy of attention.

QUESTION:

1 John 2:2 states, "And he is the propitiation for our sins: and not for ours only, but also for [the sins of] the whole world." But how can Christ be the propitiation for the sins of the whole world if the word *propitiation* means *payment*? For if Christ truly made payment for all sins, then wouldn't all sins be forgiven and everyone be saved? But obviously not all are saved. Isn't, then, 1 John 2:2 merely referring to the *world of the elect* when it uses the word *world*?

ANSWER:

The word *for* in 1 John 2:2 is the Greek word *peri*, and means *relating to*, or *concerning*. The Interlinear[116] translates it thus: "And He is the propitiation relating to our sins, and not relating to ours only, but also relating to all the world." Thus propitiation is *relating to* the sins of every man; it is not *for* in the sense of *de facto applied*. Let me offer an analogy here. I may give a panhandling drunk five dollars and tell him it is *for* a sandwich, but that hardly guarantees that the man will not consider it booze money. The money relates to his having a sandwich, but he might make other use of it. This is because the money was *given* to him, not irresistibly, but as *offered* to him. Thus he may or may not use it in the way I desire. In fact, I could buy a sandwich and hand it to him, but that wouldn't necessarily mean he would eat it; instead he might sell it and use

[116] Pocket Interlinear New Testament, Jay P. Green, Sr. (editor) Baker Book House, 1986 reprint.

the money to buy booze. In the same sense propitiation (payment) has been made *relating to* or *concerning* our sins, but the blood of Christ will not be applied to a man's account unless he receives it as such.

QUESTION:

John 15:16 says, "Ye have not chosen me, but I have chosen you…" Does this verse contradict what John says elsewhere in John 1:12, i.e., "But as many as *received* him…"? If not, what did Christ mean in John 15:16?

ANSWER:

The full verse reads: "Ye did not choose me, but I chose you, and appointed you, that ye should go and bear fruit, and that your fruit should abide: that whatsoever ye shall ask of the Father in my name, he may give it you." *If*, in John 15:16, Christ is referring to his choosing them [lit. *naming out* (them) *from among* (others)] for salvation, this is to be understood according to the definition of 'election' which involves His 'calling' (God's naming out from among others, (according to his advanced knowledge which is non-determinative), and, by implication, their response as hearers (which is in accord with the teaching of John 1:12). As Jesus said elsewhere, "Many are called (lit., *invited* or *bidden*), but few are chosen." A man does not diligently seek Christ, but Christ seeks the man. (The relevant Greek words are *eklegomai* (*to name out from among*) and *ekloge* (*the naming out of*) which have been interpreted (and dubiously translated) to mean "to elect" and "election").

Contextually, this statement in John 15:16 is one in which Christ refers back to when He named out 12 of his disciples from among others, and the service he intended for them. Mark 3:14 tells us: "And he ordained twelve, that they should be with him, and that he might send them forth to preach." [Incidentally, earlier Christ told the disciples to *abide* (*remain, tarry*) in Him. This is something all of us as professing followers of Christ are commanded to do, and the verb is active in all cases; therefore the phrase "without Me you power to do nothing," means, in context, that one powers to do nothing who remains not in Christ.] Now the statement by Christ in John 15:16 occurred at a critical time, and may have been offered as an encouragement. These words were spoken during the last supper *after* Judas Iscariot had departed, a time when Christ was alone with His true (if soon to be proven weak) disciples. Thus He refrained from telling them certain things because of their present state of sorrow (Jn. 16:12). This is the biblical context. These men, all of whom would eventually suffer death by martyrdom except for John, might have occasion in the future, because of imprisonment or other hardship, to wonder if their equipping as disciples (and therefore their preparation for such ordeals) were all on a false ground—a discipleship they themselves had initiated out of their friendship to Jesus. Of course, these friendships were ones Jesus had initiated. Still, a man near an 'end-game' circumstance might doubt his calling and discipleship, or even the Subject of his message, as had John the Baptist. Christ assures them that He first named them out from among others (based on His knowledge in advance that they would believe in Him, and also follow him), and that they themselves had not first named out Him from among others, nor named out themselves as apostles from among the other disciples.

QUESTION:

Acts 13:48 says, "And when the Gentiles heard this, they were glad, and glorified the word of the Lord: and as many as were ordained to eternal life believed." Doesn't this verse teach that God foreordains who will be saved and who will be lost irrespective of man's so-called 'choices'?

ANSWER:

In the phrase, *were ordained*, the word *ordained* can also mean *determined* (*planned*), as translated a few chapters later in Acts 15:1–2:

> And certain men which came down from Judaea taught the brethren, and said, Except ye be circumcised after the manner of Moses, ye cannot be saved. When therefore Paul and Barnabas had no small dissension and disputation with them, they *determined* [*planned*] that Paul and Barnabas, and certain other of them, should go up to Jerusalem unto the apostles and elders about this question.

Now suppose that we were to substitute the word *ordained* for *determined* in Acts 13:48, i.e., "When therefore Paul and Barnabas had no small dissension and disputation with them, they ordained that Paul and Barnabas, and certain other of them, should go up to Jerusalem unto the apostles and elders about this question." This reading sounds a bit awkward, doesn't it? Even though *ordained* in Acts 13:48 is the same word as *determined* in Acts 15:2, there seems to be something unnatural about it. Technically speaking, I would say that something seems *super*natural about it. By this I mean that the word 'ordained' is so associated with Calvinistic doctrine when God is the subject, that it makes its relation to another grammatical subject besides God seem all but misapplied. This is because

Calvinism, over the centuries, has effectually hijacked the word 'ordained' (i.e., *wordjacked* "ordained"). With little exception the KJV translators reserved this particular word for various instances when God is the subject, or when it was thought He is indirectly implied as the causative subject, and the resulting impression upon the reader has often been one of divine irresistibility.

Now observe in Acts 13 that the Antioch Gentiles had previously expressed interest in the gospel and were seeking the truth: "And when the Jews were gone out of the synagogue, the Gentiles besought that these words might be preached to them the next sabbath" (Acts 13:42). Contrasting these Gentiles of Antioch with the Gentile hearers at Athens makes an interesting comparison (Acts 17). The Athenians who said they would hear Paul "again of this matter," were either vague or mocking; (again, the Interlinear suggests that they were mocking and that in fact there was no third, neutral group among the Athenians). Now compare the Athenian response to the Gentiles at Antioch who *besought* Paul that he speak to them the very next Sabbath. These Gentiles at Antioch had scheduled Paul into their calendar, so to speak, while the unbelieving Athenians, if they even wanted to hear Paul again (though we note that the Interlinear text indicates they did not want to) could expect to hear the newcomer again when the carousel of idea-makers returned again in the course of Athenian life (as Luke says: "For all the Athenians and strangers which were there spent their time in nothing else, but either to tell, or to hear some new thing"). Thus the understanding of Acts 13:48 is that those who *had been*, or *were having been, determining unto* [Gr. *eis*, i.e., *into, unto, to, toward*, etc. (the prepositional phrase meaning, *determining themselves unto*)] eternal life, believed upon further hearing. Note also that the KJV word "ordained," like the word "fitted" in Romans 9:22, is a perfect passive participle, and therefore arguably should have been translated in the middle voice, ie., if reading a bit awkwardly here, *and as many as had been determining themselves unto eternal life, believed.* Needless to say, this is a far cry from the NAS's Calvinistic rendition of "*and as many as were appointed unto eternal life believed.*" Thus the Antioch Gentiles had grown dissatisfied with their old way of thinking about religion, and were now determining to believe, and therefore sought instruction from Paul. The converse idea about these Antioch hearers—that Luke would pull into his discussion the complicated idea of a sovereign God who irresistibly appointed Gentiles to a place in the kingdom—would certainly have required more explanation if that is what Luke meant. But the entire context of this passage simply does not support such a forced Calvinistic interpretation. Rather, Acts 13, beyond whatever other lessons it teaches, serves as a general encouragement for men to consider earnestly the gospel of Christ.

The monolithic preference, then, of translations for *were ordained* instead of *were themselves determining* in Acts 13:48, speaks more to the preconceived theological bias of translators in extant translations, than to any fair attempt to render in translation a viewpoint other than Calvinism. We have already seen this translational bias in other passages of the Bible (Rom. 9:22 especially, but also Ex. 7:13 in the KJV, etc.) and by commentaries that have offered questionable interpretations based on a Reformed way of thinking (such as we saw with Galatians 4, regarding the word *adoption*).

QUESTION:

Acts 4:26-30 speaks of Herod, Pilate, the Gentiles, and the nation of Israel rising up against Christ. Verse 28 even says that God's counsel had *determined* whatsoever He wanted them to do. Doesn't this mean that God worked with evil to accomplish His will, and thus foreordained everything done by these parties?

ANSWER:

Let us look at the passage:

> ²⁶The kings of the earth stood up, and the rulers were gathered together against the Lord, and against his Christ. ²⁷For of a truth against thy holy child Jesus, whom thou hast anointed, both Herod, and Pontius Pilate, with the Gentiles, and the people of Israel, were gathered together, ²⁸For to do whatsoever thy hand and thy counsel determined before to be done. ²⁹And now, Lord, behold their threatenings: and grant unto thy servants, that with all boldness they may speak thy word, ³⁰By stretching forth thine hand to heal; and that signs and wonders may be done by the name of thy holy child Jesus.

Consider first the presumption that is often made about this passage. Many think that verse 28 teaches that everything done by Herod *et al.* was predetermined by God. Reading these verses more carefully, however, reveals that verse 28 is not really stating this idea. Rather, it says that everything God determined that they should do, was done. This might seem to be a fine point of distinction here, but it needs to be made. Let me offer an example to clarify the difference. Suppose you work in a restaurant where you play poker after hours. One day the owner tells you to throw out a particular chair into the dumpster. After receiving these instructions you take a knife and carve some graffiti in the chair's wooden back rest, smear food into the cloth seat, and pull the underneath wooden supports out of their joints. In fact, you do these things because this has been your opponent's 'lucky' poker chair, and for several nights after work you have been losing badly at cards. Before you remove this chair to the dumpster you slice up the seat, remove the stuffing, and randomly spray paint different parts of the chair. You definitely don't want to see this chair again! Finally you shove the chair into the dumpster and close and lock the lid on top of it. So here's the question: Did you do everything the restaurant owner asked you to do? Yes, you certainly did. He asked you to throw out the chair, and you threw it out. Was everything you did, however, what the owner asked you to do? No, indeed, it was not. In fact, he never instructed you to molest the chair but merely asked you to throw it out. The point here is that the owner has an agenda you carried out, but you added your own agenda to it.

Along these lines consider what God said of the Assyrian king whom He used to destroy sinful Israel and to exile them out of their land: (Is. 10:5-15)

> [5]"Woe to Assyria, the rod of My anger And the staff in whose hand is My indignation. [6]I will send him against an ungodly nation, And against the people of My wrath I will give him charge, To seize the spoil, to take the prey, And to tread them down like the mire of the streets. [7]Yet he does not mean so, Nor does his heart think so; But it is in his heart to destroy, And cut off not a few nations. [8]For he says, 'Are not my princes altogether kings? [9]Is not Calno like Carchemish? Is not Hamath like Arpad? Is not Samaria like Damascus? [10]As my hand has found the kingdoms of the idols, Whose carved images excelled those of Jerusalem and Samaria, [11]As I have done to Samaria and her idols, Shall I not do also to Jerusalem and her idols?' " [12]Therefore it shall come to pass, when the Lord has performed all His work on Mount Zion and on Jerusalem, that He will say, "I will punish the fruit of the arrogant heart of the king of Assyria, and the glory of his haughty looks." [13]For he says: "By the strength of my hand I have done it, And by my wisdom, for I am prudent; Also I have removed the boundaries of the people, And have robbed their treasuries; So I have put down the inhabitants like a valiant man. [14]My hand has found like a nest the riches of the people, And as one gathers eggs that are left, I have gathered

all the earth; And there was no one who moved his wing, Nor opened his mouth with even a peep."
¹⁵Shall the ax boast itself against him who chops with it?¹¹⁷ Or shall the saw exalt itself against him who saws with it? As if a rod could wield itself against those who lift it up, Or as if a staff could lift up, as if it were not wood!

The key thought about the Assyrian king is found in verse 7: "Yet he does not mean so, nor does his heart think so; but it is in his heart to destroy, and cut off not a few nations." Note that God's instruction was concerning a "nation," i.e., *singular*, not plural. God had told the Assyrian king to go against Israel, not Jerusalem, but the king's motive was different than God's. The king merely wanted to plunder the nation of Israel for his own personal gain. In fact, the king was planning an entire military plan against *other* nations for the same purpose and without divine permission. Thus he seems oblivious to the fact that God had granted him a position of power for which he was responsible. Therefore God says he will judge the Assyrian king for his pride.

The implication, then, is that God does **not** use the evil of the king to bring about His glory. For if God did use it, such activity would mean that He works with evil in a cooperative way. Paul, however, says that righteousness can have no fellowship with unrighteousness, nor Christ have concord with the Devil. So it is important to understand that God does not use the Assyrian king *because* he is evil. He is simply instructing the king to carry out His judgment upon the nation of Israel. Presumably then, God presents a thought to the Assyrian king's mind, such as, *"Go down and destroy sinful Israel."* Even though the Gentile king does not know God in a personal way, God has presented to the king the power and nature of the Godhead through creation, and God has the right to give a command to any of His creatures. When God's thought is presented to the Assyrian king, however, it is filtered through the grid of the king's own sinful and selfish mind: *I will go down and destroy that bad nation, Israel. I will destroy her idols. I will do the same to other nations. I will gather all their treasures as one gathers eggs from defenseless hens, etc.* The Assyrian king could have thought differently. He could have recognized the God of Israel as the only true God, even as Cyrus the king would do in the process of carrying out God's plan for the Jews. Because Romans 1 tells us that every man is given enough spiritual light from God's creation to understand who God is, the Assyrian king had no right to say, *Well, I didn't know God, so how could I have recognized His voice?* The king *should* have recognized God's voice—that's the point. He did not, however, because he had a different agenda of his own.

Even so, those who rose up against Christ during the crucifixion had a different agenda than what God was presenting to them. They did not *have* to hate Christ to carry out his death. God did not *need* their sin. It was Messiah's death—plain and simple, and unattached with man's false railings—that God in his counsel had decided should be done and to which Acts 4:28 refers. Nowhere does Acts say that God's counsel determined *all* the words and deeds of the mob. In fact, Christ's death did not even have to be at the hand of a mob or even by a malevolent hand. Christ could have been sacrificed even if Israel had repented of their sin and believed in Christ. The brief event of Christ dying and resurrecting would not have even interrupted the prophecies regarding His coming as the great Ruler, especially if the nation of Israel had understood that this work was a necessary step in order for Christ to obtain the full glory of His Kingship as *Savior*. And so the nation *could* have understood the plan of God and with an understanding heart offered up Christ as the willing sacrifice for their sin. They could have understood from Daniel's prophecy that Messiah's life should be sacrificed after the completion of 62 weeks "from the going forth of the command to restore and build Jerusalem" (9:25) and therefore committed themselves to fulfill the prophecy with understanding. Thus God could have commanded a *believing* Israel to act on the Father's behalf to put Christ to death as the object of God's wrath and as the sacrifice for the world's sin. Herod and Pilate could likewise have been sympathetic participants in these events. It is not inconceivable that they could have repented in the weeks or months prior to the appointed hour of Messiah's death by being greatly moved by the nation itself, and have remained in governmental power long enough to have participated with all the people of Israel and the visiting Judeo-sympathizing Gentiles in presenting the Messiah (to the High Priest ?) to be offered up as the Lamb of God. The High Priest and Jewish elders *could* have likewise repented prior to this event had they merely responded positively to the ministry of Christ. Had such a scenario taken place, Messiah could have offered Himself as the sacrifice for the world's sin while surrounded by understanding, penitent sinners, in which case Christ's death would have been no less glorious.[118]

Again, the death of Christ at the hands of believing sinners need not to have been attended with any more feeling of maliciousness than Abraham had toward Isaac when the patriarch was about to slay his son upon the altar, or that Aaron the High Priest had toward the Passover lamb.

I realize that to think of Christ's death as happening in a manner where He could have been surrounded by believers is foreign to most of us. The standard explanation, however, of God using the sinful anger of man to carry out His 'sovereign' plan remains unsatisfying. It all but *requires* that men be sinners in order that righteousness be carried out. This is the kind of theology that wishes to say that 'all things work together for good,' i.e., *synergistically*. Such a turgid theology has yet to explain how God could be holy if, *in some sense* (as Boettner would put it), He determines that false accusations be leveled against His Son by crucifiers and thieves. Yet this is what the Calvinist asks us to believe—that God guides and governs all the lying words and deeds that men said and did during the crucifixion.[119] If this is the case, it remains to be explained by the Calvinist how God can be *responsible* for evil but not be *guilty* of it. But what seems left to us are the kind of explanations offered, for example, by James Spiegel, when he writes a kind of apologetic *diktat* defending Calvin and Luther's position on absolute sovereignty:

> As for the problem of evil, Calvin, again with Luther, eschews the notion that there is any problem of the sort, just because God is absolutely sovereign and therefore can do whatever he wants with his creatures. For this reason, Calvin declares, "it is sheer folly that many dare with greater license to call God's works to account, and to examine his secret plans, and to pass as rash a sentence on matters unknown as they would on the deeds of mortal men."[lix]

Sad indeed. Is a Christian really supposed to find the above explanation helpful because *Calvin* declares it? For Calvin says in effect, "How *dare* one taste to see if the Lord is good! How *dare* we presume that God's answer to the problem of evil is not inscrutably hid in unfathomable mysteries! How *dare* we think we have the ability of will to obey God's bidding to *reason* with Him, so that our sins might be washed away!" Thus, by Calvin and Luther eliminating *reasonable inquiry* into the problem of evil, they have eliminated that vehicle which God Himself claims He uses to bring sinners to the truth. Rather, Christians would do better to maintain that God *does* allow men to ask Him about the problem of evil; for how else will they understand that He is not responsible for sin nor uses the means of sin to bring about His glory? As Paul says: "And if a man also strive for masteries, yet is he not crowned, except he strive lawfully." *Are we to think the same necessity is not laid upon God, that He should choose to use evil means to obtain 'righteous' ends?*

As I think back to my upbringing in a typical fundamentalist church in the 1970s, I now understand, at least in part, why Calvinistic theology (and its view that God foreordains all things) has since taken hold across much of the Evangelical denominational spectrum. It appears that the word *sovereign* was used in sermons and in written material even outside the Presbyterian church without really defining the term closely. Nevertheless, it was invoked to describe how God brought about His own glory, though never (so far as I remember) cited in any hard-line discussion about the reprobation of the lost. Across America the deed was done, however, and once the camel's nose of God's 'absolute sovereignty' was in the door flap, it would only be a matter of time until the entire camel of Calvinistic application would threaten to stand inside the tent, toppling it over. Thus it proceeded innocently enough with statements such as the following one by fundamentalist author, Harry Rimmer, a man normally so excellent in his thinking:

> How amazed the modern research reader is, to discover that in spite of Satan's hatred and the mob's grim conduct, every word and every deed of that entire chorus declares the glory of God as truly as though they had designed to praise Him. Thus, once again God makes the wrath of man to serve Him. And this mighty chorus might almost have been under His personal direction, so thoroughly did they fulfill the prophecies and vindicate the Scriptures.
> Although devoid of any insight into the significance of their own words and deeds, they yet declared Him Whom they nailed to that cross to be the Christ Whom God promised, as definitely as though they desired to honor Him thus.[lx]

As long, then, as Evangelicals insist that God sovereignly *designs* the deeds of evil men, so long it will be that no serious Christian apologetic can be offered to the world regarding the problem of evil.

QUESTION:

Ephesians 2:8-9 says, "For by grace are ye saved through faith, and that not of yourselves, it is the gift of God, not of works, lest any man should boast." Doesn't this teach that faith is a gift that God gives us, which we cannot muster up ourselves?

ANSWER:

The key to understanding this verse is to observe the contrast Paul is making. When he says that salvation is "not of works" he is completing the contrast. Either he is comparing *grace* with works, or the *process of grace through faith* with works. I think the normal way of reading this verse would be to understand that the subject being contrasted with works is the subject of the sentence—i.e., *grace*. Recall that the apostle who wrote these verses in

Ephesians also wrote Romans 11:6 to show what element is truly to be contrasted with works: "And if by grace, then is it no more of works: otherwise grace is no more grace. But if it be of works, then is it no more grace: otherwise work is no more work."

QUESTION:

Philippians 2:13 says that God provides the will to do His good pleasure. Some commentators indicate that this refers to God's absolute sovereign activity in our lives, and that God alone must provide the willing. They say if God did not give us the *will*, we could never have this will on our own. Also (if somewhat *non-sequitur*, though I think it ultimately bears on how one interprets Phil. 2:13), throughout your book you sometimes cast aside the translations of those who are highly trained in their craft for what seems to be esoteric interpretations. Shouldn't you be concerned about coming to the wrong conclusions?

ANSWER:

I think that many of us who undertake a discussion about the nature of God's sovereignty are concerned about getting it wrong. R.C. Sproul, for example, takes a very decided Reformed position on the matter, yet expresses at the beginning of his book, *Chosen By God*, his concern about getting the issue of divine sovereignty correct. Furthermore, many of us who discuss this subject must also rely heavily on the training of linguists and their indispensable work. For example, I am completely dependent upon scholars and researchers to show how a Greek word was used in extra-biblical resources in the centuries leading up to, and including, the New Testament era. What I *have* questioned in this book, however, is the translator's and/or commentator's *logic* of application of particular Greek words in certain passages. For example, take the current question about Philippians 2:13 regarding the phrase, "to will." Because I doubted that the Calvinistic interpretation of this phrase was correct, I began with a hypothesis:

> *Does Philippians 2:13 teach that God gives us the very will (intention) itself to do what pleases Him?*

So then I considered Philippians 2:12-13:

> *Therefore my beloved, as you have always obeyed, not as in my presence only, but now much more in my absence, work out your*

own salvation with fear and trembling; for it is God who works in you both to will and to do of His good pleasure.

I began testing my hypothesis by going online and searching *Strong's* concordance. I found that there is more than one Greek word translated *will* in the KJV. Calvinists have made great use of the word *will* in Romans 9:19 ("For who hath resisted [God's] will?") to claim that man is totally subjugated to God's absolute sovereignty. It seemed natural to question, then, whether the word *will* in Romans 9:19 was the same basic word for *will* in Philippians 2:13 (where it says that God works in us *to will*). I discovered it was not. The two-word phrase, *to will*, in Philippians 2:13 is actually just one word in the Greek, i.e., *thelo*, and is defined by *Strong's* thus:

Strong's word #2309

1) to will, have in mind, intend
1a) to be resolved or determined, to purpose
1b) to desire, to wish
1c) to love
1c1) to like to do a thing, be fond of doing
1d) to take delight in, have pleasure

Following this I looked up the Greek word *will* in Romans 9:19 and saw that it was a different Greek word—*boulomai*.[120] This verb for *will* is rarely used in the New Testament compared to *thelo*. *Boulomai* is given thus by *Strong's*:

Strong's word #1013:

1) will, counsel, purpose

I then followed *Strong's* link to #1014 which gave me this:

1) to will deliberately, have a purpose, be minded
2) of willing as an affection, to desire

As for the former word, *thelo*, *Strong's* suggests the presence of a root word link between the two, claiming that *thelo* was 'apparently strengthened by an alternative form of *138, to determine*...from subjective impulse,' but noted a difference between *thelo* and *boulomai* by noting that the latter dealt more with 'objective consideration.'

As I pondered the six meanings above for the word *thelo* in Philippians 2:13, I decided that perhaps the best word that accommodated all six meanings was the verb *to want*. So I looked up the word *want* in the KJV to see if the Greek word *thelo* was used. Imagine my astonishment, then, when I found that the word *want* did not appear as a verb in the (KJV) New Testament in any form. I would never have guessed that. The word *want* occurs about a dozen times as a noun in the New Testament (from three different Greek words), i.e., as to be in *want*, etc. None of these words appeared to be related in any suggestive way to either *thelo* or *boulomai*. I reasoned then, that some other word must be used in the KJV to express the verb *to want*. The word *desire* came to mind as a likely candidate. I looked up *desire* in *Strong's*, and found the word *thelo*. I felt this was significant, since substituting the word *desire* for *will* in Philippians 2:13 now gave me an entirely different sense of the verse:

> For it is God who worketh in you to desire, and to do of his good pleasure.

Read in context *with the preceding verse of Philippians 2:12*, the *will*, spoken of in verse 13, is in fact merely the *desire* of God upon the believer who is urged to continue following the path of Christ (i.e., working out the implications of his salvation with fear and trembling), *not* a unilateral activity performed by God *upon* us or *in us* irresistibly. Thus Philippians 2:13 is talking about God working in us to both *desire* and to perform His good pleasure. *This means that God both greatly encourages us in the way we should go and equips us to do His work, that is, as we agree with the Holy Spirit's work in our lives.* This is not a work, then, that God does apart from our willingness. We *do* have the ability to resist the Holy Spirit's work in our lives, which is why Paul commanded the Christians at Thessalonica not to quench the Spirit (1 Th. 5:19). The Calvinistic idea, then, that Philippians 2:13 must be interpreted to mean that God has to give the Christian the very will itself to do what is right, is simply not biblical.

In this regard I find it interesting that the NAS would translate the Greek word *thelo* to mean "desire" in Romans 9:18 ("So then He has mercy on whom He desires, and He hardens whom He desires") but *not* translate the very same Greek word, *thelo*, to mean *desire* in Philippians 2:13. Instead, the NAS treats the verse exactly as the KJV does, choosing the phrase, *to will*. Thus, for Philippians 2:13 the NAS has:

> *for it is God who is at work in you, both to will and to work for His good pleasure.*

How subtle indeed are the nuances of translation that impute a Calvinistic interpretation for Philippians 2:13. Why, we must ask, if not for a theological agenda, did the Calvinistic KJV translators render Gr. *thelo* as *desire* seven times in 2 Corinthians and Galatians, but not do it here? Could it be, that, to have rendered *thelo* as the word *desire* in Philippians 2:13 would not have stated the case of divine irresistibility upon all men in all their acts as strongly as these translators would have liked? Rather, we maintain that the real meaning is this—that God works in us by encouraging our desire to do what He wants. Thus, *desire (thelo)* would fit the text naturally, as opposed to saying that God determined by His counsel and planning (*boulomai*) that we were going to do the things that pleased Him whether we liked it or not.[121] This latter way of paraphrasing what appears to be the intent of the KJV and NAS sounds rather severe and unfeeling, yet it seems to be the basic impression left by these translations upon its unsuspecting readers.

What compounds this error is how Calvinistic presuppositions affect even the fundamental definition of a word in contexts where it is falsely supposed that God's glory will be at stake if we allow man any predicative ability whatsoever. For notice that Strong's gives *thelo*'s primary definition as "*will*, have in mind, *intend*." Now admittedly, perhaps "to will" (understood as "*to desire into its congruent will*" IS *thelo*'s primary meaning, but some of the lexical evidence for this definition, as affirmed by *Strong's*, is doubtless based upon the KJV plethora of *English* occurrences of "to will." In other words, the KJV makes it appear that *thelo* generally means "to decide," when in fact *thelo (to want)* only includes the will IF both the near and far contexts justify that understanding. The important thing to remember is, *Context is king*. So, for example, if I said, "I do not want to go to work," but *do* go to work, then my use of "want" did not include the will. That is, I was referring to *desire* only. But conversely, if, say, a clerk behind an ice cream counter asks a child which one of the 30-odd flavors he *wants*, and the child points to the particular carton of Butter Brickle, and declares "I want *that* one," then clearly both the clerk and the child are including the will (choice) in the meaning of "want." I personally feel that the informal English word "want" is the *quid pro quo* word to Gr. *thelo*. In fact, in my own spot-search for the *verb* "want" in the works of Shakespeare, I would say, in defense of the KJV, that it appears "will" was a typical word used in the 17th century to express what today in informal English we understand by the word "want." We will come back to the point about the latitude of meaning of the verb "want" in a moment.

Now moving on, I followed a link in *Strong's* about the differences between the two words *thelo* and *boulomai*. Note that even the experts don't agree. Says Strong:

> In many cases these two words are used without appreciable distinction, meaning *conscious willing, purpose*. But frequently it is evident that a difference is intended, although there is much difference of opinion as to the exact distinction. Thayer says that *boulomai* "seems to designate the will which follows deliberation", *yelw [thelo]*, "the will which proceeds from inclination." Grimm, on the other hand, says that *yelw* gives prominence to the emotive element, *boulomai* to the rational and volitive; *yelw* signifies the choice, while *boulomai* marks the choice as deliberate and intelligent. The view of Cremer on the whole seems preferable to any other. According to this view, *boulomai* has the wider range of meaning, but *yelw* is the stronger word; *yelw* denotes the active resolution, the will urging on to action, see Rom. 7:15, while *boulomai* is rather to have in thought, to intend, to be determined. *Boulomai* sometimes means no more than to have an inclination, see Acts 23:15. Instructive examples of the use of the two words in close proximity are found in Mk. 15:9,15, and especially Mt 1:19.1[xi]

Because I believe that man has free will, I had come to the same essential position as Thayer before becoming aware of his conclusions. Since his view seemed friendly to my own, I suppose I could have (lazily) accepted Thayer's authority under the assumption that his understanding was better than anyone else's. (At length, however, I would conclude, in deference to Thayer, that *thelo* could be used to mean *bare desire* not yet culminated in the will.) I also understood that Cremer's view was friendlier to Calvinism, since it claimed that *thelo* was the *stronger* word; for plainly (we note) that which merely "urges" on to action but cannot *guarantee* action (resolution, i.e., intention), ought not to be considered as strong as that which demonstrates a consistent lexical meaning of "to plan," which *de facto* denotes intention. And thus there seems to be a doublethink in supposing that of the two words, *thelo* is the stronger. At any rate, being rather skeptical by nature, I decided to check out the claims of *Strong's* advocacy of Cremer. They seemed to involve three claims (the last being exampled by two passages).

First, a claim was made that *thelo* "denotes the active resolution, the will urging on to action." Romans 7:15 was given as a proof, and so I presumed that any verse offered in proof of this claim should be the best possible example, or at least a good example. So I looked up Romans 7:15 and read: "For that which I do I allow not: for what *I would* (*thelo*), that do I not; but what I hate, that do I." Now when I looked at *Strong's* claim that *thelo* here meant "the active *resolution*, the will urging on to action," I actually saw Paul stating something quite the opposite. Whatever it was that Paul was feeling or thinking, it did not seem to be leading him to the kind of inevitable resolution or action that proved *Strong's* point. The verse did, however, seem to suggest Paul's '*inclination*' (not to be confused with *intention*) to do something which, in fact, Paul says he ended up not doing. How then, I wondered, was Romans 7:15 a proof of Cremer's view? In fact, "resolution" and "urging on to action" are non-synonymous if, by "to," we presume *Strong's* to mean *toward*, not *into*. At best, I find *Strong's definition* confusing.

Second, Strong followed Cremer in saying, "*Boulomai* sometimes means no more than to have an inclination, see Acts 23:15." So I looked up Acts 23:15 and read, "Now therefore ye with the council signify to the chief captain that he bring [Paul] down unto you to morrow, as though ye would (Gr. *mello*) enquire something more perfectly concerning him: and we, or ever he come near, are ready to kill him." The Greek word *mello* can (it appears) mean *intend*, but *mello* and the root word from which it comes (*melo*, meaning *to care about*) are not related to either *thelo* or *boulomai* even in their root word etymologies, and so its comparison with the latter two words seems irrelevant. It remains a puzzle to me why *Strong's* would claim that *boulomai* appears in Acts 23:15.

Third, *Strong's* suggested that *boulomai* with *thelo* be compared in two passages where the two words occur closely to each other—Mark 15:9, 15, and Matthew 1:19. I found the context of the first of these particularly instructive: "But Pilate answered them, saying, Will (*thelo*) ye that I release unto you the King of the Jews? And so Pilate, willing (*boulomai*) to content the people, released Barabbas unto them, and delivered Jesus, when he had scourged him, to be crucified." Taking the hypothetical position that *thelo* means "desire" makes perfect sense here. Pilate would almost certainly not have used *boulomai* in addressing the Jews here, i.e., "Who do you *determine* (*intend*), or "who have you decided, that I release unto you?" Had Pilate asked such a question in this manner upon his initial question to the Jews, it would have carried with it *some* sense (or *a* sense) that he was simply a minion to carry out their wishes.[122] But if we take the position that *thelo* means to *desire* (i.e., *to want*, the meaning is clearer, that is, "Who do you *want* that I release…?" This way of putting the question recognizes Pilate's authority, i.e., in effect here, "What do you *desire* me to do, that I might consider it as your ruler?" Finally, in verse 15 we come to *boulomai*. Pilate was *boulomai* to content the people. We know from the Bible and Josephus that the relationship between Pilate and the Jews was an uneasy one. Pilate had mingled the blood of some of the Jewish worshipers together with their sacrifices. Yet a program of ongoing intimidation was unlikely to succeed, for rulership in Judea was a tenuous thing. In any event, the feeling was not good between ruler and ruled. It seems unlikely, therefore, that Pilate *desired* (i.e., we render *boulemai* hypothetically here to mean *desire* to test Strong's view) to do what the Jews wanted, especially regarding a man in whom he found no fault. The problem, then, in Strong's advocacy for Cremer, is that the various passages cited by Strong to explain the alleged contrast between *thelo* and *boulemai* form the 'contrast' <u>as Cremer defines it</u>. But note that Cremer defines both *thelo* and *boulemai* dialectically, since, on the one hand *thelo* is defined in its contrast as "the will urging on to action," a definition which shows Strong's and Cremer's failure to understand that the will IS the action (resolution), while on the other hand *boulemai* is defined in its contrast to mean "have in thought," which is NOT synonymous with "intend." Therefore the whole matter becomes a muddled mess when Strong tries to distinguish between *thelo* and *boulemai*, because, besides defining both terms dialectically, he and Cremer seem to think that *thelo* is the stronger word, when in fact only *boulemai* shows a consistent lexical use of "intend." To put the matter another way (and setting aside the dialectical issue for the moment), *thelo* is not shown in any of Strong's examples to include the will, much less demonstrate itself to be the stronger word. For as we just saw, *thelo* cannot mean *"intended, determined"* when Pilate first asks the Jews what they *thelo*. So then, in any discussion (i.e., Strong's) that proposes at some level to distinguish between the concepts of desire and the will as expressed through the Greek words *thelo* and *boulemai*, then by default of what *thelo* must mean when Pilate first addresses the Jews (i.e., *bare desire*), then *boulemai* must mean the approximate opposite of *thelo*, since Mark 15 is cited by Strong's as an example which in effect shows a distinction between inclination and intent. (Note that Strong ***is*** attempting a contrast, since he states Cremer's view of *boulemai* as defined "rather" as.... etc.) Frankly, while I agree with Cremer in the abstract that a single word with the meaning of "inclination" (if by this he means "bare desire" which has proven a habit of a relatively consistent type of choice, with the future expectation of the same, though *not* inevitably) *may* or *may not* include intention, I think the lexical evidence shows he has it backwards, since it is *thelo*, not *boulemai*, that demonstrates the lexical possibility of *bare desire* with the potential of reaching into resolution, depending upon context. For, in fact, a survey of the New Testament lexical use of *boulemai* show numerous instances where *boulemai* <u>must</u> mean *to intend* but not ever where it <u>must</u> mean *mere inclination* or merely *to have in thought*. [I suppose the reason Cremer ended up imagining the lexical evidence supported his dialectical view (which I doubt he even realized was dialectical) was because he accepted Calvinistic assumptions about certain key Scriptures.] At any rate, we should note that Pilate was ultimately *boulemai* (*determined*, i.e., *intending*, as having taken counsel with himself) to do as the Jews wanted, though if possible he would make them feel as though he had *relented* in doing so. The

Jewish leaders knew Pilate would not want another uproar getting back to Rome, and they played the blackmail card for all it was worth, crying out, "You are no friend of Caesar's if you let this man go." Thus Mark 15:9, 15 is a passage that substantially shows a difference of meaning between *thelo* and *boulomai*.

As for Strong's remaining comparison between *thelo* and *boulemai* found in Matthew 1:19, the distinction between the two words is not as clearly drawn *in the near context*, because the narrative in which *thelo* and *boulemai* occur is not a circumstance conducive to expressing some obvious difference in meaning. Having said that, however, we may use the far context to help us understand Matthew 1:19. "Then Joseph her husband, being a just man, and not willing (*thelo*) to make her a public example, was minded (*boulomai*) to put her away privily." Again, defining *thelo* as *desire* would render the verse thus: "Then Joseph her husband, not *desiring* to make her a public example, was *determined* (had *planned*) to put her away privately." Again, this makes perfect sense and is supported by the far context of Mark 15. On the other hand, this passage does not really provide a natural contrast in meaning, since the verse could be supposed to mean that Joseph willed not (i.e., *intended* or *decided* not) to make her a public example, but *desired* to put her away privately. So then, since Matthew 1:19 is not a passage conducive to showing a natural difference between *thelo* and *boulemai*, one ought to defer to Mark 15 for a clearer contrast.

However, it must be kept in mind that Mark 15 is merely one passage, and though *thelo* does there show a restricted meaning of desire apart from will, it does not prove that *thelo* should always be thought to have such a restricted meaning. For example, *thelo* has a meaning which includes *intention* in 2 Thessalonians 3:10, in which Paul says that "if any would (Gr. *thelo*) not work, neither should he eat." I recall someone online pointing out that, by *thelo*, Paul could not simply have meant (*bare*) *desire*, for then he would be saying that nearly all people should not eat, since nearly all people, though they work, don't particularly like their work and therefore do not *want* to work. However, the person making this observation then claimed that *thelo* obviously could **not** mean *bare desire*, by which, in fact, <u>he was implying that it could NEVER mean (*bare*) *desire* in any biblical passage that would result in challenging his Calvinistic theology</u>. This is a standard Calvinist method of argument—taking a meaning of a verb that has a wide latitude of meaning depending on its context, but restricting its meaning based on one verse (or with other verses similar to it), and then applying that restricted meaning to other verses where the context does not truly support it. This is what the Bible calls 'making a Scripture of private interpretation.' Thus the Calvinist insists on this 2 Thessalonians 3:10 meaning for *thelo* in all key passages where to understand the word differently would either mean a refutation of Calvinist theology or a failure for Calvinism to gain an advantage. The exact same approach is used by the Calvinist elsewhere, e.g., in their treatment of the word "world." For example, the Calvinist simply finds some passage where the context obviously shows that the word "world" doesn't mean "all the world" and then insists that, even so, God did not so love "all the world" but just a part of it, i.e., "the world of the elect." So too, then, does the Calvinist proceed to take the word "whosoever" to mean "whosoever of the elect," and so forth. Of course, the question begs itself why John wouldn't have simply said, "For God so loved the elect," if that's what he wanted to say? That is, Why would the Spirit lead John to make the meaning either difficult or idiomatic, in what is a straightforward and non-poetic verse like John 3:16? Again, for Calvinists to treat words in this cavalier manner stems from taking a word from another verse or verses, where the context is different, finding a meaning as justified in *those* contexts, absolutizing that meaning, and then applying that meaning to those passages whose contexts do not support that meaning and which would otherwise remain the problematic passages to Calvinism that in fact they are. The point, then, of making *thelo* of private interpretation in 2 Th. 3:10 ["this we commanded you, that if any would (Gr. *thelo*) not work, neither should he eat"], to make it mean the same thing in Philippians 2:13—i.e., to the effect that God gives us the very *will* itself to obey, when, in fact, the preceding verse to Philippians 2:13 commands believers, who, we note, ARE able to quench such a command to work out the implications of their own salvation, thus showing their ability of will—is a form of special pleading.

Now I'll come clean here and admit to (unwittingly or unheedingly) having done a similar kind of eisegesis a few years ago to my own advantage in an earlier edition of this book, when I made Luke 24:22 of private interpretation. I did this after first properly proving that *thelo* in Luke 24:22 could NOT include the meaning of will (choice) when Christ said, "Not my *thelo*, but thine be done," since Christ never chose to call for angelic rescue at the expense of His Father's will, and therefore obviously spoke of his desire apart from His will. While I believe this logical interpretation remains correct for Luke 24:22, as well as my conclusion about *thelo* and *boulemai* in Mark 15, I had not realized that *thelo*, depending on the context, did mean in some passages (such as 2 Th. 3:10) not merely the desire but also a congruent will that was present as conceived by the desire. In fact, I had simply assumed that Strong's would offer the strongest examples to show that *thelo* could have a meaning which included the will. But since such examples proved nothing of the kind to me, I assumed that *thelo* ought not to be understood as including *the will*. Thus the temptation to read a restricted meaning into a particular verb that *de facto* is not so restricted, is a transgression I now realize many a thinker has committed, myself included. Although I regret having done so, it shows the value of taking into account (as I finally did) a more persuasive opponent of my view, whose vested interest was in proving exceptions to *his* opponent's views. For while I found the *if this, then that* conclusion of his faulty, he at least showed me the deficiency in my own view as well.

Having said this, however, let me add the somewhat come-lately thought that it appears to me that *every argument assumes its conclusion*, whether true or false. As a friend of mine paraphrased this thought perhaps more clearly, *The premise IS the conclusion*. This is one reason why Calvinists and non-Calvinists simply claim that it is the other interpreter who makes various biblical scriptures of private interpretation. In the end, then, I think the matter comes down to 1) properly recognizing that the translation is not the autographa; 2) insisting on the historical-grammatical, lexical history of words; and 3) realizing by the Spirit that the proper conclusions will also generally be common sense arguments that most persons would likely understand. Such arguments might be phrased like the following three rhetorical questions: Why would God in the Old Testament often appear exasperated at unrepentant people, if they could not change their ways? Or how can we say that God changes a person's choice from what that person wants, but then call it the *person's* choice? Or how in the future will God condemn people for sinning, if they had no ability to choose differently? Such common sense arguments have led another friend of mine to say of Calvinism, "I call it the unnecessary doctrine." By this he means that it ought to be self-evident that every man creates thoughts and a will that are his own. But unfortunately the prevalence of Calvinistic theology among Christians remains, since many Evangelicals have been brainwashed by translators who in certain key passages frequently assigned false or misleading lexical meanings to words, and in so doing followed after the rudiments of this world and the philosophy of men, rather than after the Spirit.

But to move on to a final point about *thelo*, one should observe that the push by some theologians, perhaps Calvinists in particular, to make *thelo* mean "to will" i.e., "to choose," instead of "to want," in so many places in the New Testament, appears to have something also to do with the refusal to recognize that "to will" is often just assumed in the predicates of language, whether Greek or English. For one does not say, "I chose to get dressed, and then I chose to eat breakfast, and then I chose to go to work." Rather, one simply says, "I dressed, ate breakfast, and went to work." Thus "to will" is simply assumed in many predicates, whether English or Greek—indeed, even as it is assumed that man is the free will creature that he is. Therefore we ought to be inclined not to see the "to will" bogeyman behind every appearance of *thelo*, but to grant at least the possibility of "desire" in as many biblical passages as the contexts suggest. For again, the rule here, as everywhere, is: *Context is king*.

And so, to bring the discussion full cycle, it seems reasonable to conclude that Philippians 2:13, *in context* (i.e., the near context of its preceding verse and the far context of the kind of common sense objections that are implicit throughout Scripture as based upon the historical and lexical meaning of words), speaks of God working in us to *desire* and to do of His good pleasure. God does this through encouraging and affirming the intact (not seared) conscience of every believer. Furthermore, and again, since we have the ability to quench the Spirit's work in our lives, God does not simply *give* us the will, whether we want it or not, as Calvinists imply. The Calvinist, of course, will deny our contention for common sense, relying on a doctrine of human depravity that implies that man **has** no common sense, or that the "common sense" he perceives is false, and that "common sense" is rooted instead in divine mystery and therefore humanly inaccessible, inexpressible, and (currently, at least) incomprehensible.

Now the point in taking my readers through the above process in regard to Philippians 2:13 is not only to show the actual meaning of the phrase *to will*, but to explain why sometimes this book has found it necessary to question certain views of theologians and commentators regarding their logic and conclusions, since their views are often accepted by us lay persons rather uncritically. For the problem is this: many commentators treat verbs as though they are married off to nouns (typically, "God" when absolute sovereignty is at stake, or "man" when depravity is at stake). But observe that a verb, while not married to a specific noun or nouns, IS married to its historical, grammatical, and lexical latitude of meaning, as understood through the particular context in each of its given appearances.

QUESTION:

Does Philippians 1:29 teach that God gives us belief? This verse appears to state that we do not initiate the believing ourselves, but that God gives it to us. The verse reads: "For unto you it is given in the behalf of Christ, not only to believe on him, but also to suffer for his sake...."

ANSWER:

Philippians 1:29 is interpreted by Calvinists to mean that God foreordains everything the believer experiences, including his belief and suffering. We have answered in previous chapters the two questions of whether saving faith is given by God and whether all suffering is caused by God, and have answered in the negative in both cases. Philippians 1:29 is simply a generic statement about the *lot* of the Christian. That is, the path of the believer will not only involve belief, but also suffering. As Paul says elsewhere, "All they that live godly in Christ Jesus shall suffer persecution." Every Christian suffers persecution in some sense. We are hated by a world which hates Christ, and we belong to a corporate Body, the Church, which is the object of attack by the Devil and his emissaries.

QUESTION:

Paul says to the Corinthian believers, "For all things are for your sakes" (2 Cor. 4:15). That sounds like the same thought expressed in Romans 8:28, i.e., "that all things work together for good to them that love God." Does this mean that everything we are exposed to in life (including sin) is for the benefit of Christians who love God?

ANSWER:

We have already shown in this book's chapter 6 that Romans 8:28 was not translated accurately in the KJV, that is, if the translators intended to mean that all things in the world, without qualification, work together for good in the case of the believer. So we will consider just the 2 Corinthians passage. Note, then, that the context shows that the *all things* which Paul refers to is the suffering he details in the verses leading up to verse 15. In verses 8-11 Paul says that Timothy and he were "afflicted in *every way*." Paul then explains what he means by 'every way.' He and Timothy were *crushed, perplexed, persecuted,* and *struck down*. He concludes in verse 12, "So death works in us, but life in you." He then quotes a phrase from Psalm 116:10 to say that he and Timothy, like the Psalmist, still believe in the Lord in the midst of suffering. Both he and Timothy also realize that the Father who raised Jesus will one day make a presentation of them along with the Corinthian believers. At this point Paul comes to verse 15: "For all things are for your sakes, so that the grace which is spreading to more and more people may cause the giving of thanks to abound to the glory of God." Paul, in referring to "all things," is still referring to his and Timothy's endurance in the face of all kinds of suffering. Paul anticipates that the Corinthians themselves will face suffering when he adds in verse 17, "For momentary light affliction is producing for us an eternal weight of glory far beyond all comparison." The idea that suffering produces glory for the believer is not meant to be understood here as *means* being justified by their *end* (when such means come from the Enemy). The only sense that our eternal weight of glory can be understood as being produced by evil *means* in the world, is due to our *resistance* against evil. The *means* of our resistance in the Holy Spirit is what ultimately leads to our *end*, i.e., our eternal weight of glory. If Paul is saying what some claim—that every evil is really a good working for the believer—then it would make no sense for him to say two chapters later that righteousness, light, and Christ have no possibility of working cooperatively together with unrighteousness, darkness, and the Devil, respectively. Also, note that the book of 2 Corinthians actually begins with the same theme of suffering to which it returns in chapter 4. Paul states in 1:3-7, 11 that whether he suffers or is comforted, all such circumstances will benefit the Corinthian Christians as they pray for him and learn about suffering and comfort. This is yet another sense in which "all things"[123] were for the Corinthians' sakes, i.e., so that they might offer thanks:

> [3]Blessed be the God and Father of our Lord Jesus Christ, the Father of mercies and God of all comfort, [4]who comforts us in all our affliction so that we will be able to comfort those who are in any affliction with the comfort with which we ourselves are comforted by God. [5]For just as the sufferings of Christ are ours in abundance, so also our comfort is abundant through Christ. [6]But if we are afflicted, it is for your comfort and salvation; or if we are comforted, it is for your comfort, which is effective in the patient enduring of the same sufferings which we also suffer; [7]and our hope for you is firmly grounded, knowing that as you are sharers of our sufferings, so also you are sharers of our comfort…[11]you also joining in helping us through your prayers, so that thanks may be given by many persons on our behalf for the favor bestowed on us through the prayers of many.

QUESTION:

Colossian 1:15 states: "For by Him [Christ] were all things created, that are in heaven, and that are in earth, visible and invisible, whether they be thrones, or dominions, or principalities, or powers: all things were created by him, and for him." Doesn't this mean that even the Devil, the Fall, the sin of man, etc., were made to glorify God?

ANSWER:

Not at all. Colossians 1:16 is referring to all things that *were* created. In context this means all things as *God* created them *in their forms*, not in their content. Man is, in part, a form; forms are what God makes, though of course God also makes the content of His *own* thoughts. What man has become through his obedience or disobedience is a result of his content, and God did not make that content. God does try to influence our future content for good, but He does not *create* the content. (Only man can create his own content.) Indeed, if Colossians 1 was telling us that all things without exception were made *for* God, why would Paul have made the distinction four verses earlier regarding the desire of God to have us translated **from** the power of darkness into the kingdom of His dear Son? That is, if everything was created *for* God, then everything would also be part of the Son's kingdom, in which case the power of darkness would also be part of the Son's kingdom—there would be no distinction—so why would God need to translate us **from** that? But as to the anticipated Calvinist rejoinder that even the Fall, man's sin, etc., glorifies God, it ought to be observed that we have already answered these points in other portions of this book, especially with the commentary on Romans 8:28.

Furthermore, though men and fallen angels have abused their positions of power, this is not an argument that God has ever *used* their evil for good or for the good of the believer. He foreknows when evil will occur, He counters it (by limiting the degree and/or length of the trial for the sake of the believer, and the believer looks to Him). He opposes evil, and when some tremendous good has prevailed despite evil opposing it, the result may look as though God had used the evil or the evil person. But He has not. The book of Job, as we have already seen, is very instructive on this point of showing God's goodness to us, a goodness that especially arises in the midst of a believer's betimes lengthy conflict against evil.

QUESTION:

I know the Bible teaches there is a hell. But how could a man have free will if he is in hell, since he would have no choice there?

ANSWER:

Men are never without their will, e.g., without the choice to give God glory or to withhold their praise, even if they are in hell. How a man thinks of God is *never* forcibly removed from him. Until recently I thought that when an unbeliever died he woke up in torment and immediately understood the gospel he rejected. While I still believe he wakes up in torment, I no longer think it was ever correct for me to have assumed that an unbeliever truly understands the gospel after he dies. In fact, there are two passages that support the idea that after death men continue to think the same essential way they always did while they were alive. The first is found in Matthew 7:21-23, in which Christ says that many people shall come to Him in that (final judgment) day, confident in the justifying nature of their own works:

Many will say to Me on that day, 'Lord, Lord, did we not prophesy in Your name, and in Your name cast out demons, and in Your name perform many miracles?' And then I will declare to them, 'I never knew you; Depart from me, you who practice lawlessness...'

These people had gone through life convinced that the good things they did would save them from their sins. As seen in the above passage, their thinking did not change after they died. Christ said that many people would make this kind of appeal during the Judgment but be sent to hell. So we see from Scripture that men remain deceived in their thinking even after they are dead. Perhaps the most vivid example of this fact is the man described in Luke 16:19-31. This passage describes an unrepentant rich man who died and went to a place of fiery torment:

[19]There was a certain rich man who was clothed in purple and fine linen and fared sumptuously every day. [20]But there was a certain beggar named Lazarus, full of sores, who was laid at his gate, [21]desiring to be fed with the crumbs which fell from the rich man's table. Moreover the dogs came and licked his sores. [22]So it was that the beggar died, and was carried by the angels to Abraham's bosom. The rich man also died and was buried. [23]And being in torments in Hades, he lifted up his eyes and saw Abraham afar off, and Lazarus in his bosom. [24]Then he cried and said, 'Father Abraham, have mercy on me, and send Lazarus that he may dip the tip of his finger in water and cool my tongue; for I am tormented in this flame.' [25]But Abraham said, 'Son, remember that in your lifetime you received your good things, and likewise Lazarus evil things; but now he is comforted and you are tormented. [26]And besides all this, between us and you there is a great gulf fixed, so that those who want to pass from here to you cannot, nor can those from there pass to us.' [27]Then he said, 'I beg you therefore father, that you would send him to my father's house, [28]for I have five brothers, that he may testify to them, lest they also come to this place of torment.' [29]Abraham said to him, 'They have Moses and the prophets; let them hear them.' [30]And he said, 'No, father Abraham; but if one goes to them from the dead, they will repent.' [31]But he said to him, 'If

> they do not hear Moses and the prophets, neither will
> they be persuaded though one rise from the dead.'

Notice that this man never says that he has any regrets. He never says to Abraham, "I'm sorry I didn't think more about Lazarus," or "I really regret not thinking about God," or "I'm only getting what I deserve for my sin." The only concern he shows is for his five brothers. Of such concern Jesus elsewhere gave short shrift—"What reward is there in loving those who love you? Don't even the tax collectors do the same?" (Mt. 5:46). This man never got beyond his selfishness to consider how he ought to love God and his fellow man. The idea that men in hell are denied their free will to give God glory is therefore not supported in the Bible. Again, the Scripture does not give any indication that men in hell will want their thinking changed from what it was during their lifetime. Thus we should ask how a man in hell *can* acknowledge Christ if he shall remain *unwilling* to do so? And how much stronger shall a man resist truth in a place where God is no longer pulling him toward a place where he might consider the work of Christ? Thus, in hell men will still have the freedom to think of God how they will, but God will no longer be striving with them to think correctly. Such a man will be like a prisoner in jail who remains unreformed despite his punishment. This was the condition, in fact, of the rich man in Luke 16 after he died.

Finally, one might object that a man is not free to leave hell (even though he would certainly want to) and is therefore denied the freedom of his will. The Bible, however, never teaches that the *object* of our intention will always be realized, but merely that our intention (i.e., our will) shall always remain intact and free.

QUESTION:

Proverbs 16:4 states: "The LORD hath made all things for himself: yea, even the wicked for the day of evil." Doesn't this mean that God *makes* the wicked to be wicked because it pleases Him to do so as the Absolute Sovereign of the universe?

ANSWER:

God does not *make* anybody's will, and this is the case whether they are righteous or wicked. Furthermore, we have demonstrated in earlier portions of this book why God must be (and is biblically presented as) consistent in His holiness and consistent in His hatred of sin. What is in view in Proverbs 16:4 is the *end* of the wicked as judgmentally determined by God. God alone is the One who has decided what the final abode of each man shall be, according to his belief or unbelief. For the wicked it is "the day of evil," that is, the day of calamity. The unbelieving man certainly wishes that he alone could determine the final (eternal) consequence of his actions, for then there would be none that involved punishment. But God Himself (and *by* Himself) shall decide what the appropriate reward or punishment of every man shall be according to His own holy standard of *judgment*.

QUESTION:

Acts 17:26-27a states: "[God] hath made of one blood all nations of men for to dwell on all the face of the earth, and hath determined the times before appointed, and the bounds of their habitation. That they should seek the Lord…" Doesn't this verse mean that God decides who, for example, should be born in America and who should have Christian parents, etc. If I was born in India, I probably wouldn't be a Christian, because so many people there are Hindu. Hasn't God decided, then, who will be born where?

Answer:

While it is true that a child of godly parents, or the succeeding generation of a godly nation, is in a position to benefit from the godly decisions of those who have gone before them, this is because those parents or godly nations have, by their own will, responded positively to God's instruction. Conversely, a child or generation will not benefit if those who go before the child or generation are godless. Furthermore, the Bible teaches that God is not a respecter of persons, and so we should not think that God arbitrarily decides that one person or nation will be in a place of special privilege. Observe then, that in Acts 17, while it is true that Paul concludes his sermon to the Athenians by stressing the judgment of God which shall come upon all men by the Man whom God has raised from the dead, Paul's prior remark about the *habitations* of men must be understood in this light. In other words, Paul is saying that the habitations of men are subject to the judgment of God. Thus when a nation unlawfully (apart from divine instruction) goes beyond its borders to conquer another people or peoples, or fails to carry out God's judgment on His behalf (see 1 Ki. 20:42), it is subject to God's unmediated judgment. For some nations act wickedly against other nations, or refuse to carry out His judgment. But God will ultimately subject them to judgment, of which the Old Testament metaphor of the Potter and the pot directly speaks. Thus God sets the boundaries and habitations as *irresistibly* subject to judgment. That is the context and meaning of what Paul is saying.

QUESTION:

Psalm 139:16 states (NAS): "Your eyes have seen my unformed substance; And in Your book were all written The days that were ordained for me, When as yet there was not one of them." Doesn't this mean that God has ordained everything that happens in our lives, even to the exact length of our life?

ANSWER:

Of the 12 English versions of Psalm 139:16 listed on BlueLetterBible.com, two may be understood to be defining "fashioned days" are merely days that are foreseen, not "ordained", by God. But more significantly (I think), is that three versions place the Hebrew *yomw* [i.e., *days(s)*] in a <u>dependent</u> clause, i.e., "*in continuance* were fashioned" thus referring back to the (granted, implied *members*]. The Hebrew *yowm* may mean a set time, period, year, etc. Given the physiological description in the immediately preceding section ("my reins," "my mother's womb," "curiously wrought in the lower parts of the earth," "my substance"), I believe one may take the "days that were fashioned" to instead mean "the set times already developed," thus understanding the phrase as referring to the gestational times of the individual members, i.e., the "all" (v. 16) of the "substance" (v. 16).

So then, nearly half of the English translations may be understood as not teaching *predestined* days, which is what the NASB and certain other translations seem to be driving at. What all 12 versions thus demonstrate in their considerable differences (directly, or through paraphrase which assumes another's conclusions), is the *assumptions* that drive translational decisions. Indeed, is it not the case that translations vary so because translators must sometimes even discern whether a clause is dependent or independent? Such would make a huge difference. That is, Is Hebrew so restrictively defined in its grammar that there is never any question about whether a clause might be independent or dependent? Judging from the translations, it certainly does not appear so, but that much of this question lies in a translator's own judgment.

Personally, I believe the KJV got 139:16 essentially correct here, and that what is ordained is the "substance," not the "days". One objection to this view is that the word "ordained" [rather, Heb. *formed, fashioned, framed*] matches the masculine genders of both "all" and "days" and that therefore "days" is what "all" refers to.. However, the following should be noted. The word "all" can in fact refer to a noun in the plural, even though the noun may be feminine in its singular form. Further, "all" has in its component letters a pointer referring to what came *previously*, i.e., in this case the various parts which God wondrously made which the Psalmist had been describing, i.e., David's (lit.) kidneys, and also skeleton (lit. bones), embryo, and (lit.)

embroidered [parts]. All of these things, understood as a plurality, may serve as that to which "all" refers. Finally, as for "the days that were ordained *for me*", the "for me" is in italics in the NASB, supplied by the translators to make the thought clearer according to what the translators assumed the Psalmist meant. But it appears to be there because of an apparent Calvinist bias, as though the Psalmist was stating that God formed *everything* which had *any* bearing on the length of his life. Rather, the phrase about 'ordaining' should be understood as referring to the *when* of God's fashioning work. In Arabic biblical translation, for example, the phrase is treated as a *dependent* clause to the main thought that it is God who formed all these things "..., the days *they* were created." The question might be asked why the Psalmist would bother stating so obvious a thing about pregnancy taking days. Perhaps one answer lies in that David's members were not created in a single day as Adam's was, though they could have been had God willed it that way. But perhaps one reason they were not was because of the multiplication of pain and gestational period that God bestowed upon the woman in childbirth because of her disobedience, a disobedience which took place with the full compliance and knowledge of the man. Thus the Spirit of God, moving through the Psalmist, may be obliquely implying and reminding us that the fashioning of the body is not merely after the image of God, but also after the image of Adam, as the book of Genesis supports. Still, the creation of the body in its form, even along these lines, bears significant witness of God's wondrous work. Also, one other reason why "days" may be mentioned is to show the faithfulness of God pertaining to the Psalmist on a daily basis.

All this goes to the point about a theologian's assumptions driving the meaning of words and exegesis and interpretation and translation and lexicons to some vital degree. Granted, abstractly considered, Psalm 139:16 taken by itself could be (and has been) translated a number of different ways. But when I see that the persuasiveness of such Calvinistic translations in the Old Testament (e.g., that God decrees the exact length of our days, which implies He decrees in some cases that person X smokes and overeats and so shortens his life, while person Y does not), relies on other arguments from the New Testament, which here can be more easily examined for their faithfulness to the historical-grammatical hermeneutic (since contemporary Greek sources exist outside the N.T. biblical writings, which form "lexical control groups' to prevent special pleading type definitions, such as the one for "foreknew" which James White advances), I remain convinced that Calvinists are on the wrong track. And so, when I said in an earlier edition of this book that the word "days" in Psalm 139:16 should not have been rendered instead of (granted, implied) "members,", that is, the particulars of the "substance," I think the spirit of that argument remains correct, i.e., that "all [members]", not days, is what is referenced in the Hebrew, which in my opinion points to the "continuance" of formation (or, perhaps, the "set times" already developed [contextually interpreted as the gestational times of the particular members]). In short, Hebrew is sometimes in the eye of the beholder, and unless a translator walks in the Spirit while translating, most any other viewpoint can be advanced. The lesson here is clear—no Scriptural verse or passage ought to be made of private interpretation, but should harmonize with the all of Scripture in both Testaments.

<u>Footnotes:</u>

[117] God sustains the form of man and provides him with his very breath and abilities, and offers him wisdom. The king speaks as though he were independent even in the sustenance of his body.

[118] It might be objected here that not all Messianic passages in the Old Testament predict Messiah's death in a *de facto* way that makes the Messianic passage compliant with our explanation above. Such an example would be Psalm 22:7, where it says "All they that see me laugh me to scorn…" But *if* Messiah would have died at the hands of believing sinners, then such a phrase could have applied to the Psalmist alone. As Bible students know, not all Messianic passages maintain a consistent Messianic voice throughout Messianic sections, nor *must* they, since the passage is often describing the activity of another individual. Furthermore, it should be observed that where such Messianic passages describe the sinful acts of men during crucifixion, they are revealed that way because of God's foreknowledge, which is non-determinative. Had the human actions been of a different sort, the Old Testament Messianic passage would likewise have been different. Or, if the Messianic passages were still not different, then it would be understood that the Messianic aspect of the Psalm ceased or did not exist at such a point, and that the meaning should be restricted to the Psalmist himself.

[119] Psalm 76:10 does indeed predict that the "wrath of man will praise [God]," and some have thought this means that God is so absolutely sovereign that even sin praises Him (as the Designer of history). This verse, however, can be explained apart from the Calvinistic model. The anger referred to may simply mean believers who are told to be angry and sin not. Nothing in the passage suggests we must understand the verse to mean *all* the anger of *all* men at *all* times. In fact, the Bible explicitly states in James 1:20 that "the wrath of man worketh not the righteousness of God." Another possible explanation is that the anger referred to in Psalm 26:10 is that of unbelievers who will *narrowly* look upon the Antichrist after his defeat, realizing in a moment of astonishment that he failed them because he was weaker than they had imagined, i.e., "Art thou become as one of us?" (Is 14:10).

> [9]Hell from beneath is moved for thee to meet thee at thy coming: it stirreth up the dead for thee, even all the chief ones of the earth; it hath raised up from their thrones all the kings of the nations. [10]All they shall speak and say unto

thee, Art thou also become weak as we? art thou become like unto us? [11]Thy pomp is brought down to the grave, and the noise of thy viols: the worm is spread under thee, and the worms cover thee. [12]How art thou fallen from heaven, O Lucifer, son of the morning! how art thou cut down to the ground, which didst weaken the nations! [13]For thou hast said in thine heart, I will ascend into heaven, I will exalt my throne above the stars of God: I will sit also upon the mount of the congregation, in the sides of the north: [14]I will ascend above the heights of the clouds; I will be like the most High. [15]Yet thou shalt be brought down to hell, to the sides of the pit. [16]They that see thee shall narrowly look upon thee, and consider thee, saying, Is this the man that made the earth to tremble, that did shake kingdoms; [17]That made the world as a wilderness, and destroyed the cities thereof; that opened not the house of his prisoners? (Is. 14:9-17).

[120] Olson states that *boulomai* appears only once in Romans 9:19, the other occurrences being *boule*, a weaker form. Although I have followed Strong's definition of *boulomai* throughout, I don't think the argument over the contrast between *thelo* and *boulomai* (and *boule*) is affected *per se*. Nevertheless, the reader should keep this in mind.

[121] Even if *boulomai* did appear in Philippians 2:13, I do not think the near context would justify such a deterministic interpretation.

[122] John (18:39) actually does use *boulemai* instead of *thelo*, though in John the two terms are not contrasted against one another as in Mark. The explanation for John's use of *boulemai* is thus: Pilate, in the course of the tumultuous meeting between he and the Jews, asks the Jews three times what evil Jesus had done. Thus there is no reason to suppose any contradiction between John's gospel and Mark's, for Pilate presumably asked the question regarding evidence for Jesus' guilt more than once, i.e. both ways—"Whom do you *want* that I release," and "Whom do you *decide* that I release." Pilate's habit was to release a prisoner to them at a Jewish feast. This habit made for an expectation among the Jews for a political concession from Pilate. But Mark (15:8) shows that not until the Jews desired (inferior translation here; Gr. word means *begged*) did Pilate act according to his custom. Thus Pilate acquiesces to ask the Jews, *after they have shown their subordination*, who they *wanted* released (and so, too, presumably the same relative question as to whom they *decided* should be released). In this context of subordination Pilate is thus able to include the word *decided* without losing face. Then Pilate, releasing Barabbas unto them and thus fulfilling his 'obligation' according to Jewish expectations, uses the word *thelo* when asking the Jews what they *wanted* done with Jesus, that is, since he knows they could not appeal or barter from a position of further expectation. Finally, though *thelo* can mean *desirous intent* (i.e., not just mere *desire*), the context of Jewish appeal, and the contrast Pilate himself made between *thelo* and *boulamai* (actually, *boule* here, a

weaker form), indicates that *thelo* here was intended with more of (or, only) a meaning of *desire* rather than *desirous intent*.

[123] Olson has pointed out that when Gr. *panta* (things) is used with *ta* it likely has a demonstrative force. *Panta* occurs 45 times in the New Testament, with *ta* accompanying it 25 times. Arguably, then, '*ta panta*' may be translated "*all* things" or "all *these* things," *depending upon the context* (which provides the clarification). In fact, in the latter case I believe "all *these* things" can be used in a demonstrable way in which "these" may still be understood as going from the particular to the general. For example, I might, in my enthusiasm for God's display of power in creation, wave my arm to indicate my immediate surroundings, exclaiming: "*Look* at all these things!" Yet by doing so I *may* or *may not* imply that my hearer should go from contemplating the particular things to which I am drawing his attention, to contemplating the general universe of things accordingly. The fuller context of my conversation and statements before and after my exclamatory phrase would determine which meaning my hearer should infer. Thus, for 2 Corinthians 4:15, the context appears to show that Paul is referring his Corinthian readers to "all *these* things" (not "*all* things"), i.e., the things which he and Timothy had endured and which served as lessons in perseverance.

Endnotes:

[lix] Spiegel, p. 25.

[lx] Rimmer, Harry. *Calvary*. Berne, Indiana; Berne Witness, Inc., 1939).

[lxi] Strong, James. [http://www.apostolic-churches.net/bible/strongs/ref/?stgh=greek&stnm=5915].

CHAPTER 18
The Freedom of the Will

Question:

I was always taught that man is born with a sinful nature. Does this mean that man's will was corrupted by the Fall, like everything else? If so, how can you say that I can freely choose Christ or choose anything besides sin? If I'm a sinner, wouldn't I have to compulsively choose evil?

Answer:

Most Evangelicals believe that Adam plunged the entire human race into sin when he ate the forbidden fruit. Calvinists even believe that man's will was so corrupted in the Fall that man can no longer respond to God on his own *whatsoever*. Others have said that man's will was corrupted at the Fall, but that man can still respond to God. Nearly all Evangelicals, whether Reformed or non-Reformed, believe that Adam's sin (or at least the imputed guilt of Adam's sin) passed onto all his descendents. This is known as the doctrine of original sin. Interestingly enough, while Protestants and Catholics hold to a form of this belief, Judaism and Islam do not. A well-known saying encapsulates the doctrine of original sin: "We're not sinners because we sin; we sin because we're sinners." Furthermore, most Evangelicals also believe that we physically die as a result of Adam's *transgression* (that is, not merely the *consequence* of Adam's transgression) passing upon the human race.

Though nearly all my life I believed in the doctrine of original sin, I now hold to the view that what we inherit from Adam is the knowledge of good and evil—but not sin, nor imputed sin.[124] Technically speaking, I believe we inherit upon conception *the seed* of the knowledge of good and evil, not this knowledge matured. (In a moment we will go into considerable detail about what the Scripture says about the kind of knowledge which Adam gained when he first sinned.) Further, as a person mentally matures, this seed of knowledge also matures until that person can deliberate upon thoughts to form conclusions about them unto an eternal liability. By 'eternal liability' I mean the personal consequences that shall be borne eternally from God's judgment of the choices one makes. Thus, once God decides that a proper amount of time has been given for the person's maturity, i.e., such that a person's conclusions are eternally liable under God's judgment, then the person enters his probationary period. All men have sinned during this probationary period and come short of God's standard of sinless perfection. No man except Christ has ever journeyed through that probationary period and finished righteously. Therefore no other flesh has been justified in the sight of God, because all men have chosen to sin. Moreover, God in His foreknowledge knows that no man in his flesh *shall* (in the future of history) be justified (by his own works), either.

Like Charles Finney, the 19th century evangelist, I believe that we're sinners because we sin, rather than that we sin because we're sinners. At the same time (unlike Finney) I believe that man's acquisition of the knowledge of good and evil has been a disastrous thing which has made his flesh *perverse*. By *perverse*, I do not mean sin, nor imputed sin, nor sinful (some assume a substantial difference of definition in these terms), but rather *a twisted* nature, that is, a nature unbefitting man's form in which man now has *additional thoughts involving additional content about knowledge, including knowledge about sin [i.e, a body of knowledge about sin that is greater than what man would have had, had he never sinned.]* For God never intended man to have this kind of knowledge, e.g., the *vicarious knowledge* that there is pleasure in sin.

This knowledge exposes man to the various possibilities and opportunities of pleasure regarding sin, therefore distracting his mind toward a consideration of them. Such knowledge puts a tremendous testing on man as to whether he will sin, since he vicariously knows there will be pleasure in at least certain sins if he commits them. And the more he commits sin the more likely he is to have pleasure in more abominable kinds of sins. Yet, while any type of sin has the potential to allure us, allurement by itself is not sin. That is, allurement is merely our emotional response toward a desire prior to the will's involvement. And our will's choice determines our morality. If we act selfishly in response to the allurement, we have sinned. Thus James seems to draw a distinction between lust and sin, saying that when lust *has conceived*, it brings forth sin (Ja. 1:14-15). Therefore sin is not merely lust but lust *conceived*. The Greek word for lust means *to pant* after. *Lust conceived* was arguably the form of lust to which Jesus referred, when He said that a man was guilty of adultery if he lusted after another woman. For in the context of that statement, Jesus explains that if a man's will is committed to divorce his wife apart from her having committed fornication,[125] he has planned, in effect, *to sell her* for another woman whom he desires to have instead (i.e., divorcing the one to marry the other, during which presumably he intends not to suffer financial loss). That is, divorcing his wife would force his wife to commit adultery, since she would then have to seek from another man the rights she had been enjoying from her husband, (e.g., such as companionship, children, finances, sex, etc.). Thus the *guilt* of the adultery is assigned to the husband, since he has forced her to commit adultery. So if a man commits his will toward the goal of committing adultery but simply lacks the opportunity to do so, he is nevertheless judged by God to be guilty because of his intention. Therefore in this context Jesus is defining lust as lust *conceived*, since the man that Jesus describes has already committed himself to the idea of exercising his will to commit adultery.[126]

At any rate, the knowledge of good and evil, which does not befit the form of man, is now a part of him. But though this knowledge puts pressure on man, it does not *force* him to sin. That is, the knowledge of good and evil does not *determine* a man's will. Further, this knowledge is not a sin from which a man can repent. It is merely a consequence of sin, a knowledge about sin which God never intended that he should have.

This book takes the position that the knowledge of good and evil is generally referred to as the *flesh* (Gr. *sarx*) in New Testament contexts about fallen man. Sometimes the term *flesh* in the Bible refers to **non**-fallen man, i.e., man apart from the knowledge of good and evil, such as when John tells us that "the Word became flesh." I also believe that post-Adamic persons (pre-born babies and all others who have not reached their individual age of accountability) are subject to physical death because they are subject to the *consequence* of Adam's transgression. (I hasten to add that, if post-Adamic persons have brought to an end the probationary period of their accountability, they *are* spiritually dead as having actualized sin themselves.) This book defines the term 'age of accountability' as synonymous with a period of *discernment and decision*, a time in which the person is eternally liable for his decisions. During this period of accountability, Adam, for example, was on the path *toward* righteousness, but not yet accounted to be righteous. He had made correct decisions prior to his fall, but ultimately failed in *consistency*, which would have demonstrated his righteousness (see footnote 131). Furthermore, like Adam, no person but Christ has or will ever complete his probationary period unto righteousness.

Physical Death

The problem with supposing that post-Adamic man's physical death is a result of his spiritual death *per se*, is that it explains nothing about why animals and insects[127] also die, which likewise are part of God's creation.[128] Or are we to assume that ladybugs and butterflies (yes—lions, tigers, and bears, also!) all bear Adam's imputed sin along with every other insect and animal of the world? It seems unlikely. That animals in their physical death bear the consequence of Adam's sin is certain—that they are conjoined with Adam's sin is much less certain (and in my opinion not the case). Rather, the Bible's own commentary regarding the behavior of animals (or at least the serpent-animal in the Garden) suggests a degree of moral understanding and therefore an awareness and accountability before God, *though not, it would appear, of a magnitude involving* eternal *liability*. The state of the animals also suggests that they are similar to infants and(?) toddlers insofar as having no knowledge that they are naked, which would appear to be a sign of their present moral non-liability unto eternity.[129] [130] Again, as a person matures, he reaches a point where his non-liability ceases and his liability (unto eternity) begins.

Thus, regarding physical death in general, it might be said that man is under the *consequence* of Adam's sin, rather than *conjoined* with Adam's sin. To be *conjoined* with Adam's sin is essentially what the doctrine of original sin teaches. And yet this consequence of death itself appears ultimately tempered, when we consider that natural death, that terrible cloud of consequence, is nevertheless one with the golden lining of releasing the believer's soul and spirit from his body of fallen flesh—the latter being the abode of the knowledge of good and evil, which presents so much trial in this life to every believer. Thus, regarding the believer in Christ, physical death means that he enters the presence of God and no longer has that kind of knowledge known as *the knowledge of good and evil* (which man first acquired through sinning). That is the great release for the believer. In this sense [i.e., beyond the obvious sense that we enter the presence of the Lord when we die (if the Lord tarry)] the sting of physical death is taken away.

The Knowledge of Good and Evil

Our first parents obtained the knowledge of good and evil by failing to trust God consistently.[131] Again, what we inherit from Adam is fairly plain in the Lord's statement about Adam's sin, when He stated that "the man has become as one of us, knowing good and evil." Adam now had a greater *knowledge* (i.e., not *sin*, though he obtained this knowledge by sin) than what he would have had apart from his Fall. As infants we inherit, for lack of what might be a better description, the *Adamic seed* (via the *male, Adamic-line*) of the knowledge of good and evil.[132] Upon first reaching the age of *discernment (accountability)*[133] we arrive at a place where we have the knowledge of good and evil in a significantly matured form. Not until a person sins does he have the knowledge of good and evil in its full blossom. Again, this knowledge entails, at the least, *an understanding that sin (or at least certain sins) can be pleasurable* in some sense if we commit it/(them). It does not appear that Adam and Eve had this vicarious knowledge while in their probation. That is, in their original state they did not have the knowledge that there is pleasure in sin. God, in fact, did not hint to the first pair that they would find any pleasure *in sin* (though presumably they understood there would be pleasure in the fruit *as fruit*) but emphasized the negative consequence only (see footnote 134). Ever since the Fall, Adam and his descendents have had this vicarious knowledge about **sin** as they face moral decisions. Thus Adam and his descendents now also have the *additional knowledge of* **good** implied in the phrase 'the knowledge of *good* and evil,' that is, as presumably it would be defined as man's heightened awareness (i.e., *knowledge*) of the good that he sees potentially in resisting sin *despite* his vicarious knowledge that there is pleasure (if temporary) in sin. In other words, *the general knowledge surrounding* what is at stake is greater in us than what Adam and Eve knew prior to their disobedience. This means that the stakes for good and evil are contrasted more greatly in our minds than if the Fall had not occurred. For observe that the first pair in their original state had something like a mere textbook understanding of sin. As yet, they had not known sin and its pleasure experientially. Of course, they had to have *some* degree of moral knowledge, that is, a rudimentary kind that enabled them to understand God's command in the Garden, as well as to understand what *death* meant (for otherwise God's warning would have been without meaning to them)—but they did not at first have the kind of *especial* knowledge of good and evil which God had.[134] For God intended that Adam and Eve and their descendents should remain, so to speak, 'babes in the woods,' i.e., innocent of their nakedness (in the lower form in which God made them), having a simple understanding of good and evil unencumbered with the often *tireless thought* of sin's pleasurable possibilities. For God knew that such knowledge would not be *prudent* for Adam and Eve in their lower form.[135]

THE CONSCIENCE OF MAN

Man's conscience, along with his knowledge, is thus also *more intensive* now, because man's knowledge is greater than what God intended it to be. Our conscience is that part of us which has moral understanding.[136] The conscience is formed from the correct assumptions and/or conclusions we have made about *thoughts* (or *in* our thoughts), some of which thoughts we think ourselves and some of which thoughts are not ours but are presented to us by God, which we accept. *How* we beget *our* thoughts is a mystery, but *that* we beget them is certain. For to maintain our position that God and man are indeed two different persons (the former the Creator, the latter His special earthly creature), we must contend that man *himself* brings his own thoughts into existence *ex nihilo*. This means that the content of *a man's* thoughts must, by definition, be *his own*.[137] Two other persons besides himself may also put thoughts into a man's mind—God, and the Devil[138] (upon God's allowance). The man then deliberates upon the thoughts present in or presented to his mind and finally decides what he will hold to be right or wrong about each of these thoughts. Often this process takes a mere fraction of a second, such as "I need a pencil," (in which the man recognizes various truths, such as what 'I' and 'a pencil' truly are, etc.), while at other times deliberation is much drawn out in length because of the difficulty in discerning whose voice is speaking, or because a man is wrestling with his conscience about what he shall decide.

The decisions that man makes are his *intentions*, i.e., his *will*. Again, every man exercises his own will *ex nihilo (out of nothing; that is, without prior cause)*. Our will, when we judge properly the rightness or wrongness of thoughts, results in a body of conclusions that form a man's conscience. The very first thought and deliberation that a baby (in or out of the womb) thinks must therefore be good, or he could not know, i.e., affirm rightly, that, e.g., he exists (or had a thought). In this infantile state a baby is unaware of his nakedness and therefore not yet liable unto eternity for his thoughts, since he has not yet reached his probationary, accountable age. Prior to his probationary period a person's thoughts commit nothing transgressive unto eternal liability. Once a person reaches the age of accountability he will make decisions that affect his conscience negatively or positively. An *intact* conscience is maintained by agreeing with God about thoughts. A defiled conscience is formed by *disagreeing* with God about thoughts. The conscience is thus *not* the same thing as the knowledge of good and evil.[139]

The Adamic Transmission of Knowledge

A question might be raised at this point as to exactly *how* this knowledge of good and evil is passed from Adam to us. Frankly, I don't know; except to suggest that this inherited knowledge passes through Adam's *seed* via the male line. But such a response still begs the question about *how* it is passed through Adam's seed. Yet it seems to me that this mystery is no greater than *how* an infant goes from *not knowing* his left hand from his right hand, **to** *knowing* his left hand from his right hand. Again, we simply do not know why moral understanding occurs *ex nihilio*, nor how it or the knowledge of good and evil is passed from one generation to the next, nor even how thoughts originate. We may, in the end, simply have to rest upon the Bible's definitions of these things, i.e., Adam's *de facto* pre-Fall knowledge, the knowledge of good and evil, etc., as the Bible itself defines them 1) lexically, 2) contextually, and 3) according to the historical-grammatical method of interpretation—even as, for example, Thomas Edgar has done in re-discovering (for Evangelicals) the Bible's definition of *divine foreknowledge* according to the above three principles, and despite the evidence leading Edgar to a mystery about how divine foreknowledge could be non-determinative. In other words, we have the responsibility as Christians to follow the biblical and lexical evidence wherever it leads.

THE NATURE OF MAN'S KNOWLEDGE

Many people call the knowledge of good and evil, which we inherit through Adam, *the sin nature*,[140] though this latter term does not appear in the Greek, nor, would I argue, is it represented as such by other words. Again, the actual term is *flesh*, when in a context of post-Fall man. Human activity has shown that the *flesh*, i.e., the *"old man,"* is, in other words, that *state of having the knowledge of good and evil (in the flesh)* in which we may (and, in fact, *do*) act to produce sin during a probationary period in which we are accountable. Furthermore, we continue to sin after our failure in the probationary period. Most Evangelical churches do not believe there is any difference between the terms, *old man* and the *body of sin*. Paul's treatment of these terms is noteworthy, however. He says in Romans 6:6 that "our old man (NAS, *self*) was crucified with Him (Christ) in order that our body of sin might be done away with, so that we would no longer be slaves to sin…" Note that Paul's phrase *in order that* (or, *with the result that*) would seem to point to a relationship between *our old man* (KJV) and *our body of sin*, indicating they have much to do with each other but are not, in fact, synonymously defined concepts. For otherwise Paul would have presumably used a pronoun for *old man* if he understood that the same concept was returning again later in the verse. That is, why wouldn't Paul have just said, "our old man was crucified with Him [Christ], in order that **it** might be done away with…" Or else, if Paul was using synonyms, why wouldn't he have used a word approximating *therefore*, in conjunction with *our body of sin*, i.e., "therefore our body of sin might be done away," or a stronger word-indicator resulting in "this" instead of "our" (i.e., "in order that *this* body of sin is destroyed") had he meant that the *old man*[141] and *our body of sin* were synonymous? Note too that he uses the word *might* which makes the destruction of the body of sin conditional, i.e., conditional upon whether the believer yields his members as instruments of righteousness unto God. Thus, for the believer, the knowledge of good and evil has been crucified (rendered powerless) as a conditional fact, so that we *might not* (that is, *may not*) yield our members unto sin, as that which promises pleasure in accordance with the flesh. This principle of a believer facing the challenge of his flesh leads to Paul's fuller discussion of that topic in Romans 7. In that passage Paul sheds light on a *different law*, or *principle*, which he finds in his members and which wars against his true interest. The different law he is talking about is the knowledge of good and evil, and Paul finds that it nearly overwhelms him with distracting thoughts and threatens to take his focus away from God. The evident result (not *inevitable* result) is that Paul sometimes follows a sinful pleasure whose possibility had previously been presented to him through his flesh. This fact goes to the point that divinely-given additional knowledge, i.e., revelation, such as that given by God through the Mosaic Law, was designed as a counteracting knowledge which God gave to man to distract him (in a good sense) away from the vicarious knowledge about sin's pleasurable possibilities. This may account for the rather sever tone of the Mosaic Law, as God wants to warn man about the *consequences* of sin, rather than remind him of the *pleasures* of sin (which is part of what the knowledge of good and evil provides). But the severity of divine Law does not make the Law bad, but good. And yet righteousness cannot come through the Law, because man has shown that he *will* not *allow it* to come through the Law.

Now, the contrary opinion of Calvinists (and nearly all non-Calvinists) is that all men inherit Adam's sin—not just the consequences but the sin itself (or at least the *imputed guilt* of the sin). On the surface of things Psalm 51:5 appears to teach the ascription of sin upon conception; "Behold, in iniquity was I shapen [lit., "*twisted, whirled,* or in terms or childbirth, *brought forth* "], and in sin did my mother conceive me." Virtually everyone of my generation who grew up in a Bible-believing American Evangelical church was taught this view, i.e., that Adam's sin was passed down and/or imputed to every one of Adam's descendents. Romans 5:12-19, but especially verses 12, 18b-19 are generally cited in support of this view. Here, then, is Romans 5:12-21: [Certain verses (12, 18-19) are underlined and various verses subdivided with superscripted numbering.] Also, the words in brackets in verse 18 are translator interpolations, and not in the autographa.

> [12a] Wherefore, as by one man sin entered into the world, and death by sin; [12(b)] and so death passed upon all men, [12(c)] for that all have sinned: [13] (For until the law sin was in the world: but sin is not imputed when there is no law. [14] Nevertheless death reigned from Adam to Moses, even over them that had not sinned after the similitude of Adam's transgression, who is the figure of him that was to come. [15(a)] But not as the offence, so also is the free gift. [15(b)] For if through the offence of one many be dead, [15(c)] much more the grace of God, and the gift by grace, which is by one man, Jesus Christ, hath abounded unto many. [16(a)] And not as it was by one that sinned, so is the gift: [16(b)] for the judgment was by one to condemnation, [16(c)] but the free gift is of many offences unto justification. [17(a)] For if by one man's offence death reigned by one; [17(b)] much more they which receive abundance of grace and of the gift of righteousness shall reign in life by one, Jesus Christ.) [18(a)] Therefore as by the offence of one [*judgment came*] upon all men to condemnation; [18(b)] even so by the righteousness of one [*the free gift came*] upon all men unto justification of life. [19(a)] For

> as by one man's disobedience many were made sinners, <u>19(b)</u> so by the obedience of one shall many be made righteous. ²⁰ Moreover the law entered, that the offence might abound. But where sin abounded, grace did much more abound: ²¹ That as sin hath reigned unto death, even so might grace reign through righteousness unto eternal life by Jesus Christ our Lord.

Setting aside our discussion of Psalm 51:5 for later in this chapter, notice that a close examination of Romans 5:12-21 reveals that both halves of verse 18 are elliptical thoughts. By elliptical we mean that a fuller explanation is assumed by the writer without actually stating or restating it. Matthew 5:32a is an example of an ellipsis. When Jesus says, "whosoever shall put away his wife, saving for the cause of fornication, causeth her to commit adultery," He is not saying that a woman is automatically an adulteress upon the exact moment of her divorce. Rather, He understands that His hearers grant the assumption that the woman will remarry another man after her illegitimate divorce.[142] Likewise, in Romans 5:18a and 19a there is an ellipsis referring back to verse 12 which is a fuller expression of Paul's statement about sin's introduction and spreading into the world. Instead of repeating it fully in verse 18, he makes an ellipsis of verse 12's argument for the sake of brevity and to maintain the momentum of his theme, i.e., the "Even as... so too..." sentence construction (a.k.a. correlative conjunction) in verse 12, which we will examine in a moment.

Now, verse 12 reads: "Wherefore, just as through one man sin entered into the world, and death through sin, also in this manner death traversed into all men, since[143] all have sinned." [The above rendering is a more literal translation from the Greek. Note the important comparison between Adam and his descendents, i.e., that <u>even as</u> sin *entered* the world through the one man Adam, <u>so too</u> did death pass through all *because (since, i.e., on the grounds of the fact that)*[144] all have sinned. Again, a closer analysis of the sentence construction of Romans 5:12 will be discussed a little later in this chapter.] In short, verse 12 informs verse 18, not the reverse. The question, then, is what does verse 12 teach? Does it really state that all men are totally depraved *in* Adam? The answer appears negative. Note the word, *since* (Gr. *epi ho*), which explains why death is spread to all men (see footnote below). Verse 12 does not say that death spread[145] to all men *in Adam*[146] (Greek would have been "*en Adam*"), but that death spread to all men *since* (Gr. *epi ho*) all men sinned.[147] The same phrase is used in Luke 5:25 when referring to the cot *whereon* (KJV; Gr. *epi ho*) the paralytic lay. Green's Interlinear literal rendering is "taking on which he was lying," and we note that the 'that' is supplied by translators, i.e., 'taking [that] on which he was lying.'

Luke is simply stating an obvious, evidential thing, 'taking [that (cot)] since he was lying [on it],' i.e., in response to the command Christ gave to the paralytic to rise up and take his cot, that is., a command which in this context was obviously given to a paralytic man, or the Lord would not have issued such a command (as appropriate to the miracle of healing He had done), thus ("*since* he (the paralytic) lay").[148] Specifically, then, as we return to Romans 5:12, it is *since* all men sin that all spiritually die. *Epi ho* in the Greek is a prepositional phrase is which the neuter relative pronoun, *ho*, i.e. '*which*,' forms with the preposition *epi*, i.e., 'on,' 'upon,' etc., and together form the meaning of *upon which*, i.e., *upon [that] which*, i.e., (in conventional English) *on the grounds of the fact that*. According to extant Greek usage, *epi ho*, when it introduces a subordinate clause (as here in Romans 5:12) does not refer back to any textual unit larger than a concrete noun, i.e., not to a clause, paragraph, or section, as is often the case with other relative neuter pronouns used commonly for that purpose. This means that *epi ho* cannot refer back to Romans 5:12a (or some partial phrase of it) but only to one noun preceding it. The logical choice for a referent, if there is one that precedes it in this case, may be the word 'men,' which is the object of the preposition (the plural is used for 'all,' thus 'all men'). In other words, death through all men on the basis that *men* sinned. Thus the more natural meaning at the end of verse 12 is to take *epi ho* as referring *forward* to the evidential statement to which the subordinate clause testifies, i.e., 'all have sinned,' thus reminding readers of what should be to them the obvious reason why sin traversed through all men. Unfortunately, as already noted, it is not obvious to today's readers who have been taught the doctrine of original sin. Moreover, and this is important to note, even if, hypothetically, the epi ho *did* refer to something that was more than a concrete noun prior to the subordinate clause which it introduces, it could hardly refer to something so far removed as a thought expressed *prior to the 2nd part of the correlative conjunction*, especially since the subordinate clause comes **after** the 2nd part of the correlative conjunction and gives no hint suggesting that it means something mentioned *prior to* the 2nd part of the correlative conjunction. In fact, the subordinate clause does the very opposite—focusing on something granted **in** the 2nd part of the correlative conjunction [i.e., that all men sinned *similarly* (implied in *kai outws*) to Adam]. Again, this point will be further clarified shortly, when we study the correlative conjunction in more detail. Thus for the Calvinist (or even non-Calvinist) to read into the text of Romans 5:12 his own theology at the expense of Greek usage, is to distort the text for the purpose of introducing the idea of original sin. We should note that the death here spoken of in Romans 5:12, based on Paul's discussion which follows, is *spiritual* death.

On the other hand, physical death is the consequence of Adam's sin that God brought upon Adam and the rest of creation, of which Adam was steward and head. The Fall[149] of Man from that which God intended was indeed far. The knowledge of good and evil is now present within every man. But no person *has* to act in accordance with that knowledge. Furthermore, neither infants nor those with significant brain damage *can* act on the knowledge of good and evil because, again, such persons only have what might be called '*the seed* of the knowledge of good and evil' (as transmitted to them from the Adamic line). Technically, they are not spiritually dead, but they are still under the *consequence* of Adam's sin, which brings physical death. Therefore, like all persons, they too will eventually die, just like insects and animals.[150]

Deliberating upon *knowledge* (*knowledge* is defined in this sentence as that which is objectively true) for the purpose of affirming it or denying it demonstrates a discerning nature[151] and also, when an infant ultimately matures into an older child,[152] a liability unto eternity. But to give an illustration of how an infant can be born with the seed of the knowledge of good and evil and yet not be considered to be in a significant, discernable state, consider the following example. I was born with something inside me to play the piano, but it was obviously impossible for me to do so as long as I didn't know my left hand from my right. One might say that I had *the seed* of playing the piano—that is, the seeds of knowledge and ability to play the piano—but that the maturing growth of knowledge and the ability necessary to actually practice and perform on the piano had not yet come to the fore. Furthermore, no one would think to hold me responsible for not practicing the piano until I grew old enough to know my right hand from my left hand, i.e., into a maturity which would be necessary to act upon that nature within me to practice the piano. Even so, this description of a 'seed' might be the best we can offer regarding the transmission through the Adamic line to us of the knowledge of good and evil. We do not know how the seed matures in and by us, which we come to bring forth *ex nihilio*, but we recognize the process. Thus, although we (post-Fall) have the seed of the knowledge of good and evil, we do not act upon this seed unto eternal consequence until that seed matures enough, whereupon we deliberate and make choices about knowledge and behavior unto eternal liability. Moreover, not until a person actually sins does he come into the full blossom of the knowledge of good and evil. Therefore spiritual death for a post-Adamic person comes into[153] him as one who acts against his conscience unto eternal liability; and we note that, presumably, the maturing[154] knowledge of good and evil was an influence upon him.[155] Upon sinning, the person thus obtains the full blossom of the knowledge of good and evil. And so this observation in Romans 5:12, i.e., of sin spreading through all of humanity because all men sinned, is the point Paul is making.

After verses 13-17, Paul returns to his thought of the first Adam and the second Adam. He states in verse 18:

> ¹⁸Therefore as by the offence of one judgment came upon all men to condemnation; even so by the righteousness of one the free gift came upon all men unto justification of life. ¹⁹For as by one man's disobedience many were made sinners, so by the obedience of one shall many be made righteous.

While Paul ends Romans 4 with a discussion of the believer's experience, and picks up that theme at length again in chapter 6, the predominance of that theme is curiously absent in chapter 5:12-21. Note in particular the word "many" which in this particular passage literally means "the many." The Calvinist says that *"the many"*[156] who are under condemnation prior to being made righteous are the elect, i.e., those in Christ. 'The many' would thus be the 'all' of limited atonement. But Paul does not use the familiar pronouns 'us' or 'we' (i.e., believers) anywhere in his discussion of verses 12-21 when referring to those who are spiritually dead. Rather, Paul is making a more universal point about all mankind. He is speaking in a philosophically abstract way which prevents the word "all" from referring only to the 'elect.' For the Calvinistic idea—that the passage is teaching that all men are condemned to spiritual death by the one act of Adam alone—should force them to also say that all men (v. 18) are automatically saved in the obedience of Christ apart from personal commitment to Him.[157]

Again, I think the conclusion of the 19th century revivalist preacher, Charles Finney, is helpful here. Finney believed that the Bible taught that man was physically depraved but not morally depraved. To be physically depraved means that people, animals, and other creaturely life, are subject to disease and death as part of the consequence of sin by earth's representative head, Adam.[158] While God in his omniscience possesses the knowledge of good and evil apart from being a sinner, such knowledge was never intended for the lower form of man. Put another way (as previously noted), God realized it was not *prudent* that man have such knowledge. As expositor Thomas Whitelaw in the *Pulpit Commentary* notes:

> ...*To know good and evil.* Implying an acquaintance with good and evil which did not belong to [Adam] in the state of innocence. The language seems to hint that a one-sided acquaintance with good and evil, such as that possessed by the first pair in the garden and the unfallen angels in heaven, is not so complete a knowledge of the inherent beauty of the one and essential turpitude of the other as is acquired by beings who pass through the experience of a fall, and that the only way in which a finite being can approximate to

such a comprehensive knowledge of evil as the Deity
possesses without personal contact—can see it as it
lies everlastingly spread out before his infinite mind—
is by going down into it and learning what it is
through personal experience[lxii]

The age at which each of us enters into accountability certainly varies according to the individual, but each person conceived and who reaches maturity in this life is eventually declared either sinful[159] or righteous (because of their disbelief or faith in Christ, respectively). The majority of persons have survived into their probationary period; of this majority none have completed this period and not sinned.[160]

Awareness of Nakedness the Sign of Sin

Based upon Adam and Eve's *realization* to their nakedness upon eating the forbidden fruit, we can see that they sinned and (in their particular case) obtained the knowledge of good and evil, not in seed form, but as fully blossomed. It would appear that an awareness of nakedness is the sign in each of us that he has sinned. That Adam and Eve were previously *unashamed* of their nakedness suggests that their awareness of nakedness was the sign that they had sinned and gained the knowledge of good and evil. In fact (again), a post-Adamic person does not obtain the knowledge of good and evil as fully blossomed until he sins.

Here, then, is an interesting observation, i.e., not all persons are aware of their nakedness, and therefore such persons have not sinned. Along this line of assumption, we can see that Moses speaks of infants and children who did not have the knowledge of good and evil (Deut. 1:39). (This means a mature, not seed, form of the knowledge of good and evil.) In another place God reproves Jonah for not having compassion on those Ninevites who did not know their right hand from their left. Presumably, if a young child, infant, or severely retarded person does not know his left hand from his right hand, or have the knowledge of good and evil, he would not only be unaware of his nakedness but also be without discernment of an accountable nature unto eternal liability. Let us see why this is so. As a person matures, the seed of the knowledge of good and evil also begins to grow until that person reaches a level of accountable discernment, even as Adam (though apart from the knowledge of good and evil) likewise found himself at the first, i.e., in a level of accountable discernment in the Garden. This period of initial discernment unto eternal liability occurs prior to sinning, although, hypothetically, it appears it could occur simultaneously with sinning. Moreover, if a person survived a certain temporary time during his probationary period without sinning, this does not mean God has declared him righteous. It only *de facto* means that he is still under probation.[161] For Adam, too, survived a temporary probation without sinning, even communing with God in the cool of the evening. The brute fact is this—no one in his maturing flesh has, or will, complete his probationary period without sinning, and apart from satisfactorily completing his probationary period a man cannot through his own acts be declared righteous. But every person begins his life *prior* to this probationary period. For Paul himself speaks of a time when he was not subject to the law: "I was once alive apart from the Law; but when the commandment came, sin became alive and I died" (Rom. 7:9; Note: NAS's '*became alive*' (Gr. *anazao*) is to be preferred to the KJVs '*revived*,' the latter (KJV) implying an existing sin nature upon conception). Although Paul may be speaking hypothetically in an abstract philosophical way about how the law quickens his conscience, one may take this verse in its literal sense, i.e., that Paul first existed as a person without any discernment of the law or of his conscience in a way that made him subject unto eternal liability, and therefore he was in a state where he did not know his left hand from his right hand, i.e., unaware of right and wrong and therefore short of being accountable unto eternal liability. At some point he entered a period of probationary discernment unto eternal liability in which the demands of the law were plain to him, and at that point or later (seconds?, hours?, days?, etc.), during this same period of probationary discernment, he sinned, and upon that instant he spiritually died and obtained the knowledge of good and evil in its full blossom. Certainly the recognition that all persons exist first in a state of discernment that is liable temporally, not eternally, (let us call this first state a first-level discernment), would solve the problem of how God can take care of undiscerning persons (i.e., babies, the severely retarded, etc.).[162]

The Calvinistic view is that every person is conceived with imputed sin and therefore under judgment unless born into the covenantal community where they are baptized as a symbol of their covenantal status. And indeed, such an idea of salvation by parental act is not a huge leap for the Calvinist, when one considers the Calvinist's strong assertion of original sin with its assumption of parental transmission. Yet one wonders of what 'covenantal community' the infants of Ninevah could possibly have been at the time of Jonah's entrance into the city of Ninevah, that God had decided to have mercy upon them *all* so that He sent His prophet?

What the Ninevite infants show, then, as persons subject (like all humanity) to physical death, and yet not subject (unlike accountable humanity which has failed) to spiritual death, is the difference between physical and moral depravity. As for a correct definition of moral depravity, then, we find Finney's explanation helpful:

> Moral depravity is a quality of voluntary action, and not of substance… By total depravity, is not meant, that any being is, or can be, sinful, before he has exercised the powers of moral agency. By total depravity, I do not mean, that there is any sin, in human beings, or in any other beings, separate from actual transgression. I do not mean that there is some constitutional depravity, which lies back, and is the cause of actual transgression.[lxiii]

Finney is saying that a sinner is not a sinner until he sins. Evangelicalism almost universally says the opposite, claiming that a man sins because he is a sinner. Again, I held this same majority view of Evangelicals until relatively recently. I first came to question my belief in original sin when I realized that such a doctrine made it impossible to logically believe that man could freely choose between good and evil—a definition of human freedom upheld strongly throughout all the Bible. For conversely, if man was conceived by woman with a nature that *guaranteed* that he would sin even once, then his will *could not be operative* (i.e., *could not be a will*), and he would stand condemned apart from having personally chosen sin. On the other hand, the mere possession of the knowledge of good and evil does not guarantee that a man *will* sin. Every man, however, has followed, to a point of unrighteousness, the distracting presentation of the maturing (not yet fully blossomed) knowledge of good and evil, which in the context of fallen man is his maturing flesh, and sinned.[163] [164]

The Correlative Conjunction of Romans 5:12

Now, in regard to Adam's act of disobedience in Romans 5:12, a few more points must be noted to show why so many have come to believe in the doctrine of original sin.[165] First, consider the opening phrase[166] of this verse and note in particular the word "as": "Wherefore, **as** by one man sin entered into the world…" The word "as" in Greek in verse 12 is *hosper*. The NAS in the context of Romans 5:12 more succinctly and properly translates this word as "just as." (It has the synonymous meaning of "exactly like.") Thus, the NAS gives this phrase the better translation: "Therefore, *just as* through one man sin entered into the world…" Now, observe that any time the phrase "just as" appears at the beginning of a sentence, it should be evident that the sentence's resolution depends on finishing the latter half of the comparison it is invoking, i.e., "*just as* X, **even so** Y." In other words, grammatically speaking, Romans 5:12 is set forth as a correlative conjunction. It explains that **just as** sin <u>entered</u> into the world by means of one man's disobedience—and death through (the means of) sin—**so too** did death (lit.) traverse into all men, since all have sinned. And a *comparison* by definition cannot be an *exact* comparison in all respects, since a comparison also indicates *difference*. A comparison may be exactly *like*, but never exactly *is*. Thus properly speaking, one might say, "Bill and Susan's favorite color is red;" or "Bill's favorite color is red, and so is Susan's," but hardly ever the more awkward, "Just as Bill's favorite color is red, so too is Susan's favorite color red." Rather, in drawing a parallel comparison one expects to hear something like: "Just as Bill's favorite color is *red*, so also is Susan's favorite color *blue*."[167] Thus when Romans 5:12 begins by saying "Wherefore, *just as*…" one must look for the other half of the *just as*—*so too* completion of thought. Such a completing phrase will be introduced by "so too," "likewise," "even so," "so also," "in this manner also," etc. Unfortunately, most English translations simply render the completing phrase "and so" instead of one of the "so too" phrases when introducing the latter half of the thought designed to complete the comparison. The result is that the phrase "and so" in the phrase, "and so death passed upon all men" is taken by the English reader to mean "and therefore," when actually the phrase "and so" is meant to be understood as "even so," "likewise," "so too," or "so also," etc., which obviously gives the latter half of verse 12 an entirely different meaning. And the completing phrase in Greek, '*kai outws*,' literally means 'also in this manner,' or, as it would be more conventionally expressed in English by reversing the word order, "in this manner also." If we substitute for "in this manner" (*outws*) the word "so," we see that the phrase "so too" is another more common way of expressing the same thought. In this latter use, however, one must keep in mind that "so" means "in this manner," not "therefore." That 'kai' should be understood to mean 'also' instead of the usual 'and' (note: other English conjunctions for 'kai' are sometimes possible depending on the context, e.g. *but*, *yet*, etc.) is evident because of the Greek word *hosper*, which begins the first part of the correlative conjunction. The word 'kai' appears twice after the word 'hosper' in verse 12, and it is the *second* occurrence of 'kai' ("so *also* death traversed into all men, since all men sinned") which announces the beginning of the completing phrase of the correlative conjunction, since the phrase "and (kai) death by sin" is grammatically understood to be a non-essential clause and therefore essentially parenthetical to the correlative conjunction.[168] The result of ignoring the correlative conjunction has led to the following inferior translations of Romans 5:12b in the NAS, KJV, and NIV:

>(NAS) "and so death spread to all men"
>
>(KJV) "and so death passed upon all men"
>
>(NIV) "and in this way death came to all men"

None of the above really recognizes the correlative conjunction that Paul is invoking by his use of "just as" at the beginning of verse 12. This is true even though the NAS and KJV 'transliterate' the "and so." For while 'and' technically includes an aspect of meaning 'also,' and 'so' may be technically understood to mean 'in this manner,' the use of the phrase 'and so' will hardly be taken by the average English reader to mean 'also in this manner,' and thus the presence of a correlative conjunction will not be perceived as the underlying format of verse 12. Nor does the NIV's "in this manner" challenge the traditional reading which is cited to support the doctrine of original sin, since it leaves out the vital word 'also.' Ignoring the correlative conjunction, the KJV, NAS, and NIV translations thus all state (in effect): "As Adam did thus and so, *therefore* death spread to all." Thus the comparison between the action of Adam and the action of his descendents is still missing its latter half in these translations, since nothing is offered as a resolution for the "just as." Such translations are nothing short of misleading. Rather, the entire verse *should* read essentially as that given by senior editor Jay P. Green, Sr.'s *Pocket Interlinear New Testament* in the interlinear text.

> Therefore as through one man sin into the world
> entered, and through sin death, also so to all men
> death passed, inasmuch as all have sinned.

I think the NAS's "just as" near the beginning of verse 12 provides a stronger sense than the Interlinear's "as," in announcing the correlative conjunction (though the NAS fails to follow the correlative conjunction to completion). But Green's use of "as" instead of "just as" is reasonably acceptable because of the "also so" which introduces the final half of the correlative conjunction, thus contextualizing the previous "as," so that "just as" is essentially understood.[169] (One further note: Green appropriately reverses the word order in his translation of 'kai outws' at the expense of the conventional reading. Thus he renders 'kai outws' to mean 'so also,' in order to avoid the much more awkward reading, 'also so.') Conversely, observe in the first example below how the actual NAS translation of Romans 5:12 treats "just as" as nothing really more than "because," or as a mere chronological idiom or intensifier (i.e., "as in the course of events," [Adam sinned]), or "as in fact…"[170] Such assumptions have led to the traditional inference, since the word order of "and so," leaves the impression of an incorrect meaning of "therefore." The next example shows how the NAS should have been translated, so that the correlative conjunction was plainly conveyed:

Romans 5:12 (NAS):

> Therefore, just as through one man sin entered into the world, and death through sin, and so death spread to all men, because all have sinned—

Romans 5:12 as it <u>should</u> have been translated:
> Therefore, just as through one man sin entered into the world, and death through sin, also in this manner death passed (traversed) into all men, since all have sinned—

An additional point for the argument we are advancing here, is that the comparison of which we speak is actually explained more fully in verses 13-14. In fact, these verses are introduced with the word, "For," for the purpose of more fully explaining verse 12. The word, "For," as we will see later in more detail, thus grants the argument of verse 12 insofar as supporting the general sense of the correlative conjunction's "just <u>as</u>," thus stating that death, the result of sin, has traversed into every man, since all men have sinned. Thus verses 13-14 reiterate the comparison mentioned in verse 12, although, because the "just as" still implies a difference (in the minority, not general, sense of the comparison), verses 13-14 also draw a particular distinction between the kind of sin committed by Adam on the one hand, and the kind of sin committed by post-Adamic man on the other hand. An interpretative paraphrase of verses 13-14 should be helpful here to explain the point:

For prior to the [Mosaic] law there was sin in the world: (but observe that sin is not imputed when there is no law). Nevertheless, [because such men were a law unto themselves, yet failed to live up to their own consciences] death reigned over all those who lived between Adam and Moses, even over those who did not sin after the likeness of Adam's transgression [of eating the forbidden fruit, which violated the Garden Command, leading to death]; this same Adam is the figure of Him that was to come.

Thus if we understand Romans 5:12-14 properly, i.e., that the "just as" which begins verse 12 is resolved in the "so also" found later in the same verse, and that verses 13-14 give a fuller explanation of this very comparison, then much of the controversy surrounding the last, oft-debated phrase in Romans 5:12, "for that all have sinned," is clarified.

The specific controversy in view is over the Greek phrase "epi ho," translated by the KJV as "for that," in the phrase "for that all have sinned." Those who believe that Romans 5:12-21 propounds a doctrine of original sin believe that the phrase epi ho refers back to "sin [of Adam]," or "death [caused by Adam's sin]" either of which interpretations lead to the belief that men are guilty of sin in or because of Adam.[171] Nearly all Evangelicals hold this view, whether Reformed or non-Reformed.

Thus the usual argument offered by those who believe in the doctrine of original sin is that the word "that" in the phrase "for that all have sinned" refers in some way to the sin of Adam, i.e., the cause of why all men are sinners. But Paul, as we have already noted, could have written unambiguously in support of original sin by closing out verse 12 differently, e.g., "for that all have sinned in Adam," or the even plainer statement, "for that Adam sinned." Or would Paul have stated the matter unambiguously, had he expressed it as such? For when one considers, for example, that Paul (or whoever was the writer of Hebrews) uses language liberally and with every latitude to say that Levi paid tithes to Melchizedek because he was in the loins of Abraham, and then further considers that the chronological date of Abraham's offering of tithes to Melchizedek preceded the birth even of Ishmael and of Ishmael's descendents, of whom it is never reported that they tithed or understood the tithe's spiritual implications, one can hardly but conclude that Levi is only meant to be understood to have paid tithes in the loins of Abraham in the sense that his descendents, the Levitical priesthood, came to follow the same spiritual principles of their patriarch, Abraham, and so paid tithes willingly to the Lord of whom Melchizedek was a figure. The Levitical priests, not Ishmael and his descendents, did in fact give tithes unto the Lord, and thus may be figuratively understood as having paid tithes to Melchizedek while yet in Abraham's loins. That Hebrews 7:10 is actually used by some commentators to supposedly help Christians understand how all men spiritually died in Adam, shows how uncritically many theologians have received this whole idea of inherited spiritual effect.

    The second argument advanced for the doctrine of original sin is that all men sin because death is already working a sinful end in them. But it should be observed that death (Gr. thanatos) is an effect, not the cause, of sin. The Bible never says that spiritual death "works in us" or in anybody else. Rather, it is a consequence of sin. In fact, the only place in the Bible where death is said to work in anybody is when Paul said he was "always bearing about in the body the dying of the Lord Jesus, that the life also of Jesus might be made manifest in our body. So then death worketh in us, but life in you." (2 Cor. 4:11-12) But the word "death" here refers to the proper mindset of Paul regarding the Lord's call to discipleship. This was a call that could conceivably involve physical death, as the Lord Himself died.[172] Paul thought that this poignant possibility was beneficial to keep in mind. Thus the "death" of which Paul speaks in 2 Corinthians 4:11-12 does not mean a cause of sin. Therefore (spiritual) death is a result of sin, not a force that effects sin. In fact, note that James says that "sin, when it is finished, brings forth death" (1:15). The specific effect of death James is talking about is a separation from God This simple distinction between sin being the cause of death—i.e., death as a stated condition, and itself not a causative force—is almost always overlooked in discussions about Romans 5:12.

Third, and finally (in regard to the present discussion of *epi ho*), we give in the endnotes a difficult to understand but nevertheless rewarding linguistic discussion between one, Carl Conrad, professor of Classics at Washington University, and Bill Ross,[173] a discussion colleague who had queried earlier to Conrad about *epi ho* in the other occurrences in the Pauline epistles (2 Cor. 5:4, Phi. 3:12 and 4:10). Conrad's point is that the relative neuter singular Ef hWi, *when used to introduce a subordinate clause*, cannot be a referent to anything antecedent unless it be a single concrete noun (i.e., it cannot refer to a preceding phrase, clause, etc.) though it may function as an adverbial conjunction, as, in fact, it does in Romans 5:12. Conrad believes that Ef hWi's function in Romans 5:12 shows that men are individually guilty because of their own actualization of sin, and not because of any inherited guilt.[lxiv]

A Corrupted Will?

Before we end our discussion of Romans 5:12ff, we must explore the idea that man's will can be corrupted. Even non-Reformed Evangelicals who believe in the doctrine of original sin have assigned some corruption to man's will. I believe this is an incorrect view which leads to the will's annihilation. In other words, there can be no such thing as a corrupted will. For example, despite his very commendable, biblical, and scholarly book, *Getting the Gospel Right*, C. Gordon Olson embraces the common viewpoint about depravity held by most non-Reformed Evangelicals, including notable theologian Norman Geisler. Says Olson:

> "Norman Geisler suggests that extreme Calvinism has an "intensive" view of depravity, in contrast to a biblical, "extensive" understanding. The intensive view, in effect, holds that the image of God and the human will are essentially destroyed. [Geisler, *Chosen But Free*. p. 116.] The extensive view holds that the whole person of man was corrupted by sin, but that the image of God and the human will have not been destroyed but rather corrupted."

Though Olson makes many excellent points in his book supporting human freedom,[174] the specific idea (as championed today among Arminians most prominently by Geisler) that man's will is corrupted does not appear sustainable. What does it mean, for example, to say that the will is *corrupted*? It can only mean that the will is not capable of doing what the will would have been able to do prior to Adam's transgression, i.e., to choose freely in either moral direction. But the very function of the will is that it makes free choices. Thus, to say that the will is *corrupted* must mean that the will is unable to make a free choice in some sense. Observe, then, that to say that the will is *corrupted* is to say something different than that the will is merely surrounded by *vast presentation* (due to the knowledge of good and evil). We must maintain that the will is an all or nothing proposition. Either it is free to choose, or it is not free to choose and therefore is not a will. Thus, while the will is subjected to extreme stress due to various *presentations* from the knowledge of good and evil in us, the will is still totally free and operable. To maintain a lesser view is to unwittingly define man's will in dialectical terms—i.e., free to choose, yet not free to choose. To define it this way would result in the annihilation of the will, owing to an irrational (and thus mystical) definition.

As might be expected from Olson's quote, Geisler's general approach to Romans 5 in his *Systematic Theology* (Vol. III, p. 229) also supports the doctrine of original sin. For example, Romans 5:17 is cited for its observation that men *receive* Christ, but Geisler claims that no parallel comparison is taught in Romans 5 whereby a man would likewise have to *individually actualize* his sin before he could be considered a sinner.[175] Rather, it is assumed that men are sinners *in Adam*. Geisler takes this position because he believes man is already corrupted in sin upon personhood. Hence, Geisler states:

> It is important to realize in this connection that it does *not* follow from the preceding points, as some Arminians infer, that everything under "Adam" in the above chart is *also* only potential for all persons until they actualize it by their own sins.
>
> *First*, again, the phrase "not like" (vss. 15-16) differentiates the two sides of the comparison. [Geisler previously states that the "parallel" of Adam and Christ in Romans 5 "is not perfect."]
>
> *Second*, Romans 5 clearly says that some of the consequences of Adam's sin (such as physical death) are automatic, without any choice on our part (vss 12-14).
>
> *Third*, and finally, no such qualifying terms like *receive* (v. 17) are used of the consequences of Adam's sin, even though these terms are used in reference to the appropriation of the gift of salvation that Christ provided for all.

Now, let us take Geisler's points in their order. The first of his points is that the parallel between Adam and Christ recedes (or stops) with verse 15. The first part of verse 15 in the KJV reads as follows: "But not as the offense, so also (is) the free gift…" The Greek interlinear translation (without the translator help of the italicized interpolation of "is") is given below. Note how the KJV essentially (and thus properly in this case) transliterated this difficult segment:

> ἀλλ' οὐχ ὡς τὸ παράπτωμσ οὕτω καί τὸ χάρισμα.
> **But not as the offence, so also the free gift;**[176]

From the transliteration given above, it should be noted (contrary to Geisler) that the parallel is actually *continuing* the comparison begun in verse 12. (I would recommend that the reader refer to the superscripted numbered text earlier in this chapter or to have his Bible turned to Romans 5:12-21 while we discuss this passage.) While in verse 15 the phrase "not as" [Geisler, ("*not like*")] is to Geisler and the NASB a significant break from the parallel, they both seem to have overlooked that the phrase "like *also*" (i.e., lit. Gr., "*in this manner also*") actually continues the comparison. <u>Thus, the comparison **in 15a** should not be understood to be that of the transgression in *contrast* to the free gift, but of the transgression *and* the free gift in *contrast* to what is stated negatively (about those men between Adam and Moses) in relation to Adam's offense in the previous verse (v. 14), the contrast of which will prove to be carried out (see vss.15ff) in an extended discussion in regards to the free gift.</u>[177] Thus, the phrase which begins the 2nd clause in verse 15 ("so also")[178] completes a correlative conjunction as follows: even as[179] men *have not* technically participated in the similitude of Adam's transgression, and yet die, so too will men *have not* technically participated in the obedience of the One, and yet live. Again, this is Paul's thought and theology; i.e., that even as men between Adam and Moses did **not** technically break the Garden command of eating the forbidden fruit (Gen. 2:16-17) leading to spiritual death—and yet themselves obtained for themselves spiritual death—so too would all those who, technically, *did not* live a life of obedience leading to justification, nevertheless obtain justification as though they *had* obeyed (because of the free gift of God as appropriated by their faith). The reason Paul appears to have brought up the subject of post-Adamic man in verses 13-14 is because of a natural objection that arises from his statement in verse 12 (that death traversed into all men), namely, Why should anyone but Adam experience death, since only Adam broke the divine, Garden Command leading to death? Thus Paul (reminding his readers of a point in principle he already made in chapter 2) explains in verses 13-14 that post-Adamic men were *also* subject to death for having transgressed the *conscience*, since they were a law unto themselves. Thus in chapter 5 Paul is stating that this consequence of spiritual death upon the Gentile is still the case, even though post-Adamic man had no such law as had Adam. Furthermore, and in passing, we note that the consequence of physical death which was brought upon all men because of the disobedience of one (the first Adam), shall be superceded by the physical resurrection and glorification of all those receiving the free gift made efficient by the obedience of One (the second Adam). Moreover, this gift comes from a Creator whose power guarantees our security much more than if the promise came from a mere man (see v. 16). Technically, in fact, the free gift is itself the obedience of the One (Christ) put to our account.

The remaining phrases purporting to teach the doctrine of original sin [e.g., "For if through the offence of one the many be dead" (v. 15b); see also verse 17a, verse 18a, and verse 19a, all of which make similar statements, have been so narrowly contextualized as to make the understanding of them as mere ellipses of the correlative conjunction of Romans 5:12 all but impossible. Yet the two statements of 15c and 16c, teaching that justification has abounded unto the many by the obedience of the One, ought, by implication of the distinction which Calvinists claim between "all" and "the many," presumably be held by Calvinists to thus teach *universalism*, lest for Calvinists the hermeneutic for "all," which they have just established in verse 12, be now discarded in the two-fold appearance of "all" in clauses 18a and 18b *despite* the fact that these clauses are the obvious parallel summation and recapitulation of clauses 15b and 15c, in which the two-fold appearance of "the many" occurs.[180] But then of what use is such a hermeneutic? Put another way, the Calvinistic hermeneutic for "all" and "the many" in Romans 5:12ff is only as secure as the parallel between 15b-15c and 18a-18b is *not* obvious. For Arminians the dilemma (regarding original sin) is not fundamentally any different. Arminians (if they follow Arminius) likewise hold to rocking horse theology but with an emphasis on the backward rock[181] of man's freedom. The situation for an Arminian like Geisler is thus: he speaks of 'receiving' but in fact such 'receiving,' properly understood (in deference to Geisler), can only *de facto* be done by a will that is uncorrupted, a point about the will's nature which Geisler is not prepared to concede (though he *thinks* he is conceding it). Hence how is the 'receiving' spoken of by Geisler in accord with biblical definition? Thus Geisler's attempt is one in which it *appears* man's freedom is being stated, while in fact it is not. In other words, Geisler's attempt is not really any different than the Calvinist's, except that he is relatively more concerned than the Calvinist with expressing the 'freedom of man' rather than 'the absolute sovereignty of God.' Despite the confusion within both camps, the real and true biblical definition of *receiving* in verse 17 adds clarity to the interpretation of 15c and 16c. The *receiving* of verse 17 points back to verse 11 (Gr. Int. "through whom now we received the reconciliation") as the support verse which in turn makes possible the ellipses of 15c and 16c. Thus 15b,[182] 15c, 16c, 17a, 18a, and 19a are all ellipses—some of verse 11, and some of verse 12—and therefore ought to be interpreted with no more *universal* force than that implied in the referred verses themselves.

Thus in deference to what Geisler states, we can rightfully say that Paul *continues* the parallel and presents the idea that men indeed are not guilty of sin until they themselves commit it. Indeed, this view is the only one that can truly assert that every man is free in his will and is thus subject to, and judged by, God because of it.[183] *Again, I stress this point in order to recover the biblical doctrine that man's will was not corrupted by any alleged original sin that descended down from Adam. Rather, the will must be considered uncorrupted if man is truly to be free—free so that God may judge him—either of his works, or of his faith in Christ.* This answers the first of Geisler's three points. Granting this understanding, verses 15-16 seem best understood in the KJV:

> 15(a)But not as the offence, so also is the free gift. 15(b)For if through the offence of one many be dead, 15(c)much more the grace of God, and the gift by grace, which is by one man, Jesus Christ, hath abounded unto many. 16(a)And not as [like]it was by one that sinned, so is the gift: 16(b)for the judgment was by one to condemnation, 16(c)but the free gift is of many offences unto justification.

Again, in review, it should be observed that Paul's statement in verse 13—that sin is not imputed when there is no law—is not an argument that men between Adam and Moses had no imputed sin (though it is true they had no imputed sin *from Adam*) but rather implies a follow-up connection with Romans 2 (and in fact with the whole theme of unreconciled post-Adamic man in all of Paul's chapters up to this point), in which Paul states that a Gentile man was guilty even apart from the Mosiac law for having violated his own conscience.[184] For this reason spiritual death reigned from Adam to Moses, i.e., because a man's imputed sin was a man's own.

And yet let us assume, for the sake of hypothetical argument, that Paul in verses 12 and 13ff is stating the opposite idea, i.e., the doctrine of original sin. What then would he be expected to state in verse 13ff? Would he (as in fact he does) state that men who lived between Adam and Moses had NOT sinned according to the likeness of Adam's sin? No, he would hardly do that. Rather, we would expect him to state the very opposite idea, making sure to tell his readers that men between Adam and Moses HAD sinned according to the *exact image* of Adam's sin, since they had indeed sinned IN ADAM. But again, we see that Paul did not state it that way. Indeed, by verse 15 (as we have already seen) he makes it plain by stating that the free gift is *also* (i.e., *along with post-Adamic man's offense*) NOT LIKE (in the minority sense of the comparison) its respective counterpart in the respective parallels being drawn (i.e., post-Adamic man's offense to Adam's offense, and our faith in Christ to the righteousness of Christ).

As for the word "Therefore" which begins Romans 5:12, this word is actually a phrase in the original Greek which ultimately provides the key to understanding verse 12 and the rest of chapter 5. The word 'therefore' (Gr. lit. '*dia touto*') literally means, "Because of this…" and informs the correlative-conjunction format of Romans 5:12 as follows: "**Because of this**…even as X, **so too Y**." That is, Paul is about to explain the reason why sin, characterized by its effect of death, traversed through all men, not just through Adam, i.e., through him (Adam) who alone broke the specific command of God in the Garden which led to spiritual death in the day he ate the forbidden fruit. To do so, Paul points *backward* from his argument *preceding* verse 12, i.e., the 'this' in "Because of *this*…" In other words, Paul is saying (in effect), "Because of the preceding argument I have been making, we can now see the reason death traversed through all men (verse 12), including those between Adam and Moses (v. 13) who were outside the Law, even though post-Adamic men were not technically guilty of breaking God's particular command in the Garden leading to death." And, in fact, the preceding argument of Paul is one Paul has been advancing in some form since the middle of chapter one, i.e., an argument in which Adam *has never even been mentioned*, namely, that post-Adamic Gentile men who were without the Mosaic Law nevertheless were guilty of sin by transgressing their conscience, i.e., conscience as that which originally and properly existed in accordance with the creation of God which demonstrated undeniably to every Gentile the power and beneficent nature of God (Rom. 1:19-21). This fact of inexcusableness includes every man, even a *relatively* good man like Abraham (Rom. 4:2), who might have something about which to glory before men, but not before God. Thus in Romans chapter 4 Paul cites the man Abraham, who, though relatively good compared to other men, was still a sinner and in need of reconciliation with God. As such, Abraham was presumably one of those whom, as Paul states in Romans 5:6, might have dared to give their life for a (relatively) good man, i.e., a man like Abraham himself. And yet even such men as Abraham, who were of more noble character than most men, still failed in strength to love others as God loved them. This is because no man has loved God with all his heart, soul, mind, and strength, which in turn would have led him to *consistently* love his neighbor as himself. Therefore even Abraham, as one who lived between Adam and Moses (and thus lived subsequent to the Garden Command but prior to the Mosaic Law) was in need of reconciliation with God, even though he had not sinned according to the general likeness of Adam's transgression. And here again it is important to note in what sense post-Adamic man did NOT sin according to the likeness of Adam's sin: he did not transgress the Garden Command by eating the forbidden fruit. Thus (again) post-Adamic man's sin and spiritual death were attributable to some other act which was nevertheless LIKE Adam's sin *generally,* to wit, *transgression against the conscience* (since all sin, to qualify as sin, *must* be transgressive in nature). See footnote 182, which explains that in any comparison of two things in which they are *like* each other, there is, in the defining sense of the word 'like,' a particular way or ways in which the things being compared must be *unlike* each other, even though, generally speaking, they *are* like each other. By analogy, let us say that two men are found to have wronged the same company. Both are fired for cheating (fundamental kind of sin), yet one did it by stealing money from the company safe while the other stole company secrets because he was promised payment from a competing company. Thus both men cheated the company that employed them, yet their cheating took different forms. Or again, let us say that there are two university students who are extremely energetic—one who applies all his energies to the proper study of his classes, and one who puts all his energies into cheating on exams. Thus they may be compared *generally* as energetic, if that is the main point to which the one describing them wishes to draw attention, but there is still a difference within the comparison of the two students (i.e., a moral difference). So then, in any comparison there is the *general* sense in which the things being compared to each other are *alike,* while at the same time there is in the minority sense a point or points in which they are *not* alike. Even so, Paul is saying that both Adam and post-Adamic men are guilty of wrongdoing as having disobeyed their respective consciences (both of which were in accord with creation's evidences of God's power and beneficent nature), yet Adam and post-Adamic man sinned in different *forms,* the former as under a *specific* divine Command, the latter without it.

So the fact that all men *need* reconciliation, as expressed in Romans 5:1-11, though especially in verse 6, explains what Paul is doing in Romans 5:12 Notice, then, the general weakness[185] of humanity in Romans 5:1-11:

> [1]Therefore, having been justified by faith, we have peace with God through our Lord Jesus Christ, [2]through whom also we have obtained our introduction by faith into this grace in which we stand; and we exult in hope of the glory of God. [3]And not only this, but we also exult in our tribulations, knowing that tribulation brings about perseverance; [4]and perseverance, proven character; and proven character, hope; [5]and hope does not disappoint, because the love of God has been poured out within

our hearts through the Holy Spirit who was given to us. ⁶ For while we were still helpless, at the right time Christ died for the ungodly. ⁷ For one will hardly die for a righteous man; though perhaps for the good man someone would dare even to die. ⁸ But God demonstrates His own love toward us, in that while we were yet sinners, Christ died for us. ⁹ Much more then, having now been justified by His blood, we shall be saved from the wrath of God through Him. ¹⁰ For if while we were enemies we were reconciled to God through the death of His Son, much more, having been reconciled, we shall be saved by His life. ¹¹And not only this, but we also exult in God through our Lord Jesus Christ, through whom we have now received the reconciliation.

To give, then (because it seems beneficial to do), an interpretive paraphrase of verse 12, Paul is saying, "<u>Because of this (i.e., that all men have failed in strength to do the right thing)</u>, even as sin entered the world by one man, resulting in spiritual death, **also** <u>*in this manner death passed upon all men, since all have sinned.*</u>" I have underlined the first and last phrases above, because I believe this is the momentum of Paul's argument (as noted earlier). Further, I have boldened the word **also,** since the emphasis of the phrase *kai outws* appears to be on the *kai* (see prior footnote #182 on the similar phrases *kai outws* and *outws kai*). Notice, then, that the first part of the correlative conjunction[186] of verse 12 'takes a back seat' (acts parenthetical) to the general momentum of the argument. That is, "Because of this… death passed upon all men, since all have sinned." And Paul speaks of sin as a philosopher might do, *personifying it as an outside force* (along with its effect) which enters the world and then passes (lit. *traverses*) through all (the world of) men. Note that Paul would be stating something incomprehensible if he introduced verse 12 with "Because of this…" and meant that the word 'this' should refer to the word immediately preceding the opening phrase of verse 12, that is, *reconciliation*, which closes out the previous verse, and thus would have the apostle saying that *because* of reconciliation, *therefore* death spread throughout the world. Such an idea would make no sense, except in the most monstrous sense in which God might be imagined to decree good that evil might result. Thus (as we have already noted) the reader is beckoned by Paul to look backward for a statement about sin prior to verse 12 which would encapsulate his general preceding argument and explain sin's prevalence in the world. And again, the nearest statement that can be found prior to verse 12 is in verse 6, [187]which describes men as *weak* (lit. *without strength*) to do the right thing, i.e., *consistently*. (I say 'consistently' because of what we have already noted about Paul's use of *ekzetein* instead of *zetein* in Romans 3:11,[188] i.e., to seek God *diligently*). Note the similarity in Paul's statement to Jesus' statement, when Jesus says to his disciples that the flesh is *weak*. The Lord here was making a general statement about the flesh, not just the disciples' flesh; and likewise Paul observes here in Romans 5:6 that men were weak (again, lit. *without strength*) to do the right thing. Thus, because man allowed his weakness to prevail, he became in need of reconciliation, and as such was thus unable to provide his own atonement and (therefore) dead in his sins. Of course this kind of *deadness* is different than saying that man has been dead in sin *upon conception*, as the Calvinist would contend.[189]

In review then, in verse 13 Paul argues that the fact of man's *need* of reconciliation, which we note was caused by man's yielding to his weakness as alluded to in the opening phrase of verse 12, i.e., 'Because of *this*,' thus points back to the section prior, that is, particularly to verse 6, which goes to the epistle's general argument about Gentile weakness leading to sin and death. Thus sin was imputed to post-Adamic men *upon the basis of transgressing the conscience*. Again, Paul had made this point about the conscience earlier in his epistle (chapts. 2—3) while pointing out that Gentiles who had no law were nevertheless a law unto themselves. Paul had then provided examples in chapter 3 to demonstrate specifically upon what basis these same Gentiles were guilty, i.e., they had hypocritically claimed that others ought not to steal and murder yet were guilty of such sins themselves. In short, men claim that others ought not to act selfish, but every man has acted selfish in regard to others, in ways he himself condemns.

Paul soon follows this idea of "all men sinned" by a kind of umbrella-ing of the two offenses (Adam's type and post-Adamic man's type) under 'the offense of the one' spoken of in verse 15b. Paul is *now* pointing out the sense in which post-Adamic man's sin IS like Adam's sin, i.e., *sin as transgression against the conscience*. Thus momentarily, Paul appears to be combining these two kinds of offenses (Adam's and post-Adamic man's) so that he can use a rhetorical device to compare the First Adam to the Second Adam. Remember what we have already defined to be the nature of a comparison: i.e., to say that *A* is **like** *B* is to say that *A* is *generally* like *B* but at the same time is different than *B* in some particular(s). Thus in verse 18a Paul uses the word 'like' (Gr. *ws*) to speak of the similarity *and* difference between the sin of Adam and post-Adamic man. To do this Paul speaks of **sin** as a personified force which placed the *remainder* of men into condemnation (sin as *repeated* in every man). Of course, Paul is not saying that sin is an entity *apart* from the will of man, as though somehow it were an *irresistible force* acting from inside or outside Adam or post-Adamic man *to the guaranteeing* of a certain wrongful action. Rather, Paul is simply using a rhetorical device. As previously noted, Paul had already set forth the argument in verse 6 about man's weakness (under which influence men committed sin) and later identified and <u>personified</u> the choices surrounding that weakness under the nomenclature *sin* in verse 12—first as an outside force, and second, as that force's effect spreading itself through the world of men. Arguably, the use of such a rhetorical *device* to describe sin as an outside <u>singular</u> force, might lead some readers, who fail to recognize the personification for what it is, to read too much into the phrase of 15b, i.e., "through the transgression of the one," so that the notion might be imagined that Paul was speaking of sin (singular) as an irresistible causal *force* descending from Adam into all.

Note that the word 'like' (KJV 'as') is preserved along these two aspects of its meaning (alike in generality, unlike in some particularity), so that Paul in 15b (along with its approximate equivalent in 18a) is not setting up a logical contradiction with what has already been stated regarding every man being the cause of his own sin. Because most commentators have missed this dual aspect of **like,** their influence upon the casual reader has been very significant: i.e., the reader interprets 15b apart from its surrounding context, then commits the additional error of taking *epi ho* in verse 12 as supporting 15b by treating it as a referent to the *first* part of the correlative conjunction of verse 12 (even though *epi ho* comes **after** the *second* part of the correlative conjunction), and *then* commits a third error by not recognizing the 'as' in verse 18a as meaning 'like' [which, when 18a is properly taken as an ellipsis of verse 12, thus properly supports the point about *epi ho* meaning 'on the grounds of the fact that' (i.e., *since*)], and so on, ending up in total confusion of interpretation. Thus Calvinists find it easy in the overall passage to resolve the problem of 'apparent contradictions' dialectically, that is, along irrational lines, and thus conclude that 'Adam chose our choice' [as though (and we speak here with some asperity) the 'our' could really be understood to mean both *our* and *Adam's* !]. The reason Calvinists misread Romans 5:12ff, as well as many passages, stems from a simple problem—they rely too much on the English translations. Frankly, in key instances they too often refuse to recognize the loss of meaning in translation.

Of course, the natural question remains as to why Paul would make this passage complex in meaning. I submit, however, that to Paul's original readers it did not appear as complex as it does to us today. None of us, myself included, can really gauge accurately how much we have been affected negatively by the spiritual propaganda (ouch!) about original sin we formerly received, however unintentionally it was conveyed to us. The truth only strikes us Western contemporary readers as especially difficult to accept because we are on the far side of Augustine's bogus claim that the passage teaches original sin, a claim which, once it was first made with substantial force by Augustine, was then seized upon and promulgated by

Church councils and/or their minions for 17 centuries. I personally find it more than a little hypocritical that today's Protestants, who are quick enough to condemn the Catholic institution of the Pope, nevertheless regard past Church councils, or even today's seminaries, as though their repeated endorsements of the doctrine of original sin were the last, august word anyone ought to possibly say on the matter, i.e., that all these councils' *et al.* pronouncements are above not only reproach, but also analytical critique. Nevertheless, the reason Paul in Romans 5:12-21 was not so hesitant to discuss sin as a personification in the 'like, yet unlike' correlative-conjunctive manner he did, was because the Romans to whom he addressed his epistle would not have read verse 15b with any of the Augustinian baggage that would come to affect later readers. Of course, this baggage is not all Augustine's fault (though his works live after him), for every man is responsible for what he himself believes. Nevertheless, the intimidating effect of centuries of church dogma, preached by church leaders and endorsed by Church councils and supporting institutions (both Catholic and Protestant), is not to be underestimated. I can only leave it to the reader's own judgment, as he relies on the Spirit, to tell him if the resolution we advance here is a Spirit-led recovery of the biblical doctrine of the freedom of the will, or whether the Calvinist's solution of irrationalism to the annihilation of the will (and every other term and concept) is the correct one.

    Now, let us move on to look more closely at this point about the word 'as' in verses 18 and 19. In short, then, 'as' does not mean 'since,' but means 'like' (i.e., 'similar,' 'likewise') in verse 18 and 'even likewise' in verse 19. A quick online BlueLetterBible lexical search of the New Testament demonstrates the meaning of *ws* to 'like(wise)' and the meaning of *hosper* to 'even as/like(wise).' And so, because of the error of translators who ignored the lexical evidence of *ws* and *hosper*, the opening phrase of verse 18—So then, as through one transgression there resulted condemnation to all men'—is taken by most readers to mean, 'So then, *since*[190] through one transgression there resulted condemnation to all men…' But again, such a reading is lexically incorrect, for Gr. *ws* defines nothing *causatively* (which the word 'since' implies); it simply means 'like,' 'similar,' 'likewise.' Thus the opening phrase of verse 18 literally means "So, then, **like** through one transgression into all men into condemnation…" Or to put it in plainer if in somewhat translationally inferior English: "So, then, all men came into condemnation ***similarly*** (Gr. *ws*) through one transgression [i.e., the transgression which comes despite the absence of divine, revelatory Law…(verse 19)]. For ***just like*** through the one man's disobedience the many were constituted sinners, ***even so*** will the many be righteous through the obedience of the One." Again, the 'like,' in verse 18a and 'even like' in 19a, points back to the <u>*post-Adamic kind of offense*</u> which was *like* Adam's offense in the *general* sense that Paul could legitimately state that it was, that is, *as transgression against the conscience*. Further, this transgression against the conscience is Paul's explanation why all persons have traversed from their state of probation into condemnation.

This observation about *ws* and *hosper* in verses 18 and 19, respectively, bears directly on verse 15b, which states (Int., and reading somewhat awkwardly): *For if by the of the one offense the many were made sinners…*—that is, [as proven by verse 18a when Paul **summarizes** (again, note the "So then") the preceding verses including verse 15b above], Paul here in 15b avoids the word 'as' (**like**) for the purpose of using a rhetorical device to draw a simple contrast between the first Adam and the second Adam. Therefore, since 15b is proven to be more of an ellipsis than its summary in 18a, verse 15b should **not** be interpreted with any such force which would violate the more detailed summarization of it (in its echo of v. 12) in 18a. Thus the point of 15b is that Adam serves *in principle* as the one whose way leads to death, even as in 15c Christ serves *in principle* as the One whose way leads to life. And in this sense (the sense of 'as though') we observe that the similarity between Adam and post-Adamic man is never much relaxed throughout the entire passage of Romans 5:12-21, except of course in the *particular* sense in which they are distinguished from each other in verses 13-14. Again, it is more than a little disturbing that the near universal opinion of commentators has failed to draw the proper conclusions from all the evidences we have been observing in this chapter, both lexically and logically, i.e., 1) the evidence of *hosper*; 2) the various correlative conjunctions that argue against 'all in Adam' explanations; 3) the ellipses that point back to the correlative conjunctions; 4) the similarity (not contrast) showing that post-Adamic man's sin and the believer's belief both end in a result not born of themselves in regard to the Law (capital 'L'); 5) the importance of the opening phrase in verse 12, i.e., "Because of this" 6) the obvious parallel between 15b-15c and 18a-18b which shows "all" to be synonymous, if less descriptive, of "the many," etc.

But moving on further, in verse 20 Paul speaks of Law (Int.) "coming in beside,[191] that the offense might abound." 'Law,' though here without the article (with the article would be 'the Law'), would nevertheless appear to mean the Mosaic Law, for Paul has spoken earlier of the interim between Adam and Moses as a time without Law, and yet God had spoken to Noah, Job, Abraham, etc. —i.e., communication that would qualify as revelation and instruction and thus be something which we might imagine ought to called 'Law,' but apparently wrongly here, since the Bible states that post-Adamic man sinned *apart* from the Law. Therefore the 'Law' which Paul refers to in this verse must mean something more than God's revelation during this interim period. Presumably, it means Law which is accompanied by a specific divine warning the violation of which, man is told, shall lead to spiritual death.

But a further question is this: the Law came alongside *what*? The answer would seem to be that thing which Law came alongside *sympathetically*, i.e. a thing companionable *with* Law. And this would seem to be, or primarily be, man's conscience, which likewise informed man about right and wrong just as the Mosaic Law would do. Yet the introduction of the Mosaic Law also gave man more opportunity to resist God unto an abounding of sin, since it introduced a greater knowledge about God and therefore opportunity and accountability. For not since the Command in the Garden had man known a Law whose consequence was divinely stated to be spiritual death; for man's expulsion from the Garden had placed him outside the Garden Command's relevance and application, since post-Adamic man had no access to the Tree of the Knowledge of Good and Evil and the Tree of Life.

Moreover, the phrase in this verse, 'so that the offense *might* abound' does not mean 'for the purpose that sin *ought* to abound,' but rather means 'with the result that the offense would *conditionally* abound (i.e., conditioned upon the choices of men).'[192] But again, the main point here is that all men came into condemnation in a way **similar to**, not **in**, Adam. That is, Paul is following the *general sense* meaning of 15b, which has been his *primary* level of meaning in verses 12-14. Unfortunately, however, the NAS has maintained the KJV's ambiguous meaning of the word 'as' in verses 18 and 19, leaving the impression upon English readers that all men have sinned *because* of Adam. Nevertheless, despite this ambiguity of 'as' in so many English translations of Romans 5:15, 18-19, which ignore *as*'s proper meaning of 'like,' the argument ought to be conceded that any other phrase or verse in Romans 5:12-21 read so narrowly that it contradicts the objective, lexical meaning of *ws* and *hosper* as *like* and *just like*, respectively (the proper meaning of which Paul uses) in the context of verses 12, 15a, 18, and 19, is on a wrong footing, for having wrongly presupposed that Paul assumes a doctrine of original sin in the overall passage.

As for Geisler's second point, we maintain that the consequence of physical death, which descended upon all men (and creatures) as a consequence of Adam's sin, is not a proof against our rebuttal of the doctrine of original sin insofar as we have stated it. For we have already distinguished between the *physical* death which falls upon all creatures in creation regardless of the effect of original sin (granting for the moment the idea of original sin) and the *spiritual* death which comes upon every man who has violated his conscience.

Finally, Geisler's third point claims that there is no parallel to our receiving Christ in the relevant Romans 5 discussion. But as already noted in verse 12, *even as* one man's sin caused spiritual death to enter the world (and so death by sin), in this manner also death spread to all, *since* all have sinned. This statement, in the form of a correlative conjunction and as supported by the arguments we have been advancing, shows that every man *individually* has chosen to sin apart from 'sinning **in** Adam,' and thus (contrary to Geisler's claim) does in fact parallel the free will that is necessary to accept the free gift of Christ. Unfortunately (and again), most Evangelicals seem to have overlooked the "so *also*" of verse 15a, choosing instead to think that the passage is saying that the parallel ceases. Thus (again we note), the NAS's mistaken translation: "But the free gift is not as the transgression." For most Evangelicals the parallel ceases with verse 15 because they believe the comparison is found in the positive work of Christ which is said to be "much more" positive than Adam's negative sin was negative. And while certainly we would agree with the technical point that Christ, as the Creator, will so glorify the believer as to make the comparison of his glorification to his former suffering from sin in Adam's begotten sinful world an unworthy comparison, *this is not the comparison of which verse 15 is speaking*. For again, the traditional Evangelical view fails to understand that the opening words of verse 15—"But not as,"—though it rapidly moves forward the argument from the previous verse, nevertheless refers back and *implies* the prepositional phrase of verse 14 (i.e., *them* [those] born between Adam and Moses who sinned **not** after the similitude of Adam's transgression and yet had spiritually died). Thus the prepositional phrase of verse 14 *is stated only by ellipsis in verse 15's opening words, i.e., "But not as"*, lest Paul be forced to rewrite at the beginning of verse 15 the entire long prepositional phrase of his previous verse. Unless this ellipsis is understood (again, on the lexical strength of verse 15's "so *also*"), the entire meaning changes. Unfortunately, Evangelicals use translations that do not recognize the presence (and therefore the meaning) of 'so also.'

Conclusion

In summary, then, here are some key ideas to be remembered about Romans 5:12-15:

Verse 12

Because of this —i.e., Because of the preceding argument regarding sin (v. 6), which in turn encapsulates the general argument from chapter 1 and forward, which regards man as guilty as having transgressed against the conscience.
Even as sin entered into the world through one man, and death through sin, so also death traversed into all men, since all have sinned—The format is a correlative conjunction of comparison. Even as sin entered the world through Adam

(with spiritual death the result), so death traversed into men because of the same principle of violation against the conscience (i.e. conscience as in accord with God's nature), since every man has sinned.

Verse 13-14

For sin was in the world until Law, —post-Adamic man showed that he too, not just Adam, was sinful.
But sin is not charged where there is no law: but [rather, *yet*] *death reigned from Adam until Moses, even on those who did not sin in the likeness of Adam's transgression, who is a type of the coming One* —God does not put sin to a man's account unless he has broken God's law. It might seem, then, that, although Adam broke the Command that forbade him to eat of the Tree of the knowledge of Good and Evil and therefore died (spiritually) in the day he ate thereof, post-Adamic man should not die for not having broken the specific divine Command whose consequences were death. But since, in fact, post-Adamic man **has** spiritually died, it is evident he is guilty in the general way that Adam was guilty, i.e., in having transgressed against his conscience (which is in accord with God's nature), i.e., even though post-Adamic man did not sin like Adam in the same particular way of breaking the Garden Command. Despite Adam being a sinner, he is nevertheless a type of the righteous Christ insofar as being one who principled a fundamental kind of way.

Verse 15

But not as the offence, so also the free gift, —the phrase "so *also*" actually continues the comparison. Thus, the comparison should not be understood to be that of the transgression in *contrast* to the free gift, but of the transgression *and* the free gift in *contrast* to what is stated negatively about those men (between Adam and Moses) in relation to Adam's offense in the previous verse (v. 14) and as carried out in an extended discussion in regards to the free gift, respectively. Thus the phrase "so also," beginning the 2nd clause of 15a, which itself forms a correlative conjunction [in which the subject (post-Adamic man's sin)] is assumed present in the first clause ("But not as") by way of ellipsis, has in view the following: even as men *have not* technically participated in the similitude of Adam's transgression, and yet die; so too will men *have not* technically participated in the obedience of the One, and yet live.

So then, without doubt Romans 5:12ff is one of Paul's most difficult passages in his epistles to understand. Yet, once these verses are properly understood, we see that they convey interesting truths about Adam and post-Adamic man in contrast to Christ. And if we should not marvel how so difficult a passage could become easily misinterpreted by some, it should nevertheless warn us that any conclusion so much at odds with common sense knowledge, i.e., such a conclusion that would suppose that one man could forcefully choose for another man what his moral content shall be, could not also be biblical.

The rippling out of such 'original sin' theology has caused disastrous, if predictable, waves on the shore of Evangelical evangelism. For example, this insistence on 'Adamic sin in all' ironically reminds me of the time, decades ago, when I heard an Evangelical missionary tell of his difficulty in trying to dissuade the average Japanese person from identifying himself with the ancestral sin in which the Japanese person sees himself indistinguishably submerged. Indeed, what in this missionary's own Evangelical theology could have fundamentally made such a correction possible? In fact, nothing at all. Moreover, there is no use in someone claiming that even an error in Evangelical theology, such as the doctrine of original sin, can help result in an unbeliever of another culture identifying more quickly with the gospel message, since e.g., 'original sin' mirrors their own idea of ancestral sin. As Christ pointed out, only the truth sets people free. Therefore any admixture of truth with error merely weakens the overall gospel message and presentation.

Thus, the result of holding to the notion of original sin has created many problems for Evangelical theology, not the least of which is the whole confusion caused by creating permeable boundaries between the being of one person and that of another, so typical of Calvinist thought elsewhere. Did Adam choose our choice? The average Evangelical gives the same answer to this question as the Calvinist does to the question of whether God chooses our choices—*"yes but no."* This kind of answer (if *answer* it be) is ever present in a discussion with Calvinists or, for that matter, with most Evangelical non-Calvinists in any discussion about original sin. We can only hope and pray that the situation changes. For Christ said that our yea should be yea, and our nay should be nay; for whatever is more than these is of the evil one.

Question:

Psalm 51:5 states that David was conceived in sin by his mother. This seems to plainly state that David was a sinner from his very conception. Doesn't this mean, then, that he inherited this condition from Adam? And can't we understand original sin as starting out like a 'seed' just like you claim happens for the knowledge of good and evil?

Answer:

Even A.S. Barnes, the relatively well-known Reformed commentator, believed that the doctrine of original sin could not be argued from Psalm 51:5 alone. As for the idea of original sin, or a 'seed' of original sin being present but unblossomed into *de facto* sin, I can find no lexical evidence for either idea in Romans 5, which is the most thorough treatment in the Bible about the origin of sin and its spreading to all of accountable humanity. Moreover, based on our study thus far, that which may be transmitted in 'seed' from one generation to another must be, by its nature, a *form without eternally liable content* (or even *bare* content) since persons form their own content and, as they mature, eternally liable content (i.e., *what* they will believe unto eternal consequence). Thus a post-Adamic person receives from his parents the *seed* of the knowledge of good and evil (i.e., *the seed of the ability to know* about good and evil in a way similar to God) but without any content.[193]

Having shown the proper understanding of Romans 5:12-21, it remains for us to consider the meaning of Psalm 51:5, which is often cited in support of the doctrine of original sin. Again, the verse reads:

> *Behold, I was shapen (lit. brought forth) in iniquity, and in sin did my mother conceive me.*

Young's Literal translation shows the non-chronological parallelism more clearly:

> *Lo, in iniquity I have been brought forth,*
> *And in sin doth my mother conceive me.*

The best explanation of this verse appears to be what some have offered based on the nature of Hebrew poetry and other comparative Psalms. This view explains the verse as poetic exaggeration. In Psalm 51, for example, there are numerous phrases not meant to be taken literally: "*Wash me thoroughly from mine iniquity*" (that is, '*Remove* completely mine iniquity'); "*Purge me with hyssop*," [*hyssop* was a moss like plant that was dipped into blood for ceremonial sprinkling, thus *hyssop* is used substitutively in verse 7 for the substance (blood) in which it is dipped. This literary device of noun substitution is known as a *metonymy*]; "*the bones that (God) has broken may rejoice.*" Contrast these with the non-exaggerative statement, "*Deliver me from bloodguiltiness*" [Lit. *bloods*, i.e., bloodshed as *drops* of blood (the noun is in the plural form) and perhaps here meaning also the bloodshed of *men*, as Uriah was not the only one who died through the bogus battle maneuver David designed to cover up his adultery]. The idea here in these former examples is that David exaggerates in verse 5 as he does in other places in the same Psalm to emphasize his sinfulness, i.e., even as he did in Psalm 22, when the deep awareness of his sinfulness led him to exaggeratively say that he was a '*worm*.' In Psalm 22 David also says: "I was cast upon [God] from the womb: thou art my God from my mother's belly." Presumably no one uses Psalm 22:10 to argue that David had original perfection, but then what is the point of arguing one exaggeration to be literal (*in sin did my mother conceive me*) while the other is not (*thou art my God from my mother's belly*)? While Psalm 22 is Messianic and admittedly layered in meaning, it nevertheless uses less exaggeration than Psalm 51. On that basis Psalm 51 ought to be considered generally more hyperbolic of the two. In yet another Psalm (Ps. 58) David speaks of the wicked speaking lies as soon as they are born. Presumably, we are not meant to think that this happens literally. Arguably, this Psalm (which also speaks of the youthful wicked being young lions) has more hyperbole than either Psalms 51 or 22. Upon what basis, then, do we say that Psalm 22, which is *less* exaggerative than Psalm 51, and Psalm 58, which is *more* exaggerative than Psalm 51, are hyperbolic in parts while Psalm 51:5 *cannot possibly be*?

Further, consider how key texts like Isaiah 53 and Psalm 14, which are often cited in support of the doctrine of original sin, do not really assume that man is *inherently* depraved. Isaiah 53 [194] says that we have all *gone astray* unto our own way like sheep, and Psalm 14 speaks of God looking down and seeing us gone *aside* (out of the way) to do evil. This is active wandering, not a passive state. So again, the question begs itself: Gone astray from *where*—gone aside from *whom*? How can a morally depraved person, if he has been morally wayward from the time of conception, go astray **from** a state of sinfulness in which he was allegedly conceived?[195]

The chief understanding of Psalm 51:5 may thus be understood as hyperbolic. David, in the same spirit of saying, "I am a worm, and no man," uses poetic exaggeration to state his sinfulness without excuse. He expresses, in effect, his heightened sense of sin to which God has brought him to realize through the prophet Nathan: '*I have always been like this from the beginning*.' Again, as hyperbole this is not a statement indicating original sin, since that idea is contradicted in Romans 5. Indeed, to *not* take this hyperbolic approach in order to assume that "in sin" teaches 'Adamic sin upon all,' is to imperil a proper understanding of Romans 5:12-21 and to ignore (as so many translations have done) the correlative conjunction in Romans 5:12 which informs and impacts that entire passage, a point confirmed through subsequent appearances of *ws* and *hosper*.

On a personal note, and despite what God has recently been teaching me regarding 'original sin,' I struggled with giving up my old understanding of Psalm 51:5. I used it decades ago in a speech at college to argue for ensoulment at the time of conception. As ensoulment equaled personhood, I argued that the fetus ought to be considered human and therefore protected against abortion. For this reason I was not initially satisfied about understanding the verse differently. But when I considered how the overall context of the Bible resisted a Calvinistic interpretation (as we have shown throughout this book), I had to consider whether one isolated verse that seemed to point in the direction of original sin really did point there. I have discovered that, in interpreting the Bible, one either takes the *whole* of Scripture where one wants to go, or the *whole* of Scripture takes you where *it* wants to go. However, to my delight I have since realized that in the layer of Messianic (and literal) meaning of Psalm 51:5, which will be discussed in the course of this answer, the Bible **does** teach that life begins at conception.

So the above hyperbolic interpretation does not appear to be the only layer of meaning intended by the Spirit. There are at least two other layers arguably present. In some sense these layers of meaning are made possible because of the absence of Hebrew suffixes to prepositions that would have referred the reader to the identity of the subject(s) of 'in iniquity' and 'in sin.' Such grammatical pointers are conspicuously absent. Thus there are no strong indications as to who is being indicated by these prepositional phrases, i.e., where sin comes from or who is doing the sinning. Some therefore assume that, because there are no specific referents, original sin is being implied (or stated). But based on our considerations in the last question regarding Romans 5:12-21, sin is not a condition whose causative agent is *itself* but in fact is from out of the *man himself*. This in turn suggests a reason why the referent ambiguity of Psalm 51:5 does not provide restricted direction for 'in iniquity' and 'in sin'—i.e., because there is more than just the hyperbolic meaning intended here.

Now in regard to the first clause of verse 5, "Lo, in iniquity was I brought forth," it is interesting to note that the word "iniquity" involves a root meaning of "perversity," yet according to Strong's, the word can also mean *punishment* or a *consequence related to punishment*. Accordingly, 'perversity' in such instances would not mean something sinful but rather something of *punishment* or of the *consequence of punishment*. Along these lines, a pastor friend[196] of mine recently pointed out to me that the childbirth described in Psalm 51 (as post-Fall) is a perversity from that which God originally intended. He bases this on Genesis 3:16. There it implies that gestation was shorter prior to the Fall, and childbirth sorrow-free. Thus the consequence of Eve's sin was that woman would henceforth have difficulty and painful sorrow in childbirth. Young's transliteration of Genesis 3:16 shows God's irony of expression to Eve: "Multiplying[197] I multiply thy sorrow and thy conception, in sorrow dost thou bear children."[198] Therefore the first clause of Psalm 51:5, *by indirect implication*, may be understood as David acknowledging the perversity (his possession of the seed of the knowledge of good and evil) that attended his own gestation and delivery into the world as a descendent whose roots went back to Adam and Eve.

Further, although the Hebrew word *avon* is most often rendered as 'iniquity' compared to its next most frequent rendering in English, i.e., 'punishment' (220 compared to 5 in the KJV), the preference for 'punishment' in certain cases (Gen. 19:15 and Ex. 20:5) is evident. The question, then, is whether the word 'iniquity' can be legitimately translated 'punishment' or 'consequence of punishment' in Psalm 51:5? The answer appears to be *no* if understanding the verse's main hyperbolic intention, but *yes* if taking the verse literally. In other words *avon* may be intended to have a polyvalent meaning in accordance with its varied (though we presume here, divinely intended) lexical use, much like the meaning of *almah* in Isaiah 7:14, where in Isaiah God has more than one meaning in mind.[199] But first we must concede that in the near context of Psalm 51:2 David obviously has in mind the transgressive nature of *avon*, since he 1) asks God in verse 2a to wash him from his *iniquity* (*avon*), and 2) puts verse 2a in parallel with verse 2b, in which he asks God to cleanse him from sin. Moreover (regarding the possible meanings of 'iniquity') Paul, in Romans 4:7-8, quotes Psalm 32:1-2 in a similar context about sinfulness and renders the Old Testament word *iniquity* as *sin*.

The question, then, is whether there can be an additional meaning? Again, it appears so, providing that meaning is a *literal* one. Observe, for example, how the two phrases of Psalm 51:5 together form a poetic parallelism *which at least, in accordance with a literal interpretation,* points in some sense back to David's mother. Further, the Hebrew verb *khool* (*twirl/ whirl/ brought forth/ writhe*) in verse 5a is in its *passive* form, whereas the verb *yacham* (*to conceive/ get heat/ be hot/ get warm*) used in verse 5b is *active*. This distinction in verb forms shows that the parallelism of Hebrew poetry in this particular verse (i.e., as seen in clause *A*, clause *B*) form two statements that are similar to each other, but not exact, and so the parallelism of the two phrases should not be pushed to its strictest sense.

So besides the hyperbolic layer of meaning that places David as the subject and then object referent of the two prepositional phrases respectively,[200] we also have a literal layer of meaning which runs through both clauses. The first clause places David as the referent of the prepositional phrase, which in turn *implies the presence of his mother,* the justification of whose presence is the parallelism which has her clearly in view in the second clause (that is, in the particular layer of meaning we are advancing here, though also in the hyperbolic layer of meaning, but not in the third layer of meaning we will describe in a moment, which is Messianic). In the second clause, David's mother is the referent of "in sin." So Psalm 51:5, viewed literally and according to this 2nd layer of meaning, would be stating (in clause *A*) that David was brought forth in the pain and anguish of his mother, and (clause *B*) that David's mother was under the state of sinfulness when she conceived David. The real significance of this layer of meaning will become clear in a moment.

To begin with, the two phrases, though not in reproductively chronological order, are suggestive of two stated conditions of David's mother—a perversity of flesh, and a sinfulness stemming from choice. In fact, these are the two conditions that characterize every post-Adamic person who has traveled through the age of accountability.

Consider this first condition of David's mother—the perversity of her flesh, i.e., the state of her having the knowledge of good and evil. This was the result of Adam and Eve's disobedience, in which the first man and the first woman also suffered (besides spiritual death and a gaining of knowledge) separate consequences of physical punishment. For the Man it was the multiplicity of growth—weeds—so that the ground would not yield its strength. For the Woman it was the multiplicity of pain in the childbirth process, including a lengthier gestation period. These were God's ironic, divine consequences upon the original pair for choosing to multiply knowledge. For the Woman this pain is presumably to remind her that the child she bears, though generally blessed of God as made in God's image, is nevertheless not as He intended (since the child is also made in Adam's image as bearing the seed of the knowledge of good and evil). Again, the psalmist is, for the moment, primarily viewing himself within a context of childbirth, and so our attention is drawn in some sense to the stated condition of the mother. This is not because David is trying to throw embarrassing attention away from his sin. Indeed, in the course of Psalm 51, David will not excuse himself for his sin with Bathsheba. But here, in this particular layer of literal meaning, David seems to be looking beyond his particular actions in order to contemplate the larger problem of human sin in general. In effect, he appears to be asking himself, 'What are the factors affecting this general drift of man away from God, of which my sin with Bathsheba, though so great an offense, is still but one significant failing among so many in humanity?'

Thus again, the thought in Psalm 51:5a could include the idea that David's mother, in her writhing pain of childbirth which mirrors her son's own writhing as he is brought forth, bespeaks of the knowledge of good and evil as the pain's ultimate cause. This knowledge she passes in seed to her children (including David) by means of her husband Jesse, whose presence is implied in the conception mentioned in the second clause. Thus David, as a kind of 'pointer,' points generationally backwards to his mother[201] who is implied in the first clause, from whom he received a perversity of flesh, namely, the seed of the knowledge of good and evil. Moreover, David's sin with Bathsheba points to his activity according to this seed of knowledge, i.e., knowledge as having matured and to which he has acted in accord (i.e., as he walked *according to* the flesh). Hence David explores the chronology of sin and its effect from the Fall and observes its spiritual, physiological, and emotional effects, all of which he finds tragic.

Thus in his mother's begetting of him, there may be implied here (for David) a twisting of his own nature when he was formed—his mind (as a form) whirled and twirled,[202] so to speak, about his lower form as a man, i.e., with the seed of the knowledge of good and evil as inherited through his mother as a descendent from Adam.[203] Presumably, David looks back and sees that this knowledge came to mature within his nature to a point where he deliberated and made decisions about thoughts and moral judgments within a context of a fallen flesh which God had never intended for men and women. This flesh—containing the knowledge of good and evil—whirled David about with its distracting presentation, until the decisions he made were either agreeable to his conscience, or disagreeable to his conscience [and therefore in accordance with his flesh, i.e., the knowledge of good and evil (with its more intensive realization of pleasure in sin)]. His decision to commit adultery with Bathsheba was made in disagreement with his conscience, though in fact it was especially made against God, as the Supreme Law-Giver. All this is implied in David's mother's perversity of flesh and the consequence of distraction that made it difficult for David to focus upon the right decisions as he grew into maturity. That is, the reader may infer it if he understands the circumstances of David and his mother, which informs the context of Psalm 51. Thus the above considerations appear to offer a literal, if subsidiary, understanding of Psalm 51:5.

But something else should be noted about the 2nd clause in this 2nd layer of meaning, i.e., "and in sin did my mother conceive me." It has been noted that 'sin' could refer to the mother's sin if the phrase had to be taken literally. For example, in the statement, "In anger my boss fired me" the anger would be my boss's, not mine. Even so, the phrase "In sin did my mother conceive me" could mean the *mother* existed in the state of sinfulness. By this we simply mean that David's mother, like all accountable persons, was a sinner. Paul, for example, even during his apostleship, stated that he was the chief of sinners. Thus David might be implying that the human condition as trans-generational is such that people have always found a way to sin, and to have found it rather easily. Again, we note that no suffix actually refers these prepositional phrases to either David or his mother, but (we contend) this is because David is emphasizing himself in the 1st layer of meaning but emphasizing his mother in the 2nd layer of meaning, i.e., that while for David the hyperbolic meaning stresses the idea of 'the sinfulness of *me*,' the literal meaning emphasizes 'the sinfulness of my *mother*' (this latter point of which (again) appears to emphasize the sad merry*less*-go-round of sin in human experience).

Note that both layers of meaning (the hyperbolic and the literal) examined thus far are **not** in harmony with a proposed doctrine of original sin. So if in the literal meaning we grant that David's mother is an implied factor in both clauses of verse 5, we can observe that David's mother, in the second clause, could be thought *active* in the process of conceiving, in a way in which the one conceived (David, as object) would not qualify. (Remember, the verb in the 2nd clause in active, the verb in the first clause is passive.) Therefore if we take 'iniquity' to mean '[a consequence of] punishment'—such as the word means in Genesis 4:13 when Cain tells God his '[consequence of] punishment' is too great to bear—verse 5 could be rendered as follows (granting all that we have thus far established):

> "In [the consequence of] punishment was I brought forth/writhed, and in sin does my mother conceive me."

An interpretive, amplified paraphrase (i.e., not a translation) may help to show what we mean here:

> "In the midst of the consequence of punishment (as given to Eve and thus unto all future mothers, regarding childbirth) I was brought forth writhing (as syncratic with my mother's writhing), and my mother conceived me while in a general state of sinfulness."

This literal layer of meaning offers at least one additional observation regarding parallelism later in the psalm. Note the hyssop which is the carrier of atoning blood, a blood which in turn points to the blood of a righteous Christ who would become the second Adam—and how this essentially parallels David's mother as also a carrier, but of a 'perverse' knowledge whose consequence is death and which bespeaks of the first Adam and his transgression.

One further observance should be made about both these layers of meaning, as well as the following (Messianic) layer of meaning which we will examine in a moment. The conjunction, "and," connecting the two clauses of the verse has not been ignored. It is preserved in all three layers of meaning, so that the verse is preserved as a united whole.

Moving on, in the 3rd (or Messianic) layer the first phrase ("In the consequence of punishment was I brought forth") is taken to mean at least two things: 1) the Messiah was brought forth in the midst of Mary's painful childbirth even as David was brought forth, though without the seed of the knowledge of good and evil because of the Messiah's chronological priority to Adam and because of His virgin birth. Irony is evident here, since the Messiah went through pain but for the purpose of ultimately doing away with pain. 2) And very significantly, the Messiah was brought forth (by Pilate) after being subject to the consequence of punishment (which He bore as the Lamb of God); *"In the consequence of punishment was I brought forth."* The famous phrase by Pilate, "Ecce Homo" (Behold the Man!) comes to mind here, as Christ was brought before the crowd. The clause can also be seen as one in which the Son was brought forth by the Father, since it was the Father's desire, not the Son's, that the Son be sent into the world to die for the sins of the world. Note that Christ is in the passive mode in all such instances, even as the verb indicates ["...He is brought as a lamb to the slaughter...". (Is. 53:7a)]. Here the remarkableness of the Hebrew Scriptures are seen, for within the same phrase are found the different layers of meaning, the sin of the sinner at one level, and the atonement of the Redeemer on another. One should note here that the same Hebrew word is used in the Old Testament for "sin" and "sin offering." While yet David finds himself in the throes of confessing his sin, God already considers the Lamb brought forth from a woman's womb, to ultimately be brought forth to suffer an atoning death for man.

Finally, consider the 2nd clause ("and in sin did my mother conceive me") in this 3rd (Messianic) layer of meaning. Specifically, this clause goes to the point of rebuking the notion that the Messiah's mother, Mary, would be without sin. This would explain why, at the Messianic level of Psalm 51:5's textured meaning, the father is not in view, yet is, in fact, implied at the Davidic level of meaning. It goes without saying that the Immaculate Conception (the idea that Mary was herself conceived without sin, along with its implication of her acting as co-redeemer) has been one of the greatest heresies among those professing to be Christians.

Having grown up in the Evangelical faith, I understand that such a layered interpretation as suggested above for Psalm 51:5 will seem 'a stretch.' Yet certainly one reason it appears so is because Evangelicals have never really approached this psalm as the Jews do, who do not hold to a doctrine of 'original sin.' In fact, we have accepted the idea of original sin *prima facie* because the English rendering and interpretation of verse 5 has, frankly speaking, been drummed into our heads to a point of indoctrination apart from historical, grammatical, and contextual considerations, especially as regards the farther context of all the Bible (specifically Rom. 5:12ff). And so the average Evangelical quotes Psalm 51:5 as the *coup de grace* in any discussion about the doctrine of original sin and without certain essential exegetical knowledge of Romans 5. Thus he hardly suspects that in his own limited way he is employing the technique so often used by cultists—i.e., that of isolating some verse from the poetic books and performing a beheading of some important Christian doctrine—to rid, in his case, a proper understanding of the nature of man, and the Pauline view that sin is not passed from Adam upon his descendents.

Given, then, some of the latter arguments under this question for a Messianic layer of meaning, I do not see why this viewpoint could not be considered as legitimate, as coming alongside the other layers of meanings we have already observed.

Question:

You claim that all men are made in God's image, yet Genesis implies that only *Adam* was made in God's image. When Adam's son, Seth, was born, the Bible says that Seth was born in *Adam's* image. Doesn't this mean that man's free will must be lost, since Seth was not made in the image of God but merely in the image of Adam? Isn't it correct, then, to say that Seth didn't have the ability to choose good?

Answer:

Even if we granted the Calvinist's assumption about Seth, it does not help the Calvinist to explain how Adam chose to sin. It simply moves the onus of the problem of evil from Seth to Adam. In fact, it seems more problematic for the Calvinist to have to explain how an *unfallen* man (Adam) could have chosen to do evil.[204] Second, and to answer the point more directly, Seth was not merely made in the image of Adam *but also* in the image of God. The fact that persons during Noah's time continued to be born in God's image is the whole basis for God's instruction to Noah about capital punishment in Genesis 9:6: "Whoever sheds man's blood, By man his blood shall be shed; For in the image of God He made man."[205] This statement authorizing capital punishment wouldn't even make sense unless men were still made in the image of God. Thus God was making clear that, despite the sin of man, which brings divine judgment, man is still made in God's image. The difference, of course, is that Seth was also born in Adam's image, i e., with Adam's acquired knowledge of good and evil, a knowledge that greatly distracted (not controlled) his focus while making choices.

Footnotes:

[124] This view is similar to Pelagius's insofar as holding to the basic view that Adam was truly free, though in deference to Pelagius, it holds that man was not created mortal, even inheriting an effect besides physical death—i.e. the knowledge of good and evil (introduced in them as a seed of additional knowledge upon conception). Pelagius's writings are mostly secondary sourced. Furthermore, someone has stated that Pelagius sometimes speaks of 'meriting' grace. If, in fact, Pelagius believed this, he was incorrect.

[125] In Greek the word 'fornication' is *pornea*, lit. *to sell*, and in this context *fornication* means sexual intercourse apart from one's spouse. When a person commits fornication in a marriage, that person has sold their matrimonial vow—a vow publicly understood to be self-sacrificial and chaste—for their own immoral pleasure.

The 'pull' of sin, however, is not the same for all men in the same circumstances. Much of this 'pull' depends on how strong a man's conscience is, and how well he maintains it. If he has abstained from a particular sin, the 'pull' is generally less for that particular trial. Furthermore, not all pleasure is found in sins of commission. There is a kind of sinful pleasure that avoids pain, as when a man may omit doing something he ought to do, in order to avoid pain, hassle, inconvenience, etc.

[126] Moreover, there are various forms of sexual sin that are not necessarily adultery, but ones in which a man may nevertheless act selfishly within a sexual context.

[127] One might suppose, from reading 1 Corinthians 15:21-22, that the death spoken of in Romans 5:12ff is likewise a physical, not spiritual, death. I Corinthians 15:21-22 reads: "For since death is through man, also through a Man is a resurrection of the dead. For as all die in Adam, so also all will be made alive in Christ." But the contexts of 1 Corinthians 15 and Romans 5 are significantly different. 1 Corinthians 15 is a lengthy discussion about physical resurrection, while Romans 5 is a segue (footnote cont. on p. 524) (continued from p. 452) between a prior discussion in Romans about guilt, condemnation, and reconciliation (Romans 1—4) and an upcoming discussion about Christian experience (Romans 6—8). Christ's physical death and resurrection in Romans 1—7 speaks primarily to the spiritual relevance they have to man. Not until Romans 8 does Paul begin to speak in more detail about the redemption of the believer's body and his glorification. Further, if physical death is the kind Paul alludes to in Romans 5:12, then he is also stating that we physically die *because* of sin, but obviously such a statement would explain nothing about why animals and insects also die. Moreover, God told Adam that if he ate the forbidden fruit he would die *in that day*, but Adam did not *physically* die until 930 years later. While it is true that Adam obtained the *sentence* of physical death in the day he ate of the forbidden fruit, that is a different thing than death itself. Thus the Adamic death spoken of in Romans 5:12 ought to be assumed to be a *spiritual* death unless the context has in primary view the physical resurrection, which it does not. Also, the physical resurrection context of 1 Corinthians 15 arguably has in view one of the most dramatic statements Christ ever made in the gospels about the physical resurrection of both the righteous and the wicked: "Marvel not at this: for the hour is coming, in the which all that are in the graves shall hear his voice and shall come forth; they that have done good, unto the resurrection of life, and they that have done evil, unto the resurrection of damnation" (Jn 5:28-29). The point here is that all physically died because Adam had the power to bring death, even as Christ has such power that one day he will bring to life every human who has died. Adam's power, then, was of physical and consequential effect; but though Adam's choice added to us an additional knowledge we otherwise would not have had, it *determined* nothing of the moral content of who

we are, anymore than the power of Christ *determines* the moral content of those whose bodies are raised.

Furthermore, a careful reading of the immediate context surrounding Romans 5:12 likewise leads us to conclude that Paul is talking about spiritual death (see main text above). In the two sections sandwiching Romans 5:12-21 (Romans 5:1-11 and Romans 6:1ff) Paul speaks about the believer's identification with Christ's death and resurrection, and together these show that Paul was moving toward a discussion of the *believer's spiritual* life by the time he would reach Romans 6. This is not to say that the resurrection of the believer is ever far from Paul's mind in those chapters prior to 6 (including Romans 5), for the ramifications of the believer's spiritual life is solely dependent on the physical resurrection of Christ. But the primary *address* here in the first seven chapters of Romans is the *spiritual* condition of the world (unreconciled and reconciled man). As Romans 6 unfolds, the believer in this world is urged to forsake disobedience (i.e., as implied and archetyped in the disobedient one, Adam, whose actions led to sin's entrance into the world) and to follow after obedience (as archetyped in the obedient One, Christ, whose obedience makes man's reconciliation with God, and therefore eternal life, possible).

This fact of the *spiritual* element is also in view when Paul states in Romans 5:6 that Christ died for us when we were *weak* (lit. *without strength*). Paul is talking about *spiritual* weakness, not physical weakness, evidenced in every man's failure to commend his love toward sinful men in the same (neighborly) way God Himself has demonstrated. Thus man has failed to live up to the Neighborly Command (the golden rule). That is, while some men might even dare to die for a relatively *good* man, no man has loved sinful man as God has, who commended His love toward us *while we were yet sinners*. Thus God's love makes possible man's *spiritual* reconciliation *and the glorying of that fact* (Romans 10:11-12) before God (i.e., the appropriate response of a saved man in recognizing God's great work in his life, which in turn informs his walk as a believer in this world).

Finally, as an interesting side note here, while 1 Corinthians 15 uses the phrase "en tw Adam" i.e., "in Adam," to signify the physical mortality that attended Adam in the day he ate the forbidden fruit, i.e., a physical mortality inevitably passed to us, the phrase "in Adam" never technically occurs in the Romans 5 passage in which *spiritual* death is in view.*

*Note below John Calvin's statement, attempting to refute the Pelagian claim that if children inherit from Adam his spiritually *degenerate* nature, then children begotten from Christian parents ought to inherit their spiritually *regenerate* nature: Says Calvin:

> The Pelagian cavil, as to the improbability of children deriving corruption from pious parents, whereas, they ought rather to be sanctified by their purity, is easily refuted. Children come not by spiritual regeneration but carnal descent. Accordingly, as Augustine says, "Both the condemned unbeliever and the acquitted believer beget offspring not acquitted but condemned, because the nature which begets is corrupt."

Our question of Calvin is a straightforward one: Where in the Bible is it suggested that "the nature which begets," i.e., Calvin's reference to the "carnal descent,"—the sexual passion and the sexual act which Calvin implicitly connects with degenerate spirituality—is a ***morally corrupting*** act? Or, especially, why now the dichotomy between the "spiritual" and the "carnal," when the sexual activity of the parent with its ***spiritual*** effects served Calvin so well, so long as it was Adam's sexuality (and nature) and not the believer's? [Note that Calvin here does ***not*** make the argument one might expect, by supposing that Adam's parentage is the only one worthy of consideration. This is clear in his quotation of Augustine, for the word "beget" in "beget offspring" is clearly defined as the sexual reproduction of "both the condemned unbeliever and the acquitted believer," and so when Augustine proceeds to speak of "the nature which begets is corrupt," he can only be speaking of the begetting which results from ALL human sexual reproduction, not just Adam's. Calvinists would presumably attempt to solve this problem by claiming that Adam's begetting (in the moral-transfer sense) courses through the begetting acts of all his descendents. But note that this assumption introduces and conflates the moral being of Adam with the being of his descendents. But, of course, such an idea, if interesting to some, has one vital flaw—*it has no scriptural support.*] Or where now in Calvin is there an appeal to the opposite proof-texted Scripture that would say that if any man be in Christ he is a new creation wherein ALL THINGS are new? But apparently for Calvin "all things" includes all things except the "nature which begets." Put another way, Calvin's assigning of a degenerate spirituality in the course of "carnal" descent" is mere caprice, since a negative OR positive moral status could have been proposed either way, as long as ALL THINGS did not include *physical* depravity.In light of Calvin's insistence on this state of things (inherited spiritual depravity), I'll admit I found it amusing that, regarding the patristic discussion of Original Sin, Calvin himself admits that there is

> nothing more remote from common apprehension, than that the fault of one should render all guilty, and so become a common sin. This seems to be the reason why the oldest doctors of the church only glance obscurely at the point, or, at least, do not explain it so clearly as it required.

In fact, none of the early church fathers prior to Augustine supported the idea of Original Sin, which is why Augustine has been credited with recovering it (that is, by Calvinists). Apparently, it just never dawned on Calvin that his views were not sympathetic to *any* of the earliest church fathers. Indeed, as the pre-Augustinian writings demonstrate, the early fathers consistently repudiated the idea that man of his own nature could not choose God. And so, by his inferring an early fathers' puzzlement, rather than their disapproval, Calvin blithely continues his refutation of Pelagianism.

It gets worse. Calvin's appeal to Romans 5:12, Psalm 51:5, and 1 Corinthians 15:22—the three passages he cites to prove his argument for Original Sin are all stated briefly and without any analysis of the original languages or serious examination of their contexts. He ignores that the overriding question is of *physical* resurrection in 1 Corinthians 15. He also ignores the absence of prepositional pointers in Ps. 51:5, whose presence might have led some measure of credence to his position (depending on their placement); and of course he ignores his own kind of proof-texting from Psalms when it would tell against his own position, such as the converse notion of original perfection as found in "Thou art my God from my mother's belly." In brief, all his expositions are given short shrift. (See *Institutes*: Vol. 2; Chpt. 1, pts. 5-6.) In fact, because Calvin supposes that Romans 5:12 in context so obviously states the matter of Original Sin, his exposition of this crucial verse and its context extends to the magnanimous amount of 150 words in English translation, before he declares: "In this clear light of truth I cannot see any need of a longer or more laborious proof". Indeed, we should all be such diligent students of such pivotal scriptures as Calvin. Small wonder that he and his followers have never seen the correlative conjunctive format of Romans 5:12. I think, then, the matter of this most crucial section of the *Institutes* can be succinctly drawn up in a single observation about Calvin's reliance on polemics at the expense of proper presuppositions which could have led him to proper exegesis—note that one can hardly state Calvin's position in less words than Calvin's own 'exposition.'

[128] In the case of persons who have reached the age of accountability (i.e., perhaps better termed—those who have 'entered the period of accountability'), physical death is also warranted upon their own spiritual death once they choose to sin. Prior to the point where a person has sinned during his age of accountability, he is subject to physical death as a consequence of Adam's sin, just like insects and animals. [Sidebar: Someone might object here that Paul's use of the phrase "children of wrath" in Ephesians 2:3 implies original sin, and that therefore we are wrong to contend for an age of accountability. However, the word 'children' in the phrase, "children of wrath" is *tekna*, not *nerios*, denoting children that were older than infants, and thus presumably candidates for accountability. As for *nerios*, I hasten to add that babies and all persons are conceived in the image of God and therefore not equitable to animals, to be regarded, or, *dispatched* (i.e., in abortion), as such.]

As an additional note, here, consider how pre-accountable persons, in the paradigm we are suggesting, gives force to God's argument with Jonah in Jonah 4. Pre-accountable persons would not have had any more guilt (or, for the sake of argument, even *imputed* guilt) than the gourd over which Jonah had compassion. Thus Jonah could not have argued (even hypocritically) that such e.g., *infants* ought to be destroyed as having inherited Adam's guilt. God's rhetorical inquiry into Jonah's attitude put the matter clear. If Jonah, as a creature, wanted the right to have compassion over a plant he did not create, then by what reason should God, as the *Creator* of all things, not be entitled to have compassion over pre-accountable persons who had no more guilt than the gourd over which Jonah had compassion, *and* whom God had made in His image?

An objection might be raised here as to how God would be right in bringing judgment against the Ninevites, since it would have involved the death of scores of thousands of infants who were not guilty. Technically speaking, however, if the Ninevites had not repented, divine judgment would *not* have been against Ninevite infants but against the maturer Ninevites themselves as accountable persons. The point here is that God recognizes the stewardship of the Ninevites over the welfare of their infants, even as, for example, God (despite His warnings) recognized the stewardship of the Egyptians over the welfare of their cattle whom He nevertheless did not spare in the 5th and 7th plagues, even as He did not spare the firstborn of Egyptian sons and beasts in the 10th plague regardless of their age. There is, sometimes, the suffering of the blameless, whether of humans or animals in this life, because of the actions of others. (Many humans, old and young, die in a just war on the just side, for example. Further, Job's children died because of Satan's accusations, which incited God to allow Job's trial against God's wishes.) But concerning this point about stewardship, even the story of Noah and the Flood is suggestive here; for even as Noah was found faithful among men and escaped divine judgment, so too does it appear that God found it fitting to spare a single representative pair of animals as under the stewardship of Noah. Thus even as Noah's generations would continue from himself and his wife, so too would each pair of animals beget after their own kind in their generations. In this sense (of stewardship) Noah mirrors Adam, though Adam's stewardship had the greater effect of bringing physical depravity upon all human persons and all creatures (i.e., all sentient creation).

[129] The subject of animals and morality is, in fact, a difficult one. The serpent in the garden was cursed, which would imply that it had disobeyed God. (Indeed, God said to the serpent, "Because thou has done this…") For apart from disobedience there should have been no divine judgment, yet judgment was pronounced upon the snake to crawl on its belly and eat dust. (It has since been observed by scientists that snakes have the physiology that suggests that at one time they could have walked.) As for Eve not acting surprised that the serpent talked to her, it should be noted that Josephus claims that "all the living creatures had one language" at the time of creation (*Antiquities of the Jews*, Book 1 Chapter 1). Balaam's ass also talked, God having loosed her tongue, and note that the ass understood that she was being mistreated and thus had a degree of moral understanding (a degree of ability to distinguish right from wrong). Admittedly, the various conundrums that arise in trying to explain how animals might have a moral sense is difficult. Nor do I see any past theological system within Evangelicalism that has bothered about such questions. *Perhaps* the answer is in the fact (and this indeed **is** a fact) that animals, though they are creatures, are not made in the image of God. This fact may be deduced from Genesis 9:3-6, in which God gives permission to Noah to eat every living creature, while on the other hand He states that the killing of man is only allowed in cases of capital punishment. In other words, if animals were made in the image of God, then Noah would not have been allowed by God to kill them for food. Arguably, however, animals have a soul (defined here as an emotional and mental self). If they have a spirit (and I believe they do) it is not one made in the image of God (for God made persons unique in this regard). Personally, I would grant that animals are sustained past their present life here on earth, and that their bodies will one day be resurrected by God apart from any consideration regarding *eternal* guilt. Thus I believe that animals have an eternal spirit, but not one that is subject unto eternal liability (at least not after the manner of punishment to which man is subject).

As to what it means for a person 'to be made in the image of God,' I can only offer a partial answer, with the caution that what I suggest here is an answer based on what it seems to me the answer could *not* be. By default, then, it seems that man is accountable *unto eternal liability* for his actions, based on his being a God-created form in which he makes *ex nihilo* eternity-based decisions (utilizing a higher level of knowledge than that possessed by animals) about the trustworthiness of God. Man, then, occupies a realm higher than the animals.

Animals, on the other hand, appear to act within a realm of lesser accountability in which their actions may have consequences—though of a lower degree [owing in part to many (I do not say *all*) actions being born of instinct] and as one limited (it would appear) to divine judgment regarding its earthly life. (By 'instinct' we mean thoughts which the animal brings into existence *ex nihilo*, wherein each thought is supposed, or accepted and properly recognized, *prima facie* as reality, upon the same instant that the thought itself is brought *ex nihilo*.) Yet in this latter regard the same is presumably true of the beginning of thought in any of us as created persons, whose first thought in each of us must instinctually involve the granted and proper assumption of our own personal existence. But to return our thoughts to animals and their accountability, the divine judgment upon the serpent in the Garden appears to be of the limited kind restricted to its (this?) earthly life. The chief difference in animal behavior *between now and the time* of Christ's future kingdom, that is, between the current practice of certain animals killing other animals for food, versus the future state of affairs when the lion will lay down with the lamb, would seem to be 1) the current *presence* of the Devil (and presumably the demonic realm) upon earth, whose presence may have a general negative affect on the animals in a way not fully understood by us, but whose presence shall be banished during the future rule of Christ for a thousand years, and 2) the magnanimous, life-giving provisions which can only be possible in a world governed by Christ. For apart from the reign of Christ—a time when the earth shall be full of the Lord's glory—it is hard to imagine under what circumstances, generally speaking, the lion would be content to lay down with the lamb. One explanation for why animals may kill each other for food may be found in the post-Flood condition of the Earth. Since the time of the Flood, the Earth's ratio of minerals in the soil has been destroyed, a fact which may suggest why animals seek other means to obtain the minerals they need (such as killing and eating other animals). Indeed, even man was given permission to eat animal meat after the Flood. Exactly *what* in animals will sense this change of the Lord's rule, so that they will live peaceably with each other, is beyond any description I can provide, though the knowledge in animals of the Lord's presence may perhaps be inferred from the Bible's statement that even the raven's young cry out to God for food, or again, that God instructed the ravens to feed Elijah, and furthermore, that God sent his angel to shut the mouths of lions (perhaps by simple command). In short, animals (and perhaps all living creatures) appear to be aware of God in some elementary sense.

The difference in degree of animals' accountability raises the additional question of how *pre-accountable* humans, who may not even know their left hand from their right, would still fit into the *'made in the image of God'* category that is unique to humans. The answer would seem to be thus—that pre-accountable humans, like all humans, are made in the image of God with the future certainty that they will make an eternity-based choice about God's word. Even aborted babies presumably come (immediately?) into a state like that original state of Adam and the unfallen angels prior to Lucifer's rebellion, insofar as being able to exercise choice in a meaningful way. For eternity does not nullify choice. But as for *how* the image of God is present in an infant, when that infant has not yet entered his probationary period of discernment, is difficult to say, though perhaps the answer is that upon conception God recognizes that the person conceived will someday have the capability of making a choice unto eternal liability, even if it that choice occurs after this present earthly life. Again, it is difficult to say. Nevertheless, this image of God is present in persons even upon their conception, and makes humans "of more value than many sparrows," despite at this point the conscience's inactivity (or relative inactivity) within such persons.

[130] It appears that animal discernment takes place apart from any awareness of nakedness, since animals do not know they are naked. Again, note that the serpent was punished for its act in the Garden, which suggests something of accountability. But, arguably, its punishment even then was limited to its life on this earth. A further question is whether they will have life after their life on this present earth. Although I am aware of the key passages used to claim that animals do not experience an afterlife, I am not convinced that the Bible really supports this interpretation. I would, however, grant that they certainly do not have a spirit which is under eternal condemnation (as we would understand that term relevant to unsaved man and fallen angels), or that they need redemption from sin of such eternal consequence. Assuming that animals would not have died if Adam had not sinned, I hold that, because animals die in this life as under the stewardship of Adam, so too has Christ's resurrection arguably made it possible for all creatures to be restored to their former state of physical life according to the general and future restorative plan which God has for all creation. Christ has not yet exercised this right over what He has now *positionally* accomplished by His life, death, and resurrection. Indeed, it would seem of little solace to us believers today who are pet owners, if (granting the future physical immortality of animals) the only animals granted physical immortality are those living at the time when Christ shall vanquish death itself. For of what legitimate anticipation did the *past* creation share, to which Paul alluded, if that old creation waited in vain for the redemption of believers' physical bodies? (see Rom. 8:19-23). The argument that animals do not have eternal spirits, *and that therefore* they cannot experience resurrection, is to me a forced argument, since it assumes, without biblical support, that only created things which have the capacity to obey or disobey unto *eternal* human or angelic consequence (by categorical default, a liability of *persons*) is that category of creatures which can experience a physical, mental, and emotional afterlife. After all, presumably, the animals would have been physically immortal had Adam not sinned. So, while I would contend that animals are under the stewardship of Christ after this present life of theirs, they are nevertheless *not* made in the image of God, and therefore not to be valued at the same level of humans (though even in regards to this *lower* level of value, the righteous man is to regard the life of his beast, i.e., presumably meant here as

that beast that serves him in working the field or the beast that serves him as companion). As for the category of angels, it is true they also have consciences and wills as humans do; but as to this higher realm of beings and their exact nature in regards to the image of God, I am not much prepared to speak.

At any rate, until the believer dies (or is raptured), he carries within himself the knowledge of good and evil which Adam gained by disobedience. As for men who never repent and believe in Christ, it appears that they shall always have the knowledge of good and evil even after death.

[131] "Righteousness" is biblically defined, in terms of pertaining to **pre-Fall** man, as choosing consistently the path of *obedience over time* to the satisfaction of God. A person, to offer an analogy here, may be on the highway toward New York, but if he takes an exit leading south toward Atlantic City **and** travels that road *into* Atlantic City (by analogy, *disobeys*), he will not reach New York. Even so, Adam *desired*, at the first, to commune with God along the road *toward* belief, and trusted God temporarily, but at length he forsook his prior 'consistency' which was short of that consistency which God accounts for true belief. Nowhere in the Bible are Adam or Eve given any moral designation *prior* to the Fall, such as "innocent," "sinless," "righteous," etc. Righteousness is defined, in terms of **post-Fall** man [i.e., the person who has committed wrong unto eternal liability (sinned)] to be the ongoing belief in Christ, who is the man's Substitute for righteousness—a belief which shrinks not back to the point of the perdition of unbelief.

[132] Perhaps someone will object that my introduction of the term 'Adamic *seed* of the knowledge of good and evil' is a *doublethink*, that is, my attempt to say that an infant is born with knowledge, yet not knowledge. Yet while I confess freely that there is mystery about the *Adamic seed*, and how through man it transmits the knowledge of good and evil, it seems to me that this mystery is the approximate same as that of any knowledge at all, such as that seed of knowledge which Cain and Abel would have had as infants, had not their parents ever sinned. In other words, from where comes knowledge, wherein one day an infant or child does not know his right hand from his (footnote cont. on p. 528) (continued from p. 455) left, to knowing his right hand from his left? For presumably this general knowledge would have been the same for infants regardless of whether the Fall had occurred. In other words, *what*, in age progression, happens *ex nihilo* in the person, that he should cause his knowledge to come into being? Perhaps for this reason Calvinists seek a Divine Cause behind a person's every thought and act. That such an approach leads to Monism we have already established, and since the idea of Monism is false, this approach is found wholly unsatisfying to the one attempting (through an honest use of language) to preserve God and man as Creator and creature, respectively.

[133] To reach the age of accountability unto eternal liability, one must be able to decide upon some moral point that God regards as worthy of eternal consequence. And for one to so decide upon some moral point, one must often first deliberate. Presumably, a person sometimes creates thoughts as judgments, though in other cases he may hold other thoughts apart from judgment while he deliberates upon what judgments he shall assign to these thoughts. In the matter

of deciding to take Christ as Savior, one must repent—that is, have a change of mind. This choice by the sinner about whether to repent or not, can only happen with deliberation upon these two options. And one cannot contemplate two things in the same instant, therefore it would seem that deliberation precedes choice, at least in the case of repentance.

[134] Post-Adamic man in his experience simply has nothing to compare to Adam and Eve's pre-Fall experience. The irony for us today is that we can only know about the pre-Fall state of our original parents in a kind of textbook way, unless, perhaps, we have some memory of our pre-accountable period (though even then, this would hardly be equivalent to having the kind of general mental capacity which Adam experienced upon his creation).

But as for the question as to why Adam and Eve would be tempted without the vicarious knowledge that there would be pleasure *in sin*, we have only to see that it was the Devil who provided that vicarious knowledge. One might say, for example, that Adam and Eve had a textbook knowledge about the potential pleasure in eating the forbidden fruit. For Adam and Eve's anticipated pleasure in eating forbidden fruit would have been restricted to the pleasure they had already come to know from eating other fruits. In this sense their textbook (theoretical) knowledge about the potential pleasure in eating the forbidden fruit was experience-based, i.e., on the other fruits they had eaten. (In other words, there was no knowledge of the pleasure in the act of sinning, i.e., in being *selfish*.) Incidentally, this fact of Adam and Eve's pre-Fall, textbook knowledge of sin puts the whole matter of the choice God set before them very simply—i.e., 'cut-and-dried.'

So, there was no reason, before the Devil came along, for Adam and Eve to think that the pleasure possible in eating the forbidden fruit would be any more or less than that which they naturally found in other fruits. But Satan's presentation changed all that (because Adam and Eve allowed it to). For the Devil provided *vicariously* the (by definition, *intensified, higher, etc.*) knowledge about good and evil which Adam and Eve had not yet come to acquire. In fact, the Devil invoked the strategy that has since become the principal, imperative rule of all 'good' advertising—i.e., build desire in the potential consumer by trying to make him think that he's missing something, can 'belong,' can have more power which in turn will bring him more pleasure, etc., all of which, we note, is true in a distorted or temporary sense. Picture a 35-year old father 'enlightening' his 11-year old son about all the possible pleasures in sex—where to buy dirty magazines, where the brothels are, etc.—to get an idea of what I mean. Simply put, such facts for the 11-year old are not helpful to know. It's like a man driving down the highway and seeing a newly erected 'adult' bookstore; i.e., a fact he didn't know prior to seeing the building. Let us say he doesn't go in. Let us even say he has never visited such a bookstore. Alas, he will find the mere presence of the building a distraction anyway. (Of course, in real life all men miss the mark in various areas, if not regarding *this* kind, then of *some other* kind.)

But while we're on the subject of sinful *pleasure*, let me add this—I cannot help thinking that the Devil began his pitch to Eve with a wry, 'knowing laugh' that spoke volumes along with what he actually did say (indeed, laughter always gets peoples' attention):

> "Yeh, (*laugh*) really? Did God say that! [Why, I can just *imagine* that 'ol Bugger trying that trick again. You know, He just wants you to serve him! By the way, let me tell you what you'll gain by eating this fruit—you know, the gain He's not telling you about..."]

At any rate, Eve allowed her natural desire for fruit to be roused in the process of deception, until she desired the forbidden fruit. Sadly, she then chose to act in accordance with this desire. Adam, too, though not deceived, also sinned, following his newly roused desire until he committed a simple act of straight-forward rebellion.

[135] The Bible tells us that man was made lower (in form) than the angels.

[136] The conscience is not the same thing as, nor did it become (or assimilate into itself), the knowledge of good and evil. Certainly, the Fall put the will and the conscience in catastrophic circumstances, but that is a different thing than saying that they are birthed as sin. Paul says in Romans 2:15 that a Gentile's conscience either accused or excused him, and we note that this was the case even though the Gentile was without the Mosaic Law. Had the conscience been corrupted *upon* the Fall, then presumably it would have ceased to properly bear witness to the Gentile; yet the Gentile remained a law unto himself. Thus the conscience must be a good thing. Also, 1 Timothy 4:1-2 says that in the latter days some people would "depart from the faith, giving heed to seducing spirits, and doctrines of devils; speaking lies in hypocrisy; having their conscience seared with a hot iron." Thus from this statement too we may deduce that the conscience itself is a good thing, since the searing of the conscience is described as a bad thing. Again, note that it is the *searing* of the conscience, not the conscience itself, which is the bad thing. That is, if the knowledge of good and evil were merely the conscience fallen; then we would hardly expect Paul to lament over its seared state. Indeed, hypothetically speaking, the searing of a *fallen* (i.e. *totally*, which is to say, *utterly, depraved*) 'conscience' would in that case suggest something good.

[137] The Calvinist, B.B. Warfield, is quoted by Loraine Boettner as stating that God creates the very thoughts and intents of the heart. This is a way of denying that man creates his own thoughts and will. This is Calvinism at its essence, a denial of man's ability to birth his own thoughts and decisions apart from God. This is why Calvinism ends up as spiritual Monism veiled in Evangelical language.

[138] More properly speaking, the Devil also may be represented through the principalities and powers of the air, against whom we wrestle in the Spirit.

[139] A man who, hypothetically, is totally against God, is arguably one who has defiled his conscience to a point where the thoughts he brings into being *ex nihilo* are, in the same instant of their being, also accusations against God.

[140] The term 'sin nature' is itself understood variously by Evangelicals, from being a mere *inclination* to commit sin, to being *de facto* guilt *in Adam*. Generally, the understanding among Evangelicals is toward the latter, as held by Luther and Calvin, i.e., that which this book refutes. It must be noted that some theologians,

such as John Wesley, have attempted to redefine the term 'sin nature' to be something softer in effect than that held by Calvin and Luther. However, this has merely added confusion to the matter. This is because Wesley's hybrid approach is that of the Arminian who in fact holds to the same dialectical definitions as Calvinists (or at least as moderate Calvinists) though with *relatively* more concession to human freedom in their verbal and written statements. We are *relatively* glad; but thus the wry joke: What's the difference between a Calvinist and an Arminian?—Answer: *Blood pressure*. Thus Wesley might appear more congenial, but the 'softer' side of defining original sin still retains its dialectical characteristic. Thus Wesley (below) makes the following statement about sin, in which he claims we are continually 'inclined' to it (thus implying a fallen nature that is not in possession of sin *de facto*), yet also claims (in a preceding clause) that he holds human sin to be "very far gone from original *righteousness*" [(emphasis mine) and thus Wesley implies a fallen nature that is *moral*]. That is, Wesley, while properly understanding that the Pelagians were wrong to think that Adam's sin was merely a bad example which had no effect on his descendents [including an effect on knowledge, much less mortality, as Pelagius (reportedly) believed man was created mortal], fails to avoid the dialectic, since he speaks of inclination but also holds to a 'departure' which was not *merely* of prudent *knowledge*, but of *morality*, i.e., implied in his term, 'original righteousness.' And yet even here Wesley's statement is confusing, for what does he mean by *original* righteousness? For in fact Adam was not created righteous (nor in fact unrighteous) nor obtained righteousness during his probation in the Garden. Nevertheless, Wesley states:

"Original sin standeth not in the following of Adam (as the Pelagians do vainly talk), but it is the corruption of the nature of every man, that naturally is endangered of the offspring of Adam, whereby man is very far gone from original righteousness, and of his own nature inclined to evil, and that continually."

Thus the Arminian, though he holds to dialecticism, may presumably be more readily judged (that is, inferred by his readers/listeners) to be a Christian on the basis that his dialecticism is a more gentle back-and-forth rock than the violent one of the Calvinist, since the Calvinistic apologetic stresses (unwittingly) literary deconstruction* (see two paragraphs down). But a Calvinist who (hypothetically, at least) would be so extreme that he has *never* made any confession (to God) to receive Christ, would be judged by the Scriptures to hold another gospel and therefore is not saved. In the end (besides the Calvinist himself), I suppose only God can know what a Calvinist understands by the terms he uses (though even here the Body presumably may have the mind of the Spirit of Christ regarding the matter). For example, the Westminster Confessions' terms, *God*, and *man* (as these terms relate to their chief statement about the absolute sovereignty of God and the freedom of man) can only be *inferred by the reader* to be meaningless, according to the proper principles of logic and language. Yet, hypothetically, two persons could profess to believe the above Westminster statement, yet one be a Christian while the other not. For example, *Calvinist A* might truly *believe* (as God would judge it) in human freedom because at some level he sufficiently believes and confesses his need of Christ. In short, he understands to sufficient degree both what it means to receive Christ, and believes in Christ. Arguably, confession (according to Scripture) must be made before two or three witnesses for the confession to be established, yet even here one might argue that the Persons of the Trinity would suffice for that condition if the man has understood God's message and earnestly prayed to God to be saved. *Calvinist A*, despite his theology, would thus be truly born again, because, though his heart condemns him in his subsequent and erroneous doctrine about the gospel, and especially about the nature of God, God is greater than his heart, and thus the heart's *condemnation* spoken of must be the kind of *present* judgment in which double-minded Christians find themselves, i.e., a divine judgment which makes the believer subject to chastisement. That said, God knows the believer's *deception* has occurred *subsequent* to his conversion. I say 'deception,' not 'disbelief,' lest someone were to mistakenly infer from my use of 'disbelief' (and despite the context of my preceding argument) the meaning of *permanent* deception and/or confession that would belie his true state as a believer no longer under condemnation with the world for unbelief. Thus God is greater than *Calvinist A's* heart and cannot deny Himself, the Persons of the Godhead being true and bearing witness to each other of the believer's *de facto* salvation, and so *Calvinist A* is *de facto* saved. Whenever in this book I talk of the Calvinist who has made terms *meaningless*, I mean it in the sense of *linguistically meaningless to his hearers*, that is, hearers who cannot really know what is in the heart of the Calvinist. Thus by giving *Calvinist-A* his label as a Calvinist, we are referring to his *present* confession of Calvin's belief in the absolute sovereignty of God which he holds in doublethink.

Let us consider the remaining, and hypothetical, example, i.e., *Calvinist B*, a man who in his heart has *always* held the dialectical statement of the Westminster Confession's statement (see above) *to be true in its dialecticism*. That is, there has never been a time when he understood and confessed his need to God and received Christ as Savior. [I hasten to add that proper confession always involves proper (true) belief. When the Bible states that "Abraham believed God, and it was counted unto him for righteousness," the term 'belief,' used in Romans 4:3 implies, by inclusion, *confession* to God.] Thus, if such a man as *Calvinist B* has not believed unto salvation, that is, according to the most elementary sense in which it is understood that Abraham believed, *Calvinist B* is not saved. The problem, then, for readers and listeners of a Calvinist is this: how can readers/hearers really know exactly what the Calvinist believes in his heart about the theological terms he uses? In other words, does he use his terms as *Calvinist A*, or *Calvinist B*? Is he a wheat or a tare? And if a wheat, does he lately appear as a tare? And if, in any of these cases, he is a leader within a local Body—indeed, even if he is a renowned Church father who has set the course of 'Christian' apologetics for many centuries—what impact will his *confession* have on the clarity of the gospel and doctrine both inside and outside the four walls of the church?

*(from two paragraphs above) One of the problems I have with Wesley's quote is that one wonders exactly what he means by "inclined," "naturally endangered [as Adam's offspring]," "corruption of the nature of every man," etc. While Arminians differ from one another about "racial guilt," by which is meant that all men sin IN Adam, the general belief about what "inclined," etc., means, seems to be answered by the Methodist doctrine of "prevenient garce." "Prevenient" is an older word that simply means "preceding," and the idea here

is that man cannot prepare and turn Himself to God apart from God's preceding grace. Yet I find even this definition confusing, because God has always been graceful upon the world, and so we must ask what *specifically* the Arminian has in view? The answer, *specifically* then, is the will of man. Thus as one Arminian seemed to describe it to me, man is able to reject Christ, while not being "entirely free" in that rejecting, but not free to accept Christ. I find at least two faults with this view. 1) the term "man" becomes too vague to maintain proper individuation. In other words, through subtle language he implied that man's rejection is not all of man. But then, we must ask, what is "man" in the phrase "man rejecting Christ"? Therefore, the thing that becomes lost in the doctrine of prevenient grace is any proper definition of the will of man. For God's role in the will of man is the creation of its *form*, never its *content*. Once we suggest that God has to turn man this way or that way because of man's "depravity," and that this divine activity is more than mere thought-presentation, we are merely "Amen-ing" B.B. Warfield's statement that God creates the very thoughts and intents of the heart," and that man CANNOT come. So, while the Arminian thinks that God "enables" man so that he can choose in either direction, either for or against Christ, I think that "prevenient grace" becomes "irresistible grace" if people only author 'choices' of one thing (i.e., *rejection* of Christ). I suspect the Arminian has convinced himself that God either creates anew or restores(?) the form of man's will to a point where man can make the either/or choice (at least in regard to Christ). But then of course the question remains: What was the will prior to the either/or? Only a 'will' that had a 'choice' of one thing in regard to Christ, and so the will was not a will. Such a definition, if not as perniciously pursued as that Reformed brand by the Calvinist, is still irrational. So, let me offer at least one thing from the Bible to counter this idea of "prevenient grace." It is that *Christ answers the Law*. Let us insist on that. Therefore when one Arminian wrote me to say:

> "So the issue, consequent to the fall, is not so much attaining moral righteousness by way of the law but our response to the offered remedy of our sin, and the surrendering to the reality that we need God, thereby attaining righteousness through Him,"

I answered that the issue is exactly about attaining moral righteousness by way of the law, though in Christ.* Therefore, if a man is eternally liable through his rejection of the law, why would he not also have the will present within him to make choices regarding ALL OF THAT which pertains to the law? And let us note here that Christ does in fact pertain to the law; He answers the law. Indeed, all men (Adam, Christ, et al.) have answered the law, either for or against it, and continue to do so, since their knowledge of law makes relevant both sides of the choice equation. For there is no such thing as a one side choice equation. Either one has knowledge of law and therefore choice, or no knowledge and no choice. Now, readers, granted, neither we nor the heavenly angels, who desire to look into how salvation was accomplished for us, understand exactly how our salvation was accomplished; but again, I think we must insist that if a man has the moral awareness enough to be eternally liable to that which pertains to the

Law, then surely it follows that he must also understand that the law which he chose not to keep could be kept by another person other than himself—that one could satisfy the Law, be him Christ, or someone else (though Christians know that no one else besides Christ will). Of course, the sinner must have simple knowledge about the historical Christ to make a decision about Christ. But that is a matter of knowledge, not "enablement" of the will, which is what Arminians seem to claim. While I would grant the brute fact that God in all cases is the initiator of relationship with us, this does not mean that man, in his nature, is disabled in his will, such that he cannot choose Christ, that is, so long as he has simple knowledge of Christ.. Indeed, I see nothing in Genesis 3 or Romans 5 that would indicate that though man used his choice to separate himself from the Creator, his will was therefore rendered diminished or annihilated in some part. And so, while in one sense we may properly call man's separation from God "the fall," there is another sense in which we must recognize that it was a climb—into a special, inner, exalted, or higher knowledge. For that is the lexical meaning of the Hebrew word "knowledge" in Genesis 3 in the phrase "the knowledge of good and evil." The word is a somewhat different (though derived) word than the more common word used for "knowledge" in the Old Testament. So, nothing in Genesis 3 suggests that man's will was diminished but rather that his knowledge was increased. And moral awareness is according to knowledge, and we know that knowledge is wont to puff up. So, while it is evident that man sins, no act of sinning by man at any time upon any point has ever been inevitable. To state or imply, as I think Arminians are wont to do, of the nature of man as absent the influence necessary for man to have a real choice to choose either for or against Christ, is either to confuse "influence" when they mean "knowledge," OR to define the "influence" which they claim IS present in man in a way not normally understood—to wit, as an influence that cannot be resisted, hence, man's depravity. For note in this latter regard that for Arminians to speak of "influence" that can ONLY lead to "unbelief" (a 'choice' of one thing) is not to speak of something resistible but deterministic in a system where there is no choice at all. So then, such a definition of "influence" as deterministic can only be reached through an ahistorical lexical use of the word, and is therefore special pleading .

[1] Incidentally, this Arminian next replied that he agreed that the issue was exactly this, though he continued to maintain that prevenient grace was needed to accept Christ.

[141] An interesting term, since Adam's sin resulted in him and his descendents obtaining the knowledge of good and evil along with *aging*, i.e., the sign of eventual physical death. It would appear that our possession of the knowledge of good and evil is what accounts for aging (i.e., the kind of aging present in fallen Adam, not pre-fallen Adam).

[142] An ellipsis can be enormously important to observe, and the failure to note its occurrence can have grave ramifications. Calvinist James White, for example, fails to note an ellipsis in John 6:44, and consequently he argues that this verse teaches the doctrine of Irresistibility. Thus he contends that, because the word 'him' in John 6:44 must refer to the same object (since it occurs together in the

same verse, i.e., in John 6:44), this repeated word ('him') proves that God only draws those whom he shall raise [in bodily resurrection unto eternal life] at the last day. It follows, argues White in effect, that because all men are not saved, therefore God must not draw all men, i.e., "No man can come to me, except the Father which has sent me draw him; yet I will raise him up on the last day." [I have put a semicolon, not a colon, between the two main independent clauses, and translated *kai* as *yet*, since arguably the thought is that the Son has committed Himself to the welfare of those whom the Father will successfully draw, though *no man had similarly and diligently* sought God. (Remember, there was no punctuation in the original New Testament autographa. Also, *kai* can take the meaning of *but*, depending on the context). But the reader should note that Christ speaks here by way of an implied ellipsis, assuming that his hearers will understand the point, i.e., that those whom He raises in the last day will obviously be those who *responded* to his drawing. Remember that the word 'can' (Gr. *dunamai*) in John 6:44 means *will*, and that Jesus is merely saying that no man *powers himself to* (i.e., *chooses to*) come to Him "unless the Father draws him..." That is, this is not because the man *theoretically cannot* come, but because he *will* not come (see footnote 50). (Sidenote: not all Greek scholars, e.g. Carl Conrad, accept for verbs like *dunamai* the designation "deponent" verbs. In fact, he says that " "deponent" is about as useless a grammatical term as has ever been invented," and prefers the term "middle-passive" verbs. Keep in mind in the following quote that the "middle-voice" means that the subject's action has at least something of the reflexive component to it, i.e., that man's not coming to the Son is something the man *himself* wills, though, of course, it is true that God upholds the *form* of the man while the man *himself* wills what he will do:

"The terms "deponent" and "deponency" are not useful in a discussion of ancient Greek voice, a fact that has been noted at least since A. T. Robertson's big NT Greek Grammar.... In lieu of the term "deponent" I would suggest that we speak of "middle verbs." I would use this term for verbs whose primary present-tense form is middle-voice; that would include all the verbs that are traditionally or conventionally termed "deponent" but it would also include a sizable number of essentially intransitive verbs that display common middle-voice present-tense forms but also have a transitive active-voice form in the present tense... "[http://artsci.wustl.edu/~cwconrad/])

We have already seen how *dunamai* is a verb capable of one OR more verbal *aspects*, and that depending on the context *dunamai* can exhibit a middle and/or a subjunctive aspect. I think we may grant (based on N.T. usage) that *dunamai* and its negating cognate do at times respectively mean "to be able to" or "not to be able to" apart from what we normally consider is any middle (i.e., self-willed, self-intentional) quality that would account for that ability or inability. For example, Jesus spoke of not fearing those who were *able to* kill the body but not *able to* kill the soul. That is, presumably, these killers did not lack the intention to kill the soul; they simply lacked the sheer (bare) ability of soul-punishment which God has reserved for Himself alone. And yet even here it might be argued that God *could* transfer that power necessary to adjudicate souls to any person He wished, even to the Devil, if He so desired. But then of course God's kingdom would not stand, being divided against its former principles. So, a middle aspect is sometimes [if not frequently or (theoretically) always] present in *dunamai*—at least in the subjunctive sense; but perhaps more to the point here is that the near and far contexts are those things which determine what verbal aspects of a predicate are in play. In the contexts of Acts 17:19 and John 6:44, for example, the subjunctive aspect ("may") pertains to the contingency of potential hearers, though in these instances the hearing relates in turn to a 3rd party's contingency—in the former case that of whether Paul would offer his message to the Athenians, in the latter case whether God would provide the atonement through the Son which pertains to man. Hence we understand Conrad's illustration of the middle (primarily here, subjunctive) quality, in which, though on the one hand a boy is the object of others who baptize him, yet on the other hand he is the one who *himself* willingly undergoes baptism. So, the point here is that the Greek verb *dunamai* essentially acts as the word "can" in INFORMAL English, having capability of one OR more aspects, depending upon the context. And as regards John 6:44, arguably all three verbal aspects of *dunamai* are present: man does not 1) have the sheer ability to effect his atonement (*"cannot* come"); man does not will himself toward the Son apart from the Father's drawing (*"will not* come"); and may not come toward the Son apart from Father's provision of the Manna from heaven (*"may not* come"). Further, note the context of John 6:40: (lit) "And this is the will of the (One) sending Me, that everyone seeing the Son and believing in Him should have life everlasting…" Observe, then, that the person **may** see the Son contingent upon the Father's plan being realized in Christ being lifted up (which did come to pass), and so would have eternal life if he **will** believe.

Now to better understand the *will aspect* of John 6:44, an analogy of the Father's drawing may be helpful here. Suppose, for example, a son said, "Though my Dad is a local baseball team owner, no man will travel with me toward the ballpark unless my Dad woos and pulls him along with the promise of free hot dogs, while also twisting his arm by shaming him about his hitherto failure to support the local economy. Yet I will take him into the player's clubhouse after the game for signatures." Many attempts of persuasion take this form in life, e.g., when someone tries to persuade another toward some specific end. And this is done not merely by pointing out to the other person the personal advantages he can expect to enjoy, but also by appealing strongly to, or even pestering or shaming him about, his sense of duty. Even so does the word *helko* have a latitude of meaning depending on the context, even to the point of where, as Song of Solomon 1:4 demonstrates, it means *to pull along by wooing*. Arguably, John and even Jesus, as evangelists, take the full, varied approach of *helko* in the gospel of John. Thus the Father's *helko* of man may sometimes be of softer admonishments but other times of strong, urgent appeals. When we see in the gospel of John that Jesus Himself embraces both of these approaches, there is no reason why both meanings for *helko* ought not to be understood for John 6:44. Furthermore, the Calvinist argument that *helko* is used for dragging a net, and that therefore the sense of irresistible force must be the interpretation for how the Father drags men to Christ [especially since *helko* is thought by some to be used by John in this way, though, in fact, John never uses it in this way regarding the will], nevertheless fails on at least two accounts: 1) It takes no account of the near context of John 5 and 6 in which the Jews were provided physical food they could have resisted, i.e., food which parallels Christ as the Manna from heaven who may also be resisted, and 2) It ignores the defining (and therefore *lexical*) way *helko* is used elsewhere *in a willful context* in the Septuagint, where to ignore the sense of *helko*'s meaning as *pulling by wooing* would mean that the Shulamite maid is essentially asking to be *forced*. Indeed, in what sense can *helko* mean *to drag* in Solomon 1:4? For it makes no sense for the Shulamite maid to say "Drag me, and we will run after you." Furthermore, though Peter *dragged* (or *pulled along*) (helko) the net of fish ashore, the will of the fish never changed, any more than did the wills of Paul and Silas, though these apostles were dragged from Jason's house; in other words, the will of one is never *irresistibly* dragged into the will of another. It was the *bodies* of Paul and Silas that were pulled or dragged, not their wills. It was the *bodies* of fish that were pulled ashore, not their wills. Thus for the Calvinist to transfer such an application of the dragging of an inanimate fish net to the dragging of persons' wills, is to totally ignore the contextual difference between separate appearances of *helko*. In fact, by the same 'logic,' if one reversed which context was absolutized, one could make an equally absurd argument. For one could say that if God is said to *drag* a man's will to the place that He wants apart from any *physical* involvement, then when Peter is said to have *dragged* the net to shore, the Bible must likewise mean that Peter did *this* apart from any physical involvement! But returning to our baseball analogy, we see how *helko* could operate in John 6:44. In our analogy the father is both wooing (gentlemanly coercing and pulling) and even pestering each person to travel toward the ballpark. He is pulling people *toward* his desired end. Yet many men who are invited will be quite indifferent about baseball, hot dogs, and the local economy. So some will go along, but others will not. In such a circumstance the son might say, "No man will [Gr. *dunamai*, see footnote 50] come toward me to the ballpark unless my Dad woos him with the promise of free hot dogs and pulls him along by shaming him about not supporting the local economy. Yet I will take him into the player's clubhouse after the game for signatures." Now, plainly, nothing in this statement suggests that only those whom the son ultimately takes into the dugout after the ballgame for signatures will also be *only* those whom his Dad tried to persuade with hot dogs and with appeals to responsibility. To understand it in this forced way is to ignore the implied elliptical thought—i.e., the implication that those whom the son took into the dugout after the game are also those *among* whom his Dad wooed/compelled. This would be a normal assumption inferred from such a statement uttered as a manner of speaking. Why, then, as we consider John 6:44, must Jesus' statement be understood otherwise, i.e., simply because God is the grammatical subject of the exceptive clause (and thus taken by the Calvinist to mean that God's *helko is* irresistible), i.e., "except the Father draw him." In other words, I am saying that Jesus is simply granting that His hearers will understand that the one ('him') whom he raises at the last day is also him whom His Father *successfully* persuaded. (For again, by analogy, not everyone in town cares about baseball, hot dogs, or the local economy.) As Jesus said in John 5:39-40: "You search the Scriptures because you think that in them you have eternal life; it is these that testify about Me; yet (*kai*) you are undesirous to come to me so that you might have life." Again, even the context of John 5—6 (leading up to John 6:44), speaks of the many people surrounded by God's grace who failed to give proper heed to their spiritual needs, i.e., those in the Old Testament who received the physical bread provided by the Father (in the wilderness), and those in the New Testament who received bread and fish provided by the Son (in a destitute area). Many such recipients displeased God, because they did not give sufficient attention to their spiritual needs. And such divine displeasure shows that God in fact *had a right to expect* a different response, i.e., because they *could* believe and come to the Son, though they *would* not.

Now, a word here should be said about persons being liable according to their knowledge of the law.

It is generally supposed that the Bible teaches there are sins of ignorance. Various verses in Leviticus 4 (KJV) speak of those who erred through ignorance, yet were guilty. (The NAS translates the idea of doing something *ignorantly* as "unintentionally.") In this general regard note Leviticus 5:17-18 in the KJV:

> [17]And if a soul sin, and commit any of these things which are forbidden to be done by the commandments of the LORD; though he wist it not, yet is he guilty, and shall bear his iniquity. [18] And he shall bring a ram without blemish out of the flock, with thy estimation, for a trespass offering, unto the priest: and the priest shall make an atonement for him concerning his ignorance wherein he erred and wist it not, and it shall be forgiven him.

However, there are at least two reasons why we may say that the Hebrew does not support the idea of sins of ignorance, that is, as we normally understand the term "ignorance." First, while the English word "ignorance" technically means "without knowledge," the Hebrew words used in Leviticus 4 and 5 (Strong's related words #7686 and #7684) mean *to wander (thus to err)*. The idea in Hebrew is that one wanders *inadvertently*. By the word "inadvertently" here, we do not mean sheer *unknowingness* but rather *inattentiveness, unheededness*, and thus, by implication, *carelessness, negligence*, etc. The idea in Hebrew is that, though one has not premeditated to commit some particular sin **per se**, one has, nevertheless, through general carelessness committed a sin because he allowed himself to become distracted at the time. Thus the error has nothing to do with not knowing the Law itself, but of inattentiveness to the Law, i.e., a Law which the man knows. An example of the difference between *inattentive* and *unknowing* can be seen in Josiah. Over time Judah (under Manasseh) grew so inattentive to the Law that Manasseh's grandson, Josiah, was ignorant of various sins of Judah (in the sense of *unknowing*, not *inattentive*). [This is *not* to say that Manasseh was inattentive *per se*, as though the cares of the world slowly drew his attention to a point where he wandered from the Law. Rather, Manasseh's abandonment of the law seems to have been more of zeal that of any inattentiveness, the proof being the extent of Manasseh's sin despite having a godly father (Hezekiah) who ruled prior to his reign and who had led Israel into godly paths.] Another example might be a Jewish man who becomes so pre-occupied with his flocks and herds that he fails to rid his house of yeast before the Passover; thus he *knew* the law, but 'forgot,' i.e., was *inattentive* to it.

But moving on, a different Hebrew word occurs in Deuteronomy 19, which the KJV also translates as "ignorantly." The difference is most significant.

⁴And this is the case of the slayer, which shall flee thither, that he may live: Whoso killeth his neighbour ignorantly, whom he hated not in time past; ⁵As when a man goeth into the wood with his neighbour to hew wood, and his hand fetcheth a stroke with the axe to cut down the tree, and the head slippeth from the helve, and lighteth upon his neighbour, that he die; he shall flee unto one of those cities, and live: ⁶Lest the avenger of the blood pursue the slayer, while his heart is hot, and overtake him, because the way is long, and slay him; whereas he was not worthy of death, inasmuch as he hated him not in time past. (vss. 4-6)

Here, the Hebrew term translated "ignorantly" is different than that found in Leviticus 4—5. The significance is found in the example given in Scripture itself, which defines what is meant by Strong's #1097 (*without* or *lack*) with #1847 (*much* or *especial knowledge*). The idea is that one does not have significant knowledge; in other words, one has an *ignorance about something*. It does not mean that one has been *inattentive*. Indeed, based on Leviticus 4—5, if *inattentiveness* was meant by Strong's #1097 with #1847, then the ax-wielder could not be said **not** to be worthy of death. Observe also that Strong's #1847 is related to #3045, the basic word for knowledge. Tracing the lexical use of #1847 is revealing, and arguably shows that the ax-wielder did not have an especial, or additional, or 'insider's' knowledge about the danger inherent in the ax. Thus the event was an accident and could not realistically have been anticipated because of relative ignorance. An analogy of this would be, say, if a baseball batter swung at a pitch, and the bat broke and flew and hit the pitcher, killing him. Such a terrible accident would not be due to inattentiveness, but to an unknowingness on the batter's part of an inner weakness in the grain of the bat under stress, etc. Even so, the Hebrew word in Deuteronomy is essentially and adequately translated into English as "ignorantly" by the KJV here, since the ax slipped off the handle through relative ignorance, not inattentiveness. However, if, say, the ax-wielder used an ax which he already knew had the tendency to slip off upon every 4th or 5th swing, that would put the matter differently. For in such a case the ax-wielder would have had prior knowledge about the likely danger in using the ax. Thus if he used the ax and the ax-head flew off and killed someone, presumably he would be judged liable (or in some way liable) as under the same general principle of law which said that an owner was liable for a goring ox, when such an ox had gored someone in the past but the owner had not destroyed it. Finally, lest someone think that Leviticus 5:17 speaks of someone being guilty "and wist it not," the next verse demonstrates that the "wisting it not" (not knowing it) is understood in the context of *inattentiveness* (Strong's #7684), not *basic ignorance*.

Under these considerations, then, it does not appear that the Hebrew supports the idea that man is guilty even when he does not know the Law. Or to put the matter simply, it does not appear that there are sins of unknowing ignorance.

---

[143] i.e. 'on the grounds of the fact *that*,' ('that' being the neuter relative pronoun for 'on the grounds of the fact')

[144] Gr. *Epi ho* [technically here, *EF' hWi*, KJV '*for that*' (in the phrase 'for that all have sinned')] appears to have the meaning of 'since,' that is, in the sense of drawing the reader's attention more upon the *evidentiary* (that is, *obvious*) nature of the statement being made, rather than upon any *argumentative* inflection that might have been implied had Paul used a more common form of 'because.' This fact explains the apparent definition for *epi ho* which M.R. Vincent gives in his *Word Studies in the New Testament*—'on the grounds of the fact that.' In other words, *epi ho* points to the fact that the matter should be self-evident. Thus 'since' is a desirable translation, for 'since' is a form of 'because' but viewed as more obviously so (i.e., *inasmuch*). Paul, not having in mind any such thing as a doctrine of original sin, is simply making an evidential statement about how post-Adamic men came into condemnation. We ought not to expect, then, that Paul's posture of speech should stem from the kind of confrontational apologetics that one might think ought to be present if Paul were really refuting the idea of original sin. Simply put, it was never Paul's intent to do so, because it was not an issue at the time of his writing. Though Paul, in his epistles to churches, often did use an admonishing tone of (obviously, if admonitory) *argumentative* forms of 'because,' i.e., like the more common forms of 'because,' it is evident he did not do so here in verse 12. That it was never in the apostle's mind to make a refutation *per se* against the doctrine of original sin shows how self evident he assumed the matter of sin's spread (into the world) would be in his readers' minds (and in fact an assumption quite supported by the contemporary Greco-Roman concept of personal guilt, which had little or nothing to do with ancestral transference). Indeed, though other early Church fathers commented on Romans 5, none of them held to the bizarre doctrine that Augustine would state in the 4th century and which would come to have such dogmatic sway upon so many subsequent Church councils and so much thought. Personally, it seems to me that the phrase *kai outws*, which means, *also in this manner*, makes relatively plain that death traversed into the world *in a manner like* Adam's—not *in Adam*, the latter being a different concept—and thus this makes the argument about *epi ho* essentially mute, especially given, as already noted, that the position of *epi ho* introduces a subordinate clause coming *after* the 2nd part of the correlative conjunction, and therefore can hardly be thought to refer to something *prior* to the 2nd part of the correlative conjunction.

[145] The Greek word means *traverse*.

[146] Though the phrase '**in** Adam' is found in 1 Corinthians 15:22, where it refers to every man's *physical* death as a consequence originating **in** Adam, the phrase "in Adam" in nowhere found in Romans 5:12-21.

[147] Jay P. Green, Sr. (editor). *Pocket Interlinear New Testament*. (Grand Rapids, Michigan: Baker Book House, 1986), p. 365.

[148] Luke's use, however, does have a limitation for our purposes, for *epi ho* is not used in his case to introduce a subordinate clause, as it (*epi ho*) functions in Romans 5:12, where there it comes **after** the 2nd part of a correlative conjunction. This is a grave problem for supporters of original sin. Thus in Luke

the *epi ho* may likely point backward to more than a mere concrete noun, such as Christ's command. (See footnote 189 re: Carl Conrad).

[149] Of course, based on this exposition, I am using this term differently than generally accepted.

[150] At least one reason Christ was not subject to the Adamic curse is because Christ created Adam and thus preceded him (and was therefore not Adam's descendent according to technical definition). Also, Christ Himself is exonerated as the command-Giver of Genesis 2:16-17, and, further, He was never a command-*breaker*. Finally, Christ was not incarnated with the knowledge of good and evil, which in history has come through the male Adamic line. Rather, Christ bypassed the knowledge of good and evil by His virgin birth, a mysterious process in which the Holy Spirit overshadowed Mary.

[151] It appears that an infant, once he matures to a certain point, reaches a first level of accountability like animals (though he is not an animal as such, for he is made in the image of God) and is thus at first liable unto temporality (i.e., during his earthly life) but not liable unto eternity. At some subsequent point he matures to where he enters a second, or probationary, period in which his actions are liable unto eternal consequences. This we may call a person's entrance into his period of accountability. It would appear that an animal's choices are subject to this first kind of accountability (which, again, regarding its consequences, are temporal and presumably limited to this earthly life). The serpent-animal in the Fall narrative, which allowed the Devil the use of itself (it is unclear about the serpent-animal's *mate*), was sympathetic to the Devil's belief that God was selfish for wanting to keep the knowledge of good and evil away from man. Thus the serpent-animal had deliberated upon the objective knowledge that God was good, and the serpent-animal had denied it. Yet, presumably, the serpent-animal's punishment is limited to its present life on this earth, since God says nothing to it about the kind of spiritual death which God had told Adam would be the consequence of his (Adam's) disobedience. Again, presumably, this is because the serpent-animal did not act from the same kind of in-depth base of knowledge possessed by the Devil or even by the lower form, Adam, in the latter's pre-fallen state. But the point here is that human infants, as they initially mature, may at first demonstrate a kind of disobedience which is classed with that of the animals, i.e., a disobedience that is not unto eternal liability. The apparent proof of this limited kind of liability is that such disobedience has not made the maturing infant aware of his nakedness, i.e., an awareness which would be the telltale sign of his having experienced spiritual death, even as it (an awareness of nakedness) served that telltale sign for Adam and Eve.

Arguably, the serpent-animal might not have chosen what it did, had not Satan been present. And arguably one-third of the angelic host might also not have rebelled against God, had it not been for Satan. There is culpability upon all—yes. But whether these other angels besides the Devil would have sinned, that is, apart from Satan's influence, remains a question. Thus, while we do recognize that fallen angels *are* liable unto eternity for their rebellion (the Bible states that they will spend eternity in hell) we ought not to necessarily assume that animals will be subject in a future life to the kind of judgment they experience now, that is, if in fact they do have a future life (and, of course, I presume that they do for reasons already stated). At the least (and apart from the question about whether animals will be resurrected), we know that *certain* animals (e.g., the lion who lays down with the lamb) will not behave as he does now. Whether *all* animals (including the serpent-animal) will 'lay down with the lamb' is perhaps finally a question outside our ability to know, though I would hope that even this shall be the case.

[152] It appears that reaching the age of accountability also begins a person's probationary period unto eternal liability (the hypothetical length of which is ?). Furthermore, under Israel's theocracy it appears that one became accountable for different things at different times (an example follows shortly), though any breach of any level of eternal accountability presumably made the person liable unto eternity before God. This raises the question whether every level of accountability for humans is of a liability unto eternity and therefore never like the temporal accountability of animals. Again, perhaps one could argue that in very young children, the severely retarded, etc., there may be an accountability that is similar to animals, that is, a level of liability short of eternal consequence. This might explain, for example, how toddlers, presumably unaware of their nakedness, might be disobedient to their parents without necessarily being guilty before God for all eternity, or, if their motive was 100% instinct for their just survival, then without any guilt whatsoever.

Moving on, let us consider some examples which, when taken together, suggest different levels of accountability. First, many children of Israel did not die in the wilderness during the Israeli rebellion at Kadeshbarnea, because they were under the age of 20. Yet obviously at the time God judged the Israelis at Kadeshbarnea, there had been Israeli teenagers of, say, 15 years old who knew their left hand from their right hand during the time of the plagues of Egypt— knew they were naked—and were thus discerning persons unto eternal liability. Yet they were not included in the judgment of Kadeshbarnea. So the further question is this: were these younger teenagers free of accountability in all areas of their life until coming to a single instant, whereupon they became accountable for *all* areas in their life? The answer appears negative as regards this present life. For observe that one of the reasons given under the Mosaic Law regarding the capital punishment by parents against a rebellious child, is that the child had demonstrated *over time* a refusal to accept discipline. Thus the child was subject to (liable unto) *corporeal* punishment in his early years, yet ultimately subject to (liable unto) *capital* punishment if he had demonstrated a lengthy rebellion (presumably for many years). This difference in punishment would indicate that there are different levels of accountability to which God judges the person, again, at least in regards to this earthly life. God is patient with all men in this earthly life, so that some vessels will respond to His mercy. However, it would appear that this does not negate any person's eternal liability who is aware of his nakedness.

[153] That is, man commits sin *ex nihilio* (by which I mean '*out of nothing*,' or better stated (lest it be thought that I support the view that sin is privative and non-ontological) '*by his own power apart from prior cause*.'

[154] In contrast to the *seed* of the knowledge of good and evil, or, on the other hand, the *matured* knowledge of good and evil.

[155] We mean by 'influence' the normal sense and definition of the word, i.e., as an influence that is resistible, i.e., suggestion which may or may not prove successful upon its object.

[156] Paul's use of the term (lit. Greek) "the many" in Romans 5:15 is suggestive. The verse reads:

> "But not as the offence, so also is the free gift. For if through the offence of one the many be dead, much more the grace of God, and the gift by grace, which is by one man, Jesus Christ, hath abounded unto the many."

The Calvinist employs the hermeneutic of taking "the many" to mean those saved by limited atonement. Thus they claim that Paul is speaking of a subset of 'all,' i.e., 'the many,' ('the elect,') and that Paul is no longer speaking of the experience of 'all' but merely of the experience of 'the elect.' This places all elected persons first as fallen *irresistibly* in Adam, then saved *irresistibly* in Christ. This imposition upon the text, along with the assumption that unsaved man is nowhere equated in definition to be 'the many' in Romans 5, is the kind of forced, eisegetical *consistency* that the Calvinist must impose from outside the biblical text in order to make terms consistently agree with his theology. Verse 18a for example, which begins with the important (Int.) "So then," which announces the summarization of what has just been said, is an ellipsis of verse 12's correlative conjunction, and, when taken with 18b, serves as a *less abbreviated* ellipsis than verse 15b and 15c [an ellipsis, we say, because of Gr. *ws* (*like*) which implies the '*also*' aspect of post-Adamic man's *similar* performance in committing sin as had Adam]. Verse 18a and 18b also recapitulates verse 15b and 15c, thus showing the 'all' in 18b, to be a synonym (if of less implied description) than "the many" of 15c (i.e., all *accountable* persons). For one can hardly read 15b and 15c with 18a and 18b and not be struck with the natural conclusion that Paul is referring to the same persons. Needless to say, the inevitable result in Calvinist theology for the "all" is the complete annihilation of post-Adamic man's will. Further, such an interpretation does nothing to solve the problem of evil, as the dilemma is merely pushed backward a step to Adam. But the main point here is this: *Such a Calvinist position, while it fails* 1) along with every main English translation to recognize the correlative conjunction in Romans 5:12 (with its implication of the individual's *ex nihilo* culpability), and 2) to understand the limitations of reference for *epi ho* whenever that neuter relative pronoun introduces a subordinate clause, *also shows what happens when a term must be defined by Calvinists according to Calvinistic principles*—i.e., the term is defined *irrationally* (so that Adam can be claimed to have chosen our choices to be sinners).

Again, however, the correct view is wholly different than the Calvinist one. It recognizes 'the many' not as a subset of 'all,' *but a term of more specific meaning*, i.e., all *accountable* persons. (Indeed, Christ referred to *those called out from among all* as "the few," not "the many." Of what whole, then, does the Calvinist suppose the elect, i.e., "the many" are a majority?!) This is not to say that Paul was going out of his way to reprove a doctrine of original sin. Indeed, there is no reason Paul would have done so, since no such doctrine then existed among believers (as the early church Fathers prior to Augustine bear witness, some of whom wrote on Romans 5). Thus Paul simply chose language that was in keeping with his natural understanding of his subject, while the Spirit, in His inimitable way, and according to His foreknowledge, appears to have inspired Paul's language so that it would express fuller meaning to us *as argument* than it ever did to the apostle. This recovery of the definition of 'the many' means that blameless persons under the age of accountability are not under condemnation. Nor is the blood of Christ an atonement for them, as for persons for whom atonement is unnecessary. In passing, observe that in this matter of the unnecessary atonement of the *not many*, the Levitical burnt offering for a mother, having birthed a son or daughter, was an offering of atonement *for her*, not *for her baby*, implying the moral indeterminacy of the newborn as a pre-accountable person.

[157] Evangelical theologian Norman Geisler would disagree with this statement, but we will address his objections later in this chapter.

[158] Note again that, though Christ is called the second Adam in Romans 5, this describes His *office* as an unfallen man. Again, Christ is eternally existent and therefore precedes Adam and also supersedes him. (Thus Christ Himself is not subject to the consequence of Adam's fall, and thus He had to voluntarily give up His life in order to die.) Further, since Christ is called the Second Adam, we may assume that Pelagius (contemporary of Augustine) who was right to reject Augustine's doctrine of original sin, was nevertheless incorrect to hold to the idea that every man who is born is born as Adam was at the first, i.e., with *nothing* inherited that would have *affected* his freedom. For otherwise Cain and Abel would presumably have been the 2nd and 3rd Adams, and so forth. Further evidence against Pelagisus's conclusion is that Seth was made in the image of Adam, i.e., not made merely in the image of God, which suggests that Seth inherited something *additional* from Adam, though it was not something which annihilated his freedom. Thus Seth *de facto*, and in type (i.e., man since the Fall), was *affected* in his freedom, not *disabled*.

[159] The exact accountable state of those who die on earth before entering the age of accountability (aborted babies, for example) raises the question of whether these persons ever come into choice unto eternal liability. I think they must (as made in the image of God), perhaps immediately, but if not, certainly *eventually*, and presumably apart from Satanic influence, as we know from Christ's statement in Matthew that the welfare of little children is the charge of angels, and perhaps thus we may assume that they too are with God in heaven poised with choice like the angels themselves, though they are human.

[160] As a *de facto* statement, Galatians 2:6 tells us that "by the works of the law shall no flesh be justified." Presumably, here the term 'flesh' means that state in which a person has already sinned (or not yet completed his probationary period) and has the matured form of the knowledge of good and evil. Thus no such person may atone for his own sin through works of the law. No man besides Christ has

ever accomplished (or shall ever accomplish) the period of accountability unto justification.

[161] Again, in this context, we should not speak of Adam's pre-Fall actions as sufficient over time to have satisfied God's requirement for righteousness. Technically, we should not speak of Adam's "sinlessness," prior to the Fall, for he was merely on the path *toward* righteousness, i.e., a righteousness whose destination he never reached. God requires a consistency of belief unto His satisfaction, and Adam chose to miss that mark through disobedience.

[162] A person's moral choices unto eternal liability always take place in a context of understanding right and wrong; if that were not the case, that person could not be guilty unto eternal liability. This is why Paul says, "I was once alive apart from the Law; but when the commandment came, sin became alive and I died." Apart from the Law (i.e., apart from a person acting in a context of his conscience or divine law, in which his understanding has matured enough to have made him subject unto eternal liability) there is no sin unto eternal liability. Put another way, one does not simply make *bare* choices. For the person in *probation* [i.e., *testing unto a moral state*], or post-probation, there is always the context of understanding, at least while understanding is present (God being the Judge of such matters as persons with Alzheimer's, or in sleep, etc.). The failure to understand that freedom of the will is not simply the exercise of bare choices but takes place in the contexts of understanding and eternal liability has led some Calvinists to make confusing statements. For example, Calvinist and Baptist seminary professor, Bruce Ware, [http:www.youtube.com/watch?v=DeHjQHMWp1M] stated before an audience:

"Freedom is understood as this: 'An action is free, if, when that action is performed, all things being just what they are, the agent could have done otherwise.'... Well, here's the problem with this, and that is, when an action is performed, then there is no reason that is *choice specific—action specific*, for what that particular choice, why that particular action, *was done*. And so, if you ask the question: 'Why did you pull the trigger so a murder is committed. Why did you pull the trigger?' Well, any reason you give for why the trigger is pulled or any set of reasons for why the trigger is pulled, is the **identical** reason or set of reasons for why, if you hadn't pulled the trigger, you *didn't* pull the trigger. So how is that an explanation for how an action is performed? This will *not* hold up in a court of law. People look for *motives*. They look for the reason why actions are performed. So just to go on record here, don't think the compatibilist view is the only one that faces philosophical difficulties. The libertarian view faces an *enormous* problem of being reducible to arbitrary choice."

Observe, then, in the above statement by Ware, that libertarian will is treated as making *bare* choices. Ware is claiming that there is no *moral necessity* in the Arminian view [i.e., a view which he mistakenly thinks embraces libertarian will (an assumption which we will nevertheless allow for the moment for the sake of argument here)]. Thus, according to Ware, the will, if it were truly free, would have the identical reason for *committing* murder as it would for *not* committing murder.

The problem with Ware's view, however, is that the apostle Paul makes clear that a person can only exercise the will unto eternal liability if he understands the Law. In Ware's example, the subject of murder is obviously a sin unto eternal liability. But we should note that the reason one is eternally liable for murder is because the law/Law against murder is known by the perpetrator. To put the matter another way, the Bible teaches that complete ignorance of the law IS excuse in terms of eternal liability. This is why Paul goes to such lengths in Romans 1 and 2 to show that men were a law unto themselves and therefore not excusable. Thus a person who is under eternal liability for his actions knows what he *ought* to do before deciding whether or not he will commit e.g., murder. If he chooses, according to his conscience, not to commit murder because he *agrees* with the law/Law, then his *conscience* (proper reason, i.e., the understanding of right and wrong and the acknowledgement of the reality that a man is subject to God's punishment if he commits wrong, including murder) agrees with the *Law* [proper reason as defined by God as the understanding of what was, is, and shall be, real, including God's laws and their consequences, or, conversely, (where man's repentance is in view), divine grace], and thus we see that the conscience and the Law are two reasons why the man should not commit murder. And of course such reasons as these for *not* committing murder are not, as Ware claims, the same reason or reasons why one should choose *to* commit murder, since in this latter case (i.e., to commit murder) one *disagrees* with what he knows he ought to do. And so the reasons for pulling the trigger or not pulling the trigger are in fact exactly opposite to, not identical with, each other. In short, Ware is wrong for one reason—because he fails to note that by the law is the knowledge of sin.

Further, Ware's identification of the will with *performing* that will creates further confusion when motive is in view. (If Ware did make this distinction in his speech, it did not make the youtube video.) For example, suppose a person fighting in and for a just war is captured by the enemy who plans to kill him after first torturing him. Are the captors really not guilty of murder until they commit the *performance* of it? This brings us to an essential distinction which Ware fails to note, i.e., that the will, properly defined, is *intention, and/or the intention*, to perform an act, not merely the performance of the act. Thus those captors who intend to kill the just man are already guilty of murder. (This explains why Christ stated that some men are guilty of adultery even though they had not technically participated in the physical act.) But the general point here is this: a person who intends *not* to commit murder, acts accordingly because he understands *and agrees* with God that murder is wrong. It's that simple. Are you surprised that such an obvious answer—that ignorance of the law IS excuse, and that knowledge of the law is NO excuse—could escape the mind of the professing Evangelical theologian and academician? Don't be. Calvinists refuse to recognize that the finger they point at the 'enormous problem' of 'arbitrary choice' which they claim is an Arminian problem for having proposed that man exists in libertarian freedom, merely points three fingers back to the 'enormous difficulty' of proposing arbitrary choice to an absolutely free and sovereign God who elects some and damns others for the *identical* reason, i.e., that of His pleasure in *bare* choice. Here we recall A.W. Pink's view that God damns some according to His "sovereign" choice which operates apart from any consideration of "justice" or "injustice." (**See latter part of Footnote 142**, explaining further why ignorance of the Law IS excuse, and the real meaning of "ignorance" in Lev. 5:17-18.) In other words, Ware's description of man's libertarian Choice, existing in the vacuum of distinction, was a foregone conclusion for him as an alleged believer in a Sovereign Decreer of good and bad, i.e., since a Sovereign God must choose all the choices of men and their actions, some of which actions are indeed evil. Ware's accusation of man thus ought to be the same accusation he brings against God, but of course he 'escapes' this charge by appealing (we presume his response), as indeed he must as a Calvinist, to the classic Calvinist *pro Deo/ ad hominem* argument. Thus for Ware man is wrong in his 'bare' choice because he is man, but God is justified in his 'bare' choice because he is God. We are tempted to turn Ware's questions back upon himself. How does his *ad hominem/ pro Deo* presumption hold up in court? How does such an 'explanation' exonerate God's motive? Using such *sophistry* (we have a duty to call Ware's philosophy what it is), professors like Ware have helped to influence Southern Baptist seminary students until now 30% of the graduates from the combined (six) Southern Baptist seminaries identify themselves as Reformed in their theology, even though only 10% of active pastors in Southern Baptist churches identify themselves likewise. If the next generation sees the proportional difference triple again, it seems clear that Calvinism will become a *very* major issue in upcoming Southern Baptist conventions before long. Currently, there are two Calvinist presidents among the six Southern Baptist seminary presidents.

[163] Again (and not to weary the reader upon this point), this compelling nature of the knowledge of good and evil appears to be passed through the male seed, and this is why Christ needed to be born of a virgin. To truly have been the second Adam, Christ needed to have begun His life apart from the knowledge of good and evil, even as Adam had begun *his* life. Furthermore, to have the same experience of choice that Adam had, Christ had to empty Himself of His divine knowledge of good and evil which He naturally had as a Person within the Triune God. I believe this is part of the meaning in Philippians 2:7, when it tells us that Christ emptied Himself (of some of the privileges of His Divinity, though of course not of Divinity itself). Further, if Christ was truly the second Adam, then He too would have been unaware of His nakedness, even as Adam and Eve had been unaware of their own nakedness prior to the Fall. It is interesting to note that Christ never made a statement indicating that He was aware of His nakedness. Of course, He clothed himself for the sake of others, but note that the nature of the Messianic statement in Psalm 22, in which the Messiah Himself describes His unclothed self on the cross, is not really a statement about nakedness ("I can count all my bones. They look, they stare at me") but about His unclothed state as He saw and understood it as an unfallen man.

[164] One question that is often raised in favor of the doctrine of original sin is this: Wouldn't someone in all of human history besides Christ be likely to live a sinless life if all humans are not born with a sin nature but merely with the seed of the knowledge of good and evil? Yet to this I would answer that it seems more incredulous to me to grant the doctrine of original sin; for under such a doctrine God declares post-Adamic man guilty in moral matters in which man

has no more ability to choose than in the choosing of the color of his skin. But to answer the question directly, the problem here is that the knowledge of good and evil (in the matured person) is assigned too little intensity, and not at all appreciably understood for its vast influence upon the will. Doubtless, this state makes it impossible for us to fully know what it was really like for Adam to have chosen evil during a probationary period in which, during the course of his deliberation, he did **not** have the (especial) knowledge of good and evil. Basically, post-Adamic man simply has nothing with which to compare Adam's experience. But further, in practice it appears that not even ***one*** Christian among the many who live in this world to any extent has lived a spotless, unblemished, sinless life, though hypothetically the Bible tells us that ***every*** Christian has *de facto* had the power to do so. But should we conclude, because none so live, that so much contrary behavior is proof against the hypothetical? No, not at all. Then neither should we argue that because no flesh *shall* be justified, that it thus follows that no flesh *could* have been. In short, regarding all these matters, we must simply accept the Bible's statements.

[165] The question might be asked why it is important **not** to believe in original sin. The short answer is, because it is not true! A further point is that it leads to incorrect assumptions about the permeable boundaries between one person's being and another's. The matter is important, for at the heart of Christian theology there must be a true understanding of the nature of God and the nature of man. Moreover, if (as Calvinists contend) we each have sinned in Adam such that Adam chose our choice without having chosen our choice, it seems then but a small step to also say that God can choose man's choice without God choosing man's choice.

[166] Technically, the "just as" does not begin the verse. Rather, the first word in Romans 5:12 is "Wherefore" (Gr. transliteration, "Because of this") with the "just as" following immediately afterward.

[167] Even in the phrase, "Bill's jacket is *exactly like* Susan's jacket," there is still the difference of personal ownership. Otherwise the phrase 'exactly like' could not be used.

[168] The details of the first part of the correlative conjunction show this to be a natural conclusion, for observe that the first part includes sin's entrance into the world, and thus, naturally, something more should be stated about worldly effect in the second part of the correlative conjunction. Thus the phrase 'and death by sin' is used by Paul semi-parenthetically in verse 12 as a transition shifting the grammatical subject from sin to sin's effect (death), i.e., from the first part of the correlative conjunction to the second part of the correlative conjunction.

[169] Indeed, in the margin translation Green in fact renders hosper as "Even as".

[170] In English, 'as' also often substitutes for 'to be.'

[171] It would appear impossible that Paul's use of the neuter relative pronoun 'since' [on the (evidential) grounds of the fact that] could refer to any concrete noun in the first part of a correlative conjunction, since epi ho introduces a subordinate clause that comes after the <u>second</u> part of the correlative conjunction. The

natural meaning would therefore be to take either 1) the immediate preceding noun "death," which we cannot use since the Bible does not teach that death effects sin, or 2) to take the rest of the subordinate clause which <u>follows</u> epi ho, which in fact provides the natural meaning, i.e., 'on the (evidential, i.e., obvious) grounds of the fact that all have sinned.' Moreover, if Paul was using epi ho to refer to something in the first part of the correlative conjunction in order to say that we sinned in Adam, then why would Paul have stated in verse 12 that man sinned in a manner <u>like</u> Adam, and then clarify in verses 13ff what minority sense (of meaning) man sinned in a manner <u>unlike</u> Adam? Such definitions ought to exclude any interpretation that we sinned <u>in</u> Adam.

[172] By the use of 'as' in this sentence, I do not mean anything of an atoning nature but merely of the cessation of one's physical life.

[173] In endnote lxiv, showing the discussion between Ross and Conrad, we also include a brief exchange between Conrad and Steve LoVullo which occurred nearly two years later, in which the latter appears to agree with Conrad's conclusions regarding Ef hWi.

[174] (only a fraction of which I quote in this book)

[175] It should be remembered that God's provision of the free gift of salvation does not equal its automatic reception by man.

[176] Green, Jay P. (editor). *Pocket Interlinear New Testament*. (Grand Rapids, Michigan: Baker Book House, 1986). p. 365

[177] Verse 16 seems to slow down the momentum of Paul's argument just enough to allow Paul to remind his Roman readers of what should be obvious to them by this point in his book—that the free gift (of Jesus Christ) was not as Adam's contribution (which led to condemnation), but one leading to justification. Perhaps even wry irony is suggested here, i.e., that the gift of Christ to the race was not like the 'gift' ['*one*' (i.e., *of contribution*)] which Adam gave, i.e. a 'gift' that consisted of his going into the condemnation which would produce a flesh of weakness in all men. Some gift! Furthermore, the same preposition (eis) is used of the offense of Adam leading *to* [or *into*, (Gr. eis)] condemnation as that used of Christ's work leading *to* [or *into*, (Gr. eis)] justification. The point is an abstract one not to be over-literalized but to be understood in a context of human freedom and response. Geisler's claim, based on the traditional 'original sin' interpretation of verse 12—i.e., that "no such qualifying terms like *receive* (v. 17) are used of the consequences of Adam's sin, even though these terms are used in reference to the appropriation of the gift of salvation that Christ provided for all"—fails to consider that Paul is *continuing* his comparison through *all* of verse 15, as will be shown by our argument in the main text. Admittedly, sometimes commentators have forced upon the *betimes* hop-scotch, digressive, and intuitive way of Paul's thinking a template of strict, sequential argument that does not always exist (at least in some cases) and which threatens proper exegesis when such is inferred by readers. While the goal of systematizing theology may be a good one, it should be noted that the Bible, as a whole, hardly expounds its truths in so convenient a fashion, and this observation is perhaps more evident

in Paul's writings than in the writings of any other biblical author outside the poetic works. Furthermore, it does not seem to me that systematic theology has taken into sufficient account the multi-layered meanings of certain biblical passages.

[178] *kai outws* (Note to the reader: the Greek "w" is pronounced as "o" in English) is fairly straightforward in its interpretation, and means *also in this manner*. Or one may reverse the order of words for conventional English, i.e., *in this manner also*. (Even the phrase "in this manner" has an 'also' aspect to it, since it refers to some characteristic it shares with the thing with which it is being compared. Thus when *hosper* is used in conjunction with either *kai outws* or *outws kai* there is always a correlative conjunction present and a comparison being made, such that the things being compared to each other are **alike** in some general sense, yet **unlike** in some particular sense.

There are several ways *hosper* is used in its 39 appearances in Scripture. Sometimes it is used without the *kai outws* or *outws kai*, though the general thought of *also* in either of these phrases is always evident. For example, when a statement or imperative command is present, such as "Therefore be ye perfect, *just as* (Gr. *hosper*) your Father in heaven is perfect," the implication is that the believer is to be just like his Father *also*, i.e., in being perfect; other times *hosper* is used merely with *outws*, stressing the *similarity of manner* aspect, and at other times with either the phrase *kai outws* or *outws kai*. Perhaps it is a failure of my own personal study that I have not discovered any commentary on what some nuance of difference might be implied between the word order of *kai outws* and *outws kai*. At any rate, my own conclusion is that the first word in the phrase *kai outws* or in the phrase *outws kai* is the one intended by the author to be emphasized. It is rather difficult to make this argument from any one verse alone, though I believe it is more obviously the case in at least one verse, that of John 5:21, in which the issue of Jesus' equality (v. 19) would suggest that some nuance of emphasis in the phrase *kai outws* is on the *kai* (*also*), rather than on the *outws* (*in this manner*), i.e., on the fact that the Son shall give life unto the dead ALSO in the manner of the Father, rather than the fact that the Son shall give life unto the dead IN THE MANNER also of the Father. This relative emphasis on *also* instead of *in this manner* is reversed, for example, when Christ tells His disciples that they are not to pray IN THE MANNER also (*outws kai*) of the heathen, who vainly think that by repetition they shall be heard. Further, while Gr. *outws* (*in this manner*) is sometimes translated 'thus,' or 'so,' I disagree with the idea that *outws* [KJV 'so,' or 'thus' (as in *therefore*)] is properly inferred from the text to mean something causative in the way these two words 'so' and 'thus' are often taken to mean in English. Rather, *outws* merely means 'in this manner' and occurs in comparative contexts to show in *what* manner something is *like*. Therefore *outws* [*in this manner*] always acts as a referent pointing the reader's attention to a comparison in the immediate or very near context. In this sense *outws* (meaning *in this manner*) also carries with it an aspect of *besides* (i.e., *also*), and this fact explains why the two words *kai* and *outws* in certain comparative contexts might naturally occur together. Therefore the *kai outws* (*also in this manner*) should never be taken to mean an inexorable *therefore*, i.e., in a causative sense. Of further note is that *outws*, when it appears alone (without *kai*), is nevertheless always used in comparative contexts because of the 'also' aspect implicit in the word. It appears that Calvinist apologetics has not yet reached the point where our argument here about *ws* and *hosper* is sufficiently known to compel a response. If it does become known, I would expect Calvinists to rewrite the lexical history of *ws, hosper, kai outws, outws kai*, and any other word or terms that threaten their dialectical paradigm, and thus claim a wider latitude of definition, so that these terms include the implicit meaning of a <u>divine "therefore."</u> This is simply a method by Calvinists to ensure that the pantheistic quality of Calvinism is preserved. In this view *man is held to be a manifestation of the Divine, nothing more* (one recalls Warfield's statement that God creates the very thoughts and intents of the heart). This is Spinoza's man, which was held to be the finite (change) that emerges from out of the Infinite (one impersonal, unchanging Substance) and going back into it. Further, I would expect Calvinists to continue the yin and the yang of the forward and backward rocks of their dialectical rocking-horse theology, justifying the One of pantheism on the one hand, while insisting on Individuation and Creator versus creation distinctions on the other hand.

But to return to our subject, examples of the somewhat infrequent term *kai outws* are sprinkled throughout the New Testament (Lk. 24:46, Acts 17:33, Acts 27:44, Acts 28:14, Rom. 5:12 Rom. 11:26, 1 Cor. 7:17, 1 Cor. 7:36, 1 Cor. 11:28, 1 Cor. 15:11, Gal. 6:2, 1 Thes. 4:17, Heb. 6:9, and Heb. 8:15). The *also* aspect of *kai outws* is fairly apparent in most of these examples. Romans 11:26 is typical, in which the phrase "And so all Israel shall be saved" is in the context of the Gentiles being grafted in. This grafting will ultimately make Israel jealous, and so the Jews *also* [i.e. in addition to the Gentiles] *in this manner* [of desire] shall be saved. Another example typical of most examples is Galatians 6:2: "Bear ye one another's burdens, and so fulfill the law of Christ." Here the word *so* does not mean *therefore* but rather *also* [you] *in this manner* fulfill the law of Christ. Conventional English actually compels a reversal of word order here, "Bear ye one another's burdens; in this manner *also* fulfill the law of Christ." The reference is to either Christ Himself (as implied in the one authorizing His law) to whom we should *also in this manner* emulate, or, to two verses earlier, in which Paul states that the Galatians should not merely live in the Spirit *de facto*, but also *walk* in the Spirit, i.e., restoring a brother from sin and thus bearing his burden in the Christian act of one-anothering, thereby fulfilling the law of Christ. First Corinthians 15:11 is also typical: "Therefore whether [it were] I or they, so we preach, and so ye believed." Here the phrase, "*<u>also</u> in this manner* ye believed" means that the Corinthians came to also believe in the same manner in which Paul and others believed who preached to them. Thus, Paul was saying that their belief was authentic. Consider also 1 Corinthians 7:17: "But as God hath distributed [a particular marital status] to every man, as the Lord hath called every one, so let him walk. And so ordain I in all churches." Here, in the phrase "And so ordain I" the words *And so* (*kai outws*) refer to Paul *<u>also</u> in this manner* ordaining the same for all the churches, i.e., the Galatians were not being singled out as though they alone were under this type instruction. Also, consider Acts 27:43-44: "But the centurion, willing to save Paul, kept them from [their] purpose; and commanded that they which could swim should cast [themselves] first [into the sea], and get to land: And the rest, some on boards, and some on [broken pieces] of the ship. *And so* [*kai outws*] it came to pass, that they escaped all safe to land." Here the *kai outws* means that those who could not swim were *also* saved *in the same manner* of casting themselves into the sea, though these made it to land on boards or broken pieces of the ship. Another and very interesting example is Luke 24:46. Here we read, "And [Jesus] said unto them, "Thus it is written, *and thus (kai outws)* it behooved Christ to suffer, and to rise from the dead the third day." Taking our definition of *kai outws* to mean *also in this manner* would suggest a weightier texture in this passage emphasizing the deity of Christ, i.e., *ALSO in this manner* Christ was involved with the agreement with the other two Persons of the Trinity about the Messianic scripture being written by the Holy Spirit in accordance with the will of the Father. This verse helps to explain why an author might sometimes put *kai* before *outws* rather than after it. It gives a slight, relative emphasis to the aspect of *also*, rather than to *in this manner*. (Likewise, the term *outws kai*, which is more common, emphasizes the *manner* in which something *also* occurred.)

Having covered half or so of the above examples, let us consider the remaining ones (except for Rom. 5:12, discussed in detail in the main text and footnotes). Acts 17:33 apparently describes Paul as likewise mocking those who mocked at the idea of bodily resurrection, as each (Paul, and the unbelieving Athenians) departed from each other. This becomes plainer when realizing the word "others" has apparently been unwarrantedly introduced into the previous verse. Jay Green in his Interlinear (Baker Book House) transliteration also leaves out the word "others." The proper translation is: "And when they heard of the resurrection of the dead, some mocked, yet said, "We will hear thee again of this." Apparently, the reason "others" was inserted by the KJV is because of the "de" near the top of the verse, which is an adversative conjunction, corresponding to the idea of "but" or "and yet", etc. That is, "de" qualifies something previously which has been stated. And it appears the translators assumed that the statement "We will hear thee again..." was uttered by some other group than that which mocked. In fact, the text indicates they were the same group of men. Now, because we do not know the exact tone of voice of the unbelieving Atheinians, it is difficult to know whether the "de" should be taken to mean 1) that though the Athenians mocked they were serious about hearing Paul again, or 2) whether they maintained sarcasm throughout their reply, making a statement which one might suppose would ordinarily not be uttered sarcastically, i.e., that they would hear Paul again. At any rate, Paul *also in this manner* departed, apparently answering fools according to their folly in mockery of his own, lest they become wise in their own eyes; and thus Paul matched their tone throughout his like reply. In this way Paul showed himself froward to those who were froward. In the prophetic books God often takes this tone with a rebellious people. That the apostle Paul himself could be (if rarely) sarcastic even with Christians is well established. Moving on, 1 Cor. 7:36 in Green's Interlinear describes the dilemma of a male virgin [or single person?] past his prime who nevertheless still desires to marry: "But if anyone thinks *it* behaving indecently toward his virginity—if he is beyond *his* prime, and so [*kai outws*, also in this manner] it ought to be, let him do what he desires; he does not sin; let them marry." Paul is stating that in such a case a man ought to do also in the manner as those whose cases Paul has previously addressed, i.e., marry, or don't marry, according to what provides the least distraction in following the

Lord. Incidentally, since *kai* sometimes takes on an adversative aspect, it may be understood here as "yet"; that is, even though the man is past his prime, *yet in this manner* it ought to be. Note that even in this case the "yet" acts as a qualifier and so points in comparison (by implicitly *qualifying* the comparison) to something previous in the text. Yet another example of *kai outws* is found in 1 Corinthians 11:28, in which Paul tells his readers: "But let a man examine himself, and so (*kai outws*; also in this manner) let him eat of [that] bread, and drink of [that] cup." The discussion in vs. 21,22 and 29 show that the problem on either side of verse 28 points to drunkenness by many Corinthian Christians at the Lord's table. This was why many of them were sickly or slept. The point in vss. 25 and 26 is that the Lord instructed his disciples in the bread and the wine, in order that they might take them in remembrance of Him. But instead, many Corinthians came to the elements drunk, not remembering the Lord in His former distress, and so failed to recognize what the elements stood for. Thus they ate and drank judgment unto themselves. Therefore Paul urges them to imitate the attitude of Christ and His disciples during the Lord' Communion—one of cognate understanding. 1 Thes. 4:17 is our final example before we discuss two examples where the comparison seems less obvious. The verse reads: "Then we which are alive [and] remain shall be caught up together with them in the clouds, to meet the Lord in the air: and so (*kai outws*; also in this manner) shall we ever be with the Lord." The *kai outws* term points back to the way in which the dead in Christ are united with the Lord, namely, by rising into the clouds to meet Him. We, too, in this same manner of rising into the clouds, shall meet the Lord in the air to be ever with Him.

Finding what the *kai outws* refers to in two passages is somewhat more challenging. In Hebrews 6:15, for example, Abraham's patience appears to be the *also* to the given circumstance of his faith, implied in verse 12 (*a la* Galatians 5:28—'walking the walk of faith in patience, not just talking the talk'). And in Acts 28:14 the *kai outws* may refer to the renewed journey *also* proceeding in the same manner of embarking with a South wind, mentioned just one verse prior, which hearkens back a full chapter to Acts 27:13 to the time the former journey embarked just prior to shipwreck. But the more likely explanation is that Luke implicitly refers to the daily repetition of the South wind.

In conclusion, in every one of its occurrences, the term "kai outws" takes the meaning of "also in this manner" or "yet in this manner," and finishes a comparison. This should not surprise us, since 1) "and" is the most frequent translation of Gr. *kai*, and, like English, literally means, or also implies the concept of, "also"; and 2) *outws* always means "in this manner", which by definition points to something previous and comparative in the text.

Incidentally, Thayer notes what he believes is an exception to the proper completion of *wsper* ("even as") in Matthew 25:14, lit. "For even as a man going abroad…" But it should be noted that the correlative conjunctive phrase is complete if one goes to Matthew 25:1 and understands that the normal order of "even as" preceding the comparison is reversed in Matthew 25. Thus, taking the relevant clauses together from verses 1 and 14, we have "Then shall the kingdom of heaven be likened unto ten virgins…, [*even*] as a man traveling into a far country…" That is, the 'as' is understood in the words "likened unto" such that

"The kingdom of heaven shall be likened unto [i.e., *as*]..." Thus the parable of the ten virgins, which follows this introductory thought about the kingdom of heaven in verse 1, begins the correlative conjunction to which the *even as (wsper)* in verse 14 responds. The point here is that nowhere in the New Testament does the word *wsper* occur without its resolution, including Matthew 25 or, for that matter, Romans 5:12. Nor in Romans 5:12 should a delay be thought to exist as a kind of reversal of how it appears in Matthew 25, such that the resolution of *wsper* at the beginning of Romans 5:12 should seek the more usual resolution of *outws kai* which is far away *forward* in verse 15a(2), especially since *outws kai* in verse 15a(2) ["so also the offense"] points back to the immediate context of *ws* found in the preceding phrase in 15a(1) ["But not as"].

Also (and incidentally), the fact that 'men' in Romans 5:12b is the object of the preposition (upon) which points back to the subject 'death' in verse 12's compound subject (sin/death as a non-synonymous compound subject which retains its cause and effect relationship, as might be exampled, say, in the sentence, "*The theft and its effect*")—a compound subject personified by Paul in verse 12 in which he describes it as outside force coming into the world and spreading its effect throughout the world—does not affect our argument about *kai outws*, as long as we understand that Paul's personification of sin is a term of abstract convenience for the apostle's philosophical thought, and that it remains understood that *men*, not sin itself, nor death, causes sin.

Taking the above (especially former) factors regarding *kai outws* and *outws kai* into consideration, observe that the Greek word *wsper (hosper)* in Romans 5:12 would therefore suggest that the *kai* in *kai outws* be given somewhat more force than *outws*. However, it should be noted in passing that nothing crucial to the argument against original sin depends on taking *kai* with more emphasis than *outws*, since obviously both ideas (i.e., *also*, and *in the manner of*) are comparative by definition. I merely advance the idea because I think it adds a nuance of clarity to Romans 5:12. Specifically speaking, the appearance of *kai outws* in verse 12 means that the effect of death *also* (that is, along with sin) traversed into all men *in the same manner* as it had with Adam, i.e., by man sinning against the conscience.

The failure by advocates of original sin to recognize that *kai outws* is present for the purpose of completing the correlative conjunction begun by *hosper*, has given a huge boost to the false doctrine of 'original sin.' However, not *all* translators have missed the correlative conjunction. Jay Green, in the Interlinear he edited (pub. Baker), translates *kai outws* in Romans 5:12 as *so also*. I believe this is essentially correct. In contrast, the KJV and NAS translate *kai outws* "and so," while the NIV translates it "and in this manner," which is somewhat better but still not really recognizing the "also" aspect intended for completing the "even as," as it otherwise should have been translated. Note in passing that, while the last 'as' in the prior sentence of this footnote, i.e., "as it otherwise should have been translated" does not mean something causative *or even of similarity*, since the English usage also permits 'as' to be used as an intensifier of fact. This "as" thus renders the aforementioned last phrase as follows: "as in fact it otherwise should have been translated." But what I'm contending here is that the Greek words *ws* and *hosper* do not have that lexical function. They always mean "like" and "just like," respectively.

Moving on, then, below are some considerations why the KJV and NAS in particular should not have merely used "and so" for Romans 5:12. First, those who believe Romans 5:12 teaches the doctrine of original sin appear to have taken the English translation of 'as' in "Wherefore *as* by one man sin entered the world" and treated it as though it meant *since* or *because*, as in fact the word *as* may at times mean in English depending on the context and/or intent of the author. For example, in the statement "I now hope to attend college, *as* I have finished high school," the word *as* means *since* or *because*. But such an *as* is not the meaning of *wsper* nor even of *ws*, i.e., *hosper's* etymological root, according to its lexical use. That is, neither *wsper* or *ws* have a **causative** meaning. Unfortunately, the English definition of *as* in its causative sense appears to have led many English readers toward accepting the doctrine of original sin, along with the simple '*and so* ' later in verse 12, which is taken to mean in English '*and therefore*.' This assumption upon the English word *as* makes it seem as though the text is saying that all have sinned *because* of Adam. Perhaps a mistake by English readers (that we ought to mention again) is when 'as' is taken by them to be a mere intensifier of fact, i.e., "Wherefore, as in fact by one man's disobedience…", thus destroying entirely the sense that any correlative conjunction is indeed afoot.

Another proof of the presence of the correlative conjunction in Romans 5:12 is the argument of verse 13ff, in which Paul stresses that men have *not* sinned after the likeness of Adam's sin. But again, Paul does not mean a dissimilarity *in toto*, but merely a relative dissimilarity. It explains the evident reason why Paul did not use the common phrase *outws kai* (even so) which would have stressed the general sameness of manner. Instead, he used *kai outws* to stress the *relative* general sameness of manner (the *kai* taking some priority of emphasis). Indeed, it would be incongruent for Paul to draw, as he did, such a relative distinction between the act of Adam and the acts of his descendents who did *not* follow after the similitude of Adam's transgression, if the apostle actually held the idea, as advocates of original sin seem to claim, that men had imputed to them the very guilt of Adam's transgression.

[179] Technically, the word is *ws* (*as*), not the more intensive *hosper* (from *ws* and *per*, the latter intensifying *ws*), but the phrase "But not as the offence" is an ellipsis that, we note here, may include *ws* in the spirit of replacing *hosper*. If, however, Paul was intentional about using *ws* as opposed to *hosper*, it may be because the particular subjects of this correlative conjunction, i.e., the offence and the gift, are so intrinsically different in nature as to make *ws* appear somewhat more appropriate. However, in my desire to clearly articulate the argument that a correlative conjunction is introduced in 15a, I have chosen to render *ws* to be "just as," since this is the normal way in English of introducing a correlative conjunction, though technically "as" could suffice.

[180] In fact, to avoid this problem the Calvinist takes the term "all" to mean something different than "the many," whereas Paul simply meant "all the many," i.e., 'all accountable,' that is, the majority of humans who, in fact, had reached the age of accountability and also chosen to sin.

[181] See chapter 4, where a rocking horse is used as a metaphor for expressing the dialectical tension between the 'this, yet that,' i.e., the forward rock of the

absolute sovereignty of God, yet the backward rock of the free will of man. Such a dialectic finds its 'rest' only at its synthesized center of tension.

[182] Notice the phrase in 15b: "for if through the offence of the one the many did die…" This comes immediately after Paul has made the first three words of 15a ("But not as…") serve as a referent to post-Adamic sin which is contrasted in verses 13-14 with Adam's sin, a point about the former which gives Paul's readers more detail about the different *means* to how sin subsequently spread throughout the world. In other words, Paul is stating that the post-Adamic offense was not *in every particular* like Adam's sin *insofar* as involving the eating of forbidden fruit; rather, it was *generally* like Adam's sin for being transgression against the conscience (because it was committed apart from specific, divine Law). Thus what Paul states in 15b cannot be a reversal of what he just said by way of ellipsis in 15a regarding how post-Adamic man came into condemnation, or else Paul would be contradicting himself. Therefore 15b ('For if through the offense of one many be dead') ought not to be taken in its most literal sense, that is, in which its interpretation would be improperly stripped of its surrounding context. Rather, Paul has in mind merely the general, spiritual effect of Adam's sin upon humanity, when he says that through the offense of the one the many did die. *Most importantly*, while this thought is repeated with slight variation in verses 17, 18, and 19, note especially that, when Paul comes to his main summarization in verse 18a (Int. "So, then,…") to restate what in fact he has already said in verses 13-14, he re-states his position with less of an ellipsis (i.e., with more content) than that which he used in 15b:

> (Gr. lit.) "So, then, like through one offense into all men into condemnation, so also through one righteous act into all men into justification of life."

Again, Paul is here making an ellipsis of verses 13-14 to make sure that what he had said in vss. 13-14 was understood, i.e., that all men came into condemnation *like* Adam—that is, *not in the particular sense* of breaking the Garden Command (for post-Adamic man already showed that, in this regard, he was *unlike* Adam)—*but in the general sense* of transgressing against the conscience. One must always keep in mind that when Paul states in verse 18a that post-Adamic man's sin was like Adam's, that the nature of saying '*A* is like *B*,' is to say that *A* is *generally* like *B*, but in some particular(s) is unlike *B*. That, in fact, is what the word 'like' means. So, whenever Paul is discussing Adam and post-Adamic man, he has in mind that they are *generally* like each other (in that they have both committed sin against the conscience), but *particularly* [i.e. in some particular(s)] unlike each other [in the sense of the particular kind of law (or Law) against which they sinned]. This is why 15b (where the word 'like' is absent) must be taken figuratively so that Adam is representative of humanity in general, that is, if 15b is *not* taken as an ellipsis. But of course 15b *ought* to be taken as an ellipsis because 18a, in summarizing what Paul was stating by abbreviation in 15b (as stemming from vss. 12-14), and by his adding the word 'like,' shows that 15b was not meant to be taken literally, *or*, if it *was* meant to be taken *prima facie*, that it be taken *figuratively* to mean Adam representing Everyman, and how Everyman has sinned against his own conscience. Otherwise (as already noted) 15a and 15b will be in contradiction with each other. Moving on, Paul then essentially restates verse 18a in verse 19a, saying that, (Gr. lit.) 'For *even like* through the disobedience of the one man...' and here the 'even' in the 'even like' places even more emphasis on the sameness of the Adamic and post-Adamic responses of sinning against one's conscience (*the general sense* in which like is defined to be *the same*). Paul adds this slight difference (*hosper* instead of *ws*) in verse 19a to make sure the general point in his summary is not missed about the *sameness* of the nature of every man's sin as a transgression against the conscience, the primary point of verse 12. Although we have gotten a bit ahead of the main text here, this point about the dual aspect of like must be kept in mind as we move forward through the following points.

[183] This view thus also provides for a period of accountability. If the term 'age of accountability' is used, the beginning point is defined as that instant at which one *enters* the period of accountability.

[184] i.e., Paul's argument is a general one, in which the Gentile conscience is implied to have been intact (not seared) in regard to the Neighborly Command (which can only be properly understood in the context of being under the First and Greatest Command).

[185] The terms 'weakness' and 'inability' should not be confused, for to be without strength means to be without strong, not any, ability. Note the NAS's unfortunate word choice of "helpless." When Christ told Peter (Mk. 14:38) that the Spirit was eager, but the flesh was weak, He was not stating that the flesh was disabled, otherwise He would not have just asked Peter rhetorically, "Were you not strong enough to watch one hour?" (Mk. 14:37).

[186] i.e., 'even as sin entered the world by one man, resulting in spiritual death,'

[187] In fact, verse 6 characterizes the entire argument Paul has been making since the middle of chapter one—that men have sinned against their conscience.

[188] pointed out by Gordon Olson in his book, *Getting the Gospel Right*.

[189] As Carl Conrad states (see his quote in more detail on p. 676, endnote lxiv):

> "BUT I do NOT believe that EF' hWi when used to introduce a subordinate clause is EVER used to refer back to a larger textual unit (clause, paragraph, section); while you may see an instance where the hWi is masculine sg. relative pronoun referring back to a masculine antecedent noun (Acts 7:53 hWi with TOPOS) or where a hHi refers back to a feminine antecedent noun (Luke 11:22 THN PANOPLIAN AIREI EF' hHI EPEPOIQEI ...), I do not believe a clear instance will be found wherein the neuter relative pronoun object of EPI refers back to a textual unit larger than a concrete noun."

In passing, one should note the position taken by the Eastern Fathers, i.e., interpreting the spelling of EF' hWi to be masculine, thus pointing back to *thanatos* (death), and, from this, making the further inference that death passed upon all men as caused by Adam. But the problem with the view of the Eastern Fathers, besides the fact that death is defined in the Bible as an *effect*, not a cause, of sin (an argument which by itself is fatal to the Eastern Fathers' view), is that it fails to ask why Paul, if he were really putting forth a doctrine about original sin, simply wouldn't have eliminated the correlative conjunction to begin with, i.e., the whole cumbersome format about sin's entrance and subsequent traversing through all men, and eliminate also his subsequent ellipses which likewise would have presumably been unnecessary. In other words, why not just state the matter baldly from the start of verse 12 (i.e., "And all men are sinners in Adam because Adam sinned")? But that is not how the text reads, and this is why Paul states the opening phrase of verse 12 the way he does, for in stating "Because of this," he refers to a causal factor prior to verse 12 in which Adam has not at all figured *or even been mentioned.*

Furthermore, in analyzing the implications which follow from the doctrine of original sin, the charge (as already noted) may be raised that Adam and post-Adamic man are never really defined as separate *moral* beings anymore than God and Adam are defined as separate moral beings in Calvinist theology. Post-Adamic men are somehow thought to be present with Adam (i.e., in the *imagined* phrase, 'all have sinned *in* Adam') though obviously they did not yet exist as persons (or did they in some sense?—the advocates of original sin can't seem to clearly tell us); furthermore, *death* is somehow thought to cause *sin* in post-Adamic man, though on the other hand *sin* is said to have caused *death* in the first man Adam, etc. Fuzzy and circular definitions about man thus abound to a point where no moral causation is properly explained. The reason is simple—because any self-determining being other than God is never really allowed in Calvinist theology. Consequently, Adam's causative effect upon his descendents is explained with no more clarity than any other human causation. This 'back burner' insistence on God's unilateral causation is why, e.g., Calvinist John Piper concludes at the end of his article *Are there Two Wills of God?*, "I do not find in the Bible that human beings have the ultimate power of self-determination." And yet observe in passing, that Piper's use of the word 'ultimate' (in the above statement) is arguably his concession to the backward rock (of the dialectical rocking horse) in favor of man's freedom, as though there were some degree or *kind* of causation less or *other* than 'ultimate.' In fact, this explains why Piper, when about to offer an example from Deuteronomy allegedly proving that God has two wills (which Piper defines dialectically), feels enough ideological 'wiggle-room' to state that these two wills of God will be shown to be "strikingly different (not contradictory, I will argue)." In other words, had Piper stated the matter thus, i.e., "All human beings have never been, are not, and shall not be, determinative in any way whatsoever," then Piper could hardly have then used the qualifier "(*not contradictory*, I will argue)" (emphasis mine). Note, then, that such a paradigm by Piper obviously makes any *intelligible* discussion about sin, original sin, or any other topic involving causation, quite impossible.

[190] *or*, "being the state of things that"

[191] A grammatical reminder: 'beside' means *alongside*; 'besides' means *in addition to*.

[192] The early church father, Chrystotym, takes the same position as we do here, treating the Greek word *hina* i.e., 'that,' as ecbatic (i.e., *so that*, or *with the result that*) rather than telic (*in order that*). Thus, Law came alongside man's conscience, *with the result that* sin might abound.

[193] Again, it is important to understand that the seed of the knowledge of good and evil, which we inherit from Adam, is a seed of knowledge born of the consequence of Adam's sin, and is not sin itself. From Adam a person inherits this seed of knowledge that matures into a fuller knowledge presented to his mind about which he makes eternally liable decisions. Had there been no Fall, a person would still be born with a simpler kind of knowledge which nevertheless would eventually mature enough to enable the person to make decisions unto eternal liability, though apart from the distraction of a fallen flesh.

[194] In light of our observation that the Romans 5:15 term, 'the many' means accountable persons, not all persons, it is interesting to see Isaiah use the term 'many' in Isaiah 53, when stating that the Servant (Messiah) would bear the sins of *many*.

[195] This grants, of course, our earlier argument from Romans 5 that we do not sin *in Adam*.

[196] My thanks to my friend, William Cook, for this interesting insight.

[197] i.e., multiplying in knowledge and multiplying in having children.

[198] It is interesting to note that the consequences in the Fall had an aspect of undesirable gain, even as the acquiring of the knowledge of good and evil proved to be, for man, an undesirable gain. For Adam the consequence was in the field; not only would desirable plants and fruit trees grow but everything else as well. The woman, too, suffered a multiplying of hardship; gestation and pain in the childbirth process would henceforth be increased.

[199] See footnote 222, regarding *almah*.

[200] In other words, in the hyperbolic layer of meaning David is the subject in the first clause and the intended referent of the prepositional phrase "in iniquity," and is the object in the second clause in which his mother is the subject and the intended referent in the prepositional phrase, "in sin."

[201] again, at least at this particular level of meaning.

[202] It is interesting to note that the English "shapen" is the Hebrew word *khool*, which Strong defines as "to *twist* or *whirl* (in a circular or spiral manner), i.e., (spec.) to *dance*, to *writhe* in pain (esp. of parturition [childbirth]." The word is used in the Old Testament in all such senses as Strong describes it. For example, *khool* is rendered "wait" for when the dove is said to have "waited" after Noah brought it back inside the ark. It indicates not a quiet resting (as the English rendering suggests) but the kind of agitated perch-to-perch movement one sometimes sees in birds when they are caged. That is really the picture here in Psalm 51—one of *agitation*, and thus of writhing in the childbirth process; and it seems as if David's use of the somewhat flexible word *khool* is meant to invoke a

layered texture of meaning for verse 5, so that a literal, not just hyperbolic, meaning may be understood.

[203] This additional interpretation of an added layer of meaning within this layer of literal meaning of Psalm 51:5 is not necessary for the main argument for a subsidiary literal meaning. Nevertheless, we offer it as a possibility.

[204] No matter how far back the Calvinist wishes to push the problem of evil, there remains no solution for him. If Adam's sin is to be blamed on Satan, then upon whom do we blame Satan's sin? Thus the only rational solution to removing God from being the ultimate cause of evil is to insist that evil first came into existence *ex nihilio* by a person other than God.

[205] Observe that Noah in this same passage was given permission to eat animals for food. Thus animals are not made in the image of God; otherwise men who killed animals would have been subject to capital punishment.

Endnotes:

[lxii] Whitelaw, Thomas;(H.D.M. Spense and Joseph S. Excell, editors). *The Pulpit Commentary*. (London and New York: Funk & Wagnalls Company, new edition, n.d.). Vol 1 (Genesis), p. 73.

[lxiii] Finney, Charles G. Total Depravity. [www.gospeltruth.net/1836SOIS/04sois_total_depravity.htm]; Part 1.

[lxiv] Ross, Bill and Carl Conrad. "Re: FW: Ef hWi and Indicative Tenses in Greek and English."
The following exchange is dated January 5, 2000. [http://lists.ibiblio.org/pipermail/b-greek/2000-January/009388.html]

Bill:
The words EF hW are commonly translated "because." I personally object to this. In the same sentence Paul uses DIA for that purpose.

Carl:
In fact, however, DIA is not used so simply; DIA is used with TOUTO…

Bill:
I was thinking more of KAI DIA THS hAMARTIAS hO QANATOS where there is a cause and effect relationship. Here Paul says:
"DIA THS hAMRATIAS hO QANATOS"
and does not use that construction later.
Carl, are you saying that:
* DIA by itself is never used to say "because"?
* EF hW means the same as DIA TOUTO but not the same as DIA?
* EF hW cannot/will not translate to "upon which"?
* there is a grammatical reason why hW in Acts 7:53 refers back to TOPOS but hW in Romans 5:12 cannot refer back to QANATOS (or more properly, EIS PANTAS ANQROWPOUS hO ANATOS DIHLQEN)? (Paul follows this statement with a strikingly relevant subject:

Romans 5:14 ALLA EBASILEUSEN O QANATOS APO ADAM MECRI MWUSEWS KAI EPI TOUS MH MARTHSANTAS EPI TW OMOIWMATI THS PARABASEWS ADAM OS ESTIN TUPOS TOU MELLONTOS
Paul specifically tells us in the immediate context that death reigned on those who *did not transgress* as per Adam.)
* EF hW intrinsically must mean "because" and cannot mean anything else?
* that any difference between EF hW and DIA is imaginary?
The words are literally "upon which" as in Acts 7:33:
Acts 7:33 EIPEN DE AUTWi hO KURIOS: LUSON TO hUPODHMA TWN PODWN SOU, hO GAR TOPOS EF' hWi hESTHKAS GH hAGIA ESTI

Carl:
EF' hWi here is only superficially comparable to the adverbial conjunctive phrase EF' hWi; here EPI is the preposition used with a locative dative "upon" and the hWi is in this instance a relative pronoun referring back to the antecedent TOPOS.

Bill:
Is there any difference in the words? Why can't Paul be saying, figuratively, that PANTA were [standing] EP hWS [occurrence] when they sinned.
We agree that the subject is PANTA and the verb is hHMARTON is the verb. Does EF hW answer the question "why?" or "how?" or "when?" or (as I hold) "what precipitated it?" Or even, "What were the prevailing conditions?"
This leads me to the conclusion that, to Paul, the first phrase is the antecedent of the second, not the result. That is "all died, upon which [EF W] all sinned" not "all died, because [DIA] all sinned"

Carl:
Here are the four GNT texts wherein EF' hWi appears, in every one of which the prepositional phrase EF' hWi may legitimately be translated "because" or "since":
Rom 5:12 DIA TOUTO hWSPER DI' hENOS ANQRWPOU hH hAMARTIA EIS TON KOSMON EISHLQEN KAI DIA THS hAMAARTIAS hO QANATOS, KAI hOUTWS EIS PANTAS ANQRWPOUS hO QANATOS DIHLQEN, EF' hWi PANTES hHMARTON ("... because/since they have all sinned")

Bill:
"they have all sinned?" Or "all sinned?" Your translation of the aorist slants the reading of the text to require it to read in the past but that isn't the way I would understand the translation of the aorist. This verse can only be understood as "because all sinned" if, in addition to a specious idiom, we accept very strange incongruous interpretations:
* participation of all men in Adam's sin/transgression?? Then why must death "pass through" from Adam to them?
* death only to those of mankind who subsequently sin?? But death is attributed to Adam's **transgression** [PARAPTWMA], not to a multitude of sins [hAMARTIAS]

Carl:
2 COR 5:4 KAI GAR hOI ONTES EN TWi SKHNEI STENAZOMEN BAROUMENOI, EF' HWi OU QELOMEN EKDUSASQAI ALL'

EPENDUSASQAI, hINA KATAPOQHi TO QNHTON hUPO THS ZWHS.
("… because/since we don't want to strip naked but rather to put on new clothes …")

Bill:
You would read that "..we groan because/since we don't want to strip naked"?
I don't find that reasonable at all.
I prefer "We know that…we have an eternal house…we groan under our burdens. But upon this we do not desire to be unclothed, but rather to be clothed"
The UPON THIS refers back to what we know and what we have and provides the reason for the subsequent action — just as in Romans 5:12. Of course there is overlap in the sense with because, but UPON THIS is more precise in this context. We might find a meeting ground on some sense like "since this premise is true…" or "given this prerequisite" but not on "because" or "since."

Carl:
Phil 3:12 OUC' hOTI HDH ELABON H HDH TETELEIWMAI, DIWKW DE EI KAI KATALABW, EF' hWi KAI KATELHMFQHN hUPO CRISTOU [IHSOU]. ("… because/since I too have been gripped firmly by Christ [Jesus].")

Bill:
Might it not be:
"..I might also lay hold, on [account of] which also, I have been gripped by Christ Jesus"?
If so, then the sentence is one consistent thought instead of two joined by a pun. Paul is Christ's "slave" and "prisoner" and the phrase is a synonym for DIA TOUTO as used here:
1 Tim 1:16 Howbeit **for this cause** [DIA TOUTO] I obtained mercy, that in me first Jesus Christ might show forth all longsuffering, for a pattern to them which should hereafter believe on him to life everlasting.
1 Timothy 1:16 ALLA **DIA TOUTO** HLEHQHN INA EN EMOI PRWTW ENDEIXHTAI CRISTOS IHSOUS THN APASAN MAKROQUMIAN PROS UPOTUPWSIN TWN MELLONTWN PISTEUEIN EP AUTW EIS ZWHN AIWNION

Carl:
Phil 4:12 ECARHN DE EN KURIWi MEGALWS hOTI HDH POTE ANEQALETE TO hUPER EMOU FRONEIN, EF' hWi KAI EFRONEITE, HKAIREISQE DE. ("… because/since you were indeed anxious (about me) but your timing was bad.")

Bill:
Or rather, "upon which also you were thinking, but you were lacking opportunity"
or
"on [account of] which you were thinking…"

Carl:
In sum, there's all the difference in the world between DIA TOUTO and EF' hWi; the former means "for this reason" or "because of this" or "therefore", while the

latter means "because" or "since" and functions as an adverbial conjunction introducing the clause explaining the reason for what was just asserted.

Bill:
Are you setting out to show:
* EF hW has a "meaning" of "because" that must dictate the usage, or only that your notion is "plausible?"
* EF hW must always be read idiomatically as "because" or that it can be thus construed?
* EF hW is "defined" by four occurrences where "it may be legitimately translated" as "since," (while on closer inspection, such a translation is really not as good as the literal "upon which", or the idiom "on account of which")?
Do you even concede that it could be legitimately translated any other way?
Is this "idiom" of "because" an established "fact" or just a hasty theory subject to investigation?
I think we would all benefit from a dip into the classic literature for examples of the phrase. Have you a tool that could supply examples?
Bill Ross

The following exchange is dated January 7, 2000.
[http://www.ibiblio.org/bgreek/test-archives/html4/2000-01/34930.html]

Note: Bill has very wisely snipped items from a 17K off-list reply that I sent to his last on-list series of questions about our ongoing dispute over EF' hWi as an adverbial conjunction introducing subordinate explanatory clauses.
At 8:55 PM -0600 1/6/00, Bill Ross wrote:

Bill:
Carl, I've had a lot of trouble with my email. I hope this finally gets through. It keeps saying your email server doesn't exist??
Anyway, a simple question on your objection to my reading of EF hWi, that I thought might be of interest to the whole list:

Carl:
Yes. hWi in Acts 7:53 is masculine dative sg–dative to construe with EPI, masculine singular to agree with the antecedent TOPOS. Don't be confused by the fact that hWi may be either masculine or neuter. In Acts 7:53 it is masculine; in the phrase EF' hWi which I've been saying means "because" or "since" the hWi is technically neuter because TOUTWi hOTI which it represents and abbreviates is neuter.
Again, you're insisting upon "which" as a relative pronoun but aren't pointing to any noun, masculine or neuter, in what precedes that hWi could refer as to an antecedent.

Bill:
...Isn't it common for a neuter relative pronoun to refer back to a clause, paragraph, section... with no regard to gender? For example, DIA TOUTO need not refer to any particular gender, correct? The reason I ask is that this is how I am seeing hWi being used — pointing to a clause such as:
EIS PANTAS ANQROWPOUS hO QANATOS DIHLQEN

Carl:
It is indeed common to refer back to a preceding clause, paragraph, section by using a neuter relative pronoun, particularly hO/ (the accented n.sg. rel. pron. as distinguished from the unaccented article, hO) and hA/ (the accented n.pl. rel. pron. as distinguished from the n. pl. article, TA).
BUT it is more common to refer back to a larger textual unit (clause, paragraph, section) by using a demonstrative neuter pronoun, e.g. DIA TOUTO, DIA TAUTA, DI' EKEINO, DI' EKEINA, KATA TOUTO, or the like. Far more common than those is it to use the conjunction hO/TI which originated as an indirect interrogative pronoun, a compound of the relative pronoun n.sg. hO/ and the indefinite n. sg. pronoun TI. So common is this usage of hO/TI in fact that a useful convention developed (for which I'm not sure whether grammarians or editors/printers bear the greater responsibility) to distinguish the form used as a conjunction, hO/TI by writing/printing it as a single word from the form used as an indefinite relative/interrogative pronoun, hO/ TI, which was written/printed as two words. I might add that this usage of what was originally a relative pronoun as a conjunction introducing a subordinate clause is a common development in many IE languages (Latin QUOD, German DASS, French QUE, Italian CHE, English THAT, etc.).
BUT I do NOT believe that EF' hWi when used to introduce a subordinate clause is EVER used to refer back to a larger textual unit (clause, paragraph, section); while you may see an instance where the hWi is masculine sg. relative pronoun referring back to a masculine antecedent noun (Acts 7:53 hWi with TOPOS) or where a hHi refers back to a feminine antecedent noun (Luke 11:22 THN PANOPLIAN AIREI EF' hHI EPEPOIQEI …), I do not believe a clear instance will be found wherein the neuter relative pronoun object of EPI refers back to a textual unit larger than a concrete noun.
Also…

Carl [continues]:
I don't understand what you mean by "understand the TRANSLATION of the aorist;" are you trying to tell me that the aorist here is not referring to Past time? My own reason for preferring to translate the aorist here as "have sinned" is to underscore the totality of the acts of human sinning. I have no idea in the world what you mean to imply about the difference from "all have sinned" that "all sinned" implies for understanding how the aorist is used here.

Bill:
Though many allow for the addition of the word "have" for the aorist, I prefer to reserve that for the perfect. In this situation, where the question being answered is whether men sinned "at some point in time (allowing for each individually) or "upon Adam's sinning" (in the past and impacting the present) it seems unreasonable to relax the distinction between aorist and perfect.
[Note: The following, though not introduced with Carl's name, must be assumed to be his nevertheless, since he continues to state that he doesn't understand the distinction that his colleague is trying to make in the translation of the aorist.]

[Carl:]
I still don't understand the distinction you mean to draw here between "they all sinned" and "they have all sinned" for PANTES hHMARTON in Rom 5:12 DIA TOUTO hWSPER DI' hENOS ANQRWPOU hH hAMARTIA EIS TON

KOSMON EISHLQEN KAI DIA THS hAMAARTIAS hO QANATOS, KAI hOUTWS EIS PANTAS ANQRWPOUS hO QANATOS DIHLQEN, EF' hWi PANTES hHMARTON. But so long as you grant that hHMARTON does refer to the sinning of all humanity in time past, I am content.

But this does raise another matter of the difference between English and Greek tense usage that I think is worth clarifying, although it doesn't bear that directly on the question originally in dispute in the present exchange (and that's why I've added to the subject-header). I would contend that the Greek aorist form hHMARTON may legitimately be translated either as "they sinned" or "they have sinned." If so, does that mean there's no real distinction between hHMARTON and hHMARTHKASI? My own view (and I've expressed it previously in this forum) is that in actual practice this distinction between aorist and perfect to express perfective past action has largely disappeared—and that is one reason why the perfect tense is relatively rare, namely: the aorist has usurped one of the chief functions of the perfect tense. On the other hand, I think the perfect tense hHMARTHKASI retains a distinct function when it underscores the present ongoing consequence of the action referred to; thus hHMARTHKASI may be translated into English as "they have sinned" (as could also, I think hHMARTON) but hHMARTHKASI bears the additional implication: their sin—and their consequent guilt—remains in effect even now. My point, to reiterate it by stating it differently, is that there is an ambiguity in the English perfect tense form "they have sinned" just as there is in the Latin perfect PECCAVERUNT and in the Greek aorist hHMARTON in that each of these forms may represent the simple fact of past action and also the completeness of the past action. But there's a distinct sense in which these perfect tenses express resultant present state—and this sense is not so often uppermost in view as it is in Latin VIXERUNT = "Their life is over with—they're dead" or Vergil's FUIT ILIUM = "Troy has had its existence and is no more." I think that this distinct stative sense tends to be preserved in the Koine Greek perfect tense when it is actually used, but that (apart from forms like hESTHKA and OIDA which are understood and used as present tense even though their morphology is perfect-tense) the perfect tense survives the other common sense of the perfect tense—completion of action in the past—is regularly expressed in the aorist indicative. I don't really think I'm saying anything new here but that I'm simply calling attention to a fact about Koine usage of the perfect and aorist tenses that is already pretty well attested in the grammars. Wallace, for instance seems to me to be right on target regarding this function of the aorist (I don't have the page ## as I'm drawing on the AcCordance software version):

"III. Consummative (Culminative, Ecbatic, Effective) Aorist

"A. Definition

"The aorist is often used to stress the cessation of an act or state. Certain verbs, by their lexical nature, virtually require this usage.11 For example, "he died" is usually not going to be an ingressive idea. The context also assists in this usage at times; it may imply that an act was already in progress and the aorist then brings the action to a conclusion. This is different from a consummative perfect, for the latter places the stress on (a) completion of the action, not merely cessation;12 and especially (b) continuing results after the completion of the action."

*Nearly two years later there was an exchange
between Carl Conrad and Steve Lo Vullo*
[http://lists.ibiblio.org/pipermail/b-greek/2001-December/019484.html]

On Monday, December 3, 2001, at 06:40 AM, Carl W. Conrad wrote:
Steven, I think that here the hWi doesn't have an antecedent in what precedes but is rather a fairly common elliptical expression with antecedent pressed into the relative (or relative attracted into the case of the implicit antecedent demonstrative): EF' hWi = EPI TOUTWi hWI "because of this: that" or "because"; I think this EF' hWi has come to be an adverbial conjunction in its own right, much like hOTI [in] its wide-ranging usage as a conjunction derivative ultimately from a relative pronoun.
Other instances:
2 Cor 5:4 KAI GAR hOI ONTES EN TWi SKHNEI STENAZOMEN BAROUMENOI, EF' hWi OU QELOMEN EKDUSASQAI ALL' EPENDUSASQAI, hINA KATAPOQHi TO QNHTON hUPO THS ZWHS.
Phil 3:12 OUC hOTI HDH ELABON H HDH TETELEIWMAI, DIWKW DE EI KAI KATALABW, EF' hWi KAI KATELHMFQHN hUPO CRISTOU [IHSOU].
Phil 4:10 ECARHN DE EN KURIWi MEGALWS hOTI HDH POTE ANEQALETE TO hUPER EMOU FRONEIN, EF' hWi KAI EFRONEITE, HKAIREISQE DE.

[Steven:]
Carl:
Thanks for your response. Yes, these examples are pretty convincing, especially since in the first two cases there is no explicit substantive whatsoever to serve as an antecedent, and in the third example none that makes any sense. Some have proposed ANQRWPOU as the antecedent in Rom 5.12 (since hWi can be masculine), but the more I read the passage, the more unlikely this seems, the relative being so far removed (compared to, say, Acts 7.33, where EF' hWi follows immediately upon its antecedent, TOPOS).

CHAPTER 19

John 1:13 in its Historical-Grammatical Context

In the centuries-old, swirling debate between Reformed and non-Reformed theology, a discussion of John 1:13 is never far from the center of the maelstrom. Perhaps this is because Calvinists regard John 1:13 as a key text proving that man is too depraved in his will to receive Christ. The verse reads:

> "Who were born, not by blood nor by the will of the flesh nor by the will of man, but of God." (NAS)

Calvinists lay emphasis especially on these last two phrases, i.e., "the will of the flesh" and "the will of man," in an attempt to prove their argument. But, of course, to teach that verse 13 means that a man exercises no will of his own in receiving Christ is to eliminate the near context of verse 12 ("But as many as received Him"), which would seem to refute the Calvinistic claim that man is unable to respond. Nevertheless, Calvinists argue that God must change the very will itself if a man is to respond and receive Christ. As explained in principle previously and extensively in this book, the Calvinistic position (because it embraces the dialectical method) thus retains the term 'man' in the phrase "the will of man" *in name only*.[1206]

Now, as we dig deeper into the meaning of John 1:13, we concede that this verse is not easy to interpret. Part of the problem is that wrong interpretations have been 'free ranged' for many years apart from significant historical-grammatical considerations. The difficulty is in understanding John's tri-part statement, which is comprised of three things by which people are *not* born of God; these are: "blood," (lit. *bloods*), "the will of the flesh," and "the will of man."

Before interpreting this list of three things we must first establish the identity of the word "who" which begins John 1:13 (in the NAS), i.e., "who were born…" A few early church fathers (Iraneaus and Tertullian) take the phrase "who were born" to be "who *was* born," thus asserting that John 1:13 refers to Christ rather than to those who have received Christ. In fact, this view would clear up much confusion if it were true. But as A.T. Robertson points out, the phrase "who *were* born" is found in all the earliest Greek Uncials[1207] "and…must be insisted upon." The following study will take Robertson's conclusion as our starting point, i.e., that the beginning phrase is correctly rendered, "who were born" (or, "who are born." See next paragraph.)

Not of Blood

Again, the tri-part statement that follows the phrase "who were born" describes what must be understood about those born of God. John tells us that they were born, "not of blood (lit. *bloods*) nor of the will of the flesh nor of the will of man, but of God." [In the phrase "*were* born," the 'tense' is aorist, that is, without particular regard to past, present, or future time, thus "*are* born," as stating the matter generally without addressing the temporal issue per se. In other words, those who receive (v. 12) are born (v. 13).] Now in examining the first phrase, "not of bloods" (again, blood is in the plural), it is best to begin by asking two questions: 1) the identity of John's intended audience, and 2) what erroneous assumptions John was trying to anticipate in his readers' minds with the tri-part statement "not…nor…nor…"

First, then, it is reasonable to conclude that John's intended audience was both Gentile (particularly Greek[208] and Greco-Roman) and Jewish. (Even many of these latter in John's time would have had a Hellenized education—for Palestine was certainly a Hellenized culture in the first century.) John's gospel itself makes some concession to this fact of Jewish *and* Greek readership, explaining, for example, that the Passover was a Feast of the Jews, i.e., as opposed to simply stating the words, "the Passover," which is all the explanation a sole Jewish readership would have needed (Jn. 6:4). Then, of course, there is John's unfolding definition of the *Logos*, a Greek term meaning *the source and foundation of the Cosmos*[209] which went back to the time of Heraclitus (about 500 B.C.).[210] To deliberately invoke such a Greek term shows that John was using the term *Logos* as a contact point with his readers. As for the purpose of John's gospel, he tells us in 20:31 that his recording of Jesus' miracles (and therefore, by implication in one sense, *all* his gospel) is that the reader might believe in Jesus Christ and be saved.

It bears on the issue of interpreting John 1:13 to know that John's gospel was among the last books of the New Testament written, being composed around 90 A.D. By this time in early church history Paul had died, perhaps over two decades earlier, and the gospel had made considerable inroads among both Jews and Gentiles. Also, John is now very old and appears to have mellowed greatly from the much earlier time when the Lord dubbed him and his brother "the Sons of Thunder." As we look at John's epistles and gospel written toward the end of his life, the apostle's demeanor has softened considerably and comes through beautifully. In short, it is not a demeanor that *quickly* divides people into taking sides in a controversy; that is, John does not write the kind of challenging, confrontational statements Paul made in the early part of Romans, or communicated at Athens.[211] John's tendency is to use emerging definitions that *nudge* readers to keep looking and thinking. Despite John's forthright statements in his epistles identifying the antichrists of this world, etc., one always observes in John a relatively winsome approach toward "his little children." This fact of John being identified as the Apostle of Love needs special attention. For certainly John's love informs his attitude and approach throughout his gospel, though to bring the matter to a present day consideration, it appears that John's demeanor has had little impact on how certain Christian interpreters think about his books. This seems especially true of those in Evangelical cyberspace. For one sees the hard line taken by certain online Reformed bloggers anxious to state their interpretations of John 1:13—i.e., Calvinists pouncing upon the verse as though John was laying it all out there right at the beginning, caring little if he sounded contradictory to the average reader between verses 12 and 13, so long as the reader saw the truth about God beheading the dragon of free will with the *coup de group* phrase, "*nor of the will of man!*" But imagine the average Roman reader coming to the gospel of John for the first time. Probably he knows little or nothing in particular about the life of Jesus Christ. So here is the question: Would not such a reader perceive, through the beginning portion of John, that the apostle's "not…nor…nor…" statement in verse 13 was more of a diplomatic clarification rather than a forthright come-what-may statement? For certainly, John seems more gentle in his corrections than he might have been, as though he simply wishes to guard his readers against erroneous assumptions he knows his readers will likely make in the course of emerging definitions that are unfamiliar to them.

This realization of John's approach segues us into the beginning of the apostle's gospel itself, in which John uses the term *Logos* ("*In the beginning was the Logos*"). Jews and Greeks would have understood this term somewhat differently. While for the non-Hellenized Jew the *Logos* would have meant God's Communication, the Greek would have understood the *Logos* as the source of reason (not attached to a person or personality) which overarched the universe and preceded the gods and persons that had come afterward as actors in the universe. Thus John is trying to help this latter group, the Greeks, understand (in the course of the first 14 verses) that this overarching reason and principle of the universe is, in fact, a Person by whom the world was created—and who, moreover, became a Man.

In the course of this description of the *Logos*, John speaks of two groups of people: those who rejected the *Logos*, and those who received Him and became children of God. Let us consider some of the surrounding context of John 1:13, beginning with verse 9 (in the NAS):

> [9]There was the true Light which, coming into the world, enlightens every man. [10]He was in the world, and the world was made through Him, and the world did not know Him. [11]He came to His own, and those who were His own did not receive Him. [12]But as many

as received Him, to them He gave the right to become children of God, even to those who believe in His name, ¹³who were born, not of blood nor of the will of the flesh nor of the will of man, but of God. ¹⁴And the Word became flesh, and dwelt among us, and we saw his glory as of the only begotten of the Father, full of grace and truth.

Notice once more that reading John 1:13 in context with verse 12, the phrase "nor by the will of man," does not seem to be arguing *forthrightly* that man is *incapable* of volitionally receiving Christ. For again, verse 12 actually states that there *are* some who do receive Christ (though it is implied they are a minority), and here the verb means **to receive by <u>taking</u>**. The same Greek word is used in Matthew 26:26, when Christ says, "*Take*, eat; this is my body." This reading of John 1:12 (about man receiving Christ), when combined with the phrase "[not] by the will of man" in verse 13, has led certain interpreters to use a dialectical explanation in order to reconcile the supposed antinomy. Thus they claim that a man comes to God in this fashion: he passes under a doorway with a sign above it reading, "Whosoever will may come;" yet once he has passed through the doorway and looks back, he sees that the sign reads, "Foreordained before the foundation of the world." Such a dialectical explanation appears to rely on, at least in part, a misunderstanding of Ephesians 1:4-5, in which it is thought that *salvation* is what is predetermined upon certain *unbelievers*. But, in fact, Ephesians 1:4-5 is speaking of a future glorification which God has pre-planned for believers whose decisions of belief He knows in advance (see chpt. 16, discussion on *adoption*). Hence, part of the dialectical 'solution' of the hybrid view is based on an erroneous view of *adoption*, a term quite abused by many theologians (again, see chpt. 16).

But moving on, although John reveals in verse 12 that some persons have *become* [essen., *are ongoingly being* (2nd aorist Middle 'Deponent')] the children of God, *in the Roman mind this idea of being a child of God would certainly bring to mind the idea of demigods*. Thus John presumably would have acted to correct any such notion on the part of the Greco-Roman pagan that the "children of God" of whom he speaks in verse 12 were anything of the kind which they as pagans were likely to assume from their Greco-Roman mythology. For in Greco-Roman religious culture, a demigod was held to be the offspring that resulted from the pairing of a human and a god, such as those sired by the god Zeus in his philandering, conjugal activity with human women. Many such liaisons (most of them involving male gods and human women rather than female gods with human men) were recognized in Greek mythology. Interestingly enough, Alexander the Great was held by some to be a demigod, for he frequently used the title "Son of Ammon-

Zeus" which derived from his mother Olympias, who reportedly claimed that Zeus had impregnated her while she slept under an oak tree sacred to the god.[212] Caesar Augustus, somewhat similarly, claimed for himself a kind of demigod status centuries later. The cause of change happened early in his reign, when Augustus and the citizens of Rome saw Haley's Comet pass overhead. The emperor declared it was the spirit of Julius Caesar entering heaven upon his deification. As Augustus was the heir apparent of Caesar, Augustus declared himself the "son of the deified" (Latin "divi fillius"). In the polytheistic religion of Rome this title did not mean "the son of God" (Lat. "Deo fillius") but rather "a son of a god." Nevertheless, the title did assign a deification to the emperor, and the change in status helped to encourage allegiance and stabilize Augustus' reign early in the Roman ruler's career.

Considering, then, that John knew that some of his readers (Greek or Hellenized) would likely here think he was referring to demigods when he spoke of "children of God," the apostle seems anxious to clarify the point, thus stating that these he refers to are not begotten of *bloods*, i.e. not a product of human intercourse[213] nor that intercourse supposed between gods and humans. It is interesting to note in this regard that the first century Jewish historian, Josephus, speaks of the Greek belief in the *gigantes*—[mighty beings who, according to Greek religion, were the *offspring* of the two gods, Gaia (Mother Earth) and Uranus (Father Sky)]. The Greeks held that many offspring had come from various gods, some involving human parentage and some not; but presumably for the Greek, any of these offspring might be thought to be "children of divinity."[214] Josephus probably based his own view of supernatural males cohabiting with women on Genesis 6:1-4. Describing the pre-Flood culture of Noah, Josephus states: "For many angels of God accompanied with women, and begat sons that proved unjust, and despisers of all that was good, on account of the confidence they had in their own strength; for the tradition is, that these men did what resembled the acts of those whom the Grecians call giants" (*Antiquities* Book I, Chapter iii).[215] Josephus is not stating here that Greeks believed in an offspring of *angelic* cohabitation as he (as a Jew) would have defined *angelic*, but he recognizes that the Greek tradition held to something similar (the *gigantes*). In fact, the demigods were even more similar in nature to the offspring alluded to in Genesis than the race of *gigantes* that Josephus mentions, since demigods were held by the Greek to be of supernatural *and human* parentage. So, keeping Josephus's thought regarding angelic cohabitation in mind, while further noting that Paul, in his address to the Athenians on Mars' Hill, actually states that from *one* blood came all *men* and nations, it appears that John, in his use of the plural *bloods*, may have been referring also to the traditional Greek belief of *another* blood—the offspring resulting from the cohabitation of supernatural beings with humans. In fact, the concept of such cohabitation was the consistent viewpoint of all Antiquity. I myself incline to Josephus's view that angelic cohabitation did occur in Genesis, but even if John, hypothetically speaking, knew that angelic cohabitation had never occurred in history, he certainly would have wanted to refute the idea that those born of God in verse 12 were anything of the kind his readers might imagine.

The Jewish reader, on the other hand, may have taken the term *bloods* here to mean the Jews' various blood sacrifices—such as those found in Leviticus. (The idea of blood sacrifices was also common to Greco-Roman life.) Commentator John Gill (a man who occupied the same pulpit as Spurgeon but a century earlier) suggests that the term *bloods*, to the Jew, may have meant the blood of circumcision and the blood of the Passover.[216] Thus in the above cases, a misguided Jew at the time of John's writing (post-resurrection Christ) might, besides trusting in his descendency from Abraham,[217] imagine vainly that his observance of the Passover, the rite of circumcision, and (when possible) the observance of animal sacrifices under the Mosaic Law (such sacrifice ceased with the destruction of the Temple prior to John's Gospel writing), could continue to provide atonement for the hearer of the gospel of Christ, when in fact Christ had superseded and made such 'bloods,' i.e., in terms of continuing atonement, obsolete to such hearers. Note what John will clarify later in the first chapter, i.e., when he describes John the Baptist as recognizing that Christ 1) superseded Moses and the Law, and 2) was the fulfillment of the Lamb symbol in the Old Testament (vss. 17, 29). Now observe in the preceding paragraph that the general meaning of *cohabitation*, for the Greek, would also have been relevant to the Jewish mind, since the Jew likewise held the view of *de facto* supernatural cohabitation with humans; but the association of 'bloods' with cohabitation would, *for the Jew*, probably have occurred *later* to his mind than the association of the Levitical system and the Mosaic Law. In short, when he saw the word "bloods," his first thought would be of the Levitical system of sacrifice, etc. (while for the Greek it would be of cohabitation). We will come back to this point later.

It should be mentioned in passing that there are two common interpretations for "blood" in the (KJV) phrase, "not of blood." The first takes the word 'blood' to mean *race* (being ignorant, it seems, that the term is in the plural), esp. that of Abraham's particular line from which the Jews descended. In fact, many Jews of Jesus' day believed that their physical ancestry guaranteed their status as children of God. But again, regarding this view it must be remembered that Paul states to the Athenians in Acts 17 that all men descended from *one* blood, and that here in John 1:13 John uses the word *blood* in the plural. As for the second common interpretation, this holds that 'blood' (Gr. lit., *bloods*) refers to human procreation. It has been suggested that bloods in the plural might even refer to the blood of the mother plus the blood of the father. This interpretation is not *essentially* different than the above argument for *race*, and for the same reason does not therefore qualify as "bloods" [since we have no indication that John was trying to define race any differently than Paul did in the book of Acts, when Paul assigned to the idea of a line of human progeny, or *race* (presumably however segmentally considered) the word *blood* in the singular]

Nor of the Will of the Flesh

Moving along, we now come to John's second correction, i.e., that those born of God were not born "of the will of the flesh." This book takes the view that "will" (Gr. *thelo*) means *desire*, i.e., desire which, depending on the context, also may include a corresponding act of the will (i.e., *desirous intent*; see chpt. 17, question re: Phil. 2:13). The main point I wish to draw out about John's 2nd correction is this: *the term flesh in John 1:13 at one level of meaning, may be defined with due emphasis on the near, rather than on the far, context.* Some may wonder why we should do this. Here is the reason: To rely on the far context of scripture would mean defining *flesh* according to Paul's extensive treatment of the term *flesh* in Romans, in which *the flesh* is defined as that state in which a man has the knowledge of good and evil (see chpt. 18). Applying this definition of *flesh* to Christ's incarnated flesh in the verse following John 1:13 would certainly be problematic. (It would be even more problematic if one took the traditional view that Paul's Romanic use of *flesh* equals *sinful nature*.) That is, I'm saying we ought not to think that Christ was incarnated in the kind of flesh (v. 14) which Adam acquired by sinning. Nor did Adam pass down this acquired element (the knowledge of good and evil) onto Christ, for Christ preceded Adam and was therefore not subject to this aspect of Adamic inheritance in His flesh. <u>Thus, a proper lexical rendering for the word *flesh* in verse 13's phrase "nor by the will of the flesh" should mean, *at one level of meaning*, as I think it may mean in the mind of the apostle, the same *benign* form of flesh as that which the word *flesh* means in the following verse (v. 14), that is, *flesh* as it is meant to be understood when John says that the Word (Christ) became flesh.</u> (We will explain further the meaning of this interpretation in a moment).

These considerations of the term *flesh* lead us to another point regarding interpretation. There appears to be two chief reasons why Calvinists misinterpret John 1:13. First, they do not seem to take seriously John's three demarcated negations in the phrase "**not** of bloods **nor** of the will of the flesh **nor** of the will of man." All three negations are clearly delineated in the Greek. Each of these distinctions thus argue for an *essential* difference among themselves. Of course, these three categories will overlap somewhat because all three by definition share the characteristic that they cannot lead to a rebirth in God; but again, essential distinctions should nevertheless be evident among them. (In fact, they remind us of John's tri-part distinction of things that are in the world but not of God—the lust of the flesh, the lust of the eyes, and the pride of life.) Yet the Calvinist appears to see no essential distinction between the last two, i.e., "the will of the flesh" and "the will of man." In fact, Calvinists are so focused on wanting the last phrase to be understood as teaching man's total inability, that the second phrase is often taken to mean the same essential thing as the third in order to bolster their argument. This means that the 3rd phrase is subsumed within the 2nd phrase and therefore did not really need to be stated by John. Such an approach by the Calvinist is similar to the interpretation which takes the three phrases "blood," "will of the flesh," and "will of man" to mean, respectively, "natural generation," "sexual desire," and "a husband's will," thus maintaining only the barest of distinctions instead of the fairly strong delineations evident in the original Greek (because of the appearance of "*ouk… oude… oude…*"). Note that we might at first suppose that a contemporary Greek reader of John might likely, IF he believed that flesh *equaled* the state of being sexual, assume that the *Logos*, in becoming flesh, meant that the *Logos* became *sexual*, i.e., in much the same way that Zeus did when the god reputedly had children by human women. But this concept of *another blood* was already addressed and corrected in the first part of the tri-part statement. So, presumably, the reader would think John is correcting something else—to wit, the common bias held by many of his readers, namely, that the immortal God and Creator of the universe could not become human, i.e., that the divine realm could not inhabit the human realm because of the latter's humbled state. This view was held by those Jews who argued that a man could never also be deity.[218] [60 years later John was still battling this error in the form of the Gnostics, who likewise seemed to have applied a Hellenizing assumption to God and thus accepted the Platonic notion that the Ideals were incompatible with physical matter, which (Ideals), for the strongly Hellenized Jew, included God. Thus John counters by saying that the *Logos* was *not* demeaned in His incarnation but was beheld in His glory and was full of grace and truth.] Incidentally, though the term "flesh" readily connotates to today's English reader something sexual in nature, Paul's treatment of "flesh" in Romans 7 and his link with that word to Abraham's life of works ("What shall we say then, of our father Abraham, as pertaining to the flesh hath found?") arguably shows that "nor of the will of the *flesh*" would have a broader meaning for John's contemporary readers than what we might likely infer today. Second, Calvinists do not seem to have understood the lexical meaning of the word *man* in the phrase, "nor of the will of man." (At least those are my findings after visiting about 10-15 Calvinistic websites.) That is, they appear not to know that the Greek word translated *man* in John 1:13 does not mean *mankind* (i.e. gender inclusive) but means *a grown male* (e.g., *man*). And yet they all state or imply that the phrase "nor of the will of man" means that *all persons* cannot receive Christ because of their total inability. But if this is what John is stating, why would he restrict his third term to mean *the will of a male*?[219] To argue as the Calvinist does [and thus not according to the lexical knowledge of what the Greek word *aner* (*man* or *male*) means, since Calvinists seem not to recognize that here], would be to unwittingly say that John is making a special point about the depravity of *males*. Obviously, that does nothing to support the Calvinistic argument of universal *gender inclusive* depravity. Once this point is understood, it becomes evident that the phrase "[not] of the will of man" is no real argument for the Calvinistic view of universal depravity.

Up to this point we have established two things regarding the overall phrase "not of bloods nor of the will of the flesh nor of the will of man" as found in the KJV[220] and NAS: 1) The three phrases in John's tri-part statement form three *essentially* different categories wherein each is **not** to be subsumed under one of the other categories; and 2) the term *flesh* ought to be essentially consistent between verses 13 and 14, at least at one level of meaning, so that Christ is not thought to have been incarnated with the post-Adamic form of flesh.

Regarding this last point, commentators from across the denominational spectrum—i.e., those from the Reformed-based *Geneva Study Bible* (GSB) (1599) (who draw on Calvin, Zwingli, Luther, etc.) to the free will Methodist, John Wesley—seem untroubled in taking *vastly* different meanings for the two appearances of *flesh* in its successive occurrences in John 1:13-14. *Yet one can hardly expect that a contemporary reader of John's gospel might have done the same.* For although a Hellenized but nevertheless Old Testament literate Jew might understand in the context of John 1 that those born of God were men who, unlike the Logos, had a flesh intensified with the knowledge of good and evil (since they were born of the seed of fallen Adam and had acted to love darkness rather than the Light), a pagan Greek would hardly understand this point, except insofar that those born of God were previously darkened. That is, presumably, the Greek reader would understand John's formal point that man in the state of his flesh **was** in need of redemption (having rejected the Light), while the Logos **was not** in need of redemption, though the Latter too was in the flesh. And, at the least, this would challenge the Greek reader's assumption that all flesh by its material nature was imperfect. (And by "imperfect" here I do not mean that the Greek would regard the flesh to be something sinful, but rather something less fully real, as the Shadows to the Realities.) For if redemption could come by One who was in the flesh, then material nature could not also be inherently imperfect. Yet John's way of expressing the phrase might also explain why the evangelizing apostle didn't bother drawing a stronger distinction regarding the term *flesh*. For John could have stated the respective phrases in verses 13 and 14 according to normal Greek idiom, i.e., "nor the *thelo* of the flesh <u>of them</u>" and "the Word became the flesh <u>of Him</u>" (or, "the Word became the flesh as the flesh of the first man when he was created"). But to draw such a fine and contrasting distinction of *flesh* would only confuse the Greek reader, and possibly lead him to think that the kind of flesh of the Logos was too fundamentally different than that of man's flesh, for the Logos to have truly been incarnated in sufficiently human form. So then, by leaving his statement more formalized, John (or at least the Spirit of God inspiring John) seems to have tailored the phrase about *flesh* so that 1) those Jews (or Judistic Greeks) who could more readily understand such fine distinctions might do so (and, in doing so, understand Gr. *thelo* as meaning *desire* variably, see footnote 236); while 2) those who would not understand them would nevertheless be prevented from making certain unwarranted assumptions about the nature of flesh, the Logos, and man. Thus we see that John's way of expressing the phrase about *flesh* allows his different groups of readership their ongoing respective lines of proper inferences each might make.

Again, however, there is the contrary, if nearly universal, Evangelical view. In this view the term *flesh* is regarded as a <u>sinful</u> nature in verse 13 (since it refers to *man*),[221] but as a pure form of pre-Fall Adamic flesh in verse 14 (since it refers to Christ's incarnation). Typical are the statements of the aforementioned GSB, which first defines "the will of the flesh" in verse 13 as *"that shameful and corrupt nature of man, which is throughout the scriptures described as an enemy of the spirit"* to a definition for verse 14 which reads, *"That is, man: so that, by the figure of speech synecdoche, the part is taken for the whole: for he took upon himself our entire nature, that is to say, a true body, and a true soul."* This kind of fantastic turnabout in definition found in the GSB is unfortunately the common approach of Evangelicals when defining the term *flesh* in its two appearances in John 1:13-14. Yet, again, it is obvious that any contemporary reader of John's gospel, including those familiar with the Old Testament, would never have understood *flesh* to flip-flop in definition to a point of espousing a flesh that was inherently sinful.[222] The reason it seems logical to Evangelicals that *flesh* <u>*should*</u> flip-flop in such a way as they describe it, is chiefly because *tradition* has taught them to interpret these verses this way. Thus they have applied themselves to making arbitrary lexical changes whenever their theology demands it. Indeed, Evangelicals seem to act as though John's new readers will see such plain differences between what *flesh* must mean in verse 13 compared to verse 14. They will not! Neither did John's original audience; for the Jews never held to such a doctrine as original sin, and the Greeks held that *all* material creation was imperfect by its material nature, a belief hardly similar to the doctrine of original sin. Thus, besides the Greek, what John appears to be expecting the

Jew to do interpretively (regarding the term *flesh*) is to EITHER assume that the flesh referred to in verse 13 has an intensive nature regarding knowledge (i.e., had the knowledge of good and evil in accordance with the Jewish understanding of the nature of man), etc., as represented here by those born of God who, as events proved, followed after the flesh *during their probation*, and thus chose darkness, OR, to assume that the term *flesh* does **not** here flip-flop in definition, and therefore might be inferred (though improperly) to mean man as altered somehow but not per se *lost* through the course of his probation. If the latter, then such a reader may feel that he can act relatively good within what he supposes is a probationary state like man in the first form of his flesh (Adam and Eve in the Garden), in which he mistakenly thinks God weighs works in a relative, not absolute, scale. And so he strives to act like the Pharisee in the temple, who, in comparing himself to the hapless sinner, trusted in his *relative* goodness instead of in the mercy of God.[223] In any event, John's point here appears to go to an overarching argument, in which each of the three phrases of his tri-part statement will reference at least something of human involvement, namely, the history of men and women[224] which has never shown, even in its description of people in their most exalted[225] positions and activities, that people have accomplished or become that which God reasonably required of them.[226] For though a man is not in need of redemption in his pre-Fall state, redemption becomes necessary once he sins—and his rebirth is made possible only by God's grace alone as appropriated by his faith in the provision of the substitutionary death and resurrection of the incarnated *Logos*. Therefore those born of God were born not of the want (desire) (*or* desirous intent) of the flesh, because man—individual man—simply powers not to come toward the *Logos* apart from the pulling of the Father. This is evident since post-Fall man's acquired knowledge (which altered his flesh) has proven itself useless in aiding man toward his reconciliation with God. Still, while the birthing (i.e., 'midwifery') of God's children is **of God**, the taking/ receiving of God is **of man**. That is, the "of God" is not meant by John to indicate a unilateral acting of God in relation to man unto man's annihilation (i.e., annihilation because of an erasure of the will), as the Calvinist (unwittingly) proposes. It should be noted in passing that if someone should ask the question why John would, within the verse's aforementioned polyvalent meaning, be bothered to assume his reader's inference of the short-lived condition of persons under probation, it might be argued that John was slipping into the discussion the fact[227] that such a condition was indeed short-lived, and that persons have never shown a *diligent* inclination for God. This gentle, side-on challenge of John would, in fact, be consistent with the apostle's demeanor.

The Will of Man

Now if we grant that the tri-part statement in John 1:13 ought to meet the two qualifications we have been discussing, i.e., 1) that there are three *essentially* different categories in view; and 2) that there ought to be a relatively *consistent* definition for *flesh* in verses 13-14, then unfortunately we must also say that it is hard to find these criteria embraced by many (any?) translations and commentaries in common use. (I am ashamed to admit that I myself merely contributed to the confusion about John 1:13 in an earlier version of this book.) Nevertheless, let me propose what I now believe is an acceptable translation of John 1:13:

> who are born, not of bloods, nor of the want (*or* desirous intent) of the flesh, nor of the want (*or* desirous intent) of a man (or male), but of God.

By default of what each of the words 'blood,' 'flesh,' and 'man' should *not* mean, in terms of any being subsumed under one of the remaining terms, we come to establish the reasons for proper translation. The word *will* has been changed to *want* [*desire* (or desirous intent)] as contextually understood here as desire which may include the will, depending upon which path one takes within the polyvalent meaning. See chpt. 17, argument re: Phil. 2:13).][228]

Now, regarding this 3rd phrase in John's tri-part statement, "[not] of the will of man," a few things must be noted. First, the **essential differences** between the three phrases of verse 13 would appear to be thus to the Greek: The 1st speaks of a process outside his control, the 2nd of a process he may control as resourced of himself, and the 3rd of a process in which he agrees to assign control to someone else, i.e., to some 'Over-MAN' [or 'Over-MEN,' (to borrow loosely Nietzsche's term)]. Moving on, the second thing to be noted is that the word *man* in John 1:13 is singular, without the Greek article in front of it, and it is gender specific of male. While the Greek word for *man* in John 1:13 may indeed have a collective meaning (i.e., as when the word *ballplayer* in the phrase "a ballplayer's salary" may be understood in some contexts to mean "ballplayers' salaries"), it does not appear to be used in Scripture nor in John to mean *mankind*. In fact, when John 2:25 states that "[Jesus] needed not that any should testify of man: for he knew what was in man," the word *man* (Gr. *anthropo*), which appears in this verse twice, means a group composed of both sexes, i.e., *mankind* (see also Jn. 1:4, 9). But this Greek word, *anthropo*, in John 1:4, 9 and 2:25 has a different meaning than the Greek word, *aner*, used in John 1:13. (Moreover (we anticipate the objection), arguably the reference to John the Baptist as an *anthropos*, rather than an *aner*, sent from God, is not proof that John used the terms interchangably, but only that he was was intending to mean "person," to the Greek who knew nothing of Malachi's prophecy that John would be as Elijah.) The biblical commentator Thayer cites a handful of instances of *aner* (not involving Jn. 1:13) in that word's approximately 200 appearances in the New Testament, in which he believes the word means both male and female. But he notes that the commentator Meyer does not agree. Having looked up the few exceptions that Thayer cites, I personally agree with Meyer. (See Thayer's comments under Strong's word #435 (Gr. *aner*) at BlueLetterBible.com, where none of the alleged exceptions are clear examples of gender inclusivity.) So, while *aner* is translated 147 times as *man* and 50 times as *husband*, we must note that *aner* is not contested by either Thayer or Meyer to be gender inclusive in John 1:13.[229]

Unfortunately, the NAS's use of the phrase "nor of the will of man" in John 1:13 fails, along with the KJV, in bringing attention to the gender restriction of *aner*, making it appear that man means *mankind*. I have noted elsewhere (see chpt. 17 again, question regarding Phil. 2:13) that the NAS sometimes (consciously or not) seems content with rubber-stamping the KJV's long-standing phraseology if it helps to maintain a Calvinist position in a controversial passage. The NIV does better in its translation, rendering the phrase in question as "a husband's will." Thus the NIV recognizes the omission of the article in front of *aner*, while appropriately defining "man" as *male*. While the NIV rendering stands on better lexical grounds than either the KJV or the NAS, I believe it remains problematic. This is because the second and third phrases in John's tri-part statement are actually combined in the NIV to read "nor of human decision or a husband's will." The word *or* instead of *nor* before "a husband's will" between the 2nd and 3rd phrases arguably makes the tri-part statement into a two-part statement. Note the NIV: "Children born not of natural descent, nor of human decision or a husband's will, but born of God." The *or* thus refers to *either* human decision *or* a husband's will, **but not both**, unless the "or" is taken idiomatically to mean "and." But even if this were the case, "a husband's will" and "natural descent" are too close in reference to the same process to really qualify as categories of *essential* difference. Thus the NIV eliminates the idea of three separate categories of *essential* distinction. Furthermore, unless the "or" is taken idiomatically to mean "and," the NIV seems to be stating that John was *unsure* of the case, i.e., whether it were not of human decision or not of a husband's will. Or, if the NIV is stating that the phrase "human decision" is the general definition more closely and particularly defined as "a husband's will," then even here they are still contending merely for two categories, or even one. In other words, at the least, they have eliminated a 3rd category of essential distinction. But again, in the Greek, the apostle's distinction between the three categories is clear:

"ouk**(not)**…oude**(nor)**…oude**(nor)**…"

On the positive side, I do think the NIV's phrase "a husband's will" assumes it is not "*one* husband's will" but rather the will of *husbands* in general, that is, a collective subset. But again, I think the phrase "a man's (or *male's*) will," rather than "a husband's will," is to be preferred, since again, the 3rd phrase in the NIV is subsumed within at least one of the other phrases.[230] Now, if we translate the 3rd phrase to read "a man's (or *male's*) want (*or* desirous intent)," and further understand that John is using "man" (or, "*male* ") as a subset of men (or *males*), then we may assume that John is saying that those born of God (v. 12) are not born of a man's (or *male's*) want (*or* desirous intent) (v. 13)—e.g., not by the want (*or* desirous intent) of men (or *males*) who, e.g., have invented or exalted a false idea, religion, or philosophy and, while doing so, promoted the notion that by desiring (or desiring and then following) such an idea or system one becomes a child of God. All such governmental, philosophical, or religious attempts by men, (or *males*)—whose gender, most especially in John's day (e.g., various Caesars, the Pharisees, etc.) and previous to that time, seems to have given them particular opportunities to teach falsehood and become spiritual leaders of people—are the ones whom John cites as particularly failing to lead their followers into becoming children of God.[231]

It might be objected at this point that I have not maintained the essential separateness of the three categories in John's tri-part statement. I say this because it might be thought that I have already previously assigned the Jewish[232] Levitical system to the term "bloods," which, if practiced as a false religious system,[233] would also meet the criteria of the above phrase "the want (*or* desirous intent) of man." But I think the solution may be found in recognizing that these two categories—the first and the third—may actually be held in meaning for the other, that is, as long as the *order* of these two is not held to be the same for each of the two (Greek and Jewish) audiences. In other words, *a Greek reader* would presumably have understood the first clause, involving "bloods," with 'human' generation and human/supernatural cohabitation, and the third clause, involving "a male's will," with false religious/philosophical systems[234]—**whereas** a Jewish reader would presumably have understood the first clause, involving "bloods," with the (despite its destruction in 70 A.D.) Levitical system of sacrifice, and the third clause, involving "a male's will," with the kind of angelic, perverted desire and cohabitation recognized by Josephus, **or** *race*, as having arisen through "a man's (or *male's*) desire," i.e., of Abraham (Isaac, and Jacob),[235] *or*, both angelic cohabitation *and* race.

Such a view, if correct, that the first and third parts of John's tri-part statement was intended by the Spirit to speak differently to respective audiences, would thus be continuing the process that John (by the Spirit) had begun with the term *Logos*. This would account for John's not-too-closely defined and therefore somewhat flexible terms, i.e., "bloods" and "a male's want (*or* desirous intent) which ironically result, not in ambiguity, but in his contemporary readers being corrected more quickly in the first mistaken assumptions they would be likely to have as they began reading his gospel. This approach would have enabled John to have the widest possible audience as he emerged his definitions early in the first chapter, so that by the end of the chapter his readers might coalesce into a single group that could understand the nature and mission of the *Logos*.

Now, observe that the argument put forth in the preceding two paragraphs is not at all a necessary one for the general interpretation of John 1:13 as presented in this chapter. Indeed, one could just as easily say that John is correcting the Jewish reader upon the same exact points and in the same order as the Greek reader, in which case John is assigning the determination for the Levitical system by the Jew into the 3rd category of false religious, philosophical, and governmental systems, and therefore not concerning himself with culturally different viewpoints and whether everyone's first objections are immediately answered in the first clause of correction (that is, as long as they are answered in the course of the gospel). But I think this idea of the Spirit speaking differently to respective audiences through the same word symbols is a real possibility in this passage. Further, the accusation that some might bring against this possibility—i.e., that words are being treated in such an abstract and deconstructed manner that it invites the reader to insert his own particular and esoteric meaning into the text-is not a fair one. The hermeneutic I'm suggesting for the tri-part phrase of John 1:13 does nothing to violate the traditional historical-grammatical approach of proper biblical interpretation, though it may indeed offend the sensibilities of some who, perhaps through an over-zealousness for Evangelical *systematic* theology, so called, might insist that every Scripture can only have one primary meaning, that is, because it is assumed that there can only be one primary audience. While that principle would certainly be true in many cases, I do not think it applies here for the reasons already given.

Conclusion of John 1:13

Taking all these thoughts into consideration, the meaning of the phrase in John 1:13, "not of bloods, nor of the want (*or* desirous intent) of the flesh nor of the want [*or* desirous intent] of man," appears to be the following for Greek (and strongly Hellenized Jewish?) readers: Those born of God, i.e., those granted the authority by Christ to become God's children upon receiving Him, are birthed *not of bloods*—i.e., not a result of human intercourse or the cohabitation of supernatural beings with humans; *nor by the want* (or *desirous intent*) *of the flesh*—i.e., not by the want (*or* desirous intent) of any works effort through his own flesh; *nor by the want* (or *desirous intent*) *of a man (male)*—i.e., not through any man (or male) who, in particular, has thought (or thought and also sought) to lead others to think they may become children of God apart from trust in the incarnate *Logos*, Jesus Christ. [236]

Once John 1:13 is understood in its proper cultural context according to the historical-grammatical method of interpretation, it should be evident that John 1:13 is in harmony with the Scriptural view of man as a free will person able to receive Christ (see Jn. 1:12). Moreover, it should be equally evident that John 1:13 has nothing whatsoever to do with the so-called 'total depravity' of mankind as the Calvinist seeks to define it. Rather, John's overall thought for the Greek reader, as may be amplified by the apostle's implications in verses 12 and 13, is that one becomes a child and is *born* of God through receiving the *Logos*, and 1) not born by any natural or perverse procreation, 2) nor by the want [*or* desirous intent] of the flesh *as practiced inefficiently* in its consideration of the Logos, 3) nor by the want [*or* desirous intent] of men (males) who have imagined—or imagined and promoted—vain systems for the goal of Divine appeasement.

Footnotes:

[206] This fact leads to a sidebar discussion, namely this—to go from Calvinism to today's most popular spin on the gospel—the prosperity gospel—one merely needs to employ the same methodology of Calvinism but 'resolve' the dialectical emphasis in favor of *man* instead of *God*. In other words (dialectically speaking), *if A)* someone who trusts Christ by an act of his will is privileged to be a child of God; *and if B)* those who are born of God are born apart from any process involving a man exercising his own will; *then, C)* those who are said to receive Christ as His children must themselves be God, since they cannot be man. Thus they 'receive themselves,' i.e., they accept the divinity within themselves which **is** themselves. For either treatment of the two terms, "man," or "God," e.g., as shown above or as treated in Calvinism, employs the same bogus methodology whenever either of the terms "man" or "God" is absolutized 'against' the other. I say 'against' because both views actually lead to a total indistinction of definition regarding the terms *God* and *man* (as my readers up to this point will understand), so that, technically speaking, there *are* no terms to which any description can be applied, including a comparison or contrast of the one to the other.

I hasten to add that, in some Evangelical circles, the current emphases on the prosperity gospel and other similar forms of the "words are containers" movement, in which God is assumed to be *obligated* to bring to the prosperitors' lives that which they themselves *actualize* by the choice of words they use, is nothing more than the aforementioned version of Calvinism turned on its head, i.e., as just noted, the Calvinistic *method* but with the dialectical resolution upon *man* instead of *God*. Indeed, some within the prosperity movement actually teach that whatever happens to us is solely because our *thoughts* actualize it. Thus according to the prosperity gospel, one's words or thoughts—and nothing other than these—actualizes the prosperitor's history (or non-prosperitor's history, depending on the case).

Therefore the prosperity gospel is like Calvinism, insofar as regarding the world as moved only through the One. The only "difference," so imagined, is that in Calvinism this One is interpreted as "God," whereas in Prosperity the One is interpreted to be the "Self," i.e. 'the blessed Christian' (i.e., 'the enlightened one'). The term *God* or even the idea of *God* is not really necessary to the Prosperitors any more than it is to Calvinists, since God is nothing more than the ManGod's construct upon the material world. (By the term 'ManGod' I mean that *man* and *God* are defined synonymously.) (In other words, *God*, in prosperity theology, becomes one's own thought determination. Terms like "faith," "blessing," and "God," are simply kept in play and made to *sound* Evangelical. The only *real* distinctions that exist in (not between) Calvinism and Prosperity in the use of *God* and *man* in the distinctive elements of these respective theologies, are 1) the aural difference of sound when these 'words' are spoken, and 2) the visual difference on paper when seeing these 'word symbols.' Sadly, each group's followers never imagine how much they are like the other. Calvinists, for example, by far the more analytical of the two groups, hardly suspect that their intellectualized theology and the simple narcissism of prosperity gospel are the brainchildren—the mirrored twins, in fact—of the same theological method.

But to return to a consideration of John 1:13, we see that the Scripture teaches neither of these viewpoints but rather one in which God alone provides man the atonement he needs to be born of God, while allowing man to decide for himself whether or not he shall receive God's salvation. This is the only view that allows an honest use of the terms *man* and *God*.

[207] that is, the earliest copies of New Testament writings, all of which were written entirely with Greek capital letters)

[208] Though defined more closely here, throughout this chapter I generally use the term "Greek reader" to mean the Greco-Roman reader.

[209] The meaning of *Logos* was modified later in various philosophies, including Aristotle (to mean *reason*), the Stoics (to mean *the rational principle of harmony inherent in the universe*), Philo the Jew (to mean *the Platonic Realities as opposed to the 'shadows' of physical matter*), and finally by John himself (to essentially mean *the Stoic and Platonic idea of the Logos as overarching Reason, though with its full and correct realization being found in Jesus Christ, the Incarnated Son of God, equal to the Father in His eternal Deity*).

[210] Some Christian thinkers have argued that John never would have used the term *Logos* as derived from a Greek understanding of the term. In this view, Philo, the contemporary Platonic-Judaic philosopher whose thought has sometimes been claimed as influential upon the New Testament and upon John's use of *Logos* in particular, is not supposed to have influenced John toward such a pagan view, because such a Philoan view could never support the idea of Divine Incarnation. It is also claimed by some Christian thinkers that the idea of "wisdom" as personified in Proverbs 8:22-26 is the true tradition for John's concept of the *Logos*, since 1) it owes nothing to Greek influence, and 2) John was aiming to show Christ as the fulfillment of Old Testament symbol.

But I find these views inadequate for the following reasons: 1) Paul, in his speech on Mars' Hill in Athens, did not allow the Greek idea of "The Unknown God"—which, whatever form it may have been speculated by the Greek mind to involve (if theoretically, they had bothered to hypothesize about it and given it a description, in which case it surely would *not* have approximated the idea that Paul would give it)—to stop him from borrowing a rather abstract inscription from the Greeks and proceed to add and subtract from it until it reflected true Christian theology. Paul does the same thing again by quoting one of their Stoic philosophers, borrowing where he could, while not at all coming to the general conclusion of the Stoic. (The goal of bringing divine truth to man looks for such a contact point. Even God did not begin conveying His Scripture with "In the beginning God..." but rather "There was in the land of Uz a man, whose name was Job...") Why then, could not John also borrow a rather abstract term familiar to the Greek mind and add and subtract to its Stoic and Platonic form of definitions, respectively, until it too reflected true Christian theology? 2) The word *wisdom* in Proverbs in the Septuagint, while it can be argued to represent Christ in symbol, is not the word *logos*, but *sophias*. Why, then, if in fact John wanted to show that he was building his definition in John 1:1ff from such an Old Testament Judaic derivative, wouldn't he have used the word *sophias* in John 1:1-14 instead of the word *Logos*? While in one sense John *did* appeal to the Old Testament (and thus to his Jewish readers) by his use of the word *Logos* (i.e. "word" as understood in the phrase "the word of the Lord"), John's intended audience was also Greek; 3) It is not accurate to state or imply that John's goal was *only* to demonstrate Christ as the fulfillment of Old Testament symbol (i.e., at the expense of reshaping the meaning of *Logos* for the Greek). John's use of the term *Logos* and his concession to a Greek readership (Jn. 6:4, in which John bothers to define the Passover as "a feast of the Jews") clearly shows that his intended audience included Greeks unfamiliar with aspects of Jewish religion.

[211] I am not suggesting here that Paul was not led by the Spirit to have written so. I am merely pointing out the differences in personality between Paul and John at the time of their particular writings as under the full inspiration of the Spirit. Neither am I questioning Paul's demeanor toward the Early Church, for we know he was a man who admonished each one of the Ephesians for three years night and day with tears (Acts 20:31).

[212] The title "Son of Ammon-Zeus" was actually bestowed upon Alexander the Great by Egyptian priests of the god Ammon at the Oracle of the god in the Libyan Desert.

[213] This erroneous assumption was akin to that expressed by Nicodemus, who (if we assume he was not being sarcastic) had in mind the process of natural generation (or perhaps reincarnation), when he asked Christ if spiritual rebirth meant a man's re-entry into his mother's womb.

[214] (Note: John's phrase should be properly rendered in 1:12 as "children of God," not "sons of God.")

[215] The "angels" Josephus refers to would be regarded by biblical scholars (sympathetic with Josephus) as *fallen* angels.

[216] A.T. Robertson states that *bloods* (in the plural) is found commonly in the Old Testament and in that corresponding era, as, for example, in the term *bloodguiltiness* (or *bloodshed*, as in *drops of blood*), though he expresses some puzzlement for its appearance in John 1:13. But perhaps "bloods" in John 1:13 (for the Jew) refers to the bloodshed of animals in sacrifice and/or the sprinkling of blood (drops) upon the altar and upon the clothes of Aaron and his sons, etc., that is, that which involves *bloodshed* according to the Levitical system.

[217] i.e., further qualified in the sense that many Jews held that their physical ancestry to Abraham was itself the qualifying feature of being a child of God. For this reason Christ rebuked those who trusted in paternity, reminding them that others among their fathers had killed the prophets (Mt. 23:29-31).

[218] See John chapter 11.

[219] (If there *are* or *have been* Calvinists unlike those I found online, their views appear not to have affected the mainstream of their movement.)

[220] The KJV actually uses commas to set off the three categories even more decidedly, i.e., "Which were born, not of blood, nor of the will of the flesh, nor of the will of man, but of God." I believe this extensive use of the comma was the general practice of that period.

[221] ...and so, according to the demands of their theology, it *must*.

[222] Obviously, the example of *to eat* in John 6:52-53 is an exception because of its parabolic use by the Lord; but that is an entirely different thing than how *flesh* is being presented in its two appearances in John 1:13-14.

Incidentally, I am not arguing here that all of Scripture must be thought easily understandable to the unsaved man. There is a difference depending on the audience, often based on their willingness to hear the truth of a message. John assumes his readers are interested in the truthful message he relates and thus uses terms meant to be understood by his audience (or properly speaking, *audiences*). However, God's message is not always greeted enthusiastically, and in these cases, especially, it should not be assumed that the terms God uses will necessarily be understood by those in rebellion to Him. (In fact, we are told that sometimes even the Lord's prophets themselves did not understand the full implications of all that they wrote about while under the Spirit's inspiration.) In the case of Isaiah's message to rebellious King Ahaz in Isaiah 7:14, the prophecy states: "A *virgin* (Heb. *almah*, i.e., *lass* as veiled, or private) shall conceive," and the king almost certainly would not have understood that God was using *almah* as a double for something besides "lass," such that the thought would include "*virgin*." That is, God was, in fact—besides giving the king a prophecy about Isaiah's young wife ("lass") who would conceive a child (a child who, in the near aspect of the prophecy, would not reach a tender age before Damascus and Syria were judged)—also giving the king a prophecy about a Child who one day would be born of a virgin. Note that *God* named Isaiah's child Maher-shalal-hash-baz, which means "swift is the booty, speedy is the prey," but that it was prophesied that *the woman* would call the child "God with us"). Like the name "Lemuel" in Proverbs 31, which is thought by some to be a diminutive form of the name

"Solomon" which was given to him by his mother, so too may we suppose that Isaiah's wife would have called her child "God with us" upon seeing her husband's prophecy by the Spirit fulfilled in its time (i.e., that which we understand to be the prophecy's near-aspect fulfillment). Thus the appearance of the name "Immanuel" in Isaiah 8:8 may be taken as having double reference, on the one hand to Isaiah's child as born of the young lass (*almah*) who was the prophet's wife, but also to the coming Child born of a virgin (*almah*). This future aspect of *almah* reproved the spirit of the king, by stating a Messianic prophecy that Ahaz was not inclined to understand. So the insistence of theologians that *almah* be translated "virgin" in Isaiah 7:14, based on the restrictive Greek word for "virgin" in Matthew 1:23, is indeed legitimate in the sense that God Himself intended this *as one of the meanings* for "*almah*" in Isaiah 7:14, that is, when He spoke this Messianic prophecy. **But** such a restricting translation in Isaiah (solely rendering *almah* as "virgin") fails to show the near sense in which the prophecy was fulfilled in the time of King Ahaz, a layer of meaning God intended, insofar as (in the near aspect) He meant it to refer to an *almah*, "lass," who was Isaiah's young wife. Therefore this insistence on "virgin" for Isaiah 7:14 appears to have come from translational bias (stemming, perhaps, from a preference by theologians for Evangelical 'systematic' theology, which, if I'm not mistaken, esp. regarding the American form, generally believes that only one primary meaning of a passage can be in evidence). What generally fails to be seen, then, regarding Isaiah 7:14, is that there is an audience which finds the full relevance of *almah* in its *Messianic aspect* (*the Savior who was virgin-born*), but another audience which found the only relevance of *almah* in the *Ahazaic aspect* (if even in that). To insist only on one audience for "virgin" seems suspect, for it forces Isaiah's prophecy to have no real meaning for Ahaz unless the king sees the far-off view of Messiah as virgin-born. (Incidentally, Isaiah's prophetic statement about the destruction of Damascus and Samaria appears to be relevant to the prophecy's near aspect only.) This restricted meaning would practically assign God's motive in giving a prophecy about a "virgin" as that given to Ahaz to deliberately mislead him. Moreover, Isaiah's prophecy in 7:14, if it only meant "virgin," might thus be thought by Ahaz (who would have been able to know of the naming of Isaiah's newborn child, as begotten of the prophet's wife, i.e., a non-virgin) *disproven*, since a virgin in Isaiah's time never conceived (i.e., *while a virgin*). This assumes that Ahaz would not make the finer distinction we drew a moment ago, in noting a difference between the name that *God* gave Isaiah's child, and the "pet" name we presume was given him by his mother. Thus God, as it were, shows King Ahaz—a king who is summarized in 2 Kings and 2 Chronicles as one who did not do right—that He is a God able to bring appropriate judgment against those He prophesizes. I believe this thought implies an additional point God was showing King Ahaz about Himself, i.e., that God is able to judge all who are rebellious against Him, *including* King Ahaz and the nation he rules.

Now in passing one more thing should be mentioned. While it is true that Mary was a virgin at the time of Jesus' birth, I personally think the Scriptures show the propecy may have been fulfilled even if Joseph, at the bidding of the angel of the Lord, had "taken unto him" (sexually) Mary his wife *before* she had birthed Jesus, her being *already* with Child by the Holy Spirit. In other words, it seems that God did not want the fact that Mary was pregnant to cause Joseph to "burn" for Mary his wife—and thus possibly tempt him—and so the angel of the Lord bids him to go ahead according to his sexual desire; for this wouldn't matter since Mary was already with Child by the Holy Spirit. But it appears Joseph felt uncomfortable doing so, and so waited until Jesus was born. All this seems implied in the adversative Greek term "de" in the "de—kai" construction found at Mt. 1:24-25, which follows the angel of the Lord's injunction to "fear not to take unto thee Mary thy wife" (vs. 20). What the "de" shows is Joseph's qualified act of obedience—"**_yet_**" (Gr. *de*) Joseph, being raised from sleep, did *similar to what* (Gr. *hos*) the angel had bidden him, and took unto him Mary his wife—and (Gr. kai) knew her not until she had brought forth her firstborn son: and he called his name Jesus." Now, note further that Thayer states that from Homer down the Greek "parthenos" may mean, besides virgin and/or marriageable maiden, a young, *married* woman. Thus had Joseph had sexual relations with Mary *after* she was found with Child by the Holy Spirit but *before* she had given birth, the Isaiah 7:14 prophecy fulfillment would have been a more exact parallel. It's quite amazing how the parameters of definitions for Heb. *almah* and Greek *parthenos* allowed Joseph this option! Incidentally, while some claim that the adversative nature of Gr. "de" can mean merely "moreover," or "when," to sequentially move the narrative along, I think the appearance of "de" (translated "when") in Mt. 2:14 shows another case in which Joseph qualified an act of obedience. For after the angel of the Lord in Mt. 2:13 tells Joseph to "Arise…and flee," the Gr. "de" appears at the beginning of vs. 14, and may be understood to mean: "**_Yet_** Joseph arose and took the young child and his mother *by night*…" And note the repeated use of the aorist for emphasis. The implication is that Joseph *waited* until night to depart, doubtless because he wished to attract less attention to his leaving, and thus took the command to "flee" with some latitude. The "yet…by night" also implies that the command to flee was not given at night, but probably around dawn, when in fact many dreams occur. Thus in the appearance of "de" in these instances in Matthew may be gleaned something of the personality of Joseph, Mary's husband, to whom was entrusted the upbringing of the child Jesus.

[223] As to what the term *flesh* would have meant to the Greek in terms of guilt, it would have meant nothing at all. For in Greek religion there was no real distinction between the flesh of men and the flesh of the gods except that the gods were thought immortal because of a diet of nectar and ambrosia. In a religion where the gods were no more moral than the men from whom they expected homage, there was certainly no concept by the Greek, despite his view that the physical/material was imperfect, that his flesh was *inherently sinful*, nor any concern that he would give an account before a holy God because of His *nature*. Thus the Greek, while he fell short of understanding that post-Adamic man has in his flesh the knowledge of good and evil, nevertheless accepted (in the abstract) the understanding that a man's behavior, not his flesh, was the thing morally culpable.

[224] i.e., Eve before she sinned; also, women used in angelic cohabitation (which has reference to the first of John's tri-part phrase, "bloods").

[225] By "exalted," I do not mean *righteous*.

[2226] And as history has shown, all men have proved they are in need of a Savior.

[2227] (at least for the Jew familiar with the Old Testament)

[2228] A.T. Robertson also demonstrates that *thelo* can mean desire by translating it as such for the 2nd phrase. Throughout this book I have maintained that desire and will are different things. *Thelo* may correspond to eventual will, but it does not *have* to. *Thelo* is a desire that may continue during deliberation. Deliberation's completion ends in a choice, either congruent or not congruent with the desire. Further, if Calvinists were right to say that man only wills his greatest desire, then, by definition, man can never have lesser, competing desires that might lead to other choices. Thus, *vacillation* ought to be regarded by the Calvinist as man under the illusion that he could make another choice than that which he finally chooses. Furthermore, perhaps the Calvinist has never been in the position of asking a teenager to take out the trash and seeing in the boy's face the kind of greatest desire of which they speak. And assuming the further Calvinist argument that the teenager has in view the goal of gaining other privileges, and thus takes out the trash according to his greatest desire, we would respond that this greatest desire of the teenager has reference only to the other privileges and not at all to his taking out the trash, i.e., the act which Calvinists claim correspond to the boy's greatest desire. But if the matter is still disputed we have only to observe that Christ in Gethsemane *chose* His Father's desire, not His own, and that if Christ could only choose according to His greatest desire, then, according to the definition which Calvinists insist upon, we must also say that Christ was under delusion for having imagined falsely that he could have chosen something else (avoiding the cross) than His greatest desire, a course of action He clearly believed was contingently possible.

[2229] Incidentally, if one substitutes for 'husbands' the word 'men' in Jesus' statement to the woman at the well (in which John uses the Greek word, *aner*), the meaning appears clearer. In effect, Jesus was saying, "How *true* that you say that you don't have a husband; for you have had *five* men, and the man you have *now* is not your husband."

[2230] Again, if one should make the 3rd phrase read "a husband's *will*" it would subsume the 3rd phrase at least under the 1st phrase, "natural descent."

[2231] If the argument should be made that Mary Baker Eddy, for example, was the counterpart to men like Confucius, Buddha, Mohammed, Joseph Smith and Brigham Young (Mormonism), Judge Rutherford (Jehovah's Witnesses), James Jones (the "Father" of Jonestown), etc., and that John the Apostle was mistaken to think women could not create and lead significant false religious movements, it must be understood that John is simply making a statement of general observance about men and the predominant opportunities certain of them have had (and employed negatively).

[2232] Obviously, I do not mean *all* Jews.

[2233] Again, many Jews trusted in their ethnicity as from Abraham.

[2234] i.e., since he recognized that there were three distinct categories and that the sexual and race dimensions had already been addressed by the first term "bloods."

[235] The term *aner* can also mean *sir*, i.e., a term of respect, such as would be due the progenitors of the Jewish race.

[236] Someone may object that, within the polyvalent meaning of the 2nd phrase ("nor by the wanting of the flesh") in its relation to the 3rd phrase, I am, at one level of meaning (as understood by the biblically literate Jew or Judistic Greek reader), using the term *thelo* (*to want*) with different definitions in successive phrases (thus doing in principle the kind of flip-flopping I condemn in the GSB or John Wesley, in their treatment of the word *flesh*). Their argument would presumably be thus: In the phrase "the flesh's wanting," I regard the desire of a person in the first form of (continued from p. 568) his flesh as having desire *apart* from intention, but then I define the *thelo* of a male [in the phrase, "the man's (*or* male's) wanting"] as *including* intention, e.g., such as the *choice* a man makes to invent a false religion, claiming that he and his followers are the children of God. Therefore it would be alleged that I contradict myself, having claimed two different 'flip-flopping' definitions for "thelo."

In my defense are at least three considerations: 1) In accord with how the word *thelo* was understood in John's time, I have defined *thelo* (*to want*), as desire which may **or** may not come to include intention as part of that word's latitude of lexical meaning. (For note further that even one's greatest desire does not *necessitate* the will). This is different than what the GSB does with the word "flesh," for the GSB assumes, besides one definition of flesh as that pure form in which Christ was born, also the traditional and erroneous definition of "flesh" as that element in man affected by original sin, a wholly disproven assumption on their part which then informs what latitude of lexical meaning they imagine the word "flesh" may navigate, a journey they assume the reader is also obligated to make between verses 13 and 14. In contrast (regarding the word "flesh,") I am suggesting that the flesh in persons of any age in any circumstance is not inherently sinful, even hypothetically; 2) the polyvalent meanings, while harmonious with each other, *do not crisscross* with each other. That is, the meaning of "thelo" does **not** change between the 2nd and 3rd phrases insofar as that word relates to a wanting which includes intention within <u>one</u> level of meaning within the polyvalent meaning. For within this <u>one</u> level of meaning ,the meaning of the word *thelo* in the phrase, "the man's (*or* male's) *wanting* " is subject to any context already (or immediately being) established for it; and in the case of "the wanting of (a) male(s)" in John 1:13, note that *thelo* has already been established regarding a male's intention (i.e., the *males'* intention) as implied in its effect upon all persons in verses 10-11, that is, in which the *thelo* of males have established the general attitude of "the world" as rejecting the *Logos*. Thus, when the *grown* (see note following this footnote), i.e., *accountable* (that is, *no longer probationary*) male is introduced into the discussion in verse 13 under the Greek term *aner*, it has already been implied that *aner's* deliberation between desire and intention has proven itself negatively, i.e., in establishing a world that rejected the *Logos*. Thus the wanting of a male is being contextually defined as a wanting which includes a corresponding negative *intention*. That is, at this one level of meaning within the polyvalent meaning, the wanting (desire) of the male is seen as sympathetic with the wanting (desire) of all persons in their own individual wanting according to their own flesh, with the result of a universal rejection of the Logos; 3) **Whereas**, in contradistinction, the phrase "the wanting of the flesh," is, in *another* layer of meaning within the polyvalent meaning, in the process of being contextualized by verse 14 to mean *a wanting not yet established in regard to intention*. For the *Logos*, in *becoming* flesh, was yet in His probation until He underwent the baptism of His death according to the Father's will. Thus during His life the *Logos* was found as a man [i.e., Adam] in the first form of Adam's *flesh*, that is, not in the kind of flesh which bespoke of Adam's failure, but of the flesh which bespoke of the same uncondemnable kind which John invokes when he tells his readers that the *Logos* became flesh. In other words, in this *other* level of meaning, the phrase "nor by the wanting of the flesh" means that those persons born of God were not born of the wanting of the kind of flesh of Adam at the first, *because such persons would not need to be born of God (were they to exist)*. Thus the term *the wanting*, insofar as it appears to be defined differently by me, appears so only because of the polyvalent meaning which, while harmonious between its lines, is not in its lines to be crisscrossed. Finally, remember that the essential difference in phrases 2 and 3 (as already noted) is that "the want (vb.) of the flesh" refers to that resource of influence of which a person is cognizant and which influences him/ her *from within*, while "the wanting of a male(s)" refers to that resource of influence of which a person is cognizant and which influences him/ her *from without*. [**Note**: The term *aner* is used to show its distinction between women and *children* in Matthew 14:21. Furthermore, the term for the group of boys (*male children*) slaughtered by Herod is *paidos*, not the plural of *aner*. Thus *aner* must mean a *grown* male.]

Chapter 20

Calvinism and Other Pseudologies

Not that long ago, my brother and I were laying down a brick walk in front of his house, when two guys, 'Elder' McGilliam and 'Elder' Pencko,[237] crossed from the far side of the street to tell us of Joseph Smith and his message about Jesus Christ. These two young men and I began to exchange our views about Christ, and while doing so I found out that 'elders' McGilliam and Pencko were only 19 years old. Thus, in a few aspects and by Old Testament standards, they wouldn't have even been considered full adults, since a man didn't go to war unless he was at least 20, and because God didn't hold anyone responsible for refusing His command to go into the land of Canaan who was less than that age. At any rate, I felt sorry for them. Here in New Jersey they were far away from their families, the one 'elder' having kin in Idaho, and the other in California. What a shame, I thought, that the Mormon Church would limit their family contacts to four times a year during their missionary work, yet designate them 'elders' before reaching full, mature adulthood (as though on the one hand they had no wisdom to know how often they should visit their families, but on the other hand be given a church title that suggested such discernment).

Anyhow, I stayed away from the easy *ad hominem* arguments that could have been leveled against the 'glass-looking' Smith.[238] Instead, I focused on Smith's translation of certain hieroglyphic writings on some papyri that he bought in 1835. Gleason Archer in his book, *A Survey of Old Testament Introduction*, tells it best:

> Most interesting is the recently exposed fraud of the so-called Book of Abraham, part of the Mormon scripture known as *The Pearl of Great Price*. This was allegedly translated from an ancient Egyptian papyrus found in the mummy wrappings of certain mummies which had been acquired by a certain Michael H. Chandler. In 1835 Joseph Smith became very much interested in these papyrus leaves, which he first saw in Kirtland, Ohio, on July 3, and arranged for the purchase of both mummies and manuscripts. Believing he had divinely received the gift of interpreting ancient Egyptian, he was delighted to find that one of the rolls contained the writings of Abraham himself, whose signature he had personally inscribed in the Egyptian language. In 1842, Smith published his translation under the title, "The Book of

Abraham" in *Times and Seasons*. He even included two drawings of the pictures or vignettes appearing in the manuscript, and interpreted the meaning of these illustrations: Abraham sitting upon the throne of Pharaoh and the serpent with walking legs who tempted Eve in Eden.[239] For many years this collection of papyri was lost, but somehow they (or else a duplicate set of them from ancient times) were presented to the Mormon Church by the Metropolitan Art Museum of New York City on November 27, 1967. This made the translation skill of Joseph Smith susceptible to objective verification. The unhappy result was that earlier negative verdicts of scholars like Theodule Devaria of the Louvre, and Samuel A.B. Mercer of Western Theological Seminary, and James H. Breasted of the University of Chicago, and W. F. Flinders Petrie of London University (who had all been shown Smith's facsimiles) were clearly upheld by a multitude of present-day Egyptologists. Their finding was that not a single word of Joseph Smith's alleged translation bore any resemblance to the contents of this document.

'Elders' McGilliam and Pencko were unaware of these developments, but the idea that *The Pearl Of Great Price* had been proven fraudulent didn't seem to matter much to them. I also told them how Smith's claim of a blood relation between Native Americans and the Jewish race had been proven false by modern DNA testing, and that their own scholars, in fact, were now scrambling for some explanation. This too seemed not to faze them. Finally, I asked them why Jesus had said He would build His Church but then allegedly waited 1800 years before doing it through Joseph Smith. Unfortunately, that argument didn't seem to impact their thinking either. What was certain about these fellows, however, especially in 'elder' McGilliam, was a "burning in the bosom" of the Mormon message, i.e., the Smith-approved test of truth for anyone who might possibly doubt Smith's word that an angel had shown him some mysterious golden plates buried in the ground on a rural farm in New York State (which historians note occurred during Smith's 'money-digging' phase. Apparently, God had gone upscale since His Old Testament days of *stone* tablets.) And so I talked to the 'elders' while they put their particular spin on the Bible. "Jesus is a created being," they told me. When I countered that John chapter 1 says that apart from Christ nothing was made that was made, they countered with their own claim. "That just refers to the things of the universe," replied 'Elder' McGilliam. And so it went. By interjecting thoughts without any textual evidence, 'Elder' McGilliam showed his rookie partner of five-weeks on the job how to hold forth an argument with little more reason than the 'biblical' additions of Smith's internally corroborated writings. That, and with a "burning in the bosom."

I tell this incident to show how those who want to find another meaning in words *will* find another meaning. In fact, The Church of Jesus Christ of Latter Day Saints (LDS) is currently reinterpreting its own scriptures. And so proceeds the ironic element in the Mormon Church—i.e., the LDS's historical revisionism that has widened beyond the Bible to now include the Book of Mormon by Joseph Smith. Apparently, sometimes even the revisionists are subject to being revised. Because the latest DNA evidence recently showed *zero* connection between the Jews, a tribe of whom Smith alleged had immigrated to America where they became the progenitors of the American Indians, LDS scholars are now reinterpreting Smith's writings. Under one explanation, America is now *Central* America, and the Jewish tribe must have been so small that their DNA was swallowed up in the process of intermarriage with the indigenous population. While the LDS has not adopted this explanation as its official church position, there are links from the LDS official website to other sites supporting this revision of interpretation.[lxv] The effect of reinterpreting Smith's writings has effectively placed Mormon apologetics into an area beyond knowing. Indeed, this appeal to mystery is what false theologies and ideologies always seek to do. Thus in the 1830s Smith first sought to place his 'vision' in the then unknowable realm of Egyptian hieroglyphics where it could not be tested. Today, 170 years later, the LDS employs the same method to claim that all the DNA evidence that would have proven Smith's writings was irretrievably swallowed up in Central America's indigenous population, and so don't bother looking for it.

The methodology of mystical theologies or philosophies, exampled here in the LDS, is always the same. Whenever the fictional glue is threatened that holds together all the parts, a call is put out for a deeper irrationality. America has witnessed a number of these pseudologies, both religious and non-religious. For example, much later and elsewhere in America, the same kind of revisionism happened to the theory of evolution in the late 1970s, when the Harvard evolutionist, Stephen Jay Gould, anteed up to the fact (despite his colleagues) that the fossil record was absent the plethora of transitions evolutionists had promised since 1859. The evolutionary hypothesis was itself now evolving, as the original theory succumbed to another theory in the survival of the fittest. Evolution, claimed Gould, apparently happened in sporadic bursts. So whereas the theory of evolution had claimed for 120 years that evolution happened so *slowly* it couldn't be observed, in the 1970s it was being claimed that evolution happened so *fast* it couldn't be observed. But of course, it still took the same amount of eons, so that modern and post-modern man could hardly expect to actually witness an evolutionary event. Thus, like the LDS, evolutionists have likewise tried to put its 'truths' beyond knowing and therefore beyond testability. What is left in such cases for the follower of a Joseph Smith or a Stephan Jay Gould is "a burning in the bosom," whether now propagated by 19-year old Mormon missionaries beating suburbia's streets, or students-turned educators who remember listening to a 1970s Harvard professor lecturing in an Ivy League auditorium about 'punctuated equilibrium.' In the end it's all about faith, even for the atheist.

This book has tried to show that Calvinism's belief in the absolute sovereignty of God forms one of these mystical ideologies. But the difference is this: Calvinism is a false ideology that resides in the true Church. As Christian radio host Hank Hanegraaff has said, "[Calvinism] is an in-house debate." Even Hanegraaff and his (now deceased) father had disagreed with each other about the issue. And indeed the question remains as to why many Calvinists are true Christians and devoted followers of Christ despite their apologetic, since their betimes apologetic about their theological distinctives *as betimes profession* defines God and man in biblically heretical terms.[240] Perhaps it's simply the kind of disconnect from their faith all Christians tend to have in one area or another because 1) the Body of Christ is not working with 100% (interdependent) efficiency under Christ to achieve the edifying of believers unto full maturity, and, of course, because 2) our own sinfulness individually hinders us. Presumably, at least most Evangelical Calvinists really *do* accept in their heart the true biblical definitions of God and man, and so are justified in their profession of faith because the Holy Spirit is bearing witness with their new nature that 'God' is who the Bible truly says He is, even while in the midst of such profession such Calvinists alternately follow their old nature as their double-mindedness professes 'God' in Calvinistically, i.e., heretical, terms. Therefore both true and false definitions are in operation in the course of a verbal profession, and thus do Evangelical Calvinists exist in that dangerous state of double-mindedness, a condition which the apostle James indicated was a position conceivably occupiable by the Christian. And yet if we would be honest, each of us is probably double-minded about some truth in the Bible to some degree or another, even while (ironically) we find it difficult to live up to the truth that is plain to us.

At any rate, the Calvinistic doctrine of an all-sovereign God should be understood as paralleling other *pseudologies* (false ideologies and/or theologies) in its desire to change language and avoid testability. Thus, in the attempt to explain a good God who has ordained an imperfect world, Calvinists have placed their fundamental propositions into the realm of *mystery* and therefore beyond provability. Again, this appeal to the unknowable is the hallmark of all mystical ideologies (such as LDS theology and evolutionary theory). To see better how this process involving mysticism works, we will now look further into some parallels between Calvinism and certain other pseudologies.

Existentialism

The gist of Existentialism is that a person comes into *being* through an act of the will. Therefore the worst thing for a man is to fail to act. Secular Existentialism, however, does not believe there is any *real* (ultimate and therefore informing) truth to discover, so the act of the will takes place in a moral vacuum.[241] For example, suppose I see an old woman slowly crossing a busy street using her umbrella as a cane. As an act of the will I might decide to 1) go over and escort her safely to the far side of the street, or 2) go over and take away her umbrella and hit her over the head with it. In a meaningless world it does not matter what I choose, only *that* I choose in order that my *being* emerges from the Void. The question as to *why* a man should be bothered about his *being* in a purposeless universe is never answered by the secular Existentialists. It simply remains a mystery why anyone should act at all. Apparently, the moral purpose of existence itself is *being* itself, and that is supposed to be enough motivation for the person. The idea of pursuing objective truth through the Bible or by seeking God is dismissed entirely.

The connection between Existentialism and Calvinism is an interesting one. Calvinism too, cannot define moral content in any meaningful way. For example, in the statement, *"God is good"* the term 'good' is defined as everything God ordains in the world according to His good pleasure, which is every thing (and phenomena) in the world. In fact, Christians are told they ought to applaud God for it. Yet as one Christian disdainfully put the matter of Calvinism in a nutshell, 'Whatever is, one bows down to it.' As noted at the beginning of this book, this includes all the animus of human experience, including Hitler's fascism, Stalin's communism, religions that oppose Christianity, and whatever other atrocities and contradictions history may offer. The term *'good,'* then, includes all of these things, because all of these things have occurred in history, and God has ordained all of history. My point, then, is that the Calvinist is hardly concerned with *what* God does, just *that* He does. God is thus established by the *good and bad* morality implied in ordaining *all* of history, but is vindicated by simply *acting* in the world. God's *activity* in the world is the main thing in Calvinism—this is always the chief concern of the Calvinist if you listen to him closely. If we raise the objection to the Calvinist that his theology means God actively determines the reprobate acts of the worst men, our argument falls on deaf ears. We are told that Deity is an all-sovereign God who controls everything and that we cannot question Him—end of argument. Any sense of dilemma about what we must thus infer about God's holy character is brushed aside, as though the supreme view to behold is that God is always justified in all He *does*. When all the arguments and biblical passages have finally been put away at the end of the day between the Calvinist and the Free-willer, *God acting in the world* is (incredibly) the only defense the Calvinist has really offered.

We should not be surprised, then, that Calvinism is so attractive even to the Christian. Even as believers who sometimes walk according to the flesh, we often like to sin by believing the wrong thing, and sometimes we still want to believe some of the lies we once believed as former members of the world. Sadly, many are tricked into dressing up Christianity so that God and morality are so indeterminate that they are retained in name only. *As Christians, this is our current apologetic to the world.* This is the first line of explanation we offer to the unbeliever when he presses upon us the question about why God would decree suffering in the world. We offer him an Existential explanation dressed up in Christianese. We try to sidestep the question and tell him God loves him. If pressed further we give a gentle shrug of the shoulders and explain that somehow God is not so much allowing it as He is controlling it for His own ends which cannot be understood. As this is the essence of our apologetic to the world, the question must be asked—what *rational* person should accept such a faith? Indeed, what *rational* person is going to think our explanation makes *man* a sinner, and not *God* a sinner?

Catholicism

Personally speaking, Catholicism commands my respect in many ways in which Existentialism does not. At a certain social level the best of Catholicism is humanely decent, quite unlike the betimes Existentialist's narcissistic emphasis upon himself (an indulgent viewpoint technically denied by the Existentialist but one which we nevertheless observe in him). The Catholic Church's commitment to a certain integrity was something I observed firsthand while a graduate student at a formerly Jesuit-run university I attended. Of course, no culture is perfect where university life is considered—there were a great many Catholic students, for example, who did their duty by the Mass before going out to party hard on a Saturday night. But it was easy to have a certain profound respect for the university's professors. Furthermore, where one might have expected the Church of Rome in recent years to begin caving in to the pressure of the liberal West with symbolic gestures conceding pieces of theological territory, it has refused to do so and has acted in proper deference to the worst of American legislation regarding laws supporting abortion and gay 'marriage.'

"At least the Catholics were fighting it," wrote Francis Schaeffer about the legalization of abortion in *Whatever Happened to the Human Race* (co-authored with then-future Surgeon General of the United States, C. Everett Koop). Schaeffer added that, because Protestants were so slow in responding to *Roe v. Wade* in the early years following the 1973 Supreme Court ruling, there would have been no pro-life movement in the immediate aftermath of the Supreme Court's decision had it not been for the Catholic Church.

And yet the Catholic Church has had its problems with holding to biblical authority. Luther, of course, was right to fault the Catholic Church's belief that men could literally buy their way into heaven through the 'good work' of buying indulgences. This challenge went to the deeper issue of who had the authority to speak on matters that affected a man's salvation. Consequently, when the Reformation emerged from the Catholic Church it did so upon the two proper bases for which it would subsequently become famous: *sola scriptura* and *sola fide (scripture alone,* and *faith alone)*. Both Luther and Calvin denied that a man's salvation was the combined result of grace and works, and they thought to strengthen this claim by saying that God alone had provided man the necessary faith to believe Him. Therefore, as a pendulum reaction against the strong sway of the Catholic Church's emphasis on works, the Reformers stressed God's *complete* role in the salvation of the individual. This way (thought Calvin and Luther) a man could not think he had done something boastworthy, even if he had merely believed.

Calvinists today continue to embrace this idea, and we have already rebutted this particular point of Reformed theology in an earlier chapter. But what needs to be observed additionally here is the similarity of method used by both the Reformers and the Catholic Church. Both use dialecticism to argue certain points regarding man's salvation. Consider first the Catholic Church. Rome teaches that God's grace and man's works synergistically work together to effect his atonement. However, because Paul says that salvation is of grace apart from works, the Catholic emphasis on God's grace and man's works are antithetical principles (even as light is to darkness, and righteousness is to unrighteousness). To illustrate why grace and works cannot synergistically work together, consider Christ's statement about the two commandments which Christ said fulfilled all the law. The first and great commandment is to love God with all of one's heart, soul, mind, and strength, and the second is to love one's neighbor as one's self. Suppose, then, that a man fails to love God with *all* of his heart or soul or mind or strength at one point during one particular day of his life. The best he can do during the rest of the week, or even the rest of his life, is to love God at every subsequent instant during all his remaining days with all of his heart, mind, soul, and strength. This would mean the man would live perfectly after the one time he had sinned. God's standard of obedience, however, demands *total perfection <u>at all times</u>*. How, then, can a man atone for his own sin if he has sinned even once? The answer, of course, is that he cannot, and that is why he needs a Savior. Most people who trust in their works believe that God will look at some of the good things they have done and decide that these positive works make up for the bad things they have thought about or done. But can they really make up for sin? To do so would mean living *more* than perfectly during one's remaining days in order to make up the slack. And because it is irrational to say that one can love God with *more* than *all* of one's heart, soul, mind, and strength, a man cannot do good works to atone for even one of his sins. The idea, then, that a man can atone for his sin is the irrational element in the Catholic religion. It says that a man can atone for his own shortcomings, when clearly the man cannot do *more* than to love God with *all* of his heart, soul, mind, and strength after he sins.

But consider how dialecticism also appears within the *Reformed* view of salvation. It is one where God is said to impart a 'new nature' to the man, and that upon this basis the man trusts God. The term 'new nature' is not something I have ever seen clearly defined by the Calvinist, though it is the key to their entire doctrine regarding man's salvation. It is described as the 'regeneration' of the man's desire, but plainly the man's desire has been wholly *negated* in order to accommodate God's complete change in the man. What then is left of the man or his desire? Nothing whatsoever. To say, then, that God imparts a 'new nature' so that a man may (rather, *must*) trust Him, is a word game in which nothing more nor less is being said than that God chooses our choice in the matter of 'our' salvation, since the man and his desire have been negated. Thus, the Calvinist asks us to doublethink that God's implanted desire in the man in whom he negates desire can also be called the *man's own* desire. This way God can be called all-sovereign, yet in such a way so that the 'man' can be said to trust God by his 'own' will.

Hence, the *apologetic* of man's salvation, technically speaking, is not more rationally expressed in Calvinism than in Catholicism. Furthermore, such a redefining of essential terms shows Calvinism to be a false gospel, a man-constructed soteriology and thus a gospel of works created after the principles of the world, and not according to Christ. This is the great similarity between the Reformation and the Counter-Reformation. Neither movement made any advances toward rationality in the *essentials* of their apologetics. Whereas Catholicism made man's works equal to God's grace, the Reformation made man's faith a work. As the Reformation apologetic developed, it also rendered meaningless other terms, such as 'God,' 'man,' 'good,' and 'evil.' *The question remains, then, as to what moral authority the Calvinist has, that it can reprove the Catholic for the latter's amalgam of God's grace and man's works?* In other words, where is the rationality in Calvinism that makes absolute distinctions possible, so that the Calvinist might reprove the

Catholic? It is nowhere present. The Calvinist[242] would only be throwing stones in the same glass house of dialecticism in reproving the Catholic. For example, how effectively can the Calvinist say to the Catholic, *Though you may claim that my belief in God's total sovereignty and human freedom is only stating the impossibility of 'God choosing our choices,' I don't see it that way; rather, your doctrine of grace combined with works is what is actually illogical* (?) How effectively, then? Not at all effectively. And so the Calvinist remains without an effective apologetic to win over the Catholic whenever he urges a personal *receiving* of Christ by *faith* (so called) alone. One wonders how evangelization of the Catholic unto true salvation can ever be very effective, as long as (the many) Protestant Evangelicals who are following Calvinism ask Catholics to exchange *their* version of the dialectic for one of their own. Rather, only Christ as presented biblically and rationally can really challenge a man's heart and mind.

Victimization

Probably many of us know someone who suffers from acute anxiety or some other form of mental difficulty. Or maybe that someone is us. At times, many such people are prone to feel they have little, if any, control over how they feel or think. As far as most of the medical community is concerned, the whole of the person's problem is often reduced to a bio-chemical explanation apart from any spiritual consideration. This is because the science of psychology has traditionally been rooted in the evolutionary assumption that man is a physical, not spiritual, being. Though man has thoughts and emotions, a man and his mind are regarded by many psychiatrists as essentially physical products, and so the brain is understood and treated upon the same bio-chemical foundation that many professionals believe constitute the whole of the man.

The problem, then, with medicating away the symptoms in the mental sufferer is that if often fails to uncover the root problem of anxiety. Medication certainly has a positive role to play in the treatment of mental suffering. We would never deny that. Yet medication alone may also mask the real question about why the person has anxiety. Almost never is prolonged anxiety understood as a *choice*. The person's anxiety may stem from feelings of vulnerability, or prolonged anger, or fear, or frustration at unresolved circumstances in life, etc., *but anxiety is often diagnosed by the professional as the result of outside biological forces.* Unfortunately, instead of challenging the person, modern psychology tends to commiserate with them by assigning their condition to a disease over which the patient has little or no control apart from medication.

Evangelicalism, too, makes use of this same methodology. Yes, we preach against sin, but we also urge one another to understand the pressure of being human to a point where we sometimes tacitly excuse one another. The Evangelical Church has in fact become psychologized by the vast influence of modern psychology. We often excuse believers because we feel sorry for them in their circumstances, sometimes merely allowing them to take ownership of their problems without really taking responsibility for them. More often than not, the Church just allows 'problem people' to assume the victim posture. Life *is* tough, and for us to approach the oppressed with "cutting them some slack" may make us feel less accountable, should we find ourselves in similar circumstances on some future day of weakness. This tendency to "cut people slack" has a merciful ring to it, but God never administers mercy to the Christian without making clear his or her responsibility to repent ("Go and sin no more.").

Consequently, e.g., people with long-standing drug addictions in the Church are often handled with repeated 'interventions' or a series of Christian center rehab visits whenever their addiction kicks in. These may be sincere attempts to reform the addict, but they are not always in consort with a strong model of church discipline based on Matthew 18, which carries with it the greatest chance of success. Too often in today's Church a kind of milk-toast response has come to the fore. It has grown out of the Church's acceptance of modern psychology in which anxiety, addictions, and other destructive habits are given labels of *illness* (or at least *regarded* as illness) instead of being fully granted their status as sin. The result is an Evangelical posturing away from the old, harsh-sounding fundamentalists, who, *if* they had a more biblical model of discipline, nevertheless had the reputation of putting the church's reputation ahead of the person.

The similarity of victim theory with Calvinism should be fairly obvious. Viewed from the perspective that God foreordains all things, people are obviously puppets who have no control over their lives. They cannot be expected to change their behavior, since a greater outside Force is manifesting itself through them. This total governance must be true of entire nations, as well, as a simple extension of what Reformed apologist B.B. Warfield stated, i.e., that "God creates the very thoughts and intents of the soul." And so, presumably, half the time the average Calvinist will urge the person of 'will' to repent of his sin, and the rest of the time assume the sufferer is experiencing exactly what God has decreed for him. How a person is to make sense of his suffering when exposed to such a theologically schizophrenic view of God's role in his suffering, is anybody's guess. The sufferer's idea of his own responsibility will almost certainly be skewed in the midst of such ambiguity.

Multiculturalism

Some years ago ABC Television ran a Barbara Walters special called, "Heaven: Where Is It? How Do We Get There?"[lxvi] Interviews of dozens of religious leaders, as well as scientists and atheists, yielded the inevitable crop of varying beliefs. Among the many persons interviewed was an Islamic fundamentalist—a failed suicide bomber whom Walters visited inside a high-security Israeli prison. The young man told Walters that he would have had 20+ virgins[243] in the afterlife had his suicide mission been successful. (We will return to the example of this Islamic fundamentalist in a moment.) Another interviewee was evangelical pastor, Ted Haggard, who finally admitted after some dogged badgering from Walters that he couldn't be certain she was going to heaven without Jesus.[244] I think this interview would have been more interesting if Haggard had asked Walters if *she* believed in heaven, and if not, in what *did* she believe—for if she did *not* believe in heaven why bother with investigating other persons' beliefs in heaven or investigating anything else?

Presumably Walters, who professes not to have any real religious beliefs besides praying for safety when boarding an airplane, embraces by default some form of multiculturalism. This seems to be today's pop-culture, default answer for those who have no particular religious views. Among other things, such persons tend to embrace moral relativism. The great attraction toward multiculturalism in America today is the idea that everyone can be accommodated. At least, that's how multiculturalism works in theory. The reality, of course, is much different. Consider, for example, how the Christian defines *ideal existence* compared to the multiculturalist. For the Christian, ideal existence is living someday with God in heaven, worshipping Him, loving his neighbor as himself, and doing God's work (whatever the nature of that future work might be). For the multiculturalist, ideal existence is equally valuing all cultures and cultural ideas. However, the real spirit of multiculturalism never seeks to stop at merely the regional or national level, but embraces all cultures of all countries. Furthermore, nations are merely the corporate groupings of individuals; thus, to be most tolerant in the truest sense of 'multiculturalism' would presumably mean embracing every individual viewpoint in the world and granting it equal valuation, since each culture is merely the adding together of individual viewpoints. Ideal existence, then, for the true multiculturalist, would be to accept the world *as it is*. In other words, one could not cast a vote in favor of one political candidate or party over another and be a true multiculturalist, because to cast a vote would be to show prejudice in favor of one viewpoint over another and thus align oneself with one sub-group of culture over another. Furthermore, even if a person didn't vote but merely complained about somebody in regard to any matter, they would not be acting as a true multiculturalist, since they would be showing a prejudice against someone else's particular attitude about something. And even if a person managed never to complain about anyone, he could still not embrace all the viewpoints of all individuals. Some people, for example, have despaired to the point of suicide or have attempted suicide because they believed life was meaningless. How does the multiculturalist embrace *that* position while at the same time embrace the majority viewpoint that life is worth living? The premise of multiculturalism, then, is impossible to satisfy, since it is *irrational* to suggest that anyone can grant equal valuation to opposite viewpoints. Thus, it is not possible for Barbara Walters (or anyone else) to live life without having preferred views that exclude the viewpoints of some people at some time.

But let's step out of the theoretical and into the practical. If the whole machinery behind Walters's TV special is any example, it shows that TV journalism and journalists are just as opinionated as anyone else. For example, no one heard Walters say to the failed suicide bomber at the end of her interview, "Well, you know, I really think your viewpoint and the viewpoint of fundamental Islamic radicalism is as valid as anyone else's." Rather, she admitted the interview was "very frightening and very sad" and was dismayed that the Muslim interview*ee* could be so filled with "hatred and ignorance." Later, she found a different interviewee's comments "funny" and "charming."[245] So while no one really believes in multiculturalism, veteran reporters like Walters must find it terribly handy to have around when interviewing religious people stuck in the kind of exclusivity of which they, as journalists, imagine they are not a part.[246]

The connection, then, between Calvinism and (theoretical) multiculturalism is the approval of the world *as it is*. The Calvinist always says (at least while temporarily in the forward rock of the rocking horse) that God foreordains the world and all the events it contains according to His own good pleasure. Though it is a mystery how the world *as it is* reflects God's ultimate sovereignty, we are told we have the Bible's assurance on the matter, or so say Calvinists like Jerry Bridges, who assure us that "all the decisions of rulers, kings, and parliaments; and all the actions of their governments, armies, and navies serve His will.[lxvii] Their hearts and minds are as much under His control as the impersonal physical laws of nature....[lxviii] God controls the hand of both the mad tyrant and the careless officer."[lxix] Thus, as Bridges states it, God must in *every* sense approve of the world *as it is* if one is to remain true to Calvinistic principles, or else God is not really sovereign.

Eastern Mysticism

From multiculturalism to Eastern Mysticism is but a few small steps. Already the multiculturalist realizes that to prefer one view over another is "bad" (that is, insofar as the multiculturalist can believe that anything is bad). Indeed, in a world where equal consideration and valuation is attempted, nothing is thought to be ultimately good *or* bad. In terms of value, then, everything is really One. As long as people fail to understand the spirit of multiculturalism (I assume here the persona of a multiculturalist), they will mistakenly think there are differences in human expression and behavior. But though there appear to be differences, there really *are* no differences. Rather, there is only an illusion of difference. *Definition itself* is the enemy, since it makes people think in terms of difference instead of the One. Thus, to struggle against the One is to be in disharmony with the Universal. (O.k., end of persona!)

Calvinism, too, like Eastern mysticism, avoids the moral dimension at all costs, defining irrationally key subjects like *God, man, good,* and *evil.* For example, we have already seen how the phrase, *"God is good,"* is meaningless in a Calvinistic paradigm. Since God is said to ordain everything in the universe, including all the acts of human decency *and* brutality, the term 'good' is meaningless. Furthermore, since 'good' is meaningless, nothing is really being stated about the subject of the sentence, i.e., 'God.' Thus, 'God' cannot be properly posited, i.e., said to exist, since no description of 'Him' is really being made. In order to posit God, man, good, or evil, Christians must understand that true theology insists on definite and conclusive statements. But Calvinism does not provide the Christian with such definitive views. (In fact, all that Calvinism is, is the *appearance* of meaning.) Just the fact that Calvinists sense no real dilemma in ascribing to God all the activity of the world shows what little appreciation they have for Difference. Hence, terms like 'God,' 'man', 'good,' and 'evil' are indistinctly 'maintained,' and so there remains only an illusion of content. For the Calvinist the two principles of the Westminster Confessions are ultimately treated as one and the same expression, that is, when the totality of their arguments are considered. The Calvinist affirms each principle which he later denies, and then denies his denials so that he can reaffirm his dialectical principles again in a cycle of deferred 'definitions.' It is no exaggeration whatsoever to say that Calvinists, when arguing for the absolute sovereignty of God, are encouraging a kind of 'Christian' Nirvana experience through meditation of the One ('God') who comprehends all thought and experience.

Problem of the One and the Many

Now, I am not saying that those who betimes profess to believe in Calvinistic principles are not saved nor at the same level in their overall spiritual understanding as the followers of the LDS, Existentialism, Eastern mysticism, etc. Rather, I am saying that the irrationality found in Calvinistic apologetics is not fundamentally different than other expressions of irrational, non-Christian thought, and further, that such irrationality has inflicted untold damage upon the Church and the world. If we grant that Calvinists (or at least most Calvinists) believe in Christ despite their Calvinism—and I think we probably may—we must assume they are double-minded about their spiritual convictions.

At any rate, this similarity between the irrationality of Calvinism and Eastern mysticism is especially evident when we consider one of the biggest challenges to any ideological system—the problem of the One and the Many. Along with the problem of evil and the problem of epistemology (How do we know *that* we know?), the problem of the One and the Many remains a chief concern for philosophers and theologians. That is, *how are the individual things of the world related to one another?* For on the one hand it would seem that individual things are isolated things unto themselves, and that we presume a unity where there is none. On the other hand if everything is One, how do we account for individual *things*? The answer, according to Eastern philosophy, is that there is only One, and that therefore the perception of individual things is but an illusion. The act of meditating upon the One will bring the devotee into this fact so that he is in harmony with the Universal. Thus, contemplation of the One helps the mind to rid itself of itself, so that the end result is a proper absorption into the One. It seems plain to me that the underlying motive for many persons in espousing the One is to deny their creaturely status. Indeed, in this way they implicitly make for themselves an equal claim to being 'Deity.'

Now Christianity is likewise faced with this same dilemma of how to demonstrate a unity in the particulars. Yet as Reformed thinker Cornelius Van Til properly pointed out, the problem of the One and the Many is solved by the Trinity. Within one Godhead are three distinct Persons, and therefore we have unity and plurality existing in harmony together in a way in which neither the unity of the One nor the plurality of the Many jeopardizes the Other. But to Van Til's understanding we should add another fact to this model. *Within the Trinity is also the explanation of how God is good, and how choice is ever present.* Presumably, at any point in God's eternal, historical past, One of the Persons of the Godhead could have dissented against the other Two (or Two have dissented against the One).[247] Christ, for example, prayed to the Father in the Garden of Gethsemane, *"Not my desire, but thine be done,"* thus showing a different desire and will possible. Later that same night, Christ told Peter that He could have called for more than 12 legions of angels for rescue from the soldiers. Had Christ not decided to undergo the baptism of his death, how then would the Scripture have been fulfilled (i.e., that Messiah would die 62 weeks [biblically understood as 62 x 7, or 434 years (Dan. 9:26) after the going forth of the commandment to rebuild Jerusalem])? The possibility of Christ acting out of consort with the plan of the Father was thus a very real possibility, according to Christ's own testimony about His potential choices. The potential for evil has thus always been present with God, since there are separate wills able to be expressed among the Persons of the Trinity. As to the question of whether all the Persons of the Trinity would ever together act contrary to their past ideals, the answer is given in Numbers 23:19—"God is not a man, that he should lie; neither the son of man, that he should repent." (Thus, though God theoretically could deny Himself, He has not, does not, and shall not.) For the issue for the Persons of the Trinity is not just that Each acts in consort with the Others, but that together the Persons maintain the same eternal and righteous ideals of the Trinity, because in the end Each chooses to do so, not because Each *cannot* do so.[248]

I have to admit, though, that it seems strange to me to see how Van Til so admirably solves the problem of the One and the Many without seeing in his own Calvinism an implied Monism which at the same time overthrows the understanding of the One and the Many. I cannot help but again be reminded of Sproul's statement that though he (Sproul) had seen many clever attempts to solve Calvin's dialecticism (and therefore the problem of evil), he had as yet found no truly satisfying answer. We would agree, and press forward the conclusion that there can be no answer for the problem of evil when a man supposes that truth has something in common with irrationality. God must be separate from man, and good must be separate from evil if the Bible's truths are to be maintained and have effect. Conversely, an irrational apologetic does nobody good, and thus one despairs at Jerry Bridges's statement that the [absolute] sovereignty of God is found on virtually every page of the Bible.[lxx] Rather, we maintain that the Bible is not so represented on *any* of its pages. Only a God who is distinct in His creatorship, personhood, and holiness can save man. Only an upright God who is distinct from sinful man can judge him. Let us be done, then, with definitions that go nowhere except to remind us of the contradiction of bizarre human reasoning, i.e., a false reasoning which helps to form that contradiction of sinners which the Bible says Christ endured [not for His own sake, but for the Father's sake (to our benefit)]—i.e., *our* very contradiction which led Him to a cross He *despised* as an aberrant experience from the original and perfect plan of God.

Footnotes:

[237] Not their real names

[238] Smith engaged regularly in 'money-digging,' an activity somewhat common during his day. It involved pretending to divine the location of buried treasure. Smith was convicted of a "glass-looking" incident in the 1830s in which he was accused of swindling money from a farmer. Isaac Hale, the future father-in-law of Smith at the time of Smith's 'vision' of the angel Moroni, responded once to a

newspaper editor's request for information about Smith with a notarized statement (accompanied by an affidavit by his son, Alva, stating that what his father said was "correct and true"). Hale told of Smith's claim of translating a wonderful book of plates in the same manner he used in money-digging—placing a stone in one's hat and holding the hat over one's face.

[239] Ironically, the illustration that Smith claimed represented Abraham, the father of all the faithful and living, turned out to be Osiris, the Egyptian god of the Dead.

[240] Again, the true Christian who is a Calvinist expresses in some proportion truth, lie, truth, lie, etc., *ad nauseam* in this life regarding his Calvinistic apologetic. Taking the Calvinist's statements *together* would seem to form a meaningless confession to the world. Yet God is greater than the believer's heart when it condemns him, and so the Calvinist believer may be regarded as alternately expressing truth during those times when his confession occurs on what would seem to be the backward rock of his rocking horse theology, since his confession's emphasis, during these times, is on man's freedom, that is, *if he means (as God would judge it) to confess it unqualifyingly*, i.e., non-dialectically in a way in which he has abandoned rocking horse theology, thus implying a God who allows such freedom (thereby defining Deity according to a biblically rational definition). During these times of unqualified support for man's freedom (presuming there are such times as God would judge them so to be) then profession is being made to that fact. Our contention in this book about the *meaninglessness* of terms in Calvinism is this: i.e., by "meaningless" we mean the impossibility for people to infer meaning upon hearing the Calvinist express his theology in terms that condemns the Calvinist's heart.

[241] It should be noted that 'Christian' Existentialism has the same essential problem as secular Existentialism in finding meaning apart from the Self. Christian Existentialists, who take their cue from Soren Kierkegaard's philosophy, can only assume by a leap of personal faith that there is reality in the Christian faith and that God is truly good. This is an essential denial of Paul's statement in Romans 1 that God's power and munificent nature are, in fact, *objectively* demonstrated in creation *and known by man*.

[242] Again, here, as throughout the book, by the term 'Calvinist' I generally mean a person in the instance(s) of espousing *primarily* the doctrine of the absolute sovereignty of God (i.e., that all causes are divine, not secondary), and *secondarily* the theological distinctives of Calvinism (though, even if he be a believer, he does so while at present condemning his heart.)

[243] I believe an exact number over 20 was given by the Islamic terrorist, but I don't remember it, having heard that detail but once on a radio segment about Walter's project.

[244] Why any Christian leader would say he was *not* certain if one would go to heaven without Jesus ought to disturb any believer in Christ.

[245] source: www.belief.net

[246] Thus, Walters, like so many others, never thinks very critically about her own views, but simply gives lip service to some form of relativistic, pop philosophy which she selectively applies to her own personal advantage.

[247] —or all three Persons of the Godhead against God's historical position.

[248] While Titus 1:2 tells us that God cannot lie, this does not refer to an actual *inability* under every conceivable circumstance for God to lie. Rather, God cannot [Gr. lit. *powers (wills) not to*] lie because He is *set determinedly* toward exercising His will to tell the truth presently (as he has always done in the past and, we may assume, shall do so in the future). Thus, because God is set determinedly toward a truthful direction He cannot also be set toward a lying direction. Thus the inability of God to lie spoken of in Titus 1:2 is a *willful* inability, i.e., "God powers not lying." Note: Here and elsewhere, where I take the liberty of describing the Persons of the Trinity as "They" instead of "He," etc. (to advance the thought of Each Person's *theoretically* possible and separate intention), I trust it will be understood for argument's sake why I have done this, instead of adopting the biblical nomenclature of the corporate One.

Endnotes:

[lxv] [http://www.lds.org/newsroom/mistakes/0,15331,3885-1-18078, 00.html].

[lxvi] Phillips, Rebecca. "Heaven Is a Place Where You Are Happy." [www.beliefnet.com/story/181/story_18118_1.html].

[lxvii] Spiegel, p. 76.

[lxviii] Spiegel, p. 84.

[lxix] Spiegel, p. 88.

[lxx] Bridges, p. 18.

Chapter 21
Answering the Problem of Evil

The first objection thoughtful unbelievers generally raise against the Christian faith is the problem of evil. "How can there be a God?" they ask, "Just look at the state of the world!" One can certainly understand their argument, and I'm certain I would feel the same way if I were not a Christian. In fact, several years ago I heard a news story that I'm certain I would mention to any evangelist knocking on my door if I were an unbeliever. "What about that young boy, Dylan?" I would ask. Dylan Groene, nine, and his sister, Shasta, eight, were abducted by a sexual predator. As Katherine Ramsland describes the incident:

> (Shasta) told police that over the course of several days, she and her nine-year-old brother had been repeatedly sexually assaulted by their kidnapper. Then he'd taken Dylan away, tortured and shot him, burned his remains and fled with her. (Dylan's remains were found in Montana.) There's little doubt, if not for the intervention of concerned citizens, that she was next.
>
> Their abductor was James Edward Duncan III, a convicted child molester. His criminal history includes a long string of assaults against children, as well as at least one other murder. He remains a suspect in several as-yet unsolved cases, and in his online blog, he alluded to having committed murder more than once. Duncan officially began his criminal career in 1978 when he was fifteen by forcibly raping a nine-year-old boy at gunpoint. Apparently he told a therapist that he'd already assaulted at least a dozen boys in a similar manner, six of whom he'd bound. Only two years later, he was in prison for raping a 14-year-old boy.
>
> Duncan remained in prison for fourteen years, and his parole conditions stipulated that he stay away from children…
>
> In April 2005, [Joseph Edward] Duncan [III] was charged in Minnesota with molesting a six-year-old boy and attempting to molest his friend. Bond was posted and Duncan then purchased a shotgun, a claw hammer, and ammunition. He stole a Jeep Grand Cherokee and fled the state, arriving in Idaho. He

apparently spotted the Groene children in their yard, and staked out the home for a few days until he determined the right time to go grab the kids. Instead of taking them from the yard, he decided to kill three people inside the home. Even worse, rather than just shoot them, he chose instead to bind them and use the claw hammer to bludgeon them to death. Each person heard the others being killed, which bears witness to Duncan's need to inflict psychological as well as physical torture. He also described to Shasta and Dylan what he had done to their family and recorded his treatment of them for his later enjoyment.

Duncan, 42, had grown mean over the years, and viewed his treatment as unjust. He'd kept a Web diary labeled "Blogging the Fifth Nail," a reference to the nails used on Jesus Christ during his crucifixion.

In some entries, Duncan discussed the idea of right and wrong and his awareness that he did not know the difference. "God has shown me the right choice," he wrote in April 2005, "but the demons have tied me to a spit and the fire has already been lit." Duncan also expressed a great deal of anger over his social isolation, the result of his Level III sex offender status, and he wanted to strike out at society. "My intent," he wrote, "is to harm society as much as I can, and die." Apparently his aim was to kill people and grab children for his own pleasure. In one entry, just four days before the Idaho murders and abductions, he wrote, "The demons have taken over."[lxxi]

So the question I would ask the evangelist at my door, were I not a Christian, is the same one I now ask the Church as a long time member of the Christian community: *Did God foreordain in any sense the sinful activities of Joseph Edward Duncan III?*

I can imagine how a tactful evangelist might respond. Probably he would feel genuinely apologetic in having to admit it was a *mystery* to him why such things should happen. This would almost certainly be his response if he were a Calvinist or simply an average Christian attending the kind of Evangelical church where he heard a Calvinistic apologetic 'answer' about why evil exists. Probably the evangelist would hesitate to tell me what he really thought about the matter if he understood his church's apologetic at all—that in some sense God had designed that Dylan should be raped and murdered by the sexual predator who first bludgeoned most of Dylan's family to death, while yet remaining blameless in decreeing such events. "But deep down I know God is *good*," the evangelist might add, before leaving my doorstep to give a 'reason' of the hope that is in him to my neighbor down the street— "…good *all* the time."[249]

I think the Church needs to have something better—nay, *different*—than this kind of Evangelical apologetic. When Francis Schaeffer was once asked how he would approach an unbeliever with the gospel if he only had an hour to do it, he replied that he would spend 45 minutes showing the man the problem and 15 minutes showing him the solution.[lxxii] Of course, Schaeffer was referring to the problem of trying to convince the man that there was real sin in the world, and that the man was responsible for his own part in it. Unfortunately, Christian apologetics has unwittingly blame-shifted the problem of sin onto an all-sovereign God and then tried to excuse Him in order to make the gospel message more winsome to the average unbeliever. The result has been a diminished view of sin. Schaeffer was correct, however. We need an apologetic that is biblical, imposing, and impressively *truthful* about sin. And so while Christians should not endorse all the tenets of Open Theism (such as its belief that God doesn't know the future because He lacks foreknowledge), we need something other than James Spiegel's Calvinistic argument in his book, *The Benefits of Providence*, in which Spiegel argues against Open Theism's belief in human freedom. Says Spiegel:

> Open theism does not shield God against culpability for evil (assuming, for the sake of argument, that he is culpable in the classical view). According to openness theology, God allowed evil to occur in the world. Also, he has been immediately aware of it and able to prevent it. So how is he, in this view, any less responsible for evil than he would be if he ordained evil? In other words, since in the open view God is at least the indirect cause of evil, how does the insertion of an intermediate causal step (human beings and their free will) exonerate God? To do X with advance knowledge that X will lead to evil consequences is tantamount to willing the evil itself.[lxxiii]

While Spiegel is right to criticize Open Theism's claim that God had no foreknowledge about Adam's choice, his own Calvinistic system likewise fails to provide a *rational* framework for the coexistence of both God's foreknowledge and human freedom. One wonders, for example, how Spiegel's all-sovereign God is not equally guilty of the same charge which he lays at the feet of Open Theism in the above quote. Would not an *all-sovereign* God <u>also</u> have foreknown what events would lead to evil consequences (granting, for the moment, Spiegel's argument that God's foreknowledge 'led' man)? The problem here, is that Spiegel is simply mistaken to imply (presumably, unwittingly) that God is responsible for the moral content of events simply because God knows what will happen in the future. The Bible never indicates that because God foreknows the future He is responsible for it. Spiegel appears to have come to this conclusion because he has failed to see that human freedom totally removes God from the responsibility of human sin. Human freedom, we note, *by biblical definition*, means that man is the uncaused first cause of his choices, including his sin. As Jesus states (Mk. 7:20-23):

> [20]And He said, "What comes out of a man, that defiles a man. [21]For from within, out of the heart of men, proceed evil thoughts, adulteries, fornications, murders, [22]thefts, covetousness, wickedness, deceit, lewdness, an evil eye, blasphemy, pride, foolishness. [23]All these evil things come from within and defile a man."

Jesus was echoing the same thought found in Ecclesiastes 7:29: "Lo, this only have I found, that God hath made man upright; but they have sought out many inventions." Thus when Spiegel implies, in effect, that God did *X* knowing it would lead to evil, he is proposing that God is *directing* man toward sin. He views God's original creation of free will and His foreknowledge of how man would use it as 'tantamount' to God creating the evil Himself. Thus, Spiegel fails to accept at face value that Jesus recognizes no antecedent cause of man's sin other than man's own will. What has happened, in fact, is that man has taken what God has created and added evil content to it. Take, for instance, an analogy from the world of art. Spiegel's view is similar to saying that Leonardo Da Vinci would have been wrong to have painted the *Mona Lisa* had he foreknown that four centuries later the 'artist' Marcel Duchamp would take a copy of the *Mona Lisa* and paint a mustache on it as a gesture of his disdain for traditional, classical artists and their claim of upholding true principles of craftsmanship. In such a case, (we ask) should Da Vinci have not created the *Mona Lisa* simply because he knew someone would deface it? Of course not. Yet Spiegel insists, in effect, that Da Vinci's foreknowledge of someone desecrating his picture would make him responsible for such desecration along with its implied message! Thus contained within Spiegel's view of God is the subtle assumption that God's motive in creating man was to bring about evil in order to bring about good. In effect, had Da

Vinci the foreknowledge of what Duchamp would do to a copy of his picture, Da Vinci's real motive (or at least partial motive) in painting the *Mona Lisa* would have been its desecration, i.e., so that the Zeitgeist would continue its ineffable march of dialectically defining the principles of art. This is the same kind of assumption one would hold, for example, if one said that God's motive in pointing out Job's righteousness to Satan was to get the Devil to tempt Him, in order that the 'good' part of God's agenda might ultimately take place.

We don't deny here that, for *any* man to exercise his free will in this world, God must sustain the physical creation of the man and the world around him. (As Paul said (Acts 17:28) "In Him we live, and move, and have our being.") But God sustains the man apart from his sin. Again, this does not make God directly *or indirectly* responsible for evil just because He knows what man will do. When the Calvinist treats Ecclesiastes 7:29 as though it means: "The Lord hath made man upright, but he hath sought out many devices, yet the Lord hath ordained that man seek out such devices," he is being a biblical revisionist. And so despite Spiegel's claim—"To do X with advance knowledge that X will lead to evil consequences is tantamount to willing the evil itself"—we cannot find any biblical support for such a statement. Nor (to give a human example) can we imagine the likelihood that Spiegel discussed this X principle with his wife before deciding to have the three children he mentions in his book's Preface, who, precious as they doubtless are, no doubt inherited the same seed of knowledge of good and evil which all of us have inherited from the Adamic line and from which point (after later maturing) they will eventually follow during their period of accountability. For Spiegel, then, to say that people are tantamount to willing the evil itself if they do that which they know will 'lead' to evil, would all but mean that people ought not to have children (since, generally, children eventually mature and travel through the age of accountability, or, in Spiegel's view, would certainly bear the transgression of Adam even as infants).

Spiegel continues to misunderstand the true biblical definition of free will in a special chapter called "The Problem of Evil." Here he invokes a doublethink to say that God could have made man with the ability to choose, but in such a way that he would only choose good. This is apparently the flipside to the Calvinistic belief that all men can choose, but can only choose evil. Thus, in the following quote Spiegel treats irrationally the concept of choosing, i.e., by stating that there can be a choice between *one* thing:

> …is human autonomy really so valuable that it makes
> God's risking cosmic catastrophe worthwhile? Is it
> safe to assume that an omniscient being would be able

to anticipate just how devastating our evil choices might (or would likely) turn out to be, including the massive proportions of rapes, tortures, and other cruelties that human history has seen? Such misery presents a strong presumption against the idea that personal autonomy justifies it all…

…But the problems with the free will theodicy run even deeper. Even granting the premises of this approach, we may still reasonably ask why God has allowed so much evil? Couldn't he at least have diminished the harmful effects of our sins in ways that I have already suggested above?[250] Even in allowing us to run headlong into the many vices we do, surely God could have curbed the painful ramifications somehow. And couldn't he have simply made us more intelligent, such that we could more keenly anticipate the negative fallout of our wrong choices? And giving us a stronger moral imagination would have helped, so that we would have a more acute sense of what it is like to be other people. This too, would have provided a powerful buffer against evil without compromising our freedom.

To push this line of thinking even further, why couldn't God keep us from doing evil altogether? According to libertarians, this would negate our freedom. But this is not true. Much real freedom would remain for us within the domain of goodness, since there are myriad good actions one may perform in any given situation. Right now, for instance, God could build a moral hedge around me so that I could not sin in any way, yet I would still be free to do thousands of different things, from continuing my writing, to taking a walk, to starting a conversation with some students down the hall…[lxxiv]

Observe that Spiegel claims that a *domain of goodness* is possible without any attendant possibility of evil. He asks: 'Couldn't God keep us from doing evil altogether?' Thus, Spiegel makes a subtle change to the word 'us' in his question. He assumes the 'us' is present, when in fact it is not, i.e., by the same token that the 'my' in "my desire" is not present in Edwards and Sproul's theology whenever man needs to be so inoperative that he cannot *react* with real choice (in Edwards and Sproul's case, morally *positive*; in Spiegel's hypothetically stated case, morally *negative*). In effect, Spiegel is really asking, "Can't men do things without *deciding* to do them?" Well, no doubt men can be theorized to do whatever Calvinist theologians need them to do in the arena of irrational theology. After all, couldn't God have created an apple that we could have eaten without eating it? Couldn't God have created a world so that we could commit sin without doing it? Couldn't God have chosen our choices without choosing our choices? (Is anything too hard for the Lord?!) One is reminded again of C.S. Lewis's comment in *The Problem of Pain*, that, while the Bible tells us that God can do all things, such things must be *things*; they cannot be *non*-things.

And so Spiegel's view is a disturbing one, for it denies any meaning to the concept of choice or even to the concept of good. Take for instance the various activities Spiegel labels as 'good actions,' e.g., writing, walking, starting a conversation with some students down the hall, etc. But couldn't Spiegel *refuse* to do these very actions if he wanted? If he couldn't refuse to do them, then how is his *being* different from a machine? After all, a machine *performs* actions but exercises no choices.[251] So to exist in a state where choices would never be possible but where activity is said to be performed, is to be a machine. And observe that machines do not inhabit moral realms. They perform action but never *moral* or *immoral* action. One might say, "The machine is a good machine and performing well," but the machine is never understood as causing or possessing itself any *moral* good. This is because a moral designation can only be applied to persons, since obviously only persons inhabit a moral realm. To deny this distinction between men and machines is to depersonalize the moral dimension of 'good' and 'bad' and to change the words, 'good' and 'bad' into meaningless (machine) terms. The inevitable result would be a universe of existential choices devoid of any meaning, yet a universe where it might be *said* that there was 'good.' And so while we certainly recognize that God *could* have created a universe of machines instead of persons, we also recognize that the machines themselves could never be *morally* good. A robot that 'wrote,' 'took a walk,' or 'talked' to some students down the hall would not be doing *morally good* things, but merely be in motion. In fact, such a universe of indifferent machines would be far different from the universe that actually exists. God's actual creation has real persons who are able to make real choices between real good and real bad. Part of what God decided would differentiate a person from the rest of inanimate creation is this very thing—the ongoing ability to choose between good and evil unto eternal liability. But the kind of universe that Spiegel envisions as God's *ideal* creation is exactly what fallen history has provided. And so he claims that evil must exist for the greater good (Spiegel refers to this explanation of evil as *the greater good* theodicy). If Spiegel had to choose between (what would be for him) a lesser model of ideal creation, he would, according to his description, still choose the existential one he describes, in which (we note) actions are performed without any moral meaning by 'persons' without moral capabilities. That Spiegel views such a universe as even *possible*, not to mention *preferable*, to the actual creation that God originally made and which, in fact, involved human freedom, demonstrates his failure to understand what persons truly are, and can and cannot be. He imagines he is still thinking of people when he uses the word 'us,' but he is no longer describing persons. Apparently, this is because he imagines that any type of conceivable universe *without qualification* is possible with God. Thus the verse, "*With God all things are possible*," would presumably be caricatured (if unwittingly by him) to mean that God could have created a world in which God was *irrational*. This is another way of saying that "God can become other than Himself, and still be God," and of course, this is really advocating nothing more nor less than neoorthodoxy.[252]

Rather, a proper biblical view maintains that God does not exist outside the moral dimension which he defines. Neither do persons (made in God's image) exist outside the bounds of being judged by God's moral law.[253] For example, Spiegel mentions the activity of writing; but regardless of how insignificant any piece of writing might seem, the motive behind any written statement is judged either good or evil according to how God defines these concepts to be. A morally good piece of writing might be an encouraging note to a struggling friend, a letter to one's daughter away at college, or a dictionary stating accurately the definition of God. Conversely, evil writing might be the seductive advertising copy on certain billboards or a book about the equality of all religions to Christianity. In the real world there is always the moral dimension attendant with every choice, even in mundane writing, notating, or checkbook balancing. In real history there were two prisoners, one named John Bunyan who wrote *Pilgrim's Progress*, but another, Adolph Hitler, who wrote *Mein Kampf*; and while these are extreme examples to prove our point, all writing, like all human activity, embraces assumptions and motives that are right and wrong and therefore lands on only one of two sides in the moral question. To get rid of the moral dimension—to describe a 'better' creation as an existential and meaningless universe but still *say* that it has meaning and a moral dimension—is to verbally deny what a man *is*, and to deny him a culpable role in his sin.

Furthermore (in examining Spiegel's view), we find it curious that Spiegel would think that a "stronger moral imagination" would help us not to mistreat others. Indeed, is there a need for imagination here? Do we not all feel what others feel when we ourselves are sinned against? In arguing for a hypothetically better creation where a 'stronger moral imagination' would supposedly be present, Spiegel seems to have forgotten that God Himself declared that the creation of man *de facto* in Genesis was *very good*. Apparently God's own testimony about His original creation in which man was intended to remain without disobedience is not satisfying for theologians like Spiegel, who believe that any number of creation possibilities (including an existential universe) would have been better.

Then, too, Spiegel claims that more *intelligence* would have helped us with empathy, so that we would not mistreat others. Having more intelligence, however, doesn't seem to have helped Satan very much in motivating *him* to stop mistreating people, nor has it helped the rest of the demons to stop their mistreatment of fallen man out of any similar empathy, even though these emissaries of the Devil are all more intelligent than the smartest of men. Nor has having more intrinsic knowledge about good and evil ever helped Adam or any of his descendents live a godly life.

But to return to our discussion about choice, Spiegel seems to fail *entirely* in understanding that the term 'human freedom' cannot bear its opposite meaning. This principle—that a concept cannot bear its opposite meaning—is affirmed throughout all of Scripture, but specifically invoked in 2 Corinthians 6:14 ("for what fellowship hath righteousness with unrighteousness? and what communion hath light with darkness?"), Romans 11:6 ("And if by grace, then is it no more of works: otherwise grace is no more grace. But if it be of works, then is it no more grace: otherwise work is no more work"), and in Isaiah 5:20: ("Woe unto them that call evil good, and good evil; that put darkness for light, and light for darkness; that put bitter for sweet, and sweet for bitter!") The point of these verses is not that the application should stop with light *vs.* darkness, bitter vs. sweet, and good vs. evil, etc., but that it should be applied across the board to all things (including the language used to describe them) until it is understood that a particular thing (such as human freedom) cannot be *itself* and *not itself* at the same time. Furthermore, Isaiah 5:20 actually warns that God's displeasure is unto those who would traduce such terms, for God says, "*Woe unto them...*" How has Spiegel not violated this principle as set forth in Isaiah 5:20, when he tells us that God could have given man a free will that could not be exercised freely, and proceed to define other key terms in theology with similar irrationality? It is sad <u>and</u> illogical, that Spiegel actually says that things like murders, tortures, rapes, etc., are too horrific to justify the idea that God gave man the personal autonomy to unilaterally commit it, but apparently not feel that such crimes are too horrific to justify that an all-sovereign God have the autonomy to freely decree them. Obviously, the question begs itself as to how the positing of an all-sovereign God somehow justifies these crimes if sin truly displeases God. Spiegel would *deny* that such an all-sovereign God is really an argument for God criminalizing man, but, of course, such a *denial* of a logical fact in hand will always be the chief 'strength' of the one espousing an irrational position. So we should expect this procedure of Spiegel as a Calvinist, since the denial of irrationality (and rationality) is the essence of his Calvinism.

Furthermore, Spiegel laments that *"Proponents of the free will theodicy typically assume, often without justification or argument, that personal autonomy is so valuable that it makes the risk of moral evil worthwhile…"* But again the question begs itself to Spiegel why the "risk of moral evil" cannot be justified by human freedom but somehow be thought justified by an all-sovereign God. Furthermore, after each of the first five days preceding the creation of man, the Bible says that God saw that His creation was good (KJV), but after the sixth day—the day He created Adam—He looked upon the whole of creation and said "It is *very* good": Why, then, the difference in statements, unless it be that God had completed the earth's creation when a more complete expression of His nature was finally realized, i.e., Adam, and the personal free will of Adam which reflected the very nature of God and which carried with it eternal liability? Most especially, we take issue with Spiegel as to the real identity of those who would often (I should say, *always*) offer up assumptions without justification regarding the problem of evil. For we observe below his following surface treatment of Romans 9 (including his gloss-over of Isaiah 45):

> Paul's discussion of divine sovereignty in Romans 9 also suggests a compatibilist model of human freedom. In fact, in verses 19-22 he anticipates a main concern of the open theists. After underscoring God's meticulous control of human hearts, he says, "One of you will say to me: 'Then why does God still blame us? For who resists his will?'" His answer is, "Who are you, O man, to talk back to God?" And he quotes the prophet Isaiah, who likens our relation to God to that of clay in the potter's hands. We have no right to question God about his choices. It is his prerogative to use whomever he wants for whatever purposes he chooses.
>
> Note that two problems are raised in this passage. One is the metaphysical problem of reconciling divine sovereignty and human freedom. The other, which rests upon the first, is the moral question as to whether we are in fact responsible in spite of God's sovereignty. Paul's approach is to address the moral issue and seemingly ignore the metaphysical question, a strategy some find frustrating. But Paul's silence here might be the most salient feature of this passage for our purposes. Perhaps his refusal to give a metaphysical explanation suggests that we cannot comprehend the true answers. Or perhaps Paul

intends to remind us that such disputes ought not to distract us from our first order of business, which is right living. In any case, I believe this passage constitutes strong scriptural support for a compatibilist approach.[lxxv]

By 'compatibilist approach,' Spiegel is referring to what we of the opposing position have been contending is the Calvinist's embrace of a contradiction (i.e., doublethinking). But let me pause here for a moment. I feel we must congratulate whoever was first responsible for sprucing up the English language and *Christianese* with the term, '*compatibilist*,' so that a more *winsome* discussion can take place about '*compatibilism*' rather than about an *impossible contradiction* or the "*Achilles Heel of Christianity*," as R.C. Sproul was frank enough to call it. Admittedly, such words as 'compatibilism' add to the sad *tradition* of Evangelical Christian proceedings. At any rate we have already given a complete answer against Spiegel's standard Calvinistic interpretation of Romans 9 in an earlier chapter. Perhaps we should merely add that we feel genuine exasperation that the Scriptures are not handled in a more thorough and responsible way by thinkers who profess Christianity and have such obvious general intelligence.[254]

Once Spiegel advances the Calvinistic interpretation for Romans 9, it becomes inevitable that he will deny there is human freedom, even though he must still *say* there is human freedom. Again, he must *say* there is human freedom so God cannot be blamed for sin, yet *deny* there is human freedom so that God will remain absolutely sovereign. Thus Spiegel's explanation can also be added to R.C. Sproul's list of clever attempts to solve the problem of evil without giving discerning readers any real satisfaction.

By the time Spiegel's readers come to his next to the last chapter—"The Problem of Evil"—the appeal to *mystery* is reaching a climatic development. Consequently, Spiegel backs off the kind of absolutist language he uses elsewhere so that he might now describe 'evil' as chiefly a '*something*':

> Sadly, we are all well acquainted with evil. It visits us regularly and in myriad ways. Evil is typically categorized as "moral" or "natural." The former refers to the wrongful actions of free beings, such as rape, murder, theft, slander, and child abuse. Natural evil, on the other hand, includes pain and suffering that are not attributable to immorality, such as occur in earthquakes, famines, congenital defects, and infectious diseases.
>
> To define evil generally is no easy task, but the most influential definition in the West sees evil as essentially

privative, specifically a lack of being. Augustine maintained, in agreement with Plotinus before him, "that which we call evil (is) but the absence of good." Along these lines Aquinas writes:

"Being and the perfection of any nature is good. Hence it cannot be that evil signifies being, or any form of nature. Therefore it must be that by the name of evil is signified the absence of good....For since being, as such, is good, the absence of one implies the absence of the other."

This conception of evil also has been widely affirmed outside philosophical and theological circles, such as by Emerson, who declares that "Good is positive. Evil is merely privative, not absolute: it is like cold, which is the privation of heat. All evil is so much death or nonentity."

While I affirm this traditional Augustinian definition of evil, nothing that follows depends crucially upon it. One may prefer to define evil more generally as any departure from the way things ought to be, whether morally as in the case of sin or naturally as in the case of pain and suffering. The main point to recognize here is that something has gone terribly wrong in this world, and those of us who are theists have some explaining to do. Or, as some might dare to put it, the God in whom we believe has some explaining to do.[lxxvi]

Notice first that while Spiegel categorizes some evil as 'moral' and other evil as 'natural,' he does not clearly state that rape, murder, theft, etc. are *de facto* sins, i.e., *moral* evil in a way that natural disasters are not.[255] For example, suppose a man shoots another man out of malicious intent such that the victim loses his arm from the injury. The shooting we may justly call sin, but the loss of the limb, while a consequence of sin, is not at all a sin. Again, if a man were paralyzed in an auto accident we would not call his condition a sinful condition from which the man must *repent* (i.e., *change his mind*). For Spiegel, then, to lump both sin and its consequences under the heading of 'evil,' as though there was only a technical distinction between them, is a failure to define sin properly.[lxxvii] Notice too that he says that evil, generally speaking, is any departure from the way things "ought to be." But we must ask Spiegel how anything in the world can be a departure from what it "ought to be" if God is claimed to be absolutely sovereign *and good*? Such statements by Spiegel are illogical.

This vague way of defining evil continues with Spiegel's next thought in the same chapter. Here Plotinus, Augustine, Aquinas, and Emerson are cited for their agreement in defining sin. Amazingly, sin is not granted an absolute status of being, but only a *quasi-existence*, which, of course, is nonsensical. (One recalls the anecdote related by author Lloyd Douglas, accused by one critic of writing prose that was "almost ungrammatical." Douglas responded by telling his readers that he knew what "grammatical" was, and what "ungrammatical" was; but what was "almost ungrammatical"?) Sin, says Spiegel, is "essentially privative" (the West), "it cannot be that evil signifies being" (Aquinas), "Evil is merely privative, not absolute" (Emerson), etc. In a footnote at the bottom of the page Augustine is quoted: "But for good to be diminished is an evil, although, however much it may be diminished, if the being is to continue, that some good should remain to constitute the being." Note the immediate doublethink, that good can be 'diminished' to a quality other than goodness. Thus *good* is not a fixed definition in the Augustinian view. (Notice how Augustine describes evil as a nameless force acting upon 'good', i.e., "But for good to be diminished..." Yet Augustine should have asked himself the question: <u>Who</u> is it that diminishes good in an all-sovereign, divinely decreed universe? So Augustine, by defining evil as privative in nature, defines evil as the state of good being deprived. Evil, then, would have to be that state when *good* is deprived of part of *itself,* since it cannot be deprived of what it is not (in the same way that if my body lacked an arm from amputation due to a car accident, we would understand my body as being deprived of part of what (when it was complete) was properly the body *itself,* and therefore not deprived of a pair of scissors or a stapler that was never, or could never, be part of my body). In this way evil is defined by Augustine as something *within* good, not something *against* good. This makes the 'buzz' about evil, in any discussion about man's sin, appear as though it takes place in the context of good. This is a very confused way of speaking because it is a clever form of doublethink. It attempts to grant the existence of evil while denying its existence. This is why Augustine (while on the frontward rock) says evil has no being. (Again, defining evil within good mirrors the Calvinistic methodology of defining all activity as *within* God, imagining, as Calvinists must do, that they can express *one* divine will as *two* wills—a sovereign will and a 'revealed' will.) Thus, on the one hand evil is said to exist because everyone obviously experiences it, but on the other hand it is nowhere granted its *being*.[256] The result of such a contradictory definition is that no one can be the causal agent of evil since evil has no real being, a result most useful to Emersons's monism and to Calvinists trying to solve their dialectical problems. But notice what I wrote just a few sentences ago: *"On the one hand evil is said to exist because everyone obviously experiences it."* Just after writing this sentence I caught myself. I realized that I had been subconsciously adopting the passive way of describing evil in the 3rd person as do Spiegel, Augustine, Aquinas, etc. I was adopting language that states that we *experience evil*, rather than more honestly expressing the fact that we *cause evil*. I had begun to combine in my mind both sin and its consequences under one idea—'evil.' This is the danger of philosophy. We come under the subtle influence of false thinking before we realize it. It begins to make sense to our sinful desires so that we might excuse ourselves, and soon we begin thinking and talking the same way as those whose false ideas we are studying. This is why the Bible warns us to beware lest any man carry us away as a spoil of spiritual warfare through the deceitfulness of false philosophy.

The result of Spiegel taking forward this definition of evil is that he arrives at a point where the causation of evil is not much of a factor. Thus he says, "The main point to recognize here is that something has gone terribly wrong in this world, and those of us who are theists have some explaining to do." Yes, indeed, to be sure, *something* has gone terribly wrong; except we Christians used to think that this *something* was more definite— i.e., the sinful act performed by our first parents as they disobeyed God and ate of the forbidden fruit, not to mention post-Adamic man's own sinfulness besides. So much, then, for the Calvinist who might otherwise have worried about sin's causation, so that he would be forced to use the word '*evil*' in an honest fashion instead of the word, '*something*'. As long as evil is a *something* which is *nothing* the Calvinist cannot be caught on the horns of a dilemma. No more, then, does the Calvinist have to scramble to explain why an *all-sovereign* God couldn't have *sovereigned* over the formation of sin while doing so, or why man could be free to commit sin even though he and his acts are under the foreordination of God. Like Emerson, who queried in his *Essays* whether or not there was any reality outside his own mind—and thus solved the problem of tension by eliminating the particulars between which tension needs to exist—so with Calvinism the particulars of good and evil are eliminated by defining evil as a *something* that is *nothing*, so that the dialectical tension between good and 'evil' is not a tension at all (the latter being *nothing*). In this manner the tension that exists between an all-sovereign, 'good' God and the free will of 'evil' men can be 'reconciled' and placed into a cozy bed called 'compatibilism.' Thus the problem of evil is effectively swept under the Calvinist's rug. That Spiegel should be expected by our readers to go back and forth between a true biblical definition of evil and the false definition of Augustine, Aquinas, Emerson, & co., need hardly be stated. And small wonder that Spiegel claims that nothing crucially depends on whether evil is defined as privative in nature, since his other key, theological terms are meaningless deconstructions anyway.

Though Calvinists may find it necessary to make such bewildering explanations about evil,[257] an honesty is needed among all Evangelicals so that we do not shy away from a plain statement of the truth. There *is* a biblical model that is rational, logical and that explains the problem of evil—it is man's heart. The Bible demonstrates that God foreknows everything including the activity of man before He created the world, yet deemed it *exceedingly good* that man should choose his own moral content, even if it meant that content was against His will. More to the point is that God wanted man to love Him in return, a choice only a person of free will can do. Furthermore (and to return to an earlier parallel), God has been no more responsible for the desecration of man than Da Vinci would have been responsible for the desecration of the *Mona Lisa*, had Da Vinci foreknown how Duchamp would have desecrated his portrait.[258] Granted we cannot any better understand God's creation of man's free will and His non-determination of it than we can understand the same relation between God's foreknowledge of all history and His non-determination of *it*, nor both of these in regard to the additional difficulty of understanding, for example, *how* God can have an eternal past. But having examined the Scriptures and the historical-grammatical, lexical evidence of words, we may say with confidence that God foreknew the choices of all of us, including those by one, Joseph Edward Duncan III, without in any way determining or predetermining them. This is why Evangelicalism needs to turn 180° away from its meaningless and contradictory apologetic that does itself and the world no *real good*. And it needs to proceed instead unto a biblical model to explain the problem of evil, for otherwise it cannot hope to achieve a real unity within itself nor present to a skeptical world the gospel with any significant, divine power and blessing. Such falsehood always creates improper division and weakness in the saints of the Church. So let us turn away from all such false teaching. For only a God who is sovereign *over* all things, not *in* all things, can affect the malady of our time.

Footnotes:

[249] Someone recently pointed out to me that God is so good at salvaging something out of a bad situation that people think He designedly uses sin. Suppose, for example, a soloist sang in church with no other motive than to glorify himself. Even in such a circumstance God may bless the message of the song and the beauty of the music which derives its meaning and beauty from God's principles of language and music. Thus the solo may still minister to the edification of the congregation, even though the one singing will not profit *himself*. This was Paul's point in 1 Corinthians 13. Paul is not saying that the wrong motive leads to no profit *whatsoever* but to no profit for the one acting with the wrong motive, i.e., "it profiteth *me* nothing." Thus, while it may seem that God is using the sin of the soloist's motivation to bring glory to Himself, this is not really the case. Rather, God is merely upholding the form and content of language (the words of the

song) and the aesthetic form of audibly intelligible music, which is governed according to the principles of tonality and skilled structure.

[250] Elsewhere Spiegel takes the position that God could have softened the Fall so that it wouldn't have been so bad; thus the fact that God didn't ameliorate it shows how His absolute sovereignty is really a mystery (since it seems reasonable to us that He should have ameliorated it). But why (we ask) should God have ameliorated the Fall? God designed that severe consequences follow man's sin in order to show man the deep gravity of his wickedness. A lesser consequence would have said to man, *'Your sin is not so bad as that!'* God allowed severe consequences to follow the Fall for the same reason He introduced the Mosaic law— to raise man's awareness of God's determination to judge sin.

[251] A person's *choice, i.e., human freedom,* by definition means a willing, or an *eventual* willing of one thing, thought, or action above another. As for sleeping or being in a coma, it is true that persons are not always making conscious choices while in such states, but when one awakes from sleep or a coma [the latter by either being restored to health or by dying (thus regaining consciousness in the afterlife)], there is always the *eventual* return to consciousness and the making of choices, such as what the person will decide about his thoughts.

[252] —a movement which, as a mentor of mine once pointed out, is neither new nor orthodox.

[253] See chapter 18 for a discussion of persons not yet mature in age.

[254] It is interesting to note that, while throughout this book we have advocated the law of non-contradiction as a fundamental principle in the *moral* universe, it could, in theory, have been otherwise. See Letter to Ravi Zacharias beginning on p. 711.

[255] He refers to these crimes as being in the moral realm, whereas natural disasters are not; but such a distinction becomes meaningless, since 'evil' does not necessarily equal 'sin.' Spiegel, alarmingly to us, seems to treat both sin and calamity as the same, as though (for example) the KJV, in using the word 'evil' to mean both 'sin' and 'calamity,' was rightfully equating the two. In effect, Spiegel dismisses context as determining any difference of meaning for the term "evil." Nevertheless, we recognize that while the Bible regards all sin as calamitous, it does not regard all calamity as sin, and that the context surrounding each given appearance of the word "evil" determines which meaning it intends to convey.

Furthermore, Spiegel accepts Aquinas' claim that all *being* is good, rather than state that all things are good as they *were* created by God (which never included sin). Moreover, the Bible assumes and states the opposite of Aquinas' position in many places, e.g., "The heart (Heb. *leb, i.e., The heart as it really* **is)** *IS* decietful above all things and desperately wicked." Or again, as Christ stated the matter of origin in a parallelism of similarity, not contrast: "A good man out of the good treasure of his heart bringeth forth that which is good; and an evil man out of the evil treasure of his heart bringeth forth that which is evil: for of the abundance of the heart his mouth speaketh (Luke 6:45). This verse in parallelism speaks of good and evil being brought forth out of the abundance of the heart. How, then, can one suppose a lexical meaning of "brought forth" in the case of good, but "**not** brought forth" in the case of evil, i.e. evil which is claimed by Aquinas and Spiegel as having no ontological being? Why, then, did Christ express these actions as *both* coming from the *abundance* of the heart? To press the point, as Spiegel presumably would be wont to do, that it is the good of "abundance" on the one hand, but "the diminishing of abundance" on the other hand, is sheer eisegesis. So, to assume Aquinas'/Spiegel's position, one must take the verb "to be" or "brought forth" etc., to *de facto* mean "**not** to be" and "**not** brought forth" in the case of evil. Such conclusions are dialectical, illogical, and again, purely eisegetical.

[256] This notion of stating that man does evil as a thing which is no thing is the type of non-sensical statement that C.S. Lewis would have regarded as meaningless. For again, while one may correctly say that God can do all *things*, they must be *things*; they cannot be *non-things* (as Lewis pointed out). So, for example, God is not so 'great' that He cannot ever exist. Even so, we ought not to grant sin the same glib expression of non-possibility.

[257] The reason why Reformed thinkers like Spiegel deny the existence of evil is because (wittingly or not) they deny the existence of man as a distinct person from God. And, of course, if there is no man, there certainly can be no sin. By analogy the same denial would be held regarding angelic persons, that is, whenever the Reformed theologian is on the forward rock of the rocking horse.

[258] Again, Duchamp drew a mustache on a print or copy of the *Mona Lisa*, not the original.

[lxxi] Ramsland, Katherine. "Joseph Edward Duncan III: Compulsive Child Molester."
[http://www.crimelibrary.com/news/original/1205/0102_joseph_duncan_profile.html].

[lxxii] Challies, Tim. *Book Review: Pursuing God.*
[http://www.challies.com/archives/000884.php].

[lxxiii] Spiegel, p. 75.

[lxxiv] Spiegel, pp. 190-191.

[lxxv] Spiegel, pp. 71-72.

[lxxvi] Spiegel, pp. 184-185.

[lxxvii] When Christian thinkers embrace any idea built on contradictory language, it becomes impossible for them to express truth in that particular area. The resulting deception sells itself to hearers when the person advocating the contradiction makes 'explanations' that are drawn out and which contain any number of otherwise common sense statements. And that is the real danger with combining sensical statements with non-sensical statements. A man may first set up his hearers (or readers) as an unwitting patsy with common sense statements

that put his hearers off guard, such as (for example) his claim that he had a piece of apple pie at the local diner for lunch, that the pie was made with Golden Delicious apples, and that he used to pick this variety of apple on a Southern New Jersey farm when he was a boy. But then he slam dunks a non-sensical statement about once eating an apple that didn't exist, and thus he wins the game for his irrational position. Of course, the same game played out in 'theology' is on a much more subtle and sophisticated level. Thus the irrationalist, in using common sense statements, conditions his readers to think he knows what he's talking about, especially if he writes authoritatively and intellectually on his topic.

Some might still take issue with what I have said here about how a man may take the word 'apple' and treat it irrationally. One might argue, e.g., that if a man vomited an apple he ate, he really didn't eat it, even though he ate it. But this is a false way of using language. The word "eat" and "ate" in the above example ("I ate the apple I didn't eat,") is contradictory because the verb *to eat* in its two appearances is being given two different meanings. Rather, if we say that "ate" means that the apple entered the man's stomach, then we cannot also say that the apple did not enter the stomach (even if the man later vomits the apple). Similarly, if by "ate" we mean the full digestive process, then we cannot say that the apple was ever eaten if the apple goes into the man's stomach but then he vomits it. Thus by using language properly we avoid what at first appears to be "legitimate contradictions."

The same principle applies to another example I have seen used by one, Gregory Koukl, when trying to justify the idea that evil is deprivation only. He uses the idea of a donut hole. Thus he claims that a donut hole is, and is not, a part of a donut, and therefore by implication both *is* and *is not* a thing. But the confusion is cleared up once we state in what sense a donut hole IS part of the donut, and in what sense it is NOT part of the donut. First, the essential reason a donut hole IS a part of the donut is because, despite the donut hole being mere space, it is always located in three dimensional space within the outer perimeter of the donut and serves a potential function to the eater (as a finger hold). Second and contrariwise, the essential reason the donut hole is NOT part of the donut is the same reason it is not part of a bugle or a spoon, namely, it contains no donut material (dough, yeast, sugar, etc.) Once the proper meaning of words is understood, there are no "legitimate contradictions" in language. It is interesting to note that while Koukl offers the symbol of a donut hole to explain the Augustinian concept of evil, contrariwise, the most common culinary symbol that the New Testament uses for evil is yeast, a definite *thing* with an intensifying nature.

The biblical position is that evil is a real thing. Those who commit evil (i.e., commit sin) are men who use their freedom of will against God. Jesus stated that such sins arise from within men's *own* hearts. Thus, men cause their own sins, and this means that our sins are not, nor ever were, the creation of God. Christ died for these very sins so that men and women would not have to suffer eternal punishment for their own sins. If evil is a non-thing, as Augustine and his followers think, then it would mean that Christ died for nothing, which is nonsense. Furthermore, to suggest that evil is merely the deprivation of good is to use language mischievously. For example, Koukl claims that evil is the deprivation of good even as cold is the deprivation of heat. But one could claim just the opposite—that good is merely the deprivation of evil even as heat is the deprivation of cold. (I have actually had someone trying to refute me on this issue by citing the scientific *theory* of absolute cold. Yet even I, a non-scientist, understand from the Bible that creation has always involved motion, since it has a sustainedness based on God's *power*, which, in the context of a material creation that IS, must involve heat, and that therefore there can be no such thing as absolute cold.) Thus, neither Koukl's paradigm nor that paradigm turned on its head helps define evil for the Christian. In fact, if both of those paradigms were true then good, evil, cold, and heat would all be mere deprivations of their "opposites" and therefore non-things. And that would mean these "things" do not even exist. This kind of thinking ultimately leads to a theological discourse of literary deconstruction, in which definitions are circular and meaningless; all that remains is an indivisible Oneness of non-distinction and non-reality. Frankly speaking, to support definitions in this manner is to dress up Eastern Mysticism in Christianese—nothing more nor less. As Christians we must forsake these kinds of 'explanations' and insist on proper definitions for all things, including that for sin. Only then will we have a correct understanding of evil and a better appreciation for the sacrifice of Christ for our sins.

It will be helpful, in this debate about evil, if the Christian apologist prepares himself for critical responses, some of which will be aimed at him in a benign-sounding tone. I do not mean necessarily because he *must* respond to *all* criticisms; Christ did not, and neither, necessarily, must we. But for the sake of his own peace of mind, he will probably wish to know why his critics are wrong. Unjust criticisms from Calvinists have key elements that the true Christian apologist will find helpful to recognize, and I will discuss them in a moment. Criticisms will come from others claiming to be Christians (we hope they truly *are* Christians, though obviously confused). I received one such criticism after I refuted the online position of Gregory Koukl. At length I received a diplomatic response from a 3rd party person couched in difficult to understand, philosophical language. After reading and re-reading his response I began feeling stupid and wondered if I really *had* misunderstood Koukl's position in some way. I also found that the more I tried to grasp this man's criticism, the more I became confused. But at length (I believe it was many months or a year or so later) I realized (doubtless with God's help) that I was falling prey to a method of criticism I had actually warned my own readers against in this book, yet failed for a long time to catch.

My chief mistake while reading this man's criticism was my unconscious assumption that this man and I shared the same meanings about words, <u>even about the word "contradiction."</u> We did not. But I did not realize it for a great while. Consequently, the more I read the more I became confused, since I was becoming more and more enveloped in this man's 'language' as I tried to understand it. This is because he was defending his 'logic' (but, in reality, only *consistent irrationalism*, which I did not recognize at first). Interestingly enough, while he did so, he invoked the 1st principle of formal logic, i.e., that *A cannot equal non-A*, in the form of a statement to the effect that one *could* contradict one's self. The problem, however, was that in the course of his response he was defining *contradiction* in a meaningless way *once all his statements were taken into account*, and thus his statements fooled me for a great while. In short, he spotted contradictions sometimes, but not always.

First, he stated his belief that I had "gone beyond" Koukl's definition of evil. Watch out for that kind of criticism! As you confront people about their rocking horse methodology (that is, their dialectical method) you will be told (sometimes kindly, as was the case here) that you do not appear to have understood what was meant by the terms you criticized. Thus I was told that Koukl, by saying evil was a thing, was merely saying that evil was a word, symbol, idea, notion, etc. that referred to a 'thing,' but a 'thing' which had no ontological being (existence). Let my readers think of the numerical symbol "0" or word symbol "zero," both which stand for the absence of number, and I think this is what my critic meant. So, for example, if I said I had zero ducks on my farm, this would mean I had a complete absence of ducks. At this point in his attempted reproof of me, he stated that if Koukl had granted ontological being to "evil" (i.e., *nothing*), he would have contradicted himself. So far, so good. In effect my critic was stating that Koukl was merely saying that evil was e.g., a word only, and that it had no existence beyond the concept of zero that it represented. Now I don't agree with this definition of evil, of course, but I had to admit that Koukl was not contradicting himself when maintaining that non-things could have no ontological being. That much made sense. Both my critic and I understood that if Koukl had stated such a point otherwise, he would have contradicted himself. In a sense this was the pivotal point in my being deceived. For at this point my critic had me assuming that he understood, and would admit to, a contradiction *whenever it occurred*. I'll explain further what I mean in a moment. He then pointed out that Koukl states that rebellious acts are, in fact, evil against God, and that such a position agreed with my own. And, foolish person that I was, I believed him. For surely any Christian would admit that rebellious acts are against God. The problem, however, was that the phrase 'rebellious acts' and the concept 'God' meant different things to Koukl and my critic than to me, though (as events proved) it would be a long time before I realized it. So, my critic had me believing that because Koukl and I used the same words, we agreed with each other on that point.

What I missed, then, for so very long, was that two people can state the same thing but mean something entirely different. Again, I had even warned my readers of meeting people who used doublethink; indeed, I had even described how they did it. Yet because of the subtlety of my critic I did not recognize what he was doing for a long time. Now, the most obvious example that comes to my mind to illustrate how the same words can be used but with different meanings, is revealed in the response Joel Osteen once gave to Larry King when asked if Presidential hopeful Mick Romney (a Mormon) was a Christian. In effect Osteen replied that he would assume Romney was a Christian, since he said that Jesus Christ was his Savior. But as biblical apologist Hank Hanegraaf explains this incident: "It's not the words; *it's the meaning behind the words*." Hanegraaf went on to explain that Mormons do not believe that Jesus has always existed but is merely a child of one of the Father's many wives. Obviously, such a definition denies the eternality and Deity of Christ as defined by the Bible. Now to return to the point about statements made by Koukl and myself; the meaning behind the phrase 'rebellious acts' and the word 'God' are quite different. For Koukl, *rebellious acts* are non-things which have no ontological being. For me, *rebellious acts* are acts (things) which man has willed into existence *ex nihilio* (Lat. *out of nothing*, by which I mean in the particular context of our discussion here, *without prior cause*). Again, for Koukl, *God* is the only One who creates *ex nihilio*. For me, *God* is someone who made the form of creation *ex nihilio*, but not the choices of the will of man nor of angels, both of whom create their own moral content *ex nihilio* **as a thing**. For my critic, then, to state that Koukl and I *agreed* that murder and rape were rebellious acts against God, was actually false. For Koukl and I, as a more astute observer than myself would have observed at the time, actually held different meanings of what that statement meant, because we defined words differently. His Augustinian position, which disallowed any creation ex nihilio except by God, effectively disallowed *a man's will* (i.e., *intention*). Oh, to be sure he would claim otherwise, like Sproul, who thinks he solves the problem by thinking that man has freedom of will, though no liberty. But such a statement, had my critic included it in his attack, would have only demonstrated further that my critic and I held entirely different meanings. But, as I say, I was tricked for a time, scratching my head and asking myself how it was that I was not understanding exactly what this man was saying. And all because I assumed that his understanding of contradictions was of the same nature as that which the Bible defines—the one that an Average Joe's common sense tells him is a contradiction. But again, that is not the kind contradiction—i.e., an actual contradiction—in relation to *rebellious acts* and *God*, to which he was referring, *though doubtless he thought he was.*

What's the lesson in all this? It is that the Christian apologist who aims to be truthful must never assume he and a Calvinist share the same meaning of words. Most (all?) serious Calvinist apologists are so mired in the habit of trying to justify their position by appealing to their standing contradictions, that they cannot abide the reproof of common sense logic. You will not want to believe that about them. After all, they can be sincere in trying to correct you, with no hint of mocking. And you'll realize these thinkers may have just as much natural intelligence as you, if not more, and that therefore they could not possibly have allowed themselves to be led astray along such foolish lines. Don't believe it! Many persons whom the federal government recognizes as mentally slow, even to a point of vocational disablement, grasp the principles of theological common sense (which are child-like), even while these others, who can run intellectual circles around them, do not have such sense.

Thus this critic of mine claimed, through various arguments, that Koukl was not really saying that evil was a thing by merely *referring* to it as a 'thing,' and that I had misunderstood that. Later, he pointed out that Koukl claimed that rebellious acts of God were, in fact, evil. Lastly, he stated that Augustine was correct to believe that only God created *ex nihilio* (Latin, *out of nothing*). Thus evil could not be a thing, since God would not create evil. And therefore (said he) evil was merely the deprivation of good, and not a thing at all. Another trick upon my thinking lay, in part, on his clever use of the term 'deprivation,' which sounds like 'depraved.' I was tempted to think that by *deprivation* my critic meant the *moral opposite* of good; but all he really meant (though he himself surely didn't realize it, since he had to go back and forth attempting to bolster both the rational and irrational sides of his dialecticism), was the idea of 'absence,' as understood in the idea that evil is the absence of good, i.e., in the sense that evil is absent of, say, mustard. The irrationalism of this critic became clearer to me as

I examined *all* the statements he was making regarding *evil* (so called). Technically, then, there was no meaning at all in any of his statements about evil, and thus by the term "evil" he and I meant very different things (pun unintended). Moreover, since his definition of *evil* was non-sensical, therefore, technically speaking, all the terms in all his sentences which grammatically interacted with the word-symbol 'evil' also had no meaning.

Now, reader, don't tear your hair out trying to understand the 'logic' of Calvinists, because you can't. It is non-sensical. And the more you try to understand it the more you will find yourself troubled (if you are a truth-seeker), because you are trying to find meaning where there is none. The association you have with words that your detractor is using will make you think he is saying something, when he is not. Again, I myself did not realize it for a great while, and so I urge my readers to beware of the pit in which I found myself for so many months. But eventually I did realize one thing in this man's conclusion, and it began to settle my mind on the whole issue. He was claiming that only God created ex nihilio, *which, I realized, if that were the case, would eliminate the possibility that a man could ever have a will*. The *will* of a man, by biblical definition, is the bringing out by a man his own intention *ex nihilio*. Otherwise, it cannot properly be called a man's will, i.e., a man's *own* will. So, if it had been true, as the critic claimed, that only *God* could create a man's will (as Augustine implied), then we cannot refer to the will as belonging to a man, since it is a *will* in name only. A Calvinist can certainly *speak* of a *man's will*, as B.B. Warfield implies, when he claims that God creates the very thoughts and intents of the heart (i.e., heart *of man*), but such speech is nothing more than sounds without meaning. Again, technically speaking, there can be no *man* in the spirit sense (i.e., a human creature who is the sole cause of his moral content) if, indeed, God alone creates *ex nihilio*. There can only be will*less* **things**. In which case all that the Bible can mean (following Augustine) by the term *the divine judgment of man* is that God puts certain material items in the fire at the end of the age but spares other material things, like putting some logs in the fire but others not. I might proceed to show other equally absurd conclusions inevitable from the Augustinian/ Warfield view, but certainly by now my readers get the point. Needless to say, our opponents would deny this criticism of them with further fruitless 'definitions' of their own, all based on standing contradictions which have only an *appearance* of meaning Thus they could even take my own words and place them in a context of their own making, as indeed my critic did previously with my response against Koukl, until there would be no meaning to them at all. A little leaven leaveneth the whole lump.

In the end, I realized that my original article on Koukl really answered all of my objector's views. It had refuted at length the same method of irrationalism both Koukl and my critic used. Unfortunately, though my critic took some pains in thinking to correct me, he stated that he had not had the time to read through my article, and I found that neither did he indicate a familiarity with the line of objection I was taking. Also, I found it interesting that in his refutation he never really quoted scripture at all, but appealed instead to scientific *theory*, Augustine, and philosophical reasoning.

As a Christian apologist I have sometimes been overly concerned about whether and how to respond to the unending stream of conceivable arguments that people might present against my position. But it is plainly impossible for any one person to refute them all. I am slowly learning that it is not always a spiritual thing for me to respond to those who are not really searching, even though their criticism may be a public reproof of me. If you are like me, you will be tempted to think, "But if I do not respond, people will think I was dumbfounded by his arguments against me." Well, if you must, respond either privately or in a common venue with them, that is, if you are truly led by the Spirit. But I think we all need to trust God more, i.e., that His Spirit works to convince the world of sin, wayward Christian thinkers included. For it is not always our job to continue discussions. True searchers will eventually understand that you have already answered your objectors in your first detailed response. For they know it is a shame and a folly for anyone, the critic included, to answer a matter before he has really heard it. Moreover, words of wisdom are heard in quiet, and true searchers will find that corner of quiet. It is, in fact, their responsibility, even as God said—He would be found by the man who searched for him with all his heart.

Supplement

On John Piper's article,"Are There Two Wills of God?"

Recently,[259] I took the opportunity to read through John Piper's online article, "Are There Two Wills of God?: Divine Election and God's Desire for All to Be Saved"[260] That such an article should be written by any Evangelical advocating a God divided against Himself (so that two divine wills exist) is so disturbing to me that I have decided to add this Supplement.[261] My intent here is not to respond to every one of Piper's points, but only to answer what I regard as the most formidable of them.

Though John Piper is an effective communicator who writes in a non-combative tone, I find that his theology is much bolder than 'old-school' Calvinists. Whereas an R.C. Sproul, for example, might take pains to point out his own initial misgivings about the foundational irrationality within Calvinism (that is, irrationality that Sproul regards as *so perceived* because of the limited potential of human reasoning), such qualms seem curiously absent in Piper. One observes Piper's unapologetic viewpoint throughout his address, including his discussion of whether or not God takes delight in the death of the wicked. As one might suspect from the rhetorical title of his article, Piper concludes that God has two wills, and therefore delights, and does not delight, in the death of the wicked.[262] Thus about midway through his article Piper states:

> We just saw that God "desired" to put the sons of Eli to death, and that the word for desire is the same one used in Ezekiel 18:23 when God says he does not "delight" in the death of the wicked. Another illustration of this complex desiring is found in Deuteronomy 28:63. Moses is warning of coming judgment on unrepentant Israel. What he says is strikingly different (not contradictory, I will argue) from Ezekiel 18:23. "And as the Lord took delight in doing you good and multiplying you, so the Lord will take delight in bringing ruin upon you and destroying you."
> Here an even stronger word for joy is used (yasis) when it says that God will take delight over you to cause you to perish and to destroy you." We are faced with the inescapable biblical fact that in some sense God does not delight in the death of the wicked (Ezekiel 18) and in some sense he does (Deuteronomy 28:63; 2 Samuel 2:25).

[Note: last reference should read 1 Samuel 2:25]

Prior to these examples Piper cites the crucifixion as "the most compelling example of God's willing for sin to come to pass while at the same time disapproving the sin." As proof he points to the sinful activity of Satan, Herod, Pilate, the Jews, and the Gentiles, as all supporting Luke's statement that "This Jesus [was] *delivered up according to the definite plan (boule) and foreknowledge of God.*" He also cites the hardening of Pharaoh's heart as evidence that God must delight in the death of the wicked. Regarding this latter example, he points out that even Arminians admit that God hardened Pharaoh's heart at *some* point. Thus, even if Arminians are granted their argument that Pharaoh hardened his own heart at the outset of the narrative, even they are admitting that God did, in fact, harden Pharaoh's heart in the course of the plagues. (Indeed, Piper is right insofar as arguing that such a view as advanced by Arminian thinkers does concede that God *causatively* hardens Pharaoh at some point.)

Another example which Piper cites as evidence for an absolute sovereignty of God which ordains all the affairs and decisions of man is Proverbs 21:1 ("The king's heart is like channels of water in the hands of the Lord; he turns it wherever he wishes"). Certain other verses are also cited to claim that there are two wills of God to account for all the good and bad. Typical of these examples are Isaiah 45:7 ("I make peace and create woe,") and Lamentations 3:37-38: ("Who has commanded and it came to pass, unless the Lord has ordained it? Is it not from the mouth of the Most High that good and evil come?")

There are three other examples Piper cites in support of God having two wills. They are: 1) Romans 11:31-32, where Gentiles are said to have received the gospel *in order that* the Jews would be jealous of their relationship with God; 2) the numerous examples where Scripture is thought to be stating that sinful people unwittingly carry out what God had already foreordained *in order that* prophecy be fulfilled. [Examples of this last sort are found in the oft-repeated phrase, "*that* the Scripture might be fulfilled" when referring to various prophecies from the Old Testament upon becoming satisfied in the New (such as the betrayal of Judas,[263])]; and lastly, 3) Revelation 17:17, where God is claimed to have willed that ten kingdoms give their allegiance to the Satanic beast.

In responding to these arguments I do not wish to review points already cited in my book. These would include explanations about the sinful acts of men surrounding the crucifixion, the hardening of Pharaoh's heart, and the *judgmental* contexts of Isaiah 45 and Lamentations 3, all of which forbid any notion of absolute divine sovereignty and the annihilation of human freedom. Therefore I will confine my attention to the above three points, as well as to whether there is any real antinomy involving Eli's sons in 1

Samuel 2 and the house of Israel in Ezekiel 18 and 33 that the Bible would regard as "different," though "not contradictory."

Let us begin, then, by considering 1 Samuel 2 and Ezekiel 18 and 33 to see whether God delights, and does not delight, in the death of the wicked. First, observe that the context of God's judgment regarding Eli's sons and the house of Israel in Ezekiel are not the same. The context of 1 Samuel 2:22-25 is one of *impending* judgment, while the context of Ezekiel 18:23, 32 and 33:11 is *contingent* judgment. Technically, the former judgment is also contingent, but the hearts of the sons of Eli have effectually rendered it as impending. In 1 Samuel 2:12 we read, "Now the sons of Eli were sons of Belial [worthless men]; they knew not the Lord." We are told that the sons of Eli committed fornication with women involved in Temple service and also truncated the offering process in order to have red meat instead of boiled, thus despising the Lord's offering which demanded that the sacrifice be fully cooked [pointing to the comprehensive nature and efficacy of Christ's death, in which Christ's blood was intended to satisfy *God*, (not some priest's appetite)]. Their activity had become public knowledge (1 Sam. 2:23). Because they held positions of high spiritual responsibility but lived reckless and immoral lives, God promised that His judgment would come upon Eli's sons upon the selfsame day. In fact, God told Eli that this would be a sign to him of His displeasure. The phrase, "worthless fellows," is uncommonly found in the Old Testament and denotes men who have given themselves over to a particularly virulent form of rebellion. Thus divine judgment was impending, since Eli's sons showed no willingness whatsoever to repent, and this despite the admonition of their father. And so Piper's point is that the *reason* Eli's sons did not listen to their father is *because* God desired to slay them.[264] Here is 1 Samuel 2:25, the verse in question:

> If one man sin against another, the judge shall judge him: but if a man sin against the LORD, who shall intreat for him? Notwithstanding they hearkened not unto the voice of their father, because the LORD would slay them.

Now when Piper cites 1 Samuel 2:25 to say that God acts causatively to **not** restrain evil, it is his attempt to read into verse 25 a description of a divided God. But no such reading is necessary. And we should note that the Mosaic Law made provision to exact capital punishment for a child who demonstrated a lifelong rebellion against his parents. Although Eli's sons were past that age and would have been at least 30-years old to have been engaged in Temple service, they despised the commandment to honor their father as a parent (and such a parent who was the chief priest!). This fact was not lost upon the Lord, nor the fact that such immoral men who had given themselves over to various lusts—one of which nullified, the very symbolism in the burnt offering—held such esteemed positions. Thus, they were "worthless fellows" whom the Lord desired to kill.

In fact, it may be that Eli's warning to his sons about the Lord's judgment was not altogether pure in motive. For a few verses later we are told that a man of God came to Eli to reprove him for despising God's offering and for preferring his sons above God. And so perhaps Eli was warning his sons so that they would merely moderate their disobedience, so that he might still enjoy making himself fat with the choicest of every offering Israel offered to God. The situation reminds one of the time Samuel was distressed for Saul, and God told Samuel to stop mourning, seeing that He had rejected Saul. So then, God may *already by that point* have rejected Eli's sons. Indeed, men are hardly privy to the activity of God's Spirit, and how for how long He has striven to convince a man of sin and of coming judgment, before finally giving him up. But as humans we tend to over-sympathize, hardly cognizant of how long-suffering God has been toward the offenders.

The context of Ezekiel's message in 18:23, 32 and 33:11 is somewhat different, however. First, Ezekiel's address was to the house of Israel (Ezek. 18:6, 15, 25, 29-31 and Ezek. 33:7, 10-11, 20). Second, though sin was also present in the house of Israel, it does not appear that the whole of the Jewish nation during this period was so virulently engaged with sin as to make their repentance a practical impossibility. We know this because the wicked person of the house of Israel is described as *able* to "turn from his way, and live." No such thing could be expected of the *worthless* sons of Eli, however.[265] So despite the sharp language Ezekiel uses to confront his nation's sinfulness, the hearts of the majority house of Israel of Ezekial's time were not so stubborn as to have made repentance essentially impossible.

Another word needs to be said here about the degree of sinfulness which we observed earlier in certain biblical examples (e.g. Simon the Pharisee compared to the woman of many sins, or the nation of Sodom compared to Capernaum, or of Tyre and Sidon compared to Bethsaida and Chorazin). Most of Ezekiel 8 describes a prophetic vision where Ezekiel is taken to a succession of four places. The Lord calls the activity in the second place a greater abomination than that done in the first, the activity in the third worse than that done in the second, and the activity of the fourth worse than that done in the third. The four places involve various groups of Jews in a variety of idolatrous activities. The thing to be observed here is that people sin to differing degrees. The judgment of God upon the great majority of Ezekiel's people was thus *conditional*, since there was still practical hope for their repentance. Conversely and in practical effect, Eli's sons had 'sinned away their day of grace' due to the extreme hardness of their hearts. Any foundation of faith that might have been built up within them through their proper responses to God's admonitions was entirely missing. With such men God could only take delight in their deaths because there was no practical possibility of repentance, and because their deaths would simply put an end to their cancerous effect on the general populace who had become aware of their sins. As the Scripture itself warns: "A little leaven leavens the whole lump." Technically, then, Eli's sons could have still repented if they had exercised their wills accordingly—but this they would not do, for they had set their wills determinedly in opposition to God, and so God was pleased to kill them. But again, there was still hope for the house of Israel in Ezekiel's time because the hearts of these latter were more malleable. Note that the whole of the Jewish exiles are not as the last of the four groups which Ezekiel saw in his vision in chapter 8—the last group being more abominable than the first three.[266] Nor does even this last group necessarily equal in sinfulness the Israeli mother and father described in Deuteronomy 28[lxxviii] who cannibalized their offspring to maintain their physical life while apparently giving no thought to their spiritual repentance.

Piper, ignoring these considerations, puts Ezekiel into conflict with Deuteronomy. For note that the word "death" in the phrase, "I [God] take no pleasure in the death of the wicked," does not mean 'God's judgment,' but rather, 'the sinner's way.' Thus God takes a certain satisfaction and delight when He (rightly) exercises judgment in Deuteronomy, though He still takes no pleasure in the death of the wicked in the book of Ezekiel. Note that the death in Ezekiel is one from which the sinner may still repent. It states that. But when a sinner sins away his day of grace[267] and there is no remedy but forthcoming judgment only, then God may take delight in exercising His judgment.

Thus, God does not delight in the deaths of the majority house of Israel of Ezekiel's time and hopes to still bless the nation, should they repent. Following the two judgments that sent the 10 northern tribes and 2 southern tribes into exile (approx. 762 and 587 B.C., respectively) the house of Israel is now in a new probationary period. Though sin is found among Ezekiel's people their sins have not filled up their cup of iniquity. Jeremiah 18 and Romans 9 both speak of God making from the *same lump* another vessel. This means that the vessel which was being formed was *discovered* (not *created* by the Potter) flawed, and so the clay is pushed down by the Potter to be reformed into a new vessel. This means that judgment has been effected upon a particular nation, and now that nation is in a new probationary period. If at length the nation regards the Lord it shall be judged a vessel of honor, or if it rebels it shall be judged a vessel of dishonor. The individual aspect of the metaphor is found in the individuals who must be present to form the corporate aspect. Thus individual holiness is also encouraged. As a side note, and at the risk of sounding obvious, it ought to be pointed out that nowhere in Scripture, 1 Samuel 2 included, does it ever state that God delights in the *wickedness* of the wicked, but only in the deaths of particularly abominable, worthless persons whom God knows shall never repent, have had long opportunity to repent, and who, in the case of Eli's sons at least, threaten to lead *as sheep* many people into sin. When God finally afflicts the wayward sheep with judgment and grief, He never does so heartily, unless the willful rebellion of the general populace is *set* significantly and determinedly against Him (as the subjunctive case shows it to be in Deuteronomy 28, where, e.g., parents would choose to cannibalize their children). Rather, God afflicts the sheep in a way that is not from His heart, knowing, as in the case of Ezekiel's people, that the sin of the sheep is not the greater sin, at least, not significant enough for God to take delight in the judgment-killing of these sheep.[268] In Moses' long soliloquy (Duet. 28:15-68)[269] about the cursed of Israel who rebel against the Lord, it is significant that there is no mention about how such a wicked people would be able to turn from their wicked way and live. Thus Deuteronomy 28:68, though it speaks of the house of Israel, mirrors the *impending* judgmental conditions of 1 Samuel 2:25, not *per se* the *conditional* judgmental conditions of Ezekiel 18:23, 32 and 33:11.

Second, in his evaluation of Romans 11:25-26 and 11:31-32, Piper states that "[God] wills a condition (hardness of heart) which he commands people to strive against ("Do not harden your heart" (Hebrews 3:8, 15; 4:7)" Says Piper:

> Paul pictures this divine hardening as part of an overarching plan that will involve salvation for Jew and Gentile. In Romans 11:25-26 he says to his Gentile readers, "Lest you be wise in your own conceits, I want you to understand this mystery, brethren: a hardening has come upon part of Israel, until the full number of the Gentiles come in, and so all Israel will be saved." The fact that the hardening has as appointed end-"until the full number of the Gentiles comes in"-shows that it is part of God's plan rather than a merely contingent event outside God's purpose. Nevertheless Paul expresses not only his but also God's heart when he says in Romans 10:1, "My heart's desire and prayer to God for them [Israel] is their salvation." God holds out his hands to a rebellious people (Romans 10:21), but ordains a

hardening that consigns them for a time to disobedience.

This is the point of Romans 11:31-32. Paul speaks to his Gentile readers again about the disobedience of Israel in rejecting their Messiah: "So they [Israel] have now been disobedient in order that by the mercy shown to you [Gentiles] they also may receive mercy." When Paul says that Israel was disobedient "in order that" Gentiles might get the benefits of the gospel, whose purpose does he have in mind? It can only be God's.

To see Piper's remarks in relation to the biblical context of Romans 11:25-26 and 11:31-32, we will begin with Romans 10:16:

> [16]But they have not all obeyed the gospel. For Esaias saith, Lord, who hath believed our report? [17]So then faith cometh by hearing, and hearing by the word of God. [18]But I say, Have they not heard? Yes verily, their sound went into all the earth, and their words unto the ends of the world. [19]But I say, Did not Israel know? First Moses saith, I will provoke you to jealousy by them that are no people, and by a foolish nation I will anger you. [20]But Esaias is very bold, and saith, I was found of them that sought me not; I was made manifest unto them that asked not after me. [21]But to Israel he saith, All day long I have stretched forth my hands unto a disobedient and gainsaying people.
>
> **(chapter 11)**
> [1]I say then, Hath God cast away his people? God forbid. For I also am an Israelite, of the seed of Abraham, of the tribe of Benjamin. [2]God hath not cast away his people which he foreknew. Wot ye not what the scripture saith of Elias how he maketh intercession to God against Israel, saying, [3]Lord, they have killed thy prophets, and digged down thine altars; and I am left alone, and they seek my life. [4]But what saith the answer of God unto him? I have reserved to myself seven thousand men, who have not bowed the knee to the image of Baal. [5]Even so then at this present time also there is a remnant according to the election of grace. [6]And if by grace, then is it no more

of works: otherwise grace is no more grace. But if it be of works, then is it no more grace: otherwise work is no more work. [7]What then? Israel hath not obtained that which he seeketh for; but the election hath obtained it, and the rest were blinded [8](According as it is written, God hath given them the spirit of slumber, eyes that they should not see, and ears that they should not hear;) unto this day. [9]And David saith, Let their table be made a snare, and a trap, and a stumblingblock, and a recompence unto them: [10]Let their eyes be darkened, that they may not see, and bow down their back alway. [11]I say then, Have they stumbled that they should fall? God forbid: but rather through their fall salvation is come unto the Gentiles, for to provoke them to jealousy. [12]Now if the fall of them be the riches of the world, and the diminishing of them the riches of the Gentiles; how much more their fulness? [13]For I speak to you Gentiles, inasmuch as I am the apostle of the Gentiles, I magnify mine office: [14]If by any means I may provoke to emulation them which are my flesh, and might save some of them. [15]For if the casting away of them be the reconciling of the world, what shall the receiving of them be, but life from the dead? [16]For if the firstfruit be holy, the lump is also holy: and if the root be holy, so are the branches. [17]And if some of the branches be broken off, and thou, being a wild olive tree, wert graffed in among them, and with them partakest of the root and fatness of the olive tree; [18]Boast not against the branches. But if thou boast, thou bearest not the root, but the root thee. [19]Thou wilt say then, The branches were broken off, that I might be graffed in. [20]Well; because of unbelief they were broken off, and thou standest by faith. Be not highminded, but fear: [21]For if God spared not the natural branches, take heed lest he also spare not thee. [22]Behold therefore the goodness and severity of God: on them which fell, severity; but toward thee, goodness, if thou continue in his goodness: otherwise thou also shalt be cut off. [23]And they also, if they abide not still in unbelief, shall be graffed in: for God is able to graff them in again. [24]For if thou wert cut out of the olive tree which is wild by nature, and wert graffed contrary to nature into a good olive tree: how much more shall these, which be the natural branches, be graffed into their own olive tree? ²⁵For I would not, brethren, that ye should be ignorant of this mystery, lest ye should be wise in your own conceits; that blindness in part is happened to Israel, until the fulness of the Gentiles be come in. ²⁶And so all Israel shall be saved: as it is written, There shall come out of Sion the Deliverer, and shall turn away ungodliness from Jacob: ²⁷For this is my covenant unto them, when I shall take away their sins. ²⁸As concerning the gospel, they are enemies for your sakes: but as touching the election, they are beloved for the fathers' sakes. ²⁹For the gifts and calling of God are without repentance. ³⁰For as ye in times past have not believed God, yet have now obtained mercy through their unbelief: ³¹Even so have these also now not believed, that through your mercy they also may obtain mercy. ³²For God hath concluded them all in unbelief, that he might have mercy upon all.

Piper cites the NIV in verses 31-32 to obtain the phrase, "in order that,"—i.e., "*in order that* by the mercy shown to you [Gentiles] they also may receive mercy." The NIV's phrase *in order that* is merely rendered as *that* in the KJV and NAS. And the word "that" may not be so strictly observed to be "in order that" as Piper would have us believe. It appears 570 times in the KJV New Testament, 486 times as *that*, 76 times as *to*, and 8 other times. Scripturetext.com[270] gives the following definition of *that* (Gr. *hina*):

> ινα **[hina]**
>
> conjunction **hina** hin'-ah: in order that (denoting the purpose **or the result**)[271] – albeit, because, to the intent (that), lest, so as, (so) that, (for) to.

Keeping this definition in mind, consider the comparison Paul makes in verses 30-31:

> 30 For as ye in times past have not believed God, yet have now obtained mercy through their unbelief: 31 Even so have these also now not believed, **that** through your mercy they also may obtain mercy.

In the comparison, *Even as* **X**, *so too* **Y**, verse 30 acts as the *Even as* **X**, and verse 31 as the *so too* **Y**. Thus, verse 30 begins (in the KJV) with the phrase, "For as (Gr. *hosper*; "Even as," "Just as," "Exactly like")," and the comparison is completed in verse 31 which begins with the phrase, "Even so..." The point here is that the word *that* in verse 31 cannot carry with it essentially any more sense of *in order that* than what is stated in the first half of the comparison as given in verse 30. The corresponding word in verse 30 is *through*, rendered in the particular interlinear Greek text in my possession as *by*. Yet this particular preposition, as supposed from the Greek, seems to rest on the "*kai...de*" construction which often lays stress upon the *explanation* of what is being said, and not necessarily upon anything of a causative purpose. Thus the word "through" was supplied by the translators to make the sentence grammatically understandable in English. The Greek of verse 30b **does not have to** suggest a translation of "*yet have now obtained mercy* **because** *of their unbelief.*" Furthermore, verse 30 harkens the reader back to the reason Gentiles have been grafted in (as it were) into the natural olive tree. It is because of the *unbelief* of the great majority of Jewish people. Note Romans 10:21: "But to Israel [God] saith, All day long I have stretched forth my hands unto a disobedient and gainsaying people." Piper's interpretation demands that we understand that God is holding forth his hands unto a disobedient people whom God Himself has made disobedient (shut up in disobedience) in order to more universalize the gospel. In effect, Piper is arguing that God is free to do *evil* if good will result (though of course Piper does not *call* such divine actions evil, or *does* he, since he quotes Lamentations 3:38 to that intent?). Instead of resolving the tension inherent in stating that God **caused** the Jews to reject Him while holding out His hands to receive them, Piper appears to accept the contradiction with a frank, nonchalant, almost colloquial attitude. *So what* if God holds out his hands to the Jews while at the same time hardening them unto disobedience? *Whatever. So what* if God doesn't take delight in the death of sinners while at the same time taking delight in the death of sinners? *Whatever.* After all, *isn't this what the Bible teaches?* Thus, rather than resolve the tension created by such disastrous definitions of God that threaten the whole of Scripture—a Scripture that is actually opposed to any such notion that God causes evil—Piper insists that such statements that *can* be taken literally to mean that God is divided against Himself *ought* to be so taken. Of course, Piper would deny that his theology pits God against Himself because that is part and parcel of his theology. For what appears to *our* common sense as a God acting against Himself is to Piper's sense a God who acts *for* Himself. Piper's portrayal of God is one of both/and in His essence. God is not either/or. Following this logic, we can only imagine what Piper must take the Scripture to mean when it says that God is not as a man, that He should repent (change his mind). It would have to mean that

God does not change his both/and essence for one where His character is understood as *either this* **or** *that*. The result of such theology as Piper's is thus a ludicrous view where God is said not to tempt man but nevertheless assigns him to irresistible hardening! Piper's God (as he apologizes Him out) is divided against Himself, yet presumably Piper would still claim that God is *good*—but obviously this is not how a *child* would understand *good*, i.e., good in the common sense and use of the word. Piper, by adding many philosophical trappings (wrong interpretations of various scriptures) has *de facto* described God as one who authors all events and is therefore indistinct in His character. The final result for Piper is that man cannot therefore *cause* anything, that is, whenever Piper stresses the sovereignty-of-God side of his dialectical equation. Piper's inevitable conclusion occurs near the very end of his article, and of course it favors the front rock of the dialectical rocking horse:

> I do not find in the Bible that human beings have the ultimate power of self-determination.

Our inquiry, then, is a simple one. If man is not ultimately self-determinative, then who is the causal agent in man's sin? Or again, if man is not ultimately self-determinative who is it that causally "rushes" to Christ after allegedly having his desire changed, as R.C. Sproul is wont to imagine? Many Christian readers will think that Piper is stating that somehow man causates *within* God's causating, but this is really a failure to understand the force of Piper's statement. For readers doubtless imagine in their mind a man who acts in some sense—goes to church, reads his Bible, prays, goes to work, pays bills, raises a family, etc. But the idea of a man who can act—i.e., a man who in any sense can even choose for himself a single thought, is simply not permissible under Piper's definition. One cannot grant any action whatsoever under Piper's view, because even the inaugural action in any process of action is subject to Piper's statement that man himself cannot determine it. Piper's use of the word 'ultimate' is his attempt to modify the severity of his definition through a Hegelian-type synthesis of both/and, so that man can be thought to be doing it within God doing it.[272] For this 'reason' such an attempt of redefinition fails. The condition of such a 'choice' is the same as that of a woman's pregnancy—there are no half measures. We cannot speak of a half-pregnant woman anymore than, as Christian apologist Ravi Zacharias would put it, we can speak of a one-ended stick. Again, the will is an all or nothing proposition. For example, let us consider a man who is said to run a 100 yard dash. If we can suppose with Piper that the man does not do so because of ultimate self-determination, we are nevertheless obligated to apply Piper's definition to the fullest extent. Therefore even regarding the first step of the man's sprint we must say that the man doesn't choose to do even this in any ultimate power of self-determination. Even half of the first step, or one-quarter of the first step, or one-eight of the first step, etc., is not (in Piper's view) an event caused by the man himself. Thus, and likewise, the man's *decision* to begin moving his body into a first step cannot be caused by the man, for that would require ultimate self-determination. Therefore to speak of man doing anything in a causative way is not possible under Piper's definition. Again, this impossibility of causation would include Sproul's belief that man "rushes to Christ" after his desire has been allegedly changed. The only conclusion allowable in Piper's view is that God does all the acting for the man, and thus man is only 'man,' i.e., nothing more than the construct of God placed upon material creation. Incidentally, Piper never states baldly that God Himself must be viewed as similarly non-determinative if He is to escape the charge of sin. But now we see the only conclusion about sin even possible under Piper's definition. What has been regarded as sin is really only 'sin.' For since God is the only One who is ultimately self-determinate, then all experience, including sin, must be good—indeed, *goodness itself* (if we are to take Piper's position to its consistent conclusion). This is why Calvinists so often treat sin as though it were merely another tool that God also uses to accomplish His purposes. Rather than Piper simply understanding Paul's statement about shutting up the Jews in disobedience to mean that God stopped engaging them[273] because He was tired of their stubbornness—thus allowing them henceforth to be less hindered in their willfulness to be disobedient until the gospel was fully preached to the Gentiles, with the result that all Gentile nations would have a better chance to respond—(indeed, does Paul not say that the Jews were a branch broken off for *unbelief*?)—Piper reels out a definition of a God who desires and wills that men disobey Him while all the time holding out His hands **to** them. Thus, when Piper comes to Lamentations 3:33—"Though he causes grief, he does *not willingly* afflict or grieve the sons of men,"—he takes the Hebrew meaning of *willingly*, which means "from the heart," and in effect takes a position which forces the reader to interpret "not from the heart" as "without compassion" which in his system must correspond to "a will of delight," a point we will discuss in detail in a moment. In fact, Piper's position, though one he does not admit to, defines the phrase "not willingly" in such a way as to imply a divine motive essentially opposite of what really describes God's character throughout the Bible, including the passage of Lamentations 3:32-37, that is, once these verses are understood in their near and far context. In the example below by Piper, keep in mind Piper's claim that two wills operate simultaneously within God, that of NON-delight and delight in the death of the wicked:

In other words, God has a real and deep compassion for perishing sinners. Jeremiah points to this reality in God's heart. In Lamentations 3:32-33 he speaks of the judgment that God has brought upon Jerusalem: "Though he causes grief, he will have compassion according to the abundance of his steadfast love; for he does not willingly afflict or grieve the sons of men." The word "willingly" translates a composite Hebrew word (milibo) which means literally "from his heart" (cf. 1 Kings 12:33). It appears that this is Jeremiah's way of saying that God does will the affliction that he caused, but he does not will it in the same way he wills compassion. The affliction did not come "from his heart." Jeremiah was trying, as we are, to come to terms with the way a sovereign God wills two different things, affliction and compassion.

At first glance we might be tempted to think that Piper is advocating the kind of divine willing claimed by many non-Calvinists; i.e., that of God merely afflicting those whom He hopes will repent and avoid judgment. But in fact, prior to the above quote Piper cites an illustration from Robert Dabney, in which God's attitude toward the condemnation of the guilty is likened to that which George Washington felt when he reluctantly sentenced a certain Revolutionary soldier, one, Major Andre, to death for treasonous acts—reluctantly, that is, because certain of Andre's other actions were not without merit. The problem, however, is that Piper, in the above quote about Lamentations 3:33, is claiming that God *also* wills to afflict the sons of men in a *different* way than the way He wills compassion. And we have already noted that Piper's "different" will is in fact a mutually opposite will. Thus the question begs itself—If God wills His compassion, a compassion which corresponds to his NON-delight in condemning sinners, then what **_different_** divine will can it be when God, according to Piper, does *not willingly* afflict the sons of men? In can only be heart***less***ness (that is, as the word "heartless" would be normally understood in the phrase "such an act was *heartless*"). And note that "heartless" must correspond to the divine will of **delight** in God's condemnation of sinners, since Piper believes that such a will of delight must exist alongside God's other will of NON-delight. This is certainly a 'conclusion' Piper must maintain to support his argument that God **_does_**, *and yet* **_does not_**, delight in the condemnation of perishing sinners.

Yet Piper cites the illustration of George Washington's "reluctance" as the emotional desire pointing to this "different" will than that of compassion! But Washington's "reluctance" to punish was in a context of meaning which in any normal sense must indicate something more akin to a will of *compassion*, not a will of heart***less***ness! Furthermore, we note that while Washington condemned the soldier on just grounds, he acted *against* his strongest desire of compassion. That is, it is not accurate to state that Washington had both compassion and heartlessness upon Andre, or we could not speak of Washington's "reluctance" anymore than we should speak of Washington's "enthusiasm." Therefore we cannot properly say that Washington ever acted at any point from heart***less***ness, though certainly it may *appear to us* that he felt that way because of his bare decision. But of course Piper, as a Calvinist, does not believe that a man **can** act against his greatest desire. Thus for Piper, any decision (will) by God (e.g., to condemn a sinner) must involve both God's NON-delight and delight, since an all-sovereign God always acts to please Himself. Yet even here we find the Calvinistic definition of *desire* useless, for if God has two *desires/wills* of presumably equal preference, then there is no such thing as God's *greatest* desire that could lead God to will the reprobation of a man any more than to ***not*** will the reprobation of a man. And if the Calvinist claims that God's wills are beyond our comprehension and therefore ought not to invite the same kind of description men make of themselves, then of what use is it for the Calvinist to speak of God's two wills that are "different," "not contradictory," since the Calvinist is also human and therefore without the ability to define the nature of God's wills? [Such an approach reminds one of neo-orthodox theologian Karl Barth, who claimed on the one hand that it was not possible through any human conceptions to describe God, but on the other hand claimed that God nevertheless made use of human concepts to communicate Himself.] In this manner Piper spins out a kind of dialecticism within a dialecticism (i.e., a 'meaninglessness' within a meaninglessness), that is, by first citing alleged lexical evidence to combine the irrational thought that God delights in that which He does not delight upon the same object in the same instant, and then later adding a further irrationality with the Washington illustration, so that the term "delight," *as defined dialectically,* is 'understood' as being NON-delight ("reluctance," so to speak). That is, the word symbol "reluctance" is brought in to support the original doublethink of "delight"/"NON-delight," thus serving as another confusing distraction from the truth. With such reversibleness it becomes all but impossible for most Christians to realize Piper is engaging in literary deconstruction. And being further fooled by Piper's gentle demeanor, they accept his Calvinistic appeal to 'mystery' instead of identifying his irrational theology as a doctrine of demons. And so, because of these reversible meanings, Piper cannot really escape the charge that the phrase 'a will of **delight**' (that is, 'a will of **heartlessness**') might mean either a will of heartlessness or the 'opposite' of 'heartlessness' as 'heartlessness' would [as alternating moments in any dialectical system require, for the sake of *appearing* to have meaning] be dialectically defined. No doubt whichever will serve Piper in the moment will do, since neither have any actual meaning. Frankly, I don't think Piper himself really understands what he is saying, which is why he speaks of himself and his sympathizers as trying, with Jeremiah, "to come to terms with the way a sovereign God wills two different things…." The reason Piper is still trying to "come to terms," of course, is because he cannot arrive at rational definitions (and therefore proper understanding) without destroying the dialecticism that undergirds his Calvinism.

Besides a will of compassion, then, Piper speaks of the remaining will of God, i.e., the term "not willingly." And because he must assume that "not willingly" means the *opposite* of compassion (though, of course, not opposite as Piper would define it), he concludes that "not willingly" means "not compassionately." This means that without the negation of the word "not," Piper takes the word "willingly" to mean "compassionately." And the full term "not willingly" must correspond to the **delight** side of his dialectical equation, since a 'will of compassion' is thought by Piper to correspond to God's NON-delight in God's condemnation of the sinner.

And so, again, such an emotion that corresponds to that will of God which Piper claims is "different" than compassion—revealed in the implicit word "heartless"—corresponds to God's 2nd will, i.e., His **delight in non-compassion**. Thus is yielded the essential thought, 'With delight in non-compassion doth God afflict…the children of men'.

Remember, Piper makes no contextual distinctions between Ezekiel 18 and 33 on the one hand, and 1 Samuel 2 and Deuteronomy 28 on the other hand, nor *can* he if the irrational dialecticism of his Calvinism is to remain in place. Thus whenever he urges his readers to accept his definition of divine *willing* upon the wicked, he wants his readers to believe that God is both heartfelt and **un**heartfelt upon the same object at the same time. As already noted, Piper strips away all meaning and lexical use of the word *willingly*. He did this first by using the word "will(s)" as a synonym for "decree(s)," thus, Piper: "God does will the affliction that he caused, but he does not will it in the same way he wills compassion." For once Piper had admitted into his dialectical discussion of God's two wills (that are upon the wicked) the idea of compassion (that is, at the beginning of the above, paragraphed quote), he had then to find the remaining idea (or relatively synonymous idea) of NON-compassion. This dialectical approach explains his claim that God's two wills are "different," "not contradictory,"[274] though we note, in fact (as Edgar might put it), that the phrase "not willingly" is not merely *modified* by Piper, but *changed* in definition to where, we observe in this case, it becomes the mutually opposite idea of compassion, therefore making God's nature contradictory.

But the point in all this is that Piper, in doing so, has simply dismissed what the word "willingly," i.e., the cognate related to Strong's #3820 and #3824, actually means according to the consistent Hebrew use of #3820 and #3824 ***in over 700 appearances in the Old Testament,*** in which the cognate arguably demonstrates no lexical difference in meaning in relation to #3820 and #3824, besides the obvious prepositional one. And #3820 and #3824 means "<u>heart</u>," as in a "person's inner self," that is, the thoughts and/or will (and emotions) generated by the self, though, we note, not the *specific kind* of content of the thoughts and/or will and/or emotion. For we note that apart from context the Hebrew word "heart," though it denotatively indicates content, suggests nothing specific of that content, or whether that content is good or bad. And therefore examining the context of the word's every appearance is necessary. For example, the bare phrase, "the man's heart," indicates nothing about whether the man's heart is compassionate or uncompassionate, but merely what is *de facto*, i.e., the man's *real* heart. The same is true of the phrase, "God's heart," though, of course, we are reminded so often in Scripture that God is good that we tend to think of something positive in the bare term, "God's heart." But again, the term "heart" (Heb. *leb*) apart from context indicates nothing specific of the heart's *de facto* content. To assume otherwise invites serious lexical trouble. For example, when we are told in Genesis 27:41b that "Esau said in his heart, The days of mourning for my father are at hand; then will I slay my brother Jacob," we would certainly run into problems by inserting Piper's meaning of "compassion" into the verse, i.e., "Esau said in his *compassion*...I will slay my brother Jacob."(!) (Of course, we assume that Piper's meaning of the cognate would not be different from the verb(s) from which it derives, except in the obvious prepositional sense.) Thus we note that not the least of Piper's reasons for his special pleading that "not willingly" in Lamentations 3:33 ought to mean "not compassionately," is the same in principle as it always is with Calvinists, i.e., God is the grammatical subject, and so "willingly" has to mean whatever the Calvinist needs it to mean in the moment, and since the moment in Lamentations 3:33 calls for God's pleasure in reprobation, a substitute definition for the word "heart" is sought by the Calvinist to support the dialectical claim on the remaining side of the equation, with the result that God is delighted with afflicting the sons of men. Again, such an assumption by Piper relies entirely on eisegesis, not on the lexical use of the Hebrew word *leb* or its cognates. And yet Piper's kind of eisegesis is not the only kind of eisegesis that can be done. For one can also (as regrettably I did in an earlier edition of this book), assume that "unwillingly" means "not from the heart" in the sense of "his heart was not in it," i.e., "not enthusiastic," or "reluctant." (Note that this is not to be confused with how Piper defines "reluctance" in the Washington illustration, the difference in Heb. *leb* being Piper's (incorrect) definition of "compassionately" versus my former (incorrect) definition of "enthusiastically.") The explanation behind my wrong eisegesis is that I took the English colloquial understanding of what is meant behind the phrase "his heart wasn't in it," i.e., "it wasn't from his heart," and assumed that this was the proper meaning, and I did this without really understanding the lexical use and meaning of Heb. *leb* and its cognates as revealed in the Old Testament Scriptures. In other words, I assumed a wider latitude of lexical meaning for *leb* than what was really warranted, because I had not properly harmonized Lamentation 3:32-37 with enough necessary and relevant scriptures but relied instead on commentary opinion. Consequently, I misunderstood that *leb*, apart from context, indicated content, though not of what kind (including not stating the specific kind of emotional content, e.g., *enthusiasm*), though the context of Lamentations 3 showed what kind of content, i.e., that God did, in fact, take delight in His judgment of Jeremiah's irremediable generation, since that generation fit the description of Deuteronomy 28.

The problem then, as a result of this kind of (e.g., my past) eisegesis, is that the phrase, "He has not afflicted from the heart," leaves the false impression that God has *de facto* afflicted, though not from His heart, i.e., *not heartily*. In fact, this seems to be the non-Reformed interpretation. But this is misleading, since the Heb. *leb* never means, and despite whatever prepositional indicator it may take to mean *from*, the idea of "*heartily*," but is merely a bare indicator of what is *genuinely* (I do not mean *righteously*) the heart, i.e., the heart's content, that is, "of the *heart*," i.e., *of the self.*

Moreover, while the KJV infrequently translates Heb. *leb* to mean *kindly*, *comfortably*, etc., it is wrong to do so. For Heb. *leb* does not take these meanings but instead simply refers to *of the heart*. For example, when Ruth tells Boaz that he had spoken "friendly" to her, this reply came after Boaz had explained to Ruth that he had heard of her good care of her mother-in-law, and how she had left the land of her nativity. He then urged her to glean with his maidens, and to not go elsewhere for her protection. Most of Ruth 2:9, 10, 12, and 13, is taken up with Boaz' detailed conversation with, and blessing upon, Ruth. Therefore, when Ruth replies to Boaz by saying he has comforted her and spoken "kindly" (Heb. *leb*) unto his handmaid, she is simply pointing out that he has comforted her and spoken his *de facto* heart, i.e., his real heart. In other words, the Hebrew word *leb* bespeaks not merely of the form (ability) which is the heart, but also of the heart's *de facto* content, though it leaves it up to the context to explain whether that content is good or bad. So then, the word "comforted," not "heart," shows that Boaz was friendly toward her, and that when Ruth speaks of Boaz speaking (KJV) "friendly" toward her, this means that Ruth was declaring that Boaz had spoken his real heart to her, according to how he demonstrated it toward his own maidens. Thus, the translator's mistaken assumption that Heb. *leb* means "friendly" is a result of his connotative (associated), not the denotative, definition. Similarly, in Genesis 50:19-21 Joseph replies to his brothers to calm their fears that he would treat them harshly now that their father was dead. Verse 21 states: "Now therefore fear ye not: I will nourish you, and your little ones. And he comforted them, and spake *kindly* (Heb. *leb*) unto them." Here it is stated that Joseph comforted them, and so when it tells us that he spoke (Heb.) *leb*, it simply means he spoke from his *de facto* heart. The word "comforted," not "heart," is the context showing that Joseph was kind toward them. Joseph comforted them and spoke his *de facto* heart. Thus again, the translator's mistaken assumption that Heb. *leb* means "kindly" is a result of his connotative, not the denotative, definition. As a final example here, when Jeremiah says that the heart is deceitful above all things and desperately wicked, he is declaring that the *de facto* state of the heart is deceitful above all things and desperately wicked. Again, Heb. *leb* indicates the form which is the heart and bespeaks of the presence of the heart's real content and/ or emotion, but leaves it to the surrounding context to state whether that content is good or bad, or what the specific emotion is. So, in drawing a conclusion here, the idea in Lamentation 3:33 regarding Heb. *leb* is this: Jeremiah is stating that God's *de facto* heart was not, and is not, afflicting nor grieving the sons of men as a general matter of course. Stating the matter negatively, it is not that God *reluctantly* wills to afflict, but that, in the case of common, probationary periods, He *doesn't afflict at all*, i.e., <u>after the manner in which he judges men</u>. The context for *leb* in this passage about God's typical dealings with men thus goes to a question about affliction/grieving's *origin* when it occurs in such a way where it might mimic in appearance God's judgment, even during probationary periods. In other words, what is being stated is that God does **not** afflict generally, not that he **does** afflict generally though not in a certain manner. And so the passage proceeds to explain that God does not turn aside the [impl. *proper*] judgment of men or subvert the [impl. *proper*] argument of men, which, were He to do so, He would afflict and grieve the sons of men, thereby proving Himself cruel. Verse 37ff return to the subject of God's right to pronounce judgments upon men for their sins, i.e., following periods of their probation in which God's mercy, shown in His previous activity of patience, has come to an end upon all or upon the great majority.

Of further note is that the word "unwillingly" is really an English translator's attempt to render the Hebrew noun as an adverb to make the translation appear more sensical to English readers. So, in examining the Hebrew stems and tenses, while also recognizing that anything said to come *from* the heart in a way that cannot mean "heartily" must therefore simply mean *of* the heart, (i.e., of the *de facto* heart), the transliterated meaning would more accurately be something like, "for of [His] *de facto* heart [He] has not afflicted, and is not grieving, the sons of men." (This does not imply that another heart of God besides God's *de facto* heart exists; for the Bible states clearly that God is not as a man that He should repent. In other words, God is not double-willed.) Thus in more common English we might render Lamentations 3:33 thus: "His heart, as it really is, has never in the past afflicted, and still is not grieving, the sons of men."

The point here is that the Hebrew is not referring nor stating, as many commentators seem to think, that when God speaks about His judgment of Jeremiah's generation, He is stating His reluctance to judge. Indeed, Deuteronomy 28 states that God *would* rejoice over judging such a people, not be reluctant about it. Therefore within verses 32-33 there are two groups in view. The first is Jeremiah's generation referred to at the beginning of the previous verse (v. 32), i.e., those in object-relation to the activity and character of God, "For though He has caused grieving, He had [*and will have* (Heb. Piel Imperfect, allowing a polyvalent meaning here)] compassion according to the multitude of His mercies." (This means that God was mercifully patient despite Israel's unrepentant spirit, and, according to His nature, will again be merciful in the future after His judgment has passed.) Therefore at the beginning of the next verse (v. 33), Jeremiah explains why God has any mercy at all. It is because God is patient with the sons of men, i.e., by nature is not harsh with the sons of men. The "sons of men" is this second group of men. And this term, "sons of men," in context of God's activity toward them, relates to God's demeanor to men *generally*, i.e., during the typical and common, probationary circumstances of peoples, not His infrequent instances of divine judgment upon them.

Taking into consideration some of the Hebrew stems and tenses in the key phrases important to our argument here, the following is a suggested translation for Lamentations 3:32-37:

> [32]For though He has caused grieving, He had (and will have) compassion according to the multitude of His mercies; His heart (as it really is) has never in the past afflicted, and still is not grieving, the sons of men., [34]to crush under His feet prisoners of the earth, [35]to turn aside the judgment of a man before the face of the most High, [36]to subvert a man in his argument, the Lord has not considered.

Thus, of the two groups of theological commentators who approach verses 32 and 33, Calvinists like Piper miss this contrast of men under judgment versus men under probation, assume one group of object men only, and so end up with a dialectical God, ***whereas*** non-Reformed commentators likewise miss the contrast but conversely conclude that God is always reluctant in judging the wicked. And so these latter commentators miss Piper's proper point, (one which we accept as Piper basically worded it, if defined apart from Piper's definition), namely, that God IS said in Deuteronomy 28:63 to rejoice at bringing destruction upon the nation of Israel if it pursues a course of rebellion. And if some reader here wishes to steer a third course to say that God has 'mixed feelings' and therefore rejoices in His judgment while feeling reluctant in having to condemn man, thereby attempting to reconcile Lamentations 3 with Deuteronomy 28, it still remains for such a reader to prove that God *ever* in Scripture expresses reluctance to destroy the wicked who are beyond remedy.

But moving on, understandably, Piper is searching for proof in this Lamentations passage that God DELIGHTS in the destruction of the wicked who fit the description of Deuteronomy 28. That is, Piper is not content with doing what so many moderate Calvinists would do, i.e., find a 'biblical' proof text for one side of their dialectic **over here**, and then find the remaining proof of their dialectic **over there**. Rather, Piper is striving to find both sides of the dialectic in the same biblical passage. At least we see that he is trying to be consistent. In the end, however, we note that all that "remains" in Piper's wake of 'explanation' is a complete breakdown of definition about God's character, since a discussion about mutually opposite wills cannot lead to any conclusion about 'God' or 'His motive' or 'His activity,' etc. Piper has presented the matter in the same irrational way that someone might claim that God had two wills, one will that led Him **_to_** eat an apple, and another will that led him **_not_** to eat an apple. What then can be said about 'God' or 'the apple'? Nothing at all. Yet Piper attempts to persuade his readers of his doublethinking theology regarding a God who acts from a 'compassionate heart*less*ness' by 1) insisting that there is no contradiction, 2) claiming he is only following the Bible in recognizing two *different* wills of God, and 3) using lingual arguments that exchange obvious contradictions for subtler ones (i.e., exchanging the word "different" for "contradictory"). Sadly, all this passes for evangelical theology. At any rate, despite Piper's insistence that there *is* a divine will of affliction in regards to the sons of men in Lamentations 3:33, and that implicitly it is not compassionate, we state once more for the record that the Hebrew word *leb*, along with its cognates, is used hundreds times in the Old Testament to mean *heart,* or *of the heart,* defined to be *[of] the inner self of a person,* but arguably never of any specific content of thought, will and/or emotion, such as "compassion," "enthusiasm," "good," "bad," etc.

Now, since Piper cites Lamentations 3 for support of his view of two divine wills—the kind of which, we note, in a dialectical system must express morally opposite wills—his system demands both a *compassionate* AND a *delighted* willingness in condemning men, so that God can be imagined to condemn the sinner with *compassionate heartlessness*. This particular form of eisegesis is the kind of mind-numbing apologetic that has captured the minds of so many of today's Evangelicals.

So then, to review in some detail an essential point made a moment ago, Piper does make a legitimate point about Deuteronomy 28:63, since God did indeed say that He would take great delight in bringing destruction on the nation of Israel if they were to forsake Him. And, in fact, we must remember that the generation of Jeremiah's hearers fit perfectly the description of the prolonged and disobedient wicked in Deuteronomy 28 about whom God said He would delight in destroying, and therefore *did* delight in bringing destruction upon them. But again, this specific judgment against this specific people did not, and does not, reflect God's typical, 'everyday,' common demeanor toward men in general, i.e., the **sons** *of* **men**. *Note the verses surrounding verses 32-33*. These "sons of men" i.e. subsequent generations of men, or men in general, are defined in this specific context as Israel's remnant, against whom God would not retain His anger forever and so would one day return them to their own land (v. 31), and elsewhere defined as those men whose right God will not turn aside from before His presence (v. 35) and whose argument God will not subvert (v. 36). For the Lord does not intend calamity upon those He presently finds are manageable within the bounds of His *mercy*, i.e., mercy defined as God's willingness to forego judgment, at least for a time, at His own expense.

An analogy might be helpful here. Suppose, for example, you are the CEO over a huge movie production company in which employees at length prove themselves to be of two kinds—manageable and unmanageable. In that company are writers, actors, stage hands, a construction crew, a marketing department, accountants, etc. Now suppose that the writers decide they're not getting paid enough. But you realize they are paid as much as possible, and that if you paid them any more, it would jeopardize the jobs of other people in the company as well as the company itself. (For the sake of argument, we will say that your assessment is objectively true.) You try to reason with the writers, but to no avail. Meanwhile the writers go from bad to worse. They begin treating you and other employees contemptuously, show up late to work (when they show up at all), steal money from the company's safe, etc. For a long time you are merciful with them and try to reason with them. Yet you also warn them. You will have to fire them from their responsibilities and jobs if they persist in their selfish behavior. But such warnings only inflame them further, and they grow even worse in their behavior. Finally, they become unmanageable and stubborn beyond remedy. So you fire them, and they are exited from the company. Now all this time, the other departments—the actors, accountants, stage hands, etc.—did not follow the writers in becoming unmanageable employees. They were not perfect employees, of course, for they had their faults; but your common demeanor toward them remained one of patience and compassion. And even now you commit yourself to their ongoing welfare along the lines of their present *in situ*, because they did not rebel as the writers did, but accepted, and still accept, a certain degree of your management, at least sufficient enough so that you don't have to fire them and force them off the premises. You even hope that these employees will eventually come under your influence of benevolent despotism to a point where one day they regard you as a father figure instead of a boss. Thus, it could be said that while you took great delight in firing the thieving writers who were doggedly opposed to treating you and the rest of your company's employees with any sense of decency, your demeanor toward employees in general is not one of harshness, but of patience. Even so, and as we turn back our thoughts to Lamentations 3:32-33, we see that God did cause the grief that came upon Jeremiah's generation—a grief He took great delight in—but His demeanor toward men in general is one of patient mercy (love). Thus in Lamentations 3:33 the "sons of men" represent the kind of humanity [or nation(s)] that Jeremiah speaks of in Jeremiah chapter 18, a people on the wheel of probation awaiting the decision of the potter to bless or curse it, according to what that nation will come in time to prove about itself. Sometimes God breaks the pot beyond remedy (e.g., Sodom and Gomorrah) because the offense against God is too great (or the potential effects of those cities too dangerous upon other peoples); consequently, their generations will not continue after the present judgment. But oftentimes God just makes another vessel from the same lump, as He did with Israel.

So then, one reason that Piper doesn't come to these conclusions about "willingly" in Lamentations 3:32-33, besides committing the mistake of assuming that "from the heart" might mean "compassionately," is because he has a faulty view of God. As Dave Hunt has pointed out about the Calvinist in general, the Calvinist simply doesn't believe that God loves everybody. God loves Piper and a certain few others, of course, but not everyone. Thus the lexical evidence of what the word "willingly" really means is something Piper has to ignore if he is to find support for both sides of his dialecticism within this one biblical passage from Lamentations 3. And the only way he can accomplish his goal is through special pleading and through so narrow a reading of verses 32 and 33 that the overall context about God's nature is avoided in favor of dialectical conclusions. Thus he sets out both to approve and disprove that God is compassionate, for the nature of affirming both sides of the dialectic is that one must also *deny* both sides of the dialectic. This see-sawing leaves Piper open to our just charge that he assumes a lexical meaning for Heb. *leb* that is not present. But it appears Piper will not be deterred. Thus he claims with Robert Dabney that while certain objections can be raised against the analogy of Washington being reluctant about condemning Andre, nevertheless the analogy is "essentially" true. How this could be the case is truly a mystery, of course, since, besides the arguments we have been presenting here, all humans, presumably Washington and Andre as well, are claimed by Piper elsewhere not to have "ultimate" self-predication. Nor, of course (were Piper **to** grant predication), does Washington in Dabney's illustration ever demonstrate at all a delight, i.e., **uncompassionate** attitude, in condemning Andre. Of what use, then, was this analogy, that Piper introduced it?

And yet while considering this whole matter more closely, I begin to see something else. I had in fact missed how Piper's approach to irrationalism strikingly resembles the method of journalist Pico Iyer in her defense of the Dalai Lama. For even as Iyer attempted to persuade her hearers that the Dalai Lama did in fact recognize the oppression of Tibetans, but then backed away from that statement by claiming that Tibetans didn't have to be unhappy about it (thus denying, I contend, the real emotion of anger any normal person would feel if he truly believed that oppression existed), so too was Piper throwing us a red herring to convince us that he really did sympathize with those of us who can't imagine God being arbitrary in his dealings with men. Piper nearly had us fooled, talking about a reluctant God and pulling on our patriotic heartstrings with a George Washington illustration. But in fact, Piper does not really share the same concern as we non-Calvinists do about God's nature. <u>For the definition of sharing in the same concern is to share in it **consistently**</u>. For example, if Piper were a football player on Team A, he would have to share in the dilemma of winning for Team A during the duration of the game. Otherwise it could not be said that he shared in the same dilemma. But suppose he were a quarterback trying to 'win' a football game by playing on opposite sides for whatever team happened to have the ball at a given moment. In such a case he would always be on the field, playing both for, and against, both sides. This would really mean that he is not sharing in the dilemma of winning for either team; neither can he be a winner or loser. For to be a winner on Team A is to be a loser on Team B, or visa versa. Thus he cannot be called a winner or loser of the game without redefining what the words "winner" and "loser" mean.

We see then, that it is not good enough for Piper to offer his readers an illustration about Washington for the purpose of convincing us that he believes God is 'reluctant,' when in fact the entire thrust of his article denies this very thing. He is toying with us. In fact, I believe he is fooling himself unbeknownst to himself, which is why he speaks of trying to "come to terms with the way a sovereign God wills two different things, affliction and compassion." At any rate, the struggle which Piper mentions here is telling. His *coming to terms* is not a struggle born of trying to show a difference in contexts between Ezekiel 18 and 1 Samuel 2 in order to advocate for a *consistently good* nature of God, but only for a *consistent* nature of God as dialecticism defines it. And that, my readers, is the test of whether a theologian is really struggling with the truth; at least that is the case if a theologian consistently chooses the dialectical 'solution.' Never forget that. In the end, there is really no reason Calvinists like Piper can give us about why some of the *Andres* of this world are condemned and others elected unto safe keeping. For again, if man cannot predicate his own thoughts and intentions, then only God is left holding the bag to explain why He has arbitrarily condemned some but preferentially elected others in a process where only God has the ultimate power of predication. Thus, for Piper; the mirage of meaning continues, as Piper speaks repeatedly of God's two wills, yet places them both under the term "*sovereign* God" instead of "*divided* God" to leave the impression that God is still unified in one purpose and design. Furthermore, Piper insists that books that attempt a *rational* answer about God's nature are [rather, I would think that from his viewpoint, *must be*] mere metaphysical speculations without any Scriptural support. Let him think that, if he chooses. But to deny God His consistently good nature, as Piper does through dialectical spin, is to create 'definitions' about God that are not merely modified, but non-sensical. And so we have a right to say it—A failure to embrace the truth about God's nature—a failure Calvinists demonstrate through a rigorous application of irrationalism—is also a lie of the first magnitude.

This is a serious matter. By insisting on false lexical support and non-sensical definitions for God, Piper and others have, at least in some sense, blasphemed by taking God's name in vain by defining Him as *nothing*—for *nothing* is always the final result when a good God is implied to be the only person of ultimate self-determination in a sinful world.[275] And thus, in order for them to maintain a good God who does evil, they must cancel out all terms of apposition until no definitions remain. When the dust settles there is only 'good' and 'evil,' i.e., words (so-called) which have no meaning. The result is nothing but a mystical understanding (if such can be called *understanding*). One can imagine the chaos in the Church which follows in the wake of such statements. Recently, in fact, a concerned Christian friend of mine told me that his church (which does not carry with it any official designation of Presbyterian or Reformed) is teaching in their young people's group a primary goal of "looking at the beauty of Christ." He says that this is the apparent catch-phrase that has become a [the(?)] main goal of the group's experience. This, I think, is the inevitable result whenever God is stripped of any meaningful content. It aims[276] toward the old medievalist view that God can only be contemplated in His transcendence which defies description. Thus people can speak of the "beauty" of Christ while their theology *de facto* denies any reality to Christ at all. The average congregant isn't going to pick up on what is really happening in such a case, because he has no idea that when these others speak of the "beauty of Christ" they define it along Piperesque lines, which has nothing to do with the beauty of Christ as the Bible defines it. What is actually happening, then, is that young people are being encouraged to worship a man-made notion of God rather than the God of the Bible. The leaders of this young people's group who are pushing this agenda are among certain other Christians within this same church who have apparently become so identified with the study of John Piper's books that they have been referred to as "Piper heads." Whether this nickname is meant to be derisive or quasi-endearing I do not know, but of course the studying of a man's books at the expense of understanding the Bible will often lead to trouble. In this case it has been the misguidance of impressionable youth. And this is the kind of sad result a church can expect when it despises the prophetic gift and/ or gift of knowledge designed to warn it of false teaching. Thus, in a meeting meant to air out the various positions of the youth leaders and some concerned parents and congregants, two women ended up weeping at the end of the meeting because their spiritual intuition was properly telling them that something was desperately wrong with the teaching in the youth group. This whole circumstance is merely one example of what can happen when the wrong doctrine is taught in our churches.

Well, admittedly, we have traveled a long way from Romans 11, but perhaps the digression was an essential one for a fuller examination of Piper's view. Nevertheless, let us return to our previous subject before closing our discussion of it altogether, for a few more observations must still be made about the word *that* (Gr. *hina*). Some theologians, for example, have wondered if the word *that* can occasionally mean *with the result of* rather than *in order that*. In a similar vein the biblical commentator Joseph Thayer discusses the attempts of two theologians (C.F.A. Fritzsche and H.A.W. Meyer) to find in the word *that* the meaning *in which state of things* in 1 Corinthians 4:6 and Galatians 4:17. Apparently, Fritzsche and Meyer took their cue from the use of the Greek *hina* as used
1. as an adverb of Place as found in Homer and subsequent writers, especially in the poets; thus, a. *where, in what place*, b. *to what place, wither*.[277] But Thayer finds the conclusions of Fritzsche and Meyer unconvincing, and takes umbrage at the possibility of an alternate meaning, such as *ekbatikos*, which means, *with the result that*. Thus, Thayer:

> In many passages where [*hina*] has seemed to
> interpreters to be used *ekbatikos*, the sacred writers
> follow the dictate of piety, which bids us trace all them
> to God's purposes...so that, if we are ever in doubt
> whether [*hina*] is used of design or of result, we can

> easily settle the question when we can interpret the passage 'that, by God's decree,' or 'that, according to divine purpose' etc.; passages of this sort are the following:...[Romans] xi. 31 sq....also the phrase [*hina plerothe*], wont to be used in the O.T. prophecies.[278]

Despite Thayer's argument that God is the author of all events and that therefore *hina* should always be understood as supporting the doctrine of God's absolute sovereignty either directly or indirectly in doubtful passages, a few objections can be raised. First, the very nature of the phrase, *with the result of (that)*, if the Greek New Testament meant to convey this ecbatic[279] idea through the use of *hina* in certain passages, could instead, *if one so wished it to be because of one's Calvinistic presuppositions*, always be taken as pointing directly to the absolute sovereignty of God. Regarding what is relevant to our discussion here, this is because the phrase, *with the result of*, obviously cannot exist in a sentence apart from a Subject, Predicate, and the Direct Object[280] of the Subject's action i.e., the three things necessary for the Calvinist to claim that absolute sovereignty is always at work. In short, if *hina can* mean *with the result of*, how do we prove it? Put another way, how does one falsify the claim that *hina* always means *in order that*, since such a conclusion based on that claim can be read into all the appearances of *hina* by eisegetical philandering? Thus, we see the difficulty of the matter. Indeed, the Calvinist can claim a purpose every time *hina* appears, even if the only actor is Nature. Such determinists can be expected to say, "Even the moth sleeps *in order that* it might wake up—and so God is at work." Therefore the Calvinist's argument (abstractly considered) that because the phrase *in order that* may make perfect sense in every appearance of *hina*, is therefore no real argument that it must be so taken. On the other hand, a David Hume-type thinker could argue that *hina* never means *in order that*, but always means *with the result that*, and be just as consistent in his view. But we do not have to appeal to the example of Hume to argue that it is *reasonable* that *hina* may sometimes mean *with the result of*, without meaning *in order that*.[281] Thus the lexical arguments that many would bring forth claiming that *hina* so often means *in order that*, such that we ought not to doubt that it should *always* mean *in order that*, have no real value except for pointing out how a theologically deterministic agenda can drive lexical definitions in certain cases more often than most of us would care to admit. But David Hume is not among us, and, at any rate, there is no need to be so difficult as he. I would argue, however, that if one must take *hina* literally whenever it occurs, then *hina* at certain times *does* mean *with the result of*, that is, if taking *hina* to mean *in order that* would make God absolutely sovereign in decreeing sin or hardening a person unto disobedience.[282] And this conclusion we base on the message of the entire Scripture, including not a few Scriptural proof-texts we have shown in this book to be interpreted falsely by Calvinists. Indeed, it is the general message of the Bible, not a myopic, narrow focus on the immediate verse of Romans 11:31 that demands this conclusion—indeed, that also compels us to understand the *near*-context, so that when God says 1) that He has concluded all unto unbelief that He might have mercy upon all, and 2) that His gifts and calling are without any change of mind, these two thoughts taken together merely mean that God will not 'go soft' on sin because of any natural affection for the Jewish people whose patriarchs were genuine believers. Rather, God will continue declaring that sin is sin, and that sinners are sinners. And He will do this even if it means that He will stop, for a time, the great majority of His effort in trying to turn His chosen people away from their stubborn unbelief, with the result that the gospel will be preached to the Gentiles.

Still, someone may raise the question why Paul did not simply use *and* as a connective conjunction in Romans 11:31 so that there was no confusion. That is, why didn't Paul simply write, "Even so have these also now not believed, *and* through your mercy they also may obtain mercy." To use *and* instead of *that* would make it clear that no real divine purpose was afoot. But the reason such conjunctions were not used appears to be an interesting one—i.e., *such conjunctions could not convey the <u>irony</u> so very evident in the passage*, i.e., that the Jewish people rejected God *that* the gospel might be given to the Gentiles *that* the Jews might become jealous and so return to God. Let me offer an illustration to help show this irony. Suppose my neighbor saw me trashpick from his curb a rather plain-looking, antique candy jar which he did not value, but which he saw me sell at my yard sale the next day for a thousand dollars. Would my neighbor not be jealous of the money I received from something he threw out? Almost certainly he would. And certainly there would be great irony in such a circumstance. Even so have the Jewish people rejected something of immeasurable value (and apart from any so-called divine hardening[283]) which is now presented to the Gentiles. In time, the Jewish people will become (properly) jealous of the relationship God has with the Gentiles, and so turn their hearts again to God. *As irony*, then, Paul could not have restricted himself to conjunctions such as *and, yet,* or *but* to convey the *ironic* sequence of events. Thus, in Romans 11:31 *hina* can act (if we must so take it) in a literal sense of *with the result of*, and at the same time act in an ironic sense *as though* it meant *in order that*.[284]

Having now explained the difficulty of interpretation regarding Romans 11:31 owing to the use of the word *that* (Gr. *hina*), there still remains the question of prophecy, i.e., what Thayer states above as "also the phrase [*hina plerothe*], wont to be used in the O.T. prophecies." In other words, irony may work for Romans 11:31, but what (for example) of John 13:18, where Judas betrays Christ <u>*that* the Scripture might be fulfilled</u>, or John 18:32, where the Jewish leaders want Christ to die by way of crucifixion *that the Scripture might be fulfilled*? But perhaps my readers now see that *hina* in such instances can simply be taken as *with the result that*. By understanding *hina* in this way, we do not preach a God who is divided against Himself such that He would cause Judas to betray Christ *in order that* the Scripture be fulfilled. And yet one more surprise awaits us in the phrase, *that the Scripture might be fulfilled*. It is that irony is present here also! That God in the Old Testament foreknows what the future will be without Himself determining that future, is the irony of events where what God says does come to pass despite the confluence of activity which involves many unsaved people over the course of centuries—indeed, people who have no intention whatsoever of demonstrating publicly God's non-determinative foreknowledge of events in which they have freely exercised their wills! Thus, when Psalm 22 speaks of a crucifixion, a mode of death the Romans, not God, invented (centuries after Psalm 22 was written), it was foreknown by God and therefore anticipated by Him in a foreshadowing of a crucified Christ by the symbol of Moses lifting up the serpent in the wilderness (Num. 21:8). Certainly, the inventors of crucifixion and the Jewish leaders who sought to have Christ lifted up on the cross had no desire to fulfill the foreshadowed example of Numbers 21 or the Messianic prophecy of Psalm 22. Yet that is exactly what happened. And yet this is not to say that God Himself never acts to fulfill His own prophecy in a way that does no violence to the free will of His creatures. For He sent His Son Jesus, the Messiah, to die according to the time predicted in Daniel's prophecy, that is, after the 69th week[285] from the time of the commandment to rebuild Jerusalem. But again, God did not *determine* that the practice of crucifixion be extant in Palestine in the first century AD, so that the foreshadowing-type of Christ in Numbers 21 (the bronze serprent on the pole) and the prophecy of Psalm 22 (and Isaiah 53) would be fulfilled. But he did foreknow crucifixion would be extant, and He recognized the irony in such fulfillments of Scripture, that is, inasmuch as unbelievers acted *as though* they were trying to fulfill them.[286]

Having critiqued Piper's positions on the above points, we now come to the last of his arguments we will consider in this Supplement. It is that God "wills" that the ten nations in Revelation 17 give their united kingdom to the beast. Says Piper:

> Waging war against the Lamb is sin and sin is contrary to the will of God. Nevertheless the angel says (literally), "God gave into their [the ten kings'] hearts *to do his will*, and to perform one will, and to give their kingdom to the beast, until the words of God shall be fulfilled" (v. 17). Therefore God willed (in one sense)

> to influence the hearts of the ten kings so that they
> would do what is against his will (in another sense).

Those readers who have persevered through the many arguments of my book will probably recognize that when Piper uses the terms, "in one sense" and "in another sense," he is merely trying to give the appearance of a difference in *sense* regarding God's will without demonstrating, in fact, that he regards these terms as *anything except synonymous* of a single divine will. That is, Piper has been trying all along to state that God has *two* wills (which from his descriptions can only be described as mutually exclusive of each other) while claiming that God is *non-contradictory*, i.e., as implied in the necessity of God having an undivided purpose (singular). Apologist Ravi Zacharias has characterized this kind of phenomenon after observing this kind of problem in another vein, i.e., such men use the law of non-contradiction *to hammer* the law of non-contradiction. Thus Piper claims to be giving the literal translation of Revelation 17:17 when, in fact, "to do his will" actually means "to do his judgment." (Such an idea is nothing new to those who remember what God did with Pharaoh in the Exodus narrative.) Here in Revelation 17:17 the word *will* is Strong's word #1106:
1) the faculty of knowledge, mind, reason

> 2) that which is thought or known, one's mind
>
> 2a) view, judgment, opinion
>
> 2b) mind concerning what ought to be done
>
> 2b1) by one's self: resolve purpose, intention
>
> 2b2) by others: judgment, advice
>
> 2b3) decree

Strong's word #1106 (Gr. *gnome*) is rendered in translation as *judgment* more often than it is rendered as any other particular word, and is used only rarely in the New Testament. Taking together the above definitions gives us a sense of what the Greek word *gnome* means in Revelation 17:17 *if* the general message of the entire Bible is already properly understood regarding God's character. It is simply saying that God has decided to *allow* sin to run its course. That is His judgment. That is His decree. Again, such a judgment is the same type of decision that God made regarding Pharaoh after the latter's display of continued rebellion. The idea that Revelation 17:17 is somehow teaching that *God's* purpose is fulfilled by the continuance of sin, and not *man's* purpose, is the inevitable conclusion for the theologian who claims that God has two opposing wills that are not ultimately opposed to each other.[287]

In conclusion, it is a shame that in this troubled and unspiritual age in which we live—indeed, in which so many men are perishing because of their unbelief—that so much Christian effort must be directed against the false teachings of *professing Christians themselves*, when the Church is suppose to be battling the world. But, in fact, it is the *world* in the Christian, so to speak, that the Church is also fighting. Some might think our efforts in this regard are disproportional to the problem, but with such a notion we must strenuously disagree. The troubling status of the world and the weakened state in which the Church finds itself are sufficient to argue that *not enough* attention has been given to the problem of false teaching within the Church. Indeed, may we ever keep before us the Scripture which says that judgment must begin at the house of God. And may we also remember those in the early church whom Paul said desired to teach, but nevertheless disastrously affected their hearers because of their jangling (i.e., uttering of empty, senseless things). In such cases of false teaching—as Paul observed in his time, and now we in ours—the old proverb seems to hold true: "The more things change, the more they stay the same." But none of this should shake the Christian's faith, though a great many Evangelicals are heaping to themselves false teachers to tickle their ears. Such a phenomenon is simply a fulfillment of what Paul said would happen in the last days. And in light of what Paul knew of coming events, he admonished Timothy centuries ago to preserve true doctrine, and to live out the principles of faith. So, shouldn't we today, while it *is* the day, heed the same admonition?

> 5 Now the end of the commandment is charity out of a pure heart, and of a good conscience, and of faith unfeigned: 6 From which some having swerved have turned aside unto vain jangling; 7 Desiring to be teachers of the law; understanding neither what they say, nor whereof they affirm.[288]

Footnotes:

[259] At about the time of the first trade edition of this book, ca. Autumn, 2006.

[260] This article is actually a chapter from *Still Sovereign: Contemporary Perspectives on Election, Foreknowledge, and Grace*. Thomas Schreiner/Bruce Ware, editors (Grand Rapids: Baker Books, 2000

[261] —that is, I respond because Piper is so very influential these days, and because certain of his points in "Two Wills" are very cleverly constructed.

[262] found at www.desiringgod.org

[263] i.e., as seen in John 13:13-19: [13] Ye call me Master and Lord: and ye say well; for so I am. [14] If I then, your Lord and Master, have washed your feet; ye also ought to wash one another's feet. [15] For I have given you an example, that ye should do

as I have done to you. ¹⁶ Verily, verily, I say unto you, The servant is not greater than his lord; neither he that is sent greater than he that sent him. ¹⁷ If ye know these things, happy are ye if ye do them. ¹⁸ I speak not of you all: I know whom I have chosen: but that the scripture may be fulfilled, He that eateth bread with me hath lifted up his heel against me. ¹⁹ Now I tell you before it come, that, when it is come to pass, ye may believe that I am he.

[264] See Jamieson, Faussett, and Brown's commentary regarding 1 Samuel 2:25 at [http://eword.gospelcom.net/comments/1samuel/jfb/1samuel2.htm].

[265] that is, the average Israelite of Ezekiel's exile had not *set* nor exercised his will to a point of rebellion where repentance was all but impossible.

[266] —and not because there were *more* people sinning, as in fact there were only about 25 in the fourth group compared to 70 in the second.

[267] from a practical, not theoretical standpoint. We know from John 6:44 that a man *will* not come [i.e., *powers* not to come] unless God draws him. One might ask what the difference would be between the two phrases, 'no man powers to come' and 'no man comes' if the word 'powers' essentially means 'chooses,' such that there might seem to be no difference between the phrases 'no man chooses to come' and 'no man comes.' But what I'm contending here is that the Greek word *dunamai* shows us that "chooses to" (KJV 'can,' or more properly, "powers to") points to the willful, and therefore causative, nature of man, in contexts involving intention.

[268] Even in the New Testament Paul urges that not many be teachers, as God shall hold them to a stricter accountability (presumably because of their greater influence).

[269] See endnote lxxviii, for a reading of Deuteronomy 28:15-68.

[270] [http://scripturetext.com/romans/11-31.htm].

[271] emphasis mine on "or the result."

[272] See chapter 4 for a fuller explanation of Hegel's irrationality and his advocacy for relativism.

[273] Compare this similarity of circumstance with our discussion of Pharaoh in chapter 14.

[274] And yet one can almost hear how Piper himself would presumably reply to our argument here—"But I said that the "from the heart" was *different*, not *opposite* from how God exerts compassion on his chosen!" Such obfuscation of definition, then, would be our contention with Piper. For while Piper would surely retain the appearance of the rational side of definitions so that different must mean *opposite* if there are truly to be *two* wills of God wherein God can be claimed as 1) holding out His hands in invitation to Israel; and 2) hardening their hearts so that they do not come, Piper must nevertheless and all the while maintain that "different" is **not** opposite in a mutually exclusive sense, that is, in order to uphold his statement that God's character is *non-contradictory*, i.e., as when, in the context of attempting to explain his notion that God can take

delight in the death of Eli's sons while not taking delight in the death of the wicked [house of Israel of Ezekiel's time] he says, "What [God] says is strikingly different (not contradictory, I will argue)." Again, Piper, in his explanation of God delighting while not delighting in the death of the wicked, does not make final appeal to the law of non-contradiction, i.e., the law of logic which is the basis of the apologetic I have offered in this Supplement. Rather, Piper appeals to the irrationality that says that "different" **is not** defined as "opposite" while yet it *must be* defined as "opposite." For with Piper every term referring to the nature of God's will must be maintained in irrationality—as itself and its other—if God is to invite and harden at the same time the same object.

Calvinists usually trick the reader into accepting this irrationality by using synonyms that are defined as opposites (as we saw earlier, when Calvinists state that man's will is "free" but has no "liberty") or by using, as Piper more cleverly does (wittingly or not), words that can act as synonyms, but do not always have to (that is, in truly logical contexts). Thus, Piper uses the terms "different" and "not contradictory" as we saw a moment ago. It would not clarify anything, then, if a Calvinist were to object to our argument here by saying that *difference* is possible without having to be opposite, i.e., as in one woman being dressed differently than another woman while not being her opposite, i.e., a man. For such an objection would miss the point entirely, since Piper's definition requires irrationality such that the *rational* observation (God holding out His hands in earnest invitation) must also be <u>*at the same time*</u> synthesized with an *irrational* difference (God hardening their hearts so that they cannot respond to His invitation) <u>*upon the same object*</u>. Thus, again, according to Piper, God is of such character that He can only be understood, for example, as endorsing the two concepts of divine invitation and divine hardening upon the same object at the same time (i.e., a God **not** defined in mutually exclusive terms). It appears that any final appeal to logical argument has been lost on Piper for some time, now, though Piper will still use the law of non-contradiction *selectively* to hammer the law of non-contradiction. Nevertheless, he denies the consistent and unfailing usefulness of the law of non-contradiction in establishing the character of God and His will. Therefore Piper states early in his article, in response to the Arminian accusation that Calvinist assumptions involving irrationality are contradictory, "But in spite of these criticisms the distinction stands, not because of a logical or theological deduction, but because it is inescapable in the Scriptures."

[275] Please do not misunderstand the matter: when I say that Piper and other followers of Calvin are blasphem*ing*. I am not saying that Piper is necessarily a blasphem*er*. (I cannot know all his statements or any of his inward thoughts to see if he modifies his statements at all), but merely blasphem*ing*, even as I myself was blasphem*ing* for many years when I too professed to believe in the doctrine of divine absolute sovereignty. To call a man a blasphem*er* is to make an ultimate judgment upon the totality of his beliefs and confessions and to find him wanting, which is why we should be careful about making such judgments in difficult-to-discern cases. Only God can judge all the beliefs and confessions of a man, and know what a man truly believes. Thus, while we might say that a Christian acts foolishly by double-mindedly believing thus and so, we should be

careful about calling any Christian (I mean here, a professing Christian) a fool. Yet I would be less than stating the facts if I assigned to such theology as Piper's (as represented in his article "Are There Two Wills of God") anything short of blasphemy. At any rate, to be consistent with his own theology, Piper would have to conversely assign blasphemy to *my* statements in this Supplement, since from his perspective it is *I* who hold notions about *nothing* which I claim represent the nature of God. On the other hand (need I say it?), since Piper claims that man is not self-determinative, I suppose he cannot *ultimately* (to use his word) assign any causation of statements to myself.

[276] (unwittingly, no doubt)

[277] [http://www.blueletterbible.org/tmp_dir/words/2/1161343368-6447.html].

[278] http://www.blueletterbible.org/tmp_dir/words/2/1161343368-6447.html].

[279] "Denoting a mere result or consequence, as distinguished from telic, which denotes intention or purpose; thus the phrase "i'na plhrw'qh," if rendered "so that [with the result that] it was fulfilled," is ecbatic; but if rendered "in order that it might be," etc., is telic." See source: [http://www.thefreedictionary.com/Ecbatic].

[280] or, the recipient Object of the Subject's action may also be the Subject itself (i.e. reflexive).

[281] After all, we are not appealing to any principle of irrationality (though it, too, would be an equally consistent view) that would advocate the kind of purple-turtle-in-the-sky theology mentioned in chapter 2, i.e., if one were to argue, for example, that every appearance of *hina* follows, say, the scientific theory of tachyons as applied to the history of literature and interpreted through deconstruction theory, so that it would argue for backward causation. If that were the case, then when the Scripture says that the Jews rejected the gospel *that* it might be preached to the Gentiles, the real meaning of *hina* would be that the gospel was preached to Gentiles *that* it might be rejected by the Jews! Such a position would be consistent but also nonsense. Rather (and when taking *hina* in a literal sense and properly understood), while the phrase *with the result of* does not always mean *in order that*, the phrase *in order that* always includes the meaning of *with the result that*, therefore showing in this last instance the nature of difference in these phrases and therefore how easily one could *claim* that every appearances of *hina* should mean *in order that*. Thus the idea that *hina* may *sometimes* mean *with the result of/ (that)* without also meaning *in order that* is a rational possibility, that is, if one grants our argument about lexical use. Conversely, the phrase *in order that* cannot ever mean *not in order that*, since deconstruction theory is irrational and antithetical to Scripture.

[282] that is, *hardening* as Piper would define it, and not as I define it in chapter 14 of my book.

[283] that is, 'hardening' as Piper would define it.

[284] i.e., idiomatically.

[285] (biblically understood as 62 x 7 years, which is 434 years)

[286] It should also be pointed out that the phrase "that the Scripture might be fulfilled" is in the aorist passive *subjunctive*, stressing the *contingent* nature of the prophecy being fulfilled. If for no other reason, this would seem to be the case because God Himself, technically, *may* cause events or refrain from acts which would frustrate the fulfillment of prophecy. He does not do any such thing, of course, because God always chooses to maintain His eternal, historical ideals to which He acts accordingly. Nevertheless, Piper takes the subjunctive mood and subjects it, not to Possibility, but to God acting alone and irresistibly.

[287] Thus to offer another example of this kind of irrationality, Piper, would presumably have no hesitancy about stating that God had two wills for Pharaoh even as He had two wills for the Jews, inviting him to be obedient while hardening him, so that he cannot obey. Is that kind of irrationality (we ask) a problem for the post-modern, deconstructing-of-apologetics Calvinist? Piper's statement speaks for itself. In a short bulleted article called "How to Teach and Preach "Calvinism," " he states: "Be rigorously textual in all your expositions and explanations and defenses of Calvinistic teachings. Make it a textual issue every time, not a logic issue or an experience issue." The problem of course, is that Piper's 'textural issues' are all cases of special pleading argued apart from the evidence of lexical control groups. In short, textural issues involving 'definitions' of words that are without definition are meaningless. Yet so adamant is Piper about accepting this alternate form of textual 'rightness' that he wrote against J. I Packer's advocacy of mysticism some thirty years ago, all but describing it in terms of theological cowardice.

In passing, one should observe a very disturbing implication of Piper's methodological principle. It is his advocacy of two wills that (we note) allegedly occur in Scripture hundreds of years apart. Indeed, I believe Piper's methodological principle makes it possible for his followers to argue for an open canon of Scripture, which could include the Koran, as well as the works-based soteriology of Catholicism, etc., *ad nauseam*, (even including various historical religious beliefs of certain pagan peoples). For since a span of 900 years separates Moses' Deuteronomy from Ezekiel's writings (and 400 years Samuel from Ezekiel), *and since the principle of irrationality does not bother Piper*, any statement in the New Testament book of Revelation that could be taken to mean that the canon of Scripture is closed, and that therefore one ought not to add to the words of this book (understood in its near context as referring to the book of Revelation and in its far context as the entire Bible), *can also*, if one follows the methodological principle of Piper, argue that, e.g., the Koran is part of the ongoing revelation of God. For why should any who follow Piper be bothered with the idea of an ongoing divine revelation that *logically* refutes itself hundreds of years later, since to Piper and his followers such refutation might only appear to be refutation because of the limits of fallen, human reasoning? Christ may thus be taken to be the exclusive Savior of the world and only begotten Son of God, yet also just a man who was not God at all (i.e., merely a human prophet of some importance). For why could we not say that the Koran is a different, yet not contradictory, divinely given text awaiting its own Calvinistic imprimatur, based not on logic but on 'textual issues'? Indeed, no more essential span of time separates John and his book of Revelation from Mohammed and the Koran than does separate Moses from the writer of 1 Samuel and Ezekiel, and thus no charge of heresy about the nature of Jesus can be sustained, as long as one consistently applies Piper's principle of irrationality. In effect, we on the East Coast of the United States are told by Piper, "Go West, young man!" only to observe that Piper stops at Chicago (so to speak) while his followers are free to travel the full road of irrationality all the way into the Pacific Ocean, should they wish to do so. O Pshaw, that we thought Ecunemicalism a bad thing!

[288] 1 Timothy 1:5-7

Endnotes:

lxxviii

Deuteronomy 28:15-68:

[15]But it shall come to pass, if thou wilt not hearken unto the voice of the LORD thy God, to observe to do all his commandments and his statutes which I command thee this day; that all these curses shall come upon thee, and overtake thee: [16]Cursed shalt thou be in the city, and cursed shalt thou be in the field. [17]Cursed shall be thy basket and thy store. [18]Cursed shall be the fruit of thy body, and the fruit of thy land, the increase of thy kine, and the flocks of thy sheep. [19]Cursed shalt thou be when thou comest in, and cursed shalt thou be when thou goest out. [20]The LORD shall send upon thee cursing, vexation, and rebuke, in all that thou settest thine hand unto for to do, until thou be destroyed, and until thou perish quickly; because of the wickedness of thy doings, whereby thou hast forsaken me. [21]The LORD shall make the pestilence cleave unto thee, until he have consumed thee from off the land, whither thou goest to possess it. [22]The LORD shall smite thee with a consumption, and with a fever, and with an inflammation, and with an extreme burning, and with the sword, and with blasting, and with mildew; and they shall pursue thee until thou perish. [23]And thy heaven that is over thy head shall be brass, and the earth that is under thee shall be iron. [24]The LORD shall make the rain of thy land powder and dust: from heaven shall it come down upon thee, until thou be destroyed. [25]The LORD shall cause thee to be smitten before thine enemies: thou shalt go out one way against them, and flee seven ways before them: and shalt be removed into all the kingdoms of the earth. [26]And thy carcase shall be meat unto all fowls of the air, and unto the beasts of the earth, and no man shall fray them away. [27]The LORD will smite thee with the botch of Egypt, and with the emerods, and with the scab, and with the itch, whereof thou canst not be healed. [28]The LORD shall smite thee with madness, and blindness, and astonishment of heart: [29]And thou shalt grope at noonday, as the blind gropeth in darkness, and thou shalt not prosper in thy ways: and thou shalt be only oppressed and spoiled evermore, and no man shall save thee. [30]Thou shalt betroth a wife, and another man shall lie with her: thou shalt build an house, and thou shalt not dwell therein: thou shalt plant a vineyard, and shalt not gather the grapes thereof. [31]Thine ox shall be slain before thine eyes, and thou shalt not eat thereof: thine ass shall be violently taken away from before thy face, and shall not be restored to thee: thy sheep shall be given

unto thine enemies, and thou shalt have none to rescue them. ³²Thy sons and thy daughters shall be given unto another people, and thine eyes shall look, and fail with longing for them all the day long: and there shall be no might in thine hand. ³³The fruit of thy land, and all thy labours, shall a nation which thou knowest not eat up; and thou shalt be only oppressed and crushed alway: ³⁴So that thou shalt be mad for the sight of thine eyes which thou shalt see. ³⁵The LORD shall smite thee in the knees, and in the legs, with a sore botch that cannot be healed, from the sole of thy foot unto the top of thy head. ³⁶The LORD shall bring thee, and thy king which thou shalt set over thee, unto a nation which neither thou nor thy fathers have known; and there shalt thou serve other gods, wood and stone. ³⁷And thou shalt become an astonishment, a proverb, and a byword, among all nations whither the LORD shall lead thee . ³⁸Thou shalt carry much seed out into the field, and shalt gather but little in; for the locust shall consume it. ³⁹Thou shalt plant vineyards, and dress them, but shalt neither drink of the wine, nor gather the grapes; for the worms shall eat them. ⁴⁰Thou shalt have olive trees throughout all thy coasts, but thou shalt not anoint thyself with the oil; for thine olive shall cast his fruit. ⁴¹Thou shalt beget sons and daughters, but thou shalt not enjoy them; for they shall go into captivity. ⁴²All thy trees and fruit of thy land shall the locust consume. ⁴³The stranger that is within thee shall get up above thee very high; and thou shalt come down very low. ⁴⁴He shall lend to thee, and thou shalt not lend to him: he shall be the head, and thou shalt be the tail.

⁴⁵Moreover all these curses shall come upon thee, and shall pursue thee, and overtake thee, till thou be destroyed; because thou hearkenedst not unto the voice of the LORD thy God, to keep his commandments and his statutes which he commanded thee: ⁴⁶And they shall be upon thee for a sign and for a wonder, and upon thy seed for ever. ⁴⁷Because thou servedst not the LORD thy God with joyfulness, and with gladness of heart, for the abundance of all things; ⁴⁸Therefore shalt thou serve thine enemies which the LORD shall send against thee, in hunger, and in thirst, and in nakedness, and in want of all things: and he shall put a yoke of iron upon thy neck, until he have destroyed thee. ⁴⁹The LORD shall bring a nation against thee from far, from the end of the earth, as swift as the eagle flieth; a nation whose tongue thou shalt not understand; ⁵⁰A nation of fierce countenance, which shall not regard the person of the old, nor shew favour to the young: ⁵¹And he shall eat the fruit of thy cattle, and the fruit of thy land, until thou be destroyed: which also shall not leave thee either corn, wine, or oil, or the increase of thy kine, or flocks of thy sheep, until he have destroyed thee. ⁵²And he shall besiege thee in all thy gates, until thy high and fenced walls come down, wherein thou trustedst, throughout all thy land: and he shall besiege thee in all thy gates throughout all thy land, which the LORD thy God hath given thee. ⁵³And thou shalt eat the fruit of thine own body, the flesh of thy sons and of thy daughters, which the LORD thy God hath given thee, in the siege, and in the straitness, wherewith thine enemies shall distress thee: ⁵⁴So that the man that is tender among you, and very delicate, his eye shall be evil toward his brother, and toward the wife of his bosom, and toward the remnant of his children which he shall leave: ⁵⁵So that he will not give to any of them of the flesh of his children whom he shall eat: because he hath nothing left him in

the siege, and in the straitness, wherewith thine enemies shall distress thee in all thy gates. [56]The tender and delicate woman among you, which would not adventure to set the sole of her foot upon the ground for delicateness and tenderness, her eye shall be evil toward the husband of her bosom, and toward her son, and toward her daughter, [57]And toward her young one that cometh out from between her feet, and toward her children which she shall bear: for she shall eat them for want of all things secretly in the siege and straitness, wherewith thine enemy shall distress thee in thy gates. [58]If thou wilt not observe to do all the words of this law that are written in this book, that thou mayest fear this glorious and fearful name, THE LORD THY GOD; [59]Then the LORD will make thy plagues wonderful, and the plagues of thy seed, even great plagues, and of long continuance, and sore sicknesses, and of long continuance. [60]Moreover he will bring upon thee all the diseases of Egypt, which thou wast afraid of; and they shall cleave unto thee. [61]Also every sickness, and every plague, which is not written in the book of this law, them will the LORD bring upon thee, until thou be destroyed. [62]And ye shall be left few in number, whereas ye were as the stars of heaven for multitude; because thou wouldest not obey the voice of the LORD thy God. [63]And it shall come to pass, that as the LORD rejoiced over you to do you good, and to multiply you; so the LORD will rejoice over you to destroy you, and to bring you to nought; and ye shall be plucked from off the land whither thou goest to possess it. [64]And the LORD shall scatter thee among all people, from the one end of the earth even unto the other; and there thou shalt serve other gods, which neither thou nor thy fathers have known, even wood and stone. [65]And among these nations shalt thou find no ease, neither shall the sole of thy foot have rest: but the LORD shall give thee there a trembling heart, and failing of eyes, and sorrow of mind: [66]And thy life shall hang in doubt before thee; and thou shalt fear day and night, and shalt have none assurance of thy life: [67]In the morning thou shalt say, Would God it were even! and at even thou shalt say, Would God it were morning! for the fear of thine heart wherewith thou shalt fear, and for the sight of thine eyes which thou shalt see. [68]And the LORD shall bring thee into Egypt again with ships, by the way whereof I spake unto thee, Thou shalt see it no more again: and there ye shall be sold unto your enemies for bondmen and bondwomen, and no man shall buy you.

(Letter excerpt to Christian Apologist, Ravi Zacharias)

March 29, 2009

*Dear Dr. Zacharias,

    Some time ago, I saw a youtube interview of you with D. James Kennedy, in which you stated that the most frequently asked question among university students was how God could be good if there was evil in the world. You gave an example of one such Harvard student who asked this question. And I agree with your answer—that the student was trying to *dis*prove, not prove, God, yet could only pose the question hypocritically, since he had to assume moral law, a moral law Giver, etc., all at the expense of his own system. However, I hope you will consider one other thought, for it ultimately bears on the Christian apologist's general approach to the skeptic.
    I believe it is possible, based on the decision that Christ faced at Gethsemane, that among the eternal, Divine Persons—The Father, the Son, the Holy Spirit—there *could* have existed (if history had proven differently) a both/and **moral** system, not one of either/or. [I use the phrase "among the eternal, Divine Persons," rather than "with God," because in the hypothetical case of moral division the Trinity would no longer be a **unity** in the *moral* sense [as normally granted and understood in the singular, corporate term "God." Nevertheless, I hereafter use the term "God" with the assumption (argument following) that He has the possibility of becoming morally divided.] The point is an important one and goes directly to the question of whether in theory God can/could be divided against Himself *morally*. Arguably, *at some level* this may have been the sub-conscious question the student was asking you. For even Presbyterian pastor and radio minister, James Boice, facing terminal cancer some years ago, asked the same essential question when he told his congregation that while he certainly believed God was *sovereign* in his circumstances, he saw that one might nevertheless be tempted to question whether God was a *good* God.
    Essentially, I think that Christ also mulled over this same question in Gethsemane. That is, facing the baptism of His death, Jesus, in effect, asked Himself whether He would obey the Father so that the oneness of God would remain good. Indeed, this accounts for something of Jesus' struggle in Gethsemane. And ultimately, it appears He took courage in knowing that the Father would remain true to His own self-sacrificial nature. "Could [the Son] not," Jesus asked Peter rhetorically, "immediately be granted 12 legions of rescuing angels from His Father if He so asked Him?" I

especially note here that Jesus had this confidence of the Father even at the expense of Scripture being fulfilled. That is, the Father would grant the request of Christ's will even to such a point, not because the Father Himself desired it, but because the Father allowed the free will of the Son to such a point of *effect*.

Now the point here about free will goes directly to the word 'can' in the New Testament. For a close study of the word 'can' in Greek (i.e., *dunamai*), finds that the verb (contrary to standard lexical assumption) can mean *to will*, and thus in contexts of the Will, means *to power the will*, i.e., *to choose*. For how else can we explain Christ's other statement earlier in John's gospel, when He says that He *can* (Gr. *dunamai*) do nothing of Himself, except that which He sees the Father do (Jn. 5:19)? For, as stated, this would seem to contradict Christ's statement in Gethsemane, when Christ implied that He *could* avoid death and thus do something which His Father did not show Him nor which the Spirit prophesied of Him*

The answer, then, to what at first appears to be a contradiction between these two statements of Christ, is that Christ's will was congruent with His Father's will *at the time* Christ made the earlier statement, but *undecided* about His Father's will at the *beginning* of his trial in Gethsemane, hence the Son's prayer to the Father in the Garden, "Not my *desire* [Gr. *thelo*, defined in this particular appearance to be *bare desire* (apart from intention), as proven by the context], but thine be done." (A careful observation of the lexical spectrum of *thelo* in the N.T. shows that the closest *quid pro quo* word in English is the verb *want* as used ***in***formally in English, which, depending on the context, either implies the presence OR the absence of intention.) In brief, *desire* and *will* are not the same things, despite what e.g., Reformed theologians claim, who use these terms synonymously, if slightly distinguished *sequentially* in regards to their *ordo salutis* (and thus irrationally). "*Irrationally*," I say, because they do this by defining "regeneration" as *desire changed* **prior** to "rushing to Christ" instead of defining "regeneration" to be that *instant* of conversion—i.e., in which God bequeaths His Spirit to the one believing in Christ *in* the first indivisible instant of that belief. (which, pertaining to the future, the true believer *wills* to endure unto the ages). In other words, by extension, I am saying that the only basis upon which the Scripture can say that God *cannot* lie is at it relates to *when* the will of the Persons of the Godhead are the same. In short, God's '*cannot*' (*lie*) is not a question of sheer ability. To put the matter negatively and in human terms, how *can* a husband be a good husband if he *will* not to be a good husband? Or stated positively and in divine terms, how *can* God be an evil God if He *will* not be an evil God? In Gethsemane Christ thus shows that the whole matter of goodness ultimately lies in the sphere of the will alone (not desire). That is, He denied His greatest desire and *chose* to act in accordance with the Father's desire. And this fact—of the sphere of the will alone being that which determines obedience or disobedience to the known, divine, moral law—brings us to the further question about how God *could* have been good in eternity past if He did not have the possibility of choosing evil. And the answer (far from the Reformed view that evil is merely privative in nature as having no ontological being), is that each Person within the Godhead has, in fact, always had that choice, but has never chosen to act selfishly in regards to the other Two Persons of the Godhead; nor has God changed His ideal that this self*less*ness within the Three Persons of the Godhead is good. Thus in this sense, God *cannot* lie, and He does not change. This is the proper understanding of the Trinity—that while the Divine Persons do not always **enter** conference with the same desires, they **leave** with the same decision. And thus we properly refer to the Divine Persons under the singular term "God," and rightly call Him so.

This fact of God's eternal love and constancy gives me a newer appreciation for the question about evil asked of you at these universities. As students look at the evil world which so many (Reformed-leaning) Christian theologians nevertheless would tell them is God's foreordained plan for HIS purposes (one thinks of Baudelaire's statement, 'If there is a God, He is the Devil'), they are, in effect, being told that God is the kind of God that God would have been *had Christ NOT gone to the cross*. That is, if Christ had been selfish and chosen NOT to die, then the Godhead would have been a morally indeterminate Being. And therefore in this world one would expect good ***and*** evil (as God has eternally defined these terms for Himself, and to which principles He properly subjects man to judgment) to be God-approved. If the contingent history of what Christ could have chosen had actually happened, God, of course, would have remained One in terms of His shared, eternal past and Creator-hood as Persons. That much, at least, could not change. But He would have ceased to exist as One being *morally*. In other words, if Christ had disobeyed the Father out of selfishness (and again, let us remember that the Bible demonstrates that such a choice by Christ of such a contingent history was indeed possible) God would have become a selfish/unselfish, i.e., a morally both/and God. And in such a case the definition of 'moral law' for God would be **both/and**, since the Persons of the Godhead would be morally divided. Put another way, *moral law* would cease to have any meaning as we *now* (rightfully) understand and know this moral law to mean and to *de facto* exist for God and for those of us who follow Him. But for any person outside God, he has become his own Lawgiver, as James says (though such persons are subject to God's punishment because of it), and so I think we must be careful by using the term, "Absolutes," since they are only universal in regards to divine judgment, not to all persons' convictions.

Now, understandably, a God who is claimed by so many <u>Christian</u> theologians to have ordained **all** events, including all the animus of human experience, confuses university students. As a man of letters, you will doubtless recall that this theological antinomy was a chief complaint of Deists in the 18th century, and remains so today of later skeptics. Possibly, some of these men from the Enlightenment might have even become defenders of the Christian faith, had not Calvinism, which they thought synonymous with (non-Catholic) biblical faith, impressed them as strikingly irrational. **Instead, such skeptics** [as *Benjamin Franklin*—in referring to Boyle's lectures; *Thomas Paine*—in railing against the Calvinistic interpretation of Romans 9:18-21 (an interpretation he assumed was congruent with Pauline thought); *Voltaire*—in decrying against Leibniz's Optimism, an ideology, in fact, identical to the 'greater good theodicy' of today's Reformed theology; and *Freud*—concluding his 2nd chapter in *Civilization and Its Discontents*, in which he states that the believer's appeal to God's 'inscrutable decrees' for the purpose of explaining evil is a detour the believer should avoid in the first place, since it is merely an appeal for an unconditional submission] **all felt legitimate in walking away from the Bible.** They did so because they believed, at least in part, even as in fact R.C. Sproul (in his own way) expressed the matter at the beginning of his book, *Chosen By God*, <u>that there is NOT a satisfying answer to the problem of evil intelligible to the human mind</u>. But, of course, there ***is*** an answer, for Christ stated in the gospel of Matthew that sins arise from man's heart, i.e., from man *ex nihilo* (by which I mean *without prior cause*). At any rate, the predominance of unbelievers linking Calvinistic principles *synonymously* with Christian doctrine has always confused students, both young and old. And this linking seems evident whenever students ask you that first question at major universities.

Even 30-odd years ago, this very assumption—that Christianity was synonymous with Calvinism—was brought home personally to me with special force, when an SAT question asked me to identify the 'paradox' of Christianity. I refused to answer the multiple-choice question, since clearly the expected answer was *'the [absolute] sovereignty of God and the free will of man.'* I realized then, as I do now (though sadly, not for an interim of years subsequent to attending a Reformed College), that the paradox is actually a *contradiction of Calvinism*, not *a paradox of Christianity* (as though the Christian faith were dialectical and therefore at odds with itself). And so I hold firmly to what you have implied often about the both/and system not being *reality* [though I might add that it is *God's* reality and the reality of those who follow him (but **not** the reality, sadly, for those who have become their own Lawgivers and disbelieve God)]. Further, I am encouraged to continue my hope in God, for if ever there was a historical moment when God could have turned away from remaining morally One, it was when Christ was wrestling in Gethsemane; and since Christ was Victor there (in the most trying of circumstances), I may rest assured, as a Christian believer, that He shall remain faithful to me in the future.

The tragedy, then, is that many past skeptics did not have this same hope because of what so many Christian theologians <u>themselves</u> have often taught about God. Even in our own generation certain influential, Christian apologists (e.g., John Piper) have turned aside to the fable that God exists in 'self-centeredness'—a term he defines in such a way so that each Person within the Godhead does **_not_** have a self-sacrificial role in relation to the other Two Persons of the Godhead. Consequently, his false claim that God is *selfish* (again, generally expressed by Piper under the more winsome and diplomatic term, 'self-centeredness') continues to inform his apologetic while also sharpening the foil of the skeptic's question: 'Is God good, evil, or both?' I do not know your exact position on this general matter of 'paradox,' and perhaps I am not even entitled to know; but I hope the histories of Franklin, Paine, *et al.* will be kept in all our minds in all our exchanges with skeptics who ask legitimate questions about evil. I have been a long-time admirer of you, and hope you share this feeling toward Christian apologetics. Perhaps what I am also expressing here is my real dismay, as I gallop toward the advancing age of 50, to find that only *now* have I truly become sympathetic to that first question of the skeptic. May we all, then, as Christian apologists, continue to see the *legitimacy* of questions about evil. And may we also feel ashamed of what excuses Christian theologians have betimes offered, instead of giving the earnest skeptic a full and truthful answer. More than any other public figure in Christian apologetics, it seems to me you have given the proper answer faithfully, and I thank you for that.

Sincerely in our Savior, Jesus,

Daniel Gracely

cc: excerpt to www.xCalvinist.com

* (Jn. 5:19 in Gr.) "The Son powers [Himself] to do nothing of Himself unless what He may see the Father doing." Moreover, though R.C. Sproul believes that "can" ought not to be confused with "may" (Sproul: "Who has not been corrected by a schoolteacher for confusing the words *can* and *may*?"), such insistence on the **formal** English distinction between "can" and "may" (versus the **in**formal English use of "can," which (to wit) *can* include "may,") is not observed in the Greek verb *dunamai*. For example, when the Athenians asked Paul to share his thoughts, they said, "May (*dunamai*) we know…?" Substituting the word "can" for *dunamai* makes no sense here. Or are we to suppose that Sproul thinks the Athenians were asking Paul if they "can" know, i.e., have the mental capacity to understand an argument?!

SAMUEL J. ANDREWS
CHRISTIANITY AND ANTI-CHRISTIANITY IN THEIR FINAL CONFLICT
PART III
Tendencies in Our Day Preparing the Way of the Anti-Christ.
(Pub. by The Bible Colportage Institution: Chicago, 2nd edition, 1898.)

<u>An Introductory note from Daniel Gracely:</u>

The following four chapters from *Christianity and Anti-Christianity in Their Final Conflict*, by Samuel J. Andrews, trace the effect of pantheistic thinking upon Western philosophy, and, in turn, that part of the Protestant Church which at length embraced modern Christian liberalism. Andrews picks up the trail from Spinoza on, discussing a variety of thinkers or movements. This includes German higher criticism, in which terms like "incarnation," "Son of God," etc., all became linguistically deconstructed by that movement's religious or philosophical thinkers. Some, perhaps even much, of this shift in theological thinking happened during Andrews' own generation, at least insofar as the brand of pantheistic language the Higher critics used, which owed considerable debt to German Idealism. Reading and studying this section has personally helped me to see that Calvinism is merely one *expression* of pantheism and thus not unique at its core. By *"expression"* (in this context) I mean the language symbols (sounds or 'words') that are peculiar to one type of pantheist-espousing religious or philosophical group of thinkers. Such language symbols which are pressed into service for pantheism nevertheless change appearance among different pantheistic thinkers or movements (as it does in Barthianism compared to Calvinism, for example). But, of course, the principle of pantheism in all these movements remains the same—the loss of individuation in its terms. This principle is perhaps most notably seen in the repeated emphasis (implicit or forthright) endorsing the divinization of the Mind of man. Since I found Andrews' chapters striking and, further, germane to the subject of my book, I have included them on the website.)

The following content is by SAMUEL J ANDREWS
(Note: footnotes in this section come after each chapter respectively)

[Chapter 1]
Modern Pantheistic Philosophy

We can readily see in the early departure of the Church from the primitive order through the loss of the first love, what the line of subsequent development must be if there were no repentance and return. The Head unable to exercise the full prerogatives of His Headship; the Holy Ghost unable to life up His voice to warn and instruct; the Church thinking to build up a kingdom in this world, and to rule in it; here are all the elements of a history full of peril and struggle. Of this history for eighteen centuries we are not now to speak. Looking backward, we may see its winding course, its mingled good and evil, the growth of the tares and wheat. But passing over the time intervening, we fix our attention upon the present tendencies and movements in the Church and in Christendom, and ask, To what goal are hey leading? To know this, we must consider the new conceptions of God, of Creation, of the Incarnation, of the Person and work of Christ, of the relation of the Church to the world, and of the coming of the kingdom of God. As the marked tendency in our day is in Philosophy and Theology to spiritual Monism, we begin with Philosophy, that through it we may better understand the principles underlying and directing modern religious thought, and determining its outward expression.

The relation of philosophy to religion is in itself a very close one; and in modern Germany philosophy is equivalent to speculative theology. Philosophy has for its problem to bring all existence into unity, to find some first principle which is the ground of all, and embraces all. It looks behind phenomena to learn their causes; through the ever changing to find the unchanging; through the many to the One. The object of its search is the first great Cause, the ultimate Essence, the Absolute Being, or God; and thus get rid of all dualism. As philosophy necessarily affects the conception of men respecting God, and therefore the conception of their relations to him, and of His actings toward them, it must affect their religion; hence we see the importance of our present inquiry: What does the most recent and current philosophy teach us of God?

It will hardly be questioned by any one competent to judge, that the tendency of modern philosophical thought is to undermine the faith of men in a personal God; and, in general, in all that system of religious doctrine which has the Incarnate Son as its center, and is embodies in the Catholic Creeds, It needs scarcely be said that, so far as this is done, the way is being prepared for him who "exalts himself above all this is called God, or that is worshipped." So long as men have faith in a personal God, the Creator of the worlds and of man, One who governs all things according to His will, and exists apart from all, no man can seat himself in the temple of God "showing himself that he is God"; such a claim would be instantly rejected as both blasphemous and absurd. Before such a claim could be listened to, there must be wrought in many minds such a change in their conception of God that this claim of Divinity would not offend them as something strange and incredible, but be accepted as wholly consistent with what they believe of the Divine nature, and of its relations to humanity.

The purpose of this enquiry, therefore, is to ascertain how far the orthodox Christian conception of God as personal, the Creator and Ruler of all, is being effaced, and that of an impersonal God substituted for it. So far as this is done, the conception also of the Incarnation of the Son of God as held by the Church is radically changed. Instead of the union of "the two natures in one Person," the essential unity of the Divine and human natures is asserted, and the way, and the way thus opened for the deified man, our enquiry relates chiefly to the tendencies toward the denial of the Father and the Son as seen in Agnosticism and Pantheism, but a few words must be said also of Atheism.

Atheism. The term Atheist is often applied to those who deny any supreme Being with intelligence and will, the Creator of the world, and distinct from it. It is often also applied to those who say that, if such a Being exists, we can have no knowledge of Him. But this is to confound Atheism with Pantheism, on the one side, and with Agnosticism, on the other. We can, strictly speaking, call only those atheists who deny any design or order in the universe, any first principle or cause, personal or impersonal.. These may be classed as idealistic and materialistic atheists; the idealistic, who affirm God to be an idealistic fiction, an idea of their own minds; the materialistic, who affirm that all that exists is matter and motion, "atoms and empty space"; and that we need only atoms and their properties to explain the universe.

Atheism has never had any great number of advocates, for it is repugnant to the laws of our intellectual nature, and to all noble moral aspirations. Yet, in recent times, a good many scientific men have professed themselves materialists, finding support for their belief in the newly-discovered properties of atoms, and the supposed fact of the conservation of energy. Tyndall defines matter as "that mysterious thing which accomplishes all the phenomena of the universe," and in which is "the potency of all life." Huxley says, though his utterances are often inconsistent that "the physiology of the future will gradually enlarge the realm of matter and law until it is coexistent with knowledge, with feeling, and with action." The materialistic school in Germany has been, of late years, especially aggressive, and ahs largely affected the popular mind, Probably the number of those who affirm matter to be self-existent, and find in it the substance of all being, is now considerable, The atoms are their God, and for a Creator and moral Ruler they have no need.

Atheism thus sets aside, not only the Christian religion, but all religion. As it has no ultimate spiritual principle, nothing but physical forces, there is nothing to worship. And, as there is no future life, as much as possible must be made of the present. According as it prevails among the people there must be seen increased devotion to material interests, with growing disregard of the intellectual and spiritual. Science, because it craves absolute and unchangeable law, is favorable inclined to materialism. It dislikes any Divine interposition; its aim is physical, not moral.

Agnosticism: This term, claimed by Professor Huxley as a word of his coinage, is used to express man's necessary ignorance of God. In itself it is a negative rather than positive term. Agnostics do not, like atheists, deny absolutely that there is a God, but say, we cannot know whether He exists or not; and, if He exists, we do not know that we have any true knowledge of Him, The central principle of Agnosticism is thus the unknowability of God arising from the limitations of our minds. As this is a mode of thought already quite general, and bears directly upon the main point of our enquiry, we must briefly consider it; first, in its philosophical principle, secondly, in its religious applications.

Going no further back than to Hume (d. 1776), who has been called the father of modern Agnosticism, we find him denying that we have any true knowledge of the attributes of God, whose existence, however, he did not deny. But all our ideas of Him are, and must be, anthropomorphic. "The whole is a riddle, an enigma, an inexplicable mystery."

This Agnosticism was the logical result of the philosophical principle then generally accepted, that all knowledge is based upon experience.

It was reserved to Kant (d. 1804) to make Agnosticism an integral part of his philosophy. He affirmed that all we can know of things external to us is their phenomena; of what is back of these phenomena, and underlying them, we are, and must be, ignorant. Of the three great objects of knowledge, God, Nature, and Man, we can affirm nothing certain, Kant gives three antinomies—contradictory propositions—which, he affirms, can neither be proved not disproved. 1."There exists, either as a part of the world or as the cause of it, an absolutely necessary Being; *Contra,* An absolutely necessary Being does not exist." 2."The cosmos had a beginning, and is limited in space; *Contra,* The cosmos had no beginning, and is not limited but infinite." 3."The soul is an indissoluble and indestructible unity; Contra, The soul is dissoluble and transitory." (critique of Pure Reason. Meiklejohn's Trans.)

Thus, according to the Kantian philosophy, reason is unable to attain any certainty as to these vital points; "it is hemmed in by a press of opposite and contradictory conclusions." It is true that Kant attempted in another way to prove the existence of a God, but only s a postulate or pre-supposition, made necessary in order that man may keep the moral law, which is imperative. God exists because a necessary means to enable man to gain the victory over evil. It is generally admitted that this attempt is unsuccessful, and that any positive affirmation of God's existence is inconsistent with the leading idea of his philosophical system. Dorner says of this system that "it leaves to the Divine, as compared with the Human, merely the semblance of existence." Professor Seth ("Scottish Philosophy") remarks: "Kant is the *fons et origo* of the most cultured agnosticism of the day." Religion with Kant is simply morality, and Christ's significance is only that of a moral Ideal; and, therefore, our faith in Him is moral, not historical. "A rational theology must be founded upon the laws of morality." Humanity is the true Son of God. Whether the Scriptures are historically true or not, is a matter of no real importance, since the ideal of reason alone has validity.

Thus Kant, by denying that we can have any true knowledge of God, of the world, or of man, laid the foundation of an universal skepticism. As the mind can think only under its limitations, our conception of God must be anthropomorphic, and, therefore, both unreal and unworthy. Nevertheless, "the notion of a Supreme Being is in many respects a highly useful idea."

As bearing upon this point of Agnosticism, two later writers should be mentioned, Hamilton and Mansel. The purpose of Hamilton, in opposition to the German pantheists, was to show that the Infinite and the Absolute are beyond the limits of our knowledge. He affirms that "All we immediately know, or can know, is the conditioned, the relative, the phenomenal, the finite." "We cannot know the Infinite through a finite notion, or have a finite knowledge of an Infinite object of knowledge." Hamilton thus placed himself in direct opposition to all who think that they can define and understand the nature of God. In this sense he was an agnostic; but he also affirmed that,"through faith we apprehend what is beyond our knowledge." "When I deny that the Infinite can by us be known, I am far from denying that it must, and ought to be believed."

Mansel ("Limits of Religious Thought") takes in substance the same ground. "The conception of the Absolute and the Infinite, from whatever side we view it, appears encompassed with contradictions." "To speak of an absolute or infinite Person, is simply to use language to which, however true it may be in a superhuman sense, no mode of human thought can possibly attach itself." Yet Mansel believed in such an absolute and infinite Person. "We are compelled by the constitution of our minds to believe in the existence of an absolute and infinite Being." And this being is personal. "The highest existence is still the highest personality; and the source of all being reveals Himself by His name, 'I am.'" Thus Mansel agrees with

Hamilton that "Belief cannot be solely determined by reason." The seeming contradictions between reason and belief may exist only in our minds, and prove simply the limitations of thought.

But, however good in themselves the motives of these philosophers, it cannot be denied that their affirmations of the necessary ignorance of men in regard to God have given a strong impulse to Agnosticism.[1] The inference is that, as we can know so little of Him because of our mental limitations, it is useless to carry on the search. And, it is also objected, that to affirm faith without knowledge is credulity. Let us, then, they say, resign ourselves to ignorance. Some of those who thus speak are, doubtless, willing to be ignorant, and glad to find some philosophic grounds on which to stand; but there are others, in their hearts seekers after God, who are burdened and perplexed by the intellectual difficulties which all questions connected with the Infinite and Eternal must present.[2]

Pantheism: As to know rightly this form of error is of the highest importance in our enquiry, it is necessary to state as clearly as possible its leading principle and to illustrate it; this will be best done by a brief outline of its modem historical development

The essential element of Pantheism, as stated by Saisset ("Pantheism"),"is the unity of God and nature, of the Infinite and the finite, in one single substance." The Infinite is not swallowed up in the finite, nor the finite in the Infinite, but both co-exist; and this co-existence is necessary and eternal. Thus we have the One and the many, the Absolute, the All. It will have no dualism, it will unify nature, man, and God. Let us trace the development of this principle, and for this purpose it is necessary to speak of Spinoza.

Descartes (d. 1 650), the founder of modem philosophy, who distinguished God from nature as its Creator, divided nature into the two created substances, extension and thought. But these have nothing in common, and thus arose a dualism that he was not able to reconcile. Spinoza (d. 1677) attempted to set this dualism aside by affirming one Substance, embracing both thought and extension, both God and nature. This Substance, infinite and absolute, has an infinity of attributes; but of these we know only the two, thought and extension, each of which has an infinity of finite modes. This Substance, the permanent reality under all transient phenomena, is ever changing; all finite things are only passing modes of its being, transient manifestations of its essence, coming out of it and again absorbed into it Spinoza called this substance God. Man, as to his body, is simply a mode of the Divine extension; as to his soul, of the Divine thought. Both are individualizations of the Infinite.

If this Substance be God, embracing in Himself all existence—the Absolute, the All in all—we ask, Has He consciousness, intelligence, will? No, says Spinoza. These are elements of personality, and He is impersonal We cannot ascribe to Him purpose or design; He is with out feeling; He cannot love or pity, reward or punish; of His own will He creates nothing; all things eternally exist, and are in a perpetual flow. He is the universal and impersonal principle of the universe, which has neither beginning nor end.

Thus there is one Substance in which co-exists the Infinite and finite. But here the problem meets us: How does the Infinite become the finite; the Absolute, the relative; the One, the many? How does the one impersonal Substance become personal in man? The dualism of Descartes is not set aside; God and nature, extension and thought, soul and body, remain distinct as before.

This pantheistic philosophy of Spinoza was for a time little understood, and generally regarded as atheism. That it wholly denies the Christian belief respecting God, need not be said. Man is not a creature of God made in His image, but a part of Him, a finite manifestation of His infinite essence; he has no free will, and cannot be morally responsible. No finite thing has any reality, all reality is in God.

So well satisfied was Spinoza with his philosophy that he could say:" I have explained the nature of God;" and modem German philosophers have called him," The god-intoxicated man."

The attention of philosophers following Spinoza was chiefly given to other questions, such as the origin of our knowledge, and the nature of our mental powers. Of Kant and his teaching notice has already been taken so far as is necessary for our purpose. He left the dualism between thought and being, subject and object, phenomenon and noumenon unsolved. Indeed, his distinction between the pure and the practical Reason made it more conspicuous.

Fichte (d. 1814) took up the problem, affirming that all things must be derived from a single principle, and solved it by making the subject or the Ego supreme; it creates the object. Everything external to itself exists only in the consciousness of the Ego, a form of its productive activity. Nature is reduced to a non-entity. "The conception of a particular substance is impossible and contradictory" The universe, and even God Himself, are of the mind's creation, so that Fichte could say to his class: "Gentlemen, now we will create God." The supreme Being in his system is no more than the Moral Order of the world: "We need no other, and can comprehend no other." This moral order is what Mr. Arnold calls "the Power that makes for righteousness."

This idealism of Fichte was in its principle rather atheistic than pantheistic, but became pantheistic in its later development. For our purpose it is important to note how it tends to the exaltation of man, on the one side, and to the annihilation of God, on the other. Of his philosophy Bomer says: "Each man per se is immediately, not through the mediation of Christ, but by nature, God. . . God is the only reality in any one." Christ has, indeed, an unique place as the first born Son of God, but "all men are equal to Him in that which constitutes their proper reality." It is said by Morell (Hist, of Phil.),"With Fichte the idea of nature and the idea of God absolutely vanished; self became the sole existence in the universe, and from its own power and activity everything human was constructed"; and to the same effect Prof. Seth: "Self, as the eternal sustaining subject of the Universe, formed the beginning, middle, and end of the system."

In Schelling (d. 1854) the pantheistic element comes much more clearly into view. Of the two factors, subject and object, thought and being, God and nature, he will not with Fichte allow the one to swallow up the other; but will identify them in one primary and eternal essence or first Principle, which is hardly to be distinguished from the Substance of Spinoza. This first Principle is ever developing itself, or "embodying its own infinite attributes in the finite." Thought and being cannot be separated, for thought is shown to be in all nature by the presence of law. But there are degrees of thought from unconscious matter to conscious man, and the law of the development of the infinite Essence is from lower to higher. "It develops itself sometimes with, and sometimes without self-consciousness."" Nature," says Schelling," sleeps in the plant, dreams in the animal, wakens in man."" Mind in man is nothing else but nature gradually raised to a state of consciousness." The universal Divine life runs through a process, but can manifest itself only in finite forms, and so comes under limitations, each individual form being necessarily imperfect. But as being the Divine life in each individual, the finite is not merely finite; it is that in which God has His historical life." It is God in his growth." The collective finite, or the world, is the Son of God. This incarnation of God in Nature is the principle of philosophy, everything is to be explained by it. But it is in man that this absolute essence, or God, comes to the full possession of itself, or to self-consciousness; and man, therefore, is the highest of beings. In him the process of the Divine development comes to its culmination. Of this development Morell remarks that "all difference between God and the universe is entirely lost. Schelling's pantheism is as complete as that of Spinoza." Of some later modifications of his philosophy it is not necessary here to speak.

It is at this point that Hegel (d. 1831) took up the problem, accepting much from his predecessors. He begins with pure undetermined being, or, what is equivalent, with Nothing with zero; and this he calls the Idea, or God; and out of this must all things come. Creation is not an act. "Without the world God would not be God." It is, therefore, only an eternal process of becoming which he has to explain. He finds the law of this process to be the law of thought. As thoughts alone are real existences, and are creative powers, the laws of thought are those of being. Thus the two kingdoms of thought and being, or of spirit and nature, are one. In individual things there is no reality, man is a passing phenomenon; the only reality is in the first Principle, the Idea; in other words, in God. In all its determinations this first Principle determines itself; in producing differences, it produces itself in them. The Infinite becomes the finite; the Absolute, the relative. In all these determinations there is progress, but man only of finite things attains to self-consciousness. In him the self-determining Principle, or God, who is everywhere in nature, comes to know Himself, or to self-realization; as distinct from the world, He has no self-consciousness; He attains to this in man. Thus man is both one with nature and with the absolute Spirit, and, therefore, the highest of beings, the last in the chain of development; in fine, man is God.

Thus we have, according to this philosophy, a spiritual principle or essence called God, which is eternally differentiating itself, or eternally becoming. All finite, or differentiated existences are simply necessary modes of His existence,—progressive manifestations of the One Infinite Essence. The law of this progress Hegel lays down as, "The identity of contradictions." It is not necessary to our purpose here to speak of this; we are now concerned only with the nature of the relation which he makes to exist between the Infinite and the finite, between God and man. And we see here his advance upon Spinoza. With Spinoza there is no real progress, man is but one of the transient forms of finite being; with Hegel, he is the end of the series. Only in man does God folly realize Himself.

It is true, and should be said, that there has been much dispute among the students of this philosophy whether Hegel meant to absolutely deny the personality of God, and the immortality of man, or not But the most competent and impartial interpreters so understand his philosophy. It has been very recently said by Professor Seth ("Hegelianism and Personality") "If the system leaves us without any self-conscious existence in the universe beyond that realized in the self-consciousness of individuals, the saying means that God, in any ordinary acceptation of the term, is eliminated from our philosophy altogether the self-existence of God seems to disappear. . . Evidently this is to renounce the idea of anything like a separate personality or self-consciousness in the Divine Being." "As to immortality, Hegel shelves the question."

With Hegel the climax seems to be reached, the last word to be spoken. All dualism is resolved, God alone exists. He is the All, both the Infinite and the finite, the Absolute and the relative, the Eternal and the temporal. His life is an Eternal process of self-development. We know the law of His development, and that its ultimate term is man. Humanity is the consummation of Divinity.

Of the later developments of the Hegelian Philosophy in Germany it is not necessary here to speak. Its three great divisions into Right, Middle, and Left, are well known. The first attempts to reconcile this philosophy with the personality of God, and the immortality of the soul; the second holds

God's personality "in a general pantheistic sense," but denies immortality, and the Christ of the Church; the last knows no God apart from the world, no immortality, and no Incarnation but that in which all men alike partake. In this school are Strauss and Feuerbach, whose position will be examined in another place.

Pessimism: The chief representatives of this philosophy are the Germans, Schopenhauer and Hartman. The fundamental principle, as said by Professor Bowen ("Modern Philosophy"), is that "there is an universal, all-pervading Will, a blind, and incognitive, and unconscious God; coinciding in this respect with the one universal substance of Spinoza." Of this Will every individual human existence is but a transient phenomenon, and death is its annihilation. Christianity as a religion Schopenhaur wholly rejects, as, indeed, he does all religions except that of the Buddhists, which denies the existence of a God. He says (Religion and other Essays, Trans. 1893) that" Everything true in Christianity is found in Brahmanism and Buddhism." The world is the worst of all possible worlds; nothing is so God as to cease to be." All qualities are innate, the bad as well as the God," and" a man's acts proceed from his innate and unalterable character"; they cannot be other than they are. Of Hartmann, Professor Bowen says: "He is a thorough-going monist;" his unconscious "Principle" is the equivalent of Spinoza's "Substance" and Schopenhauer's "Will." In the universe is no mark of an intelligent free will. The world, if not the worst possible, is so bad that we are "to will the annihilation of all things, and thus get rid of the misery of existence." "The blissful repose of nothingness" is the consummation, the haven of rest, to which we look forward.

That this pessimistic philosophy is gaining an increasing hold upon the public mind, seems to be shown by the larger circulation of its writings, both in Germany and elsewhere; but, if so, this must be ascribed chiefly to the loss of faith in God, and of the hope of a higher future life. None of its advocates openly commend suicide; but this mode of ending a miserable existence is one which must naturally suggest itself, and be more chosen as the gloom of the last days darkens over the earth.

Of the bearings of this pessimistic philosophy on morality, something will be said later.

Neo-Kantianism, or Hegelianism: Of this philosophy, which has within a recent period appeared in Scotland and England, and whose chief representatives are the late Professor T. H. Green, and the Professors E. and J. Caird, some words may be said. So far as we are here concerned with it, it does not differ in any essential point from original Hegelianism. Its central tenet, as we are told by Professor A. Seth ("^ Hegelianism and Personality") is "the identification of the transcendental self with a Divine or creative Self"; or, in other words, the identification of the Divine and the human self-consciousness. As regards this Divine Self, or, as it is frequently called, "Spiritual Principle," there is much vagueness of expression. Professor E. Caird ("Evolution of Religion") speaks of it as "a self-determining Principle manifesting itself in all the determinations of the finite." It is said to be "somehow present and active in each individual." Is this "Spiritual Principle" the Christian God ? Does it exist for itself, with a distinct self-consciousness, and with all that constitutes personality? Apparently not. Its self-consciousness is that of the individual man, separated from which it is nothing. But this takes away the individual self-consciousness; and, as said by Professor Seth, "man's selfhood and independence are wiped out with a completeness which few systems of pantheism can rival." "There is only one self—the Universal or Divine—and this all-embracing subject manifests itself alike in the object and in the subject of human consciousness; in nature and in man. Both are God, though they appear to be somewhat on their own account."

Of the pantheistic character of this Neo-Hegelian philosophy, it is said by Professor Upton ("Bases of Religious Belief"), writing of Professor E. Caird's "Evolution of Religion" : "So far as I can understand his position, it is simply unmitigated pantheism, for, according to it, every moral decision to which man comes, noble or base, is an act for which no human being but only God is responsible." "Sin, repentance, moral responsibility, become only empty words."

Evolutionary Philosophy: Of this philosophy Mr. H. Spencer is the chief representative. He must be classed among the agnostics, as affirming that no definite conception of the Infinite or Absolute is possible. For a personal God he substitutes a Force or Energy which he calls "The Unknowable," but of which, he says, we have a dim but positive consciousness. We know it "to exist," to be a "reality," "the first cause of all," "the source of power"; in a word, "an infinite and eternal Energy by which all things are created and sustained." Yet he tells us, also, that it is "utterly inscrutable," "absolutely incomprehensible," " forever inconceivable."

In what relation does this Energy stand to the universe? It is its cause. There has been no act of creation, but an eternal evolutionary process, passing in endless cycles from "the imperceptible to the perceptible, and back again from the perceptible to the imperceptible." The law of this process is "the continuous redistribution of matter and motion." Nothing that exists can be other than it is; all life, intellectual and moral, as well as animal, comes under this law.

We are here concerned with this philosophy only as it bears upon religion. Having substituted for a personal God "an infinite and eternal Energy," can we worship it? Mr. Spencer thinks that the feeling of wonder and awe which it inspires, is worship. It has, indeed, no positive attributes, it is not God, or wise, or merciful, or just; it is merely a force working unconsciously and blindly; but we are told that this is better than the Christian God, and that if we cannot pray to it, or bow down in worship, we can fear and wonder as we behold its mighty workings in the universe.

It is apparent that belief in such a dynamic force can have no more practical bearing upon the moral conduct of life than the belief in gravitation. It has in it no religious element. It not only denies the personality of God; but the personality of man also; and presents to us only nature, and man, as under a process of Evolution which has neither beginning nor end. For immortality there is no place. Man being only one of the forms of expression of the Universal Energy, has no free will, and no moral responsibility. It need not be said that with this philosophy revealed religion has no possible points of contact, and least of all has Christianity.

Of the Hegelian philosophy a recent writer says "In itself it is unmixed anthropotheism, not the exaltation of a creature into the place of God, but the assertion that the creature is the sole and essential God... Alas! Herein lies its bad excellence, that while utterly expunging from creation, as a popular representation, a present Deity; while rejecting an Incarnate Saviour, an indwelling Spirit, an inspired record, a coming day of judgment; its subtlety is such that there is no point of Christian verity, no office of the adorable Trinity, no text of Holy Writ, for which it has not an appropriate niche in its temple of lies. It contradicts nothing, it stultifies everything; it confounds, neutralizes, and eliminates all objects of present faith. It is the first truly philosophical system which, denying the life to come, eternizes the present... The thought of man is the fountain, the judgment of man the judge, of all things... And man, though as an individual born and mortal, is as man the eternal essence." A German writer says of it that it is "a paganism dressed up anew, and sublimed to a self-adoring worship of mind." A very recent writer, Professor Wenley ("Contemporary Theology and Theism") says: The warring of the pantheistic and monotheistic tendencies, both implicitly present in Hegel, ended, unfortunately, in a complete victory for the former."

In examining the anti-Christian influences now at work, we find the current pantheistic philosophy the most fundamental and powerful. Beginning with the century, it has now penetrated all regions of human thought. Theology, Literature, Science, Art, all bear its impress. Its growing influence has been often noted. It is said by J. S. Mill (1840):" The philosophical writings of Schelling and Hegel have given pantheistic principles a complacent admission and a currency which they never before this age possessed in any part of Christendom." Buchanan (1857) says: "The grand ultimate struggle between Christianity and Atheism will resolve itself into a controversy between Christianity and Pantheism." Saisset (1868) speaks of Pantheism "as having made, and daily making, the most alarming progress." "This is the beginning and end of German philosophy, it begins with skepticism, it ends with Pantheism." It is said by E. Caird (1888):" In the scientific life of Germany there is no greater power at present than Hegelianism, especially in all that relates to metaphysics, and thus to the philosophy and history of religion." Fairbaim observes ("Place of Christ in Modern Thought"): "It were mere folly to attempt to understand modern movements in theology without Hegel, especially those that circle around the history of Christ." Christlieb ("Modern Doubt"): "Fichte and Schelling made the idea of Divine personality to be absorbed in an all-confounding idealistic Pantheism, which received from Hegel its last development. This philosophy appears in German literature from Schiller to Heine. Hence, we meet at the present day so many educated persons whose faith in a personal Deity has resolved itself into faith in the moral order of the universe, or in some universal law or principle."

But no proof need be given of what is universally confessed. A mighty wave of Pantheism, beginning in Germany, has been sweeping over Christendom during the present century; and now finds but little to resist it. As Greek philosophy developed when the popular religions were in a process of disintegration, so is it now. It was then an attempt to replace the old faith by a new philosophic religion. So today, Christianity being regarded in many quarters as incapable of giving a satisfactory theory of the world and of human life, philosophy steps in and undertakes the task. It will give us a new religion based upon a new conception of God, a new Christianity based on a new conception of Christ, a universe evolved, not created. How far the new will supplant the old, time only can show us, for we do not know how far faith in the Christian Creeds has been silently undermined. But Christianity meets a new enemy, a philosophic religion which boasts itself able to satisfy, as Christianity is not able to do, all the demands of the intellect; a religion more suitable to our advanced culture than one transmitted from an ancient and half-civilized people. It is a religion which many will gladly welcome, for it opens a wide gate and a broad way in which all men, of whatever race or belief, may walk without jostling one another.

Andrews's footnotes to chapter 1:

[1] It is said by Pfleiderer ("Development of Theology") that "in the course of the next decade, upon this agnosticism Matthew Arnold based his ethical Idealism, Seeley his aesthetical idealism, and Spencer his evolutionism; three theories which, with all their dissimilarities, have this in common, that they all regard the impossibility of a Divine revelation, and of a revealed religion, to be the necessary consequences of the incognizability of God."

[2] It should be observed that many who call themselves agnostics, are not really such. The real agnostic simply affirms that he does not know about God, he is in doubt; this is a purely negative position. But to affirm or to deny a God is a positive act. The true agnostic neither affirms nor denies, he has no belief one

way or the other; he simply doubts. How far from this position, for example, is Mr. Leslie Stephen in his recent book, "An Agnostic's Apology." He affirms that the limits of human intelligence exclude all knowledge that transcends the narrow limits of experience. Theology is thus excluded, God is unknowable, the universe is a dark riddle. There is no revelation, no miracle, nothing supernatural, no future life. These are not negative, but positive affirmations; not those of an agnostic, but of a gnostic, of one who knows. The old Creeds, all statements in the Church symbols as to the nature of God, the Trinity, the Incarnation, he affirms cap now" produce nothing but the laughter of skeptics, and the contempt of the healthy human intellect." And he affirms that "Agnosticism is the frame of mind which summarily rejects these imbecilities." Mr. Matthew Arnold is equally positive. He affirms that we cannot believe in God or angels, because "we absolutely have no experience of one or the other." He knows that God is not a Person, but merely a Force or Power. And, in general, it may be said that no men are more dogmatic in their utterances than most of the professed agnostics.

[Chapter 2]
Modern Philosophy and The New Christianity

We have seen the attempt on the part of modem philosophy to get rid of all dualism, and to bring all things into unity. Regarding this philosophy as the characteristic and most potent antichristian influence of our time, we are here especially concerned with its bearings upon Christianity; but its influence is seen in all spheres of human thought, in Biblical criticism, in Science, in Literature, in Sociology, and in Art. We are now to consider only the two chief modifications of Christianity springing from this attempt to unify God and man; and which are becoming familiar to the Christian ear under the general name of the "New Christianity," though sometimes called the "New Religion," the "New Theology," the "New Reformation," the "New Orthodoxy," and other like terms.

What is this New Christianity? and who are the Neo-Christians? As yet no very clear and positive answers have been given. There is a vagueness of statement, or, perhaps, in some cases, an intentional reserve, which makes it difficult to distinguish between the new and the old. It is said by one of them: "The time has not come for writing the New Theology." But all its advocates affirm that Christianity is in a transition state. Theological knowledge, like all other knowledge, must be progressive. Thus, we are told by a recent writer, (Allen, "Continuity of Christian Thought"), that "the traditional conception of God which has come down to us through the middle ages, through the Latin Church, is undergoing a profound transformation. A change so fundamental involves other changes of momentous importance in every department of human thought, and, more especially, in Christian theology. There is no theological doctrine which does not undergo a change in consequence of the change in our thoughts about God. "It is said by another: "We need a new theology constructed on a new foundation."

If there is such a change going on, and one so momentous, in Christian Theology, we are bound to give it the most careful consideration. We are not dealing, we are repeatedly assured, with merely verbal distinctions, old wine in new bottles; if this be all, it is not a matter of vital importance. The body is more than raiment. But it is much more than this. As was recently said by one of its representatives: "We can not keep the new wine in old bottles: this can end only in destroying the bottles, and spilling the wine."

But when we seek to know more accurately the fundamental principles and distinctive features of the New Christianity, we find that, in fact, there are two doctrinal systems, differing widely in their conceptions of God, and in their Christologies, yet reaching substantially the same result—that Divinity and humanity are one. Let us examine them successively, and learn what is distinctive in each. We begin with that school which makes distinctive the doctrine of the Divine immanence in man.

I. The Divine immanence in man.

We are told by this school of Neo-Christians that "the idea of God as transcendent, is yielding to the idea of Deity as immanent in His creatures." It is said ("Progressive Orthodoxy"): "We add a single remark upon the general philosophical conception of God in His relation to the Universe, which underlies these Essays. It is a modification of the prevailing Latin conception of the Divine transcendence by a fuller and clearer perception of the Divine immanence. Such a doctrine of God, we believe, is more and more commending itself to the best philosophy of our time, and the fact of the Incarnation commends it to the acceptance of the Christian theologians."This Divine immanence is the fundamental fact on which this school of Neo-Ohristians builds its theology.

As transcendence and immanence are philosophical terms, we must note their meaning in philosophy.

It was the doctrine of the pantheist, Spinoza, that all that exists, exists in God. He is immanent in the universe, and cannot in any act pass out of Himself, or transcend Himself.[3] God and the universe are one. "All the energy displayed in it is His, and therein consists His immanence." "A being acting out of himself, is a finite being." Creation, being a transcendent act, is impossible.

If we may not charge this school of Neo-Christians can understand the Divine immanence in nature and man? Is there an immanence, distinct from that indwelling of God in man through the Holy Ghost of which the

Bible speaks, which is not pantheistic, but preserves the essential distinction of the Divine and human natures, and of the personalities of God and man? It is here that we meet great vagueness of expression. It has been defined by one as "such immanence that the human mind is one in principle with the Divine mind"; and by another, as "absolute oneness with God"; by another, "that man and God and the universe are fused into one"; by an- other, that "humanity is consubstantial with God." Are we here taught that God and man are of the same essence or substance? Or, are we to take a distinction between unity and identity? Can we say that we are one with God in kind, and yet not identical with Him?

It may be answered by some that this unity means no more than that communion of man with God of which the Lord and the Apostles speak, such unity that "we dwell in God and God in us"; and that "in Him we live, and move, and have our being." But that this, and like expressions, are not to be taken in a pantheistic sense, is shown by the whole tenor of the Bible. Man made in the image of God, and so capable of communion with Him, is still distinct from Him; not God, but a creature of God. If this unity with God be all, the New Christianity gives us nothing new. Its immanence is only the indwelling of the Holy Spirit in man, and preserves his personality and responsibility.

We have, then, still to ask, what other meaning we are to give to the term immanence that is not pantheistic? Perhaps we may learn this by asking the meaning of other terms, in frequent use, as expressing the relation of men to God, "Divine Sonship," and "Divine Humanity." The word Divine is confessedly ambiguous; it may mean simply likeness, or it may mean identity of essence. That man was made in the image of God, affirms likeness; and on the ground of this likeness, he may be called Divine. So man, as made by God, is His son, and this sonship may be called Divine; and the same term be used of our humanity. But neither term of itself affirms identity of essence. Man may be Godlike and not God; if a creature of God, he cannot be God.

Thus we are still left uncertain in what sense our humanity and our sonship are Divine. But we may obtain light by asking what place these Neo-Christians give the Lord Jesus—the Incarnate Son? What was His Sonship? in what sense was it Divine? We are told by an eminent writer of this school—Pfleiderer—that He does not differ from others "because of an unique metaphysical relation between Him and God." The peculiar and exclusive place given Him in the Creeds, as the one pre-existent and only-begotten Son, does not belong to Him. The relation of sonship is a general one; "all men having the same Divine origin and destination." As immanent in all, all are God's sons, and He is Son of God in the same sense in which all men are. The relation is an ethical one, and, therefore, universal. The Incarnation is, as said by one, "a race fact." His distinction is not one of nature, but simply that He was the first to recognize the common filial relation, and to fulfil the duties it imposes. He thus became the religious, Ideal, the perfect Son, whose example others are to follow. Knowing as a Son His union with the Father, He could say: "I and my Father are one." All men, as they stand in the same filial relation, may have the same consciousness of sonship, and affirm the same unity; and this consciousness of our Divine sonship is "the essence of Christianity."

Thus in regard to the Person of the Lord and His Divine Sonship, we reach the result that He differed from other men only so far as He was more conscious of God immanent in Him, and so could reveal Him in word and work; and that all men are in the same sense Divine, for God is imminent in all. If we speak of Deity as especially incarnated in Jesus, it is only as a larger pitcher may hold more water than a smaller, or as one star may be brighter than another.

The question returns: How is this universal immanence of God in humanity to be distinguished from Pantheism? Many attempts have been made to draw a clear line of distinction between them by those who affirm the essential unity of the Divine and human. One of the latest of these attempts, known as "Ethical Theism," is by Professor Upton ("Bases of Religious Belief"), who speaks of all rational beings as "so many differentiations of God," or as "those created by Him out of His own substance"; and yet he would preserve man's free will and substantial individuality. But if of "one substance with God," "differentiations of Him," how is it possible to maintain distinct individual existence?[4]

We must call any system Pantheistic which denies man's free will, and makes the individual self to be swallowed up in the universal Self. It is on this ground, as we have seen, that Professor Upton declares the philosophy of the Absolute Idealists or Neo-Hegelians to be "unmitigated Pantheism."
[5]

It is only when the fact of the creation of nature and of man by an act of the Divine will is clearly held, that Theism can be clearly distinguished from Pan- theism. Nothing that God by an act of His will brings into being, can be a part of Himself. The Creator cannot be the created. Any philosophy which makes the universe to be of the Divine Substance, or an eternal or necessary manifestation of God, and any theology based upon it, must be pantheistic. If, as said by Hegel, and repeated by many since, "God without the world would not be God,"the world is an integral part of Him, without which He would be imperfect; and, therefore, if we affirm Him to be perfect, it must be co-existent and eternal.

But it is our purpose here only to state beliefs and show their bearings, not to disprove them. We are concerned only to note how the attempts to get rid of all dualism between God, nature, and man, all tend to pantheistic identity. If the orthodox doctrine of the Incarnation be set aside, and that of a universal incarnation under the name of Immanence be substituted for it, the Neo-Christians are right in saying that "our conceptions of God, and of His relations to men, are undergoing a profound transformation." Especially this transformation is seen as regards the Person of the Son. It is said by Dorner: "The characteristic feature of all recent Christologies is the endeavour to point out the essential unity of the Divine and the human." The dualism of the two natures in Christ must be got rid of. We are told by one of this school that "the peculiar power and truth of Christ's humanity will not be reached till this anomalous division and composition of His Person be abolished."

Thus, if we accept the teachings of this new theology, the old distinction of the Divine and the human must be given up. As said by one: "We are passing over from the conception of God as another Self existing over against the human self, to the more spiritual view of God as the Self-immanent, not only in nature, but also in the worshipper's own soul"; and it is this view "which, in the present day, most commends itself to cultivated minds." It is said by another: "This idea of the Immanence of God underlies the Christian conception . . .and is an idea involved in all modern philosophy and theology. It may well be called a new Christianity. At any rate it is the only religion that will fully realize the idea of religion, and so meet the wants of the new time." The relation of this form of the New Christianity to the current pantheistic philosophy is obvious. We have seen that modern philosophical thought has spent its strength on the problem how all things may be brought into unity, and that Hegelianism professes to give it its final solution. Philosophy and theology are at one: the first affirms that God came to self-consciousness in man; the second bases on this a universal Incarnation. It is said by Professor Seth: "Hegelianism has attempted to find a unity in which God and man shall be comprehended in a more intimate union, or living interpenetration, than any philosophy had succeeded in reaching." This unity it finds by making God and man essentially one. Thus Dorner says of Hegel's Christology: "The unity of God and man is not an isolated fact once accomplished in Jesus; it is eternally and essentially characteristic of God to be, and to become, man. His true existence, or actuality, is in humanity; and man is essentially one with God." As the Divine impersonal Principle or Idea first fully realizes itself in man, man is the real God, the culmination of the Divine development. It need not be said that between this philosophic Pantheism carried to its last results, and the Christianity of the Creeds, there is a chasm, broad, and deep, and impassable. But as always between the old and the new there are some who attempt to mediate, so is it now. Between those who hold fast to the old historic Christianity and its Creeds, and those who teach the new religion of absolute Pantheism, appears a mediating party, the Neo-Christian. To the pantheistic spirit it will make large concessions. It will not affirm boldly that man is God, but in effect effaces any real distinction between them by its doctrine of a Divine immanence, making humanity Divine; and on this basis will reconstruct Christian theology.

Let us now briefly sum up the bearings of this new form of Christianity on the relation of men to God, and on the work of Christ as man's Saviour.

1. If God and man are not separated by any real distinction of natures, it is idle to speak of our humanity as fallen and corrupt The Divinity in us may be obscured, but is indestructible.

Our sin and misery lie only in the unconsciousness of our Divine Sonship, and our redemption is in our awakening to a consciousness of it. It is a process within every man's own spirit, and is effected when he realizes his Sonship. There is no need of any sacrifice for sin, or of any mediator outside of our humanity. "As directly united with God, man possesses his full salvation within himself." Jesus did not redeem us from the law of sin and death by His sacrificial death; but from Him, as from all prophets and religious heroes, goes forth " a redeeming force," only in a far higher degree, because "He, among all the ethical and religious geniuses and heroes of history, occupies the central place. . • As He possessed the new and most exalted ideal of man, so He presented it in His life with impressive and educating power." His work in our salvation was not to bear our sins in His body on the tree, and by resurrection to become the source of a new life; but to furnish an ideal for men, and to educate them by His earthly example. As said by the writer last quoted: "The true redeeming and saving faith of the Christian consists in his adopting this ideal as the conviction of his heart, and the principle of his whole life."

2. As the work of Jesus was completed by giving in His earthly life a moral and religious ideal, His relations to us since His death have no real importance. His life on earth was a historical demonstration that God and man are essentially one, and having taught men their Divine Sonship, His work was done. As to His bodily resurrection, some of the Neo-Christians are silent, but some affirm its belief to have been a hallucination of the early disciples. As an historical fact, it is not important. He is not now fulfilling any priestly functions in Heaven, or any work of mediation between God and man. He is not the second Adam, giving His resurrection life to man. The Church does not exist as His body, it has no living Head. It is the community of all the sons of God, in which He has no supreme place. It is the ethical principle of the Divine Sonship perfectly illustrated in Him, which makes church-unity; and as this Sonship embraces all men, so the Church embraces all. It is as large as humanity. We enter it by natural birth, we enter into its full communion when the consciousness of our sonship is fully awakened within us; and this not by the Spirit of Christ sent by Him,

and working in any supernatural way, but by the redeeming force of His ideal. As there is no living Head of the Church whose life and grace are conveyed through sacraments and ordinances, these have only such value as a man's own spirit may give them.

3. If Christ is not now carrying on any redemptive work in Heaven, will He have any work in the future? Clearly, He Himself believed this, for He continually spoke of His return, and of His work as King and Judge; and this is affirmed in all the Creeds. But we are told that, while He was from one point of view far above His time and surroundings, from another He was the child of His time, and of His people; and, therefore, we must not be surprised at His belief that He would return to set up His kingdom, and be the King and Judge. In this He shared the mistaken Messianic expectations of the Jews. The Church is now outgrowing this illusion, and sees in the Messianic King descending from heaven to establish His kingdom, only "a earned conception of that spiritual-ethical kingdom" which will be realized only when all come to a consciousness of their Divine Sonship.

II. A Divine humanity in God.

Before considering this we may be reminded of the orthodox faith, that man was created by God in His own image, but is absolutely distinct in his essence from his Creator. It was this created nature which the Son took when He came into the world and became man; He came under the law of death, but rose from the dead, and in the risen and glorified form of this nature He now abides. As opposed to this faith, this school of Neo-Christians affirms that the Incarnation, as realized in Him, was not a union of two natures, but "the development or determination of the Divine in the form of the human." This has been otherwise expressed as "an eternal determination of the essence of God, by virtue of which God in so far only becomes man as He is man from eternity." Again: "The Incarnation is a revelation of the essential humanity of God, and of the potential Divinity of man."

Thus there is in the Godhead a human element" and, as the Godhead is incapable of change, it must be an eternal element; and, unless we affirm a dualism in the Godhead, this human element is itself "a determination of the Divine in the form of the human." Thus we get an eternal Divine-human element, "an uncreated humanity."

In what relation does this Divine-human element stand to Christ, the Incarnate Son? It was the teaching of F. D. Maurice[6] (see Haweis, Contemporary Rev., June, 1894): "That Jesus Christ was the coming forth of something that had always existed in God; it was the coming forth of the human side of God, God manifest in the flesh." In general, those of this school agree that before the Incarnation, or before any act of creation, the Divine-human element had in the Son its eternal embodiment. On this ground He is called by one, "the Archetypal man," and His humanity, "the Archetypal humanity"; by another, "the Eternal Prototype of humanity," "the Eternal Pattern of our race." It is because He was the archetypal man that humanity is what it is. "His humanity is more real and true than ours because it is the original from which ours is derived." "The Pat tern of man," it is said by Bishop Brooks, "existed in the nature of Him who was to make him." "Before the clay was fashioned, this humanity existed in the Divinity; already was there union of the Divine and the human, and thus already there was the eternal Christ." The word "Christ includes to our thought such a Divinity as involves the human element... Of the two words, God and man, one describes pure Deity, the other pure humanity. Christ is not a word identical with either, but including both." This special Christ-nature, the Divine-human, has existed forever; and it was because this Christ-nature existed in the Godhead that an incarnation was possible. Being already man. He could manifest Himself as man; as a Son of man, He could become the Son of Mary.

We thus reach a new conception of the Person of Christ, and a new doctrine of the Incarnation. As regards His Person, we are told that the term Christ includes, to our thought, such a Divinity as involves the human element. Is this eternal Divine-human element in the Son alone, or is it an integral part of the Godhead? The first is impossible, for then the Father and Spirit would be pure Deity, the Son Deity plus humanity. We must then believe that an eternal Divine-human element has forever existed, which, though common to all the Divine Persons, finds its embodiment in the Son. It was to reveal this humanity, and thus to teach men that it has always existed and is Divine, that the Son came into the world.

Being thus " the pre-incarnate Man," the Incarnation could not be the assumption of a new, created humanity, but merely the revelation of that which the Son already possessed. And this revelation was made by the taking of a mortal body, thus bringing His Divine humanity under certain limitations. Thus we meet the humanity of the Lord imder two different conditions; as it eternally pre-existed in Him, and as it was in Him when He was on earth. What was the nature of this change from the higher condition to the lower, and how effected ? We are told by one, that "possessing already an essential affinity, he enters into a flesh and blood affinity"; or "changes His condition of being by the assumption of a mere human body. "How vague and superficial this is, need not be said. But it rests upon the assumption everywhere made by this school, that there was no such fall of man, no such corruption of nature, as the, Church has held. The Divine humanity cannot be separated from God, and cannot become really evil; and therefore the work of the Son on earth was not to offer Himself a sacrifice for the sins of men, but "to present us with a perfected specimen, the type, the promise, the potency, of the entire race of tempted, suffering humanity." The sacrificial aspects of the Atonement vanish; no element of humiliation enters into the Incarnation. "It was the actual manifestation of God in the human, so that Jesus of Nazareth became the revelation of God in His absolute glory." A future and more glorious revelation of Him is not promised or to be expected. The world is already redeemed, He has made all things new, we are living in the new heaven and earth.

Thus the end of the Incarnation was not, by the Lord's assumption of our nature and by His death, "to condemn sin in the flesh," and to bring in through resurrection a new and immortal form of humanity, as has been always taught by the Church; but to "show men that the eternal Divine-humanity possessed by the Son is theirs as their birthright, and that to regain it is the perfect life. As said by Bishop Brooks, the work of Christ was "to build a bridge on which man might walk, fearfully but safely, back into the Divinity where he belonged." As said by another: "He descended into the race to renew or recreate it after the original Divine image." He established no new Divine relation between God and man, He simply restored the old. He had, as the risen and glorified Man, no new and higher life to impart.

When the Lord left the earth, having finished His work, He regained His place as "the archetypal man," "'His pre-incarnate state of fullness and immortality." His mission was ended when He had shown in his own Person the eternal Divinity of human nature, and set before men the heavenly ideal; it was now for them to realize it.

Let us now note some of the bearings of this doctrine of the Divine humanity.

1. The distinction between the Church and the world is effaced. As "the eternal Prototype," He, not Adam, is the Head of humanity. Our humanity is derived from Him, and is the same in all men; therefore, all stand in the relation of sons to God. We are told that when "He came unto His own," He came not to the Jews, or to any elect portion of men, but unto all men; when He uses the figure of the vine and the branches. He speaks of Himself and of the whole human race. In like manner, when St. Paul speaks of the Church as His body, he does not mean a part, more or less, of men, but the totality of men regarded as an organic whole. As said by one: " The Church belongs to all, and all to the Church." "The whole family in heaven and earth is the Church." "The appearance of the Son of God is the sanctification of the human race." We wrongly narrow the meaning of the term Church when we speak of it as composed of the baptized. "Every man by virtue of his birth is called. Humanity is the ecclesia, called out and away from the old animal life from which it sprang." All are, in virtue of the Divine humanity, the sons of God; and we are told that "the belief of the

Church that God has only one Son, and that all others, as fallen and sinful, must become His sons by regeneration and adoption, is no longer preachable or credible among thinking men." As all are children of God and partakers of the Divine nature, "every man must belong to the Church, and the Church to him, whether he knows it or not." It was said by Maurice: "The truth is, every man is in Christ," and if so, a sharer in His perfect humanity.

2. The distinction between the Church and the world being thus, as to its essence, effaced, we may no longer say that the Church is set to save men by gathering them out of the world, but is set "to save the world." This salvation it effects by showing men the Divinity of their nature, and by teaching them that, therefore, all human interests are heavenly and Divine; and that what is needed is their development. Christ, being immanent in the world, His life pervades humanity. Through Him all things are now holy. The kingdom of God, which began at His advent, enlarges with the development of the Divine humanity in all its manifold forms and earthly interests; or, in other words, with the progress of a Christian civilization. How directly this tends to help on, or rather to serve as a foundation for, the present sociological movement, is obvious; and also the place it gives to the Church as the leader in them. If the Church is to save the world by developing and perfecting it, then it must address itself with all its powers to the work of Christian socialism, for, as said by Maurice: "This is the assertion of God's order."

3. It ministers to the pride of man by thus making him the partaker of a Divine humanity by natural birth. As the Divine-human, our nature cannot become really corrupt, or be eternally separated from God. Sin is but the passing obscuration of the sun, the dirt upon the image of the coin: the cloud melts away, and the sun shines bright again; the dirt is washed off, the image reappears distinct. When made fully conscious of our Divine origin, we rise to a true sense of our dignity and power as men. As said by one: "The most glorious and perfect Godness is, in the deepest sense of the word, natural to man." "Christ came to help me to realize myself to be a man." "Whatever man does in his true human nature, is Divinely done." Since the Son came, "no man has a right to say. My race is a sinful, fallen race, . . because he is bound to contemplate his race in the Son of God."

4. While it claims greatly to exalt Christ, in fact it puts Him out of sight as the living, ruling Lord, and Head of the Church. If it does not deny His present Priesthood, it makes little or nothing of it; and ignores, if it does not deny, His return to earth to complete His redemptive work, and to lift up His saints into the glory of the resurrection life. All that is to be expected is the gradual awakening of men to a consciousness of their

natural participation in His humanity, and thus lead to amelioration of present evils; and somewhere in the indefinite future, to a universal Church.

As the eternal Christ came to restore humanity to its original goodness, and not to give to it a new higher life through resurrection; all sacraments and ordinances appointed by Him look backward rather than forward. They restore the old, but give nothing new. "Baptism merely tells me that I am God's child." It is the acknowledgment on our part that we are already by natural birth, sons of God. (See F. W. Robertson's Sermons on Baptism.) In like manner, all sacraments are but recognitions of pre-existing relations, His incarnation reveals to us the fact of our sonship, and the acknowledgment of this fact is regeneration.

5. The doctrine of a Divine humanity in the Godhead, cannot be distinguished in its bearings upon the relation of God to man from Pantheism. If we have two essential and eternal elements in the God-head, we have Dualism. But God is absolutely one. His personality excludes all mingling of elements. In the Eternal Word made man, the Divine and the human co-exist, but mingle not—"perfect God and perfect man." This is possible only in Him. His humanity, made immortal in the resurrection, and glorified by the Spirit of glory, is purely human, and of this we are made partakers through regeneration. To speak of humanity "as consubstantial with God," and to say that "God and man are essentially one," is pantheistic. When it is said by one (Rev. Dr. Parks' "Theology of Phillips Brooks"): that there is a sense in which the words of the Nicene Creed of the Incarnate Son, that 'He is God of God, Light of Light, very God of very God, begotten, not made, of one substance with the Father,' may be applied to humanity"; how can the Divinity of man be more distinctly affirmed? The writer adds: "If this be not true, I do not believe that the doctrine of the Incarnation can be justified, or at least can have any vital meaning for us."

In this outline of the New Christianity we must keep in mind that, in both its forms, it attempts to hold a mediating position between the orthodox faith as represented in the great Creeds and the strong pantheistic tendencies of our time; and therefore may be presented under varying aspects as one element or the other may predominate in the mind of the writer. Doubtless, there are many who are quite unaware how far their theology is pervaded by the pantheistic leaven; but any one who reads our more recent theological literature with open eyes, will not fail to see that a doctrine of a Divine humanity,—a humanity eternally existing in God, or of a general Incarnation under the name of immanence, is rapidly supplanting the doctrine of a humanity created by God in His image, but now fallen and sinful and alienated from God, and to be redeemed only by the atoning sacrifice of His only-begotten Son, the Word made flesh. It is plain that the doctrine of the immanence of God in man, and that of a human element in God, each lays a broad basis for the deification of man, and so serves as a preparation for the Antichrist.

Andrews's footnotes for chapter 2:

[3] *Deui ut omnium rerum causa immanens, non vero transiens.*

[4] This Professor Upton does by affirming that "the universe, with its centres of energy and personal selves, is called into existence by a partial self-surrendering of His own essential being; and God thus creates a cosmos, in one aspect distinct from Himself, in which only rational souls are possessed of freedom of will. God is living and immanent in all; and thus a universal Self, which we can distinguish from the finite self. This is the incarnation of the eternal, present in every finite thing." This is a wide application of the doctrine of the Kenosis, or God's self-limitation. All finite things are of one substance with God, but partially sundered from Him by His own act. Man, though a part of God, is free because "God withdraws Himself from identity with his will" and thus gives him some degree of independent reality.

This attempt to make man of the substance of God. and yet preserve his personality and freedom, and thus to avoid pantheism, can scarcely be called successful. It is not easy to see how "Ethical Theism'" by dividing Deity into perfect and imperfect, unlimited and limited, can escape being called pantheistic.

[5] Professor J. Seth speaks in the same way: "Professor Caird maintains explicitly the entire immanence of God in man as well as in nature. The immanence of God precludes His transcendence; His unity with man makes impossible that separateness of being which we are accustomed to call personality."

[6] Of Maurice's theology Dr. Hartineau said: "It was an effort to oppose the pantheistic tendency, and is itself reached and touched by that tendency." "It owes its power not less to its indulgence than to its correction of the pantheistic tendency of the age."

[Chapter 3]
Deification of Humanity

In our examination of the words of St. Paul (2 Thess. ii, 4), where he speaks of the man of sin as "sitting in the temple of God, showing himself that he is God" and claiming Divine honour, we found reason to believe that the Apostle did not speak of a deification like that of the Roman emperors, but of one far higher, and resting upon a very different ground. This point we shall now consider in the light of what has been said of the current philosophical pantheism, and its influence upon the religious movements of our time.

In our examination of the tendencies of modern philosophy we have seen that all tend to deify man. As all roads were said of old to lead to Rome, so all present movements, social, political, religious, find their centre in humanity. Philosophy teaches man that he is Divine, and he is quite ready to believe it, and to act accordingly. Science, which shows the greatness of the universe, and which should teach him humility, only enlarges his conception of the greatness of the intellect which is able thus to search out Nature's mysteries. What eulogiums are daily pronounced upon the dignity and excellence of Humanity, and what unbounded possibilities of development are before it! If Science is able now to explain in large measure the universe, its origin, its laws, its evolution, what limit can be set to future possible discoveries? If Philosophy is competent to solve the problem of the Divine existence" and reconstruct the Godhead in thought, and define the law of its beings this itself gives proof of man's potential Divinity. It is upon the consciousness of this Divinity that the religion of the future must be founded.

The great obstacles to these tendencies to deify humanity lie in the facts of the creation of man with limited and defined powers; and of the Incarnation, as given in the Creeds, and held by the Church. Of creation we shall have another occasion to speak. As regards the Incarnation, it is obvious that so long as the absolute distinction between Christ and other men is held—"His two natures and one Person"— no man affirming that he is God, can be received by the Church. But this dualism of the two natures in one Person, which the Church does not attempt to reconcile, but accepts as a reality in Jesus Christ, is offensive to the philosophical pride which is not content till it has reduced all things to unity. It is willing, as we have already seen, to admit that He is Divine if all men are equally Divine. If we may say that God is incarnate in all as in Him, or that all partake of the Divine-human element manifested in the Son, then all are alike the sons of God; and the distinction of Jesus Christ is made one of degree, not of kind.

These two forms of neo-Christianity, although differing widely as to the Person of Christ, agree in the result that man is essentially one with God. In the first, Christ is Divine, not as the eternally pre-existing Son of God "made man" by His birth of the Virgin, but as simply man through the immanence of God in Him. God being immanent in all men, all are Divine in the same sense in which He was Divine. In the second, we have in the Son an eternal, "" archetypal " man, of whose Divine humanity we are partakers, and are thus brought into unity with Deity. We are, as said by one, " consubstantial with Him, and 80 consubstantial with God."

It is the deposition of the Lord from His place as the One Incarnate Son through the assertion of the incarnation of God in the race, which removes the first great obstacle in the way of the reception of the Antichrist; for it is as the representative of our common Divine humanity that he will demand the homage of the world. By a belief in a general incarnation, as affirmed by one school of the neo-Christians, Christ is no more God-man as to His nature than all are God-men.

If one may suppose this belief to have spread widely in Christendom, the questions must arise: To whom, as the best representative of our Divine humanity, shall men pay their homage—to one who lived many centuries ago, when humanity was comparatively undeveloped, or to one of our own day,—the product of its highest culture? Why, it is now asked by not a few, should Jesus of Nazareth stand forever as the great example of the Incarnation? Can we affirm that the fulness of our Divinity has been realized in any one man, or at any past time? . Are we not rather to expect a higher realization of it in some one to come? If humanity is under the law of dynamic evolution, or if a Divine Principle is ever developing itself in men, must there not be a continual upward religious progress? We cannot, therefore, believe that a man of the distant past is to be regarded as the final term of man's evolution, or the highest manifestation of God. Whether Christ or another will hold the higher place as the Divine man, is a matter which time only can decide. But the strong presumption is that we are to look forward rather than backward, and that it is unreasonable to regard any religious or moral type of the past as perfect and unsurpassable.

It is also to be remembered that in rendering homage to one who appears as the rival of Christ, men will not do homage to one who differs in his nature from themselves, and superior to them; but to their own nature as embodied in him. In exalting him, they exalt themselves. Yet the community of nature does not forbid that they recognize in him one in whom is a larger measure of Divinity, and so capable of taking the place of a supreme religious leader. While distinguished above others, yet is he in closest sympathy with them. He is not, like the Christ of the Church, a superhuman being coming down from heaven, and returning thither, but a true son of man; nor does he stand in special relations to a few, as does the Head of the Church, but is the representative of universal humanity.

It is, indeed, hard for many reared from childhood under the influence of the Christian faith, but now accepting more or less clearly the pantheistic theory of God's continuous self-development in humanity, or of its continuous evolution, to set Christ aside as its highest realization, and to believe that any one higher than He can come. Yet, this logical conclusion is more and more forcing its way, and demanding assent. Of this we may see many signs. The time may not be far distant when multitudes will say what a few now affirm: " It is a dishonour done to human nature to teach that in any man of the past it has reached its culmination." The path of humanity is upward and onward; the Divine element in it will manifest itself more and more, and we may not go back eighteen centuries to find the Ideal man.

Of the growing depreciation of Christ, and His rejection as the Ideal which we of to-day are to reverence and imitate, some proofs will be given later.

As illustrative of the present tendencies to deify humanity, and thus deny the special place of Christ, we give some extracts from representative writers; showing how rapidly these are preparing men's minds to receive the coming Antichrist. We begin with some writers who best represent logical Hegelian pantheism; and first with Strauss, taking the translations from Mill's "Mythical Interpretation":

> "The infinite Spirit is alone actual when He shuts himself up in finite spirits. The union of the Divine and human natures is real in an infinitely higher sense when I apprehend the whole of humanity as its subject of operation, than when I set apart a particular man as such. Is not the incarnation of God from eternity a truer thing than one in an exclusive point of time? Taken as residing in an individual Godman, the properties and functions which the Church doctrine ascribes to the Christ are inconsistent and self-contradictory; but in the idea of the race of men, they harmonize together. Humanity is the union of both natures, it is God made man, the Infinite manifesting itself in the finite. . . Humanity is the miracle-worker. . . It is the sinless one. . .It is that which dies and rises again, and ascends toward Heaven. Through faith in this Christ, and especially in His death and resurrection, is man justified before God. A dogmatic theology which, in handling the topic of Christ, rests in Hun as an individual, is not dogmatic theology, but a sermon."

Thus, according to Strauss, the human race as a whole is the Godman—the Incarnate Son—the true Christ—its history is the Gospel. It comes from God, and returns to Him; ever dying to the old, and living to the new; making progress upward forever. Individuals die, but the race lives; this is the eternal life.

The race being thus the ideal Christ, we ask what is the significance and importance of the historical Christ? It is only this, that " by means of His personality and destiny. He became the occasion of bringing the union of the Divine and human into universal consciousness; the uncultivated mind being unable to contemplate the idea of humanity except in the concrete figure of an individual. . . In this way the Church has unconsciously made the historic Christ the full realization of the idea of humanity in its relation to God; whereas, in any individual we should see only the temporary and popular form of the doctrine."

Feuerbach is still more outspoken ("Essence of Religion," translated by Miss Evans): "Religion in its heart, its essence, believes in nothing else than the truth, the Divinity of man." "Its true object and substance is man." "Man, adoring a God, adores the goodness of his own nature." "The nature of God is nothing else but the nature of man considered as something external to man." "Man has his highest being, his God, in himself."

Renan speaks in the same strain. "There has never been in nature or in history any fact caused manifestly by an individual will superior to that of man." "The Absolute of justice and reason exhibits itself in humanity alone. . . The Infinite exists only as it is clothed in a finite form." What account he gives of the Lord in his "Life of Jesus," is well known. He is presented not only as a weak enthusiast, but as conniving at falsehood.

Leslie Stephen affirms that " Christ was simply man, and His character quite within the range of human possibilities. There is no need of postulating an incarnation."

Professor Clifford uses bolder language. "The allegiance of man may not be diverted from man by any Divinity. . . A helper of man outside of humanity, the truth will not permit us to see." "The dim and shadowy outline of the superhuman Deity fades slowly away from before us, and as the mist of His presence floats aside, we perceive with great and greater clearness the shape of a yet greater and nobler figure, of Him who made all gods, and shall unmake them. From the dim dawn of history, and from the inmost depth of every soul, the face of our father Man looks out upon us with the fire of eternal youth in his eyes, and says: "Before Jehovah was, I am.' "

Let us listen to B. W. Emerson: "Jesus saw that God incarnates Himself in man, . . and in a jubilee of sublime emotion said, " I am Divine, through me God acts, through me speaks. Would you see God, see me, or see thee when thou thinkest as I now think.' Jesus would absorb the race, but Tom Paine, or the coarsest blasphemer, helps humanity by resisting the exuberance of the power." This is to say that all men are equally Divine as Jesus; and that every one, even the coarsest blasphemer, who denies His exclusive claims, does a service to the race.

If we now turn to the philosophical representatives of Evolution, we see that they also give to humanity the highest possible place. Thus Mr. John Fiske says: " The Darwinian theory shows that the creation and perfecting of man is the goal toward which nature's work has all the time been tending. . . On earth there will never be a higher creature than man. . . Not the production of any higher existence, but the perfecting of humanity, is to be the glorious consummation of nature's long and tedious work. • . Man is the chief among God's creatures." This leaves no place for Christ as the Incarnate Son, the second Adam, and the Head of the new and glorified humanity. It is said by another that "Human history is the record of the process of the evolution of the Divinity out of the humanity." Another says: " Divinity is humanity raised to its nth power." "The individual man is partly the animal from whom we have come, and partly the God who is coming into him."

The ideal man, the consummation of the evolutionary process, is thus he in whom the primitive animal element is extinguished, and the Divine fully manifested. Let the race, as said by Tennyson,

> "Move upward, working out the beast.
> And let the ape and tiger die."

In this process upward the law of continuity is not broken; there is no place for a supernatural inter- position, and a heavenly humanity of which the risen Lord is the source. There is only a simple unfolding of the natural, beginning with chaos and ending with the cosmos. Man begins a beast and ends a God.

These extracts, which might be indefinitely multiplied, serve to show that the line of distinction between the Divine and the human, God and man, if not openly denied to exist, is being rapidly effaced. The world is learning, and is quite ready to believe, that human nature has in itself, and in its own right, the possibility of many future Christs; and the world may rightly expect them.

We see how broad and deep a foundation is thus laid in the philosophical teachings of the essential unity of the Divine and human natures, for the deification of the Antichrist. The belief of this unity has not yet fully penetrated the popular mind, and most shrink from the name of pantheists; but the spirit of pride which it begets, is already everywhere manifest. A recent writer says: "A most notable sign of our time is the growing faith in man. . .For superhuman revelation we may put human discovery of the truth; and declare all religions, all Bibles, to be the outgrowth of human nature. As man takes the responsibility of evil, so also he provides the remedy. In place of supernatural grace converting the sinner, and trust in the atoning merits and sacrifice of a Redeemer, he substitutes the human ability to put away sin, and to do what is right and God. . .In a word, in place of the descent of God, he puts the ascent of man."

Where this spirit of pride prevails it is idle to preach the offence of the Cross. To say that man is a sinner and needs a Saviour, is pessimism, and offensive; to say that he is a god, is optimism. Man has no confession of sin to make, he needs no atoning sacrifice, no Divine teacher, he accepts no Divine lair as supreme over him; the assertion of his own Divinity is his creed, to live in the power of it is his religion. As said by one: "Man can obey the law of righteousness without any Divine interposition/' No revelation that God has made of Himself and of His will in past generations, is authoritative for us; our God is within us, and our guide; no book can bind us; and no prophet can be our master. As one has sung:

> "I am the master of my fate,
> I am the captain of my soul."

Conscious of the Divinity within us, we teach and are not taught. To worship God aright, we must pay homage to man. To-day is Lord of all the past, and man is Lord of to-day.

This is the spirit that prepares the way for the Antichrist. Christ being deposed from His place as the only Godman; all men being as to nature equally with Him Godmen, the nations are prepared to welcome one who will prove to the deceived and wondering world his Divinity by his mighty acts, wrought in Satanic power; and will say, " This man is the great Power of God." As the representative of deified humanity, he will seat himself in the temple of God, and all "the children of pride" will worship Him. And thus the kingdom of Man will come, and the world will say, this is the kingdom of God, this is the King.

[Chapter 4]
Tendencies of Modern Biblical Criticism

It is well known that biblical criticism has greatly changed its character within a few years. It is said by Pfleiderer ("Development of Theology") that the year 1835 marked an era, three works then appearing by Vatke, Strauss, and F. C. Baur, so fundamentally differing from earlier works, and showing so predominantly the new element, that "we are justified in taking from these the special character of the biblical criticism of to-day."

Let us ask in what consists the special character of the biblical criticism of to-day. We find it in the attempt to adjust the statements of the Scriptures, doctrinal and historical, to certain new ruling ideas, pantheistic, agnostic, evolutionary, scientific; and to reject all that cannot be thus adjusted. We may divide the critics of whom we here speak into the two general classes, 1. Those who deny a personal God, or any knowledge of Him, if he exists; 2. Those who reject some fundamental facts or principles affirmed in the Bible, thus destroying its unity, and undermining the faith of men in it as the revelation of a Divine purpose and will.

I. It needs scarcely be said that all criticism of a book purporting to be a historical account of the actings of God with men from the earliest times, must take its character mainly from the critic's conception of God, and of His relations to men. If the critic conceives of Him in the pantheistic way, as Absolute Spirit, impersonal, unconscious, without will or purpose, or as the unknowable Force of the Agnostics, the Bible is on the face of it incredible. No man can accept it as credible who does not believe in such a God as it sets forth, — One who is in the fullest' sense personal, who has made and rules all things according to His will, who has a purpose in human history which He makes known to men, who can give them ordinances and rites of worship, and reward or punish them as they obey or disobey. If there be not such a God, making known His truth to those whom He chooses, and inspiring them to teach others, the Bible is a record of what could not possibly have taken place. Its Jehovah is a being who does not exist, and all its accounts of His dealings with men are idle fictions.

When, therefore, a critic sits in judgment on the Bible, we ask him, first of all, what he believes respecting God and His relations to men. Can these relations, as presented in it, be true? If his conception of God be such that he starts with the assumption of the necessary untruthfulness of most important points of the biblical record, it is idle to consider his criticism in detail; if, indeed, that can be called criticism which assumes the necessary falsity of the statements criticised.[2]

We may then exclude from the class of true biblical critics all those who, denying a personal God, make thereby the fundamental statements of the Scriptures, dogmatic and historical, impossible. And the agnostic must also be excluded, since his affirmation of the unknowability of God is, in substance, a positive assertion that the Bible, as a revelation of His character and will, cannot be true. Of its essential falsity to the atheist, it is not necessary to speak. The critics of these several classes are thus set free from any inquiry as to the reality of the great facts on which biblical history rests — the creation, the relation of Adam to the race, the fall, the redemption, the Incarnation. Its foundation truths denied in advance, the Bible ceases to be a sacred and authoritative book, and has an interest for the critic only as the sacred books of other peoples have, that he may show its origin, its gradual growth, how its statements came to be believed, and what influence they have had in moulding modern religious belief. Its study is mainly a matter of antiquarian research, and its chief value is as an illustration of one conspicuous form of religious development.

It may seem strange that pantheists, agnostics, and atheists should think it worth while to employ themselves upon such a work of supererogation as to attack the Bible in detail, when they have already condemned it in the gross; but many books of this kind of pseudo-criticism are yearly written.

We may take as an eminent example Strauss in his "Life of Jesus." With his pantheistic conception of God and of His relations to men, he could not accept the Gospels as possibly true. Such a man as the Incarnate Son, the Christ of the Church, could never have lived. Undoubtedly there lived the man Jesus, a super-eminent religious genius, yet in nature a man like other men, without supernatural powers, a son of His age; and the work of criticism is to separate the nucleus of historical truth in the gospel narratives from the encrustations that have grown up around it. The reader, knowing his philosophical starting point, knows from the first to what conclusion Strauss will come; and that, even if there were absolute agreement among the Evangelists as to the details of the Lord's earthly life, the more important of their statements would have been rejected all the same.

Again, let us take the agnostic, Mr. M. Arnold, with his critical presuppositions, as he has expressed himself in his " God and the Bible." The God of the Bible is the " Eternal Power that makes for righteousness;" not personal, not a Being who thinks and loves. All that we know of this Power we " know in the same way we know of the force of gravitation, by its effect upon us; we know no more of the nature of one than of the other."[8] All the miraculous statements we are to regard as poetry or legend; and so, also, what be calls the materialistic features — the supernatural birth and bodily resurrection of Jesus, the expectation of a Messianic kingdom, and of a new heaven and earth. The fall of man is a legend, Satan an imaginary being. " Theology goes upon data furnished by a time of imperfect observation and boundless credulity."

There being so little of doctrinal and historical truth in the Bible, we ask with some surprise what Mr. Arnold can find in it to commend it to popular reading, for he fells us, "the world cannot be without it, and we desire to bring the masses to use it." After taking away all that it teaches of a personal God, of His Incarnate Son, of creation, of sin, of atonement, of resurrection, of judgment, we wonder to be told that we may still retain in the expurgated book " the elements of a religion more serious, potent, awe-inspiring, and profound, than any which the world has yet seen."

II. Of the critics who do not wholly deny the truthfulness of the Bible on a priori grounds, and yet only partially accept its statements, no classification can be made. They are of all shades of opinion, according as their criticism is determined by their philosophy, their science, or their feelings. Many, coming to the Scriptures with a philosophical theory of the order of man's religious development, will make this order the test of truth, and reject all statements that do not conform to it. It is on the principle of "a psychologically possible process of development " that much of the more recent criticism of the Old Testament is based. Some affirm that the Hebrews could not have been monotheists in Moses's days, for Monotheism must have been a later development; and that Jehovah was simply a tribal God, and the Hebrews polytheists. Nor could the Mosaic ritual have been given so early, since ritual presupposes a long period of religious development, and comes at its end, not at the beginning. We may not, therefore, speak of "the Law and the Prophets," but of the Prophets and the Law. The account of the Covenant with the Jews cannot be true, since the selection of one people would be "particularism," and make the Deity partial; and, therefore, Jewish history is no more sacred, and of no more real importance as a revelation of God, than the history of any other people. And, in general, we may not speak of any "falling away" from a Covenant relation, of any decline from a higher spiritual condition to a lower; but rather of a continual upward progress in Jewish history. In the destruction of the first temple, and the cessation of its worship, the Jews suffered no loss. It was, in fact, we are told, a religious gain. They entered thereby into a larger liberty, and a more spiritual service. So, also, in the destruction of the second temple; the synagogue was a great advance upon it.

Others base their criticism mainly upon scientific grounds, into which more or less pantheistic elements enter. We are told by some evolutionists that we must give up the Mosaic cosmogony, and the idea of a creation. The uniform persistence of Force in nature puts miracles and all Divine interpositions out of the question; and biology refutes the biblical account of man's formation, and shows his development from the lower animals. As there is a natural law of progress in humanity, the account of the fall cannot be accepted. Nor are we to accept the supernatural birth of the Lord, since nothing can come into humanity from without; all is developed from within. And the future of humanity must be in the same line as the past; no break of dynamic continuity, no resurrection, no day of judgment, no new creation.[2]

Others still reject the Bible on the ground that in many things it affronts their moral sense. An all-powerful God, being Love, could not have done in the treatment of the nations what He is said in the Old Testament to have done, nor does He punish individuals or nations for disobedience to His will. Redemption from sin and evil by the death of His Son, as related in the Gospels, does not satisfy their injured feeling, for why should sin and evil exist at all ? We must choose, they say, between imperfect goodness and imperfect power; and, whichever taken, the Bible ceases to be authoritative.

But underlying all hostile criticism, and giving it a force which it could not otherwise have over the popular mind is the feeling which is in the air, that the Bible is a superannuated book. Transmitted to us, for the most part, from a remote past, and embodying the religious conceptions of an uncultured people, what authority has it over us? It reflects, as we are incessantly told, the crude beliefs of a people living in the early age of humanity, when men's conceptions of the Supreme Being were necessarily narrow and very anthropomorphic; a time when any scientific study of nature was unknown, when legends were everywhere received as facts, and dead heroes were magnified into gods. It is not possible for us of this century to go back to such undeveloped forms of religious belief. We have outgrown them. Our religion must be conformed to the advanced philosophy and science of our own time, to the modern ideas of man and nature. The Bible is, indeed, valuable as a record of what men have believed, but its conceptions of God are the conceptions of childhood, and must now be greatly enlarged, and our relations to Him be determined by our wider knowledge of nature and of humanity.

Many illustrations might be given of the growing disposition to regard the Old Testament as superannuated, having little historical value, and no religious authority. Thus it was said a half-century ago by Theodore Parker, who, in this matter, represents a multitude: "The Old Testament contains the opinions of from forty to fifty different men, the greater part of them living from four to ten hundred years before Jesus, and belonging to a people we should now call half-civilized... It, therefore, has no authority, and if an appeal is made to some command in it, we answer that nobody knows when it was given, by whom, or to whom. The physics of the Bible are shown to be a false science, its metaphysics false philosophy, its history often mistaken."

A very recent writer, Professor Goldwin Smith, in a magazine article (1895) entitled "Christianity's Millstone," affirms the Old Testament to be this millstone. The New Testament must be separated from the Old; the two should not be bound up in the same volume. "The time has surely come when, as a super-natural revelation, the Old Testament should frankly, though reverently, be laid aside, and never more allowed to cloud the vision of free enquiry, or to cast the shadow of primal religion on our modern life."[10]

It is probable that some of those who are under* mining the faith of men in the Old Testament, are desirous of preserving a measure of faith in the New. But the two cannot be separated. We can explain the appearing of Jesus and His teachings only by accepting the covenant relation of the Jews, the law and ritual as Divinely appointed, and the Divine inspiration of their prophets. Taken as a whole, there is a beautiful unity, God's purpose in the Incarnation running like a golden thread through all. There is a beginning, middle, and end, but the end separated from the beginning is unintelligible.

It is a loud modern cry that we give up the traditional Christ of the Church, and go back to the historical Christ. We must rediscover the long-lost Jesus. We must by criticism of the gospels learn who He was, and how much of what He is reported in them to have said and done. He did, in fact, say and do. We can regard nothing as settled; all must be examined anew. Endless questions here arise: who the writers of the several Gospels, the time of their composition, their relations to one another, their accuracy, the rule of interpretation, and the like. The same questions arise as to the Epistles. The discussions of learned scholars have been minute and long drawn out, and, we may add, almost fruitless, because without any agreement of results as to the one point in question, the person of the Lord.[11]

It is a striking illustration of the separation between the Head and the Church, that after eighteen centuries its scholars are going back to the records of His earthly life to find out who He was! If it had continued in the heavenly fellowship to which He exalted it, it would be able to tell the world with one voice both what He was and what He is.

There is another school of critics who come to the Gospels in the Kantian spirit, and who make very little of facts; the idea is all. Having the ideal Christ, we need no more. It is unimportant whether there was a real man corresponding to the ideal. It is not, it is said, by His acts as a Mediator between God and us that Christ saves us, but as the representative and example of the idea of self-sacrifice. This idea once gained through Him, it must be separated from His individual person that it may become universal. He may wholly disappear from memory; but the idea remains ever active, and we need not go back to its origin.

But we may not go here into details as to the several critical schools. The critics, writing from all points of view about the Lord's person and work — historic, philosophic, scientific, agnostic, evolutionary — each determining by his own pre-accepted criterion what measure of truth there may be in the gospel narratives, have filled the minds of their readers with confusion and perplexity. Almost any modern commentary is an illustration of the critical spirit of the times, and of the perplexity which it brings to the common reader.[12]

Nor in saying this do we disparage the service which genuine criticism may give to the better understanding of the Biblical records. Every kind of knowledge, geological, archeological, historical, scientific, linguistic, is valuable for the light it may cast on these records, and let there be no suppression of the light; but it is to be remembered that the real point at issue between Christianity and anti-Christianity is not the verbal accuracy, or the general infallibility of the Bible.

We can suppose the possibility of the destruction of every copy of the Bible now in existence, but this would not be the destruction of Christianity. It lives in the living Head of the Church: and however valuable the sacred records of the past, their loss would bring no limitation of His prerogatives, or of His ability to manifest Himself to men. Whilst, therefore, gladly acknowledging the aid which criticism, the higher and lower, may furnish to the elucidation of the Bible, we remember that the book is only a means to an end; and that its value is in opening to our knowledge the purpose of God in His Son so far as it has been accomplished, and preparing us to be His helpers in what remains to be done. To one whose eyes are steadily fixed upon the risen Lord, a great deal of the current biblical criticism will seem trifling, if not wholly useless. In the multitude of details unity is lost, the goal is not seen; men's hearts are set upon the past while God desires present action. Only one question is of supreme interest to us: Is the Virgin's Son, raised from the dead, now at God's right hand, having all power in heaven and earth? If the critic says, "He is not, He sleeps in some unknown grave," of what value are his laboured and wearisome efforts to prove small contradictions or errors in a book which can have for us only an antiquarian interest? If the critic says, "He is now living and Lord of all," why trouble himself to refute what, in the nature of the case, is of very small importance, and which the Lord may at any moment refute by His acts?

Can any one think that honest and earnest men will long remain in this state of doubt as to the truthfulness of the Scriptures, or profess to believe what they do not in fact believe? Most will say: "The Bible must be taken as a whole, or rejected as a whole. We will take it as the Church has received it, in its entirety, or we will cast it away altogether." No protestations of biblical critics that they can tear out a page here and a page there, that they can substitute abstractions for Persons, "Eternal Verities" for Father and Son and Spirit, legends for facts, speculations for prophecy, and still keep all that their spiritual needs demand, will satisfy him who will have realities, not idle words. He will say: "I will put the book away, I will not perplex and weary myself in attempting to separate the truth from the error. When biblical scholars have come to some fixed conclusion as to what the Bible is, and what it teaches, and the Church has put the finally ascertained truth into her rewritten Creeds; then I can read it with some assurance that I am not deceiving myself with empty beliefs."

No building can long stand when the foundation is undermined; the first rude shock makes it fall. Many, indeed, may continue to profess great reverence for the Scriptures, as did the Jews of the Lord's day, and study them much, simply because they interpret them in the spirit of the time, and find in them what they wish to find. And we have reason to believe that there are many who, like Mr. Arnold, sing the praises of the Bible long after it has ceased to have for them any authority, or any theological value. They think that it has for the masses an ethical value, and fancy that, while scholars and cultivated people like themselves find much of it out of date, its ideas of moral order and right will keep their hold upon the popular mind, and help to preserve social peace.

Looking to the future, we may not attempt to conceal from ourselves the real character of much of the current biblical criticism. Formerly, accepting the Scriptures as a revelation from God, showing His purpose in nature and man, it limited itself to pointing out some discrepancies, or apparent contradictions; errors affecting particular points, historic or dogmatic, but leaving their general truthfulness unimpeached. The special criticism of our day is far more aggressive and destructive. It affirms on a priori grounds, philosophical and scientific, that very considerable parts of the Bible cannot be true.

It would, of course, be unjust to say that all, or even most, of our biblical critics go to this extent. Not a few attempt to stay the destructive work; but that this work goes steadily on, becoming more and more aggressive, no one acquainted with the more recent critical literature can doubt. Nor can we doubt that it has more and more the tide of popular feeling with it. One of these critics, well qualified to judge, has very lately said: "We rise from the survey of this exegetical literature with the feeling that we have only begun the critical history of the biblical writings." Even now the process of biblical disintegration has gone so far that we see in the "Polychrome Bible" all the colours of the rainbow.

This overthrow of the faith of men in the Bible is a great step forward in preparing the way for the Antichrist. It is of comparatively less importance in the Roman Catholic than in the Protestant communion, since the former makes the Church itself to be an infallible teacher; and to those thus believing, what the biblical critics may say is a matter of indifference. Still it is abundantly manifest that in the Roman communion the loss of faith in the Scriptures is greatly weakening the faith of many in the Church. But to the Protestant, the loss of faith in the Bible points to a great religious change. It leaves him without any guide or teacher, for his choice must be between the biblical teachings of God and of His relations to the Universe and to man, and the teachings of Pantheism. Men are too nobly constituted to be atheists, nor can they long be agnostics. They cannot remain in the pains of doubt, or emptiness of unbelief.

To reject or ignore the Bible on whatever grounds is to be ignorant of God and of His purpose in man and thus to be exposed to the most dangerous form "of delusion, that of self-deification. In proportion as unbelief in the Scriptures increases, the Person of the Incarnate Son, who, as the First and Last, the Beginning and the End, alone gives it unity and meaning, recedes from our sight; and, as He recedes, darkness deepens over both present and future. "For years the most unobservant has seen how within the ' Church the study of" prophecy has been greatly disparaged, — a sure sign of that decay of faith which, beginning here, extends itself to history and doctrine, and ends in their final rejection.

Thus the Bible, made up, as we are told, of disconnected and discordant parts, emptied of all historical unity, revealing no Divine purpose, neither explains the past nor casts light upon the future. Why retain it? Put it among other sacred books, call it literature, keep it for its teachings of ethics, and as illustrating the evolution of religion; but the new age must have its new Bible, one reflecting its advanced knowledge of God and man and nature. It was said by Thomas Carlyle (" Essays") "A Bible is the authentic biography of noble souls." "To each nation its believed history is its Bible; not in Judaea alone, or Hellas, or Latium, but in all lands and in all times." We may, therefore, look for a new Bible which will not narrow its records to the life of one covenant people, but be the history of the evolution of the idea of God in all the noble spirits of the race; and thus be the sacred book of a universal religion!

Andrews's footnotes to Chapter 4:

[7] In Jewish history, as presented by the pantheistic critics, we have not the dealings of God with the Jews, but the evolution of their conception of God. The historical statements have value chiefly as illustrative of the growth of spiritual ideas. God is not a Person making known to them in gradual revelation a purpose in which He calls them the workers together with Him, but an impersonal spiritual Principle developing itself in them. It is on this ground that such histories of the Jews as given by Kuenen, Reuss, Renan, Menzies, and others, although they may have value for the critical student, tend to weaken the faith of the general reader in the Biblical history. If this does not conform to the historian's philosophy of God and of man's religious development, the conclusion is foregone that the events could not have taken place as narrated.

[8] Mr. Arnold is unwilling that this Power should be called the Unknowable, for he feels the absurdity of saying: "The Unknowable is our refuge and strength, a very present help in trouble." "Out of the depths have I cried unto Thee, O Unknowable." He explains the Jehovah of the Hebrews by affirming Him to be "the unconscious deification of the law of righteousness."

[9] A very recent illustration of the disposition to adjust the teachings of the Bible to modem scientific theories is seen in "The Place of Death in Evolution," by Dr. Newman Smyth, 1897. We are told by him that death had originally no moral significance, but gradually acquired one. In itself it is both useful and beneficent, and necessary in evolution. It lifts man into a higher stage of life, and, therefore, will in the end be universally welcomed. Of course there can be no bodily resurrection, and the resurrection of the Lord was an expression to His disciples of "His spiritual identity." When a man dies, death is no more; and when all are dead, death will disappear forever. Dying is " passage out of death into life." When there is " complete detachment of the soul from atomic matter, and it is brought into new and better connection with the elemental forces, the natural is completed in the spiritual." This is the resurrection. Thus the earth is made a birthplace for souls, which, transported at death into some other world, have there their growth and development.

Dr. Smyth thinks that "the coming defender of the faith once given to ike saints will be a trained and accomplished biologist."

[10] Some are now making an attempt to accredit the Bible by presenting it as a book for literary study. It is said that by "a Judicious selection" of its most graphic and eloquent passages it may be made a source of literary, as well as spiritual, stimulation. As expressed by one writer: "Who shall say that it is not to be

included in the curriculum of polite learning as a theme, perhaps of equal moment with Shakspeare? "This is meant to do the Bible high honour. But how could we find a more significant sign that it is ceasing to be regarded as an inspired book, unfolding to men the character and purpose of God. His mercy and grace in His Son, salvation from sin, and the terrors of judgment? Instead of being read as a book in which the voice of God is heard calling all to repentance, to obedience, and to righteousness, a voice which no man may disregard but at the peril of his soul, we are told to read it as literature, — a collection of elegant extracts, of biblical masterpieces. Doubtless the purpose is by appealing to the literary taste, the imagination, the sense of the beautiful and sublime, to obtain for the Bible a new hold upon the attention of cultivated people. But its sacred character is thus lost. It is merely a book among books— of value for intellectual culture, but no more the one book, able to make us wise unto salvation, to which we come upon the bended knee, praying for that light from the Spirit who inspired it, without which we read in vain.

[11] It is to be noted that those who reject the personality of God make the knowledge of Him to be intellectual only. As said by one: "Theology is not a matter of faith, but of intellectual grasp and careful scholarship." And this is necessarily the case if, as we are told, we must study all forms of religion to learn "the self-evolution of the Idea "in them, and thus come to the knowledge of God. If God be a Person, then can we all, learned and unlearned, come into personal communion with Him and know Him as our Father. But this approach to Him is not alike open to all without regard to spiritual character. As it is in the power of a man to make himself known to some and not to others, much more is it in the power of God. Those who dare to rush unbidden into the Most Holy to find Him, will find only thick darkness. To the weary and the heavy-laden, the meek and penitent, the Incarnate Son says: *'Come unto me," and they shall see His face; but to the proud and presumptuous who say: " Bring Him to our tribunal, and we will sit in Judgment on Him," He is invisible. The critic who feels no need of a Redeemer, may scan the pages of the Evangelist with his microscope, but will find no Son of God.

[12] We may take, as an instance, Godet on the Gospel of John (English Trans.) In the first volume of five hundred closely printed pages we find two hundred and fifty-five occupied in preliminary discussions quite beyond the reach of one not especially versed in such themes. The natural effect is to awaken doubts in our minds, for those must be very serious objections which demand such elaborate replies.

Printed in Great Britain
by Amazon